① Jan 22
pages
1-46   12?

D1446301

The Many Legalities of Early America

Jan 29
47-77

Feb. 12
337 - 356

Feb 19.
78 - 96
357 - 387

The Many Legalities
of Early America

EDITED BY CHRISTOPHER L. TOMLINS

AND BRUCE H. MANN

Published for the Omohundro Institute of Early American

History and Culture, Williamsburg, Virginia,

by the University of North Carolina Press,

Chapel Hill and London

The Omohundro Institute of Early American History and Culture is
sponsored jointly by the College of William and Mary and the Colonial
Williamsburg Foundation. On November 15, 1996, the Institute adopted
the present name in honor of a bequest from Malvern H. Omohundro, Jr.

© 2001 The University of North Carolina Press
All rights reserved
Manufactured in the United States of America

The paper in this book meets the guidelines for permanence and
durability of the Committee on Production Guidelines for Book
Longevity of the Council on Library Resources.

Library of Congress Cataloging-in-Publication Data
The many legalities of early America / edited by Christopher L. Tomlins
and Bruce H. Mann.
p. cm.
Papers presented at the November 1996 conference.
Includes index.
ISBN 0-8078-2632-4 (cloth: alk. paper)
ISBN 0-8078-4964-2 (pbk.: alk. paper)
1. Law—United States—History—18th century—Congresses. 2. Law—
United States—History—17th century—Congresses. I. Tomlins,
Christopher L., 1951– II. Mann, Bruce H.
KF361.A2 M36 2001
349.73—dc21
00-048930

05 04 03 02 01 5 4 3 2 1

ACKNOWLEDGMENTS

THIS COLLECTION of essays has benefited from the labors of many individuals and the sponsorship of several institutions. We wish to thank them all.

First, the individuals. The program of the November 1996 conference, "The Many Legalities of Early America," that spawned this collection was created under the supervision of a committee that united this volume's editors with Fredrika J. Teute, Editor of Publications at the Omohundro Institute of Early American History and Culture, who also oversaw the initial steps moving the collection beyond the realm of "conference papers" and into that of "book." James Horn brought the process to painstaking completion in his capacity as the Institute's Visiting Editor of Publications. The original conference program included several contributions—papers and commentaries—that, regrettably, could not be included here. Marjoleine Kars and Steven Wilf each decided that the demands of finishing their respective books would prevent them from revising the papers they had presented and therefore withdrew them from consideration. Jack P. Greene and J. R. Pole each provided stimulating concluding reflections on the prospects for early American legal history that we could not include for reasons of space. The conference's four invited commentators—Michael Zuckerman, Christine Heyrman, Allan Kulikoff (in absentia), and John Murrin—all offered probing discussions that improved the papers at which they were directed. In the course of chairing the conference's opening and closing sessions, Stanley N. Katz and Linda K. Kerber respectively went to considerable lengths to orient the conference's proceedings to general developments in the field of early American history. Other sessions were chaired by members of the conference committee and by Peter Hoffer. At the OIEAHC, Beverly Smith, Sally Mason, Gil Kelly, and Virginia L. Montijo all made major contributions to the success of the conference and to production of the subsequent volume. Much of the secretarial work generated by the conference program and by the revision and editing of essays was undertaken by Diane Levin, formerly of the American Bar Foundation. Finally, we are deeply grateful to Kevin Butterfield and Kathryn Burdette for their patience and expertise in copy-editing.

Second, the institutions. The original "Many Legalities" conference would not have been possible without the enthusiastic support, intellectual and financial, of the Omohundro Institute of Early American History and Culture and its Director, Ronald Hoffman. Nor would it have been possible without the intellectual and financial support of the Institute of Bill of Rights Law of the Marshall-Wythe Law School, College of William and Mary, and its then-Director, Rodney Smolla. The success of the conference, and of the subsequent editing and production of this volume, also owes much to the generous support of the American Bar Foundation and its Director, Bryant G. Garth.

The essay by David Barry Gaspar, " 'Rigid and Inclement': Origins of the Jamaica Slave Laws of the Seventeenth Century," was not part of the original conference program but was commissioned after the event. We are grateful for Barry Gaspar's willingness to join our enterprise halfway through. The introductions to the four sections into which the essays are organized are written by Christopher Tomlins, with important critical input from Bruce Mann.

CHRISTOPHER TOMLINS
The American Bar Foundation, Chicago

BRUCE H. MANN
University of Pennsylvania, Philadelphia

CONTENTS

Acknowledgments v

Christopher Tomlins
INTRODUCTION
The Many Legalities of Colonization:
A Manifesto of Destiny for Early American Legal History
1

PART ONE
Atlantic Crossings

James Muldoon
Discovery, Grant, Charter, Conquest, or Purchase:
John Adams on the Legal Basis for English
Possession of North America
25

Mary Sarah Bilder
Salamanders and Sons of God:
The Culture of Appeal in Early New England
47

David Barry Gaspar
"Rigid and Inclement":
Origins of the Jamaica Slave Laws
of the Seventeenth Century
78

David Thomas Konig
Legal Fictions and the Rule(s) of Law:
The Jeffersonian Critique of Common-Law Adjudication
97

The Many Legalities of Early America

CHRISTOPHER TOMLINS

INTRODUCTION

The Many Legalities of Colonization

A Manifesto of Destiny for Early American Legal History

> Laws in their most general significance are the necessary
> relations arising from the nature of things.
> MONTESQUIEU

> Whether this is Jerusalem or Babylon We know not.
> WILLIAM BLAKE

W HEN THE Institute of Early American History and Culture asked me to consider how one might frame a conference to assess the state of early American legal history, it happened that I was in the grip of an extraordinary book, *Remembering Babylon*, by my compatriot David Malouf. *Remembering Babylon* is an account, nominally fictional, actually mythopoeic, of Europeans' colonization and settlement of a remote land. But in particular it is about the epistemology of colonial encounter—about meetings with landscapes, vegetation, animals, climate, and people all unutterably different from anything the settlers had before experienced, about settlers' capacities to comprehend their situation under circumstances so challenging to the conceptual categories, the imaginative and linguistic resources, the very means to construct knowledge, that their memories furnished them. It is about how strangers in new lands are imaginatively distant from their new surroundings, handicapped in their abilities to see or hear or feel what is in fact immediately present all around them. It is about how encounter confounds memory itself, how new unfamiliarities may play havoc with brought sensibilities by

My thanks to John Murrin, whose comments at the Williamsburg conference gave me the title for this essay; to Jack Greene and Jack Pole for stimulating remarks on the same occasion; to my coeditor, Bruce H. Mann, my colleagues, Bryant Garth and John Comaroff, and James Horn, all of whom offered helpful advice; and to the Institute's referees for their reactions. It is appropriate to state that the arguments advanced are the conclusions of the author alone.

An earlier version of this essay has been published as *American Bar Foundation Working Paper*, no. 9723 (Chicago, 1998), under the title "Colonization and the Subject: A Manifesto of Destiny for Early American Legal History."

casting doubt upon remembered realities. It is about how in such situations new realities are constructed—and how they in turn are remembered.[1]

Remembering Babylon seemed to me at the time—still seems now—to portray the experience of colonial settlement in a profound and compelling way. That the time of Malouf's encounter was the mid-nineteenth century rather than the seventeenth, that its place was the Pacific coast of North Queensland, not the Atlantic coast of North America, struck me as incidental. It seemed to me essential that a conference treating aspects of a colonial society attempt to draw in some way upon so powerful an evocation of colonization.

What was there in Malouf's rendition of colonial encounter, however, that could possibly help frame the specifics of inquiry into a phenomenon as apparently remote from its primary experiential colors, as apparently arcane, as early American law? In fact, the answer bursts off his pages. Legality has a sustained hold on the lives and discourse of Malouf's protagonists. In a situation of extreme fluidity, even confusion, legality furnished many of the terms upon which they interacted with their setting. Legality established a grid of new imposed realities to which the law's institutional technology of recorded word, deed, and authoritative delivery could give real, if often brittle, effect. That is, legality provided an epistemology for the colonial encounter. In English processes of colonization and possession, Patricia Seed has reminded us, legality always had.[2]

By talking of legality here rather than simply of law, I mean to try to alter our focus twice over. First, my intention is to counter what has always seemed to me law's enviable capacity to evade the historian's grasp by trumping critique with timeless and self-legitimating values—universality of application, singularity of meaning, rightness. Law tends always to slip through historicist clutches. Legality, in contrast, is a condition with social and cultural existence; it has specificity, its effects can be measured, its incarnations investigated. In their Foucauldian sense, legalities are the symbols, signs, and instantiations of formal law's classificatory impulse, the outcomes of its specialized practices, the products of its institutions. They are the means of effecting law's discourses, the mechanisms through which law names, blames, and claims.[3] But legalities are not produced in formal legal settings alone. They are social products, generated in the course of

1. David Malouf, *Remembering Babylon* (New York, 1993). Malouf at once echoes, and builds upon, Paul Carter's magisterial *Road to Botany Bay: An Exploration of Landscape and History* (New York, 1988), as does Donna Merwick in *Possessing Albany, 1630–1710: The Dutch and English Experiences* (New York, 1990).

2. Patricia Seed, *Ceremonies of Possession in Europe's Conquest of the New World, 1492–1640* (Cambridge, 1995), 6–7.

3. I take this turn of phrase from the title of William L. F. Felstiner et al., "The Emergence and Transformation of Disputes: Naming, Blaming, Claiming . . . ," *Law and Society Review*, XV (1980–1981), 631–654.

virtually any repetitive practice of wide acceptance within a specific locale, call the result rule, custom, tradition, folkway or pastime, popular belief or protest.[4] As Ann Plane demonstrates in her essay in this volume, ideologies of legality also supply the conceptual frames that we use to interpret practices and invent legalities for, and of, others.[5] And of course legalities generate illegalities, for the two are necessary conditions of each other's existence. Law, after all, makes outlaws, not law's absence. Their cheek-by-jowl intimacy, in fact, helps explain how easily, and frequently, legality and illegality trade places.

Unless purposefully embodied in description and argument, however, the simple substitution of *legalities* for the singularity of *law* adds up to little more than rhetorical cleverness. Fortunately, *Remembering Babylon* offers us certain clues how the idea of legalities may be made somewhat more concrete, and in ways—because of the book's subject—that are particularly germane to the investigation of law in colonial settings. In Malouf's encounter, for example, legalities are what define who is who: who is a British subject, who is not, and how the resources and terms of interaction given to each arise from that initial point of difference. Further, in a fashion not unlike that explored by Richard Bushman in this collection, legalities also help form the material terrain that protagonists inhabit.[6] Together these legalities of self, other, and place then define who should appropriately be where (and where not) on that terrain. Finally, legalities, so powerful, are also fragile and contingent. They define action and actors epistemologically, but they do not necessarily determine action behaviorally. One may begin, lightly enough, with the pub, the central institution in Malouf's remote unnamed gaggle of shacks. It was unlicensed. Did that make it functionally any less of a pub? Consider, more seriously, the general contingencies of legality's functional capacity to rule, particularly in a country like this where

4. In *Law for the Elephant: Property and Social Behavior on the Overland Trail* (San Marino, Calif., 1980), 361–362, John Phillip Reid concludes that "a pattern of behavior based on mutual expectations concerning duties and rights may as accurately be labeled 'legal' behavior as may behavior dictated by fear of police enforcement." "What their words and conduct tell us is that for nineteenth-century Americans the definition of binding 'law,' vesting rights and imposing obligations, was not limited to a command or set of commands from the 'sovereign' backed by threats or by force. Nor was 'law' some abstraction discovered or justified by appealing to 'natural' or universal rules of ideal deportment. Law was the taught, learned, accepted customs of a people."

5. See Martin Chanock, *Law, Custom, and Social Order: The Colonial Experience in Malawi and Zambia* (Cambridge, 1985).

6. See Richard Lyman Bushman, "Farmers in Court: Orange County, North Carolina, 1750–1776," below. More generally, on the relationship between surveying, land management, land law, and colonization, see Edward T. Price, *Dividing the Land: Early American Beginnings of Our Private Property Mosaic* (Chicago, 1995); Roger J. P. Kain and Elizabeth Baigent, *The Cadastral Map in the Service of the State: A History of Property Mapping* (Chicago, 1992), particularly 265–344; Matthew H. Edney, *Mapping an Empire: The Geographical Construction of British India, 1765–1843* (Chicago, 1997).

"the nearest named place . . . was twelve miles off." Consider, on the other hand, that the name of that place—Bowen—invoked all the specific authority of the governor of Queensland himself, Sir George Bowen, "the figure in an official uniform . . . and the Crown he represented, which held them all, a whole continent, in its grip," the governor whose task it was to bestow names on the nameless, to found towns, to lay down laws, and in these and other ways fulfill his civilizing commission "to call into existence a new self-governing state."[7]

Consider, most seriously of all, the centrality of legality to the pivotal definitional experience in the whole process of colonization and settlement—the struggle to transform strangeness into familiarity and to fix authority on the outcome, so that henceforth that outcome would prevail and no other:

> Out here the very ground under their feet was strange. It had never been ploughed. You had to learn all over again how to deal with weather: drenching downpours when in moments all the topsoil you had exposed went liquid and all the dry little creek-beds in the vicinity ran wild; cyclones that could wrench whole trees up by their roots and send a shed too lightly anchored sailing clear through the air with all its corrugated iron sheets collapsing inward and slicing and singing in the wind. And all around, before and behind, worse than weather and the deepest night, natives, tribes of wandering myalls who, in their traipsing this way and that all over the map, were forever encroaching on boundaries that could be insisted on by daylight—a good shotgun saw to that—but in the dark hours, when you no longer stood there as a living marker with all the glow of the white man's authority about you, reverted to being a creek-bed or ridge of granite like any other, and gave no indication that six hundred miles away, in the Lands Office in Brisbane, this bit of country had a name set against it on a numbered document, and a line drawn that was empowered with all the authority of the Law.[8]

Law stretches right into faraway places, to claim and to name, to plant authority amid strangeness, to declare with portentous certainty what the reality of a remote spot shall be. Yet how vulnerable to other authority—of nature ("which knew nothing, cared nothing either, for the little laws of men"), or of the native, who might be made to answer to law only by means of a good shotgun. And therefore how strong the need for a yet more absolute possession, for a final destruction of the strangeness, for the cre-

---

7. Malouf, *Remembering Babylon*, 3–5, 168.
8. Ibid., 9.

ation of a new reality, material as well as ideal, so that at last one's metaphysic of legality would be grounded on established facts; all this because you knew

> that, just three years back, the very patch of earth you were standing on had itself been on the other side of things, part of the unknown, and might still, for all your coming and going over it, and the sweat you had poured into its acre or two of ploughed earth, have the last of mystery upon it, in jungle brakes between paddocks and ferny places out of the sun. Good reason, that, for stripping it, as soon as you could manage, of every vestige of the native; for ringbarking and clearing and reducing it to what would make it, at last, just a bit like home.[9]

It has become a commonplace of modern historical and anthropological examinations of colonization, John Comaroff and Jean Comaroff tell us, to insist upon "the centrality of law in the colonization of the non-European world . . . to assert 'its' role in the making of new Eurocentric hegemonies [and] in the creation of colonial subjects." In this literature, where once theorists of underdevelopment and modernization saw Western law as an essential component of progress, law's "dark side" has increasingly become the uppermost—the presentation of the colonizer's legal institutions and procedures "as tools of domination and disempowerment; blunt instruments wielded by states, ruling classes, reigning regimes." That law has served to introduce such sensibilities and practices into colonizing processes, the Comaroffs do not dispute. Nevertheless, their discussions of the role of law in colonization suggest that to give such dominance to the dark side is conceptually crude. Colonization's legalities were not an instrumental facilitation of a "linear, coherent, coercive process" between clearly defined protagonists, one expansive and metropolitan, the other subordinate and local. The whole encounter was "a good deal more ambiguous, less audible, murkier." One should not doubt that legality entered centrally "into the making of modern history," but one must allow that it did so "imaginatively" and "in inherently ambivalent, contradictory ways."[10]

To investigate the history of law's part in the colonization and settlement of early America is to discover history ensconced, at least until recently, in a conceptual world very different from that described by the Comaroffs, a world whose agenda has for the most part borne so little relation to what elsewhere has become commonplace as perhaps actually to stand in tempo-

9. Ibid., 9–10, 187.
10. Jean Comaroff and John L. Comaroff, *The Dialectics of Modernity on a South African Frontier* (Chicago, 1997), 365–367, vol. II of *Of Revelation and Revolution;* John L. Comaroff, "Foreword," in Mindie Lazarus-Black and Susan F. Hirsch, eds., *Contested States: Law, Hegemony, and Resistance* (New York, 1994), ix–xiii.

rary need of a dose of the crudities they seek to move us beyond. The legal history of European colonization and settlement of the Atlantic's western shores has generally been told in terms hedged by the later, greater, and, it would seem, distinctly American story of national formation. It has been a history, first, largely defined chronologically (which is to say politically) as a story of events in a separate colonial period rather than as the initial episode in a history of processes that continued throughout the nineteenth century. It has been a history, second, that has been far more an interior history of colonies—of European settlements and their affairs—than of colonization. And it has been a history, third, that, notwithstanding (or perhaps because of) "Americans' pervasive sense that their society is uniquely lawbound," has subjected law to relatively little critical attention.[11] Rather than, for example, find themselves challenged (as elsewhere) to pursue, or refute, claims of law's blunt instrumentality in visitations of oppression or its role in the making of Eurocentric hegemonies, historians of law in colonial America in the main traveled quieter roads, free to parse doctrinal receptions, trace institutional inheritances, and generally pursue trails of ideas from old country to new. The mainstream of the subject was the "sources" and "origins" of the American legal tradition, its theme carryover and adaptation—what the American tradition reproduced or mimicked, where it departed that of the "mother country," when it began to show signs of "maturity" and under what impetus. Its cap and explanatory exclamation point was usually the late eighteenth century's Revolutionary-constitutional climacteric.[12]

The legal history that resulted remains useful—a substantial body of carefully researched, if occasionally technically abstruse, scholarship. Unfortunately, as Stanley N. Katz pointed out in 1984, that scholarship did not result in the establishment of anything that could be recognized as a legal-historical perspective capable of bearing decisively on the general interpretation of early American history, a perspective that could convey how the law traced so carefully had actually made a difference. The critique was polite, but nonetheless it was devastating: colonial legal history had never established critical interpretive presence for itself as history.

As Katz explained it, part of the problem was the field's prevailing narrowness of vision.[13] Part, however, was the scholarly headwind that for more

11. Stanley N. Katz, "The Problem of a Colonial Legal History," in Jack P. Greene and J. R. Pole, eds., *Colonial British America: Essays in the New History of the Early Modern Era* (Baltimore, 1984), 465.
12. Ibid., 476, 480.
13. Ibid., 457–468. Just a few years after Katz, another critic, Michael Bellesiles, put the matter rather more bluntly. Citing a number of well-known works published during the preceding twenty-five years as representative of the mainstream of early American legal history, Bellesiles castigated their authors for various failings, notably for echoing the traditional conception of law and order as phenomena "generated principally from above"

than half a century had blown from the nineteenth century. In the 1930s, Roscoe Pound located American law's formative era in the period "extending from independence to the time of the Civil War," and American historians had followed that cue ever since, finding virtually nothing of relevance to "American law" at any time before the later eighteenth century's Revolutionary stirrings.[14] Pound's approach—primarily jurisprudential and internal—glorified the guiding role of the legal intellectual in the development of the American legal tradition and owed much to the efflorescence of domestic written sources (case reports, legal texts) that indubitably was a feature of his period. Perhaps a socioeconomic interpretation would result in a different assessment. It did not. Twenty years after Pound, James Willard Hurst of the University of Wisconsin led a generation of law scholars in a breakout from their traditional "internalist" focus on law as an autonomous box of doctrine, constructing in its stead a history that placed law firmly in a social and economic context.[15] But, like Pound, Hurst's Wisconsin School found nothing "formative" before the first half of the nineteenth century. American law, Hurst argued, was a creature of nineteenth-century modernity, pragmatic and instrumental, devoted to the realization of liberal ends of freedom and individualism—the release of "individual creative energy," freedom from "arbitrary public or private interference," the provision of "instruments or procedures" to effect "man's creative talents." The unforgettable account of the creation of the Pike River Claimants Union that Hurst used to open his best-known work, *Law and the Conditions of Freedom in the Nineteenth-Century United States,* effectively identified the origins and essence of American legal culture with the 1830s Mississippi Valley frontier more than a half-century after the endpoint of the colonial period and many hundred miles to the west of any of the mainland colonies. Little from the previous two centuries engaged him. Colonial law was "communal, conservative and moralistic"; real American law "was creative, expansive, and pragmatic." The colonial period was a preliberal past, of no interest or current relevance, simply a curiosity from which the real America had long since departed.[16]

---

and for writing about "the direct transportation of common law to the American frontier as though every settler carried a copy of Blackstone in his luggage." See Michael A. Bellesiles, "The Establishment of Legal Structures on the Frontier: The Case of Revolutionary Vermont," *Journal of American History,* LXXIII (1986–1987), 897.

14. Roscoe Pound, *The Formative Era of American Law* (Boston, 1938), 3; Katz, "Colonial Legal History," in Greene and Pole, eds., *Colonial British America,* 469.

15. For an appreciative assessment of Hurst's innovations and their historiographical context, see Robert W. Gordon, "Introduction: J. Willard Hurst and the Common-Law Tradition in American Legal Historiography," *Law and Society Review,* X (1975), 9–55.

16. See James Willard Hurst, *Law and the Conditions of Freedom in the Nineteenth-Century United States* (Madison, Wis., 1956), esp. 3–10; Katz, "Colonial Legal History," in Greene and Pole, eds., *Colonial British America,* 470–471. Hurst's ascendancy represented,

Interpretively, not much has happened in the mainstream of American legal history to alter decisively early America's segregation.[17] The result has been a legal history of the colonial period condemned to the status of a tolerated but mostly ignored "poor relation within the family," an idiosyncratic preoccupation of a relative handful of specialists. There can be virtue in isolation, and Katz's 1984 critique was not all lament. As individuals, early American legal historians had shown themselves to be vigorous and talented scholars—"We know more than we ever did about the context and nature of colonial legal behavior." Still, he was unable to find in vigor alone the seeds for the "coherent and compelling interpretation" that he believed possible. The field's larger conceptual problems, whether of its own making or the making of others, were simply too debilitating.[18]

For all the severity of the critique, the remedies Katz canvassed did not suggest as decisively as one might have wished how the situation could be changed. Although, for example, he recognized both the salience and the artificiality of the periodization that marginalized the colonial period, and rejected it, he did not offer any particular strategy for overcoming it. Katz properly criticized Pound for his Whiggishness and Hurst for his modernism but failed to delineate in any detail the continuities that he thought could be counterposed to the late-eighteenth-century intellectual (or socio-

---

in effect, a triumph of law school–centered historical "presentism" over a previous generation's somewhat antiquarian doctrinal predilections. But it was also a legal-historical presentism of a particular political genus, one that contrasted pointedly with the more collectivist presentism of Richard B. Morris, for whom early America was certainly not an irrelevance. Contrast, for example, Hurst's moral narrative (nineteenth-century lawmaking shows that American law's essential service to democracy lies in its capacity to shoulder aside obstacles to "the release of energy") with Morris's in *Government and Labor in Early America* (New York, 1947) (examination of early American law suggests long-term historical continuities that link eighteenth-century ideologies of social and economic regulation to twentieth-century state interventionism). Hurst's ascendancy eclipsed Morris as inevitably as it eclipsed the colonial period. See Christopher Tomlins, "Why Wait for Industrialism? Work, Legal Culture, and the Example of Early America—An Historiographical Argument," *Labor History*, XL (February 1999), 5–34.

17. To be an American legal historian, Lawrence Friedman long ago observed, was to be "either a Hurstian or a reviser of Hurst." See Aviam Soifer, "Reflections on the Fortieth Anniversary of Hurst's *Growth of American Law*," *Law and Social Inquiry*, XVII (Winter 1992), 168. Both major syntheses of law in the later colonial/early national periods—William E. Nelson, *Americanization of the Common Law: The Impact of Legal Change on Massachusetts Society, 1760–1830* (Cambridge, Mass., 1976), Morton Horwitz, *The Transformation of American Law, 1780–1860* (Cambridge, Mass., 1977)—conform themselves to a Hurstian periodization that contrasts a period of dynamic and changing American law after the 1780s with stasis and communitarianism before. For the most influential challenge to this view to emerge to date, see Bruce H. Mann, *Neighbors and Strangers: Law and Community in Early Connecticut* (Chapel Hill, N.C., 1987).

18. Katz, "Colonial Legal History," in Greene and Pole, eds., *Colonial British America*, 457, 467, 474.

economic) ruptures that Pound and Hurst and their followers had decided cut American law off from whatever had preceded it. Second, notwithstanding the hunger for large-scale reinterpretation that appeared in Katz's concluding plea for theory in colonial legal history, he expressed mostly caution in discussing the possibilities inherent in actual theories. Critical legal theory, law and economics, reformist Marxism and historical anthropology all had their uses; embracing them would represent "a step forward in sophistication" for legal historians. But the explicit embrace of theory would also launch historians into arenas where they were "not ordinarily very adept." The dangers, hence, were "as great as the opportunities." While rejecting doctrinal history and antiquarianism, therefore, Katz pursued conceptual innovation only indirectly and consequentially. In fact, his main recommendation was methodological: a call for the pursuit of an explicitly sociolegal history. Overall, the new "intellectual agenda" Katz proposed did not suggest a recasting of the interpretive orientation of the field so much as identify topics that had not yet been investigated—the roots of the functional bifurcation of legislation and adjudication, the rise of the legal profession, the legal status of women—and offer a new way of investigating them. Katz hinted at the possibility that resort to sociolegal methods of inquiry in investigating those topics might breed results with broad conceptual implications for the field as a whole; inquiry into women's legal status, for example, could lead to exploration of "the coercive (or at least socially confirming) role of law in colonial society." Interestingly, however, his analysis identified (accurately) the stimulus for that exploration as one initiated in women's history, not legal history.[19]

Katz's 1984 essay is properly recognized as a watershed in the field of early American legal history. Much of the scholarship produced since has demonstrated the wisdom of his recommendations for the way forward. The methodology to which he pointed, sociolegal history, has helped to invigorate the field as never before. Most of the essays in this volume bear its mark. Yet, despite all this, as a field of study early American legal history has remained wedded more to detail than to worldview. It has neither achieved the larger objective of "a coherent and compelling interpretation" of early America nor overcome "the discontinuity of colonial and national law" that sustains its relative isolation.[20] Both failings remain, stubbornly, central characteristics of the field. It is our responsibility to tackle them.

As this essay's title and opening already have suggested, I believe that consideration of law as a central actor in processes of colonization offers early American legal history a chance to resolve its problems—to develop the

19. Ibid., 474–484, esp. 480, 483.
20. Ibid., 474.

compelling overall narrative that it has lacked and to overcome the imputed irrelevance of colonial to national law.

It is worth noting that colonization is not entirely bereft of earlier and promising attention in colonial American legal history, albeit the attention lies at a considerable remove and its promise was only partially realized. Between 1900 and the 1930s, historians of the so-called Imperial school, Herbert Levi Osgood, George Louis Beer, and Charles M. Andrews, developed an approach to American history in which law and empire supplied the dominant frames of perception. As John Higham has pointed out, their approach was an original contribution to the study of imperialism—"English historians had largely neglected the study of imperial organization: the Americans now told the Old World something new about itself." Osgood was the initiator, stressing that "the growth of a system of imperial administration" was the "central thread" of the seventeenth and eighteenth centuries, consciously seeking a wide transatlantic context for American history. But it was Andrews who developed the perspective to its fullest extent. For Andrews, America could be understood only as an instance of imperial expansion. Not interested (at least at the outset) in "adding another account to the existing histories of the thirteen original colonies," he sought instead to establish a "genuinely comprehensive and unprovincial" frame for early American history by locating it as one element in the history of "the whole Anglo-American Empire," including "all England's colonial possessions in the West that were founded in the seventeenth century." His goal was "to discover what our colonial history" was really all about by examining the colonies "not from within, as is commonly done, but from without . . . disregarding all preconceptions based on later events."[21]

There were clear blind spots in Andrews's field of vision. First, his imperial perspective was resolutely Anglophone. He looked westward, at the formation of American empire, but "his design did not call for . . . attention to the non-English empires and peoples that contributed to" early American history.[22] Second, and more serious, Andrews's design was institutional rather than social. He stressed the colonies' status as "subordinate and dependent communities legally subject" to sovereign metropolitan authority but paid little attention to distributions of subordination, dependency, and

21. Charles M. Andrews, *The Colonial Period of American History*, 3 vols. (New Haven, Conn., [1964]), I, *The Settlements*, xi; John Higham, *History: Professional Scholarship in America* (New York, 1965), 162–164.

22. Higham, *History*, 164. This was not a failing unique to Andrews or to the American Imperial school. See, for example, Carter's biting critique of the Imperial school of Australian history in *Road to Botany Bay*, xiii–xxv.

authority within.[23] Andrews, the rival progressive historians objected, wrote about early American communities "in a 'legalistic' spirit, touched only incidentally on economic developments . . . ignored sectional conflicts, and paid little heed to the common man." The critique was merited, but ironically the progressives' own ascendancy largely forestalled the possibility that it would be absorbed in a revised colonial history, for the progressive historians were not much interested in the colonial period at all. "Progressive historians saw the colonial period as a time of origins, and their attention tended to move from that starting toward what followed. Most of them neglected the origins of American history in favor of the changes it subsequently underwent."[24] It was in their spirit that Pound and, especially, Hurst constructed the strain of American legal history that for more than half a century excluded the colonial period.

A new colonization synthesis that absorbs rather than ignores the social has the potential fully to meet Katz's desire for a coherent and compelling interpretation of early American legal history. That potential is on display in this volume. As a theme for legal history, colonization has two primary aspects, one centered on the interaction and transformation of peoples, the other on the occupation and transformation of places. In the last fifteen years, an early American legal history of the first of these aspects has begun to be broached quite thoroughly and is well represented in the essays in this collection. Take for example the transforming relations of contact between settler and indigenous populations, of possession and conquest, legitimation and accommodation, pursued in the essays by James Muldoon, Katherine Hermes, James F. Brooks, and Ann Marie Plane.[25] As they indicate, law was integral to European encounter. Law provided the means and the language for the actual construction of European social realities—facts on the ground, as it were—in America. It also provided a context in which Europeans encountered, reconstructed, and eventually displaced the competing legalities, or, to borrow Hermes's useful term, the jurispractices, of indigenous others. As in early American history in general, legal history has tended to concentrate predominantly on the social dynamics internal to Euroamerican, particularly Anglo-American, settler cultures. Yet these dynamics, we have begun to realize, are themselves decisively shaped by continuing interactions occurring across boundaries both of culture and settlement. Across the earliest frontiers, multiple cultures mean multiple legalities.

23. Andrews, *Colonial Period of American History,* I, xiv.
24. Higham, *History,* 186–187.
25. Readers will find more elaborated comments on the individual essays included in this collection in the introductions to each part of the volume.

There is, nevertheless, good historical reason for the tendency of historians of Anglo-America to give most of their attention to the internalities of the English colonies. In other colonized settings, European elites pursued the transformation of indigenous inhabitants for essentially extractive purposes. In early North America, however, systematic exploitation of the indigenous population was incidental to English ambition. The English in fact "had comparatively little interest in preserving indigenous peoples; their presence constituted a barrier to English occupation."[26] The English colonial project was one more of accumulation through clearance and settlement than through extraction, a transference of population rather than the seizure of one. Thus, to a greater extent than in the case of other European powers, the English project became one of self-colonization, a labor of transformation wrought largely upon themselves and upon other, non-English, migrant minorities.[27] This characteristic is illustrated in many of the essays collected in this volume, in the legal construction and reconstruction of social identities and social disciplines, in law's mediation and stabilization of economic, moral, and racial relations, in its development of the rudimentary classificatory schema and categorizations that created a population increasingly differentiated in legal subjectivity. It is on display in David Barry Gaspar's essay on the development of Jamaica's slave codes and in Christine Daniels's careful unpacking of the actual legal mediation of master-servant relationships. It is developed most thoroughly, perhaps, in Holly Brewer's work on the legal identities of children. Exploration of the theme's practical implications—that is, for law's capacities to determine

26. Seed, *Ceremonies of Possession*, 187.

27. The creation of disciplined labor forces in overseas colonies through transportation or migration of surplus populations is a theme of English colonizing discourse from the younger Richard Hakluyt onward. See, for example, Richard Hakluyt, "Discourse of Western Planting," in *The Original Writings and Correspondence of the Two Richard Hakluyts*, Hakluyt Society, 2d Ser., LXXVII, doc. 46 (1935), 211–326, esp. 233–239. English historians have noted, moreover, how colonization's aspect as the transformation of peoples extended simultaneously to the "internal" colonization (geographic, social, and intellectual) of the British Isles. On this, see, generally, Richard Helgerson, *Forms of Nationhood: The Elizabethan Writing of England* (Chicago, 1992). For more specific treatments, see Michael Brogden, "An Act to Colonize the Internal Lands of the Island: Empire and the Origins of the Professional Police," *International Journal of the Sociology of Law*, XV, no. 2 (May 1987); Robert D. Storch, "The Policeman as Domestic Missionary: Urban Discipline and Popular Culture in Northern England, 1850–1880," *Journal of Social History*, IX, no. 4 (Summer 1976), 481–509. By the late eighteenth century a dialectic between metropolitan and colonial social transformation had already become explicit in the work of police/political economy theorists like P. Colquhoun. See, for example, his *Treatise on the Police of the Metropolis*, 2d ed. (London, 1796), and *A Treatise on the Wealth, Power, and Resources, of the British Empire, in Every Quarter of the World . . .* (London, 1814). This point is hinted at in Tomlins, *Law, Labor, and Ideology in the Early American Republic* (Cambridge, 1993), 74–80. It is developed in greater detail in Comaroff and Comaroff, *Dialectics of Modernity*, 310–322, vol. II of *Of Revelation and Revolution*.

outcomes as well as to influence the definition of interactions—are not ignored in any of these essays. They are tested most explicitly, however, in the essays by Linda L. Sturtz and by John G. Kolp and Terri L. Snyder investigating the extent of economic and political space that law afforded women in seventeenth- and eighteenth-century Virginia. In all these examinations of the internal sociolegal order of the settled colonies, we encounter settlers engrossed in local legal construction, ordering the societies they established for themselves, engaging sometimes in innovation both piecemeal and systematic that departed Anglocentric norms, sometimes in efforts to reproduce what they imagined to be those norms, and often in behavior that tended to subvert or at least evade the very legal forms to which they had expressed allegiance.[28]

Other essays offer critical examinations of law's capacity to stabilize social formation and cultural perception. Mary Sarah Bilder, David Thomas Konig, Richard Lyman Bushman, Cornelia Hughes Dayton, A. G. Roeber, and William M. Offutt, Jr. variously offer paths into the conceptual and material bases of early American legal cultures. Their essays chart the legal resources to which settler-inhabitants resorted in the course of their social, economic, and political practices; assess to what extent usages signified reliance on imported beliefs and doctrines and from what cultural contexts examples of appropriate practice were sought; debate whether legal texts and ideas were employed instrumentally or to furnish enduring maps or means of self-orientation and cultural reference; and investigate the influence of other systematic patterns of belief, notably religion, in the construction of legal meanings and practices.

These essays show us something of Europeans' reliance upon law to project European social and physical circumstance onto novel American environments, but they also underscore that settlers' orientations to law were not singular but plural, exposing further sources of the multiplicity that characterized early American legal culture. Take, for example, differences in the expression given Christianity in legal culture. As Dayton and Roeber both stress, Christianity was of major significance in influencing the form and culture and responsibilities of the early American state. Illustrating

---

28. Several of the essays combine to raise by collective implication a further theme equally worthy of debate, in their contrasting of intellectual and procedural formality with an implicitly popular tradition built upon rougher-hewn ideas or ideals of substantive justice—call it a jurispractice of results, *derecho vulgar*, communal ideal, or simply a different form of equity. A preference for substantive informality over formal rationality is not a new theme in the sociolegal history of any period. But it is well worth addressing here, particularly because some essays buttress the preference in detail, while others—that by Daniels, for example—instead find justice in formal procedure; and still others, for example Sturtz and Kolp and Snyder, expose degrees of ambiguity or flexibility in formal procedure sufficient to enable the facilitation of apparently just outcomes.

change over time, their individual papers point in distinct directions, however, in assessing the precise nature of Christianity's intersection with law.
Dayton shows us that godliness in seventeenth-century New Haven meant
godly government and an interventionist legal culture. By the eighteenth
century, and even more by the early nineteenth, Roeber suggests, the legal
culture of the North Atlantic region was exhibiting far greater ambivalence
over the question whether a compelling state interest in the achievement of a
properly Christian society should trump the values of privacy and commercial fungibility increasingly prominent in all social spheres—a prominence,
both authors show, that was clearly a departure from the seventeenth century's more communitarian impulse. William Offutt's longitudinal model of
colonial litigation, meanwhile, offers a different illustration of plurality.
Seeking a systematic measure of the role of courts in the transmission of
authoritative norms and, generally, of the stability of colonial legal regimes,
Offutt finds considerable variation in different social groups' participation
in litigation, suggesting substantial differentiation in rates of agreement on
and adherence to legal norms according to the nature of the dispute being
litigated and according to the litigants' social background. Offutt also suggests that measures of participation may allow legal historians to track the
contribution of legal institutions to value consensus in colonial society and
indeed to map the penetration of values across disparate populations. Not
the least significant aspect of his argument, in my view, lies in underlining
that consensus may be achieved as much by exclusion as by inclusion.[29]

  We have seen less exploration, thus far, of the legal history of early American colonization in its second aspect, namely the appropriation, occupation,
and transformation of place. But its centrality is clearly displayed here, in
James Muldoon's essentially institutionalist discussion of the legal basis of
English claims to possess and Richard Bushman's sociocultural perspective
on the legal implementation of possession, farm formation, and "improve-
ment" in Orange County, North Carolina. Substantively, one may of course
also draw here on the wide-ranging research of the Imperial school.[30] Elsewhere, the work of scholars like David Grayson Allen, William Cronon, and
Patricia Seed confirms the cultural importance of the physical transformation of places in understanding the impact of law. Cronon, though not a
legal historian, leaves us in little doubt of the instrumentality of legalities in
English attempts to colonize the landscape—to give it system, regularity,
purpose, familiarity. Claiming, using, granting, and owning the land all

  29. For related monographic work already published by several of these authors, see
Cornelia Hughes Dayton, *Women before the Bar: Gender, Law, and Society in Connecticut,
1639–1789* (Chapel Hill, N.C., 1995); A. G. Roeber, *Palatines, Liberty, and Property: German
Lutherans in Colonial British America* (Baltimore, 1993); Offutt, *Of "Good Laws" and
"Good Men": Law and Society in the Delaware Valley, 1680–1710* (Urbana, Ill., 1995).
  30. See Andrews, *Colonial Period of American History,* I–III.

invoked a legal culture that gave land distinct transactional identities for specific mundane outcomes. As Seed has shown, they also invoked basic cultural conceptions of legitimacy that authorized the act of colonizing itself. English enactments of authority overseas had cultural legitimacy in English eyes because they were grounded in familiar conceptions of lawful authority derived from rightful possession of place through usage. By facilitating usage, law became the means whereby the larger legitimacy of colonization was displayed.[31]

Precisely because the history of colonization is the history of a process and not of a period, it also offers a means to overcome the imputed irrelevance of colonial to national law. We have seen that, for Willard Hurst, what lent American law its originality and constituted its point of departure from the experience of the previous two centuries was its capacity to facilitate the realization of human creativity through freedom of choice. Hurst grounded this character in the demands of a particular socioeconomic context: westward movement. But there was nothing unique to westward movement seen from the perspective of colonization. Nineteenth-century themes—taking possession, transforming peoples and places—differed little from what had gone before. Take, for example, the lead participants in Hurst's emblematic Pike River Claimants Union. They had previously joined together in a Western Emigration Company to remove from Oswego County in New York to what would eventually be Kenosha County, Wisconsin, territory they described as a "new country." Their effort of removal itself gave them entitlement to reward, they said, because it was a transforming journey, conducted on behalf of civilization, into a void. "We have left our friends, deprived ourselves of the many blessings and privileges of society, have borne the expenses, and encountered the hardships of a perilous journey, advancing into a space beyond the bounds of civilization." Their civilizing mission was to transform that space, through labor, from open prairie hunted by Indians to enclosed agricultural smallholdings, the exclusive possession of which would be signified by the erection of "a house body, or frame of sufficient dimensions for a family to dwell in, or half an acre ploughed, or a piece enclosed with at least 100 rails." They considered their place of settlement fruitful, but perilous, "a state of nature" prone to "anarchy, confusion" often leading to "bitter quar-

31. David Grayson Allen, *In English Ways: The Movement of Societies and the Transferal of English Local Law and Custom to Massachusetts Bay in the Seventeenth Century* (Chapel Hill, N.C., 1981); William Cronon, *Changes in the Land: Indians, Colonists, and the Ecology of New England* (New York, 1983), 54–82; Seed, *Ceremonies of Possession*, 16–40. See also James T. Lemon, "Spatial Order: Households in Local Communities and Regions," in Greene and Pole, eds., *Colonial British America*, 86–122. See, generally, Merwick, *Possessing Albany*, 68–133, 188–219, 286–295; Carter, *Road to Botany Bay*; David Hackett Fischer, *Albion's Seed: Four British Folkways in America* (New York, 1989); Carol M. Rose, *Property and Persuasion: Essays on the History, Theory, and Rhetoric of Ownership* (Boulder, Colo., 1994), 1–162, 265–304.

rels, even bloodshed." In advance of government instrumentalities their "protective union" was constituted to resolve disputes among themselves and to guard their claims against others: from other migrants, "malignant . . . unprincipled, avaricious," the "mob"; from the "unfeeling speculator"; and also from Indians, whose presence was threatening legally, "as the country had not yet been surveyed," whose competing uses were threatening physically—they "fired the prairies . . . for hunting purposes" and endangered the settlers' farms—and whose proximity meant thieving and a "constant desire for whiskey" that was both repugnant and troublesome.[32]

The claimants' intimations of moral superiority masked their own illegality, for as Hurst acknowledges they were trespassers, "in defiance of law, ahead of official survey, without color of title," whose protective unions were, in their relationship to nonmember outsiders (like all colonizing governments), but assemblages of force. Hurst recognized something of their moral ambiguity but perceived—in their impatient determination to meet "the challenge of the unexploited continent" and their seizure of law and the state as instrumentalities to be put to work in that service—a historical inevitability that dwarfed, or at least muted, moral ambiguity. By enabling and then regulating transactional behavior, law and the state would assist in the generation of material benefits that would tame the mob and actually put the unfeeling speculator to good use. In what was a brilliant observation, Hurst wrote of contract's "capture of the land" as its "first and most dramatic victory." It could have been a more telling insight yet had he remarked on those from whom the land had been captured. As it was, he rested its significance entirely on the land's capture by one intra-European principle (market exchange) from another one (a rather vague "feudal type of tenure") rather than from its prior occupants.[33]

The larger point here, however, is that in none of these respects was law doing anything very different than it had done for the previous two hundred years. If social functionality is one's touchstone, then, as the essays in this volume suggest, early American law was no less functional in facilitating transformations of peoples and places than law in the nineteenth century. If the touchstone is structural resilience imparted by enduring institutions and ideologies, then, David Konig argues, early American law can make formative claims that counter quite concretely Pound's dismissals.

One may find this lack of difference hinted even in the "extrinsic and formal" history of the Imperial school. Though in no sense a social historian, Charles M. Andrews nevertheless planned to build a new history of the

32. Rev. Jason Lothrop, "A Sketch of the Early History of Kenosha County, Wisconsin, and of the Western Emigration Company," *Wisconsin Assembly Journal,* IX (Madison, Wis., 1856), app. 14, 450–479, esp. 461–464, 472–479. I am very grateful to Arthur McEvoy for making this material available to me.

33. Hurst, *Law and the Conditions of Freedom,* 3–32, esp. 5, 12.

eighteenth century on the back of his investigations of colonization. This history would explore the interior of colonial life—its "social, economic, educational, domestic, and religious, and in some respects political" dimensions. Responding, perhaps, to his critics, Andrews described his project as an inquiry that would reveal "trends and divergencies" from English patterns over the course of the eighteenth century indicative of "a progressive movement . . . an Americanizing process." He died before he began the task (it was to have been the fifth of a projected seven-volume history, only the first four of which were completed), so one cannot be sure how it might have turned out. But an extended essay that to some extent foreshadowed the entire work, *The Colonial Background of the American Revolution*, suggested that Andrews saw a crucial relationship between his external institutional history of the imperial relationship and the internal social history of the conditions for growth of Americanization in the eighteenth century. None of it cut much ice with the progressives, who preferred to see America as the creation of its founding and the antithesis of its European settlement. Nor, consequently, did Andrews have any impact on the Pound-Hurst "formative era" thesis. Yet, when Andrews wrote of the "fearless and aggressive individualism" of the eighteenth-century settlement frontier, of the spreading eighteenth-century belief in "every man's natural liberty to use his power to his own advantage," of the colonies' exemplification of "a law of general evolution of human society toward higher and broader forms of government and social relations," what he appeared to be perceiving was the birth of an Anglo-American civic modernism in the course of an eighteenth-century imperial and colonial expansion. It is of course precisely that modernity, "the forging of the nation-state, conceived as a moral community . . . its reliance on a culture of legality—built on rights of person and property, of constitutionality and contract—in imagining the body politic" and its invention of "the right-bearing, responsible, 'free' individual whose very condition of possibility was the nation-state itself," that Hurst celebrated. But in its most salient aspects civic modernity ("civilization") had become colonization's central gesture, and retort, to the non-European world long before the Reverend Jason Lothrop and his companions arrived on the Pike River and established its westernmost microcosm in his Claimants Union. This is what makes it impossible to segregate "colonial" from "national" or transoceanic expansion from pancontinental. The one is the condition for the existence of the other.[34]

34. Andrews's plans for his fifth volume are quoted in Leonard W. Labaree's foreword in Andrews, *Colonial Period of American History*, I, xi. See also Andrews, "On the Writing of Colonial History," *William and Mary Quarterly*, 3d Ser., I (1944), 33–38. On Andrews and the birth of civic modernism, see his *Colonial Background of the American Revolution: Four Essays in American Colonial History*, rev. ed. (New Haven, Conn., 1931), 180–203, esp. 196, 202, 208. On modernity, see Comaroff and Comaroff, *Dialectics of Modernity*, 365.

Fragments recovered from the Imperial school's largely forgotten legacy thus suggest an earlier attempt to draw attention to colonization's import for American legal history. We can usefully employ the Imperial school's example, and at least some of its substance, in carrying forward our own project. But obviously the Imperial school is a precursor only in general orientation, not in specific interpretation. For whether one takes one's history from Andrews or Hurst one will find little replication in either case of the negative implications of legality and modernity that exist in current historical discourses on other colonizations. In Malouf's Queensland, the importation of the sensibilities and practices associated with an Anglocentric rights-bearing individualism and the creation of legalities to sustain them are recognizably coercive intrusions upon a very distinct culture. In the American case, the history of contract's capture of land and of people is far more likely to be treated as a study in liberation.

As, in an important sense, it was (and, we should remember, in that sense it long had been—at least for some).[35] For, as I noted at the outset, we should not allow the dark side more than a temporary corrective ascendancy. We want to bring law's place in colonization up to speed in the American case, not accelerate it injudiciously into another reign of error. As the Comaroffs' analysis of nineteenth-century southern Africa reminds us, to look at the culture of legality in the context of colonization is certainly to discover blunt instrumentality but also to discover that discourses of rights and consent can underpin both transformation and resistance to transformation. They may even allow a measure of power to the colonized subject—once transformed.

Law was very much a two-edged sword. On one hand it was a devastating weapon of warfare, like no other in its capacity to annihilate and dispossess without being seen to do anything at all. And yet the appeal to rights was a means that, over the long run, came to be used by black South Africans in self-protection. Not always successfully, but not always in vain either. More to the point, it often seemed to be the *only* real means to hand, since it was part of the technology of rule on which

35. This theme has illustration in this volume, notably in the essays of Christine Daniels and Holly Brewer. As these essays show, contract's freedoms were not the invention of the nineteenth century; its liberating capacities may be detected substantially earlier in the context of particular forms of social relation. On this (in the realm of labor contracts) see also my own *Law, Labor, and Ideology* and "Exploring the Legal Culture of Work in Early British America," *American Bar Foundation Working Paper*, no. 9505 (Chicago, 1996). As I try to indicate in these works, we should not regard freedom as a necessary or inevitable accompaniment of contract as a legal form, but rather as the distinctly conditional product of the struggles for which law provides a useful and influential site. For work particularly expressive of the ambiguities of contract freedom in social and cultural context, see Amy Stanley, *From Bondage to Contract: Wage Labor, Marriage, and the Market in the Age of Slave Emancipation* (New York, 1998).

rested the inequalities and disablements from which they suffered. This is why the language of the law is reducible neither to a brute weapon of control nor simply to an instrument of resistance. The inherently contradictory character of the colonial discourse of rights, the multiplicity of its registers and the forms of consciousness to which it gave rise, ensured that it would be engaged, on all sides, in the effort to forge viable moral communities, identities, modes of being-in-the-world. It still is. Everywhere.[36]

Those who would embark on the writing of legal history for early America must of course understand early America's many legalities on their own terms. But they are also obligated to offer some explanation why anyone now should care. No historian would think it appropriate to approach the history of law, or of any phenomenon, as if its significance lay only in the extent to which it could be shown to connect with what was to come after, let alone to the present. To treat the past as if it were wholly separate unto itself, however, is not simply to risk obscurity but to covet it. Legal historians have now demonstrated that there exists enormous scholarly opportunity in opening up for examination the rich variety of innovation and transformation in social practice and daily occurrence that characterized the legal cultures of seventeenth- and eighteenth-century settlement. As we pursue that history, however, let us not forget that early American legal history can also tell us much about what was to follow: the continuously unfolding colonial encounter that, throughout the nineteenth century, as it opened possibilities on its European flank, most forcefully closed them on others. In my view, in exploring the great continuity of European colonization of America we will discover how to establish the significance of early American legal history, not merely significance for itself but for American history as a whole. We will discover, not, as Hurst contended, that early American law was preliberal and hence uninteresting, nor, as later scholarship has sometimes implied, that it was a modest precursor of a liberalism to come, but instead that it was an essential condition of the unfolding nationalism, the manifest destiny, that in the later nineteenth century climaxed the colonial encounter begun more than three hundred years before.[37]

To begin to understand what was bequeathed to the nineteenth century,

36. Comaroff and Comaroff, *Dialectics of Modernity,* 404, vol. II of *Of Revelation and Revolution.* It is also appropriate to note here that David Malouf's moving conclusion to *Remembering Babylon* (at 200) is above all about reconciliation: "The vast continent appears, in touch now with its other life."

37. See generally Anders Stephanson, *Manifest Destiny: American Expansionism and the Empire of Right* (New York, 1995); Eric Hinderaker, *Elusive Empires: Constructing Colonialism in the Ohio Valley, 1673–1800* (New York, 1997).

our legal history—no less than any other genre of early American history—must be focused by the essence of what America was. It was a colonized space upon which Europeans, notably (in our case) the English, had planted themselves, transforming both it and themselves. In examining their encounter, the essential lesson to be learned, for the legal historian, is that the social world is fundamentally a human construct and that law furnishes one of the most powerful technologies of construction. In the early American case, as in other colonial cases, one finds further that the act of construction is simultaneously one of destruction, notably the destruction of strangeness—essential to making new worlds, in David Malouf's words, "a bit like home."[38]

In the internal legal history of the settler cultures, the extent to which early American law was or was not "a bit like home" and how that changed over time, and when, is of the first importance. But let us not forget what Malouf brings metaphorically to our attention, that rendering early America even a bit like home entailed the ending of what it had been before, the destruction of its awful strangeness so that Europeans could live in it.

In the American case the destruction of strangeness was so successful that ultimately it made possible the imagining of a new unitary American legality that, in intellectual conception at least, could be pancontinental. Charting and idealizing the subsequent progress of that single legal order so dominated the agenda of the academic enterprise of American legal history that for many years, as Stanley Katz noted, it diverted attention almost completely from the very period with which we are now concerned. But the fragmentation of the liberal model in modern legal history, as in other fields of American history, has created an opening. Collections like this, in pushing through it, may demonstrate that there is more to find beyond. Here is where we will rediscover the non-European world that law helped subsequently to remake. We will discover, too, the multiplicity of the European worlds that law helped to create. We will discover, as the Comaroffs suggest, that those worlds exhibited law's instrumentalities and its resistances, and in both we will discover law's murkiness and its ambiguities. In all this, we will discover that modern Americans' "sense that their society is uniquely law-bound" is indeed both historically justified and historically grounded, but in ways even more singular—and more binding—than the sentiment commonly has conveyed.

38. As Michael T. Ryan observes so acutely, "The assimilation of the new worlds . . . involved their domestication." See "Assimilating New Worlds in the Sixteenth and Seventeenth Centuries," *Comparative Studies in Society and History,* XXIII (1981), 523.

Atlantic Crossings

AMERICAN LEGAL HISTORIANS have long treated the relationship between early-modern English law and early American law as
their point of orientation for the first two centuries of American
history—a dominating backdrop that both locates their subject
in a wider Atlantic world and serves as a fundamental point of departure for
much of what they study on the provincial mainland stage. Methodologically, whether the preferred trope is one of formal doctrinal receptions, of a
more pragmatic "carryover and adaptation" of learned traditions, of a mi-
metic impulse redolent of cultural dependency, or of the obverse—rude self-
sufficiency born of self-imposed isolation— exploration of law's Atlantic
crossings has always bulked large in the literature of early American legal
history. Conceptually, through its comparative aspect, the perspective has
long served as a valuable means of disciplining the field's conclusions.

Given this heritage, it is appropriate to begin this collection with four
essays each of which in its own fashion takes very seriously the transatlantic
context of early American law but also explores that context in new ways,
collectively revealing the ideological and conceptual multiplicity at the roots
of the legal culture of early America.

In the first of the essays in Part I, James Muldoon shows how debates over
legalities frame the very act of colonization. Muldoon notes that Anglo-
colonial understandings of the basis for legitimate occupation of North
American territories were first articulated at length during the constitutional
crisis that heralded American independence, but he situates those understandings in a much older, self-justifying, Catholic expansionist tradition
that founded claims of colonial legitimacy in papal grants authorized by
medieval canon law. Muldoon demonstrates the intimate historical connections—conceptual and linguistic—that existed between canon law and
common-law discourses of English colonization. He demonstrates how, at
the moment of colonial independence, both exerted a profound influence
on attempts to render legitimate the American state emerging from colonial
settlement.

In the second essay, Mary Sarah Bilder offers a similar emphasis on the
diversity of influences manifested in early American legal culture. By retrac-

ing the routes followed by procedures as familiar to modern audiences as the appeal, she shows how one may expose quite unexpected points of conceptual and institutional provenance—in canon and civil law, not common law, in the internal workings of corporations and franchises, not of the monarch's courts. Her essay describes the existence in New England of a "culture of appeal," comprising a set of perspectives and attendant legal meanings broadly related to matters of equity and authority and distinct both in origin and significance from the common-law review procedure of the writ of error, to which the idea of appeal has often been attributed. Bilder traces the history and expression of appeal within Roman law, ecclesiastical law, and English history, its transmission to New England via the corporate jurisdictional practices of English trading companies, and its manifestation in colonial political and legal culture. The existence of this broad culture of appeal, she argues, suggests an orientation among New England colonists less to English common law than to a larger transatlantic western European legal culture. That is, like Muldoon's discoveries, Bilder's point up both the plurality of formative influences on early American law and its broad, Atlantic (rather than specifically English) cultural orientation.

The third and fourth essays in this section focus on the dynamics of specifically Anglo-American legal influence. The third essay, by David Barry Gaspar, inquires into the relative importance of the several factors steering the evolution of Jamaica's statutory police laws of slavery in the second half of the seventeenth century—precedents culled from Barbados, precedents from England, and the particularities of Jamaica's independent development. Gaspar's work helps correct a common tendency to assume that the law of slavery was in some sense different from other Anglo-American law, sui generis and locally determined rather than transatlantic in meaning. Regional and local contexts are of course important: Gaspar demonstrates the early influence of models borrowed from elsewhere in the region (that is, from Barbados), and he indicates how, as the colony developed and the slave population increased, its slave laws began to respond to specifically Jamaican circumstances in developing a police response to fugitive and rebellious slaves. But he also shows that English law provided for lessons in the control of rebels and of plantation subordinates, and the significance of the turn to English example is heightened by evidence of the more general interest in Jamaica in developing an English legal culture for the colony. In this light the notion that English law somehow does not accommodate slavery looks somewhat formalistic; slave law's purely local invention seems less tenable. Gaspar shows us that English law had a part in the construction of plantation slavery in English colonies.

If Gaspar's essay suggests that the segregation of slavery from English law depends on too formalistic an understanding both of English law and slavery, the last essay in this section, by David Thomas Konig, demonstrates that law's formalism has rich and meaningful and controversial purpose. Konig's careful investigation of the concept of the legal fiction tells us that even within familiar and ostensibly singular strands of common-law reception there lie major complexities. Tracing the genealogy of an apparently arcane technical concept leads one in this case to distinctly nonarcane purposes—the creation of means to manage conflicts—and on to yet deeper meanings, notably those inherent in the competition between adjudication and legislation, alternative locales of constitutive authority that promised radically different conceptions of lawmaking, and hence radically different sources of legitimacy for rules of law in American life. Law, in Konig's argument, is an enduring structure in American society, formed in the unceasing rivalry between judge-made law and statute. Legal fictions epitomize the judicial power to intervene: extrapolation from one set of circumstances extends one's reach to others. To Thomas Jefferson, however, fictions epitomized arbitrariness—a "law craft" that undermined notions of legality based on the sovereignty of the people. Through their authority to create or deny fictions, judges established themselves in the position of gatekeepers of American legality. Contrasting popular will to juridical supremacy, Jefferson inaugurated the long tradition of legislative counterpoint to the authority of adjudication in American jurisprudential debate.

Discovery, Grant, Charter, Conquest, or Purchase

John Adams on the Legal Basis for English Possession of North America

O NE OF THE MOST striking aspects of the Spanish conquest of the Americas is the enormous number of treatises that Spanish intellectuals generated in the debate about the legitimacy of the conquest. It is, of course, easy to reject this debate as little more than pious hypocrisy. But doubting the sincerity of the Spanish and questioning the practical value of the debate among intellectuals is too facile, too simple a response. For reasons that are not fully sorted out, Spanish philosophers, theologians, lawyers, and bureaucrats discussed the issue of conquest seriously, at great length, and in enormous detail. There has never been a fuller consideration of the right, even the responsibility, of one society to intervene in the internal affairs of another than the Spanish writers of the sixteenth and seventeenth centuries provided.[1]

In contrast to the Spanish world, English occupation of North America did not generate much of a debate about its legitimacy. But the English were not simply more honest in dealing with naked aggression. Although no scholarly debate inspired their efforts to rationalize and legitimize their conquests, the English still made use of much of the same rhetoric as the Spanish. Even though the English intellectuals did not compose treatises on the legitimacy of the conquest and generate a debate like the one that occupied dozens of Spanish intellectuals over two centuries, the literature of English overseas expansion echoed some of the concerns found in the Spanish literature. Official documents such as the charters of Virginia and Massachusetts

I wish to thank Kevin Butterfield for his careful editing of the text and for his suggestions for improving it.

1. One reason that has been suggested for the debate is that at the time of the discoveries Spanish universities were undergoing significant growth, the period of the Second Scholasticism. The discovery of the New World provided the leading intellectuals with a moral and legal issue of enormous significance upon which they could focus their energies. See James Muldoon, *The Americas in the Spanish World Order: The Justification for Conquest in the Seventeenth Century* (Philadelphia, 1994), 4–5. The fundamental work on the Spanish debate is Lewis Hanke, *The Spanish Struggle for Justice in the Conquest of America* (Philadelphia, 1949).

and promotional literature encouraging the English to undertake colonization often contained concepts and even language drawn from the texts that
formed the core of the Spanish debate about the legitimacy of conquest.
The handful of English materials relating to the legitimacy of possession
of North America did not stir up an extensive debate about the conquest,
because there were no vociferous critics of English colonization.[2] There was
no English Las Casas, for example, to arouse spirited defenses of English
colonial policies and practices. The English can easily appear to have taken
for granted the legitimacy of what they were doing. English intellectuals did
utilize Spanish arguments about the legitimacy of conquest, but the limited
use of these ideas might appear to be little more than the borrowing of some
pious rhetoric to clothe predatory claims to the Americas. One might conclude that English Protestant intellectuals would have no use for the arguments that Spanish Catholics employed. But, although the writings of Spanish philosophers and theologians who produced much of the literature
about the legitimacy of the conquest were rejected, the medieval legal tradition was not. As Garrett Mattingly pointed out many years ago, it was the
canon lawyers of the twelfth and thirteenth centuries who had first begun to
examine the nature of Christian relations with infidels, and it was through
the legal tradition Catholics and Protestants shared that these ideas continued to develop.[3]

During the seventeenth and eighteenth centuries lawyers came to play an
ever-increasing role in the development of theories about the nature of
international relations. This was the start of the great age of international-
law thought, the beginning of the modern attempt to create a legal regime
that would govern the relations among the emerging nation-states of Europe
and between European states and non-European societies. Clearly it was the
legally trained who played the central role in shaping the terms of political
discourse in the early modern world as it concerned international relations,
not theologians or philosophers.[4]

2. Chester E. Eisinger, "The Puritans' Justification for Taking the Land," Essex Institute,
Historical Collections, LXXIV (1948), 131–143; Wilcomb E. Washburn, "The Moral and
Legal Justifications for Dispossessing the Indians," in James Morton Smith, ed., Seventeenth Century America: Essays in Colonial History (Chapel Hill, N.C., 1959), 15–32; John T.
Juricek, "English Territorial Claims in North America under Elizabeth and the Early
Stuarts," Terrae incognitae, VII (1975), 7–22; Robert A. Williams, Jr., The American Indian
in Western Legal Thought: The Discourses of Conquest (New York, 1990), 121–192.
3. Garrett Mattingly, Renaissance Diplomacy (Boston, 1955), 284. For a concrete example
of the use of legal materials within a philosophical context, specifically Francisco de
Vitoria's De indis, see James Muldoon, "A Canonistic Contribution to the Formation of
International Law," Jurist, XXVIII (1968), 265–279.
4. James Muldoon, "The Contribution of the Medieval Canon Lawyers to the Formation of International Law," Traditio, XXVIII (1972), 483–497. See also Brian Tierney,
"Aristotle and the American Indians—Again," Cristianesimo nella storia, XII (1991), 295–

It should come as no surprise that when the question of the legitimacy of English possession of North America did arise it was lawyers who raised it and debated it—although not in the sixteenth and early seventeenth centuries when colonization was beginning, but on the eve of American Independence. In the months leading up to the Revolution, John Adams, lawyer, Revolutionary, and future president, became embroiled in polemical combat about English policy toward the colonies that caused him to consider the legal basis for English occupation and possession of parts of North America, briefly providing a faint Anglophone echo of earlier Spanish disquisitions.

The immediate cause of Adams's interest in the basis of English possession of North America was the publication of a series of seventeen letters in the *Massachusetts Gazette* between December 1774 and April 1775. The author of these letters, known to contemporaries only as Massachusettensis (in reality Adams's old friend and fellow lawyer Daniel Leonard), presented a forceful defense of the English claim to parliamentary jurisdiction over the North American colonies. Writing as Novanglus, Adams responded to deny such jurisdiction.

At the heart of the debate about the extent of Parliament's jurisdiction was the question of the nature of British government. Was there a single political or constitutional unit known as the British Empire coextensive with the territories that the king of England ruled in conjunction with his Parliament, or were there a number of territories ruled by the king, not all of which were subject to Parliament's jurisdiction? If there were a unitary empire, then the American colonies were subject to Parliament's authority. If there were no such empire, then the Americans could legitimately claim to be subject to the king but not to Parliament, whose jurisdiction was limited to the kingdom of England unless specifically extended to other lands by agreement or statute.

Massachusettensis had begun his series of essays with a flat statement of the unitary nature of the British Empire and the consequent subordination of the American colonies to Parliament's jurisdiction.

> However closely we may hug ourselves in the opinion, that the parliament has no right to tax or legislate for us, the people of England hold the contrary opinion as firmly. They tell us we are a part of the British empire; that every state, from the nature of government, must have a supreme, uncontrolable power, co-extensive with the empire itself; and that power is vested in parliament.[5]

322; Donald R. Kelley, "Law," in J. H. Burns and Mark Goldie, eds., *The Cambridge History of Political Thought, 1450–1700* (Cambridge, 1991), 66–94, esp. 71–72.

5. John Adams and Jonathan Sewall [Daniel Leonard], *Novanglus, and Massachusetten-*

There followed a much more detailed analysis of the first charter of the Massachusetts Bay Colony. Leonard saw no need for any act or statute formally incorporating American settlements into the British Empire or bringing them under the jurisdiction of the English king and Parliament. All one had to do to demonstrate the existence of Massachusetts within the British Empire was to examine the original charter of that colony.

> Our charter, like all other American charters, are under the great seal of England; the grants are made by the king, for his heirs and *successors*. . . . It is apparent the king acted in his royal capacity, as king of England, which necessarily supposes the territory granted, to be a part of the English dominions, holden of the crown of England.

This led him to draw what he considered the logical conclusion about the relationship of the colonists to England: "For if we are not annexed to the crown, we are aliens, and no charter, grant, or other act of the crown can naturalize us or entitle us to the liberties and immunities of Englishmen."[6]

Adams began to publish his response in the Novanglus letters six weeks after the first of Leonard's essays had appeared. In the third letter, Adams raised what he saw as the fundamental issue involved. To the argument that the British North American colonies were part of the British Empire, Adams replied:

> The terms "British Empire" are not the language of the common law, but the language of newspapers and political pamphlets; . . . the dominions of the king of Great Britain have no power coextensive with them. I would ask, by what law the parliament has authority over America? By the law of God, in the Old and New Testament, it has none; by the law of nature and nations, it has none; by the common law of England, it has none, for the common law, and the authority of parliament founded on it, never extended beyond the four seas; by statute law it has none, for no statute was made before the settlement of the colonies for this purpose.

In effect, Adams was arguing that there was no legal or historical basis for the claim that the Parliament sitting in London possessed the right to legislate for any place outside Great Britain, that is, to act as an imperial legislature.[7]

---

sis; or, Political Essays Published in the Years 1774 to 1775 (1819; rpt., New York, 1968), 143. The citations to Massachusettensis are from this edition. The citations to Novanglus are from Charles Francis Adams, ed., *The Works of John Adams,* 10 vols. (Boston, 1850–1856). As late as the 1819 edition of these letters Adams believed that Jonathan Sewall, a friend and fellow lawyer, had written as Massachusettensis. In 1821, however, he learned that another Boston lawyer and old friend, Daniel Leonard, was in fact the author (Adams, ed., *Works of John Adams,* IV, 5–10, esp. 10 n. 1).

6. Adams and Sewall [Leonard], *Novanglus, and Massachusettensis,* 174, 177.

7. Adams, ed., *Works of John Adams,* IV, 37.

If Adams was correct in denying the existence of the British Empire as a legal reality, what then was the nature of the relationship of the colonies to England? For this, Adams, like Leonard, turned to the historical record. Analyzing the charters of Virginia and Massachusetts, Adams concluded that these colonies "had precisely the same sense of the authority of parliament, namely,—that it had none at all." The colonists received their charters from the king of England, not Parliament, and so were not subject to Parliament's jurisdiction except "by our own express consent." The only area in which the colonists had given this express consent was the Navigation Acts. The result, according to Adams:

> We are a part of the British dominions, that is, of the King of Great Britain, and it is our interest and duty to continue so. It is equally our interest and duty to continue subject to the authority of parliament, in the regulation of our trade, as long as she shall leave us to govern our internal policy, and to give and grant our own money, and no longer.[8]

Adams also argued that, as there was no legal entity known as the British Empire, so too there was no consideration of colonies in English common law. "There was no provision made in this law for governing colonies beyond the Atlantic, or beyond the four seas, by authority of parliament; no, nor for the king to grant charters to subjects to settle in foreign countries."[9]

The only action that an English king could take regarding potential colonies was to issue a writ of *ne exeat regno,* forbidding those wishing to leave his kingdom from doing so. This common-law writ punished those who violated it by the seizure of any lands the individuals had left behind in England and by the imposition of fines if they ever returned. If the king did not protest the act of leaving, then the potential colonists took with them when they left England "all the rights of nature." Furthermore, each colonist retained the "allegiance [that] bound him to the king, and entitled him to protection."[10]

In Adams's opinion, the colonists came to the New World with the rights of Englishmen and still offering allegiance to the king of England. They could erect any form of government they chose, and, as long as they did not bear arms against the king, they retained those rights and remained entitled to his protection. On the other hand, if they did nothing to maintain their relationship with England, "their children would not have been born within the king's allegiance, would not have been natural subjects, and consequently not entitled to protection, or bound to the king." To Leonard's claim

---

8. Adams's narrow, legalistic definition of the term "empire" reflects the fact that the term had a variety of meanings in the eighteenth century. His definition was as narrow as Leonard's was expansive. See Adams, ed., *Works of John Adams,* IV, 112–113, 120–121.

9. Ibid., IV, 121.

10. Ibid., IV, 122.

that the American colonies were annexed to the realm of England and so were subject to laws passed by the English Parliament, Adams responded:

But will any man soberly contend, that America was ever annexed to the realm? to what realm? When New England was settled, there was a realm of England, a realm of Scotland, and a realm of Ireland. To which of these three realms was New England annexed? To the realm of England, it will be said. But by what law? No territory could be annexed to the realm of England but by an act of parliament. Acts of parliament have been passed to annex Wales . . . but none ever passed to annex America.[11]

Having demonstrated to his own satisfaction that the English Parliament possessed no jurisdiction over North America, Adams moved to consider Leonard's argument that, if the Americans were not subject to Parliament, they were at the mercy of the king's absolute power. According to Adams, just as there was no basis upon which Parliament could construct a claim to jurisdiction over North America, there was no basis on which the king of England could claim possession of North America on his own authority either. The claim that the discovery of North America by English sailors was a basis for English claims to possession was, in Adams's opinion, no basis at all. "Discovery . . . could give no title to the English king, by common law, or by the law of nature, to the lands, tenements, and hereditaments of the native Indians here." The ancestors of the eighteenth-century inhabitants of Massachusetts "were sensible" of the right of the native Indians to the ownership of their lands, so the first English settlers "honestly purchased their lands of the natives." In Adams's argument, the charters that authorized the settlement of the colonists did not transfer ownership of Indian lands to the colonists. Such lands could be acquired legitimately only by purchase. Adams admitted that, if an English king "had sent an army here to conquer King Massachusetts, and it had succeeded, he would have been sovereign lord of the land here." But, as no English king had done so, there was no basis for an English claim to North America based on feudal law.[12]

Also to be rejected, Adams argued, were claims derived from the papal

11. Ibid., IV, 122–123. Unlike Scotland in 1707 and Ireland in 1800, Wales had been annexed to England by means of several statutes, not by an Act of Union. See John Davies, *A History of Wales* (London, 1993), 231–235. The relevant documents are in C. H. Williams, ed., *English Historical Documents, 1485–1558* (New York, 1967), vol. V of David C. Douglas, ed., *English Historical Documents,* 554–562.

12. Adams and Sewall [Leonard], *Novanglus, and Massachusettensis,* 170–171; Adams, ed., *Works of John Adams,* IV, 124–125. Adams derived his notion of feudalism from William Robertson, *The History of Scotland . . . ,* 3 vols. (1759; rpt., London, 1809), I, 216. Adams's definition of feudalism stressed possession by conquest. He discussed feudalism at greater length in his *Dissertation on the Canon and the Feudal Law* (1765), in Adams, ed., *Works of John Adams,* III, 447–464.

pretension to "a sovereign propriety in, as well as authority over, the whole earth," a claim rooted in medieval canon law doctrines that asserted "a right to all the countries and possessions of heathens and infidels." When Henry VIII had taken upon himself the powers of the papacy by asserting his claim to headship of the church in England, Adams noted, "he and his courtiers seemed to think that all the rights of the holy see were transferred to him." All this meant, however, was that English defenders of royal power were perpetuating "the most impertinent and fantastical ideas that ever got into a human pericranium, namely,—that, as feudal sovereign and supreme head of the church together, a king of England had a right to all the land his subjects could find, not possessed by any Christian state or prince, though possessed by heathen or infidel nations."[13] Indeed, apparently such fantastic ideas had "deluded the nation about the time of the settlement of the colonies," but not even these ideas, if accepted, "gave or inferred any right in parliament, over the new countries conquered or discovered." In Adams's opinion, the only role that the kings of England had played was to authorize the migration of their subjects to distant lands. Subsequently, as a result of this desire to associate themselves freely with the king, these adventurous Englishmen had made a compact with him, accepting his overlordship in return for his protection. In sum, then, according to Adams, "it follows from thence" that George III is also "King of Massachusetts, King of Rhode Island, King of Connecticut, etc."[14]

Adams's argument is interesting because it turned attention to the ultimate basis upon which English possession of North America rested. In that sense, Adams provided in a brief compass the kind of debate in which Spanish intellectuals had engaged two centuries earlier.

The starting point for any discussion of the legitimacy of English possession of North America must be the charters that English kings granted to potential colonizers in the sixteenth and seventeenth centuries. As Adams recognized, these charters contained claims rooted in papal theories of European relations with non-European peoples. In fact, the language that English monarchs used in the charters they granted to the American colonists was derived from Pope Alexander VI's *Inter caetera* (1493), the legal basis for Spanish possession of the Americas (except Brazil). Underlying this bull was a body of legal theory stretching back to the middle of the thir-

13. Adams, ed., *Works of John Adams*, IV, 125. Adams was rejecting arguments about the legality of the conquest of infidel nations by Christians that went back to the thirteenth century. In fact, the papacy did not make the claims that Adams mentioned here, but some extreme defenders of papal power did (James Muldoon, *Popes, Lawyers, and Infidels: The Christian Church and the Non-Christian World, 1250–1550* [Philadelphia, 1979], 10–12, 16–17). On the king's ecclesiastical powers, see John R. H. Moorman, *A History of the Church in England* (New York, 1954), 178–179.

14. Adams, ed., *Works of John Adams*, IV, 114, 125.

teenth century. The language of *Inter caetera* articulated in brief, in a kind of shorthand, the nature of Christian relations with non-Christian societies. In the case of the Americas, what this shorthand stated was that the peoples of the Americas whom the Spanish had encountered possessed the right to govern themselves and to own property, rights of which the Spanish could not on their own authority legitimately deprive them. On the other hand, because all mankind is subject to the pope in spiritual matters and he is responsible for the salvation of all mankind, the pope may authorize Christian rulers to enter the lands of infidels, even those who pose no direct military threat to Christians, in order to ensure that missionaries can preach there in safety. Only the pope has this authority, as Ferdinand and Isabella recognized when they requested *Inter caetera*.[15]

Adams was aware that the English monarchs and the draftsmen who drew up their charters used the language of *Inter caetera* in the charters granted to the American colonists. The draftsmen did this, not because they simply copied Alexander VI's letter mindlessly, but because the English monarchs deliberately chose to justify their claims to possession of North America in these terms and because the language contained ideas that the rulers wished to employ in the creation of their overseas domains. The language of the papal documents was, so to speak, the standard language of European overseas expansion.[16]

Three clauses of *Inter caetera* relate directly to the charters of the British colonies in North America. The first concerned the regions that the Spanish monarchs claimed on the basis of Columbus's first voyage. The second concerned the rationale that the pope used to justify the grant of the Americas to Ferdinand and Isabella. The third concerned the monopoly of trade with the newly discovered lands that the pope granted to the Castilians and to the Portuguese.

With *Inter caetera*, Alexander VI granted to Ferdinand and Isabella "all and singular the aforesaid countries and islands thus unknown and hitherto discovered by your envoys and to be discovered hereafter, provided however they at no time have been in the actual temporal possession of any Christian

15. For an analysis of this bull, see James Muldoon, "Papal Responsibility for the Infidel: Another Look at Alexander VI's *Inter Caetera*," *Catholic Historical Review*, LXIV (1978), 168–184.

16. Legal scholars now point to a *ius commune*, a common law employed throughout Europe as a result of the medieval revival of the Roman legal tradition. Roman legal concepts affected the development of all medieval and early modern legal systems, even in England where lawyers of the common law rejected it but where it was still found in equity and admiralty courts. See R. C. van Caenegem, *An Historical Introduction to Private Law*, trans. D. E. L. Johnston (Cambridge, 1992), 45–85, esp. 70–71; Manlio Bellomo, *The Common Legal Past of Europe, 1000–1800*, trans. Lydia G. Cochrane (Washington, D.C., 1995).

owner, together with all their dominions, cities, camps, places, and villages, and all rights, jurisdictions, and appurtenances of the same."[17] Like the rest of Alexander's bull, this phrase had a long history. For several centuries, the papacy had been authorizing European Christian rulers to occupy various lands for reasons associated with the church's spiritual mission. Indeed, there were more than one hundred papal bulls dealing with Portuguese and Castilian exploration and colonization in the Atlantic Ocean, beginning in 1420.[18] In these letters, various popes granted to the Portuguese and, subsequently, to the Castilians as well the right to occupy any lands they encountered. The assumption of these letters was that such lands would be occupied by enemies of the true faith. For example, in the bull *Romanus pontifex* (1455), Nicholas V granted to the Portuguese the right to explore and conquer lands and islands found in the Atlantic along the west coast of Africa. By the terms of the bull, the Portuguese were authorized

> to invade, search out, capture, vanquish, and subdue all Saracens and pagans whatsoever, and other enemies of Christ wheresoever placed, and the kingdoms, dukedoms, principalities, dominions, possessions, and all moveable and immovable goods whatsoever held and possessed by them and to reduce their persons to perpetual slavery . . . in order that King Alfonso himself and his successors and the infante may be able the more zealously to pursue and may pursue this most pious and noble work . . . since the salvation of souls, increase of the faith, and overthrow of its enemies may be procured thereby.

The basis for Portuguese possession of these lands was the assumption that these lands were occupied by enemies of the Christian faith who posed a direct military threat to Christians. Thus, the occupation of these lands was an exercise of legitimate force under the terms of the theory of the just war. There was no need to add any clause exempting lands already possessed by Christian rulers from the terms of this bull because there was no reason to assume that there were any such lands in the regions involved.[19]

17. Francis Gardiner Davenport, ed., *European Treaties bearing on the History of the United States and Its Dependencies*, 4 vols. (Washington, D.C., 1917–1937; rpt., Gloucester, Mass., 1967), I, 62. This volume contains the two *Inter caetera* bulls as well as the related bull *Eximiae devotionis* and some of the earlier bulls on overseas expansion.

18. Charles Martial de Witte, "Les bulles pontificales et l'expansion portugaise au XVe siècle," *Revue d'histoire ecclesiastique*, XLVIII (1953), 683–718, XLIX (1954), 438–461, LI (1956), 413–453, 809–836, LIII (1958), 5–46, 443–471. For the argument that the language can be traced back to the mid-eighth century, see Luis Weckmann, *Las bulas alejandrinas de 1493 y la teoriá del Papado medieval* (Mexico, 1949).

19. Davenport, ed., *European Treaties*, I, 23. The fundamental book on the medieval theory of the just war is Frederick H. Russell, *The Just War in the Middle Ages* (Cambridge, 1975). For a discussion of papal letters dealing with Portuguese and Castilian conquests in the Atlantic, see Muldoon, *Popes, Lawyers, and Infidels*, 88–91, 103–104, 119–131, 133–136.

Furthermore, to support the work of defeating the enemies of the faith and converting the native peoples, the pope granted the Portuguese a monopoly of trade with these regions. Without "payment of a certain tribute and with an express license previously obtained from the said [that is, Portuguese] king or infante, [no one] should presume to sail to the said provinces or to trade in their ports or to fish in the sea." Thus, the work of discovery, the defense of Christendom, the spiritual work of missionaries, and the monopoly of trade fitted together neatly, at least in the mind of the pope and the Portuguese monarchs.[20]

By 1481, however, when Pope Sixtus IV issued the bull *Aeterni patris* to confirm previous letters authorizing a Portuguese monopoly of exploration and colonization in the Atlantic, it had become necessary to add a clause exempting some lands from the Portuguese monopoly. The reason was that the Castilians had acquired the Canary Islands, and by the terms of the Treaty of Alcaçovas (1479) the Portuguese had agreed not to contest that fact. The result was that, when Sixtus IV confirmed the Portuguese monopoly of the Atlantic regions, his bull included a clause exempting the Castilian-held Canary Islands from the grant.[21]

The recognition of Castilian possession of the Canary Islands was one root of the subsequent clause in *Inter caetera* that exempted lands already possessed by Christian rulers from occupation by the Castilians or the Portuguese. This was not, however, the only reason that Alexander VI's bull contained that clause. Columbus had, after all, claimed to be seeking a direct water route to Asia. He and other knowledgeable Europeans took for granted that Christian peoples existed in Asia. The pope was only underscoring the fact that, if such Christians did exist, any kingdoms they possessed would not be the object of European expansion. This did not, of course, mean that such kingdoms, their rulers, and their people were not subject to papal spiritual jurisdiction. What it did mean was that papal jurisdiction over non-Christians and their lands was of a different order from papal jurisdiction over Christians.[22]

These fifteenth-century bulls also explained that the grant of jurisdiction over the lands and peoples in the regions indicated was rooted in the papal responsibility for the salvation of all mankind and for the physical security of Christian society. For example, in *Romanus pontifex*, Nicholas V stated that the Portuguese had a responsibility not only for restraining "the savage excesses of the Saracens and of other infidels, enemies of the Christian name, but also for the defense and increase of the faith [and to] vanquish them and

---

20. Davenport, ed., *European Treaties*, I, 22.
21. Ibid., 44, 53.
22. J. R. S. Phillips, *The Medieval Expansion of Europe* (Oxford, 1988), 251.

their kingdoms and habitations." Already, as a consequence of the Portuguese efforts, "many inhabitants or dwellers in divers islands situated in the said sea, coming to the knowledge of the true God, have received holy baptism, to the praise and glory of God, the salvation of the souls of many, the propagation also of the orthodox faith, and the increase of divine worship."[23]

In *Inter caetera*, the link between exploration and conquest on the one hand and the conversion of the peoples whom the Europeans encountered on the other was even more emphatically stated. The pope pointed out in the opening section of the bull:

> We have indeed learned that you [Ferdinand and Isabella] . . . for a long time had intended to seek out and discover certain lands and islands remote and unknown and not hitherto discovered by others, to the end that you might bring to the worship of our Redeemer and profession of the Catholic faith their residents and inhabitants.

It should be noted, however, that Columbus's original agreement with the Spanish monarchs made no mention of converting the peoples he encountered, and no missionary accompanied him on his first voyage. What he presumably intended was to establish a trading post that would enable Castile to participate in existing Asian trade routes. When he reached islands whose inhabitants were clearly not part of the Asian trade network and who themselves did not engage in trade, the legal basis on which he had expected to legitimize his activities was useless. Subsequently, Ferdinand and Isabella requested *Inter caetera* in order to obtain moral justification for occupying the lands that Columbus had found. The only way in which they could legitimately claim possession of the Americas now was to assert their desire to ensure the conversion of this newly encountered people to Christianity. The subsequent Spanish claim to possession of the Americas and to a monopoly of trade there always had as its legal base Alexander VI's grant of these lands to Ferdinand and Isabella in 1493. In effect, papal bulls provided the Spanish with legal title to the Americas.[24]

When we turn to the English in the New World, we find royal charters that parallel the papal bulls. Where the pope had granted authorization for exploration and conquest, the English monarchs now provided the sanction. In doing this, English monarchs were asserting jurisdiction derived from their role as Supreme Head of the Church of England. The various acts that separated the Anglican Church from the jurisdiction of the pope transferred to the king of England responsibility for administering the church.

23. Davenport, ed., *European Treaties*, I, 21.
24. Ibid., 61; James Muldoon, "Columbus's First Voyage and the Medieval Legal Tradition," *Medievalia et humanistica*, N.S., no. 19 (1993), 11–26.

Just as Henry VIII had asserted his independence of any superior temporal authority by claiming that "this realm of England is an empire," a phrase rooted in the medieval legal tradition that was a forerunner of the modern notion of sovereignty, so too, by asserting his headship of the church, he was laying claim to the jurisdictional powers of the pope. Having papal power of jurisdiction, so to speak, enabled him to use the papal legal language with regard to the settlement of the New World.[25]

One might also ask why the English monarchs bothered with charters at all. Why not simply take what lands were available and forget about formal justification of the action? The obvious reason is that, by the sixteenth century, possession of property clearly required a formal, written record. If the English were to occupy part of North America, they would need a title deed. As far back as the reign of Henry II, possessory assizes settled disputes about the possession of property in royal courts. Subsequently, as a means of avoiding litigation over property, the formal charter became the basis for asserting rights and privileges. Since the thirteenth century, English kings had required that nobles prove their right to "franchises," or "privileged jurisdictions," by means of so-called quo warranto proceedings. The muniment rooms of noble houses attest to the importance of keeping good records of the rights and privileges, lands and offices that the family had acquired over the centuries.[26]

Furthermore, as sixteenth- and seventeenth-century English kings and their Catholic critics well knew, English monarchs relied upon papal authorization, specifically the papal bull *Laudabiliter* issued in 1155, in order to occupy Ireland in the twelfth century. The English solution to this dilemma was to suggest that the papacy had played only a small role in the acquisition of Ireland, stressing instead that the Irish themselves had suggested that the pope grant overlordship of Ireland to Henry II. In this version of the story, the pope only confirmed an arrangement that the English and the Irish had already made. In either case, however, the occupation of Ireland was justified in terms of a legal title.[27]

25. Act of Appeals, in G. R. Elton, ed., *The Tudor Constitution: Documents and Commentary*, 2d ed. (Cambridge, 1982), 353–358. Imperial language also appeared in other acts of Henry VIII (ibid., 37, 360). Elton also notes, "As supreme head, Henry VIII acquired all the administrative episcopal powers of the papacy and none of the sacerdotal ones: he was as much of a bishop as a man can be who is no priest" (*England under the Tudors*, 2d ed. [London, 1974], 162–163). On England as an empire, see Walter Ullmann, "This Realm of England Is an Empire," *Journal of Ecclesiastical History*, XXX (1979), 175–203.

26. M. T. Clanchy, *From Memory to Written Record: England, 1066–1307*, 2d ed. (Oxford, 1993), 36. For the development of muniment rooms, see 168–172.

27. Muldoon, "Spiritual Conquests Compared: *Laudabiliter* and the Conquest of the Americas," in Steven B. Bowman and Blanche E. Cody, eds., *In Iure Veritas: Studies in Canon Law in Memory of Schafer Williams* (Cincinnati, 1991), 174–186, esp. 181. For the text of this bull, see Edmund Curtis and R. B. McDowell, eds., *Irish Historical Documents, 1172–*

Having rejected the papacy and its claim to the right to authorize a Christian monarch to occupy the lands of non-Christians, the English had to find another legal form to justify the occupation of land in North America. Their solution was to assert the right of any Christian ruler to authorize the conquest of lands occupied by infidels, in effect laying claim to the papacy's power. Even this was not a new claim invented in the sixteenth century to justify the conquest of the Americas. In the mid-thirteenth century, when Pope Innocent IV developed the basic legal theory behind the papal bulls dealing with the conquest of the Americas, he had raised the issue of whether Christian rulers could occupy the lands of infidels without papal authorization. Innocent IV rejected this possibility, insisting that only the pope could provide the authorization necessary. The only justification for occupying the lands of infidels who posed no threat to Christians, in his view, was to make possible the conversion of the inhabitants to Christianity. Only the pope, who was by virtue of his office responsible for the spiritual well-being of all mankind, had the right to authorize such an occupation. Sixteenth-century Spanish defenders of Spanish possession of the Americas restated the same point. Francisco de Vitoria, for example, pointed out that the Spanish could be seen as the pope's designated agents for the conversion of the peoples of the New World. The pope could designate one nation as responsible for the work of conversion simply to ensure that the work was done in an orderly manner. This was, in effect, what fifteenth-century popes had been doing when they authorized the Portuguese monopoly of trade with West Africa and the Atlantic islands.[28]

The Protestant Reformation removed the pope from the role of arbiter of the Christian world, but it did not mean the end of Christian universalism, nor did it relieve Christian rulers of religious responsibilities, such as spreading the Christian message. In the absence of papal oversight, however, individual Christian rulers could determine when and how their responsibility to spread the message of Christ was to be accomplished. One consequence of this assertion of sovereignty in both temporal and spiritual matters by European rulers was the development of modern international law and relations. With the end of the nominal papal role as arbiter among Christian kingdoms and between Christian and non-Christian societies and in the absence of any overarching authority, the kingdoms of Europe, the emerging sov-

---

1922 (1943; rpt., New York, 1968), 17–18. On the Irish response, see Muldoon, "The Remonstrance of the Irish Princes and the Canon Law Tradition of the Just War," *American Journal of Legal History*, XXII (1978), 309–325.

28. Francisco de Vitoria, *Political Writings*, ed. Anthony Pagden and Jeremy Lawrence (Cambridge, 1991), 259. See also Muldoon, "'*Extra ecclesiam non est imperium*': The Canonists and the Legitimacy of Secular Power," *Studia gratiana*, IX (1966), 551–580, esp. 573–575. See also Muldoon, *Popes, Lawyers, and Infidels*, 12, 148.

ereign nation-states, had to develop a set of agreed-upon rules that would enable them to deal with one another and with the newly encountered peoples of the New World in some rational way.[29]

As Dorothy Owen and Richard Helmholz have pointed out, Roman canon law did not suddenly disappear from England once Henry VIII declared himself Supreme Head of the Church of England. It was logical for the English to claim possession of the New World in the language that the pope had employed. At the same time, however, the language of the documents of English exploration and colonization reveals the emergence of new justifications upon which the occupation of the lands of infidels could be based. Like many other documents of the sixteenth and seventeenth centuries, these charters were transitional documents, often containing medieval language understood in new ways.[30]

One of the earliest English statements concerning the English right to lay claim to part of North America appears in the records of Sir Humphrey Gilbert's attempt to establish a settlement in Newfoundland in 1583. A member of that expedition, Edward Hayes, explained the basis upon which Queen Elizabeth had authorized the expedition.

> Sir Humphrey Gilbert undertook the western discovery of America and had procured from her Majesty [in 1578] a very large commission to inhabit and possess at his choice all remote and heathen lands not in the actual possession of any Christian prince.

This language clearly echoes the language of Alexander VI in *Inter caetera*. That is to say, claims to possess vast regions based on papal or other documents had no value unless backed up with settlement, functioning government, and other signs of actual control. Thus, although Alexander VI had authorized Spanish possession of the Americas from pole to pole, the English could occupy lands within the alleged Spanish zone of jurisdiction if the Spanish had not taken actual control of them. In practice, the English were interested in occupying lands well north of effective Spanish control, implying that the English accepted the legitimacy of Spanish possession of South America and, in return, assumed that the Spanish would accept English possession of parts of North America.[31]

At the same time, Hayes recognized that the French had explored the

---

29. George H. Sabine, *A History of Political Theory*, 3d ed. (New York, 1961), 422.

30. The Reformation did not automatically end the use of Roman canon law in the Church of England. See Dorothy Mary Owen, *The Medieval Canon Law: Teaching, Literature, and Transmission* (Cambridge, 1990), 43–65; R. H. Helmholz, *Roman Canon Law in Reformation England* (Cambridge, 1990).

31. Edward Hayes, "The Voyage of Sir Humphrey Gilbert to Newfoundland, Anno 1578," in David Freeman Hawke, ed., *Hakluyt's Voyages to the New World: A Selection* (Indianapolis, 1972), 47–66, esp. 49.

region in which Gilbert proposed to settle and organize a colony. Indeed, he admitted that most of what was known about these northern regions was the product of French exploration. But, because of the civil wars that had roiled their land, the French were unable to convert their knowledge of North America into effective possession. The English, on the other hand, would be able to take effective control of these lands because of the peace that England enjoyed.[32]

The English also possessed a claim to the northern lands of the Americas because of the voyages of John Cabot and his son. Hayes claimed that the English possessed "those islands which we now call the Newfoundland, all which they brought and annexed unto the crown of England" as a result of the Cabots' voyages. This did not provide effective possession, however, as Hayes went on to point out.

> Since when, if with like diligence the search of inland countries had been followed . . . no doubt her Majesty's territories and revenue had been mightily enlarged and advanced by this day. And which is more, the seed of Christian religion had been sowed amongst those pagans . . . which must be the chief intent of such as shall make any attempt that way.[33]

With Sir Humphrey Gilbert's expedition, however, the English were about to make effective their claim to a part of North America that lay between the areas over which the French and the Spanish had actual possession. The British Empire in North America would exist, so to speak, in the interstice between the French and Spanish Empires. At the same time, the English would accomplish what the occupation of the New World was expected to accomplish—the enriching of the English people and the conversion of the native inhabitants to Christianity, goals stated in *Inter caetera*. We may even see in the remarks about conversion a challenge to the Spanish. The English would do what the Spanish had failed to. They would bring these infidels to the true faith, that is, to Protestant Christianity. Furthermore, like the Spanish, the English claimed a monopoly of contact with the regions they were to occupy. Seen in this light, the English claim to Newfoundland and adjacent areas paralleled the Spanish claim to all of the Americas.

Curiously, Gilbert's failure to establish a colony in Newfoundland and his presumed death when the ship returning him to England disappeared with all hands led to the publication of "perhaps the Elizabethan era's most

32. On French claims to North America, see L. C. Green and Olive P. Dickason, *The Law of Nations and the New World* (Edmonton, Alta., 1989), 25–34. The issue of the legitimacy of French and English possession of Canada remains an important issue in Canadian law and politics.

33. Hayes, "Voyage of Sir Humphrey Gilbert," in Hawke, ed., *Hakluyt's Voyages,* 48–49.

systematized elaboration" of the legal basis for English claims to North America. Sir George Peckham, a Catholic who had supported Gilbert's colonizing endeavor in order to provide a refuge for his persecuted coreligionists, wrote what he labeled *A True Reporte* of Gilbert's venture in order to encourage doubters to continue the work. The full (and lengthy) title of this work refers to "possession, taken in the right of the Crowne of Englande, of the Newfound Landes" and to "her highnesse lawfull Tytle thereunto," thus emphasizing the legitimacy of English possession of these lands.[34]

The main lines of argument that Peckham developed in the *True Reporte* appear to have come from the Spanish Dominican writer Francisco de Vitoria, whose *De indis* first appeared in print in 1557. Peckham was careful not to identify Vitoria as the source of his arguments for obvious reasons, but otherwise Vitoria's "discourse was appropriated, suppressed, and, in essence, colonized by the Catholic Englishman." Central to Vitoria's argument and a theme that Peckham adopted and developed was the opinion that "Christians may lawfully travaile into those Countries and abide there . . . in respect of the mutual society and fellowship between man and man prescribed by the Lawe of Nations." Peckham went on to explain the benefits that would accrue both to Englishmen and to the inhabitants of North America as a result of this peaceful contact. There would be trade in goods that each required, and the Indians would be introduced to Christianity.[35]

Peckham also argued that late-sixteenth-century English occupation of North America was based upon acts of discovery dating back to the twelfth century, when a Welsh prince, Madoc, sailed west and reached North America. In addition, at the end of the fifteenth century, John Cabot and his sons made voyages of discovery licensed by Henry VII. The result, according to Peckham, was that English monarchs had a title to possession of North America that "is as much, or more then any other Christian Prince can pretende to the Indies before suche time as they had actuall possession thereof."[36]

The attempt at colonizing Newfoundland failed, but the legal basis upon which the English might claim portions of North America remained. In the early seventeenth century, as Englishmen sought to establish settlements farther south, the language of *Inter caetera* is again found. The first three charters of Virginia, 1606–1612, for example, used Alexander VI's language. The first and the third charters restated the exemption of any land actually

34. Williams, *American Indian*, 172; George Peckham, *A True Reporte . . .*, in David Beers Quinn, ed., *The Voyages and Colonising Enterprises of Sir Humphrey Gilbert*, 2 vols. (London, 1939–1940), II, 435–482, esp. 435.

35. Williams, *American Indian*, 168; Peckham, *A True Reporte . . .*, in Quinn, ed., *Voyages of Gilbert*, II, 450.

36. Peckham, *A True Reporte . . .*, in Quinn, ed., *Voyages of Gilbert*, II, 460.

occupied by Christians from English settlement. According to the first charter, the colonists could legitimately occupy any land "not now actually possessed by any *Christian* Prince or People." The third charter permitted the colonists to claim any land "not actually possessed or inhabited by any other *Christian* Prince or Estate." As for the motives underlying the Virginia settlement, the initial charter pointed with favor to the incorporators' desire to propagate the *"Christian* Religion to such People, as yet live in Darkness and miserable Ignorance of the true Knowledge and Worship of God, and may in time bring the Infidels and Savages, living in those Parts, to human Civility, and to a settled and quiet Government." The second charter was even more explicit about the religious motives of the future colonists: "The principal Effect, which we can desire or expect of this Action, is the Conversion and Reduction of the People in those Parts unto the true Worship of God and Christian Religion."[37]

In addition to these traditional justifications for occupying the lands of infidels, the patent of the Council for New England (1620) added a new one. The explorers who had visited the coast of New England noted, "Within these late Yeares there hath by God's Visitation raigned a wonderfull Plague, together with many horrible Slaughters, and Murthers, committed amoungst the savages and bruitish People there, heertofore inhabiting, in a Manner to the utter Destruction, Devastacion, and depopulacion of that whole Territorye, so that there is not left for many Leagues together in a Manner, any that doe claime or challenge any Kind of Interests therein, nor any other Superiour Lord or Souveraigne to make Claime unto." This is not to say that some of the original inhabitants did not remain. What people did remain, however, were "wandering in Desolacion and Distress," a situation that the English planned to remedy by "the reducing and Conversion of such Savages as remaine . . . to Civil Societie and Christian Religion."[38]

When the patent described the devastating population decline in New England, it did so, not to express horror at that turn of events, but to explain why the English had a right to settle there. God had caused these lands to be

37. William MacDonald, ed., *Select Charters and Other Documents Illustrative of American History, 1606–1775* (New York, 1899), 2–3. 16–18. In addition, the colonization of Virginia also generated a defense of its legitimacy. Some time after 1622, Samuel Purchas, continuator of Hakluyt's work and enthusiastic promotor of colonization, wrote a piece to encourage continued support for the settlement of Virginia in one of its darkest hours. He justified English occupation of Virginia in terms quite similar to those that Peckham had employed four decades earlier: see his *Virginias Verger . . .* , in *Hakluytus Posthumus; or, Purchas His Pilgrimes . . .* , 20 vols. (Glasgow, 1905–1907), XIX, 218–268. One scholar has suggested that Purchas might have derived his arguments from "Richard Hakluyt's much more famous (though never published) 'Discourse of Western Planting.'" See Loren E. Pennington, *"Hakluytus Posthumus:* Samuel Purchas and the Promotion of English Overseas Expansion," *Emporia State Research Studies,* XIV (March 1966), 1–39, esp. 39.

38. MacDonald, ed., *Select Charters,* 25.

"deserted as it were by their naturall Inhabitants" so that the English could occupy them. This description of the destruction of the indigenous population meant that the English planned to settle unoccupied or vacant land. In addition, by claiming that no organized society existed in New England, the patent avoided the question of whether the inhabitants of the New World possessed a right to the land that the English had to respect. For all practical purposes, New England was empty, open to anyone who would settle there.[39] One consequence of this definition of *possession* was that Europeans who seized lands defined as vacant because there was no permanent settlement, agriculture, and an organized state were obliged to strive for the "reducing and Conversion of such savages as remaine wandering in Desolacion and Distress, to Civil Societie and Christian Religion." In other words, it was incumbent upon the English colonists to assist the surviving indigenous population to return to the normal and natural way of life for human beings, settled agricultural existence.[40]

The 1620 patent of New England paid only slight heed to the question of converting the Indians because, for all practical purposes, there were none to convert. The first charter of Massachusetts Bay (1629), however, gave close attention to the subject. In addition to repeating the usual exemption of lands "actuallie possessed or inhabited by any other Christian Prince or State," the charter also stated that the conversion of the Indians to the "knowledg and obedience of the onlie true God and Savior of mankinde, and the Christian fayth . . . is the principall ende of this plantation." This was, of course, a sentiment with which Alexander VI would have been in full agreement. Furthermore, the assertion of conversion as a prime goal of the colony was not simply repeating standard colonizing rhetoric. Although it is generally overlooked, the Puritans of Massachusetts Bay devoted some of their energies to civilizing and Christianizing the Indians they encountered, although they had only limited success. In the so-called praying towns, some Puritan divines attempted a process of acculturating Indians to European Christian life that was similar to the more famous Jesuit reductions in

39. Ibid. True possession of land depended on the existence of a stable, settled society, a concept rooted in Aristotle's notion of civilized people. Early defenders of the occupation of Indian lands in North America classified "land occupied by migratory and semisedentary peoples as *terra nullius* or, perhaps more precisely, *vacuum domicilium*, in the phrasing of Massachusetts Governor John Winthrop. . . . The land of prestate people . . . was therefore legally vacant" (Green and Dickason, *Law of Nations*, 235). The Spanish used a similar argument: see Muldoon, *The Americas*, 66–72. On the importance of settlement and agriculture in English thought, see Patricia Seed, *Ceremonies of Possession in Europe's Conquest of the New World, 1492–1640* (Cambridge, 1995), 16–40.

40. MacDonald, ed., *Select Charters*, 25. "Reducing" in this context meant bringing back to the natural way of living as Aristotle defined it, that is, living in organized, settled communities. The word is from the Latin *reduco*, "draw back or lead back."

Paraguay. The outbreak of King Philip's War in 1675, however, virtually ended these missions to the Indians.[41]

Throughout the seventeenth century, English charters authorizing the occupation of North America thus continued to employ the language of *Inter caetera* and the concepts of the medieval canonists that underlay Alexander VI's letter. To some extent, the English monarchs' adoption of formulas derived from Alexander VI and the canonists reflects the fact that their interests had a great deal in common. What then of Adams's assertion that the colonists purchased their lands from the Indians? The *Records of Massachusetts Bay* do mention the purchase of land from Indians but not in the sense that Adams meant. In 1633, for example, the General Court ordered that "noe p[er]son whatsoever shall buy any land of any Indean without leave from the Court." Individual colonists did purchase land from Indians, but the right of the colonial government to order the regulation of such transactions did not depend on some prior purchase from Indians, but depended on the royal charter for the colony. Furthermore, after defeating the Pequot tribe, the colony claimed possession of that tribe's lands "by just title of conquest."[42]

The General Court of Massachusetts continued to dispose of land on the basis that it was "vacuum domicilium" even after the original settlement. Any Englishman who received a grant of land and did not build a structure on it or otherwise improve it within a space of three years would lose it. On the other hand, in 1648, the Court recognized the title by "vacuum domicilium" of one John Thomson to an island in Massachusetts Bay that his father had taken "actuall possession of" in 1626 because it was "vacuum domicilium." Having erected the "forme of an habitation" there, he had taken legitimate possession of it as far as the Court was concerned.[43]

From a modern-day perspective, one might think that the English would have been anxious to distance themselves from the medieval papal legal tradition as a basis for justifying their occupation of the New World and instead employ the legal concepts associated with the new international law,

41. Ibid., 39, 42; Henry Warner Bowden, *American Indians and Christian Missions: Studies in Cultural Conflict* (Chicago, 1981), 111–133. See also James H. Merrell, "'The Customes of Our Country': Indians and Colonists in Early America," in Bernard Bailyn and Philip D. Morgan, eds., *Strangers within the Realm: Cultural Margins of the First British Empire* (Chapel Hill, N.C., 1991), 117–156, esp. 146–152. The English experience in Ireland affected the way the Indians were perceived and were dealt with by the English. See Muldoon, "The Indian as Irishman," Essex Institute, *Historical Collections*, CXI (1975), 267–289.

42. Nathaniel B. Shurtleff, ed., *Records of the Governor and Company of the Massachusetts Bay in New England*, 5 vols. in 6 (Boston, 1853–1854), I, 112, 216. In effect, the Puritans were invoking the medieval theory of the just war to defend their possession of the land.

43. Ibid., I, 114, II, 245.

constructed on the principle of state sovereignty that Hugo Grotius was beginning to describe at the beginning of the seventeenth century. The new international law specifically denied to the pope any role in international relations; thus, Grotius's ideas might seem acceptable to any monarch interested in creating a legal basis for overseas expansion that could ignore papal involvement. In fact, however, the English found Grotius's ideas in conflict with their own interests and found the medieval papal position more acceptable.

The reason for this English unwillingness to adopt Grotius's position on international relations was that his ideas clashed with their desire to maintain a monopoly of trade with their colonies in North America. In his anonymously published *Mare liberum* (1608), Grotius argued that the seas were open to all and that no one, least of all the pope, had the right to award the lands of infidels to a single nation that would then acquire a monopoly of trade with the land involved. Grotius wrote his *Mare liberum* to refute Spanish and Portuguese claims to a monopoly of trade with the East and the West Indies based on *Inter caetera*, framing the basic issues this way:

Can any one nation have the right to prevent other nations which so desire, from selling to one another, from bartering with one another, actually from communicating with one another? Can any nation give away what it never owned, or discover what already belonged to some one else? Does a manifest injustice of long standing create a specific right?

Grotius went on to locate the right to freedom of trade and travel in Creation itself. God gave to mankind communication skills "in order that they might recognize their natural social bond and kinship." That being the case, the "most specific and unimpeachable axiom of the Law of Nations . . . [is]: Every nation is free to travel to every other nation, and to trade with it."[44]

At precisely the same time as Grotius was proclaiming the freedom of the seas and the invalidity of any claim to monopoly of trade with any part of the world by any nation, the English government was asserting its absolute domination of the seas around it, a claim specifically directed against Dutch shipping in the North Sea. In 1617 or 1618, the English lawyer John Selden wrote the *Mare clausum*, eventually published in 1635, to defend the English claim to these waters. The English were claiming monopoly control of the seas just as Alexander VI had in effect done in *Inter caetera*. Thus, from the

44. Hugo Grotius, *Mare Liberum/The Freedom of the Seas* . . . , ed. James Brown Scott, trans. Ralph Van Deman Magoffin (New York, 1916), 1–2, 4, 7. See also Muldoon, "Hugo Grotius, Medieval Canon Law, and the Creation of Modern International Law," Ninth International Congress of Medieval Canon Law, Munich, July 13–18 1992, *Proceedings* (Vatican City, 1997), 1155–1165.

English perspective, if their claims to a monopoly of trade with their American colonies were to be respected, other nations' claims to similar monopolies would have to be recognized. They found themselves in the awkward position of having to accept Spanish claims to a monopoly of trade with the southern regions of America in return for at least tacit acceptance of their monopoly of trade with their North American regions.[45]

Some conclusions about John Adams's discussion of the legitimacy of English possession of North America are now in order. In the first place, as Adams made clear, the reasons that Alexander VI gave for authorizing Castilian possession of the Americas continued to serve the interests of other European monarchs, including Protestants, for more than a century. The motives for expansion contained in the words of the papal bull had not changed substantially. Protestants, no less than Catholics, accepted the responsibility of Christian monarchs to strive for the conversion of infidels and could justify trade monopolies based on that responsibility. Furthermore, the English monarchs recognized that their land claims in the New World did not override the existing claims of other Christian rulers to territory in the Americas. The kings of England were not especially eager to fight wars with those European monarchs who had already staked out claims to parts of the Americas, so their charters repeated the papal exemption of lands already possessed by Christians from settlement. Here, of course, the English were shifting the meaning of the words to mean the Spanish in America, not Christian kingdoms in Asia. The English stressed that such possession must be effective, that is, any Christian ruler who claimed land in the Americas must be able to demonstrate such possession by the presence of permanent inhabitants firmly entrenched. Waving a papal bull awarding all of the Americas from pole to pole to Castile was not enough to claim possession. Thus, English monarchs had no hesitation about awarding the lands around Chesapeake Bay to the Virginia Company, although both Spanish and French explorers had visited the region and the Spanish had attempted (unsuccessfully) to settle there.[46]

In authorizing occupation of North America, the monarchs of England were acting as the pope could act according to the canonists. Henry VIII had asserted that "this realm of England is an empire," the king possessing within his kingdom the powers of the emperor within his empire. The language of the charters of exploration and settlement is a reminder that,

45. W. E. Butler, "Grotius and the Law of the Sea," in Hedley Bull, Benedict Kingsbury, and Adam Roberts, eds., *Hugo Grotius and International Relations* (New York, 1990), 209–220, esp. 210–212.

46. J. H. Parry, "The Spaniards in Eastern North America," in David B. Quinn, ed., *Early Maryland in a Wider World* (Detroit, 1982), 84–102; Green and Dickason, *Law of Nations*, 220.

within his kingdom, the king was also the pope, possessing the powers that the pope possessed within the church.

What then of John Adams's assertion that English possession of North America arose from purchase of the land and the contract that the colonists made with the English monarchs, and not from royal grant? It was of course true that the North American colonists purchased land from Indians. The *Records of the Governor and Company of the Massachusetts Bay in New England* contain evidence of such transactions. But the original colonists had not purchased all of the land specified in their charter from the Indians. The legal tradition on which the original charters were based assumed the Indians held *dominium,* or the right to possess property and govern themselves, only if they occupied fixed habitations, just as the English settlers did.

The charters of Massachusetts and Virginia, rooted as they were in the medieval legal tradition, were much more than writs of *exeat.* They provided a legal and moral basis for English settlement of North America. Furthermore, the charters protected the colonists somewhat, placing them under the protection of the English king from the beginning. At the very least, the possession of a charter meant that no other Englishmen could occupy the lands outlined in the charter without the approval of the colonists who were already there.

The Novanglus essays serve as a reminder that medieval discussions of legitimacy had become a part of the common legal vocabulary that eighteenth-century writers employed in political discussions. John Adams was part of a legal tradition that stretched back to the twelfth century and encompassed not only the common law but canon and Roman law as well. To appreciate fully the political debates of the age of the American Revolution, it is necessary to understand the place of this tradition in the intellectual formation of the Revolutionary generation. John Adams might not have interpreted the medieval tradition correctly, but he was well aware of it and its implications for his own political situation. The standard language of European overseas expansion was drawn from papal documents and was based on medieval legal concepts. What we have in the English colonial charters and the subsequent discussions about the possession of North America, then, are examples of the way in which medieval legal language and ideas continued to shape the early modern world and how English lawyers and American Revolutionaries employed legal concepts from this tradition in the development of their own systems.

Salamanders and Sons of God

The Culture of Appeal in Early New England

"Whenever yet was your appeal denied?"
WILLIAM SHAKESPEARE, *Henry IV, Part 2*

THROUGHOUT THE seventeenth century, William Harris of Rhode Island appealed. He appealed to the General Court of Trials. He appealed to England. He appealed to a specially convened inter-colonial court. And, again, he appealed to England. In fact, Harris traveled at least three times to England to appeal to authorities for assistance with his land claims. He stopped appealing only upon his death—within three days of reaching London after being ransomed from pirates. Roger Williams referred to Harris as "the salamander always delighting to live in the fire of contention as witnesses his several suits in law." Not today's little newts, salamanders were mythical lizards that endured fire without harm. And Harris was not the only salamander. New England abounded with men like him. Rhode Island's Roger Williams and Samuel Gorton and Massachusetts's John Wheelwright and Robert Child made leaders like John Winthrop worry about the appeal; indeed, Edward Winslow's *New-Englands Salamander* bewailed such dissenters. Nevertheless, although the appeal seemed to encourage the colonists to behave as salamanders rather than peace-loving "Sons of God," Massachusetts, Rhode Island, and six other colonies initially adopted the appeal as the review procedure for their court systems.[1]

My thanks to Bernard Bailyn, Alfred Brophy, Daniel Coquillette, David Hall, Frank Herrmann, Morton Horwitz, Ray Madoff, Bruce Mann, John O'Keefe, Kathryn Preyer, James Rogers, Aviam Soifer, Christopher Tomlins, Kevin Van Anglen, the participants of the "Many Legalities of Early America" conference, and the late Elizabeth Clark. Research was supported by a Boston College Research Incentive Grant and the Boston College Law School's Dean Fund.

1. *Harris Papers,* Rhode Island Historical Society, *Collections,* X (1902), 78; Edward Winslow, *New-Englands Salamander Discovered* (1647), in Massachusetts Historical Society, *Collections,* 3d Ser., II (Boston, 1830), 110–145. I use the word "appeal" figuratively in this paragraph; not all of Harris's complaints were technically framed as appeals (*Harris Papers,* 25–42). For other salamanders, see Charles M. Andrews, *The Colonial Period of American History* (New Haven, Conn., 1934), I, 492 n. 2. On the history of the salamander,

Despite the colonists' love of the appeal, historians have found its existence interesting only as part of the story of the antinomian struggles and
the Puritans' confrontational stance toward England. Legal historians' interest in the colonial procedure has been greater but also limited to locating the appeal within the existing story of the development of American common law. Influenced by the frontier thesis of Frederick Jackson
Turner, Roscoe Pound perceived the appeal as part of a "simple system"
that was natural to the "circumstances of pioneer communities." Julius
Goebel, in the grasp of his local-practices theory of transmission, argued that the "so-called appeal" had been a justice-of-the-peace practice
brought to the colonies from "the backwaters of the mainstream of common
law."[2]

I disagree with those studies that present the appeal as a mere procedure
and situate it solely within the common law. Here, I follow a path laid by
cultural historians who have explored and explicated "how structures of
meaning emerge, circulate, and are put to use." In describing seventeenth-
century New England, David Hall notes, "For many, the meaning of a
situation could be expressed in a word or two—a word that may be meaningless to us . . . but that resonated with significance in the context of this
culture." By bringing the resonating significance of the appeal to the surface,
this essay sketches the beginnings of a different story of colonial legal

see *Brewer's Dictionary of Phrase and Fable,* 15th ed. (New York, 1995); *Oxford English Dictionary,* 2d ed. (Oxford, 1989). On the adoption of the appeal, see Julius Goebel, *Antecedents and Beginnings to 1801* (New York, 1971), vol. I of *History of the Supreme Court of the United States,* 119–126. Williams referred to the "peace makers" as the "Sons of God" (*Winthrop Papers* [Boston, 1929–], V, 298).

An earlier and longer version of this material with detailed notes was published as "The Origin of the Appeal in America," *Hastings Law Journal,* XLVIII (1997), 913–968. Readers interested in additional background and references should consult that version. I have silently modernized many spellings, added apostrophes, and deleted many italics and final ellipses.

2. On the Antinomian controversy and dissent in the 1640s, see David D. Hall, ed., *The Antinomian Controversy, 1636–1638: A Documentary History* (Durham, N.C., 1990), ix–23; Charles Francis Adams, *Three Episodes of Massachusetts History: The Settlement of Boston Bay, the Antinomian Controversy, a Study of Church and Town Government* (1892; rev. ed., New York, 1965), 363–532; Philip F. Gura, *A Glimpse of Sion's Glory: Puritan Radicalism in New England, 1620–1660* (Middletown, Conn., 1984); Andrew Delbanco, *The Puritan Ordeal* (Cambridge, Mass., 1989), 118–148; Janice Knight, *Orthodoxies in Massachusetts: Rereading American Puritanism* (Cambridge, Mass., 1994), 13–33. For legal historians' writings regarding the appeal, see Roscoe Pound, *Organization of Courts* (Boston, 1940), 57; Goebel, *Antecedents and Beginnings,* 1, 5, 19. Other bodies of scholarship that implicate the appeal include the work of Barbara Aronstein Black, for example, her article, "The Concept of a Supreme Court: Massachusetts Bay, 1630–1686," in Russell K. Osgood, ed., *The History of the Law in Massachusetts: The Supreme Judicial Court, 1692–1992* (Boston, 1992), 43–79; Edith G. Henderson, *Foundations of English Administrative Law: Certiorari and Mandamus in the Seventeenth Century* (Cambridge, Mass., 1963), 1–7.

culture—one that locates the colonists within a transatlantic English and western European legal culture.[3]

The appeal emerges with a set of meanings that should cause us to pause over our lingering belief that the colonists possessed only a low-level understanding of English common law. These meanings arose from the long heritage of canon and civil law in which a commitment to equity—to individualized justice—required that a higher tribunal must be able to rehear and redecide both the facts and law of an individual's case. The acceptance of this set of meanings betrayed the colonial leaders' careful knowledge of English corporation law and their agreement with the broader, more flexible, and more equitable theory of review and redress that the appeal reflected. In the political struggles over the location of supreme authority that haunted the early seventeenth century, the appeal became an integral part of the legal culture as its meanings continued to represent elusive ideas about the structure of authority.

To connote and emphasize these underlying subtleties and complexities of the early colonial concept of the appeal, I use the phrase "culture of appeal." I mean by this phrase to suggest that the specialized technical use of the word "appeal" in legal spheres was inseparable from its more colloquial use in the political sphere and that the term also referred to a set of broader meanings and practices. I also intend the phrase to allude to a culture of understanding about the appeal that transcended national and colonial boundaries. Moreover, the phrase should help readers, for whom the word "appeal" carries modern common-law connotations, to remember that the colonists' initial choice of the appeal represented a moment of "deep cultural reorientation" away from English common-law culture. Finally, the phrase should remind us that even the most technical of legal procedures, beneath their surface reflections, are embedded in the rich culture of their time.[4]

I. The English Culture of Appeal

Although the New England appeal represented a departure from the English common law, it lay neatly within part of the English legal tradition. Since the fourteenth century, England had possessed two legal cultures. One, that of the common law, saw itself as the product of an indigenous development through custom by common-law practitioners and judges. The other, that of the civil law, proudly traced its roots to the grand tradition of Roman law as

3. David D. Hall, *Worlds of Wonder, Days of Judgment: Popular Religious Belief in Early New England* (New York, 1989), 69–70, 245.

4. A. G. Roeber, *Faithful Magistrates and Republican Lawyers: Creators of Virginia Legal Culture, 1680–1810* (Chapel Hill, N.C., 1981), xv.

applied in the ecclesiastical and civil law courts by the civilians. Not only did these cultures have different stories of their origins; they had different procedures for redress. Although the word "appeal" actually appeared in both cultures, it referred to very different legal procedures.[5]

The civilian lawyer John Cowell explained in his 1607 suppressed dictionary, *The Interpreter*, the difference between the understanding of the appeal possessed by the civilian students of Roman, or canon, law and their common-law colleagues. Cowell noted that "appeal" "is used in our common law divers times, as it is taken in the civil law: which is a removing of a cause from an inferior judge to a superior as appeal to Rome. . . . But it is more commonly used for the private accusation, of a murderer by a party."[6]

As Cowell's phrase "divers times" indicates, the civil and common-law worlds were not completely separate, and the civil law meaning of the word "appeal" had already begun to drift into the common law. Yet throughout the early seventeenth century the concept of the appeal was recognized as having its origins in the civil and canon law. During the seventeenth century, as the power of the theory of redress represented by the appeal began to invade the common law, these differences were not lost on the New England colonists.

The Culture of Redress within the Common Law: The Writ of Error

Good sixteenth- and seventeenth-century lawyers of the common law, and perhaps a wider spectrum of English readers, knew that the appeal did not refer to common-law redress procedures. In 1628, Edward Coke noted, *"Appellatio*, is a removing of a cause in any ecclesiastical court to a superior." He emphasized, however, "But of this there needeth no speech in this place." In a popular book on English government, Queen Elizabeth's secretary of state, Thomas Smith, similarly stated, "As for provocation or appeal which is used so much in other countries, it hath no place in England."[7]

What most common-law practitioners who looked up "appeal" would have found was a discussion of felonies. The entry under "appeal" in the popular edition of John Rastell's *Difficult and Obscure Words and Terms of the Law of this Realm* (1579) referred to an indictment by a private citizen for mayhem, rape, robbery, murder, or other felonies. Indeed, Smith acknowl-

---

5. William Holdsworth, *A History of English Law*, 7th ed., I (London, 1956), 213–214; Frederick Pollock and Frederic William Maitland, *The History of English Law before the Time of Edward I*, 2d ed., 2 vols. (Cambridge, 1968), I, 664.

6. John Cowell, *The Interpreter; or, Booke Containing the Signification of Words* (Cambridge, 1607), s.v. "appeal."

7. Edward Coke, *The First Part of the Institutes of the Lawes of England*, 2 vols. (1628; rpt., New York, 1979), II, 287; Thomas Smith, *De Republica Anglorum: A Discourse on the Commonwealth of England*, ed. Leonard Alston (1583; rpt., Shannon, Ireland, 1972), 108. The sentence in Coke appears under appeals of felony.

edged England's eccentricity: "That which in England is called appeal, [is] in other places [an] accusation."[8]

In the sixteenth and early seventeenth century, English common law had no word to describe the ability to seek redress from the decision of an inferior court in a superior court. At that time the common-law culture did not imagine a world in which "inferior" and "superior" courts were an important distinction. English legal theory tended to see law as "a system of reasoning" working within a "system of remedies."[9] The crucial issue was the availability and applicability of various pleas and writs. The fascination was more with the correctness of the process than the justness of the result. During the seventeenth century, Coke and then Hale would develop increasingly elaborate understandings of the common law, but it remained a system in which pleas to the judiciary required addressing "reason"—"the faculty acquired by training that extracted some workable rules from a formless body of immemorial knowledge"—rather than appealing on the basis of what any ordinary person could claim was justice, equity, or mercy.[10]

Within this culture, therefore, disagreeing with the judgment was tricky. If the law is what reason or custom is—or, at least, what judges think it is (and they tend to "think" in a funny version of Latin and French)—then how is the lowly litigant to complain about the result? During the Middle Ages, one possibility for redress involved accusing the jury or judge of giving a false verdict. In essence, the aggrieved party claimed that the judge or jury had lied about what was known to be the correct verdict. Given the realities of socioeconomic power, accusing the judge (the writ of false judgment) was unlikely to seem fruitful. And, although accusing the jury (the writ of attaint) remained an option for a longer period of time, by the beginning of the seventeenth century it had fallen into disuse.[11]

The other possibility for redress was the "writ of error," the claim that an error had been made in the various writs and pleas of the case. Limited to the

8. John Rastell, *An Exposition of Certaine Difficult and Obscure Wordes and Termes of the Lawes of This Realme* (1579; rpt., New York, 1969), 19–20; Smith, *De Republica Anglorum*, ed. Alston, 113–115. In a later edition, Rastell included the word "appeal" to refer to ecclesiastical proceedings under "Arches" ([Rastell], *Les Termes de La Ley; or, Certain Difficult and Obscure Words and Terms of the Common and Statute Laws of England, Now in Use, Expounded and Explained* [1812; rpt., Littleton, Colo., 1993], 37).

9. Michael Lobban, *The Common Law and English Jurisprudence, 1760–1850* (New York, 1991), 7.

10. Alan Cromartie, *Sir Matthew Hale, 1609–1676: Law, Religion, and Natural Philosophy* (Cambridge, 1995), 17. For similar discussions, see Gerald J. Postema, "Some Roots of Our Notion of Precedent," in Laurence Goldstein, ed., *Precedent in Law* (New York, 1987), 9, 16–17; Charles M. Gray, "Parliament, Liberty, and the Law," in J. H. Hexter, ed., *Parliament and Liberty from the Reign of Elizabeth to the English Civil War* (Stanford, Calif., 1992), 155–158.

11. See Henry Finch, *A Summary of the Common Law of England* (1654; rpt., New York, 1979), table 47; Coke, *First Part of the Institutes*, I, 130; Pollock and Maitland, *History of English Law before the Time of Edward I*, I, 667–668.

record, the writ of error permitted only a narrow scope of review. The aggrieved party was not supposed to bring in new evidence; indeed, the only debatable errors about factual matters involved facts that would show that no judgment should have been entered in the first place. One example was to prove that the original plaintiff had been a minor or a woman. Review was, in essence, limited to errors of law. Even the inquiry concerning errors of law was narrow, because "errors" had to be in the record and the "record" usually contained only the writ, the pleadings and issue, the jury process and verdict, and the judgment. A party who felt that "manifest injustice" had occurred had to find justice by "proof of a technical error (verbal or pro-cedural) in the previous trial."[12]

The common-law theory of law also meant that the common-law courts did not operate in a strictly hierarchical fashion. If the law was what judges thought it was, then one particular set of justices had no supreme claim on knowing it. Consequently, by 1600, the reviewing authorities for the writ of error operated under a horizontal system of "mutual review." Although decisions of local courts of record were reviewed by the King's Bench, the three central courts reviewed each other's decisions in a complicated man-ner. The review did not involve a rehearing of the case, and reviewed cases were returned to the original court for further proceedings or new trials. As one modern author comments, common-law "appellate review had nothing to do with whether justice was done."[13]

The Culture of Redress outside Common Law: The Appeal

The common-law courts, however, were not the only courts in England. Justice on the merits was the point of redress elsewhere, and redress else-where was by the appeal. In his 1607 dictionary, Cowell described the appeal as "a removing of a cause from an inferior judge to a superior as appeal to Rome." His definition once again embodied many of the cultural under-

12. G. R. Elton, ed., *The Tudor Constitution: Documents and Commentary*, 2d ed. (Cam-bridge, 1982), 149. On the procedure, see Goebel, *Antecedents and Beginnings*, 19–20; J. H. Baker, *An Introduction to English Legal History*, 3d ed. (London, 1990), 60–61, 163–164; Edward Coke, *The Second Part of the Institutes of the Laws of England*, 2 vols. (1797; rpt., Buffalo, N.Y., 1986), II, 427. Unlike the appeal, the writ of error was an original proceeding with the writ issuing from chancery. The bill of exceptions permitted inclusion of addi-tional errors, but only if the judge recorded the ruling in writing at judgment (Roscoe Pound, *Appellate Procedure in Civil Cases* [Boston, 1941], 44–46).

13. Gray, "Parliament, Liberty, and the Law," in Hexter, ed., *Parliament and Liberty*, 165; Robert J. Martineau, *Appellate Justice in England and the United States: A Comparative Analysis* (Buffalo, N.Y., 1990), 6. On the process, see Smith, *De Republica Anglorum*, 156–169; Holdsworth, *History of English Law*, I, 244–245; Baker, *Introduction to English Legal History*, 158.

standings of the appeal. Cowell associated the act with the civil law and Rome, and, indeed, the appeal dominated the ecclesiastical and civil law courts. Within these courts, the appeal served as a flexible form of redress based on an increasingly important understanding of equity advanced by the civilians. Cowell's use of the word "remove" emphasized the power of the appeal to permit a complete rehearing of both law and fact. His description of the removal from an "inferior" to a "superior" judge hinted that the legitimacy of the appeal rested ultimately on a supreme authority—often the authority of God. Moreover, Cowell's casual mention of Rome signaled that the appeal carried a set of political memories. First as a symbol of Rome's authority and then as a symbol of the king's, the appeal had been entwined into English political history.

Equity, Authority, and the Appeal in Ecclesiastical Courts

As of the seventeenth century, the appeal's origins stretched back as far as the Catholic Church could remember. By the time of Justinian, Roman law had developed an appeal, which was basically a rehearing that permitted the production of new evidence. An early instance of this Roman appeal is the recounting of Paul's journey from Jerusalem to Rome found in Acts. At a crucial moment, when it appeared that Paul would be sent back from Caesarea to Jerusalem for trial, Paul stated, "I appeal to Caesar." Festus and the council accepted Paul's appeal and sent him to Rome.[14]

As a legal device, the Roman appeal melded well with church hierarchy. By the eleventh century, Pope Gregory VII clarified that "the pope stood supreme above all others." Although the pope therefore "had to listen to *all* complaints," Gregory emphasized the system of appeal to permit the delegation of cases while maintaining papal judicial supremacy. By the end of the twelfth century, "the Church and its legal administrators had constructed a transnational hierarchy of tribunals, with the pope at its apex." The appeal was part of this pyramid. Within England, an appeal moved from the local diocese courts, to the archbishops' courts, and then to the pope's courts. This appeal had few procedural requirements. William Holdsworth notes that an "almost unlimited right of appeal to the Pope" existed and "the system of appeals and rehearings was, or might be, never ending." Indeed, with a new pope, cases often could be reappealed.[15]

14. See H. F. Jolowicz and Barry Nicholas, *Historical Introduction to the Study of Roman Law*, 3d ed. (Cambridge, 1972), 444; Brian Rapske, *The Book of Acts and Paul in Roman Custody* (Grand Rapids, Mich., 1994), 48–56. See Acts 25:11–12; see also Johannes Munck, ed., *The Anchor Bible: The Acts of the Apostles*, rev. William F. Albright and C. S. Mann (New York, 1967), 234.
15. John Gilchrist, "Canon Law Aspects of the Eleventh-Century Gregorian Reform

The appeal's association with papal power meant that the cultural understanding of the appeal involved far more than simply seeing it as a procedural device. The appeal was at the center of two significant political
struggles between the English crown and Rome. The first conflict involved
Thomas à Becket, archbishop of Canterbury. In 1164, Henry II proposed the
Constitutions of Clarendon. The eighth article substituted the king for the
pope as the place of appeal in cases where the archbishop failed to do
"justice." Not surprisingly, Becket protested the attempt to end the pope's
appellate jurisdiction. Becket maintained the pope's authority to hear appeals, but at a price—violent death at the hands of the king's men at Christ-
mas in Canterbury Cathedral.[16]

Almost four hundred years later, the English kings resurrected the struggle in a more successful, if not less bloody, fashion. Pressured by the desire
for a legitimate male heir and for an end to his marriage with Katharine of
Aragón, Henry VIII needed to prevent any future appeal by Katharine to the
pope. The act For the Restraint of Appeals passed in 1533 reached beyond
Henry's particular situation and ended all appeals to the pope. Drafted
by Thomas Cromwell, the act declared the king the supreme head of the
Church of England. Using language that would become part of the cultural
rhetoric for anyone complaining about appeals, the act stated that appeals
would be restrained because they were often brought for "the delay of
justice" and created "great inquietation, vexation, trouble, cost and charges."
Moreover, the "great distance" meant that necessary proofs, witnesses, and
"true knowledge of the cause" could not be known and therefore the grieved
party would be "without remedy."[17]

Programme," in *Canon Law in the Age of Reform, 11th–12th Centuries* (Aldershot, Hampshire, 1993), 27–30; Baker, *Introduction to English Legal History*, 147; Holdsworth, *History of
English Law*, I, 603. On the court structure of the church, see Martin Ingram, *Church
Courts, Sex, and Marriage in England, 1570–1640* (Cambridge, 1987), 35–37; G. I. O. Duncan, *The High Court of Delegates* (Cambridge, 1971), 1–31.

16. Constitutions of Clarendon, art. 8, in William Stubbs, ed., *Select Charters and Other
Illustrations of English Constitutional History from the Earliest Times to the Reign of Edward I*, 9th ed., rev. by H. W. C. Davis (1921; rpt. Littleton, Colo., 1985), 165. On the
controversy, see David Knowles, *Thomas Becket* (Stanford, Calif., 1971), 88–92, 171; Charles
Duggan, *Canon Law in Medieval England: The Becket Dispute and Decretal Collections*
(London, 1982), I, 370; William Holden Hutton, *Thomas Becket, Archbishop of Canterbury*,
rev. ed. (Cambridge, 1926), 153–178.

17. 24 Hen. VIII, c. xii; 25 Hen. VIII, c. xix. On the act, see Duncan, *High Court of
Delegates*, 6–13; R. H. Helmholz, *Roman Canon Law in Reformation England* (Cambridge,
1990), 34–38; Ralph Houlbrooke, *Church Courts and the People during the English Reformation, 1520–1579* (Oxford, 1979), 153–178; James C. Spalding, *The Reformation of the
Ecclesiastical Laws of England, 1552* (Kirksville, Mo., 1992), 14–18; G. R. Elton, *The Tudor
Revolution in Government: Administrative Changes in the Reign of Henry VIII* (Cambridge,
1953), 362–364. For a discussion of the drafting of the statute, see Elton, "The Evolution of
a Reformation Statute," *English Historical Review*, LXIV (1949), 174–197.

Ending appeals to the pope did not end the enormous influence of the ecclesiastical courts and the ecclesiastical appeal procedure. It had "simply varied the place to which appealed causes finally went." The "omnipresent" courts continued to handle causes involving marriage and separation, probate and intestate estates, and slander and defamation as well as heresy, witchcraft, usury, profanity, and sexual offenses. With only one brief interruption during the reign of Mary, the ecclesiastical appeal continued into the seventeenth century with the crown as head of both spiritual and temporal jurisdictions. As popular legal writers from William Lambarde to Edward Coke noted, appeals now ran from the courts of the archbishop to a new body commissioned by the crown, the Court of Delegates. The delegates maintained civil law procedures of the ecclesiastical system: the appeal was conducted in writing, in English, with depositions and interrogatories. It was understood as a rehearing of both law and fact.[18]

Beyond standing as the symbol of fundamental political struggles and the vast jurisdiction of the English church over daily life, the appeal represented an equitable theory of justice arising from medieval Roman canon law. In the medieval ecclesiastical system, "the aspiration to do full justice between the parties led to an appellate process in which all questions were open that had been open in the proceeding appealed from." After the Henrician Reformation, ecclesiastical justice was explicitly linked to equity. One popular writer noted, "Where the *ius civile* establishes equity and the *ius canonicum* formality, the *ius civile* prevails even in the ecclesiastical forum." Similarly, in one of the sixty-one chapters regarding the appeal in the 1552 proposed revisions to the canon law in England, thirty-two of England's most prominent common lawyers, civilians, bishops, and divines wrote: "Appeals are procured not for the sake of oppressing anyone's justice, but so that imposed grievances inflicted may be repaired, and to correct injustice, and the unskillfulness of the judge, and sometimes to come to the aid of the ignorance of the afflicted one himself. . . . For what has been omitted in the first instance frequently has a place in the second." The connection between equity and ecclesiastical law lasted into the seventeenth century. In 1607, Sir

---

18. Helmholz, *Roman Canon Law,* 38; Ingram, *Church Courts, Sex, and Marriage,* 1–69. On the ecclesiastical courts and appeals, see William Lambarde, *Archeion; or, A Discourse upon the High Courts of Justice in England,* ed. Charles H. McIlwain and Paul L. Ward (1635; rpt., Cambridge, Mass., 1957), 14; Edward Coke, *The Fourth Part of the Institutes of the Laws of England* (1797; rpt., Buffalo, N.Y., 1986), 339–340; Duncan, *High Court of Delegates,* 1–31; Ingram, *Church Courts, Sex, and Marriage,* 2–3, 35–41; Helmholz, *Roman Canon Law,* 45–47, 155–156; John Dawson, *The Oracles of the Law* (Ann Arbor, Mich., 1968), 188; Patrick Collinson, *The Religion of Protestants: The Church in English Society, 1559–1625* (Oxford, 1982). The changes were reversed under Mary Tudor. The first act of Elizabeth's reign, however, restored the restraint on appeals and supremacy of the crown in temporal and spiritual jurisdictions (1 Eliz. I, c. i).

Thomas Ridley's *View of Civile and Ecclesiastical Law* noted that the study of
civil and ecclesiastical law was called "Aequitas Canonica" because of the
"cases of Equity and Conscience."[19]
Indeed, in the sixteenth century, the civilians practicing in the ecclesiastical courts had developed an elaborate theory of equity and its companion,
conscience. "Equity" was an ancient word—Aristotle and Aquinas had discussed *epieikeia*. "Conscience" had a similar rich intellectual heritage, reaching back as far as the fourteenth century. Both words, however, became
ubiquitous after 1530 with the civilian writer Christopher St. German's publication of *Doctor and Student* in English. This influential work defined
equity as "a righteousness that considers all the particular circumstances of
the deed which also is tempered with the sweetness of mercy." St. German
theorized that "equitable interventions in the name of good conscience,
which were sometimes necessary to mitigate the rigor of the common law,
were designed to reinforce, not to contradict, general legal principles." Unlike Aquinas, who thought equity should be reserved for exceptional interventions, St. German argued that equity was "a part of the law not something outside of it." Equity "followeth the law in all particular cases where
right and Justice reign." Equity arose from conscience: "And as a light is set
in a lantern that all that is in the house may be seen thereby so almighty god
hath set conscience in the midst of every reasonable soul as a light whereby
he may discern and know what he ought to do: and why he ought not to do."
Conscience was more than the distinction between right and wrong; it was a
form of "applied knowledge," an "art of translating" the distinction into
"specific rules of conduct to be followed in particular situations." Judgments
in the ecclesiastical and civil law courts were to be based on equity and
conscience.[20]

19. Robert E. Rodes, Jr., *Ecclesiastical Administration in Medieval England: The Anglo-
Saxons to the Reformation* (Notre Dame, Ind., 1977), 142; Robertus Maranta, *Speculum
aureum et lumen advocatorum praxis civilis*, part III, no. 76 (Venice, 1556), quoted in
Helmholz, *Roman Canon Law*, 17; Spalding, *Reformation of the Ecclesiastical Laws*, 246–
247. For the Ridley quotation, see J. Dodd, *A History of Canon Law* (1884; rpt., Littleton,
Colo., 1987), 50–51.
20. Christopher St. German, *St. German's Doctor and Student*, ed. T. F. T. Plucknett and
J. L. Barton (London, 1974), 95, 97; J. A. Guy, *Christopher St. German on Chancery and
Statute* (London, 1985), 19–20, 73; Barton, "Introduction," in St. German, *Doctor and
Student*, ed. Plucknett and Barton, xxvi. On the history of equity and conscience, see St.
German, *Doctor and Student*, ed. Plucknett and Barton, xx–li; Guy, *Christopher St. German*, 71–75; D. E. C. Yale, ed., *Lord Nottingham's Chancery Cases*, 2 vols. (London, 1957), I,
xxxvii–cxxiv; John Spelman, *The Reports of Sir John Spelman*, ed. John H. Baker (London,
1978), 37–43; Edward Hake, *Epieikeia: A Dialogue on Equity in Three Parts*, ed. D. E. C. Yale
(1603; rpt., London, 1953), xiii–xxv; Norman Doe, *Fundamental Authority in Late Medieval English Law* (Cambridge, 1990), 84, 101–107; Baker, *Introduction to English Legal
History*, 122–124; Peter Hoffer, *The Law's Conscience: Equitable Constitutionalism in America* (Chapel Hill, N.C., 1990), 7–12.

Into the seventeenth century, these understandings of equity and the appeal remained linked. Even a common lawyer like Coke grasped the essential meaning. In Coke's discussion of ecclesiastical courts, he stated that the "appeal is a natural defence" and cannot be taken away "by any prince or power." He added, if the appeal is "just and lawful, the superior judge ought of right and equity to receive and admit the same, as he ought to do justice to the subjects." Common lawyers and civilians alike knew that, as one modern historian notes, the appeal considered "the merits of the whole cause."[21]

The Ripples of Appeal

This understanding of the appeal as equity and justice, as superior and inferior courts, as rehearings of law and fact, rippled into other areas of English legal life. The martial and admiralty courts had long relied on the appeal and its meanings because of their reliance on civil law procedures. During the late sixteenth and early seventeenth century, this meaning of the appeal as an equitable rehearing in front of a superior authority began to spread to other areas of English law. The gradual association of the appeal with two areas that emphasized the appeal's association with equity and the delegation of authority—courts of chancery and franchises—demonstrates that a "fairly coherent, though hardly articulated" theory of law had grown up around the appeal.[22]

At the beginning of the seventeenth century, the word "appeal" began consistently to appear in conjunction with discussions of the chancery courts. The chancery courts, theoretically originating from the crown, did not use common-law procedure. Like the ecclesiastical courts, chancery emphasized the importance of equity and an examination in English into the peculiar circumstances of the party. Indeed, the civilians had so often used "equity" to justify chancery jurisdiction that, by the seventeenth century, the two words seemed interchangeable. William Lambarde's popular *Archeion* (1635), a text on English legal institutions, simply titled one section "The Court of Equity, or Chancery."[23]

21. Coke, *Fourth Part of the Institutes*, 340; Duncan, *High Court of Delegates*, 43.
22. Coke, *Fourth Part of the Institutes*, 123–125, 340; Gray, "Boundaries of the Equitable Function," *American Journal of Legal History*, XX (1976), 223.
23. See William West, *The First Part of Symboleography* (1647; rpt., New York, 1979); Hake, *Epieikeia: A Dialogue*, ed. Yale; Thomas Ashe, *Epieikeia* (London, 1609). Chancery usually heard cases through subpoena and the "English bill." On chancery procedures, see Tho[mas] Powell, *Attourneys Academy; or, Manner and Forme of Proceeding Practically . . .* (London, 1623), 1–5, 38; Yale, ed., *Lord Nottingham's 'Manual of Chancery Practice' and 'Prolegmena of Chancery and Equity'* (London, 1665), 45–48; William J. Jones, "Due Process and Slow Process in the Elizabethan Chancery," *Am. Jour. Leg. Hist.*, VI (1962), 129–130; Baker, *Introduction to English Legal History*, 119–130; Donald Veall, *The Popular Movement for Law Reform, 1640–1660* (Oxford, 1970), 32–36; Lambarde, *Archeion*, ed. McIlwaine and Ward, 37.

The precise date during the early seventeenth century when "appeal" became the descriptive word for grievances brought to and taken from the chancery courts is not clear. The phrase "appeal to the kings court of chancery" appears as early as the Henrician act For the Restraint of Appeals. According to one contemporary treatise, chancery heard appeals from maritime and martial matters and from the "mayor of the Staple." And, in 1591, a petition in chancery stated that the appeal was the proper device when complaining about a difference between the facts and the judgment.[24]

By the early seventeenth century, as a series of discussions in the House of Lords demonstrates, the appeal also had become linked to the idea of broad equitable redress in chancery. In the 1620s, the Lords began to discuss whether, and with what scope, they could review chancery decisions. The issue was framed as whether they could hear appeals. In 1620, a petition brought to the House of Lords employed the word "appeal," giving rise to a discussion "whether it be a formal appeal for matter of justice or no." Lord Say argued that it was an appeal and that there was "no appeal from the Chancery but hither." The committee concluded that it could not find "that the word 'appeal' is usual in any petition for any matter to be brought hither." Nonetheless, the house heard the accusation, and a "number of members expressed a willingness to consider the substance of the case, as an appeal," that is, to hear the merits of the cause. By the middle to late seventeenth century, the "appeal in equity" was well ensconced within chancery's practice, and, in 1675, the House of Lords accepted jurisdiction over "appeals in equity" from chancery.[25]

The meaning of "appeal" is also revealed as it spread beyond the ecclesiastical courts into the quasi-governmental entities that English legal culture referred to as "franchises." Franchises were "a miscellaneous lot"—the palatine of Durham, the county of Chester, and various local warrens and corporations. These franchises were all "exercises of the king's rights by private persons"; they involved the "delegation of various *jura regalia*." Crucial to the franchise was the patent or charter, a document that literally was

24. 25 Hen. VIII, c. xix; "A Treatise of the Maisters of the Chaunceries" [c. 1596–1603], in Francis Hargrave, ed., *A Collection of Tracts relative to the Law of England* (London, 1787), 310; *Sames v Beecher* (July 23, 1591), in Cecil Monro, *Acta Cancellariae; or, Selections from the Records of the Court of Chancery* (London, 1847), 129–130.

25. Samuel Rawson Gardiner, ed., *Notes of the Debates in the House of Lords . . . A.D. 1621* (Westminster, 1870), 107–108, quoted in James S. Hart, *Justice upon Petition: The House of Lords and the Reformation of Justice, 1621–1675* (New York, 1991), 46–47; Matthew Hale, *The Jurisdiction of the Lords House, or Parliament, Considered according to Antient Records*, ed. Francis Hargraves (London, 1796), 195. The legitimacy of the appeal from chancery to the House of Lords was finally settled in 1675 in *Shirley v Fagg*. Goebel noted that the colonial appeal could not "have been in imitation of the English Chancery appeal, for this was still, so to speak, *in ventre sa mere* when the first American enactments were put on the books" (*Antecedents and Beginnings*, 26).

to be kept under lock and key. Subject to the document, however, the franchise could develop its own system of courts. A number of franchise courts
had long employed the appeal. The corporate university courts of Oxford
and Cambridge had used appeals to review internal cases. Another kind of
franchise court, like the stannary courts of Cornwall and Devon, did not
permit reversals by writ of error to the king but only by the appeal. The
islands of Jersey and Guernsey similarly had appeals to the King-in-Council.
Within these franchises, the appeal represented the hierarchy of authority of
the delegated powers.[26]

In the late sixteenth century, franchises like the English trading companies also began to use the appeal to describe the relationship between the
crown and the company. The charters to the trading companies delegated to
the governor and company the power to do justice and to pass laws not
contrary or repugnant to the laws of England. In some cases, the crown
acknowledged that the company had complete legal authority by specifically
barring appeals beyond the company. John Wheeler's famous *Treatise on
Commerce* (1601) described the Merchant Adventurers' power to "end and
determine all Civil causes, questions, and controversies . . . without Appeal,
provocation, or declination." The charter to the King's Merchants of the
New Trade stated that there would be no "further appeal or provocation
whatever" from the power and authority of the Company and Fellowship.
The Levant Company's 1615 charter permitted fines for anyone who appealed to Turkish authorities.[27]

Not only was the appeal used to indicate the delegation of power from
crown to corporation, but it also began to be used to delegate power within
the corporation. The judicial structure of the corporations was governed by
internal acts passed by their General Court. In at least one known case, that
of the Eastland Merchants, a trading company active in the Baltic since the
fifteenth century, internal ordinances established the appeal. Their 1579
charter established a governor, deputy, and twenty-four assistants. As merchants from all over England joined the company, they demanded local
courts. The London court agreed but retained control over the local courts

26. Donald W. Sutherland, *Quo Warranto Proceedings in the Reign of Edward I, 1278–
1294* (Oxford, 1963), 2; Cecil T. Carr, ed., *Select Charters of Trading Companies*, A.D. 1530–
1707 (London, 1913), xxvii; Duncan, *High Court of Delegates*, 40; Coke, *Fourth Part of the
Institutes*, 227–230; Holdsworth, *History of English Law*, I, 156–158, 520; Joseph Henry
Smith, *Appeals to the Privy Council from the American Plantations* (1950; rpt., New York,
1965), 3–38.

27. Douglas R. Bisson, *The Merchant Adventurers of England: The Company and the
Crown, 1474–1564* (Newark, Del., 1993), 3; John Wheeler, *A Treatise of Commerce*, ed.
George Burton Hotchkiss (1601; rpt., New York, 1931), 156; Carr, ed., *Select Charters of
Trading Companies*, 88; Mortimer Epstein, *The English Levant Company: Its Foundation
and Its History to 1640* (1908; rpt., New York, 1968), 103.

by regulating the appeal. The Privy Council approved an appeals ordinance
in 1617, although it might have recodified a similar, older one. The ordinance
discussed in "what cases appeals are made," noting that it was intended for
the "avoiding of needless and unjust appeals." The ordinance distinguished
among appeals on monetary amount, prohibiting appeals from the local
courts in amounts below twenty "dollours." Appeals for matters above forty
"dollours" had to provide security and appeal within six months.[28]

The use of the appeal by the trading companies emphasized the delegation aspect of the appeal—that justice lay in the ability to seek redress of
decisions in a superior power. The appeal to the pope and then to the
English ecclesiastical authorities had emphasized this point. With the rise of
the Stuarts, the appeal began also to be associated with the king's supreme
authority. James I explained the relationship between king and judge in the
infamous Star Chamber: "As Kings borrow their power from God, so Judges
from Kings: And as Kings are to accompt to God, so Judges unto God and
Kings." And in *Archeion,* Lambarde wrote: "Let no man in Suit appeal to the
King, unless he may not get right at home; but if that right be too heavy for
him, go to the King to have it eased. By which it may evidently appear, that
even so many years ago there might Appellation be made to the King's
Person, whensoever the Cause should enforce it."[29]

The Appeal of the Appeal

What appealed to the king should not have appealed to the Puritan colonists. The Stuart theory of the divine right of kings and of the "king's powers
to remedy grievances" rapidly came under attack in the early seventeenth
century. The use of the prerogative court of Star Chamber against Puritan
opponents called into question the very existence of prerogative courts and
their discretionary powers. The increasing use of chancery to rehear cases
decided in common-law courts called into question the legitimacy of a court
without juries and the unbounded discretion of the chancellor. And the
continued power of the ecclesiastical courts led Puritan reformers to criticize
the courts as "relics of the popish past" and led common-law courts to
attempt to restrain the courts' jurisdiction.[30]

28. Maud Sellers, ed., *Acts and Ordinances of the Eastland Company* (London, 1906), xiii,
ix–xi, lxi–lxii, 52–54. The "Orders and constitutions" are similar to those of the East India
Company, although the East India Company's orders do not contain an appeal provision
(*The Lawes or Standing Orders of the East India Company* [London, 1621]).

29. James I, "A Speech in the Starre-Chamber," quoted in John Dykstra Eusden, *Puritans, Lawyers, and Politics in Early Seventeenth-Century England* (New Haven, Conn.,
1958), 59; Lambarde, *Archeion,* ed. McIlwaine and Ward, 58.

30. Elton, ed., *Tudor Constitution,* 163, 233–238; Ingram, *Church Courts, Sex, and Marriage,* 4–5; Veall, *Popular Movement,* 30–44; Eusden, *Puritans, Lawyers, and Politics,* 89–

Yet the attacks on those courts did not translate into an assault on the legitimacy of equity or the belief that justice should come from the supreme authority in the land. Although Puritans disagreed with its origins, they found the idea of equity essential to bring men's "imperfect" laws into line with the "perfect and absolute" laws of God. They disagreed on the application of "conscience," but it remained a crucial concept in their vocabulary. And, although they were concerned about the Stuart notion of a king-centered hierarchy, the "conviction that there were ultimate authorities ruling through laws determined the function and relationship of all institutions for Puritans and lawyers."[31]

Perhaps most important, these attacks never became an attack on the appeal; instead, "appeal" became an increasingly powerful word in popular culture. From widely read political tracts to popular plays by William Shakespeare, the appeal made its appearance. A popularizer of the perils of Puritanism, Richard Montagu, recalled Paul's appeal in the title of his work defending the divine right of kings: *Appello Caesarem: A Just Appeale from Two Unjust Informers* (1625). The Puritan John Yates's response to Montagu, *Ibis ad Caesarem*, also embraced the appeal. Yates addressed the pamphlet to the king: "The Supreme and Sovereign Judge over all Causes and Appeals in his Majesty's Dominion." His title, *Ibis ad Caesarem*, quoted Festus's words to Paul: "Hast thou appealed unto Caesar? Unto Caesar shalt thou go" (Acts 25:12). Yet Yates also was eager to go before the king in this literary appeal. Paraphrasing Paul, he wrote, "I think my self happy (o King) because I shall answer this day before thee." To both men, the appeal provided the opportunity to bring all the facts before a new, higher authority. Even

---

94. On Puritan law reform, see Nancy L. Matthews, *William Sheppard, Cromwell's Law Reformer* (Cambridge, 1984); David Sandler Berkowitz, *John Selden's Formative Years: Politics and Society in Early Seventeenth-Century England* (Washington, D.C., 1988), 96–134; G. B. Warden, "Law Reform in England and New England, 1620 to 1660," *William and Mary Quarterly,* 3d Ser., XXXV (1975), 668–690. On the church courts and the Puritans, see Ingram, "Puritans and the Church Courts, 1560–1640," in Christopher Durston and Jacqueline Eales, eds., *The Culture of English Puritanism, 1560–1700* (New York, 1996), 58–91.

31. William Perkins, *Epieikeia; or, A Treatise of Christian Equitie and Moderation* (Cambridge, 1604), in Edmund S. Morgan, ed., *Puritan Political Ideas, 1558–1794* (New York, 1965), 66–67; William W. Beach, "The Meaning and Authority of Conscience in Protestant Thought of Seventeenth-Century England" (Ph.D. diss., Yale, 1944); David Little, *Religion, Order, and Law: A Study in Pre-Revolutionary England* (New York, 1969), 101–131; George L. Mosse, *The Holy Pretence: A Study of Christianity and Reason of State from William Perkins to John Winthrop* (Oxford, 1957), 48–87; Margo Todd, *Christian Humanism and the Puritan Social Order* (Cambridge, 1987), 176; Eusden, *Puritans, Lawyers, and Politics,* 141.

The publication and republication of works addressing the jurisdictional hierarchy of courts in the 1630s and 1640s attests to the fascination with the location of authority. Coke's *Fourth Part of the Institutes* was printed in 1644; Lambarde's *Archeion* was printed in 1635; Crompton's *Jurisdiction of Courts* was reprinted in 1637; Thomas Smith's *De Republica Anglorum* was reprinted in 1635. See Cromartie, *Sir Matthew Hale,* 53.

Shakespeare chose the device of the appeal in a crucial scene in the play
that seemed an explicit comment on the reigns of Elizabeth and James I,
Henry VIII (1613). Shakespeare retold the story of Katharine of Aragón's
appeal to the pope. To the king and Cardinal Wolsey, Katharine states:

> . . . that again
> I do refuse you for my judge and here,
> Before you all, appeal unto the Pope,
> To bring my whole cause 'fore his Holiness,
> And to be judg'd by him.

Like all appellants, Katharine knew the appeal would provide a rehearing of
her "whole cause" before a judge whose authority she was willing to accept.
From Paul to the Puritans, the appeal permitted a second chance to cry
injustice.[32]

II. The Culture of Appeal in Massachusetts and Rhode Island

The cultural power of the word "appeal" rippled into New England. Even in
colloquial references, "appeal" connoted the search for justice by a rehearing
before a higher authority. In 1632, the Company of Husbandmen sought
to resolve a monetary dispute by writing Governor John Winthrop in an
"appeal . . . for Justice." In 1636, William Leigh wrote that he "appeale[d]" to
the governor's brother as to the fact that he was a diligent preacher. In the
spring of 1638, Roger Williams wrote John Winthrop that, with respect to
their disagreements, Williams desired "to rest in my Appeal to the most
high." In an autumn 1638 treaty, Miantonomi and Uncas pledged, not to seek
revenge for injuries, but "to appeal to the English" who were "to decide." In
these references, "appeal" signaled the acceptance of authority—whether of
God, the governor, or, more questionably, the English—in return for the
promise of a just decision. In each instance, the appeal promised an investigation into the facts and merits of the particular case. The power of this
meaning of the appeal persuaded the Puritan colonists to overlook the
word's heritage, which embodied all that the Puritan colonists despised—
Rome, the Anglican ecclesiastical system, the king—and accept the appeal
after it arose out of colonial corporate practice.[33]

---

32. Richard Mountagu, *Appello Caesarem: A Just Appeale from Two Unjust Informers* (London, 1625); [John Yates], *Ibis ad Caesarem; or, A Submissive Appearance before
Caesar . . .* (London, 1626); *Henry VIII,* act 2, scene 4. The "appeal" appears twice more in
Henry VIII: act 2, scene 4, and act 5, scene 1.
33. *Winthrop Papers,* III, 102, 311; Roger Williams, *The Correspondence of Roger Williams,*

The Corporate Practice of Appeal

By the 1640s, the appeal became a central component in the legal system of Massachusetts Bay and Rhode Island. Two explanations exist for the peculiar colonial appearance of the appeal. Roscoe Pound argued that the appeal was the result of crude colonial practice. Julius Goebel argued that it was modeled on the practices of justices of the peace. Both theories implied that the colonial system of redress had been based on rudimentary, common-law legal practices and involved no substantive theory of justice.

Pound provided no evidence for his explanation, and Goebel relied on justice-of-the-peace statutes that were passed after the English Revolution. In fact, Goebel's uncertainty about his own theory is apparent throughout his argument. He explicitly acknowledged it when he wrote that the effect of the justice-of-the-peace experience "had, *we believe,* much more to do with establishing in men's minds ideas about the 'right of appeal,' . . . than did the older forms of review."[34] He did not cite any sixteenth- or early-seventeenth-century manuals for justices of the peace that used the term "appeal" to describe a petition for redress, and, thus far, I have been unable to find one. Although the word "appeal" was eventually attached to the statutes providing for the justice-of-the-peace sessions review procedure, the earliest version of these statutes was passed between 1597 and 1601 and did not use the term. Moreover, if the justice-of-the-peace practice had been as well known as Goebel speculated, then the failure of Rhode Island initially to adopt it is somewhat inexplicable. The mid-seventeenth-century use of the word "appeal" to describe these procedures likely came from the larger cultural understandings of the appeal.

A more persuasive, simpler explanation for the origin of the appeal in America is that the culture of appeal passed to the colonists through the

---

ed. Glenn W. LaFantasie et al., 2 vols. (Providence, R.I., 1988), I, 149; Elisha R. Potter, *The Early History of Narragansett* (Providence, R.I., 1835), 177.

34. Goebel, *Antecedents and Beginnings,* 25 (emphasis added). Prior to 1640, the manuals were quite explicit on the use of writs of error after judgment or certiorari for interlocutory moves to the central courts. See, for example, William Lambard, *Eirenarcha; or, Of the Office of the Justices of Peace in Foure Bookes,* 4th ed. (London, 1599); Michael Dalton, *The Countrey Justice* . . . (London, 1618 ed., 1619 ed., 1626 ed., 1635 ed.). Indeed, Goebel acknowledged in a footnote, the "term 'appeal' in the statutes begins after the Restoration" (Goebel, *Antecedents and Beginnings,* 24–25 n. 73). By the eighteenth century, the procedure was termed an "appeal" (Joseph Shaw, *Parish Law; or, A Guide to Justices of the Peace,* 6th ed. [1748; rpt., Littleton, Colo., 1991], 168–169). Before the Elizabethan statutes, there was no right of appeal. "The remedy, in so far as one was available, was to have the proceedings reviewed by the prerogative writ or to have the justices tried and punished for misconduct" (Thomas Skyrme, *History of the Justices of the Peace,* I [Chichester, England, 1991], 137–138). Skyrme views the Elizabethan statutes as the earliest possible right of appeal to the quarter sessions. However, as noted above, neither statute contained the word "appeal" (39 Eliz. I, c. iii; 43 Eliz. I, c. ii).

corporate structure of the trading companies. The story of Massachusetts's transition from company to colony is a familiar one: the General Court of shareholders becoming the legislative body; the governor of the company becoming the colonial leader; the assistants becoming the Council; the freemen, the citizens. To this list, one should add that the appeal within the company became an appeal within the country.

The appeal became known in Massachusetts most likely through the Virginia Council—although perhaps via London instead of Jamestown. In 1619–1620, the Council for Virginia in England published a small pamphlet entitled *Orders and Constitutions*, which, like the Eastland Merchants' *Acts and Ordinances* (1617), described the company's internal regulations. Within these ordinances, "partly collected" from the patents, "partly ordained upon mature deliberation," the Virginia Council included chapter 88 on appeals: "The particular Members of the Company shall be subject to the general Courts, in matters concerning the Company or Plantation. If any man find himself aggrieved by a lesser or ordinary Court, he may appeal to a great and Quarter-Court, where the matter shall be heard and finally ordered. If any man refuse to obey both the one Court and other, he shall be disfranchised." In 1624, the Virginia Colony further adopted the corporate understanding of the appeal as a method of delegation when it established monthly courts "in the corporations of Charles City and Elizabeth City" "with reservation of appeal" to the governor and Council.[35]

Massachusetts's appeal procedure appears to have been modeled on the Virginia Council's corporate appeal procedure. Lawmakers in Massachusetts were aware of Virginia law. In March 1633, Edward Howe sent John Winthrop, Jr. a "book of the Laws established for Virginia" to present to his

---

35. *Orders and Constitutions, Partly Collected Out of His Majesties Letters Patents, and Partly Ordained upon Mature Deliberation, by the Treasuror, Counseil and Companie of Virginia . . . Anno 1619 and 1620* (London, 1620), reprinted in Susan Myra Kingsbury, ed., *The Records of the Virginia Company of London*, 4 vols. (Washington, D.C., 1906–1935), III, 340–365. The pre-1620 laws do not appear to include appeals (Kingsbury, ed., *Records of the Virginia Company*, III, 158–177 [July–Aug. 1619]); David H. Flaherty, ed., and William Strahey, comp., *For the Colony of Virginea Britannia: Lawes Divine, Morall, and Martiall, etc.* (1612; rpt., Charlottesville, Va., 1969); David Thomas Konig, "'Dale's Laws' and the Non–Common Law Origins of Criminal Justice in Virginia," *Am. Jour. Leg. Hist.*, XXVI (1982), 354–375. The 1619 "complaint in nature of an appeal" found throughout the Virginia records was a typical use of the appeal within the martial courts to address a jurisdictional issue: the "question whether Marshall law be a justiciable proceedings" (Kingsbury, ed., *Records of the Virginia Company*, I, 217, 219, 222, 226, 230). Andrews suggests that the *Orders and Constitutions* were not sent over until 1621 with Governor Wyatt (Andrews, *Colonial Period of American History*, I, 187). However, in February 1620, references to laws of the company being 120 in number in 18 chapters appear in the records. The *Orders* had 18 chapters and headings identical to those discussed (Kingsbury, ed., *Records of the Virginia Company*, I, 301–304 [Feb. 2, 1620]). For the 1624 statute, see Kingsbury, ed., *Records of the Virginia Company*, IV, 582.

father. A few years later, in April 1636, Governor Winthrop wrote his son that, in March, the General Court had ordained "quarterly Courts" and "4 Courts in the year at Boston for greater Causes, and for Appeals." The March 1636 legislation provided: "If any persons shall find himself grieved with the sentence of any of the said Courts, he may appeal to the next great Quarter Court." The similarity between the Massachusetts appellate procedure and the Virginia Council's *Orders and Constitutions* suggests that the Howe volume might have been a copy of the Council's published orders. Like the procedure used by the Eastland Merchants, the Massachusetts appeal structured the delegation of judicial power to lower courts in towns.[36]

After 1636, the appeal appeared repeatedly in Massachusetts legislation as a method to delegate authority. In September 1638, the General Court passed an act to end "small causes" by permitting a magistrate or two men to hear and determine small matters with the exception: "If any of the parties shall find themselves grieved with any such end or sentence, they may appeal to the next Quarter Court, or Courts of Assistants, etc." When the court deputized the towns to take land for highways, it authorized an appeal. When it granted William Pynchon a commission to hear cases at Springfield, it also authorized an appeal to the court of assistants. And when it created quarter courts in Ipswich and Salem, it once again authorized an appeal.[37]

Indeed, the appeal remained even when the corporate origins of it began to disappear. In John Cotton's draft of "Moses His Judicialls," Cotton included appeals from the town courts to the "Court of Governor and Assistants" and then to the General Court. The governor was to "direct in all matters, wherein appeal is made to them from inferior Courts." Cotton justified the appeal as "agreeable with the word of God" by simply citing sections of Exodus and Deuteronomy. His choice of references was not original. In a 1618 English pamphlet, Nathaniel Ward had cited the same biblical passages as a reminder to Chancellor Francis Bacon that chancery should "elect, direct and correct inferior Magistracy." By 1641, Ward was in Massachusetts, and references to the Mosaic law had become contested. Thus Ward's scribal edition of Massachusetts laws, *The Body of Liberties*, included the liberty of appeal and this time suggested it was equally compatible with "humanity, civility and Christianity." By 1648, the appeal was an accepted part of Massachusetts law. The colony's first printed code, *The Laws*

36. *Winthrop Papers*, III, 115 (Mar. 18, 1632/3). The editor of the Winthrop Papers has suggested that Howe's book "was a manuscript copy of the revision of the laws adopted by the General Assembly in September, 1632." The editor, however, cites no additional proof for the theory (*Winthrop Papers*, III, 115 n. 2). See also *Winthrop Papers*, III, 255 (Apr. 26, 1636); Nathaniel B. Shurtleff, ed., *Records of the Governor and Company of the Massachusetts Bay in New England* (Boston, 1853–1854), I, 169 (Mar. 3, 1635/6).

37. Shurtleff, ed., *Records of the Governor and Company*, I, 239, 280, 321–322, 325–326.

and Liberties of Massachusetts, contained an entire chapter entitled "Appeal."
The law permitted appeals to the court of assistants and a jury if the appeal
involved a matter of fact. Into the 1660s, long after Massachusetts had abandoned its outward commitment to the corporate form, the appeal, with its
promise of rehearings, remained central to the judicial system.[38]

The corporate origin of the appeal explains the initial absence of appeals
in Rhode Island. This absence did not arise from lack of legal knowledge
about the corporation. Roger Williams knew that corporations had courts.
He noted, "A Corporation, Society, or Company of East-Indie or Turkie-
Merchants, or any other Society or Company in London" can "hold their
Courts, keep their Records, hold disputations; and in matters concerning
their Society, may dissent, divide, break into Schisms and Factions, sue and
implead each other at Law." The communities of Rhode Island, however,
were not corporations. As Williams observed, they had "no Patent." Thus,
they had no appeals.[39]

Nevertheless, the appeal began to appear in Rhode Island. The first mention of the appeal appears in 1640, when Portsmouth and Newport merged.
The appeal solved the problem of delegating authority between each town's
courts and the new unified court structure. From the town courts, the new
law authorized "appeals to the Quarter Sessions" courts consisting of magistrates and a jury. In 1647, Roger Williams communicated instructions to a
Providence committee on a new colonial government: there should be "an
exact and orderly way open for appeals unto General Courts, that so, if any
shall be justly grieved, at any sentence passed, or otherwise, he or they may
make their lawful charge for relief there." Although the 1647 laws did not
include such appeals, the colony by 1651 had passed legislation permitting an
appeal from the town courts to the General Court of Trials. As in Massachusetts, the appeal permitted a rehearing of the case. The General Court
of Trials consisted of an assistant from each of the four towns, the town

38. [John Cotton], *An Abstract; or, The Lawes of New England, as They Are Now Established* (London, 1641), 1–2; Shurtleff, *Records of the Governor and Company of the Massachusetts Bay in New England,* 175; Samuel Ward, *Jethro's Justice of Peace* (London, 1618), A4;
William H. Whitmore, ed., *The Colonial Laws of Massachusetts . . . Containing Also, the
Body of Liberties* (Boston, 1889), 41; Max Farrand, ed., *The Laws and Liberties of Massachusetts* (Cambridge, Mass., 1929), 2; John D. Cushing, comp., *The Laws and Liberties of
Massachusetts, 1641–1691* (Wilmington, Del., 1976), 72. Nathaniel Ward's pamphlet included his brother Samuel's sermon, *Jethro's Justice of Peace,* which made use of the same
biblical passages mentioned above. The Wards' connection to the Jethro sermon suggests
that the dichotomy between Cotton's and Ward's approach might not have been as great as
has been suggested. Both were influenced by and could cite biblical law and secular law.
On Cotton and Ward, see Theodore Dwight Bozeman, *To Live Ancient Lives: The Primitivist Dimension in Puritanism* (Chapel Hill, N.C., 1988), 174–182. The 1635 edition of Lambarde's *Archeion* also referred to Jethro's ideas of the judiciary (11).

39. Roger Williams, *The Bloudy Tenent of Persecution . . .* (1644), ed. Samuel L. Caldwell,
in Narragansett Club, *Publications,* III (Providence, R.I., 1867), 73; Williams, *Correspondence,* ed. LaFantasie et al., I, 53 (Aug. 25, 1636).

magistrates from the town in which the court sat, and a jury. Despite legislative changes almost annually to the court system during the 1650s, the appeal remained a constant part of Rhode Island law. In 1663, Rhode Island became the first colony to include in its new charter a provision expressly permitting "the GOVERNOUR and Company" to appeal to England in matters of "public controversy" between it and other colonies.[40]

The Meaning of Appeal: Equity and Conscience

Although the corporate origins of the appeal meant that it was adopted in the two colonies at different moments, the meanings surrounding the culture of appeal in England were understood and shared by the colonists of Massachusetts Bay and Rhode Island. Colloquial references to the appeal demonstrate that the colonists associated it with a request for broad, equitable justice. Thus William Piggott made an "appeal" to Winthrop "not doubting, but to receive ample satisfaction" to rescue his son from an abusive indentureship. They also associated the appeal with conscience; indeed, the words seemed to belong together. Thomas Larkham "appeale[d] with a good conscience" to God in a matter of religious dispute. John Cotton stated that he would "appeal to Mr. Williams his own Conscience," if it were "not leavened with overdeep prejudice." Williams dared to "appeal to Master Cotton's conscience," and, in his *Address to the General Court of New England*, he made an "appeal to the consciences of God's most knowing servants."[41]

The colonists repeatedly confirmed their belief in the importance of equity in deciding controversial causes. Sir Henry Vane offered to give John Winthrop, Jr. his advice to settle a matter "according to the Justice and the Equity of the cause." John Cotton complained that Samuel Gorton had refused to "shew the right, and equity" of his cause and, with regard to Roger Williams, declared the "equity of his Banishment." Roger Williams was no different. He noted that some of Cotton's accusations had a "want of Equity." Williams even explicitly condoned the equity of chancery courts, justifying "men [who] see cause to ordain a Court of Chancery, and erect a Mercy-seat to moderate the rigor of Laws, which cannot be justly executed, without the

40. John Russell Bartlett, ed., *Records of the Colony of Rhode Island and Providence Plantation, in New England*, 10 vols. (Providence, R.I., 1856–1865), I, 106–107; Williams, *Correspondence*, ed. LaFantasie et al., I, 230 (May 18, 1647); Bartlett, ed., *Rhode Island Colonial Records*, I, 143–146, 237, 191–192, 203, II, 20. On the unpublished 1647 laws, see G. B. Warden, "The Rhode Island Civil Code of 1647," in David D. Hall, John M. Murrin, and Thad W. Tate, eds., *Saints and Revolutionaries: Essays on Early American History* (New York, 1984), 142, 144. On the 1650s changes, see Bartlett, ed., *Rhode Island Colonial Records*, I, 222, 237, 242, 357; for 1664 appeals law, see II, 30–32.

41. *Winthrop Papers*, V, 155 (May 4, 1647), IV, 319 (Feb. 1640/1); John Cotton, *A Reply to Mr. Williams His Examination*... (1647), ed. J. Lewis Diman, in Narr. Club, *Publications*, II (Providence, R.I., 1867), 31; Roger Williams, *The Bloody Tenent Yet More Bloody*... (1652), ed. Samuel L. Caldwell, in Narr. Club, *Publications*, IV (Providence, R.I., 1870), 29, 98.

moderate and equal consideration of persons and other circumstances!" Indeed, other colonists thought equity was the point of the justice system. Samuel Symonds observed a trial in which, after the "rest was pleaded . . . , point of Chancery or equity was pleaded." And Edward Parks described a trial against a Mr. Cooke, whose "friends carried it against justice and equity." Moreover, procedural characteristics of both colonies' judicial systems reinforced the importance of equity. The colonial court systems did not separate equity courts like chancery from common-law courts. Rhode Island's General Court of Trials heard cases without distinction. In Massachusetts, as Thomas Lechford noted in *Plain Dealing* (1642), the general and quarter courts had the "power of Parliament, King's Bench, Common Pleas, Chancery, High Commission and Star-Chamber, and all other Courts of England."[42]

Both colonies made this promise of equity a reality by allowing rehearings before superior authorities. In Rhode Island, although no "appeal" initially existed, both the arbitral system in Providence and the judge-and-elder structure in Pocasset guaranteed rehearings by a larger section of the community. In Providence, a document signed by members of the community, including apparently two women, ensured that a party who disagreed with the decision of the five arbitral "desposers" could have the clerk call "the Town together . . . for a Trial." In Pocasset, "the Judge and Elders" had to report to the assembly of freemen of the town, every three months, "all such cases, actions and Rules which have passed through their hands, by them to be scanned and weighed by the word of Christ." If "the Lord" had "dispensed light to the contrary of what by the Judge and Elders hath been determined, that then and there it should be repealed."[43]

In Massachusetts, the infamous case of Goody Sherman's sow, *Sherman v. Keayne*, demonstrates the broad acceptance of rehearings. Mrs. Sherman had sued the merchant Robert Keayne for allegedly killing her husband's sow. After his acquittal, he sued her for slander and recovered a monetary judgment. When Sherman's case reached the General Court on petition, the court completely reheard the case over a seven-day period. After this hearing, Winthrop even suggested that the case could be reargued once again. Indeed, the theory behind the suggestion of rehearing demonstrates the wide-

42. *Winthrop Papers*, III, 282 (July 1, 1636); Cotton, *A Reply*, ed. Diman, in Narr. Club, *Publications*, II, 16, 67; Williams, *Bloody Tenent Yet More Bloody*, ed. Caldwell, in Narr. Club, *Publications*, IV, 466, 486; *Winthrop Papers*, V, 151 (Apr. 28, 1647), 187 (Oct. 6, 1647); Thomas Lechford, *Plain Dealing; or, News from New England* (1640), ed. J. Hammond Trumbull (Boston, 1867), 63. On Rhode Island courts, see *Rhode Island Court Records: Records of the Court of Trials of the Colony of Providence Plantations, 1647–1670*, 2 vols. (Providence, R.I., 1920–1922).

43. Howard Millar Chapin, *Documentary History of Rhode Island* (Providence, R.I., 1916), 48–49, 113; Bartlett, ed., *Rhode Island Colonial Records*, I, 63–64.

spread belief in the importance of equity and the particular circumstances of the parties. Winthrop notes in his journal that many people wanted the case to be reheard because the defendant's "being accounted a rich man, and she a poor woman, this so wrought with the people." Winthrop thought these feelings to be "unreasonable compassion"; nonetheless, he noted, despite the uncertain result, the General Court decided to try to persuade Keayne to restore whatever money he had obtained from Sherman.[44]

Both colonial systems ensured that the rehearing would be on the facts by usually requiring the presence of a jury on appeal. In Massachusetts, the 1648 *Laws and Liberties* required that a jury be present in an appeal to the Court of Assistants if the appeal was in matter of fact. Similarly, Rhode Island's General Court of Trials appears to have almost always provided for a jury. The appeal's association with this common acceptance of equity on rehearing strengthened its presence in the colonial judicial systems.[45]

The Meaning of Appeal: Authority

The acceptance of the culture of appeal in New England allowed the appeal to become the central motif of numerous debates over the location of authority. In seventeenth-century New England, no question was more difficult than determining who held authority. Avi Soifer writes: "Intrigue and ceaseless disputation about what gave anyone legitimate authority to claim to be in charge pervaded life among the first colonists in Virginia and New England. . . . Sovereignty always was uncertain." Yet rejecting or restructuring authority was not without its hazards and could lead to imprisonment or even death. Moreover, authority was often hard to recognize and, therefore, sometimes even harder to reject. The appeal mediated these difficulties. Unlike the writ of error, with its static insistence on the authority of the court, the appeal engaged the litigant in the acceptance of superior authority. The appeal represented an exchange wherein the litigant promised to recognize authority in return for the case's being reheard. Authority was constructed at the moment of the appeal. Thus, by talking about the appeal, the colonists could safely discuss their understanding of the location of supreme authority.[46]

The New England colonists knew that the culture of appeal carried with it the belief that justice lay in a series of hierarchically arranged superior powers. Thus it is not surprising that they used the word to convey their

44. *Winthrop Papers*, IV, 349–351 (July 15, 1642); James Kendall Hosmer, ed., *Winthrop's Journal: History of New England, 1630–1649*, 2 vols. (New York, 1908), II, 64–66, 118–119.

45. Farrand, ed., *Laws and Liberties*, 2; *The Early Records of the Town of Portsmouth* (Providence, R.I., 1901); *The Early Records of the Town of Warwick* (Providence, R.I., 1926); *Rhode Island Court Records*, I, II.

46. Aviam Soifer, *Law and the Company We Keep* (Cambridge, Mass., 1995), 7, 24.

recognition of a superior authority. In the spiritual realm, where the supreme authority was relatively uncontroversial, they appealed to God. Roger
Williams "appeale[d] to the Searcher of all Hearts." Samuel Gorton also
"appeale[d] unto God the searcher of hearts," and he "appeale[d] unto God
the judge of all secrets." On occasion, they used the appeal to designate God's
delegated authority. John Winthrop, for example, thought seven members a
better number to constitute a church congregation, because "an appeal was
allowed from three." Sometimes they even used the appeal to worry about
the relationship of church and God. Winthrop noted that, if "the Church
should become the supreme Court in the Jurisdiction, and capable of all
Appeals," then it would be exalted above God.[47]

In the 1630s, when the location of supreme political authority—Massachusetts Bay—also appeared relatively uncontroversial to many colonists,
the appeal was often absent or only hesitatingly asserted. In 1636, the banished Roger Williams did not appeal to England. A few were less agreeable.
Edward Winslow warned Winthrop from New Plymouth that, if "new England will afford no Justice," he would "appeal further." Yet, in 1637, when
John Wheelwright appealed to the king, he "relinquished his appeal" on
being told by the court that "an appeal did not lie; for by the king's grant we
had power to hear and determine without any reservation."[48]

With the onset of the English Revolution, the issue of who held supreme
authority was no longer so quietly accepted. Roger Williams noted, "In this
present storm of England's sorrows, one of the greatest Queries in all the
Kingdom [is] who are the true Officers, true Commanders, true Justices,
true Commissioners." As Williams's "true" suggested, authority was a slippery idea. In England, as John Winthrop learned, "books entitled Appeals to
the people are put forth by Lilburne and others" to persuade "the people,
that all power and sovereignty is devolved and came back to its first subject,
viz: themselves." Like John Lilburne, the American colonists employed the
legal meaning of the appeal as a literary device to signal the rejection or
acceptance of authority. But the culture of appeal, with its blurred boundaries between the literary, the legal, and the political, meant that the appeal
could also be used actually to accept or reject political authority—without
dangerous confrontations.[49]

47. Williams, *Bloody Tenent Yet More Bloody*, ed. Caldwell, in Narr. Club, *Publications*,
IV, 465; Samuel Gorton, "Samuel Gorton's Letter to Nathaniel Morton (June 30, 1669)," in
Peter Force, comp., *Tracts and Other Papers*, IV, no. 7, 9, 11; Hosmer, ed., *Winthrop's
Journal*, I, 173 (Feb. 1, 1636); *Winthrop Papers*, III, 505 (c. November 1637).

48. Hosmer, ed., *Winthrop's Journal*, I, 162–163; Williams, *Correspondence*, ed. LaFantasie et al., I, 21–22; *Winthrop Papers*, III, 274; Hosmer, ed., *Winthrop's Journal*, I, 239–240.

49. Roger Williams, *Mr. Cotton's Letter Lately Printed, Examined and Answered* (1644),
ed. Reuben Aldridge Guild, in Narr. Club, *Publications* (Providence, R.I., 1866), I, 332;
Winthrop Papers, V, 212–213 (Apr. 10, 1648).

Within New England in the 1640s, Thomas Lechford was among the first to take advantage of this culture of appeal by using the procedure to represent his acceptance of English authority and Massachusetts Bay's defiance of it. Lechford's discussions of the appeal in *Plain Dealing* appear in amendments he apparently made to his manuscript in late 1641 after leaving the colonies. Their substance and tone suggest that they were Lechford's response to the *Body of Liberties*. Lechford noted that, although there was "no appeal" from the General Court in Massachusetts to England, he "presume[d] their Patent doth reserve and provide for Appeals, in some cases, to the King's Majesty." The words "Patent" and "Majesty" underscored that the proper location of authority was the king, not the colony, and, in essence, accused Massachusetts of defiance. Yet Lechford also used the device of the appeal to emphasize that, unlike Massachusetts, he accepted such supremacy. He "appeale[d] to his royal Majesty, and his honorable and great Counsel" as to the truth of his comments. Safely in England, Lechford was not worried about his defiance of Massachusetts authority.[50]

But, in a situation where one was actually challenging a very present authority, the appeal could establish defiance without leaving one dead or imprisoned, as the story of Rhode Island religious dissident Samuel Gorton demonstrates. In the minds of Massachusetts authorities, Samuel Gorton was an old troublemaker. Banished to Rhode Island in 1639 for heretical lay preaching, Gorton once again became the subject of complaints in 1641 and 1642. The following year, Massachusetts sent an armed force into Warwick, Rhode Island, to capture him and a number of others. In Gorton's mind, the Massachusetts leaders presumed too much authority; therefore, he made an "appeal to the honorable State of England." Another letter, in describing the incident, emphasizes Gorton's appeal as defiance without bloodshed: "The resolution on both sides being so hot, that we thought immediately the Battle would have began; they did then appeal to the highest Court in old England, for the trial of their right."[51]

Even after Massachusetts took him by force, Gorton continued to express his defiance by declaring that he appealed to England. His appeal was a literary one. He had yet to be tried; the point of his appeal was to demonstrate that he saw England as possessing authority over Massachusetts. The colony's leaders were aware of the meaning of his appeals—and refused to acknowledge them. Like Lechford, Gorton argued that Massachusetts's mere denial of his appeal signaled a graver denial of English authority. Mas-

50. Lechford, *Plain Dealing,* ed. Trumbull, xxxviii–xl, 64, 67.

51. Gorton, *Simplicity's Defence against Seven-Headed Policy* . . . (London, 1646), 40, 42, 55. The pamphlet also appears in Rhode Island Historical Society, *Collections* (Providence, R.I., 1835), II. On Gorton, see Gura, *A Glimpse of Sion's Glory,* 194–95, 276–303; Lewis G. Janes, *Samuell Gorton: A Forgotten Founder of Our Liberties* (Providence, R.I., 1896).

sachusetts could try him only "by virtue" of the judicial power given them from the "State of old England." The colony's denial of his appeal thus "must either presuppose a superiority in them that deny it, or an equality at the least, with the State appealed unto." Freed eventually by the General Court, Gorton sailed for England to complain. In England, his publication of *Simplicitie's Defence* (1646), with its endless recounting of his appeals, allowed Gorton to continue to express his defiance of Massachusetts's erroneous belief in its supremacy.[52]

The link between the appeal and supreme authority haunted even those who would have preferred to disregard the culture of appeal for reasons of practical politics. Roger Williams and John Winthrop—two of the greatest political leaders and intellectuals of the seventeenth-century American colonies—confronted the same political struggle over authority. For Williams, Rhode Island's famous religious dissenter, the problem lay in Massachusetts Bay's prosecutions and threats of prosecutions of religious dissenters who disagreed with the religious and political authority of the colony. For Winthrop, the leader of Massachusetts Bay, the problem lay in these dissenters' perpetual attempts to complain to England that the prosecutions proved that the colony had usurped English authority. The practical solution for both men was simple: Williams needed to justify appeals in cases of religious dissent; Winthrop needed to deny appeals without angering England. In justifying these ends, both men further explored and elaborated the relationship between the appeal and supreme authority.

Roger Williams and the Appeal

Roger Williams wanted to reconcile the practical reality of the need to appeal to England with his theory of the separation of civil and spiritual authority. Williams believed that the civil realm of government did not have authority over the spiritual, or religious, realm. Yet Williams understood that the appeal designated supreme authority: "For in appealing to an higher Judge, a man always presupposeth (if not skill perfect, yet) competent skill, and a true power committed from God, to judge in such cases." Thus, if appealing signaled the acceptance of authority, how could the dissenters complain about Massachusetts's treatment of them? Would not appealing prove that they accepted the civil government's authority over spiritual matters? Williams was clear that, in spiritual matters, if civil authorities lacked power to prosecute, then they also lacked power to be appealed to for wrongful prosecution. He acknowledged "that stumbling block which many fall at, to wit, Paul's appealing to Caesar." If Paul had appealed to Caesar in spiritual things, he had committed five evils. Indeed, when Williams described his

52. Gorton, *Simplicity's Defence*, 40, 42, 55.

own actions after his banishment, he emphasized he had appealed, but not to civil authorities: "I humbly appeale[d] unto the Father of Spirits for witness of the upright and constant diligent search my spirit made after him." The ever politically adept Williams realized, however, that appealing to God would not stop Massachusetts's threats.[53]

Williams's desire to justify appeals and his dislike of the Massachusetts government's assertion of authority led him to redefine the type of persecution experienced by dissenters and the proper location of authority in the civil state. In *The Bloudy Tenent* (1644) and *The Bloody Tenent Yet More Bloody* (1647), Williams argued that Paul had not appealed in spiritual matters: "And yet Caesar (as a civil supreme Magistrate) ought to defend Paul from Civil violence, and slanderous accusations about sedition, mutiny, civil disobedience, etc. And in that sense who doubts but that God's people may appeal to the Roman Caesar."[54]

Williams later emphasized, "Paul never appealed to Caesar as a Judge appointed by Christ Jesus to give definitive sentence in any spiritual or Church controversy, but against that civil violence and murder . . . , Paul justly appealed." Given that the church-state structure of Massachusetts resulted in linking spiritual disagreements to sedition and civil disobedience, Williams's theory, in essence, condoned appeals in all cases. Indeed, by 1647, Williams explicitly stated that "persecution for matters of conscience" was, not a spiritual matter, but "a violence against the civil state" from which the "supreme officer" was "bound to protect the bodies, goods, or good names of his subjects." By redefining the underlying matter, Williams could have both the appeal and a theory of separate authority.[55]

Yet this discussion of the appeal also provided Williams with an opportunity to redefine the location of civil authority. Although God reigned supreme in the spiritual realm, Williams suggested that the English king might not be the supreme power in the civil realm. In certain cases, "the last

53. Williams, *Bloody Tenent Yet More Bloody,* ed. Caldwell, in Narr. Club, *Publications,* IV, 161; Williams, *Bloudy Tenent,* ed. Caldwell, in Narr. Club, *Publications,* III, 120, 157–59; Williams, *Mr. Cotton's Letter,* ed. Guild, in Narr. Club, *Publications,* I, 340; Williams, *Correspondence,* ed. LaFantasie et al., I, 22. Among books on Williams, see Perry Miller, *Roger Williams: His Contribution to the American Tradition* (Indianapolis, Ind., 1962); Edmund S. Morgan, *Roger Williams: The Church and the State* (New York, 1967); Samuel Hugh Brockunier, *The Irrepressible Democrat: Roger Williams* (New York, 1940); W. Clark Gilpin, *The Millenarian Piety of Roger Williams* (Chicago, 1979); Edwin S. Gaustad, *Liberty of Conscience: Roger Williams in America* (Grand Rapids, Mich., 1991); Orla Elizabeth Winslow, *Master Roger Williams* (New York, 1957).

54. Williams, *Bloudy Tenent,* ed. Caldwell, in Narr. Club, *Publications,* III, 159.

55. Ibid., 243; Williams, *Bloody Tenent Yet More Bloody,* ed. Caldwell, in Narr. Club, *Publications,* IV, 161, 273–275. Wheelwright's appeal echoed almost precisely Paul's words. See Irving Berdine Richman, *Rhode Island: Its Making and Its Meaning* (New York, 1902), I, 46–47.

Appeal must come to the Bar of the People or Commonweal, where all may personally meet, as in some Commonweals of small number, or in greater by their Representatives." The people, Williams implied, were the supreme authority. Williams's almost culturally relativist list of authorities that could be appealed to—"the Roman Caesar, an Egyptian Pharaoh, a Philistian Abimelecke, an Assyrian Nabuchadnezzar, the great Mogol, Prester John, the great Turk, or an Indian Sachim"—suggests that Williams saw both Caesar and the king as drawing their authority from the commonweal. Like Lilburne, Williams used the appeal to construct a theory of authority that rested with the people.[56]

With his understanding of authority redefined, Williams supported the appeal. When he returned from England in 1647, he was moderator for the Providence town session that instructed the assembly to create appeals in Rhode Island. In 1666, he praised the "inestimable Jewels" in the new 1663 Rhode Island charter, which explicitly permitted appeals to England in cases of public controversy between colonies. In 1670, Williams made apparent that all of these understandings were linked to the appeal. He described Rhode Island's decision to seek redress in a boundary dispute by use of the charter's appeal provision as "the Case of Paul appealing to Caesar."[57]

John Winthrop and the Appeal

Unlike Williams, who wanted to justify appeals, John Winthrop needed to legitimize his government's denial of dissenters' complaints and appeals to England without appearing to imply the colony was separating and rejecting England's supreme authority. The stumbling block for Winthrop was that the colony was a corporation that had been delegated authority from the crown and therefore had a right to appeal implicit in the charter. Winthrop knew this argument well in the form of Dr. Robert Child's "logic": "Every corporation of England is subject to the laws of England," and "this was a corporation of England, ergo." Winthrop could do little to argue that the colony was not a corporation, although he suggested that "though plantations be bodies corporate . . . yet they are also above the rank of an ordinary corporation." Even if such a hierarchy of corporations had existed, it did little to alter the historic precedents that suggested crown patents had delegated specific judicial powers and did not need explicitly to reserve the right of appeals.[58]

56. Williams, *Bloudy Tenent,* ed. Caldwell, in Narr. Club, *Publications,* III, 159, 356. For Williams on appeals to magistrates and governors, see 174.

57. Williams, *Correspondence,* ed. LaFantasie et al., I, 233 nn. 13–14, 535, 618.

58. Hosmer, ed., *Winthrop's Journal,* II, 304–305. Winthrop wrote to his son in 1646 that the Child petitioners "did presently appeal to the Parl[ia]ment, etc: so as we are like to proceed to some Censure for their appeal, if not for the Petition" (*Winthrop Papers,* V, 120

In attempting to justify the denial of appeals without renouncing English authority, Winthrop tried to reinterpret the appeal as a common-law creation. First, he tried to turn the corporate patent from the king into a common-law document. If the patent was a common-law document, he could claim that any reservation as to a right to appeal had to be stated in the patent. Winthrop advanced this argument in a number of different settings. He suggested this textualist understanding of the patent in numerous discussions with the deputies. Winthrop's journal entry on Wheelwright's appeal likewise argued that the patent denied appeals. And, in his 1644 recounting of the Wheelwright appeal, *A Short Story*, Winthrop emphasized:

> Upon this he appealed to the Kings Majesty, but the Court told him an appeal did not lie in this case, for the King having given us an authority by his grant under his great seal of England to hear and determine all causes without any reservation, we were not to admit of any such appeals for any such subordinate state, either in Ireland, or Scotland, or other places; and if an appeal should lie in one case, it might be challenged in all, and then there would be no use of government among us.[59]

But by 1644, Winthrop seemed to grow uncertain about the patent reservation argument. In his journal account of the Wheelwright appeal, he had simply added an ambiguous "etc." to his argument. In *A Short Story*, Winthrop explicitly expanded the "etc.": "Neither did an appeal lie from any Court in any County or Corporation in England, but if a party will remove his cause to any of the King's higher Courts, he must bring the King's Writ for it; neither did he tender any appeal, nor call any witnesses, nor desired any Act to be entered of it." Parallel to the common-law reservation argument, Winthrop thus advanced a common-law understanding of redress. To remove a case, one had to bring a writ of error, not an appeal. If one had failed to follow the proper procedures, then the appeal must never have existed. Winthrop seemed to hope that he could define away the appeals.[60]

All these technical common-law arguments, however, could not convincingly disguise the fact that the refusal to permit appeals appeared to deny England's supreme authority. Winthrop's efforts did not stop the English commissioners for foreign plantations from investigating the Gorton situa-

---

[Nov. 16, 1646]). Child referred to his "Appeal before Parliament" and hoped that his "Cause may be heard before indifferent Arbiters" (*Winthrop Papers*, V, 160 [May 14, 1647]).

59. John Winthrop, *A Short Story of the Rise, Reign, and Ruine of the Antinomians, Familists, and Libertines* (1644), in Hall, ed., *Antinomian Controversy*, 256–257. On the patent and corporations during the negative vote debate, see *Winthrop Papers*, IV, 382.

60. Hosmer, ed., *Winthrop's Journal*, I, 240–241; Winthrop, *A Short Story*, in Hall, ed., *Antinomian Controversy*, 257.

tion or from showing interest in another group of dissenters who wrote the
Child remonstrance. The culture of appeal was too strong to be redefined or
reinterpreted away.[61]

Finally, in a 1646 petition to the commissioners, Winthrop abandoned the
common-law arguments. Accepting the culture of appeal, he confronted the
issue of authority. He explicitly stated that the colony recognized the supremacy of England. In an eerie historical twist, Winthrop actually referred
to the Henrician act For the Restraint of Appeals. Winthrop's petition stated
that "the records" showed the wisdom of "our ancestors," who "acknowledged a supremacy in the bishops of Rome in all causes ecclesiastical, yet
would not allow appeals to Rome." Borrowing language from the preface to
the Henrician act, the petition stated that appeals "would be destructive to
all government" because the colony would have to follow the "delinquents"
to England "where the evidence and circumstances of facts cannot be so
clearly held forth as in their proper place," and the expenses would be great.
If the Puritan leaders of Massachusetts were Henry VIII, then England could
only be Rome. Winthrop must not have thought much of the commissioners—the analogy betrayed the precariousness of the argument: when
Henry VIII had barred appeals, he had ended the supremacy of Rome.[62]

Massachusetts, however, had acknowledged English authority, and the
commissioners returned the favor by writing a response that seemed to
support Massachusetts's practice. In 1647, the commissioners wrote, "We
intended not . . . to encourage any appeals from your justice, nor to restrain
the bounds of your jurisdiction to a narrower compass than is held forth by
your letters patent," and, the commissioners wrote, we "leave you with all
that freedom and latitude that may, in any respect, be duly claimed by you."
Whether the patent implicitly reserved appeals was left unclear. Nonetheless,
Massachusetts took the response as a sign that the denial of appeals was
compatible with English supremacy. Into the 1660s, the colony would proclaim its ability to deny appeals to England even as it clung tight to the
culture of appeal.[63]

In places as diverse as Rhode Island and Massachusetts, the appeal sur-

---

61. The fear of the Gorton and Child appeals twice sent Edward Winslow to England.
His effort to stop Gorton, *Hypocrisie Unmasked*, did not address the appeals issue (*Hypoc-
risie Unmasked: A True Relation of the Proceedings of the Governor and Company of the
Massachusetts against Samuel Gorton of Rhode Island* [1646; rpt., Providence, R.I., 1916]).

62. Hosmer, ed., *Winthrop's Journal*, II, 312.

63. Ibid., 337. Hugh Peter mysteriously wrote Winthrop shortly before the answer of the
commissioners that "appeals will hardly be overthrown," and they should not be troubled
by such appeals (*Winthrop Papers*, V, 159 [May 5, 1647]). A 1661 General Court order stated
that the governor and other officials in Massachusetts had "full power and authority" over
"ecclesiastics and civils, without appeal." See "Act of the General Court," June 10, 1661,
Shurtleff, ed., *Records of the Governor and Company*, IV, 24–25.

vived with the help of people as ideologically different from one another as Williams and Winthrop. As numerous other incidents during the 1640s in Massachusetts and Rhode Island demonstrate, the appeal signified the acceptance of authority to such a degree that discussions of the appeal provided a space to construct and recognize authority. American Indians such as Pumhom used the appeal to indicate which colony's authority they would temporarily recognize. John Winthrop and the Massachusetts deputies discussed the appeal as they struggled to agree upon the precise composition of the supreme authority of the General Court, asking, "Is there not a clear way of help in such cases, by Appeal, or Petition to the highest Authority?" Robert Child and the remonstrants used the appeal to suggest that supreme authority should be relocated in the fundamental laws of England instead of "arbitrary government." And the Rhode Island towns adopted the appeal to the General Court of Trials as a way of signaling their belief that "the Sovereign power of all Civil Authority is founded in the consent of the People."[64]

The appeal did not fade as the corporate structure of the colonies disappeared, because it carried with it a larger vision of law's relationship to the world. The colonists adopted a word that they used in everyday life to structure relationships with each other and with God. They accepted a word that envisioned a justice of equity, of rehearings on the merits, and of individual redress. They came to embrace a word that reconfirmed the structure of authority each time it was used. And, perhaps most important, they accepted the appeal because each grievance became a new bargain: the acknowledgment of authority for the guarantee of equity. In the end, they adopted a word whose ancient heritage might have reminded them that, rather than remaining salamanders far from England, they could aspire to the culture of the sons of God.

64. *Winthrop Papers*, VI, 246–247 (Aug. 15, 1648); *Winthrop Papers*, IV, 468, 477. On the Child remonstrants, see Gura, *A Glimpse of Sion's Glory*, 196–204; George L. Kittredge, "Dr. Robert Child the Remonstrant," in Colonial Society of Massachusetts, *Publications*, XXI, *Transactions* (Boston, 1919), 1–146; John Child, "New Englands Jonas Cast Up at London" (1647), in MHS, *Colls.*, 2d Ser., IV (Boston, 1846), 110–120; Thomas Hutchinson, *Hutchinson Papers* (1865; rpt., New York, 1967), 214. On the Rhode Island towns, see Williams, *Bloudy Tenent*, ed. Caldwell, in Narr. Club., *Publications*, III, 214, 249, 355, 367. Initially, each town had a representative on the General Court of Trials as well as the town judges from whichever town the court sat in; town members were also on the jury.

"Rigid and Inclement"

Origins of the Jamaica Slave Laws
of the Seventeenth Century

B Y 1700 SEVERAL English plantation colonies had been established in North America and in the Caribbean. The economies of these mainland and island colonies were generally based on the exploitation of African slave labor for the large-scale production of exportable staples, but reliance on slave labor was most pronounced in the Caribbean colonies that produced primarily sugar. Varying in size and cultivable acreage, these colonies, scattered through the archipelago that separates the Caribbean Sea from the Atlantic Ocean, also varied in the stages of evolution of their plantation complex—Barbados was the most advanced, followed by the Leeward Islands, and then Jamaica. All of them, however, can be classified as slave societies, because all were irrevocably tied to sugar and black slavery and subject to the powerful influences that these exerted on social, economic, political, and cultural relations.

Slavery was the sine qua non of the so-called Sugar Revolution that overtook the island colonies, starting in Barbados during the 1640s. It did not take long for plantation owners and the island legislatures to begin to acknowledge that the steady increase of the slave population through importation from Africa was a two-edged sword. Slavery supplied much-needed labor for the laborious tasks of sugar production, but at the same time it raised troublesome questions about the control of the enslaved workers. Among the various measures that the island authorities adopted in constructing their elaborate apparatus of control were slave laws.[1]

I would like to thank Philip J. Schwarz, Cynthia Herrup, Mindie Lazarus-Black, and the editors of this volume for their comments on versions of this essay. All dates are Old Style, but with the year made to start on January 1 instead of March 25.

1. For a general discussion of the development of the English plantation colonies of the Caribbean, see, for example, Richard S. Dunn, *Sugar and Slaves: The Rise of the Planter Class in the English West Indies, 1624–1713* (Chapel Hill, N.C., 1972); Richard B. Sheridan, *Sugar and Slavery: An Economic History of the British West Indies, 1623–1775* (Baltimore, 1973), 124–232; Robert Carlyle Batie, "Why Sugar? Economic Cycles and the Changing of Staples on the English and French Antilles, 1624–54," *Journal of Caribbean History*, VIII (1976), 1–41; Carl and Roberta Bridenbaugh, *No Peace beyond the Line: The English in the Caribbean, 1624–1690* (New York, 1972); Richard Pares, *Merchants and Planters* (Cam-

This essay discusses the origins of the police component of the laws concerning slavery, with particular reference to Jamaica during the seventeenth century, based on the premise that statutes are culturally and historically determined. Building on the work of Richard S. Dunn, it traces the origins of Jamaica's laws for the control of slaves to the Barbados precedent, the English precedent, and the particularities of Jamaica's independent development. Initially, Barbadian and English influences were prominent in the police laws that dealt with slaves as persons. Slave laws that reflected conditions or considerations generated by or within the colony did not emerge fully until the end of the seventeenth century. The exploration of Jamaica's early slave laws therefore seeks to throw light on the beginnings of a colonial slave society.[2]

I

Jamaica became an English colony in 1655, when it was captured from the Spanish and placed under the military government of General Edward D'Oyley. Serious efforts to develop a plantation economy in the captured colony did not commence until after the Restoration in 1660, and sugar became a major product during the 1670s. In the early 1660s the imperial government in England made a firm decision to keep Jamaica and devised new policy for the fledgling English colony that, situated "commodiously for Trade and Commerce" and of "a pleasant and most fertile Soyl," possessed the potential to generate "great Benefitt and Advantage" to the empire. The new policy for the colony's development took shape during the governorships of Edward D'Oyley, Thomas, Lord Windsor, Sir Charles Lyttelton, Sir

bridge, 1960); Jack P. Greene, "Society and Economy in the British Caribbean during the Seventeenth and Eighteenth Centuries," *American Historical Review*, LXXIX (1974), 1499–1517.

2. Elsa V. Goveia, "The West Indian Slave Laws of the Eighteenth Century," *Revista de ciencias sociales*, IV (1960), 75–105; William M. Wiecek, "The Statutory Law of Slavery and Race in the Thirteen Mainland Colonies of British America," *William and Mary Quarterly*, 3d Ser., XXXIV (1977), 258–280; Alan Watson, *Slave Law in the Americas* (Athens, Ga., 1989), 63–82, 115–133; Bradley J. Nicholson, "Legal Borrowing and the Origins of Slave Law in the British Colonies," *American Journal of Legal History*, XXXVIII (1994), 38–54; Dunn, *Sugar and Slaves*, 238–246; Jonathan A. Bush, "Free to Enslave: The Foundations of Colonial American Slave Law," *Yale Journal of Law and the Humanities*, V (1993), 417–470; Patricia Seed, *Ceremonies of Possession in Europe's Conquest of the New World, 1492–1640* (Cambridge, 1995), 6; Thomas D. Morris, *Southern Slavery and the Law, 1619–1860* (Chapel Hill, N.C., 1996); Philip J. Schwarz, *Slave Laws in Virginia* (Athens, Ga., 1996); Mindie Lazarus-Black, "Slaves, Masters, and Magistrates: Law and the Politics of Resistance in the English-Speaking Caribbean, 1736–1834," *American Bar Foundation Working Paper*, no. 9124 (Chicago, 1991); Michael Craton, *Empire, Enslavement, and Freedom in the Caribbean* (Kingston, Jamaica, 1997), 68–103, 463–470.

Thomas Modyford, and Sir Thomas Lynch. In December 1661 a proclamation from the king outlined a number of conditions under which settlement
and expansion might be pushed forward. As an inducement to settlers, the
proclamation declared, for example, "All children of any of our Naturall
born Subjects of England to be born in Jamaica shall from their respective
Births be reputed to be, and shall be free Denizens of England and shall have
the same priviledge to all intents and purposes as our free born Subjects of
England." Many settlers arrived subsequently from the other Caribbean
island colonies of Barbados and the Leeward Islands. In about 1660, Jamaica's population was estimated at 3,360 whites and 514 blacks; the number
of acres planted was 2,588. In 1664, after a few years of piecemeal legislation
related to the slowly growing but restive slave population, the Jamaica legislature passed the colony's first truly comprehensive slave act for the better
control of slaves. It had taken about a decade for Jamaica to move to this
higher level of slave legislation and to acknowledge particular problems of
control that the use of slave labor spawned. The legislature of Barbados had
passed fragmented legislation for nearly two decades before it approved a
comprehensive slave act in 1661. Jamaica thus moved much more quickly in
making use of a comprehensive slave act.[3]

This situation can be explained by the particular internal circumstances of
the colony at the Restoration, when "New Foundations, as well as a new
structure of government, had there to be built" to replace the "anarchy and
confusion" that followed its capture from the Spanish. During the early
1660s the emphasis was on creating order within the colony and placing it on
more secure footing. One troubling problem that the authorities faced in
those years was how to pacify or destroy the blacks who had taken to the
interior when the English invaded in 1655. Even after the last of the Spanish
defenders vacated the island around 1660, these blacks remained in rebellion
against the English, establishing the foundations of the Maroon, or fugitive
slave, phenomenon that was to plague Jamaica so intensely until 1739. During the second half of the seventeenth century, the development of Maroon
resistance was greatly facilitated by the growth in the number of plantations,
by the increase of the slave population, by the flight of slaves, and, most

3. Dunn, *Sugar and Slaves*, 46–116, 149–187, 224–262; "A Proclamation for the Encour-
ageing of Planters in His Majesties Island of Jamaica in the West Indies," Dec. 14, 1661,
Colonial Office 139/1, Public Record Office; A. P. Thornton, *West-India Policy under the
Restoration* (Oxford, 1956), 22–66; Great Britain, P.R.O., *Calendar of State Papers* (hereafter cited as *CSP*), Colonial Series, *America and West Indies* (London, 1860–), XII, *1685–
1688*, no. 2014; Orlando Patterson, *The Sociology of Slavery: An Analysis of the Origins,
Development, and Structure of Negro Slave Society in Jamaica* (London, 1967), 70–93, 260–
283; Richard Hart, *Slaves Who Abolished Slavery*, 2 vols. (Mona, Jamaica, 1985), II, 1–31;
Mavis C. Campbell, *The Maroons of Jamaica, 1655–1796: A History of Resistance, Collabora-
tion, and Betrayal* (Granby, Mass., 1988), 14–43.

important, by the "extreme environment" of Jamaica's difficult topography and its large size (4,411 square miles), both of which encouraged slave rebellion and flight. The contrast with Barbados (166 square miles) in this regard is very striking. An important element in the construction of Jamaica's first comprehensive slave act, therefore, was the almost immediate appearance of persistent and collective slave resistance.[4]

The legislation and various orders of government passed or released before 1664 illustrate how the Jamaica authorities intended to cope with rebellious plantation slaves and the Maroons. In 1661 D'Oyley released at least three orders directly or indirectly related to control of plantation slaves. The first mandated that "whatsoever Person Shall Presume to Carry a Stick of fire or a Pipe of Tobacco Lighted through a field of Caynes," and was convicted, faced a fine, half of which went to the informer and the rest to the public treasury. A second order also imposed a fine on "whosoever Shall entertayne any Bought servt or Slave in their house or Plantacon" for more than one night "after hee Shall Know him Soe to bee." The third order observed, "It hath been by dayly experience found that Many Great Mischeifes have risen in this Island to the Particular Masters of familyes by Wandring of Servants and Slaves, One Sundayes, Saturdayes in the afternoone, and other dayes, wherein the Said Servants and Slaves doe not Worke, And for such Tymes, as they Can gett out of their Masters Plantacons, By Stealing and filching their Masters goods And Provisions, Bartering and Selling the Same." The order outlined a number of measures to remedy the situation.

In 1663, the Jamaica legislature under Deputy Governor Sir Charles Lyttelton (successor to Thomas, Lord Windsor, who spent only ten weeks in the government to which he had recently been appointed), came to an agreement with Juan Lu-bola, leader of a palenque, or Maroon refuge, on the island. By this agreement, the new civil government of Jamaica pledged, among other things, to grant the Maroons freedom in return for their voluntary submission. Other fugitive slaves were also pressed to surrender and "receive the said Benefitts, Previledge and Immunities" offered to the Lu-bola group, "there being no Enemy now in the Island." This was probably a reference to the Spanish, but the Jamaica authorities also no doubt wished to avoid turning the Maroons and other fugitives into a new enemy. At any

4. Thornton, West-India Policy, 22–66; David Barry Gaspar, "'With a Rod of Iron': Barbados Slave Laws as a Model for Jamaica, South Carolina, and Antigua, 1661–1697," paper presented at the Comparative History of Blacks in the Diaspora Conference, Michigan State University, East Lansing, April 1995. On the Jamaica Maroon context, see Richard Price, ed., Maroon Societies: Rebel Slave Communities in the Americas, 2d ed. (Baltimore, 1979), 1–30, 227–292; Campbell, Maroons of Jamaica; Patterson, Sociology of Slavery; George Metcalf, Royal Government and Political Conflict in Jamaica, 1729–1783 (London, 1965), 33–59. See also the discussion on slave rebelliousness in Barbados and Jamaica during the seventeenth century in Dunn, Sugar and Slaves, 238–246, 256–262.

rate, in the records of the Jamaica Council the arrangements of 1663 were written down both in English and Spanish. Other measures were taken by the English in 1663 to curb slave rebelliousness. An order was issued that, "if any negroes shall raise a mutiny, any two justices of the peace may order their masters to sell or send them off the island." Another order obligated owners of small boats to secure them to prevent slave flight. Whatever might have been the immediate effect of such measures, they indicate that the authorities realized that slave rebelliousness was a multidimensional phenomenon that was not easy to bring under control.[5]

Early in 1664, after an elective assembly was organized, the Jamaica legislature passed an act "for the Punishing and Ordering of Negro Slaves." Its title notwithstanding, the act was by no means comprehensive. It was, however, the first enactment of any length on record that provides useful insight into the concerns of the authorities regarding slaves and conditions in frontier Jamaica. The preamble to the act read:

> Whereas there is now uppon this his Magesties Island Numbers of Negroes and more Dayly expected and that it is utterly impossible to make and continue Plantations without such Slaves as aforesaid. And that the orderly and regular Commanding and punishing the aforesaid Negro Slaves will tend verry much to the generall advantage of Settlers. And that the said Planters and Masters of Slaves cannot Mortally punish or afflict these offending Slaves by any due and formall Process of Law this Island being exceeding Great and the Law expensive.

The four factors mentioned in the preamble represented the foundation on which the act was constructed. Together, they confirmed the formative stages of development of a plantation society based on slavery. The problem facing the Jamaica legislature was how to promote (in the face of black rebelliousness that plagued them since the capture of the colony) white settlement and the growth of plantations worked by slaves. In 1664 the legislature sought to resolve the problem, trying to bring order to a situation that it did not wish to see get out of hand for want of a regulatory system. The Assembly's goal, bluntly, was to create an effective means for policing a restive slave population that was sure to get larger.[6]

5. D'Oyley's orders of Aug. 27, 1661, Nov. 15, 1661, C.O. 139/1; Thornton, *West-India Policy*, 51–60. For the Lu-bola order, see Feb. 1, 1663, C.O. 139/1. The document in English and Spanish can be found in Feb. 1, 1663, C.O. 140/1. See also Minutes of the Council of Jamaica, Oct. 23, 1663, G.B., P.R.O., *CSP*, Col. Ser., V, *1661–1668*, no. 573, and Oct. 23, 1663, C.O. 140/1.

6. For reference to the slave act, see *Journals of the Assembly of Jamaica*, January 10, 1664–April 20, 1709 (Jamaica, 1811), I, microfilm, Library of Congress, Washington, D.C. A copy of "An Act for the Punishing and Ordering of Negro Slaves" in manuscript can be found in n.d., C.O. 139/1.

Because slaveowners were not "Competent and equall Judges" in disciplining their own slaves, the act established rules for the control and punishment of all slaves. Thus, the master of a slave who committed any offense "worthy of Death" (in the master's mind) should deliver the slave to a justice of the peace and two "sufficient Neighbors as an Inquest," where they would pass "small Judgment or Sentence to death or otherwise." Such a sentence was declared to "stand good in Law." The act also discouraged masters from harboring desperate fugitives who might have enticed other slaves to follow their example. Masters were authorized to employ severe measures, including chaining and hamstringing, to secure such fugitives, or they were to chase these slaves away. If they did not, they could be fined. The act was also quite emphatic that no one should purchase or encourage the purchase of "any Spanish slave." However, the act was lenient toward fugitive "New Negroes" or recent arrivals from Africa. The article in the act regarding fugitives did not apply to them in the case of their first offense of flight.[7]

Apart from supplementing masters' discretion on their plantations by systematizing procedures for dealing with slaves accused of particularly heinous crimes or felonies, the act was aimed most specifically at problems related to fugitives and Spanish slaves. This fugitive crisis troubled the authorities during the early period when the Jamaica police slave laws, like those of Barbados, were still enacted piecemeal. For instance, under Colonel Sir Thomas Modyford of Barbados, who replaced Lyttelton as governor in mid-1664, the legislature passed "an act declaring war against the outlying Spanish negroes, unless they submit to the government." The act called attention to "divers rebellious Spanish Negroes that have bin offerd theire Libertyes and all the Priviledges of Englishmen if they would come in and submitt" to the government, but who persisted in "theyre Disobedience and contempt haveing murthered sume and threatened others" among the white people. Modyford also addressed other familiar problems of slave resistance. In June 1664, the month Modyford took his oath of office, the governor and Council ordered a "commission to be drawn empowering Capt. Rutter to reduce the runaway negroes on the north side" of the island. Rutter was authorized "to assemble a number of persons for apprehending certain runaway blacks from Barbadoes who have committed murder and other felonies . . . and in case of resistance to slay and kill said slaves." Captured rebels who had no masters were to become the property of their captors "and their heirs for ever." A monetary reward was also offered for taking rebels who had Jamaican owners.[8]

7. "An Act for the Punishing and Ordering of Negro Slaves," C.O. 139/1, preamble.
8. Dunn, *Sugar and Slaves,* 81–82, 154–156, 242–243; Thornton, *West-India Policy,* 60–66; Sheridan, *Sugar and Slavery,* 208–215; James Knight, "The Naturall, Morall and Politi-

Modyford was well qualified for the job of "perfecting the settlement of the island of Jamaica" under the revived English colonial plans of the Restoration government and approached his duties as new governor with great vigor, determination, and imagination. A Barbados magnate and planter who had been deeply involved in high-level politics in that colony, Modyford also acted as factor there for the Company of Royal Adventurers. A number of other Barbados residents accompanied him to Jamaica, some of them bringing along slaves. Among the various duties spelled out in his commission as governor, Modyford was authorized: "To choose a standing Council of 12 persons or to continue that already established; to make laws with the advice of five or more of said Council, so as they do not extend to taking away the right or interest of any persons in their freehold goods and chattels or to loss of members, such laws to be speedily sent home, and if disallowed thenceforward to cease. To erect courts of judicature, administer oaths, and appoint judges with salaries. To muster and command military forces, and ordain martial law." Modyford was also given the "power to call Assemblies, and with their consent to make laws, reserving to himself a negative voice; also to levy monies: said laws to agree with those of England, and to be in force for two years only, except they be confirmed by the King."[9]

' On matters of legal administration, Modyford was directed in his more expansive instructions as governor "to examine carefully the constitucon of such Judicatories for civil and criminall Affaires as are established there, and if they bee any way defective with the advice of the Councell cause them to bee amended in such manner as may bee most proper to keep the Peace of that Our Island and determine all causes Civil and Criminall matrimoniall and Testimentorie yet soe as noe mans Freehold Life or member be taken away or harmed but by established and knowne Lawes not repugnant to but as much as may bee agreeable to the knowne Laws of this Our Kingdome of Engld." In both his commission and instructions, therefore, Modyford received guidance on the importance of English law and a functioning judicial system for getting Jamaica on its feet as a plantation colony. It was a challenge from which he did not flinch. In meeting it Modyford was helped enormously by the latitude allowed him in his instructions to act, with the

---

call History of Jamaica and the Territories Thereon Depending; from the Earliest Account of the Time to the Year 1742," in Add. MSS, British Library, Department of Manuscripts, London; *Journals of the Assembly of Jamaica*, I, List of Acts passed Oct. 11, 1664–Mar. 16, 1665, act 8. For a manuscript copy of the act, see n.d., C.O. 139/1. See also Minutes of the Council of Jamaica, June 9, 1664, G.B., P.R.O., *CSP*, Col. Ser., V, 1661–1668, no. 746, or in C.O. 140/1.

9. Thornton, *West-India Policy*, 60–66; Sheridan, *Sugar and Slavery*, 211. For Modyford's commission etc., see G.B., P.R.O., *CSP*, Col. Ser., V, 1661–1668, nos. 629–635, 656, 687, 762, 764, 767.

advice of the Council, in "extraordinary cases" for which no specific instructions had been issued. Modyford could not have asked for more.[10]

II

The new governor of Jamaica did much to promote the expansion of plantation production and to chart a more steady course for the development of the colony. Under Modyford (1664–1670) Jamaica planters cultivated ginger, indigo, pimento, cotton, sugarcane, and cacao, which was the main crop until a blight destroyed the planters' dreams for riches from it in 1670. Sugarcane then replaced cacao and injected new life into the economy of Jamaica. Before this happened, however, Modyford introduced Jamaica's first truly comprehensive slave act in November 1664. In his first six months in Jamaica, Modyford led the legislature in passing twenty-seven important acts, including one for "dividing the island into several parishes and precincts," another "declaring the Laws of England in force in the Island," and the slave act.[11]

Jamaica's first major slave act of the seventeenth century, the comprehensive act "for the better ordering and Governing of negro slaves," was not a Jamaican creation, and it did not bear any signs of Spanish influence. According to Richard S. Dunn, it was copied "lock, stock, and barrel" from the Barbados slave act of 1661, with which Modyford would have been familiar. It served the colony well for a number of years. Even before the arrival of Modyford, the island legislature had been quite comfortable borrowing laws established at Barbados, then the most advanced English sugar colony. In 1661, for example, the legislature ordered that "certain Acts of Barbadoes be in force here, viz., servants under 18 years to be bound for seven years, and over 18 years for five years; that such as lay violent hands on their masters shall serve two years after their time; and such as beget a woman-servant with child, shall serve her master three years. That no ship shall unload until her master hath been with the Governor; no person leave the island without his name be up in the Secretary's office 21 days, all underwritings cleared; and that any servant marrying without his master's consent, shall serve four years after time."[12]

10. "Instructions for Col. Muddiford," Feb. 18, 1664, C.O. 1/18.

11. Sheridan, *Sugar and Slavery*, 211–214; J. Harry Bennett, "Cary Helyar, Merchant and Planter of Seventeenth-Century Jamaica," *WMQ*, 3d Ser., XXI (1964), 53–76; Bennett, "William Whaley, Planter of Seventeenth-Century Jamaica," *Agricultural History*, XL (1966), 113–123; Minutes of the Council of Jamaica, Nov. 1664, G.B., P.R.O., *CSP*, Col. Ser., V, *1661–1668*, nos. 836, 882; Thornton, *West-India Policy*, 60–66.

12. "An Act for the Better Ordering and Governing of Negro Slaves," Nov. 2, 1664, C.O.

The adoption of the Barbados slave act suggested more such following of precedent, but conditions in the two colonies were only roughly similar. Jamaica certainly had greater potential for development into a plantation colony than did Barbados, and, throughout the last four decades of the seventeenth century, the authorities made every effort to encourage exploitation of that potential. It was natural and sensible for frontier Jamaica to borrow from developed Barbados. If Barbados had to start from scratch in framing its slave laws, largely because there was no tradition of slavery or slave law in England to draw from, then Jamaica, borrowing from Barbados, could bypass a similar extended period of legislative experimentation. Jamaica was able, at least in this sense of the application of statute law, to accelerate its drive to organize a slave society. But had Barbados really started from scratch in developing its slave laws? If, as Alan Watson has pointed out, "borrowing is the nature of the legal game," and, since Barbados could not have borrowed from a nonexistent tradition of English slavery, was there some other tradition that the early colonial lawmakers might have drawn on? "Those making the law in whatever capacity," Watson noted, "whether as legislators or as subordinate, restricted judges or jurists, shape the law in part through their own tradition."[13]

In a section of his history of Jamaica bearing the title "Remarks on the Negroe Regulations," the Jamaica planter-historian Edward Long observed:

The Negroe code of this island appears originally to have [been] copied from the model in use at Barbadoes; and the legislature of this latter island, which was the first planted by the English, resorted to the English *villeinage* laws, from whence they undoubtedly transfused all that severity which characterizes them, and shews the abject slavery which the common people of England formerly laboured under.

Long cited laws of the reigns of Edward III, Richard II, Elizabeth I, and Edward VI to support his claim. He concluded,

The modes of punishment in these statutes, and the general provisions contained in the statute of Edward VI, have so near an affinity to the Barbadoes law respecting Negroe slaves, as to leave scarcely any doubt

---

139/1; Thornton, *West-India Policy*, 22–39; Dunn, *Sugar and Slaves*, 151, 243. For the Barbados slave act, see "An Act for the Better Ordering and Governing of Negroes," Sept. 27, 1661, C.O. 30/2. See also Gaspar, "'With a Rod of Iron,'" 18–19. For 1661 policies, which borrowed heavily from Barbados, see Orders of the Governor and Council of Jamaica, July 2–3, 1661, G.B., P.R.O., *CSP*, Col. Ser., V, *1661–1668*, no. 123.

13. Thornton, *West-India Policy*, 60–125, 214–252; Dunn, *Sugar and Slaves*, 149–187; Watson, *Slave Law in the Americas*, 63–65, 69. See also Watson, *Legal Transplants: An Approach to Comparative Law*, 2d ed. (Athens, Ga., 1993), 95–121; Morris, *Southern Slavery and the Law*, 17–57.

but that the legislature of that island transcribed from these precedents, which they found in the mother state.[14]

Long cited various regulations connected with villeinage, but he did not systematically trace the descent of the Barbados slave laws from them, although he implied continuity. The truth is that Long was simply guessing at a connection between the two systems to explain the provenance of the slave laws, noting that their severity and general character were "undoubtedly" derived from the laws of villeinage to which they bore "so near an affinity." But, as Thomas Morris has pointed out, similarities between bodies of law may be important, but they do not "necessarily signify influence." Such similarities "can mean that certain generalizations about social relationships will hold true without regard to different historical experiences." Further indication of the conjectural nature of Long's explanation of the origins of the slave laws comes from his observation that "the first emigrants to the West-Indies, it is natural to think, carried with them some prejudices in favour of the villeinage system, so far as it might seem to coincide with the government of Negroe-labourers." Morris and Jonathan Bush have argued persuasively that the sources or roots of colonial slave law can be traced, not to villeinage, but to "the common law of England, as well as the equitable principles used in English chancery courts," though these were not "transferred whole" to the colonies.[15]

Long also pointed to other sources of Barbados slave law, including English Star Chamber judgments and other practices and laws related to the "regulation, discipline, and punishment" of vagabonds, laborers, apprentices, soldiers, seamen, and workers in coal and salt mines. In England in 1547, enslavement became a punishment for vagabonds or for "the refusal to work," but two years later the statute was repealed. Even without a usable tradition of slavery and slave law to draw from in English society, Barbados lawmakers evidently still had sufficient access to English statutes aimed at the social control of restless segments of society. Bradley J. Nicholson supports this view, arguing that colonial slave law was not created "in the colonies out of whole cloth." The police laws of slavery in Barbados and Virginia came to be "composed of practices well-known in England, and

14. Edward Long, *The History of Jamaica*, 3 vols. (1774; rpt., London, 1970), II, 493–505; George Wilson Bridges, *The Annals of Jamaica*, 2 vols. (1828; rpt., London, 1968), I, 507–510. On Long, see Elsa V. Goveia, *A Study on the Historiography of the British West Indies to the End of the Nineteenth Century* (Mexico, 1956), 52–64.

15. Thomas D. Morris, " 'Villeinage . . . as It Existed in England, Reflects but Little Light on Our Subject': The Problem of the Sources of Southern Slave Law," *Am. Jour. Leg. Hist.*, XXXII (1988), 95–134, 137; Morris, *Southern Slavery and the Law*, 37–57; Bush, "Free to Enslave," *Yale Journal of Law and the Humanities*, V (1993), 423–425. On villeinage and slave law in America, see Winthrop D. Jordan, *White over Black: American Attitudes toward the Negro, 1550–1812* (Chapel Hill, N.C., 1968), 48–56, 62, 67.

based on England's previous experience with problems of social order in the sixteenth century." "The colonists found the sixteenth century experience valuable because the legal dimension of slavery was foreshadowed by the problem of 'masterless men' in England during the previous century." English authorities associated such people with the spread of vagrancy or vagabondage, which, according to A. L. Beier, was "the most intractable social problem" of Tudor and early Stuart England.[16]

If Barbados was able to draw upon English precedent or a background of experience, albeit one that was only roughly analogous to what confronted slaveowners, Jamaica did too—indirectly—through its borrowing from the Barbados slave act of 1661. The same could be said for the British Leeward Islands in the Caribbean as well as South Carolina on the North American mainland. In short, through "innovative borrowing," the slaveowners of all of these slave societies pieced together their slave laws by drawing selectively upon English precedent or principles of law: the common law, especially as it related to property; apprenticeship regulations; martial law; treason law; and the police laws of the sixteenth century directed at greater control of the lower strata of English society.[17]

Clearly, Barbados played a critical role in the colonial world of Anglo-America in the seventeenth century as a legal "culture hearth," defined by D. W. Meinig as "an area wherein new basic cultural systems and configurations are developed and nurtured before spreading vigorously outward to alter the character of much larger areas." Nevertheless, it is not enough to say simply that Jamaica and other areas of Anglo-America adopted in whole or in part any of the slave acts of Barbados. It is also important to make the link with English precedent. In 1664 the Jamaica legislature underscored its intention to draw directly on English precedent in framing the colony's laws when it passed the act "declareing the Laws of England in force" there, only

16. Long, *History of Jamaica*, II, 495–496; Watson, *Slave Law in the Americas*, 148 n. 1; C. S. L. Davis, "Slavery and Protector Somerset: The Vagrancy Act of 1547," *Economic History Review*, 2d Ser., XIX (1966), 533–549; Nicholson, "Legal Borrowing," *Am. Jour. Leg. Hist.*, XXXVIII (1994), 39–41; A. L. Beier, *Masterless Men: The Vagrancy Problem in England, 1560–1640* (London, 1985); Beier, "Vagrants and the Social Order in Elizabethan England," *Past and Present*, no. 64 (August 1974), 3–29.

17. Gaspar, "'With a Rod of Iron.'" Nicholson asserts that the Barbados slave act of 1661 was "accepted by the other major slave holding colonies, except Virginia and Maryland." These exceptions need to be explained. Nicholson, "Legal Borrowing," *Am. Jour. Leg. Hist.*, XXXVIII (1994), 41. See also Thomas J. Little, "The South Carolina Slave Laws Reconsidered, 1670–1700," *South Carolina Historical Magazine* (hereafter cited as *SCHM*), XCIV (1993), 86–101; M. Eugene Sirmans, "The Legal Status of the Slave in South Carolina, 1670–1740," *Journal of Southern History*, XXVIII (1962), 462–473; Morris, "'Villeinage in England,'" *Am. Jour. Leg. Hist.*, XXXII (1988); Nicholson, "Legal Borrowing" *Am. Jour. Leg. Hist.*, XXXVIII (1994); Watson, *Slave Law in the Americas*, 63–82.

one week after passing the slave act. This new act declared that "all the Laws and Statutes heretofore made" in England "for the publique weale . . . And all the liberties previledges immunities and freedoms conteyned therein have allwayes bin of force and are belonging unto all" the king's subjects in Jamaica "as theyre Byrthright and that the same ever were now are and ever shall bee accepted used and executed" in Jamaica "in all points and at all times requisite according to the tennor and true meaning of them." The act indicated further that some English laws would not come under this ruling and that the others could be "mittigated altered lessened or enlarged according as the constitution of this place shall requyre," or as the Jamaica Assembly saw fit. Nevertheless, the declared reliance on English law and legal principles meant clearly that the foundations of an *English* colony in the Caribbean were being laid, even though the circumstances of construction might be unusual (in regard to English background) in some ways.[18]

To contextualize the seventeenth-century police laws of slavery in Jamaica, two other sources that helped to shape them must be borne in mind: the early military character of the government of the colony under D'Oyley (1655–1662) after it was taken from the Spanish, and the perception of the early settlers that Africans were "wild and savage." This second influence on statutory law in particular suggests that the substance of the police law should be traced to the more specific circumstances, especially in regard to master-slave relations, of the emerging slave society of Jamaica. Thus, changes in particular circumstances may best explain modifications in the laws. The preamble to the comprehensive Jamaica slave act of 1664 gives clear indication about multiple roots of the slave laws in general and provides a summary statement about their character. It must be emphasized that, because the Jamaica act was transplanted whole from Barbados, it does not necessarily mirror nascent Jamaica slave society. It represents more accurately perhaps the legislature's presumption of a rough fit that could help their aggressive drive to create a prosperous slave society. This notwithstanding, some slight alterations in the text suggest the Assembly had considered the act in light of Jamaican particularities, a feature not hitherto pointed out by historians.[19]

The whole preamble of the act deserves to be quoted:

18. D. W. Meinig, *The Shaping of America: A Geographical Perspective on 500 Years of History,* I, *Atlantic America, 1492–1800* (New Haven, Conn., 1986), 52–53, 250–253. See also Greene, "Colonial South Carolina and the Caribbean Connection," *SCHM,* LXXXVIII (1987), 192–210; "An Act Declareing the Laws of England in Force in This Island," Nov. 10, 1664, C.O. 139/1.

19. Long, *History of Jamaica,* II, 496–497; Bridges, *Annals of Jamaica,* I, 508. For the period of military government under D'Oyley, see, for example, Thornton, *West-India Policy,* 39–58.

Whereas heretofore many good Lawes and ordinances have bin made
for the governing regulating and ordering the Negroes Slaves in this
Island and Sundry punishments appointed for many theire Misdemeanors Crimes and offenses which yet have not met the effect hath
bin desired and might have reasonably bin expected had the Masters of
familyes and other the Inhabitants of this Island bin soe carefull of their
obedyence and complyance with the said lawes as they ought to have
bin and these former Lawes being in many clauses imperfect and not
fully comprehending the true constitution of this Goverment in rela-
con to theyre Slaves especially the Negroes an heathenishe brutish and
uncertaine and dangerous kind of people to whome if surely in anything wee may extend the legislative power given us of punishionary
Laws for the benefit and good of this Island not being contradictory to
the Laws of England there being in all the body of that Law noe perfect
track to guide us where to walke Nor any expert rule sett us how to
governe such Slaves as wee have or as Negroes are Yet wee well know by
the right rule of reason and order wee are not to leave them to the
arbitrary cruell and outragious will of every evill disposed person But
soe farr to protect them as wee doe many other goods and chattels
and alsoe somewhat further as being created men though without the
knowledge of God in the world Wee have therefore upon mature and
Serious consideracon of the premisses thought good to renewe and
revive whatsoever wee have found necessary and usefull in the Laws of
England concerning the governing and ordering of Slaves and to add
thereunto such further Laws and ordinances as at this time we thinke
absolutely Needful for the publique Safety and may prove in the future
behovefull to the Peace and Utillity of this Island.[20]

The rationale contained in the preamble for the enactment of the slave
code covers a number of points that follow the Barbados text exactly. Devia-
tions from the Barbados text in the Jamaica preamble suggest, however, that,
although it fully intended to copy the Barbados act, the Jamaica legislature
probably read it carefully enough to decide that minor modifications were
appropriate. The two references in the Jamaica preamble to the laws of
England are of special pertinence here.

The first reference indicates that, because of the special circumstances of
slavery and because African slaves were a "heathenish brutish and an uncertaine and dangerous kind of people," special laws for their control should be
passed. The laws were not to be "contradictory to the Laws of England there
being in all the body of that Law noe perfect track to guide us where to walke

20. "An Act for the Better Ordering and Governing of Negro Slaves," Nov. 2, 1664, C.O.
139/1, preamble.

Nor any expert rule Sett us how to governe such Slaves as wee have or as Negroes are Yet wee well know by the right rule of reason and order" that the slaves ought not to be exposed to the arbitrary will of masters but should be offered protection by law as human chattel. The Barbados preamble followed the same line of reasoning, but it was somewhat less deliberate and precise in reference to the laws of England, citing that "in all the body of that Lawe" there was "noe track to guide us where to walke nor any rule sett." The insertion by the Jamaica legislature of the adjectives "perfect" and "expert" in reference to the absence of precedents in English law for governing slaves suggests that the legislature gave this part of the act very careful consideration. However, the precedents they were unable to find related to slaves in particular; they were free to draw upon other areas of English custom and social legislation. In that sense, the slave laws were seen to be not "contradictory to the Laws of England." The whole preamble of the Jamaica slave act attempts to outline an argument for the compatability of the slave laws with English law, even if they were intended for the special situation of colonial slavery. Indeed, a few years later, in 1680, an English official who examined the Barbados slave laws for 1660–1672 (which were similar in substance to those of Jamaica) found them "good," even if "not always consonant with the laws of England, as, for instance, that negro slaves are to be tried for capital offenses not by a jury but summarily before two justices of the peace, and that negroes are punishable more severely than others for like offences." The slave laws were "reasonable, for by reason of their numbers they [the slaves] become dangerous, being a brutish sort of people and reckoned as goods and chattels."[21]

To judge from the preamble of Jamaica's 1664 slave act alone, one might conclude that Jamaica slaveowners were even more conscious than their counterparts at Barbados in 1661 of the need to buttress their slave laws with English precedents. Otherwise, careful examination and comparison of the two slave acts show little difference. For instance, they were equally comprehensive in their focus on the police regulation of slaves. Four prevailing perceptions of slaves dominated that focus: their rebellious behavior, their growing numbers, their status as property, and their striking difference in culture. The twenty-one clauses or articles of the Jamaica slave act covered several broad areas of concern: relations between all whites and slaves, relations between masters and their slaves, noncriminal and criminal disciplining of slaves, and protection of slaves. The act was ordered to be read and published in all of the colony's churches on the first Sunday of every March

21. See the preamble to the Barbados act, "An Act for the Better Ordering and Governing of Negroes," Sept. 27, 1661, C.O. 30/2; Gaspar, " 'With a Rod of Iron' "; Samuel Baldwin to Lords of Trade and Plantations, [June 14?], 1680, G.B., P.R.O., *CSP,* Col. Ser., X, *1677–1680,* no. 1391.

and September. It was modified several times during the seventeenth century under the pressures of emerging conditions in the rapidly developing
colony, particularly in regard to slave rebelliousness. Between 1673 and 1690,
several slave rebellions occurred in different parts of the island, and they
each had their roots in persistent slave flight and Maroon activity that had
started to flare up threateningly in the late 1660s. In 1667 the governor and
Council, taking "into serious consideration the many mischeifs that have
been done by such Men Negroes as are taken upon the Spanish Coasts and
brought into this Island and sold here," issued orders regarding preventive
measures.[22]

Here, the second reference in the Jamaica preamble to the laws of England
should be noted. The preamble declared the legislature's intent to "renew
and revive whatsoever wee have found necessary and usefull in the Laws of
England concerning the governing and ordering of [our] Slaves." The equiv-
alent Barbados reference said simply: "to renewe and revive whatsoever wee
have found necessary and usefull in the former Lawes of this Island." Jamaica's explicit reference to the laws of England, rather than to earlier local
laws, probably indicates an awareness by their legislature that in fact there
were not many local laws to draw upon or to modify. The reference in the
opening words of the preamble to the "many good Lawes and ordinances"
(repeated from the Barbados act) that had been passed already was merely
exaggeration or perhaps a rhetorical flourish.

The Jamaica authorities, then, were more concerned than those of Barbados to tie their law to English legitimation. There were also very practical
limits to how much "borrowing" from Barbados they would tolerate. In
1675, "on reading advices from Barbadoes concerning a late rebellion attempted by the negroes there, and on consideration of the dangers that
might accrue to this island by the ill-government of negroes," the Jamaica
Council ordered, "No negres concerned in the late rebellion or convicted of
any other crime in Barbadoes be permitted to be bought or sold, and that
the Collector at Port Royal examine all masters of ships from Barbadoes on
their oaths, and take bond of them in 50l. that they will not put ashore any
such criminal or convicted negroes." Increasingly during this period in the
evolution of Jamaica slave society and slave law, it was the particularities of
the island's social, economic, and political environment that began to play
major roles rather than any Barbados model.[23]

22. Dunn, *Sugar and Slaves*, 243, 259–262; Campbell, *Maroons of Jamaica*, 14–43; Minutes of the Council of Jamaica, Nov. 26, 1667, C.O. 140/1. See also the minutes for 1668 in
C.O. 140/1.
23. "An Act for the Better Ordering and Governing of Negro Slaves," Nov. 2, 1664, C.O.
139/1, preamble; Minutes of the Council of Jamaica, Sept. 3, 1675, G.B., P.R.O., *CSP*, Col.
Ser., IX, *1675–1676*, no. 661.

III

During the last quarter of the seventeenth century, slavery and plantation agriculture, particularly in regard to the cultivation of sugarcane, expanded quickly in Jamaica. Large numbers of Africans were imported, and the slave population grew from 9,504 in 1673 to 40,000 in 1698. In the latter year there were only 7,375 whites in the colony. The number of sugar plantations increased from 57 in 1671 to 246 in 1684. Other plantations produced primarily cacao, indigo, and cotton; altogether there were 690 plantations in 1684, compared to 146 in 1671. Slaves also worked cattle ranches, which numbered 73 in 1684.[24]

With the expansion of the slave-based economy came more slave rebelliousness during the 1680s. When an "act for regulation of slaves " (which imposed a fine "on all such as wilfully and wantonly kill a negro") was sent to the king for approval, the Lords of Trade and Plantations advised the governor of Jamaica, Sir Thomas Lynch, in 1683, "The King will not confirm this clause, which seems to encourage the wilful shedding of blood. Some better provision must be found than a fine to deter men from such acts of cruelty." What better provision? Three years later, when the Jamaica Council convened again to consider "means of suppressing the rebel negroes who are now more formidable than ever before," its proposals were no more careful of blacks' lives than before. "On the advice of the Governor, it was ordered that twelve parties be forthwith raised out of the several regiments, each of eighteen men with suitable officers, that those guilty of neglect of duty should be called to serious account, that petty offences should be punishable by officers commanding parties, with other provision for discipline and quarters, that every party have a good gang of dogs, and be empowered to impress hunters and dogs. Every man killing a negro to have £20, or, if a servant, his freedom; every man taking a negro to have £40; any party killing a negro to divide £20 round."[25]

These rulings were to be "heartily commended to the next Assembly for confirmation." Anxieties regarding slave discipline and rebelliousness persisted into the 1690s and raised disquieting questions about the substance and functioning of the slave laws. In 1694 the Jamaica Council ordered that armed parties be sent out after outlying rebellious blacks, "that a list of free

24. Noel Deerr, *The History of Sugar*, 2 vols. (London, 1949–1950), II, 278; Dunn, *Sugar and Slaves*, 155, 169; Trevor Burnard, "Who Bought Slaves in Early America? Purchasers of Slaves from the Royal African Company in Jamaica, 1674–1708," *Slavery and Abolition*, XVII, no. 2 (August 1996), 68–92; Burnard, "European Migration to Jamaica, 1655–1780," *WMQ*, 3d Ser., LIII (1996), 769–796.

25. Lords of Trade and Plantations to Gov. Sir Thomas Lynch, February 17, 1683, G.B., P.R.O., *CSP*, Col. Ser., XI, *1681–1685*, no. 948; Minutes of the Council of Jamaica, Feb. 2, 1686, G.B., P.R.O., *CSP*, Col. Ser., XII, *1685–1688*, no. 560.

negroes be made, and that all negroes now out shall be reputed rebels unless they come home in a month." Forty shillings was to be paid to the parties out hunting rebels "for every head of a dead rebel sent in."[26]

In 1696, the Jamaica legislature passed another comprehensive slave act at a time when their minds were obviously still sharply focused on keeping rebellious blacks in check. As the final comprehensive slave act of the seventeenth century, the 1696 measure superseded all others. This act too was said to have been modeled after the Barbados slave acts. It contained forty-nine clauses or articles and indeed did bear a close resemblance to the Barbados slave act of 1688. This feature, however, does not by itself conclusively establish provenance or influence, only a strong likelihood, particularly when the overall history of slave legislation and settlement of Jamaica is taken into account. Nonetheless, unlike the Barbados slave act of 1688, the Jamaica slave act of 1696 did not include an elaborate preamble but identified immediately the most pressing problem with which Jamaica whites were confronted, and therefore also the main justification for its creation—slave rebellion. The preamble stated: "Whereas it is found by Experience, that the often Insurrections and Rebellions of the Slaves within this Island have proved the Ruin and Destruction of several Families: To the End therefore that they may be punished according to their Demerit, and their bloody and inhuman Practices."[27]

Several tough provisions were introduced in the 1696 act that, in their emphasis on prevention as well as deterrence, had no parallel in the Barbados model of laws. In regard to feeding slaves, for example, the Barbados slave act simply connected underfeeding with slave unrest and punished masters who contributed to it. The Jamaica slave act, however, required masters to have an acre of land "well planted" with provisions for every five slaves on the plantation. This was one nonpunitive way (in regard to the slaves themselves) in which Jamaica authorities sought to deal with slave rebelliousness. Another new law dealt with slave trials. In Jamaica these trials were generally similar to those of Barbados, but the new law ruled that

26. Minutes of the Council of Jamaica, Feb. 2, 1686, G.B., P.R.O., *CSP,* Col. Ser., XII, *1685–1688,* no. 560.

27. Minutes of the Council of Jamaica, Dec. 16, 1694, G.B., P.R.O., *CSP,* Col. Ser., XIV, *January 1693–14 May 1696,* nos. 1603, 1604; "An Act for the Better Order and Government of Slaves," 1696 (hereafter Jamaica slave act, 1696), act 70 in John Baskett, comp., *Acts of Assembly, Passed in the Island of Jamaica, from 1681, to 1737, Inclusive* (London, 1738), 73–82. See also "Appendix" regarding the slave laws of Jamaica, in Sheila Lambert, ed., *House of Commons Sessional Papers of the Eighteenth Century,* 145 vols. (Wilmington, Del., 1975), LXIX, 231–240. On the Jamaica and Barbados acts, see Dunn, *Sugar and Slaves,* 243; but see also Morris, *Southern Slavery and the Law,* 37. For the Barbados act that preceded the Jamaica act, see "An Act for the Governing of Negroes," August 8, 1688, act 82 in Richard Hall, comp., *Acts, Passed in the Island of Barbados, from 1643, to 1762, Inclusive* (London, 1764), 112–121.

pregnant slave women could not be executed until after giving birth. Another new measure provided that, when several slaves were found guilty of crime collectively, only one was to be executed "as exemplary to the rest." Special laws were included in the act to cover poisoning ("The Consequences of which secret way of murdering may prove fatal, if not timly prevented"). Free blacks, unlike whites, could also be tried using testimony of slaves. And, although Christianization of slaves was supported, it was not understood to bring them any closer to freedom. In general the Jamaica slave act of 1696 was more thorough and more focused on policing the slaves than the act of 1664. It was also a more mature police apparatus in that it had transcended indiscriminate brutality to achieve disciplined coercion.[28]

Conclusion

When at the end of the eighteenth century Edward Long turned his attention to evaluate the Jamaica slave laws, he observed, "The Africans, first imported, were wild and savage to an extreme: their intractable and ferocious tempers naturally provoked their masters to rule them with a rod of iron." Long added that the earliest slave laws were thus understandably "rigid and inclement, even to a degree of inhumanity." If, however, this response of masters to slave intractability was unavoidable, according to Long, so too was slave resistance to bondage. From the very start of the English occupation of Jamaica, in fact, whites faced problems of control over the black population. In the frontier environment of the seventeenth-century Caribbean, the impulse to recruit ever-increasing numbers of slaves from Africa for forced labor could only exacerbate their situation. The slave laws, with their heavy emphasis on police measures, were created primarily in response to this context. Or, to put it differently, the chief emphasis of most of the slave laws was on slave rebelliousness, which involved perception of the slaves as persons. It is not that difficult to appreciate why, in a tropical frontier environment such as Jamaica's, where there were so many forces over which slaveowners had little or no control, they should strive so hard to maintain control of their slaves, whom they regarded as the sinews of the plantations, and who could, they thought, be broken or subdued with the use of sufficient force.[29]

Under these circumstances, the Jamaica legislature, with the experience of Barbados before them, did not bother to invent or create its own compre-

28. "An Act for the Governing of Negroes," art. 16, in Hall, comp., *Acts of Barbados,* 119; Jamaica slave act, 1696, arts. 6, 23, 26, 32–33, 40, in Baskett, comp., *Acts of Jamaica,* 74, 77–80.

29. Long, *History of Jamaica,* II, 497. See Dunn, *Sugar and Slaves,* 263–334.

hensive slave act during the early 1660s, but instead borrowed the Barbados slave act of 1661. The two acts differed very little in substance, probably largely because Sir Thomas Modyford, the new governor of Jamaica who had come from Barbados, wished to place his government in good order quickly. He thought the Barbados act would work well enough as a starting point, adding more substance to the few Jamaica slave laws then in operation. The Barbados laws, however, cannot be read as if they were an accurate reflection of conditions within the other colonies to which they were applied. It would therefore be an error to extrapolate conditions in Jamaica from its borrowed slave act of 1664.

By 1696, on the other hand, when Jamaica's last comprehensive slave act of the seventeenth century came into being, conditions within the colony had clearly begun to play a much greater role in shaping the slave laws. The slave acts contained several laws other than those of a police nature, but all were drawn to respond to local conditions and contained indications that they were meant to reflect the spirit, if not the substance, of English law. Hence, Jamaica's insistence on the value of English social and legal precedent in the preamble of the slave act of 1664 is of considerable significance. It shows how, in taking steps to legitimize their actions, the Jamaica legislature also intended to construct an English plantation colony in which black slavery and English law were established, side by side, as central and essential institutions. In other words, the evidence suggests that English law was not segregated from the law of slavery in Jamaica (and indeed in the rest of the English sugar islands) during the seventeenth century. English law was thus implicated in the creation of Caribbean slavery in ways that historians have not often recognized. In 1695 Governor Francis Russell of Barbados understood the connection. In a report to the Lords of Trade and Plantations, Russell noted that among the most suitable men whom he considered to fill vacancies in his advisory council was one who had "great knowledge of the laws" and another who was "very well versed in the law." In addition, Russell asked the permission of the officials in England that, "as I have no training in the law, the Attorney and Solicitor-General may be allowed to sit in the Council Chamber, so that I may be able to consult them at all times, as is done in Jamaica."[30]

30. Gaspar, " 'With a Rod of Iron' "; Russell to Lords of Trade and Plantations, Mar. 23, 1695, G.B., P.R.O., *CSP,* Col. Ser., XIV, *January 1693–14 May 1696,* no. 1738.

Legal Fictions and the Rule(s) of Law

The Jeffersonian Critique of Common-Law Adjudication

I

ESPITE THE venerable common-law maxim, "Justice is a constant and perpetuall will of rendring unto every one their Due," Virginia attorney Edward Barradall argued vainly in a 1737 case that justice would "clash with a Rule of law" and be denied to the man he represented. His client, an estate administrator, would have to pay a decedent's debt from his own pocket if the court deemed the obligation to be a debt on a specialty rather than on a simple contract. Both types of obligation derived from written promises, Barradall argued, and the only difference between them was the seal affixed to the former. In reality, "there is certainly no natural Difference between a Debt by Specialty and a Debt without but there may and often is more Justice and commonly more Charity to satisfie a Debt of the latter Sort [o]ther than the former. . . . the Difference is meerly artificial introduced upon Reasons that now no longer subsist." The court refused to accept his argument that the two debts were "of equal Dignity" and that any legal distinction was "absurd"; instead, it relied on an ancient rule of law that the specialty, being a legal agreement in the form of a sealed instrument, created an obligation of a higher order. This rule, in effect for centuries, rested on an archaic distinction—"the magic of the seal," it has been called—that transformed the obligation from a promise to pay into a confession of a legal debt. Because of the seal, the law presumed that "consideration" had been made and left the defendant with very limited and difficult defenses to plead.[1]

The author wishes to thank Stuart Banner, Barry Cushman, Robert Gordon, Bruce Mann, Stanton Krauss, Richard Ross, and participants in legal history workshops at the University of Chicago, Yale University, and the University of Pennsylvania for their helpful criticisms.

1. John Cowell, *The Institutes of the Lawes of England . . .* (London, 1651), 1; *Corbin v Chew's Adm'rs* (1737), in R. T. Barton, ed., *Virginia Colonial Decisions: The Reports by Sir John Randolph and by Edward Barradall of Decisions of the General Court of Virginia, 1728–1741*, 2 vols. (Boston, 1909), B240–241 (hereafter cited as *Colonial Decisions*, with pagination preceded by "R" for Randolph's reports and "B" for Barradall's); J. H. Baker, *An Introduction to English Legal History*, 2d ed. (London, 1979), 292. According to S. F. C.

Lawyers in Britain's common-law courts on both sides of the Atlantic debated such matters of archaic and "artificial" legal rules. Barradall's argument, in fact, closely paralleled a plea made four decades later in a King's Bench lawsuit at the House of Lords: "In reason, there is little or no difference between a contract which is deliberately reduced into writing and signed by the parties without a seal, and a contract under the same circumstances, to which a party at the time of signing it puts a seal or his finger on cold wax." In 1740, this legal distinction again confronted a Barradall client: if the court treated the obligation as a debt on a simple contract, it could not take real property in execution and award damages to his client, as it could if the instrument were sealed and thus a specialty. Only by circumventing the common-law rule with a bill in equity did Barradall obtain a decree in chancery "that the House and Lots should be sold to satisfie the Pltfs. Debts," a judgment he deemed "founded both in Charity and Justice."[2]

Legal terms and rules might outlive the reality that had produced them, but in theory their constancy imparted predictability, prevented greater inconvenience and uncertainty, and restrained judges within known boundaries. For this reason, even the dead language of Law French (a legal variety of Anglo-French dating back to medieval times) survived in common-law terminology. As Thomas Jefferson learned in his legal studies, such archaic terms "are grown to be *vocabula artis*, vocables of art, so apt and significant to express the true sense of the laws, and are so woven in the laws themselves, as it is in a manner impossible to change them, neither ought legal terms to be changed." To those who took pride in the common law, the rigidity of its language and timeless precision of its rules embodied justice itself, and its jurists proudly insisted that they acted only to find and speak law (*jus dicere*) and not to create or give law (*jus dare*).[3]

Milsom, the seal created "a formal contract analogous to the Roman *stipulatio:* you go through the appropriate magical steps and you are magically bound" (*Historical Foundations of the Common Law* [London, 1969], 214). For the theory by which the seal created "a duty from an executed consideration" rather than from any promise, see Benjamin J. Shipman, *Handbook of Common-Law Pleading*, 3d ed. (St. Paul, Minn., 1923), 264.

2. Kevin M. Teeven, *A History of the Anglo-American Common Law of Contract* (Westport, Conn., 1990), 132; *Burwell v Ogilby etc.* (1740), in Barton, ed., *Colonial Decisions*, B106. The Virginia General Court possessed the authority to act as a court of chancery, an "extraordinary court," according to Sir William Blackstone, that "mitigated the severity or supplied the defects of the judgments pronounced in the courts of [common] law, upon weighing the circumstances of the case" (*Commentaries on the Laws of England*, 4 vols. [1765–1769; facs. rpt., Chicago, 1979], III, 49–50).

3. Sir Edward Coke, *The First Part of the Institutes of the Laws of England; or, A Commentary upon Littleton* (1628; Philadelphia, 1853), I, xxxix. Jefferson noted his reaction to the "old dull scoundrel" Coke as he began his legal study on leaving the College of William and Mary (Jefferson to John Page, Dec. 25, 1762, in Julian P. Boyd et al., eds., *Papers of Thomas Jefferson* [Princeton, N.J., 1950–], I, 5).

Critics of the vaunted constancy of the common law might well fault such reasoning, which concealed the potential for the arbitrary judicial behavior—or, at least, the capricious discretion—that it claimed to eschew. The seemingly illogical retention of archaic and mischievous rules such as those locked in the seal provided considerable grounds for protest. Even after Parliament enacted the Statute of Frauds in 1677, traditionalist judicial decisions chipped away at the statute's effectiveness and undermined much of its purpose.[4]

Rigidity might have petrified the common law and rendered it unable to adapt to or provide remedies for new situations, but common-law jurists proudly pointed to the maxim *ubi jus, ubi remedium*—"where there is a legal right there is also a remedy." "It is taken absolutely for granted," explained the nineteenth-century jurist Sir Henry Maine, "that there is somewhere a rule of known law which will cover the facts of the dispute now litigated." If no rule came immediately to mind, "the necessary patience, knowledge, or acumen" would find one, or additional facts could be identified to place the problem within a given body of rules.[5]

But what if the necessary facts did not truly exist for the court to apply a known rule, or compelled the court to treat the claim under a theory of liability and a set of rules that inconvenienced the parties? In such cases, the common law allowed facts to be contrived to fit the rule; known to all concerned as "fictions," they were legal and thereby accepted by the court. A legal fiction was a "feigned Construction of the Law . . . when in a similitudinary and colourable Way the Law construeth a Thing otherwise than it is in Truth: And therefore *Fictions* were formerly termed an *Abuse* of our Law; but have been a long Time thought necessary, and allowed of in several cases."[6] The commercial world required forms of action to allow recovery of moneys owed when no express promise had been made, and the courts accordingly accepted the fiction that the defendant, being "indebted," "undertook" to pay, describing his fictitious act as an "indebitatus assumpsit" that would be decided by a jury.[7] Similarly, the courts created a form of

4. 29 Car. 2, c. 3; Teeven, *Common Law of Contract*, 88. The Act for Prevention of Frauds and Perjuries had attempted to correct much of the inconvenience of this rule by legitimating several types of written contracts not bearing seals.

5. Blackstone, *Commentaries*, III, 23; Sir Henry James Sumner Maine, *Ancient Law: Its Connection with the Early History of Society, and Its Relation to Modern Ideas*, 5th ed. (New York, 1873), 30.

6. Giles Jacob, *A Law Grammar; or, Rudiments of the Law . . .* , 4th ed. (London, 1767), 199. One modern legal dictionary concisely defines the legal fiction as "a contrived condition or situation; the simulation of a status or condition with the purpose of accomplishing justice, albeit justice reached by devious means" (*Ballentine's Law Dictionary*, 3d ed. [Rochester, N.Y., 1969], 468).

7. This fiction was brought into common-law pleading by *Slade's* case (1602), referred to in Blackstone's *Commentaries*, III, 167. The fiction behind it is described by Arthur Allen

action by allowing a plaintiff to aver—falsely—that he had "casually lost" property, which the defendant had found and converted to his own use. In this action, known as "trover" (from the Law French, "to find"), the property had not been lost or found, but that untruth, wrote Sir William Blackstone, "is therefore now totally immaterial"; though it had been pleaded only to satisfy the necessary wording of the writ, it could not be traversed by the defendant. "The form of action is a fiction," explained Lord Mansfield, chief justice of England's Court of King's Bench, more bluntly and approvingly in 1756.[8]

Historically, the rule of law has depended on fictions to maintain political authority and stability. To do so, it has made use of constitutional fictions such as the king's two bodies—by which "the king is esteemed to be immortal, invisible, not subject to death, infirmity, nonage, etc.," so that legal succession is never interrupted—as well as "Big Fictions" such as "the social contract." These grand fictions have received incisive analyses that have given them their due in history, and the present essay approaches the legal fiction as a more narrowly technical, though no less influential, concept.[9] It examines within the legal tradition of colonial Virginia the use of, and debate over, legal fictions as a "modality of rule" in the courtroom and thus in society. This debate was a contest of competing legalities over what rules should constitute the law and who should rule by making them, and it involved the long-term contest between adjudication and legislation in England *and* in America, before as well as after the Revolution.[10]

Routine fictitious pleadings brought considerable procedural advantages to those seeking redress otherwise slowed by the archaic requirements of feudal institutions and the cumbersome wording of the common law's writ

---

Leff, "The Leff Dictionary of Law: A Fragment," *Yale Law Journal*, XCIV (1985), 2082–2083.

8. Blackstone, *Commentaries*, III, 150–152; *Cooper v Cutty* (1756), in James Oldham, *The Mansfield Manuscripts and the Growth of English Law in the Eighteenth Century*, 2 vols. (Chapel Hill, N.C., 1992), 1175.

9. *Calvin's Case* (1608). Coke reports his own opinion in vol. VII of *The Reports of Sir Edward Coke Knight in English . . .* , 13 vols. (London, 1727), at 1a, with quotation at 18. See also Ernst H. Kantorowicz, *The King's Two Bodies: A Study in Medieval Political Theology* (Princeton, N.J., 1957). Social contract: Fuller, *Legal Fictions*, ix. Fuller provides a more systematic classification in chap. 1, "What is a Legal Fiction?" The definition of "legal fiction" used in the present essay excludes such fictions as the false assumptions or erroneous reasoning of social constructions, of whose falsity the historical creators may not have been aware at the time. That used here, then, is the stricter sense described by Fuller, *Legal Fictions*, 5–14.

10. For an extended discussion of law as a "modality of rule," see Christopher L. Tomlins, *Law, Labor, and Ideology in the Early American Republic* (Cambridge, 1993), 19–34. Among twentieth-century discussions, John Hart Ely, *Democracy and Distrust: A Theory of Judicial Review* (Cambridge, Mass., 1980), remains a classic delineation of the conflict between legality as embodied in statute and as judicially constructed.

system. To save a plaintiff the time and money required in other courts, the Court of King's Bench issued a "bill of Middlesex" to take jurisdiction (and lucrative fees) over a broad range of civil litigation formerly handled elsewhere. It did so by accepting the legal fiction that a defendant had once been in Middlesex, where King's Bench sat, but had fled and was "lurking" (in Latin, "latitat") in another county. In so doing, this "Supposal or Fiction" served as a "Pretence of easing the Subject, and expediting Justice"; not unintentionally, it also attracted ample court fees otherwise collected by a rival jurisdiction.[11] Rivalry between courts in the seventeenth century also figured, in part, in the creation of the most ingenious fiction of English law, the action of ejectment to try land title and avoid the crippling technicalities of existing, ancient forms of action. "This new method entirely depends upon a string of legal fictions," wrote Blackstone after its perfection by a series of judicial decisions; "no actual lease is made, no actual entry by the plaintiff, no actual ouster by the defendant." To effect its purpose, the common law welcomed before its bar the fictitious figures John Doe and Richard Roe and accepted pledges from the fictitious John Den and Richard Fen. By the time Blackstone wrote, it also had allowed "Fairclaim" to commence an action against "Shamtitle."[12]

The undeniable utility of these judicially encouraged "procedural pretenses" should not mask the political or self-interested uses that attorneys and court officers might make of them, nor the challenges they provoked. From the thirteenth century through the nineteenth, English private law changed little by statute compared to its alteration by judicial action, and in the inherent rivalry between court and legislature, the creation of fictions might be seen as a debatable intrusion of judicial authority into an area of law marked off by legislative provision. Thus, when the judges of common pleas in 1472 accepted a fictitious tenancy and established the rule in *Taltarum's* case that created a collusive "common recovery" to end an entail (for example, to allow land to be sold), they were not only exerting a profound impact on the economy of England and transforming society but were also weakening noble families by breaking up the large estates of potential rivals.

11. John Cowell, *A Law Dictionary; or, The Interpreter of Words and Terms*. . . . (London, 1727). This writ, the "latitat," was a common legal fiction. See also the law dictionary most commonly used in colonial Virginia, Giles Jacob, *A New Law-Dictionary: Containing the Interpretation and Definition of Words and Terms Used in the LAW*, 5th ed. (London, 1744), s.v. "fiction of law." On the popularity of Jacob's work, see William Hamilton Bryson, *Census of Law Books in Colonial Virginia* (Charlottesville, Va., 1978), xvi.

12. Blackstone, *Commentaries*, III, 203; he provides a long explanation of the creation of this "contrivance" on 200–207 and an example of the writ bringing the fictitious parties into court in appendix 2. For an actual case litigated under the names "Fairclaim" and "Shamtitle" in 1762, see A. W. B. Simpson, *An Introduction to the History of the Land Law* (Oxford, 1961), 139.

In addition, they were challenging legislative power and effecting an obvious judicial repeal of a parliamentary statute—in this case, the famous *De donis conditionalibus*, which had created the entail and exerted a powerful influence on the disposition of land since 1285. Lauding the court for its ingenuity, Blackstone described the case's "fictitious proceedings" as "a kind of *pia fraus* ["honorable deceit"] to elude the statute *de donis*, which was found so intolerably mischievous, and which yet one branch of the legislature would not then consent to repeal."[13]

The political competition between legislature and judiciary was not, however, the only tension spawned by the legal fiction. False or artificial averments enabled the central common-law courts to expand their jurisdiction at the expense of the many competing legalities of English culture. Local courts, often biased or under the direct control of local magnates, lost jurisdiction when the courts at Westminster accepted the fictitious plea that "force and arms" had been involved in a dispute. The violence so alleged would bring a grievance within the king's jurisdiction as keeper of the peace in the realm—a ploy contrived in the reign of Edward II when a plaintiff ingeniously pleaded that he had left a cask of wine with another man, who "with force and arms, to wit with swords and bows and arrows" drew off a quantity of wine for his own use and watered down what remained.[14]

Though demonstrably useful, the making of legal fictions did not escape harsh criticism and drew repeated attacks on the legitimacy of the common law. Especially to those who lost jurisdiction, the expansion of the common-law courts was likely perceived, not inaccurately, with distrust, in the way that many twentieth-century Americans have come to regard the expansion of federal jurisdiction. Oliver Wendell Holmes said it well in 1927 when he observed that treating a particular situation as "affected with the public interest" might be seen as "little more than a fiction intended to beautify what is disagreeable to the sufferers." Similarly, seventeenth-century English civil law jurisprudents attacked the legal fiction as "an Assumption of Law upon an Untruth, for a Truth, in something possible to be done, but not done."[15] Assailing the averment of a fictitious location to bring a grievance to common-law courts, a critic called it a "new-coyned untraversable fiction"

13. Lon L. Fuller, *Legal Fictions* (Stanford, Calif., 1967), 5 n. 17; Charles Howard McIlwain, *The High Court of Parliament and Its Supremacy: An Historical Essay on the Boundaries between Legislation and Adjudication in England* (New Haven, Conn., 1910), 267–268. *Taltarum's* case is more fully analyzed by Simpson, *Land Law*, 122–129, and the statute at 78–96. For the latter, see also Blackstone, *Commentaries*, II, 117.

14. Milsom, "Reason in the Development of the Common Law," *Law Quarterly Review*, LXXXI (1965), 502.

15. *Tyson and Brother v Barton*, 273 US 418, 446 (1927), cited by Aviam Soifer, "Reviewing Legal Fictions," *Georgia Law Review*, XX (1986), 882; Jacob, *New Law-Dictionary*, s.v. "fiction of law."

that operated by "transporting whole Kingdoms, Countries, Cities, Rivers, Ports, Creeks, Shores, in foreign parts into Cheapside in London, or Islington in Middlesex; (which no Miracle or Omnipotency itself can do, because a direct contradiction, repugnant to nature, experience, Scripture, and Gods own constitution)." Criticism continued into the eighteenth century, as law reformers pilloried the legal fiction as epitomizing judicial usurpation of the people's voice in the legislature. When asked, How was the "fiction of use to justice?" Jeremy Bentham responded acidly, "Exactly as swindling is to trade." Bentham's critique reminds us that the establishment of particular legal fictions has been historically contested and has brought into opposition competing concepts of the rule of law.[16]

The legal tradition of eighteenth-century Americans was profoundly influenced by the bloody constitutional struggle between crown and Parliament in the preceding century. Out of that conflict, the central courts at Westminster assumed a role of leadership in legal reform led by two giants of the common law—Lord Mansfield, who served as chief justice of King's Bench from 1756 to 1788, and Sir William Blackstone, who held the Vinerian chair at Oxford from 1758 to 1766 as the first professor of English law and who wrote the widely influential *Commentaries on the Laws of England.* Mansfield (as Solicitor General William Murray before his knighthood and presidency of King's Bench) had assailed statute as inferior to the common law, whose "rules drawn from the fountain of justice" made it "superior to an act of parliament." Mansfield's many judicial opinions, bringing major changes to English commercial law, prompted protest. Not only did they "undermine and alter the whole system of jurisprudence in the Court of King's Bench," one contemporary complained, but in so doing they usurped a function more properly left to legislators. Such opponents, however, could not reverse the trend, which too efficiently served the mercantile needs of the time.[17]

Blackstone's *Commentaries* spread the common law, and with it his era's skepticism of legislation, into the legal hinterlands of North America. He viewed statute law as merely a supplement, an instrument of policy less

16. William Prynne, *Brief Animadversions on . . . the Fourth Part of the Institutes . . .* (1669), 95, cited by Lionel H. Laing, "Historic Origins of Admiralty Jurisdiction in England," *Michigan Law Review,* XLV (1946), 180. Bentham: Fuller, *Legal Fictions,* viii; Eben Moglen, "Legal Fictions and Common Law Legal Theory: Some Historical Reflections," *Tel Aviv University Studies in Law,* X (1990), 35. For the enduring force of the contest over legal fictions, see Richard H. Fallon, Jr., "The 'Rule of Law' as a Concept in Constitutional Discourse," *Columbia Law Review,* XCVII (1997), 1–56.

17. David Lieberman, *The Province of Legislation Determined: Legal Theory in Eighteenth-Century Britain* (Cambridge, 1989), 90–91. The definitive source on Mansfield's legal career is the enormously learned collection, with comment, by Oldham, *Mansfield Manuscripts.* Mansfield's method and impact are concisely described by Michael Lobban, *The Common Law and English Jurisprudence, 1760–1850* (Oxford, 1991), 98–114.

worthy than judge-made common law, which he compared to "other venerable edifices of antiquity." The edifice of the common law might (with its legal fictions) appear needlessly complex at first glance, but closer examination would reveal a suitable and useful structure. Common-law adjudicatory "expedients" were now well recognized and appreciated; as he explained further,

> The only difficulty that attends them arises from their fictions and circuities, but, when once we have discovered the proper clew, that labyrinth is easily pervaded. We inherit an old Gothic castle, erected in the days of chivalry, but fitted up for a modern inhabitant. The moated ramparts, the embattled towers, and the trophied halls, are magnificent and venerable, but useless. The inferior apartments, now converted into rooms of convenience, are chearful and commodious, though their approaches are winding and difficult.[18]

Nevertheless, the ascendancy of Blackstonian common-law adjudication at Westminster and in the colonies should not obscure the tenacious counterarguments advanced against it, even as the new Vinerian professor delivered his first lectures at Oxford. Listening to them, the young Jeremy Bentham immediately set out to refute their entire basis. "As a system of general rules," he wrote in his *Comment on the Commentaries,* "the Common Law is a thing merely imaginary." Emphasizing his distaste for what he regarded as an unfounded mass of inconsistent and arbitrary judge-made expedients, he asked: "Once more, to give a gross idea of it, what is the Common Law? What, but an assemblage of fictitious regulations feigned after the images of these real ones that compose Statute Law."[19]

At the center of the opposition was a belief in the greater potential for arbitrary abuse by the courts. To challengers such as Bentham, the common law was unwritten and therefore manipulable and uncertain, notwithstanding Blackstone's protestations to the contrary; it "is made not by the people but by Judges," complained Bentham, "the substance of it by Judges solely; the expression of it, either by Judges or by Lawyers who hope to be so." The common law was, moreover, unreasonable law whose articulation by "four men appointed by the Crown" was not nearly as reliable as the opinion of "many hundred men chosen the greater part of them by the people." For Bentham, the solution was to vest in the legislature, as the agent of the people's sovereign commanding voice, the responsibility of bringing reason, certainty, and justice to the law: "The Common Law must be digested into

18. Blackstone, *Commentaries,* I, 10, III, 268.
19. Lieberman, *Province of Legislation Determined,* chap. 11, 119–120.

Statute," wrote the man who would later coin the term "codification"; "the fictitious must be substantiated into real."[20]

The use of—and opposition to—legal fictions in colonial America must be placed within a transatlantic context and the "longue durée" of legal history.[21] Throughout the history of the colonies, legal fictions served needs created by the novel conditions and pressures of settlement. Still, the challenge to judicial gatekeeping was especially acute in colonial Virginia, where the extent of judicial authority raised questions for the legitimacy of what has been called the "mechanisms of control in a purportedly democratic society."[22] The artful use, and willing acceptance, of sham pleadings bred distrust of legal institutions in a culture that distrusted sophistical reasoning and the encumbering artificiality of archaic procedures. Their application to areas of public policy, moreover, conferred on them a political dimension that invited still more resentment.

II

No one better appreciated this debate than Thomas Jefferson, whose investigations into Virginia's legal past exposed him to the ambivalence that its

20. Ibid., 159, 223, 320.

21. The "longue durée," or long endurance of historical forms, is a term devised and elaborated on by Fernand Braudel, *La Méditerranée et le monde méditerranéen a l'époque de Philippe II*, 2 vols., 2d ed. (1949; Paris, 1966), I, 325. That such fictions have gone unexamined—indeed virtually unnoticed—in the writings of historians of early American law is remarkable, given the widespread utility of legal fictions. Occasional reference to the use of legal fictions appears in the scholarship, but not in the corpus, of early American history. Legal scholars (as distinguished from nonlawyer historians) have possessed a near monopoly on this important question. In addition to Moglen, "Legal Fictions," *Tel Aviv University Studies in Law*, X (1990), and Soifer, "Reviewing Legal Fictions," *Georgia Law Review*, XX (1986), see, for example, Tejshree Thapa, "Expounding the Constitution: Legal Fictions and the Ninth Amendment," *Cornell Law Review*, LXXVIII (1992), 139–161; Andrea C. Loux, "The Persistence of the Ancient Regime: Custom, Utility, and the Common Law in the Nineteenth Century," *Cornell Law Review*, LXXIX (1993), 183–218; John Edward Barry, "Oneida Indian Nation v. County of Oneida: Tribal Rights of Action and the Indian Trade and Intercourse Act," *Columbia Law Review*, LXXXIV (1984), 1852–1880; Sanford A. Schane, "The Corporation Is a Person: The Language of a Legal Fiction," *Tulane Law Review*, LXI (1986), 563–609. That these scholars have identified the importance of legal fictions in Anglo-American legal history from the Middle Ages to the present, and in areas ranging from corporate law to American Indian land claims, attests to its role in this longue durée of historical jurisprudence. Among historians, exceptional is Harold M. Hyman, "Federalism: Legal Fiction and Historical Artifact?" *Brigham Young University Law Review*, 1987 (1987), 905–921; otherwise, one must recur to the nineteenth-century work of Maine and to McIlwain's 1910 masterpiece.

22. Jan Lewis, "Variations on a Theme by Jefferson . . . ," *Reviews in American History*, XXII (1994), 32–38, esp. 35. See also, generally, A. G. Roeber, *Faithful Magistrates and Republican Lawyers: Creators of Virginia Legal Culture, 1680–1810* (Chapel Hill, N.C., 1981).

jurists held. He came to regard the two giants of eighteenth-century common law, Mansfield and Blackstone, as twin demons whose judicial alterations violated the deepest principles of popular sovereignty and the legitimacy of the rule of law. Frustrated by resistance to more radical law reform
in the 1780s, Jefferson blamed the "sly poison" of Mansfield, which had been
"admirably seconded by the celebrated Dr. Blackstone." But his misgivings
had begun much earlier, with his law studies, and had intensified when his
legal expertise drew him into the imperial debate. In his personal critical
examination of this issue, no less than in his later public career, he expressed
doubts that run throughout the American legal tradition and illustrate a
significant issue in the contested nature of early American law.[23]

Jefferson's skepticism about legal fictions operated at every level of their
use, from the grand constitutional fictions to the minute fictions of mundane legal practice. Certainly he would have approved, along with other
Virginians, of the fiction that Virginia lands were deemed to be held as
though they were legally of the manor of East Greenwich in Kent, since such
lands bore the lightest feudal exactions. But he staunchly rejected another
fiction—that of the English conquest of North America, by which the king's
prerogative would be established over the colonies through a fictitious war
and military triumph—and insisted that English law in Virginia derived
from the literal text of James I's letters patent as well as from the active
consent of the settlers. Indeed, one of his most famous statements, "that the
earth belongs in usufruct to the living," is a direct refutation of a well-known
maxim based on a fiction: "A body politick is a body in fiction of law that
endureth in perpetual succession."[24]

But it was Jefferson's acquaintance with legal fictions in his private law
practice that brought this contested tradition most clearly into focus. It
cannot be emphasized strongly enough that early American jurisprudence
was a provincial practitioners' jurisprudence. Until the imperial crisis, the
quotidian realities of the practitioner shaped the course of the law, and,

23. Jefferson to John Brown Cutting, Oct. 1788 ("sly poison"), *Papers of Jefferson*, XIII,
649; Jefferson to Philip Mazzei, Nov. 28, 1785, IX, 70–71 ("celebrated Dr. Blackstone").
Studies of Jefferson's attitude toward Blackstone have placed their attention on his constitutional criticisms. See, for example, Julian S. Waterman, "Thomas Jefferson and Blackstone's Commentaries," *Illinois Law Review*, XXVII (1933), 629–659.

24. Charles M. Andrews, *The Colonial Period of American History*, I, *The Settlements*
(New Haven, Conn., 1934), 86–87; Thomas Jefferson, *Notes on the State of Virginia*, ed.
William Peden (Chapel Hill, N.C., 1982), 132; Sir Henry Finch, *Law or a Discourse Thereof
in Four Books* (London, 1759), 87. Jefferson, to the contrary, believed that the body politic
reconstituted itself naturally every nineteen years and "that between society and society,
generation and generation, there is no municipal obligation, no umpire but the law of
nature. We seem not to have perceived that, by the law of nature, one generation is to
another as one independant nation to another" (Jefferson to James Madison, Sept. 6, 1789,
in Boyd et al., eds., *Papers of Jefferson*, XV, 392–397).

when the crisis did erupt, so did American legal protests.[25] Although Jefferson has left us with an account of his legal study that is open to question, his attention to the requirements of pleading is clear. The primary substantive concern shown in the reported Virginia cases that Jefferson studied was, not surprisingly, property, including the legal problems of slaves as property.[26] Altogether, the cases that Jefferson grappled with required close attention and inquiry not only because they involved extremely complex and abstruse points of law but also because they contained the tension between adjudicatory authority and legislative intent, the conflict of mandatory legal rules and the intent of the individual, and the presence of legal fictions that made no innate sense outside the artificial reason of the law.

Jefferson entered a jurisprudential landscape that had been occupied for centuries. At first a dutiful and conventional student, he constructed his study according to the ways of thinking in the common law. After plodding through Coke's *Institutes,* the authoritative basis for law as practiced in the common-law courts, he continued with the published reports of English cases, an approach that recognized and accepted the use of judge-made rules, including such legal fictions employed in Virginia courts as the feigned location of a grievance.[27] He took due note of the benefits conferred by the use of the collusive common recovery to bar entails and of the method by which the courts had responded to legislative enactments with "a feigned suit" against "an imaginary warrantee worth nothing . . . and tho' it was imaginary they were not permitted to impeach it." He accepted, too, the fiction that a seal on a bond imported consideration; that is, it made the bond a deed, which presumed that possession of property had transferred,

25. No better example exists of this influence than the many studies of the Revolutionary crisis by John Phillip Reid, especially *In a Rebellious Spirit: The Argument of Facts, the Liberty Riot, and the Coming of the American Revolution* (University Park, Pa., 1979), esp. 30–32.

26. The best examination of Jefferson's questionable account of his legal study is Frank L. Dewey, *Thomas Jefferson, Lawyer* (Charlottesville, Va., 1986), 9–17. Jefferson's common-law notes are contained in his manuscript legal commonplace book, now at the Library of Congress. Though parts were published in Gilbert Chinard, ed., *The Commonplace Book of Thomas Jefferson* (Baltimore, 1926), most legal materials were omitted, referred to only by titles that Chinard's copyist gave to the topic. For this reason, the unpaged manuscript will be cited as LCB, followed by the entry number Jefferson assigned.

To those manuscript reports compiled by Randolph and Barradall, he added some made by William Hopkins and reported nine cases he observed and two that he argued between 1768 and 1772; these were published by his grandson, Thomas Jefferson Randolph, as Thomas Jefferson, comp., *Reports of Cases Determined in the General Court of Virginia, from 1730, to 1740, and from 1768, to 1772* (Charlottesville, Va., 1829).

27. Jefferson began his commonplacing with William Salkeld, *Reports of Cases Adjudged in the Court of King's Bench . . .* , 3 vols. (London, 1717–1743); George Andrews, *Reports of Cases Argued and Adjudged in the Court of King's Bench . . .* (London, 1754); Robert, Baron Raymond, *Reports of Cases Argued and Adjudged in the Courts of King's Bench and Common Pleas . . .* (London, 1743); LCB, no. 522.

whether or not it had. This situation sufficed to make the defendant liable, even if the bond were not dated or had "an impossible date," and gave the bond the procedural advantages noticed by Edward Barradall.[28]

As a young practitioner, Jefferson also recognized the value in impeaching the authority of an opponent's precedents. From the start of his common-placing, therefore, he carefully identified dubious common-law reporters of "small authority" or "of no authority." "That part of Popham's reports reported by an uncertain author," he recorded, "ought not to be regarded." In another case, he noted "an error" and quoted Lord Chief Justice Holt's comment on the matter: "See the inconvenience of these scambling reports; they will make us appear to posterity for a parcel of blockheads." Mansfield had read this same case but had drawn a very different lesson: he used Holt's comment to justify his own ignoring of precedent and to craft his own judi-cially innovative rules. Holt's embarrassment touched a raw nerve among the common lawyers, who were sensitive to the charge that judge-made law lacked the consistency and clarity of statute; moreover, it brought judge-made common law perilously close to the arbitrariness and inconsistency that its law officers had attributed to their rivals in the courts of equity. Again quoting Holt, Jefferson observed that another reporter's cases con-tained "many bad precedents" despite someone else's comment that that same collection was "a pretty judicious book." How was one to be certain, especially if the student or judge encountered a case "wrong reported"? "What the court is made to say in relation to keeping a bastard child," Jefferson reminded himself in one entry, "is plainly mistaken" by its re-porter, and might even be so by counsel in the case. Jefferson might not yet have been confident in his ability to distinguish correct reporting from the misleading, but the weakness of the reporting system and the latitude given to judges were obvious to him.[29]

As he gave closer attention to the printed reports he had taken with him to study in the mountains at Shadwell, misgivings crept into his thinking. He observed, for example, that in theory the wide jurisdiction of King's Bench, brought about by a series of fictions, served "not only to correct errors in judicial proceedings, but other errors and misdemeanors extrajudicial, tending to breach of peace, oppression of the subject, or any kind of mis-government: so that no wrong, public or private can be done, but redress may be here obtained by due course of law." Although he approvingly noted that the cited cases demonstrated the laudable principle that "the law will not oblige any custom tending to the support of arbitrary power," he ques-

28. LCB, 189, 189 nn. 1–5, no. 583.
29. LCB, nos. 14, 402, 506, 515, 516, 523 (Jefferson inadvertently numbered two different entries "516"; that referred to here is the second so numbered); Oldham, *Mansfield Manu-scripts*, 102–103.

tioned their force in practice: because in one of them "judgment was reversed," he queried whether its "reversal . . . shall impeach the authority of
these" others.[30]

In grappling with the problematic nature of judicial latitude, Jefferson
was not discovering anything new. It was, in fact, a familiar subject in
England, a stock in trade of writers literary as well as legal, and he encountered it in his reading for pleasure as well. A voracious reader, he had come
to enjoy the work of Laurence Sterne, whose novel *Tristram Shandy* made
numerous references to the courts and the law. One of these references,
which Sterne included from his own sermons, offered the reader an ironic
comment on the superiority of English justice: Those who aspire to follow
the law must act "not like an Asiatick Cadi, according to the ebbs and flows
of his own passions,—but like a British judge in this land of liberty and good
sense, who makes no new law, but faithfully declares that law which he
knows already written."[31]

In 1768, Jefferson complemented his commonplacing of English legal
decisions with the reports of Virginia cases and with those he observed at the
General Court in Williamsburg. In Virginia, the debate over legality not only
brought into conflict the common law and the statute but laid bare a contest
within the common law itself. In October 1735, the General Court heard a
case that posed a simple and easily settled question—on the surface. Five
years before her husband Edward Myhil died, Anne Myhil had deserted him
and "lived in Adultery" with another man, by whom she bore a male child.
In his will (made after the desertion and the birth), Edward had entailed his
land to his heirs male. He took note of the "unspeakable Grief" that Anne's
actions had caused him and provided that "not having had carnal Knowledge of my said Wife for several Years last past . . . I do not think fit to give or
bequeath any Part of my Estate real or personal to my said Wife or her
Child." When grown to maturity, however, Anne's child sued for his right
and secured Edward Barradall to take the case.[32]

The issue rested on the nonrebuttable legal presumption that the child
was the natural offspring of the testator. That is, it accepted a legal fiction
deemed to be true and conclusive in every instance and not subject to factual

30. LCB, no. 245.

31. Laurence Sterne, *The Life and Opinions of Tristram Shandy, Gentleman* (1759–1767),
ed. Ian Campbell Ross (New York, 1983), 112. Jefferson almost certainly had read this
quotation by the time he finished the first round of commonplacing, around 1768. On
Jefferson's enthusiasm for Sterne, and on his purchase of his sermons in 1765, see Douglas L. Wilson, *Jefferson's Literary Commonplace Book* (Princeton, N.J., 1989), 182–184. The
quotation cited appears in book 2, which had been published in 1760, the year Jefferson
came to the College of William and Mary.

32. *Doe Lessee of Myhil v Myhil,* in Barton, ed., *Colonial Decisions,* B161–166, esp. 161–
162.

denial even if manifestly false in a particular case. The law did so because the question of adjudicating paternity is a very slippery slope, and an assured line of inheritance was vital as a matter of policy to the stability of property inheritance. This common-law rule therefore ignored any lack of actual cohabitation or access and asserted that if the husband and wife remained within the king's jurisdiction all "Issue is legitimate and no Proof shall be admitted that it is a Bastard," absent any "apparent Impossibility of Procreation as [for example that the husband was] but eight years old." Barradall rested his case firmly on this conclusive presumption of fact, despite his candid admission that it was a fiction tolerated by the common law; indeed, it tolerated more, as in a case where "a Child is born but one Day after the Marriage and the Child was begot by another[,] such Child is legitimate and no Proof or Averment will be admitted ag't the Legitimacy." Implying that rules on inheritance were adventitious creations, Barradall noted that they varied "almost in every Country" and, though not based on any principle of natural justice, must be followed.[33]

Sir John Randolph represented the defendant, whose factual denial of Edward Myhil's access to his wife would have to be accepted to rebut the plaintiff's presumption of legitimacy. Randolph argued strenuously against the common-law rule, but not out of disagreement with its practical necessity or the policy considerations it represented. Rather, he sought to undermine the legitimacy of this particular legal fiction by tracing its origin to a discredited jurisprudence; namely, that it had been "introduced by the Superstition of Rome upon the Opinion and Doctrine that Marriage was a Sacrament." Even the authority of Sir Edward Coke, he argued, did not suffice to legitimize the succession of such a claimant; the common-law Rule in Shelley's Case, pleaded by Barradall to allow possession and title to vest immediately in the plaintiff as heir, was "only Cokes Opinion and was a groundless Distinction inconsistent with Right, Reason and common Sense." Remarkably—because the judges were acting in their common-law, not equitable, capacity—the court agreed: the child was a "Bastard" and thus "excluded by the Will."[34]

Randolph's direct contradiction of Coke and, moreover, of one of the common law's most celebrated opinions, testified as much to the competition between legalities as it did to that between two of the colony's most eminent lawyers. The common law could be a supple tool in the hands of Virginia jurists—and for attorneys like Barradall, who might argue one way and then another as his client's interests dictated. On the one hand, Barradall could agree that a rule should be disregarded because it had "no Foundation in natural Justice" and that "no natural Difference" existed between two

33. Ibid.
34. Ibid., B164–166.

types of obligation and thus there should be no legal distinction. On the other, he was, as in Myhil, capable of maintaining "the Reason and Principles of the Common Law" over Randolph's point that such were "inconsistent with Right, Reason and common Sense" as well as being the "Superstition of Rome."[35]

The adaptability of the common law through the legal fiction was especially evident in the area of property rights in human beings. "That peculiar relation between persons and things, signified by the term 'property,' is one of the great objects of law," Kames wrote and Jefferson later recorded. To establish their rights in their slave property—that is, to secure in law the rules they wished to apply with regard to their slaves—white Virginians in 1705 reclassified slave property from chattel to real property. This was an eighteenth-century legal fiction building on a seventeenth-century injustice perpetrated under color of law: slaves had none of the natural qualities of immovable real property, whatever the common-law status of chattel had imposed. This would later provoke direct legal challenge, but the fictitious legal classification of slaves as real estate was accepted because it was congruent with efforts to stabilize slave property.

The goal of the legislature had been to bring into operation those common-law rules that determined how slaves should "descend unto the heirs and widows of persons departing this life, according to the manner and custom of land of inheritance, held in fee simple." But because the act also provided that "all such slaves shall be liable to the paiment of debts, and may be taken by execution, for that end, as other chattels or personal estate may be," slave property was not as tightly controlled as some owners wished it to be, and they sought to protect their slave holdings from debt forfeiture by entailing them. The lawfulness of this stratagem was unclear, however; no definite rules existed to determine if slaves could be entailed or whether, if entailed, they could be forfeited for debts. By 1727, the result was that "many mischiefs have arisen, from the various constructions, and contrary judgments and opinions, which have been made and given thereupon, whereby many people have been involved in law suits and controversies, which are still like to increase." That year the Assembly attempted to clarify the situation by enacting that slaves could be entailed if "annexed" to the land by a simple declaration, but it left them liable to forfeiture. Unfortunately, this law did not end the "law suits and controversies," because it also provided that slaves could not be forfeited unless the land to which they were annexed "is, should, or might, be forfeited."[36]

35. *Field a[gainst] Cocke* (1735), ibid., B186, B186 n. 2.
36. LCB, no. 559; William Waller Hening, comp., *The Statutes at Large: Being a Collection of All the Laws of Virginia, from the First Session of the Legislature, in the Year 1619*, 13 vols. (1819–1823, reprint, Charlottesville, Va., 1969), III, 333, 334, IV, 222, 223 (where not liable), 225 (how annexed to land), 226 (where liable). What precise interest would have

Not surprisingly, the law of 1727, as interpreted by the various courts of the colony, "was attended with such doubts, variety of opinions, and confusion, that new points are even yet started, and undetermined." Accordingly, the Assembly in 1748 recognized that "it was thought best to reduce them [slaves] to their natural condition" and not treat them as chattel for some purposes and resort to the legal fiction of realty for others. That year it enacted "that for the future, all slaves whatsoever shall be held, deemed, and taken, to be chattels personal." Unfortunately for this attempt to use statute to clarify legislative ambiguity as well as adjudicatory disagreement, the Privy Council disallowed the law.[37]

One aspect of the 1727 law, however, had seemed clear: it expressly provided that slaves might be annexed to, and thereby entailed with, land. But were entails of slaves made before this law (that is, under the act of 1705) retroactively legal? The question reached the General Court in 1768, where Jefferson witnessed and reported a contest that pitted Attorney General John Randolph and George Mason against George Wythe and Edmund Pendleton. This question of slave entails had come before the court in chancery in 1751, been dismissed in 1758, appealed to the Privy Council in 1759, and argued there in 1762. No clear decision had emerged, and even the precise matter in issue was unclear.[38] As Jefferson reported when the entailability of slaves once again came before the General Court in 1768, "Slaves had been entailed between the years 1705 and 1727, without being annexed to lands, and the question was, whether the entail was good?" Randolph and Mason argued for the plaintiff that entails of slaves, even if not annexed to land, were lawful, while Wythe and Pendleton argued for the defendant and denied their lawfulness. The contest also brought into collision rival conceptions of legality; the validity of both turned on a single legal fiction.[39]

---

been forfeited in such a case is not clear and poses one of the great unanswered questions of Virginia legal history. A likely result would be the creation of a less than complete estate, limited to possession by the creditor during the life of the tenant-in-tail. For a fuller appreciation of the law's interpretation through the creation of an estate *pour autre vie,* I am grateful to Professor J. Gordon Hylton of Marquette University Law School.

37. Ibid., V, 439, 441. The Assembly did retain one aspect of realty: that slaves might be forfeited for debts only "in such cases where the lands and tenements of the person incurring the forfeiture are, should, or might be forfeited" (443).

Making matters worse, this executive meddling with legislation occurred after the two-year suspending clause had expired, and notification of the disallowance arrived only after the law was printed in a revisal of colony statute law (432).

38. *Blackwell v Wilkinson* (1768), in Jefferson, comp., *Reports,* 73–85; *Burwell et ux. v Johnson et ux.* This case is not reported in Virginia materials but is analyzed by Joseph Henry Smith, *Appeals to the Privy Council from the American Plantations* (New York, 1950), 504–506. No decision of the Privy Council survives, and Virginians differed as to its meaning.

39. Jefferson, comp., *Reports,* 73.

Randolph insisted that slaves, though "having the natural properties of personal estate," had been given all the "legal qualities" of realty by the statute and thus "should be considered as real estate" for every purpose. This "transmutation of properties" conferred on them not only the expressly named qualities of descent and dower but "every quality" attached by the common law to real property. Whether the slaves had been annexed to land did not matter; Randolph asserted that he had it "from good authority" that the Privy Council in Burwell in 1762 had made its decision as if the slaves had been entailed separately, and that the entail there was good.[40]

Wythe rejected Randolph's version of the Privy Council's determination and insisted that explicit annexation of the slaves to land was necessary for the entail to be valid. Arguing a strict construction of the statute, Wythe was raising as a question the problem of how broadly a legislatively created legal fiction should be construed by the judiciary. Whatever the narrow lawyerly goal of pleading his client's case to the best of his ability, Wythe (tersely supported by Pendleton) was taking sides in a persistent debate in Anglo-American jurisprudence. He emphasized that the statute had expressly mentioned only descent and dower as applying to slaves as real estate. To do otherwise and to apply all "the adventitious or collateral qualities of land" would be doing violence to the legislative intent, which must be construed narrowly where a legal fiction was involved. Mason, to the contrary, had called the effort to determine legislative intent "absurd." "When they have enacted a law," he stated of the legislature, "their power ceases, they have done their part, and then the judges are to take it up, and say what was the meaning." For Wythe, plaintiff's counsel was asking the bench to misuse the common-law method of reasoning by analogy and extend a limited conferral of real property law to an area unjustified by right reasoning. Wythe's insistence on strict construction and limitation of the "transmutation" fiction won the day: the court decided, eight to three, for the defendant. In effect, the General Court had decided against judicial expansion of a rule, but the legislative incapacity of the colony to revise the law clearly on this matter left the status of slaves as property in a curiously "amphibious nature," as Jefferson's law teacher Wythe described it in 1772.[41]

The more Jefferson observed of the General Court, the more he distrusted the judiciary and adjudication. What he saw of it before he suspended his commonplacing in 1772 not only reinforced this inclination but pointed toward the positions he would take as a public official. Before leaving the practice of law, Jefferson reported a case he had argued, *Howell* v. *Netherland* (1770), where, among other issues, he vociferously maintained that an act of

40. Ibid., 73–79, 85.
41. *Herndon v Carr* (1772), ibid., 134.

the legislature denying the freedom of a mixed-race bastard had to be construed narrowly. No court, he insisted, could deny freedom where statute
was unclear. Only "some future legislature, if any shall be found wicked
enough" could so "extend" the law through its own express enactment.[42]

After he turned to politics, this opposition to broad judicial expansion
reappeared and led him to report "a Disquisition of my own on the most
remarkable instance of Judicial legislation, that has ever occurred in English
jurisprudence, or perhaps in any other": the "adoption in mass" of Christianity into the common law "by usurpation of the Judges alone, without a
particle of legislative will having ever been called on, or exercised towards its
introduction or confirmation." Throughout, his comments assailed numerous great figures from the English legal past whose opinions had transformed a "false quotation into a maxim of the common law," but Blackstone
and, especially, Mansfield stood out among the most recent authorities receiving criticism. The latter, Jefferson wrote, at least "qualified it a little, by
saying . . . that 'the essential principles of revealed religion are part of the
common law.' But he cites no authority, and leaves us at our peril to find out
what, in the opinion of the judge, and according to the measure of his foot
or his faith, are those *essential* principles of revealed religion, obligatory on
us as a part of the common law."[43]

Jefferson's disapproval of judicial discretion grew directly out of his Virginia experience and, more particularly, through his acquaintance with the
abuse of legal fictions. The tension that he perceived between legislation
and adjudication gives greater meaning to the colonial period of American law by reaching back into the long tradition in Virginia that had led
William Beverley at the turn of the eighteenth century to condemn reliance on the "Crooked Cord of a Judge's Discretion," as well as forward
to today. This conflict appears clearly in Jefferson's first great political work,
A Summary View of the Rights of British America (1774). Among the vil-
lains of his attack were those "Norman lawyers" who had "found means to
saddle" the lands of the Saxons with the contrivances of "feudal burthens"
based on the "fictitious principle that all lands belong originally to the
king." This "error," which the English "were early persuaded to beleive real,"
endured as a judicial deception that had arrogated from "society" an authority to do that which only "may be done by themselves assembled collec-

42. Jefferson, comp., *Reports,* 96.

43. Jefferson, "Preface," in Jefferson, comp., *Reports,* vi, with text as appendix, at 137–
142, esp. 138. This is drawn from LCB, nos. 873, 879, from the 1770s and perhaps as late as
1781. Jefferson's critique has been the subject of several excellent analyses, from those of
John Quincy Adams and Joseph Story to the twentieth century; see Edward Dumbauld,
Thomas Jefferson and the Law (Norman, Okla., 1978), 76–83; Stuart Banner, "When Christianity Was Part of the Common Law," *Law and History Review,* XVI (1998), 27–62.

tively, or by their legislature to whom they may have delegated sovereign authority."[44]

Jefferson's hostility to the fiction of "feudal burthens" and his belief in legislative priority over matters of land were apparent in another matter in 1774, shortly before he wrote the *Summary View*. In May, he and his wife Martha submitted a petition to the House of Burgesses for "docking the Intail and settling lands" she had inherited through her mother. In 1705, the judicial remedies for doing so had been abolished, requiring anyone wishing to free real estate from the restrictions of entail to do so by petition and private bill. Although the private bill introduced for them by Richard Bland passed, it failed to receive Governor Dunmore's signature before he dissolved the House.[45]

Jefferson's aversion to entail was strong and abiding, and he opposed it for reasons not only personal but deeply ideological. He viewed it as a corruption of nature and quoted Scottish jurist Lord Kames in his commonplace book: "Land-property naturally one of the greatest blessings of life, is thus converted into a curse" by entail. Above all, Jefferson saw entail as an instrument for the "accumulation and perpetuation of wealth, in select families," who formed an artificial aristocracy in Virginia; its abolition by statute, he predicted, would be part of a planned "system by which every fibre would be eradicated of antient or future aristocracy; and a foundation laid for a government truly republican."[46]

Such a goal challenged the very bedrock of landed authority and the stability of real property that assured the political ascendancy of the great property owners, who recognized the import of the abolition bill. Before his bill became law in the fall of 1776, Jefferson's efforts ran into strong opposition from men such as Landon Carter, who denounced them as the product of a "midday drunkard."[47] Foremost among his legal opponents was Ed-

44. "An American" [William Beverley], *An Essay upon the Government of the English Plantations on the Continent of America* (London, 1701), 23; Boyd et al., eds., *Papers of Jefferson,* I, 132–133.

45. Ibid., 105; Hening, comp., *Statutes,* III, 320.

46. LCB, no. 559; Thomas Jefferson, "Autobiography" (1790), in *Thomas Jefferson: Writings* (New York, 1984), 44. The extent to which real property was encumbered by entail in colonial Virginia has been vastly underestimated, thereby diminishing the impact of Jefferson's efforts. On the true significance of this reform, see the important study by Holly Brewer, "Entailing Aristocracy in Colonial Virginia: 'Ancient Feudal Restraints' and Revolutionary Reform," *William and Mary Quarterly,* 3d Ser., LIV (1997), 307–346.

47. This struggle is summarized in Dumas Malone, *Jefferson the Virginian* (Boston, 1948), 251–256, vol. I of *Jefferson and His Time.* The impact of Jefferson's campaign can be appreciated by the endurance of vilification well into the next century. Writing more than eighty years after the reform, Henry S. Randall remarked of the lingering animosity, "*Class hate*—the rage of a permanently injured *profession*—never dies!" (*The Life of Thomas Jefferson,* 3 vols. [New York, 1858], I, 202)

mund Pendleton, with whom Jefferson engaged in a spirited correspondence on the matter. To the elder lawyer, who had been "beating my brain"
over the question, Jefferson held firm. "The opinion that our lands were
allodial possessions is one which I have very long held," he insisted, "and had
in my eye during a pretty considerable part of my law reading which I found
alwais strengthened it." The matter was clear: "feudal burthens" were a
"mere fiction" and "afterwards made an engine of immense oppresion."[48]

Jefferson continued to express his distrust of judges and his preference for
legislative certainty as the awareness of the need for a new legal system in Virginia became apparent. Turning to the Italian law reformer Cesare Beccaria,
Jefferson copied into his commonplace book some time after 1773 passages
whose distrust of judicial discretion sounds very much like a twentieth-
century legal realist. Jefferson chose to begin his long extract from Beccaria's
essay on crimes and punishments, very significantly, with the fourth chapter,
which dealt with the interpretation of laws. He noted Beccaria's warning of
the effect of judicial discretion: "si apre la porta all'incertezza [the door is
opened to uncertainty]." Judges were only human, and they reflected human
unpredictability in their decisions. Beccaria continued, "Each man has his
point of view, each man in different times has a different one. The spirit of
the law would thus be the result of good, or wicked logic of a judge of an easy,
or indisposed digestion; it would depend on the violence of his passions, of
the infirmity of which he suffers."[49]

When it came time to take definite steps toward reform in the 1780s,
therefore, Jefferson placed his trust in legislative rulemaking. What stability
the common law possessed, he was confident, would be the product of
statutory precision. To Philip Mazzei, he extolled the way that "the Common
law . . . has been enlarged from time to time by acts of the legislature," and he
urged that any rules developed in chancery be legislatively approved and
codified. No advocate of static rules, Jefferson had seen the Virginia legislature create legal fictions of its own. Nevertheless, he trusted the legislature
more than the judges. Like Bentham, who had urged codification in 1776 so
that "the fictitious must be substantiated into real," Jefferson that same year

48. Pendleton to Jefferson, Aug. 3, 1776, Jefferson to Pendleton, Aug. 13, 1776, in Boyd et
al., eds., *Papers of Jefferson*, I, 484–485, 491–492.
49. Cesare Bonesana, marchese di Beccaria, *Dei delitti e delle pene*, 2d ed. (Munich,
1764); LCB, no. 806, citing ibid., 12–13. In its original Italian, the second Beccaria quotation reads, "Ciascun uomo ha il suo punto di vista, ciascun uomo in differenti tempi ne ha
un diverso. Lo spirito della legge sarebbe dunque il risultato di una buona, o cattiva logica
di un giudice di una facile, o malsana digestione; dipenderebbe dall violenza delle sue
passioni, della debolezza di chi soffre." Beccaria's reference to indigestion calls to mind
Robert M. Hutchins's comment, "The law may thus depend on what the judge has had for
breakfast" ("The Autobiography of an Ex-Law Student," *American Law School Review*, VII
[1934], 1054).

began an effort to codify Virginia's law. The effort fell far short of his goals, but in 1812 he still hoped for the complete "exclusion from the courts of the malign influence of all [English] authorities" after 1760, which "would add the advantage of getting us rid of all Mansfield's innovations, or civilizations of the common law."[50]

Jefferson ultimately despaired of any hope that Virginians might purify the common law and place it beyond the reach of the judges, however. Any effort "to reduce the common law, our own, and so much of the English statutes as we have adopted, to a text," he conceded, is "a question of transcendant difficulty." Had the attempt been made, "the meaning of every word of Blackstone would have become a source of litigation, until it had been settled by repeated legal decisions." Case reports would have piled up, producing "the same chaos of law-lore from which we wished to be emancipated, added to the evils of the uncertainty which a new text and new phrases would have generated."[51]

He thus placed his faith in elected representatives whose implementation of legality rested on what he believed to be the more legitimate foundation of popular sovereignty. In the same spirit that had led Bentham to write *Introduction to the Principles of Morals and Legislation* (1789), Jefferson turned to that subject and compiled *A Manual of Parliamentary Practice* in 1800. Opening his work with the section "The Importance of Adhering to Rules," he praised them for their effectiveness "against the attempts of power." Legislators, like judges, might not be able to devise fully rational rules; indeed, whether these rules "be in all cases the most rational or not, is really not of so great importance," he believed. "It is much more material that there should be a rule to go by, than what that rule is." Who would make that rule and how they would do so, however, would remain as contested as ever.[52]

50. Jefferson to Mazzei, Nov. 28, 1785, in Boyd et al., eds., *Papers of Jefferson*, IX, 69–70; Jefferson to Judge John Tyler, June 17, 1812, in Andrew A. Lipscomb and Albert Ellery Bergh, eds., *The Writings of Thomas Jefferson*, 20 vols. (Washington, D.C., 1905), XIII, 166.

51. Jefferson to Judge John Tyler, June 17, 1812, in Lipscomb and Bergh, eds., *Writings of Jefferson*, XIII, 167.

52. Thomas Jefferson, *A Manual of Parliamentary Practice: For the Use of the Senate of the United States*, 2d ed. (1812), reprinted as *Jefferson's Parliamentary Writings: "Parliamentary Pocket-Book" and "A Manual of Parliamentary Practice,"* ed. Wilbur Samuel Howell (Princeton, N.J., 1988), 357.

PART TWO

Intercultural Encounters

S OCIAL AND CULTURAL histories of colonialism the world over have, in recent years, given increasing attention to the dialogic aspect of colonization. Matters once approached as if they consisted of little more than the rapid and overwhelming imposition of European ways on unfamiliar landscapes, in which the fate of indigenous cultures was simply to be transformed or obliterated, have been reexamined for signs of the agency of the colonized. The change has yielded histories that present colonial encounters as processes at once more tentative than previously thought, and with effects mutually rather than singly transforming. The three essays in Part II extend to early American legal history the model of intercultural encounter as at least in part an instance of negotiation.

In the first essay, Katherine Hermes suggests that, for much of the seventeenth century in New England, a shared concept of reciprocity mediated the conflict between Algonquian and Anglo-European legal cultures and that law thus provided a forum in which European settlers and Algonquian inhabitants were able to pursue a fragile and limited but nonetheless real accommodation of differences that arose between them. Jurisdictionally the forum was the colonizer's; Hermes does not suggest that the two sides achieved their working relationship through a mutual yielding to an indifferent third party. Yet she argues that Algonquians entering Anglo-European courts could have an expectation of fair dealing, extending even to the substance of decision making, because certain concepts—notably reciprocity—had independent resonance in the *jurispractices* (the combination of attitudes and behaviors in legal situations on the part of ordinary people) of both cultures. Indeed, Hermes suggests that, by encouraging the settlers' exploration of their own understanding of reciprocity, Algonquian legal practices might well have influenced the development of New England legal culture in ways previously unacknowledged. By the second half of the century, changes in colonial policy, the Christianization of some Indians, frustrations arising in Algonquian dealings with colonists, and ultimately King Philip's War meant an end to the effectiveness of reciprocity and an Algonquian population that exercised legal authority for itself only at European sufferance. Sensitivity to law's place in the extended encounter between

Europeans and Algonquians, however, suggests a more complex story than an inevitable extinguishment of Algonquian autonomy. For three-quarters of a century, Hermes argues, substantive justice was a two-way street.

In the next essay, James F. Brooks explores the dynamics of intercultural relations on another nondominant frontier, that of the New Mexico borderlands between 1700 and 1821, through examination of a series of cases in which the region's *genízaro* slave caste employed the various means at its disposal (extralegal popular protest, claims to customary or traditional rights as slaves or Indians, diplomatic ties to nomadic Indian allies) to negotiate their status vis-à-vis developing colonial legal and economic structures. Law, according to Brooks, clearly stands as an instrument of domination but also offers the subordinated tools of resistance. These mutually antagonistic capacities create in law the possibility of a medium in which interactions among different groups—in this case representatives of empire, *vecino* settlers, genízaros, Pueblo Indians, *los indios bárbaros* beyond the frontier—can be mediated, precisely because no one is fully in control. This is particularly the case in borderlands. Though powerful, Spanish colonizers were by no means in complete ascendancy in the region. Though vulnerable, the genízaros could at times exert influence well beyond their status by dint of their key position in the borderlands political economy. By pursuing claims of group entitlement of one kind or another (gifts and grants, privileges, rights) and by taking advantage of frontier political-economic circumstance, they and other subordinated populations were hence able to negotiate varieties of accommodation for themselves, contributing to the development of a regional species of *derecho vulgar* (customary justice) that allowed the marginal, vecino as well as Indian, a degree of local autonomy from the colonizer's control. By the early nineteenth century, Brooks finds, Bourbon reforms liberalizing the commerce and social structure of the borderlands had narrowed, although they had not destroyed, the opportunities for a fragile local autonomy enjoyed by genízaros and others. The contingencies of reform underlined the ever-present uncertainties of power in colonial borderlands.

Finally, Ann Marie Plane's essay returns us to the Atlantic coast settlements, notably eighteenth-century Rhode Island. Plane uses a long and involved dispute over the marital status of a deceased Narragansett sachem, Charles Ninegret, to explore in detail how a now-dominant Anglo-European legal culture went about creating (in the guise of discovering) the customary law of indigenous inhabitants. The exercise had a practical stimulus— disputes fueled by settlers' pressure on tribal land created intratribal competition that turned on the legitimacy of lines of succession. But it also stands as an important example of the existence in the early American case of phenomena to date more commonly explored in the nineteenth-century heyday of imperialism: namely, the demand, created by colonization itself, that a colonized population have a discoverable customary law from which acts undertaken on its behalf in concert with, or in relation to, the colonizers, may gain standing; and the colonizers' assiduous application of themselves to the task of constructing the practices—inventing the traditions—that will bring the desired "native" customary law (a vital constituent of native identity itself) into being. By examining the structure of testimony regarding Narragansett customs governing royal marriage and succession, Plane shows how the very concepts mobilized to construct custom owed their existence to the influence of English legal culture and to the social context of eighteenth-century colonized Rhode Island. As dialogic as colonial encounters may be, Plane's essay demonstrates how fragile the accommodations achieved by the colonized always are, how easily they may be made the unwilling, sometimes unwitting, subjects of the colonizer's scripts.

"Justice Will Be Done Us"

Algonquian Demands for Reciprocity
in the Courts of European Settlers

I N 1651, AFTER the English colonization of New England had been
under way for more than two decades, a sachem of the Mohegans,
Uncas, appeared before the Particular Court of Connecticut to make a
complaint. An unnamed Long Island Indian had purchased a stolen
Mohegan canoe from a Connecticut settler. The Mohegan owner of the
canoe then took it back. Uncas was in court to complain about the settler's
theft, despite the return of the object to its owner. He wanted satisfaction,
not for the canoe itself, since that was recovered, but for the Long Island
Indian who had lost money in the illicit transaction. The court awarded the
Long Island Indian, on Uncas's complaint, nine shillings.[1]

Considering Uncas's friendship with the English, it is not too surprising
that one finds him seeking justice through an English court. What surprises,
at first glance, is his demand that satisfaction be given to an Indian not of his
tribe. Yet, Uncas was doing what Indians and colonists both agreed was the
right thing: he was an Indian looking after another Indian. Moreover, the
Indians and the English also agreed that, when colonists hurt Indians, colonial courts would punish the offender. Uncas did not have to go to court by
any English dictates; he could easily have let the situation pass. Algonquian
societies did not take intrusion lightly, however, and expected wrongs to be

I would like to thank Christopher Tomlins, Bruce Mann, Ann Marie Plane, and Michael
Zuckerman for their helpful commentary and criticism regarding methodology as well as
sources. If this essay has improved at all through its several drafts, it is due largely to their
efforts to stimulate my thought about the historical issues raised here. I am grateful to the
other participants in the "Many Legalities of Early America" conference at the Omohundro
Institute of Early American History and Culture, November 1996, who also provided many
useful suggestions and raised important questions; the University of Otago, Dunedin, New
Zealand, for its support for my research; Megan Cook, for her research assistance; and
Alexandra Maravel, for her advice and encouragement. This essay is dedicated to the late
Marie Butler, for her strength, virtue, and love.

1. *Records of the Particular Court of Connecticut, 1639–1663*, Connecticut Historical Society, *Collections*, XXII (Hartford, Conn., 1928), 98. The Particular Court heard cases having
to do with individuals rather than cases dealing with matters pertaining to the colony. Its
procedures and the kinds of cases it heard were similar to those of county courts.

righted.[2] So Uncas went to court to make sure that what was taken away was given back. He would have demanded the same of anyone, Indian or settler. The record of the case takes up only a few lines of the court's records, but it speaks volumes about the way in which Indians and colonists could and did resolve disputes during a period in which historians have more frequently noticed violent encounters. By looking more closely into the judicial settlement of grievances of Algonquians against colonists, one sees a more complex picture of the postcontact period than has been drawn previously. One can see the clash of legal systems rather than weapons. One can see the demands, concessions, negotiations, compromises, and unique approaches of postcontact dispute resolution. One can see the reflection of Indian concepts of justice in colonial court cases as a new stage in the postcontact shift in power. The first century after contact was a period of sovereign interaction that gradually mediated the transition from military conquest to the dominance of Anglo-European governance.

A three-way governance over the northeastern coast of North America formed over the course of the seventeenth and eighteenth centuries. Algonquians ruled themselves as usual, but they also came to French and English colonial courts in certain matters and became the quasi subjects of European international law. The interaction of Algonquian and Anglo-European governance of people, chattel, issues, and land is a complex subject that has been rendered more simple by a pervasive historical model: invasion and conquest. My objective here is to question the accuracy of that model and to suggest ways in which we may move toward a more complex understanding of colonization as a gradual process rather than an event. The Algonquian Indians were not simply the victims of conquest or the recipients of European culture, goods, and ideas. To just what extent native American traditions persisted in postcolonial society must remain speculative for the time being. Yet, it is worth considering the possibility that the current conquest narrative in which native American society was "wiped out" is simply wrong. By trying to understand what the Indians were doing before and

2. The Algonquians were, in the colonial period, coastal peoples of the Chesapeake, Middle Atlantic, and northward, as well as some western neighbors in New England and Canada who shared a linguistic element, some customs, and stories of origin. See T. J. C. Brasser, "The Coastal Algonkians: People of the First Frontiers," in Eleanor Burke Leacock and Nancy Oestreich Lurie, eds., *North American Indians in Historical Perspective* (New York, 1971), 67, for a map that basically represents the tribes termed "Algonquian" or "Algonkian." This paper is concerned most specifically with the Lenni Lenape tribe northward to the Abenaki and the Europeans who settled in the areas that those tribes inhabited. Sometimes it has not been possible to identify the precise tribe of the litigants owing to the nature of the colonial record. Although my describing these many tribes under one rubric is problematic, it is justified, I think, by the fact that no major tribal differences regarding legal practices or governance appear to have existed among the Algonquians north of Delaware.

during the colonial period, acting alongside the Europeans, the emergent narrative looks less like a rapid, uninterrupted conquest and more like a relationship in which the deterioration of one party and the dominance of the other was neither linear nor absolute.[3]

I. Reciprocity as a Legal Principle

Law is an area of Algonquian-settler relations that aptly illustrates many of the complexities omitted from conquest narratives.[4] The legal landscape

3. It may seem obvious to state that Indians were actors just as much as Europeans in the story of the European settlement of America, but historians have not generally written as if that were the case. Even sympathetic and revisionist histories have emphasized European rather than Indian acts. Trying to tell the story from "an Indian perspective" is rarely attempted, for numerous reasons. Some historians are skeptical that the use of western sources can produce an unbiased or balanced account of native life. Native Americans have credited their oral history traditions, but many professional historians do not. There is also an ongoing argument about the authority of non-Indian authors to represent their work as "from a native perspective." For a recent critique of this trend, see David Murray, "Through Native Eyes? Indian History/American History," in Deborah L. Madsen, ed., *Visions of America since 1492* (London, 1994), 57–71. See also Clifford Geertz, "'From the Native's Point of View': On the Nature of Anthropological Understanding," in Geertz, *Local Knowledge: Further Essays in Interpretive Anthropology* (New York, 1983), 55–70, esp. 56.

Since 1990, even authors of "conquest" interpretations have relented in their tales of destruction to emphasize "recovery" among tribes. See, for example, Francis Jennings, *The Founders of America: How Indians Discovered the Land, Pioneered in It, and Created Great Classical Civilizations; How They Were Plunged into a Dark Age by Invasion and Conquest; and How They Are Reviving* (New York, 1993). Yet note that in Jennings's title all stages are in the active voice with the Indians as actors, save one: the invasion and conquest.

4. In fact, conquest narratives rarely examine law or legal structures beyond the mention of territorial jurisdiction. Interactions between native Americans and settlers that are described in detail include mainly war, trade, and diplomacy. One particular book—which is also one of the finest syntheses—never mentions law or legal systems despite covering with extraordinary breadth most areas of Indian-European relations; see Colin G. Calloway, *New Worlds for All: Indians, Europeans, and the Remaking of Early America* (Baltimore, 1997). One example that appears on 123 describes the death of three colonists and some cattle at the hands of Wicomesse Indians: "The governor of Maryland demanded that the killers be handed over to the English for punishment, but the Indians offered to give wampum in atonement," telling the settlers that they should conform themselves to Indian customs rather than vice versa. For Calloway, the above incident is about negotiating customary differences and learning how to conduct business in a new colonial world. But, viewed more precisely, the incident demonstrates that the Wicomesse settled some legal disputes with payments to the aggrieved party and anticipated that Europeans would accept the payment as a just settlement. It was not a business transaction but rather punishment for a crime, a matter of law, in which the two parties were involved. Compare Neal Salisbury, "Indians and Colonists in Southern New England after the Pequot War: An Uneasy Balance," in Laurence M. Hauptman and James Wherry, eds., *The Pequots in Southern New England: The Fall and Rise of an American Indian Nation* (Nor-

shows ways in which Indian-European interactions were handled with mini-
mal violence and provides a glimpse into periods when compromise and
mediation attenuated the colonizing process. Although violence was no
stranger to colonization, neither were attempts on both sides to control it,
mediate it, and adjudicate it.[5]

A common misunderstanding is that "there was no law in the European
sense" among the Algonquians, or indeed among any other Indian tribe in
North America before contact. There was, historians and anthropologists
have alleged, "tribal custom" or the "primitive law" of "reciprocity" or
"something like law," but not law itself.[6] Colonists themselves often pronounced the Indians to be lawless. A closer examination of definitions of law
and Algonquian societies disproves such a notion. Not only did Algonquians
have legal systems possessing features in common with contemporary European systems, but Europeans, particularly English Puritan sects, were ex-
perimenting with concepts and procedures already present among some
Algonquian tribes. Moreover, as a result of contact, a set of indigenous legal
rules emerged, especially with regard to personal and subject matter jurisdiction, interpretation, and final resolution of conflict. The very interaction
of legal systems and recombinant emergence of new legal approaches to
uniquely colonial problems exemplify the new narrative of relationship.[7]

---

man, Okla., 1990), 81, which argues that, to understand Indian-European relations, historians must look beyond war and at legal relations, among other things.

5. My argument is, not that courts always and everywhere serve as fora in which
violence can be curbed, but that, in this period of the history of the North Atlantic, they
did. Violence between strangers in a close community has unique characteristics, though,
when compared to either violence between people who know each other well or violence
between people who in some way are able to insert distance between themselves. Colonial
society lurched its way through each of these types of interactions, but was in the main, to
borrow a phrase and a concept, a "neighborhood of strangers" (Sally Engle Merry, *Urban
Danger: Life in a Neighborhood of Strangers* [Philadelphia, 1981]).

6. Howard S. Russell, *Indian New England before the Mayflower* (Hanover, N.H., 1980),
19. William Starna, "The Pequots in the Early Seventeenth Century," in Hauptman and
Wherry, eds., *The Pequots in Southern New England*, 42, describes all the major tribes in
the region as operating on a "system of reciprocity." For a standard generalization about
prehistorical societies, see Grant Gilmore, *The Ages of American Law* (New Haven, Conn.,
1977), 1.

Even a reconstruction of the Algonquian language omits any word for law (see John
Hewson, index to *A Computer-Generated Dictionary of Proto-Algonquian* [Hull, Quebec,
1993], 265). There are, however, words for "to judge; he judges" *(tepaxkwenewa; tipasko-
new)* and "a judge; judge, lawyer, he passes judgment" *(tepaxkwenikewa; tepahkkonekew)*
(197). As this is a reconstruction, no historical etymologies are included. Yet the Indians
appear to have had a word. Abraham Pierson used *pákkadtawáuwunk* as "the law," which
seems to incorporate the proto-Algonquian root (*Some Helps for the Indians . . .* [Cam-
bridge, Mass., 1658]), 29.

7. Gregory Evans Dowd, *A Spirited Resistance: The North American Indian Struggle for
Unity, 1745–1815* (Baltimore, 1992), esp. 2, argues for the Indians' positive approaches to

There is evidence that Algonquians shared certain legal concepts, particularly that of reciprocity, with some groups of colonists. Reciprocity, simply put, is the idea of mutuality, or give-and-take.[8] For Algonquians involved in disputes with Europeans, the concept was usually literal; they expected that, if they had to pay a fine or damages, the European litigant would have to pay as well. The idea was that the sides exchanged something, so that in the end both parties had a material and a psychological "gift." In the colonial setting, reciprocity meant that, when Indians appeared in European colonial courts, they received "the same" treatment they would have if they had been Europeans. In most cases, the concept worked as a mixture of Algonquian and European modes. Although Europeans retained a definition of fairness from imported customs that sometimes overrode the *jurispractice* of "give-and-take," many colonial courts tended to act in accordance with Indian expectations.[9] A New Haven court thus bowed to the request of Wash, an Indian assaulted brutally by an English seaman, to receive medical treatment for his injuries at the seaman's cost rather than money damages, which the court first offered as compensation. The court ordered a doctor to try to heal him; Wash later reported satisfaction with his cure.[10]

From among the colonial court records, diaries, correspondence, travel accounts, and town records, it is possible to sift out the words of the Algonquian Indians who lived in what was known to Europeans as French Canada, New England, and the Middle Colonies. Europeans wrote down not just their own impressions about native American life but also Indian words. Algonquians have left oral traditions and the occasional written record. All

------

innovation in general. See Mark D. Walters, "Mohegan Indians v. Connecticut (1705–1773) and the Legal Status of Aboriginal Customary Laws and Government in British North America," *Osgood Hall Law Journal*, XXXIII, no. 4 (Winter 1995), esp. 829.

8. *Black's Law Dictionary*, 4th ed. rev. (St. Paul, Minn., 1968), 1435.

9. The word *jurispractice* is my own, but I think it accurately encapsulates, more than either *jurisprudence* or *legal system*, what these societies were engaged in. Their ideas were not yet of the level of jurisprudence, for these were ordinary people, not great legal thinkers, implementing ideas about law. Their practices and procedures were more rudimentary than *legal system* implies, for all groups were highly informal. *Jurispractice*, in this sense, is similar to *mentalité*, for it is a mixture of thought and action taken by ordinary people to construct the law without elaborate legal theories but with definite understandings about the nature of law and its purposes. The concept of jurisculture might seem applicable here, concerned as it is with the ordering of institutions based on a society's unified patterns of behavior, but it focuses upon culture as a shaper of law. *Jurispractice* better describes, in my view, what goes on in a specifically legal setting wherein the law is a funnel for a variety of cultural norms upon which it imposes rules. See Abraham Edel and Elizabeth Flower, "Reflections on the Concept of Jurisculture," in Sava Alexander Vojcanin, ed., *Law, Culture, and Values: Essays in Honor of Gray L. Dorsey* (New Brunswick, N.J., 1990).

10. Franklin Bowditch Dexter, ed., *New Haven Town Records, 1649–1662* (New Haven, Conn., 1917), 36–37, 135 (1652), vol. I of *Ancient Town Records*.

of these sources, taken together, provide an adequate, though not rich, account of what Algonquians thought about law, dispute settlement, and justice.[11]

Both Algonquian and European shared the jurisprudential precept that substance (the fairness of the decision) was valued over form (procedural process). The native American culture united with an Anglo-European legal experiment in the colonial period to produce the conditions under which ideas of substantive justice flourished. "Lett them have justice," William Penn wrote of the Delaware Algonquians, "and you win them." And so justice, if not always practiced, was at least recognized as a tangible objective. Justice often hinged on a sense of fairness, which in turn rested on an idea of mutuality and trust.[12]

Reciprocity, the term most frequently used for the type of mutuality that developed in contact culture, was independently a principle of all three systems of law prevailing in the relevant region: Algonquian, French, and English-Puritan law. For the Algonquians, in their dealings with Europeans, the principle resulted in their demands for the Europeans to own up to the problems for which they were responsible, namely alcohol and guns.[13] For Europeans generally, including the English, reciprocity was at minimum applicable to international law, for it regulated the relationship of states. Foreigners, on entering another nation, had privileges similar to subjects of that nation. For a significant number of Puritans, the principle came from Scottish law and was part of their radical legal experiment to create a community in which consensus, rather than adversarial relations, ruled in court.[14] The legal scholar Torstein Eckhoff has noted in his consideration of modern-day adjudication that, the fewer normative factors that two parties have in common, the fewer their chances for resolving a dispute without third-party intervention. There were no third-party mediators between colonists and Indians, but clearly within some settler-Algonquian contacts

11. For an ethnographic approach to probate records of Christian Indians, see Kathleen J. Bragdon, "The Material Culture of the Christian Indians of New England," in Mary C. Beaudry, ed., *Documentary Archaeology of the New World* (Cambridge, 1988), 126–131. On written and oral Indian records, see David McCutchen, trans. and annot., *The Red Record (The Wallam Olum): The Oldest Native North American History* (Garden City Park, N.Y., 1993); *Natick Town Records: Original Known Indian Records, Earliest Date 1700,* roll 6, book 3, Town Clerk Records, Morse Institute Library, Natick, Mass.

12. Richard S. Dunn and Mary Maples Dunn, eds., *The Papers of William Penn,* II (Philadelphia, 1981), 454.

13. Peter Mancall, *Deadly Medicine: Indians and Alcohol in Early America* (Ithaca, N.Y., 1995), 80, notes that Indians all over French Canada and the English colonies considered the alcohol itself to be more criminal than their behavior. There were other matters, such as livestock, that were particularly labeled as European problems and thus matters for their jurisdiction. See also discussion below.

14. Edward Dumbauld, *The Life and Legal Writings of Hugo Grotius* (Norman, Okla., 1969), 61. See also Katherine A. Hermes, "Religion and Law in Colonial New England, 1620–1730" (Ph.D. diss., Yale, 1995), esp. 14–17, 25–29, 103–105.

there was a common normative concept (reciprocity), although in others there was not. Whether this common norm existed had great implications for how individual Algonquians and their tribes would fare in their own demands when they entered colonial courts.[15]

The concept of reciprocity needs critical reassessment. It was first defined and interpreted as the system of primitive law in Bronislaw Malinowski's *Crime and Custom in Savage Society* (1926), in which he argued, against predecessors in anthropology such as Sir Paul Vinogradoff, that all societies had law and legal forms. Malinowski believed that organic law, embedded in social functioning rather than in historical jurisprudence, could still qualify as systematic, even if it was primitive. He generalized that primitive law was rooted in the principle of give-and-take. Historians have reiterated that the "idea of reciprocity became the core" of an Indian's existence. They have lumped together such diverse activities as sharing food and selecting political leaders under the rubric of "reciprocity."[16]

This general theory of primitive law as reciprocity and reciprocity as the basic value or idea of indigenous peoples remains a fundamental concept of historians, despite considerable development in anthropology, ethnography, and theories of human relations. It is extremely limiting, superimposing a picture of sharing that threatens—although anthropologists have repeatedly warned against such a tendency for the better part of sixty years—to make all aboriginal societies seem generic and simple.[17]

15. Torstein Eckhoff, "The Mediator, the Judge, and the Administrator in Conflict Resolution," in Geoffrey C. Hazard, Jr. and Jan Vetter, eds., *Perspectives on Civil Procedure* (Boston, 1987), 2. It is probable that, in Virginia, for example, the colonial law did not recognize reciprocity as a value (Helen Rountree, "The Powhatans and the English," in Rountree, ed., *Powhatan Foreign Relations, 1500–1722* [Charlottesville, Va., 1993], 201). Algonquians of the Powhatan Confederation did not appear to have used English courts in the same ways as their northern counterparts. In the early colonial period, they largely were absent from court records, except in references to Indian attacks or to Indian servants (*York County Court Orders Beginning in 1633*, DOW 1–3, Colonial Williamsburg Foundation Library Archives, Williamsburg, Virginia). (DOW 2 contains most of the debt and criminal cases; 1 and 3, the inventories, deeds, and wills, although the division is not absolute.) Rountree refers to one case in which a Powhatan took an Englishman from the Eastern Shore to the colonial court and won, but she does not cite the record and gives no details of the case (193). At the turn of the century, there are examples of Indians' agreeing to come to the English courts to show "good faith" when charges were laid against them. The Virginia colonial government, moreover, did not use the courts for dispute resolution but rather for retribution (Gwenda Morgan, *The Hegemony of the Law: Richmond County, Virginia, 1692–1776* [New York, 1989], 36–38).

16. D'Arcy McNickle, "Americans Called Indians," in Leacock and Lurie, eds., *North American Indians in Historical Perspective*, 56; Laurie Weinstein, ed., *Enduring Traditions: The Native Peoples of New England* (Westport, Conn., 1994), xvi.

17. There is some evidence of change in the historiography. See Dowd, *A Spirited Resistance*, 3, who states that "power lay at the center of all concerns." This may be substituting one overriding principle for another, but at least it looks in another direction. See also Ruth Benedict, *Patterns of Culture* (1934; New York, 1946), 46; Geertz, "Local Knowledge: Fact and Law in Comparative Perspective," in Geertz, *Local Knowledge*, 179.

Reciprocity was, not the fundamental law of Algonquian societies, but simply one principle.[18] Nevertheless, it was a principle that had resonance for colonists who were founding their societies as consensus-based communities (and for whom equity was taking on a significant legal meaning devoid of its English connotation of torturous inquisition) or for Europeans already steeped in a civil law tradition. It was a principle that the two societies, Algonquian and Anglo-European, had in common during the period of contact and shortly thereafter—and one on which the two groups often were able to agree as a basis for their legal relationships.

The principle of reciprocity also aided another legal goal that the two communities shared: coming to the substantively, rather than procedurally, correct decision. Algonquian groups held long deliberations in councils, turning out decisions only after each councillor had spoken his mind about the issue. English groups, for example, experimented with legal methods such as conventing, a procedure infamous during the Antinomian Controversy in Massachusetts but more positively allowing for the unrestricted gathering of information to obtain the truth.[19] The Puritans also codified a procedure of dispute resolution that roughly corresponded to the Algonquian emphasis on result over form and ritual, the Massachusetts *Body of Liberties* (1641) declaring, "No Summons pleading Judgement, or any kinde of proceeding in Court or course of Justice shall be abated, arested or reversed upon any kinde of cercumstantiall errors or mistakes, If the person and cause be rightly understood and intended by the Court."[20]

The claim that reciprocity was not the law of an indigenous people but merely a principle within it must be subjected to scrutiny. In order for a principle or set of principles to form the "law," the formation has to be immutable except by an agreed-upon means of change; if violated, there must be an enforcement provision and procedure to impose sanctions. Mere custom, if it can be violated at will or if it is subject to intentional change

18. It is worth exploring further whether there was an oral jurisprudence in some nonliterate societies; whether reciprocity was an underlying principle in all jurispractice of any given society; or whether legal reciprocity was always peculiar to certain forms and factual situations. Furthermore, we need to know more about how the rules that governed societies engaging in reciprocity were formulated and applied.

19. Conventing is a procedure based in Roman law, canon law, and civil law that is unknown in English common law. In a convention, private individuals or the state make out a complaint against a defendant, who then has the chance personally to answer charges before the community of complainants and witnesses. There is a tribunal presiding over the court, but procedure is rather informal, allowing all to speak without limitations due to one's position, relationship to the individual on trial, or rules of evidence. Its use in the Antinomian Controversy in a uniquely Puritan form is discussed in Hermes, "Religion and Law in Colonial New England," 122–132.

20. Hermes, "Religion and Law in Colonial New England," 126–127; John Cushing, ed., *The Laws and Liberties of Massachusetts, 1641–1691,* facs. ed. (Wilmington, Del., 1976), app. 3, 693.

with no clear method for effecting it, cannot be considered law without diluting the definition to meaninglessness. The Indians' dealings in land showed that they could bridge their cultural divides with the colonists by using principles other than reciprocity, such as usufruct rights. Within their own communities, moreover, Algonquians regulated such customs as marriage and divorce with legal rules different from reciprocity that included, for example, reliance on principles of hierarchy and status.[21]

On the Anglo-European side, some colonial societies, such as Rhode Island, were not interested in a reformed equity jurisprudence; neither were they as interested in developing a legal relationship with the Indians based on reciprocity. Relations with Rhode Island were arguably the best in New England in terms of tribal satisfaction. Rhode Island as a colony preferred to deal with individuals through their sachems, a practice that corresponded to Narragansett rules of foreign diplomacy, whereas the other New England colonies dealt with individual Indians as persons in their own right, albeit usually with a sachem present. In Rhode Island courts, however, Indians followed English law, a practice that, because of the adversarial nature of English law, left individual Indians much less satisfied than those who went to Massachusetts, Connecticut, or New Haven courts or to the courts of New France. In the latter instances, the less-formal nature of legal practice allowed for a more flexible process and a substantive outcome that conformed more readily to Indian ideas of fairness.[22]

Once one recognizes that Algonquian legal systems continued after contact, one can begin to look at demands for reciprocity through the lens of legal analysis. It is a matter of the evolution of law in a prolonged period of contact between different systems and different peoples, not merely the disposition of individual disputes between Indians and colonists. Indians did not lose their legal concepts at contact, nor did they willingly relinquish their legal autonomy or demands for accountability in the succeeding years.

II. Jurisdiction and Legal Rules

Once the Europeans began to establish settlements, the Algonquians voluntarily placed themselves within the jurisdiction of European colonies, but

21. Geertz, "Local Knowledge," in Geertz, *Local Knowledge*, 168; William Cronon, *Changes in the Land: Indians, Colonists, and the Ecology of New England* (New York, 1983), 62–63. Cronon links usufruct rights with mutuality; each goes toward a similar aim. The concepts are nevertheless distinct. See also Chrestien Le Clerq, "Micmac Modesty," in James Axtell, ed., *The Indian Peoples of Eastern America: A Documentary History of the Sexes* (New York, 1981), 83–87; Daniel Denton, *A Brief Description of New York . . .*, facs. ed. (Ann Arbor, Mich., 1966), 10.

22. Paul A. Robinson, "A Narragansett History from 1000 B.P. to the Present," in Weinstein, ed., *Enduring Traditions*, 82–83.

only in certain circumstances. One of those circumstances was conflict resolution, leading the Algonquians to enter a very particular part of the English domain—the courtroom. The Algonquians pursued their own ideas of
right in their contact with the settlers; they did not appear in colonial
courts simply because the magistrates commanded them to. Nor did the
tribes rely on Anglo-European legal institutions to resolve or settle all problems. Rather, the use of colonial legal power was by negotiation and consent.
The Algonquians demanded that the colonists take responsibility in some
cases, but, in other cases, they simply accepted the colonists' prerogative
for deciding a given issue. The Algonquian experience in the colonial legal sphere yields an important story of accommodation between sovereign
powers in a newly shared environment.

Language was an initial point of accommodation rather than submission.
Algonquians did not learn European languages any more immediately than
most colonists learned Algonquian, but leaders of both groups ordinarily
took it upon themselves to learn some of the other's language.[23] Still, professional interpreters were central to the conduct of legal business between
Anglo-Europeans and Indians. The French quickly trained interpreters in
Algonquian and Iroquoian languages by settling young Frenchmen with the
Indians. William Penn mentioned the English settlers' use of interpreters for
relations with the Lenni Lenape (Delaware), although he noted that problems could arise when the interpreter was neither English nor Indian.[24]

Both sides employed interpreters whenever they discussed a matter of
importance, and interpreters were present in most legal situations until the
latter part of the seventeenth century.[25] Their roles were defined by the needs

23. All records in Natick, the original praying town, were initially kept in the Massachu-
set language, and books published for Indian instruction, if they used English at all, often
had English on one side and the appropriate Indian language on the other. See *Natick
Town Records*, roll 6, book 3; John Eliot, *The Logick Primer* (Cambridge, Mass., 1672);
Cotton Mather, *Wussukwonk en Christianeue asuh peantamwae Indianog/An Epistle to the
Christian Indians* (Boston, 1700).

24. On French interpreters, see Mason Wade, "French Indian Policies," in Wilcomb
Washburn, ed., *Handbook of the North American Indians*, IV, *History of Indian White
Relations* (Washington, D.C., 1988), 21. See also Yasu Kawashima, "Forest Diplomats: The
Role of Interpreters in Indian-White Relations on the Early American Frontier," in *Ameri-
can Indian Quarterly*, XIII (1989), 1–14. Nancy L. Hagedorn, " 'A Friend to Go between
Them': The Interpreter as Cultural Broker during Anglo-Iroquois Councils, 1740–70,"
Ethnohistory, XXXV (1988), 60–80, discusses the difficulty of training interpreters. Her
study focuses on the latter half of the eighteenth century, when much of the "need" for
interpreters had moved westward and into Iroquois territory, but a European's settlement
with the Indians for "immersion" in their language, and Indian attendance at colonial
schools or service in settlers' homes, were the preferred methods of training. On Penn and
interpreters, see Dunn and Dunn, eds., *Papers of Penn*, II, 452.

25. Thomas Stanton was Interpreter General to the United Colonies for the Indian
Language, an official office, and numerous other interpreters of quasi-legal or semipro-

of the parties: in Puritan New England, where lawyers were not used in court, interpreters acted as translators, but, in Rhode Island, and doubtless in other territories that had an adversarial system of law, interpreters sometimes took on the role of attorneys. The varying demands had some implications for gender relations within both groups, because Indian interpreters frequently were women. Perhaps out of deference to Anglo-European custom, or repeated failure to get colonial cooperation, the Indian tradition of female interpreters was abandoned in colonial courts. It persisted, however, in treaty negotiations when Indians and Europeans met outside the jurisdiction of one party or the other.[26]

The resolution of disputes was an area of some difference between the practice of most European colonial courts and that of the Algonquians. Indian tribes had existing customs regarding the final resolution of a legal case. Anglo-European writers commented upon the length of time Indians spent in deliberation and the sachems' consultation of their counselors in all matters.[27] The Indians accepted the use of juries in English colonial courts, but under varying conditions. If a criminal case arose between a white person and an Indian, juries were often composed of six Indians of the same tribe as the defendant or victim and six Englishmen. William Penn stipulated in a treaty with the Lenni Lenape that this would be the usual procedure, after explaining to them how the jury system worked. The Lenape readily complied. Cotton Mather recorded the use of a mixed Indian/English jury in the controversial trial of three Wampanoag Indians for the murder of a Chris-

---

fessional status existed. See E[dward] W[inslow], "Relation," in Alexander Young, ed., *Chronicles of the Pilgrim Fathers of the Colony of Plymouth, from 1602 to 1625* (Boston, 1841), 366 (notes the specialists who "daily converse with us"); Pierson, *Some Helps for the Indians,* title page; Margaret Connell Szasz, *Indian Education in the American Colonies, 1607–1783* (Albuquerque, N.M., 1988), 111–118 (on the roles of Cockenoe, Eliot's interpreter for ten years, and of Nesuton, a Massachuset who taught at Natick and who later helped give linguistic authority to Eliot's Indian books).

26. John Winthrop, *The History of New England from 1630 to 1649,* ed. James Savage (reprint, Salem, N.H., 1992), II, 120–121 (the interpreter in this case was Benedict Arnold, translating for Sacononoco and Pumham); *Rhode Island Court Records: Records of the Court of Trials of the Colony of Providence Plantation, 1647–1670* (Providence, R.I., 1920–1922), I, 57 (hereafter cited as *RICR*). Thomas might have been the first native American to act as an attorney in a colonial court. It is the earliest reference I have found. On the continuation of the Indian tradition in treaty negotiations, see Stephanus Van Courtlandt and Nicholas Beyard, *A Journal Kept . . . in Treating with the Indians of the Five Nations* (New York, 1693), 5 (regarding the 1693 Deerfield, Massachusetts, massacre); James H. Merrell, *Into the American Woods: Negotiations on the Pennsylvania Frontier* (New York, 1999), 68–71; Francis Jennings, *The Invasion of America: Indians, Colonialism, and the Cant of Conquest* (Chapel Hill, N.C., 1975), 112.

27. Karen Ordahl Kupperman, *Settling with the Indians: The Meeting of English and Indian Cultures in America, 1580–1640* (Totowa, N.J., 1980), 53–54; Dunn and Dunn, eds., *Papers of Penn,* II, 453; Daniel Gookin, quoted in editor's note, in Young, ed., *Chronicles,* 360–361 n. 2; Denton, *A Brief Description of New York,* 12–13.

tianized Indian, John Sassamon. Rhode Island also impaneled mixed juries, though how often and with what consistency is unknown.[28]

The Algonquians did not have juries in their own councils/courts as far as can be determined, and it is likely that the mixed jury was not a colonial compromise but drew upon old English invention for dealing with foreigners.[29] Yet, Indian assent to the mixed jury was paramount. Penn was clear that he and the Lenape agreed between them on the use of the jury. Mather, in contrast, notes the protest in the Sassamon case: according to Indian critics of the trial, because all defendants and the victim were Wampanoag, no English should have been on the jury. Some of the Indian interpreters left the English as a result.[30] The importance of the matter is clear. The procedural conduct of Sassamon's trial and the perceived substantive injustice of the convictions of the Wampanoag defendants were catalysts for the outbreak of King Philip's War in 1675, discussed below.

The Indians do not appear to have demanded that European settlers come to their councils even if a European committed a criminal offense against them, despite their agreement to send Indian offenders to colonial courts. According to William Bradford of Plymouth Colony, the first treaty drawn up with Massasoit of the Wampanoag stipulated, "If any of [Massasoit's people] did any hurte to any of [the settlers], he should send the offender, that they might punish him." The Plymouth settlers and Wampanoag did have reciprocal agreements concerning the return of stolen property and assistance in war against other Indian tribes. On one occasion, for instance, the Plymouth settlers offered to make restitution for corn they had taken, giving the sachem, Manamoick, the choice whether the colonists should bring him the corn or he would come for it. Manamoick chose to come.[31]

28. Dunn and Dunn, eds., *Papers of Penn*, II, 454; see also the same account in abridged form, Albert Cook Myers, ed., *William Penn's Own Account of the Lenni Lenape or Delaware Indians*, rev. ed. (Wilmington, Del., 1970), 40; Cotton Mather, *Magnalia Christi Americana; or, The Ecclesiastical History of New-England*, ed. Thomas Robbins (Hartford, Conn., 1855), II, 560. The "mixed" jury would have been a recognized, even standard, English practice. On Rhode Island's mixed juries, see *Rhode Island Record Book, Newport County*, Rhode Island Judicial Archives, A, 37–38 (1674), 209 (1702); *RICR*, II, 509 (1673). These cases were homicides; all involved Indian defendants. No mixed juries were impaneled for less than capital crimes or crimes committed by English people against Indians. See *Rhode Island Record Book, Newport County*, Rhode Island Judicial Archives, A, 197–198 (1712). Two Indian trials for murder did not have mixed juries.
29. See Marianne Constable, *The Law of the Other: The Mixed Jury and Changing Conceptions of Citizenship, Law, and Knowledge* (Chicago, 1994), esp. 124–127.
30. Szasz, *Indian Education*, 118, notes that Christian Indians James Printer and Nesuton, who helped translate John Eliot's books, joined King Philip's protest.
31. William Bradford, *Of Plimoth Plantation* (Boston, 1898), 115; League of Peace, quoted in N[athaniel] S[altonstall], "A Continuation of the State of New England," in C. H. Lincoln, ed., *Narratives of the Indian Wars, 1675–1699* (New York, 1913), 69; William Bradford, "History of Plymouth Colony," in Young, ed., *Chronicles*, 217.

The absence of any evidence that Indians demanded settlers come to their councils for transgressions against them does not mean that Indians had no say in what happened to offending settlers. Conceivably, the settler's punishment was considered more important than a jurisdictional claim over him. Colonies sometimes initiated claims in their own courts for damage committed by settlers to Indian property. The townspeople of an area south of Hartford "propounded to the Magestrates" that reparation should be made to the Indians for destruction of their crops by a herd of cattle. At the next session, an individual Indian, Tetabon, sued, "in an action of the case," six colonists for the destruction of his corn. Taken together, these two actions suggest that various means of initiating complaints and obtaining damages existed in Indian-settler disputes.[32]

Francis Jennings has argued that jurisdiction, because of the nature of land transfer in a colonial enterprise, was a one-way street in which Indians might come under English jurisdiction, but the English would never submit to Indian jurisdiction.[33] The statement is true on its face, but this view ignores the possibility that Indians chose to place themselves, or certain subject matters, under English jurisdiction. Indians did place limits on the kinds of jurisdiction the English (and other Europeans) could have. When Pumham, the sachem of Shawomet, and Sacononoco, sachem of Patuxet, agreed to live "under the govrmt and jurisdictio" of the Bay Colony and its laws, they stipulated that the laws would apply "so farr as wee shalbee made capable of understanding them."[34]

Indians went to colonial courts only when an Indian was somehow involved in a legal problem with a European.[35] They did not recognize the right of jurisdiction over their persons or with regard to subject matter that involved only other Indians.[36] Even those Indians who chose to live among

32. *Records of the Particular Court of Connecticut*, XXII, 208. "Action on the case" refers to a form of trespass and was often used when livestock or animals caused the harm.

33. Jennings, *Invasion of America*, 129.

34. May 10, 1643, in Nathaniel B. Shurtleff, ed., *Records of the Governor and Company of the Massachusetts Bay in New England*, 6 vols. (Boston, 1853–1854), II, 40 (hereafter cited as *MCR*).

35. Edgar J. McManus, *Law and Liberty in Early New England: Criminal Justice and Due Process, 1620–1692* (Amherst, Mass., 1993), 124, distinguishes between "Indians [who] lived under the white man's laws" and "self-governing tribes." This distinction is false. Those Indians who resided with whites nevertheless lived under their own laws before 1675. His interpretations of events also discussed in my paper, below, often differ markedly. See McManus, *Law and Liberty*, esp. 123–128. His is one of the few books that deal extensively with Indians and colonial law as part of a monograph on one colony's legal system.

36. One effect that this refusal to recognize English jurisdiction may have had was to change the way in which Indians thought of themselves. It is debated whether, before European arrival, there was any identification beyond the tribe. In Connecticut by 1658, for example, the word "Eansketambaug" seems to have distinguished Indians from Europeans (Pierson, *Some Helps for the Indians*, 4). Over time, certainly, by arguing that

the colonists usually reserved the right of autonomy in legal matters, and the colonists did the same. In 1647, when Massachusetts Bay Colony first set up a court for the Indians who lived among the settlers, the law specified that the court would hear only cases between Indians. The Indians had the power to issue summons to their own people and conduct the court themselves. They could not summon English persons. One thus sees a solid rule in the years immediately following contact where intra-Indian disputes remained matters for Indians to resolve.[37]

Disputes between praying Indians at Cambridge were a lonely but important exception to this rule. At Cambridge, Daniel Gookin was designated the justice of the peace in charge of hearing all cases "among themselves, or between them and the English."[38] The exception reflects a change that was occurring in the English attitude toward jurisdiction that did not correspond with Indian ideas. The English began slowly to think of the praying Indians as more like themselves than other Indians.

In New England, it was not until 1676, after King Philip's War, that other Indians found themselves on Jennings' proverbial one-way street. Even then the trajectory downhill was not as rapid as historians have sometimes assumed.[39] Before 1676, Indians were able to establish their own terms for dispute resolution. After 1676, they were able to maintain their own laws for the most part, but without the security of knowing for certain when to expect interference from the colonial powers.

III. Rules and Reciprocity

The contact of cultures required both Algonquians and Anglo-Europeans to make the most of whatever common ground existed between them. Certain tenets held by the colonists helped alleviate some of the inherent violence of colonialism. The Puritans of Massachusetts, for example, believed in a category of "all men" to whom God had given rights and upon whom he had imposed duties. The General Court was thus able to justify its refusal to

Europeans had no de jure right of jurisdiction even in intertribal disputes, tribes began to see a relationship between themselves as against Europeans. In reality, Europeans did broker intertribal disputes or intervene without invitation even in the seventeenth century, but the rule that they ought not to was clear. Europeans did occasionally attempt to exercise such jurisdiction, with disastrous results. See the discussion regarding the death of John Sassamon and the trial of three Wampanoag Indians.

37. May 26, 1647, in *MCR*, II, 188–189.

38. N[athaniel] S[altonstall], "The Present State of New-England with respect to the Indian War," in Lincoln, ed., *Narratives*, 37.

39. McManus, *Law and Liberty*, 126, also dates King Philip's War as a turning point in Indian self-government, though he claims it ended there, whereas I see it continuing but with limitations.

prohibit the sale of wine to the Indians, because "it is not fit to deprive the Indians of any lawful comfort wch God aloweth to all men." The Court could, though, prohibit the sale of "strong water" and the use of guns, which were not given as a matter of right to all people and which the English considered dangerous in Indian hands.[40]

As noted earlier, the legal principle of reciprocity was common ground. The colonists' interest in reciprocity was genuine, but it was not always applied in the literal, Algonquian sense. Some cases did not involve a mutual exchange of penalties. For example, several Connecticut Indians living on the outskirts of the town of New Haven broke into a locked warehouse full of liquor. They drank some and poured the rest out. The owner of the warehouse, John Winston, filed a complaint with the town court. Tom, the Indian principally responsible for the break-in, confessed and was fined fifty shillings; he and another Indian had to pay a bond for good behavior. The court, unable to find any responsibility on the part of Winston and unable to extract a confession from Samuel Andrews, an alleged accomplice, reminded Tom and his fellows that the English suffered them to live so close to New Haven only to protect them from the Mohawks. The court's pronouncement enunciated the principle of mutuality but phrased it in terms of responsibility: the Indians should be grateful for English protection and in turn should behave themselves. Nevertheless, a New Haven woman who breached the peace by striking an Indian was told her act "was not to be borne" and that the court would "do justice as well to indians as English." At Warwick, Rhode Island, a complaint by the settlers that Indians had killed their swine led the court at Newport to inform Sachem Pumham and his tribe of the terms of coexistence. The settlers agreed to hold a "Legall Tryall according to equity and Justice in o[u]r Courte when occasion is presented."[41]

Liquor was the primary cause for Indian appearance in colonial courts. The Indians considered alcohol to be part of the Europeans' world. Therefore, problems associated with it rightly came to Anglo-European courts. One Algonquian Catholic complained that the French governor was "killing us by permitting people to give us liquors." The French accepted their joint responsibility for Indian drunkenness by fining the sellers as well as punishing the drunk.[42]

The English also adopted the principle of reciprocity where liquor was

40. Sept. 7, 1630, in *MCR*, I, 76 (law forbidding colonists to let Indians use guns); Jul. 2, 1633, 106 (law forbidding sale or trade of liquor to the Indians); Nov. 13, 1644, II, 85.

41. Dexter, ed., *New Haven Town Records, 1662–1684* (New Haven, Conn., 1919), 127–128, 197, vol. II of *Ancient Town Records; RICR*, I, 5. Pumham had been in an alliance with the Bay Colony, but his territory fell within lands claimed by both the Bay and Rhode Island.

42. Quoted in Mancall, *Deadly Medicine*, 142; Colin G. Calloway, *The Western Abenakis of Vermont, 1600–1800: War, Migration, and the Survival of an Indian People* (Norman, Okla., 1990), 50.

concerned. Plymouth Colony fined its colonists who sold liquor to Indians twenty pounds, and all colonies had laws prohibiting the sale or trade to some degree.[43] Indians were frequently punished for breaching the laws against drunkenness if they did so in colonial settlements, but they also received damages upon their counterclaims for any injuries caused to them. By 1672, the General Court of Massachusetts attempted to turn the practice on its head by passing a law that in essence codified both the jurisdictional practice and the practice of the Indians to make counterclaims but that in reality undermined Indian autonomy. This law mandated that the Indians "confess" who had given them alcohol and threatened them with imprisonment if they did not.[44]

Guns and ammunition also brought the Indians to court. Colonial laws often restricted the sale of arms and ammunition to the Indians, making exceptions for certain friendly sachems. For example, the Squaw Sachem, who later accepted English jurisdiction and Christianity, petitioned the Massachusetts General Court to have her gun fixed. So did the Sagamore of Agawam. Since the Indians had obtained these items in trade with the English, it was apparently the obligation of the English to repair the guns when they did not work.[45]

Despite the existence of mutual recognition of the power of colonial courts over certain claims and under certain terms and despite the colonial application of the principle of reciprocity, over time Algonquians began to withdraw from the initial accommodation that had previously won their trust. Occasionally, Indians would refuse to appear in court when summoned, even when the dispute was between an Indian and an English person. Some of these might have been renegades from their own tribes or, especially as time went on, dissidents who wanted no contact whatsoever with the English. In June 1658, the sachem of the Narragansetts, Coginaquont, who had posted a bond guaranteeing the presence of Casseejuwasuck at the Newport court, forfeited his surety when the defendant did not appear. There were also instances when courts were prepared to use force to

43. Mancall, *Deadly Medicine*, 105. Throughout his book, Mancall notes objections by chiefs and sachems about colonists' sales of alcohol to their tribal members (see esp. 116–117), but overall Mancall sees alcohol as part of a trade that the Indians desired and that colonial authorities deplored and punished (see esp. 43). The subject of alcoholism among Indians, as Mancall's book shows, is complex. Whether Indians wanted alcohol or not (and there is no doubt many did), they realized it was a European commodity. They did not produce their own alcohol (43).
44. Jan. 18, 1664/65 (Tom's case, above), in Dexter, ed., *New Haven Town Records, 1662–1684*, vol. II of *New Haven Town Records*, 127–128; Feb. 5, 1666/67, 197. Wawatt received 3s, 4d., though he was warned to "carry it more peaceably for the future" or to stay out of Englishmen's houses. On the counterclaim law, see *Massachusetts General Laws* (1672), 77–78.
45. June 14, 1642, May 10, 1643, Oct. 7, 1646, all in *MCR*, II, 16, 36, 163.

bring an Indian in, usually in felony cases. Rhode Island threatened to "Fetch" Quisuckquonch if he refused a third summons. Most often, the colonies reserved force for serious felonies, such as murder.[46]

By the 1650s, many of the Indians had developed a fear of English justice. Indian fugitives from English justice told the magistrates they ran away because they were afraid, not of the court, but of those—sometimes other Indians—sent to arrest them. Taphanse, an Indian suspected of the murder of John Whitmore of Stamford in the New Haven Colony, told the court that another Indian had urged him to run away (even though he, Taphanse, was innocent), because "Uncus would take him and carry him away."[47]

Cases where the English compelled Indians to appear in court also show changes in Indian reaction over time. At first, Indians were defiant and uncooperative when brought to court. After the first two decades, however, they became more compliant. When before the court, by the 1650s, Indian defendants had plainly learned the formulaic expressions of repentance that seasoned the statements of English defendants. When he admitted his guilt in running away, for instance, Taphanse told the court he was "sorry he soe did, for he did evill and gave just cause of suspicion."[48]

Although one may discern a general pattern of resistance, accommodation, and eventual erosion of dispute settlement measures worked out between Algonquians and colonial powers based on the shared principle of reciprocity, one must also recognize fluctuations in the pattern. The court records of the various colonies show different levels of cooperation between Indians and Anglo-Europeans in court proceedings. In New Haven, Indians often vigorously pressed their own claims when called to court, and often they received at least a partial judgment in their favor. In Connecticut's courts, an Indian could as easily be the plaintiff as the defendant in a civil suit. In the autumn of 1648, Tantomheage sued two settlers for damages; the jury awarded him ten pounds plus court costs. Fourteen years later, a colonist sued Tantomheage for debt and won a judgment of two pounds and ten shillings.[49]

Rhode Island judgments more often went to English plaintiffs. In sepa-

46. *RICR*, I, 44–45, 54.

47. Charles J. Hoadly, ed., *Records of the Colony or Jurisdiction of New Haven, from May, 1653, to the Union* (Hartford, Conn., 1858), 458–463, 460 (hereafter *N.H. Col. Rec.*). Uncas was a close ally of the English in Connecticut and New Haven. The English used their Indian allies whenever possible if the business at hand involved other Indians, according to Jennings, *Invasion of America*, 125. Yet Indian initiative might have been responsible for the cooperation of one tribe against another. See Eric S. Johnson, "Uncas and the Politics of Contact," in Robert S. Grumet, ed., *Northeastern Indian Lives, 1632–1816* (Amherst, Mass., 1996), 33.

48. *N.H. Col. Rec.*, 460.

49. *Records of the Particular Court of Connecticut*, XXII, 52, 256.

rate cases, English plaintiffs obtained damages from both Coginaquont and Moeallicke in actions of debt. No counterclaim is recorded for either defendant. Despite a disclaimer by Roger Williams that "Sachims . . . will not conclude of ought that concernes all, either Lawes, or Subsides, or warres," in Rhode Island it appears individual Indians dealt with the English through the sachems, who assumed ultimate responsibility for any infraction against the English and who often posted bonds with the court.[50] Indians in New Haven and Connecticut, on the other hand, faced the court one-to-one.

The initial response of the Indians to court proceedings shows both a willingness to try to work with the colonists and an occasional failure to master the necessary rituals. In an early case, the Narragansett tribe in Rhode Island, which sought to proceed against a Warwick man for damages for desecrating and robbing the grave of an Indian woman, failed to show up for the prosecution. The court then dropped the case. The court had seized the defendant's goods until the trial, and the Indians might have assumed they had done all they needed to. In a short time, however, the Indians learned most of the procedural technicalities, and, in an October 1659 case, the Sachem Wamsutta was represented by an Indian attorney.[51]

The practice of Indians' having sole control over legal matters between Indians was tested from time to time. In the early 1640s, relations between the Narragansetts and the English of Massachusetts Bay deteriorated. In a set of circumstances that can only be described as double-dealing, Massachusetts colluded with Uncas, sachem of the Mohegans, to kill Miantonomi, sachem of the Narragansetts. The Bay Colony accused Miantonomi of hiring a Pequot youth to assassinate Uncas.[52] The Massachusetts court found the Pequot guilty but was willing to give Miantonomi the youth to deliver to Uncas for punishment. Instead, Miantonomi himself severed the boy's head. Uncas then captured Miantonomi and took him to Hartford, Connecticut, to the English, who said they did not have grounds to execute the sachem, although Uncas had jurisdiction. Uncas and his brother executed Miantonomi.[53] This series of events technically preserved the boundaries of En-

50. *RICR*, I, 75–76; Roger Williams, *A Key into the Language of America* . . . (1643), quoted in Jennings, *Invasion of America*, 113. For court cases in which sachems acted on behalf of individual Indian defendants, see *RICR*, I, 52–53, 57.

51. *RICR*, I, 9, 57.

52. Narragansett dealings with the Pequot after the war in 1637 (in which the Narragansetts had sided with the English) became the subject of much controversy. The assassination of Miantonomi was not an isolated act. See Paul Robinson, "Lost Opportunities: Miantonomi and the English in Seventeenth-Century Narragansett Country," in Grumet, ed., *Northeastern Indian Lives*, 23, 28.

53. Isaac Backus, *A History of New England with Particular Reference to the Baptists*, 2d ed. (New York, 1969), 102; Winthrop, *History of New England*, II, 130–134 and editor's notes. The treachery of Massachusetts is undoubted, but the events at the time were confusing to those outside of the council of the United Colonies.

glish/Indian jurisdiction but certainly put pressure on them. Nevertheless, they would hold for thirty more years.

The jurisdictional lines finally broke in 1675. A praying Indian of the Massachuset tribe, John Sassamon, who had grown up among Christian Indians at Natick and studied at Harvard, died on his way to Marshfield, Plymouth Colony, under suspicious circumstances. The colonists became convinced that Sassamon was murdered on his way to warn them of the conspiracy against the English organized by Metacom, also known as King Philip. Originally it looked as though Sassamon had fallen through ice on a pond and become trapped. Soon, however, rumors connected three Wampanoag—Mattashunnamo, Tobias, and Wampapaquan—to Sassamon's death. The three were arrested and tried before a jury in Massachusetts Bay. The jury was composed of at least six Englishmen and six Indians (though of what tribe is unknown). When the Massachusetts jury convicted the three men and the colonial authorities hanged them, Metacom was outraged.[54]

The English understood that they had thwarted Indian claims of right and a long-standing precedent. As one English narrator put it, "This so Exasperated King Philip, that from that Day after, he studied to be Revenged on the English, judging that the English Authority have Nothing to do to Hang any of his Indians for killing another." Perhaps because Sassamon was a praying Indian and one born to converts (and so probably baptized as an infant), the English considered him "Christian" and not Indian.[55]

The English were moving in an ever more consistent direction toward the Anglicization of their colonial society. This trend affected their relationship with the Indians both socially and legally. As the colonies adjusted to changes in their mother country, the development of colonial Indian policy moved beyond even the brutal domination that Metacom saw on the horizon. More and more, the English behaved as though the Indians were theirs.[56] The court records of Massachusetts are filled with instances of

54. Mather, *Magnalia Christi Americana*, II, 559, 560; Szasz, *Indian Education*, 125; Jennings, *Invasion of America*, 294–295.

55. Saltonstall, "Present State of New-England," in Lincoln, ed., *Narratives*, 25. On John Sassamon's relationship with John Eliot, see Jill Lepore, *The Name of War: King Philip's War and the Origins of American Identity* (New York, 1998), 28–31.

56. Conquest and even Christianization may not be the only relevant explanations for the English belief, especially as it does not appear to have been shared by the French. Scholarly research into John Eliot's missions and the "Hebraist" or "Judaist" literature in England between 1633 and 1660 suggests that some Puritans accepted the idea that the Indians were lost tribes of Israel or were like the Israelites (and thus part of Christianity historically and culturally, whether "converted" or not). See, for example, Claire Jowitt, "Radical Identities? Native Americans, Jews, and the English Commonwealth," *Seventeenth Century*, X (Spring 1995), 101–119; David S. Katz, *Philo-Semitism and the Readmission of the Jews to England, 1603–1655* (Oxford, 1982), esp. 151–152. The "appropriation" of the Indians could be linked to these ideas.

Indians submitting (from the English point of view) to colonial jurisdiction. The purchase of huge tracts of Indian land left many tribes living right on the edge of English settlements. John Eliot and Thomas Mayhew, the missionaries to the Indians, had established several praying towns. Socially, it seemed, Indians and colonists were merging their societies into the English model.

Legally, too, the English came to expect eventual union. They believed their courts offered the same justice to Indian as to English persons, and the court records often show direct reference to that fact by the magistrates. English laws were published and read to the Indians in the area so the tribes would be familiar with the code.[57] The praying Indians of Cambridge had their English justice of the peace, Daniel Gookin, and operated under English principles of justice. Hence, it probably seemed reasonable to the English to bring the Sassamon case, involving a Christian Indian, into their court. But what seemed reasonable to the English seemed intolerable to the Wampanoag and Narragansett Indians. Still angry over his brother's ignoble treatment by the colonists and his suspected murder at their hands two years earlier, Metacom needed little provocation to rage against further magisterial intrusions.

Thirty years after the Sassamon case, the emergent, Anglicized legal landscape became evident. In her travel journal in 1704, Madam Sarah Knight recorded the case of a theft by a black slave and a praying Indian. Although Knight's journal contains the story because the author herself thought it funny, the events were, in all likelihood, no joke. The slave had stolen a hogshead, which he sold to the Indian, who in turn sold it "in the neighbourhood." The theft and the resulting sales were discovered, whereupon

> the Heathen was seized, and carried to the Justices House to be Examined. But his worship (it seems) was gone into the feild, with a Brother in office, to gather in his Pompions [pumpkins]. Whither the malefactor is hurried, And Complaint made, and satisfaction in the name of Justice demanded. Their Worships cann't proceed in form without a Bench: whereupon they Order one to be Imediately erected, which for want of fitter materials, they made with pompions.[58]

The justices interrogated the accused slave and Indian, apparently speaking to each of them in a specific pidgin tongue, for the Indian objected that he "no stomany," that is, did not understand. Not only had the court foregone a formal approach to the Indians, once a prerequisite to their appearance; this court (and doubtless others) dispensed with interpreters.

57. McManus, *Law and Liberty*, 125–127.
58. Sarah Kemble Knight, *The Journal of Madam Knight* (Boston, 1920), 34–35.

Colonists and Indians now conducted at least some of their judicial business in the real language of neither party.[59] The change was more than superficial. It represented the erosion of mutually accepted accommodations and a critical shift in legal power.

By the eighteenth century, then, a tremendous transition had taken place in jurisdictional arrangements between the Indians and the English. Indians who lived on the outskirts of towns fell into a twilight zone between their own laws and those of the English, the once predictable border shattered by King Philip's War. The English no longer worried about the implications of seizing an Indian and bringing him to summary justice. Indian court cases required neither additional protocol nor a special venue. The local justice of the peace could preside over a hearing that only a quarter of a century earlier would have required at least a tribunal, an interpreter, and perhaps a sachem.

Madam Knight noticed on her journey "every where in the Towns as I passed, a Number of Indians." She was appalled by their condition. In some places they still possessed land of their own "and Govern'd by Law's of their own making." But, by the turn of the century, New England had already begun a different system of containing the Indians and their way of life: the reservation. The praying towns that Eliot had envisioned as settlements of Anglicized Indians were, perhaps unwittingly, the prototypes. The praying towns themselves gradually yielded to English rule. English selectmen replaced the Indians in town government, although Indians were able to elect the (English) selectmen as late as the mid-eighteenth century.[60] Their own law had been whittled away, no longer the law of the land, merely the law of a ragged group on the edge of town. They now kept their laws at English sufferance, and when the English demanded jurisdiction, the Eastern Indians were, more often than not, in no position to refuse.

---

59. Knight, *Journal of Madam Knight*, 35–36. See the great formality and the use of an interpreter in the same jurisdiction in the case of Taphanse, October 1662, *N.H. Col. Rec.*, 458–463. Massachusetts has also been in the habit of issuing formal summonses for all offenses, from drunkenness to stealing to capital crimes *(MCR)*. The Indian, Tatapa, in Madam Knight's case was a praying Indian, but in earlier times even he would have been spoken to in his own tongue by the missionary or teacher in charge of the group, usually another Indian.

Calloway, *New Worlds for All*, 176, says Massachusetts Indians spoke English by the mid-eighteenth century but points out that a distinctive "Indian English" has persisted. How well New England Indians spoke English even by 1750 is anyone's guess, but in 1700 missionaries to the Indians still found it necessary to learn Algonquian languages. The Natick Church Records change from Massachuset to English around 1719 (*Natick Town Records*, roll 6, book 3 [about 15 pages of microfilmed text]).

60. Knight, *Journal of Madam Knight*, 39; Kawashima, "Legal Origins of the Indian Reservation in Colonial Massachusetts," in Bruce A. Glasrud and Alan M. Smith, eds., *Race Relations in British North America, 1607–1783* (Chicago, 1982), 78.

Neither did European magistrates in the eighteenth century feel the need to consult kinfolk or sachems for cases in which, in earlier days, it would have been absolutely necessary to involve all parties to resolve the dispute. When settlers killed a member of a New Brunswick tribe in 1786, the English court tried the settlers for murder. The dead man's killers were punished, but without any Indian serving as a complainant or representative. Nor was reparation even an issue, as it would have been in the seventeenth century. In the course of a century, the European colonial courts had gone from one extreme of respect for Indian sovereignty to another extreme of colonial legal dominion in their dealings with the Algonquians.[61]

It has become increasingly common to recognize that, when two cultures come into sustained contact with one another, both change. The meanings of even the most fundamental concepts needed to be questioned and re-defined in order to meet with practical contingencies of the colonial world.[62] Historians have described the exchange of agricultural products and pro-cedures, and even styles of warfare, but one area in which few will acknowl-edge change is that of the Anglo-European legal institutions. Yet, why would law or legal institutions necessarily have been exempt from the types of changes, large and small, that permeated so many institutions and social customs in the colonial period?

The first colonists in Massachusetts had been interested in creating a legal system distinct from that of England, one based on primitivist notions of religion and law. They were receptive to the idea of mutuality, and, in the early decades when their idealism was strong, the Indians might, unwit-tingly, have helped them realize it in their courts by demanding it of them as a matter of course. That the Algonquian tribes did demand the right to make claims against Europeans is reflected in French accounts as well. In one instance in 1646, when a Frenchman's cow trampled an Indian field and the Indians killed the cow, the Indians agreed to pay reparation for the animal. In addition, though, the Indians forced the French to agree that "when [the Indians] should complain, Justice would be done them" in the courts of the French.[63]

Anglo-Europeans and native Americans shared a legal precept that al-lowed them to live together for a time without being drawn into the endemic conflict that two such different cultures might otherwise have suffered. While mutual recognition of reciprocity prevailed, it allowed for the accom-

61. L. S. F. Upton, *Micmacs and Colonists: Indian-White Relations in the Maritimes, 1713–1867* (Norman, Okla., 1990), 145; Karen Anderson, *Chain Her by One Foot: The Subjuga-tion of Native Women in Seventeenth-Century New France* (New York, 1991), 151.

62. Marshall Sahlins, *Historical Metaphors and Mythical Realities: Structure in the Early History of the Sandwich Islands Kingdom* (Ann Arbor, Mich., 1981), 8.

63. Jesuit account quoted in Alfred G. Bailey, *The Conflict of European and Eastern Al-gonkian Cultures, 1504–1700: A Study in Canadian Civilization,* 2d ed. (Toronto, 1969), 94.

modation of competing legal systems. When mutual recognition of reciprocity failed, the Anglo-European legal system and the power it represented began the ascent to dominance.

IV. The Cultural Clash

The greatest impediment to sustaining the concept of reciprocity in relations between the two cultures was a physical barrier impossible to lift. While the Europeans had a complete view of Indian life, limited only by their own failures of imagination and understanding, the Indians could see European culture only in its rudimentary form. Behind the colonists, back in England or France, there was a complex culture that informed the settlers' lives and behavior but that was entirely a mystery to all but a very few Indians.[64] The independence of different cultures sustained, in part, by a legal accommodation based on a shared principle of mutual legal respect could not withstand the greater pressures of cultural conflict. The Atlantic Ocean was more than a symbol of the distance between Algonquian and Anglo-European culture.

The distance of England or France became an increasing source of tension for Anglo-European relations with the Algonquians. It seemed that, whatever the Indians knew or did not know, Europeans could always find a way to confound them with European customs. Treaty making suffered especially from the lack of mutuality. For example, both Canonchet and Metacom (King Philip) of New England pressed the colonial leaders to give them someone of equal status, that is, a prince, with whom to treat. They wanted to meet Charles II face-to-face, believing that only this would resolve the inequities they felt were building. Their lack of knowledge of English diplomacy made negotiations on their terms impossible. Europeans often referred to the power of England, itself not visible to most Indians, to overwhelm them. Sometimes, however, the Indians found the tables turned on them because they did have knowledge of Europe. When the Iroquois sachem Donnacona complained to Jacques Cartier that the Europeans carried weapons while the Indians carried none, Cartier explained that Donnacona's son, Taignaogny, well knew the French custom as he had been to France. Once again, European assertion of custom prevailed, frustrating Indian attempts to curb the invasion of such customs.[65]

Having missionaries among them also angered many of the Indians, seemingly because the missionaries added to the imbalance of European-

64. A few Indians, like Squanto, who first befriended the Plymouth colonists, had been to England, but his experience was a rarity (Bradford, *Of Plimouth Plantation*, 114–115).

65. Saltonstall, "A Continuation of the State of New England," in Lincoln, ed., *Narratives*, 73, 91. Dom Agaya and Taignaogny, two Stadaconans, made the trip to France and back after being kidnapped by the French explorers (Ramsay Cook, ed., *The Voyages of Jacques Cartier* [Toronto, 1993], xxiii–xxv, 52–53).

Indian relations. Missionaries were another force, sent in with stories of an unseen god "to amaze and scare us of our old Customs, and bring us to stand in awe of them."[66] That one purpose was to "wipe us of our Lands, and drive us into Corners" appeared obvious to the steadfastly unconverted. The Indians had no counterpart to the missionaries to offer the settlers, and, although praying Indians remained a small part of the Algonquian population of the Northeast, the Algonquians felt besieged. There was no doubt that they were increasingly dependent upon European manufactures and trade, if not religion. Even in praying towns, Christian Algonquians found themselves at odds with, and eventually giving way to, European customs of landholding, officeholding, and inheritance.[67]

Algonquian culture slowly yielded to Anglo-European ways of living. One legal example is that of testate succession. Before and during the early period of contact, in Algonquian society status could be matrilineal, and property descended without the legal documentation that characterized Anglo-European succession. By the end of the seventeenth century, some Algonquian women adopted the custom, albeit not always successfully, of leaving their property through the use of both nuncupative and written wills. Algonquian men appear to have been less likely to leave wills, but their estates were subject to the colonies' rules of inventorying and administering estates.[68]

This is not to say that Algonquian culture disappeared. If one looks closely at the wills, estate administrations, and statements of guardianship, one sees a deliberate attempt to hold the line against colonial encroachments upon their lands and their persons. Indian women directed that their real prop-

66. Unnamed Indian of Nashauneog, in John Eliot, ed., *Indian Dialogues, for Their Instruction in That Great Service of Christ* . . . (Cambridge, Mass., 1671), 3. These dialogues were between praying Indians and their heathen kin. The speeches of the praying Indians are somewhat suspect owing to their formulaic nature and the fact that Eliot was supervising their missionary work. The words of the "heathen" Indians seem more trustworthy, in my view; although they are invariably hostile at first to the ministrations of the Christian Indian and thus predictable, their words vary in form and content to a greater extent. Eliot states the book is "partly Historical" and "partly Instructive" (1).
67. Ibid. The commissioners of Charles II were unimpressed by the number of converts, believing too that the colonists paid Indians to attend sermons (Isabel MacBeath Calder, *The New Haven Colony* [New Haven, Conn., 1934], 177). On the Indians' dependence on European manufacture, see Calloway, *The Western Abenakis*, 40; Mancall, *Deadly Medicine*, 25. On the Christian Indians' giving way to European customs, see Daniel Mandell, "'Standing by His Father': Thomas Waban of Natick, circa 1630–1722," in Grumet, ed., *Northeastern Indian Lives*, 182–183.
68. Hermes, ed., "'By Their Desire Recorded': Native American Wills and Estate Papers in Colonial Connecticut," *Connecticut History*, XXXVIII, no. 2 (Fall 1999), 154–168; Ann Marie Plane, "Putting a Face on Colonization: Factionalism and Gender Politics in the Life History of Awashunkes, the 'Squaw Sachem' of Saconet," in Grumet, ed., *Northeastern Indian Lives*, 156.

erty be inherited by relatives rather than sold on the open market, possibly to colonists. Other women directed that their minor dependents be raised by Indian guardians rather than leave the decision to the discretion of a colonial court, which might appoint an Anglo-European guardian. When a relative was already the servant of a colonist, a will helped to ensure distribution to the Indian relation. Although native women saw a dramatic decrease in power after 1676 and became more vulnerable to gender-specific Anglo-European laws, they also were able to use the colonists' laws to help some of their own culture survive.[69]

Despite the eventual dominance of Anglo-European culture, during the period of transition colonists might have been affected by Indian customs of all kinds. Some of the customs bore on legal matters. As Madam Knight toured the countryside, she commented that male Indians often divorced their wives with little bother, telling them to "*stand away.*" As an after-thought, she added, "Indeed those uncomely *Stand aways* are too much in Vougue among the English in this (Indulgent Colony)."[70] Her simple observation does not make for proof of influence, and it seems unlikely that the Puritans wanted to copy any such practices from the Indians. Divorce was an issue that had been debated hotly in England during the Civil War years. Nevertheless, gender roles were altered by contact, and definitions of proper marital behavior were altered by both colonization itself and contact with another culture that, by all accounts, gave women a greater share of the responsibility for economic production, political decision making, and familial and community organization. Defensive about the superiority of their culture, European men may have responded to Algonquian ridicule by putting their wives to work in the fields like Indian women, even while they tried to make Algonquian men take their own wives out of the fields.[71] The

69. Will of Pampenum, an Indian woman, May 20, 1697, in Hermes, ed., "'By Their Desire Recorded,'" *Connecticut History,* XXXVIII, no. 2 (Fall 1999), 156–157. This will gives Pampenum's brother a life estate in two-sevenths of her island; his son, Seemook, would eventually inherit that share, with the rest distributed among her cousins, a grandson, and a woman (friend) and her son. The will clearly stipulates that the land will pass to more than one generation. See also Declaration of Mary Mcumpas, Sept. 27, 1692, Nuncupative Will of Sarah Onepenny, May 1713, ibid., 155–156, 165. On the decrease in power for native American women, see Plane, "Putting a Face on Colonization," in Grumet, ed., *Northeastern Indian Lives,* 141–142, 151; Anderson, *Chain Her by One Foot,* esp. 25.

70. The idea of reciprocal influence is not new, but it is not as developed as 2the literature about African American influences upon European Americans. See Bruce E. Johansen and Donald A. Grinde, Jr., "The Debate regarding Native American Precedents for Democracy: A Recent Historiography," *American Indian Culture and Research Journal,* XIV, no. 1 (1990), 61–88. For Madam Knight's comment, see Knight, *Journal of Madam Knight,* 39. See also Jennings, *Invasion of America,* 49, regarding divorce among Indians, which he describes as "easy."

71. Among the Algonquians, women could be chiefs, interpreters, and kingmakers. They were responsible for agricultural production and in some tribes for the construction

similarity in their views on divorce may also reflect, though, the once similar nature of their legal outlooks, where the substance of a marriage mattered more than its formal existence.

Possible reciprocal cultural influence aside, Algonquian culture did not withstand the pressures of Anglo-European culture. The gradual reduction of Algonquian culture is reflected in the eventual demise of the legal accommodation between separate sovereigns based on shared principles of mutual recognition. The demise of this accommodation does not, however, undercut the importance of its very existence in the first century after contact.

V. The Significance of the Legal Relationship

It was not clear at the beginning of contact that Anglo-European law would devour that of the Algonquians. For most of the first century of contact, a shared principle of law for both Algonquians and Europeans enabled them, once in a while, to settle differences. The Restoration of Charles II in 1660, however, helped make possible a change in English colonial policy toward the Indians because it caused a debate within colonial society about the degree to which the colonies would become once again like England. The push to re-Anglicize from some quarters of the society was a powerful factor in the desire to eliminate cultural difference. Changed relations between colonists and Indians were also key steps for the Anglophiles in New England who saw their colonies as part of a unified English empire. French law was not similarly affected, and the Algonquians maintained their autonomy to a greater degree until the Seven Years' War stripped it away.[72]

Violent encounters between Indians and Europeans are well documented and well recounted in the annals of American history. Peaceful encounters also have their place in historical literature, but mostly as rare and rather mythic episodes. The appearances of Algonquians in European colonial courts were neither violent nor peaceful. They signify negotiations for peaceful resolutions to conflict. As individual episodes, they are interesting, although no more significant than many other "odd" cases. Only when

---

of the dwelling houses. See, for example, Jennings, *Invasion of America*, 112. Thomas Lechford, a lawyer who came briefly to New England in the Great Migration, believed it was the presence of the English that had caused Indian men to treat their wives better. He admits that Indian women thought English women were lazy (Lechford, "An Account of the New England Indians" [1642], in Albert Bushnell Hart and John Gould Curtis, eds., *American History Told by Contemporaries* [New York, 1897], I, 318–319).

For the division of labor and changes in English women's work in colonial New England, see Gloria L. Main, "Gender, Work, and Wages in Colonial New England," *William and Mary Quarterly*, 3d Ser., LI (1994), 39–66. Main says that colonial women often did hoeing in the garden "wherever families could use existing Indian fields" (53).

72. Calloway, *The Western Abenakis*, 182.

viewed as a pattern of interaction do these cases demonstrate their importance. They provide examples of the gradual process of colonization, its unevenness, and its occasional humanity. When the relationship of legal systems is recognized, the complexities of the gradual shift in power from Algonquian sovereignty to Anglo-European dominance can emerge from the shadow of the conquest narrative. When the legal story is included as a part of the metanarrative of Indian-European relations, the intricacies of these human relationships can also emerge.

"Lest We Go in Search of Relief to Our Lands and Our Nation"

Customary Justice and Colonial Law in the New Mexico Borderlands, 1680–1821

AN UNUSUAL AUDIENCE occurred in the Sonoran town of Arizpe, seat of the Comandante General of the Interior Provinces of New Spain, early in the summer of 1780. Bentura Bustamante, "Lieutenant of the *Genízaro* Indians of the Villa of Santa Fe in the Kingdom of New Mexico," laid a bold challenge before Spain's highest-ranking representative in the provinces, the newly appointed Teodoro de Croix. Speaking in the name of thirty-three petitioners, four of whom accompanied him, Bustamante swore that, unless the comandante general addressed their community's grievance, they faced little choice but to "go in search of relief to our lands and our Nation." As is too often the case in Spanish colonial legal proceedings, neither the exact nature of Bustamante's complaint nor the remedy he and his companions had in mind was ever explicitly mentioned. But Bustamante asserted his community's right to make a claim without hesitancy. As *yndios genízaros,* he argued, his people had been delivered from infidelity into the mysteries of the Holy Catholic Faith by their Spanish "parents and masters." After that, they had purchased lands, built houses, and "remained obedient to the Royal Service for campaigns and war activities," even when to do so meant they had "betrayed their own Nation." For "loyal Christian Indians" to confront their superiors in such a manner seems unusual. But it becomes startling when we consider that the threat to desert the colony and find succor within their "own Nation" issued from peoples who were, legally speaking, its slaves.[1]

I wish to thank Christopher Tomlins and Bruce Mann for their invitation to participate in the "Many Legalities of Early America" conference and their astute recommendations toward revision of this chapter. Ira Berlin, Amy Turner Bushnell, Emory Evans, and James Henretta each influenced my revisions, while the anonymous reviewers for the Institute offered important criticisms and insights for which I am grateful. Finally, Institute manuscript editor Kathryn Burdette deserves much credit for whatever gracefulness of style and strength of argument exists herein.

    1. Petición de Bentura Bustamante, June 20, 1780, in *Spanish Archives of New Mexico* (hereafter cited as *SANM*), I, no. 1138, roll 6, frames 323–325, New Mexico State Records Center, Santa Fe. I thank David H. Snow for bringing this case to my attention. The

This essay addresses Bustamante's case and the role of genízaros in colonial New Mexico, but these immediate details frame a guiding question: in cultural borderlands where neither indigenous nor colonial peoples could dominate the other completely, how did various actors assert and resist power in the interests of law, order, and justice? Scholars have long recognized that New Mexico constituted a particularly volatile "non-dominant frontier" where, despite the exceptional success of Pueblo Indian revolts between 1680 and 1696, neither colonial New Mexicans nor the numerically superior indigenous peoples proved able (or willing) to subordinate or eject the other completely. Despite nearly a century of research and debate, a comprehensive picture of just how these culturally complex borderlands actually functioned remains elusive.[2]

However unstable power was in the region, law provided much of its means of contestation. Legal historians have made major contributions to our understandings of the colonial legal structures underpinning Pueblo Indian and Spanish village land grants. The Spanish crown granted *mercedes reales* (royal gifts) to nominally Christianized Pueblo Indians, which cynically confirmed the "already acquired rights of indigenous peoples found in lands discovered by Spain." The conveyance of title to long-occupied lands was but one of the artifices by which Spain asserted her rights of conquest in the New World. Spanish *vecinos* (tithe-paying citizens) also received royal gifts in the form of mercedes, which contained communal lands, individual allotments for houses, and irrigated fields. In addition to community grants, individual private grants for livestock grazing were conferred upon favored royal subjects. Nevertheless, local Spanish administrators took some pains to protect Pueblo Indian lands against encroachment and to adjudicate vecino disputes in the interest of larger community harmony.[3]

---

nominal definition of *genízaros*, by which we may begin our discussion, was offered by Frances Leon Swadesh in 1974, who described them as

> detribalized Christian Indian[s] living under the control of colonial authorities. The term was primarily used to apply to Indians of various tribes not native to New Mexico who had been ransomed from captivity among the nomadic tribes and placed as servants in settler households. In practice, many *Genízaros* were Pueblo Indians who had been expelled from the home village for being overly adaptive to Hispanic culture.

See *Los Primeros Pobladores: Hispanic Americans of the Ute Frontier* (South Bend, Ind., 1974), xviii. The following pages will address several necessary additions to this understanding.

2. Frances Swadesh (Quintana) first proposed the "non-dominant frontier" concept in "Structure of Hispanic-Indian Relations in New Mexico," in Paul M. Kutsche, ed., *The Survival of Spanish American Villages* (Colorado Springs, Colo., 1979), 53–61. For a modern synthesis of the Spanish borderlands that expands this thinking, see David J. Weber, *The Spanish Frontier in North America* (New Haven, Conn., 1992).

3. See G. Emlen Hall, *Four Leagues of Pecos: A Legal History of the Pecos Grant, 1800–1933*

The trust relationship between the Spanish crown and its Indian subjects extended beyond issues of land tenure. Once the crown took cognizance of Bartolome de las Casas's argument that the natives of the New World were indeed humans, although "poor and wretched" ones, the royal conscience required that some real efforts be made to protect those who, in the eyes of the law, were equal to minors. In New Mexico as elsewhere in New Spain, this concern translated into the office of the *protector de indios,* a royal appointee who acted as advocate for aggrieved Indians. And, as elsewhere in Spanish America, local Indians proved quick to acquire their own legal acumen and often drove the courts to distraction with their litigiousness.[4]

We know less about the day-to-day workings of the law among the vecino population, but even a cursory look through indexes of the Spanish Archives of New Mexico reveals a society in which property disputes, personal assaults, and illegal trading demanded the regular attention of both the governor and local *alcaldes mayores* (district magistrates). Far away from the learned jurists of Mexico and Spain, New Mexicans drew upon Castilian legal customs, *derecho indiano criollo* (law promulgated in the New World), and local traditions, including those of Indians, to initiate litigation and reach resolutions.[5]

(Albuquerque, N.M., 1984); Victor Westphall, *Mercedes Reales: Hispanic Land Grants of the Upper Rio Grande Region* (Albuquerque, N.M., 1983); Charles L. Briggs and John R. Van Ness, eds., *Land, Water, and Culture: New Perspectives on Hispanic Land Grants* (Albuquerque, N.M., 1987), esp. 72; John R. Van Ness, ed., "Spanish Land Grants in New Mexico and Colorado," *Journal of the West,* XIX, no. 3 (July 1980), 3–128; Malcolm Ebright, ed., "Introduction: Spanish and Mexican Land Grants and the Law," *Journal of the West,* XXVII (July 1988), 3–11; Ebright, *Land Grants and Lawsuits in Northern New Mexico* (Albuquerque, N.M., 1994); Ebright, "Frontier Land Litigation in Colonial New Mexico: A Determinant of Spanish Custom and Law," *Western Legal History,* VIII (1995), 211–214; Ebright, "Advocates for the Oppressed: Indians, Genízaros, and Their Spanish Advocates in New Mexico," *New Mexico Historical Review,* LXXI (October 1996), 305–339.

4. For the debate over Indian humanity, see Lewis Hanke, *All Mankind Is One: A Study of the Disputation between Bartolomé de Las Casas and Juan Ginés de Sepúlveda in 1550 on the Intellectual and Religious Capacity of American Indians* (DeKalb, Ill., 1974). For the *protector de indios* in New Mexico, see Charles R. Cutter, *The Protector de Indios in Colonial New Mexico, 1659–1821* (Albuquerque, N.M., 1986).

Ross H. Frank's work reveals the sophisticated and culturally specific legal tactics employed by Pueblo Indians to conceal "criminal and subversive" activities from Spanish administrators in the late eighteenth century, aspects of the cultural compartmentalization for which Pueblos became renowned in the eyes of twentieth-century American ethnographers. See "From Settler to Citizen: Economic Development and Cultural Change in Late Colonial New Mexico, 1750–1820" (Ph.D. diss., University of California, Berkeley, 1992), 358–388; Edward H. Spicer, "Spanish-Indian Acculturation in the Southwest," *American Anthropologist,* LVI (1954), 663–684; Edward P. Dozier, *The Pueblo Indians of North America* (New York, 1970).

5. See Cutter, *The Legal Culture of Northern New Spain, 1700–1810* (Albuquerque, N.M., 1995), for a comprehensive treatment of *justicia real ordinaria* (ordinary royal jurisdiction) in the northern provinces of New Mexico and Texas. Angelina Veyna's work on women's *testamentos* (wills) in New Mexico illustrates the markedly superior legal status

Moreover, we have also moved closer to an understanding of the military and diplomatic dance in which Spanish governors and powerful Indian groups like the Apaches, Navahos, Kiowas, and Comanches engaged for more than two centuries. Here the question was, not that of land tenure or protections against everyday labor exploitation, but that of the complex of punitive raids, diplomatic alliances, and intercultural commerce employed by Spanish and *los indios gentiles* ("heathen" Indians) alike to achieve some measure of stability. Although the *Recopilación de Indias* of 1681 (a compendium of laws governing colonial/Indian relations) made clear that just war doctrine applied to any heathens who failed to submit to Spanish authority, thereby legalizing their murder, pillage, and enslavement, actual relations in New Mexico proved much more complicated than those laws implied. Far removed from the military resources of Mexico, the garrison in Santa Fe never exceeded 140 poorly armed-and-mounted soldiers. In a colony surrounded by highly militarized equestrian Indian groups who could field thousands of accomplished fighters at short notice, Spanish governors like Tómas Vélez de Cachupín and Juan Bautista de Anza seldom risked major military campaigns. Their diplomatic efforts drew sustenance from parallel strategies pursued by their Indian counterparts, leaders like the Comanche captain Ecueracapa, who knew full well that Comanche power rested in part on their access to Spanish firearms, powder, and shot.[6]

But Bentura Bustamante's complaint hints that Spanish-Indian power relations in colonial New Mexico were even more multistranded than the foregoing summary suggests. Land rights, Indian rights, and intercultural

---

that women maintained in that colony as compared to their sisters on the eastern seaboard of North America. See *"Hago, dispongo, y ordeno mi testamento:* Reflections of Colonial New Mexican Women," paper presented at the Annual Meeting of the Western History Association, October 1991, Austin, Texas. David H. Snow's research on colonial land tenure systems suggests a shift from large-scale *estancias* and *haciendas* in the pre-1680 period to smaller-scale, but more numerous, communal mercedes in the eighteenth century. This seems consistent with an expanding *vecino* population and a desire to project Spanish settlement outward, both defensively and commercially, into territories ranged by indigenous nomads and pastoralists known collectively as *los indios bárbaros.* See David H. Snow, "Ownership and Uses of Lands in Seventeenth-Century New Mexico," paper presented at Annual Conference of the Historical Society of New Mexico, April, 1994, Taos, New Mexico; Snow, "Rural Hispanic Community Organization in Northern New Mexico: An Historical Perspective," in Kutsche, ed., *Survival of Spanish American Villages,* 45–52.

6. Alfred Barnaby Thomas, trans. and ed., *Forgotten Frontiers: A Study of the Spanish Indian Policy of Don Juan Bautista de Anza, Governor of New Mexico, 1777–1787* (Norman, Okla., 1932); Thomas, *The Plains Indians and New Mexico, 1751–1778* (Albuquerque, N.M., 1940); Charles L. Kenner, *The Comanchero Frontier: A History of New Mexican-Plains Indian Relations* (1969; Norman, Okla., 1994); Thomas W. Kavanagh, *Comanche Political History: An Ethnohistorical Perspective, 1706–1875* (Lincoln, Nebr., 1996). For *la guerra justa* and Indian slavery, see Silvio Zavala, *Los esclavos indios en Nueva España* (Mexico City, 1967), esp. 40–45.

diplomacy all appear in his complaint. Yet we will see that the genízaro question draws us into a larger analysis of social inequality, ethnic identity, political economy, and customary justice in the region. When Bustamante presented himself as Lieutenant of the Genízaro Indians and "in the name of" his thirty-three companions, he did so as the representative of a slave community. When he claimed that his community had embraced Catholicism and had performed as a loyal militia in the service of the Spanish crown, he spoke a truth designed to solicit Croix's sympathies. And when he threatened that, should his community's grievances not be redressed, they might desert the colony and find succor in "their lands and their Nation," he likely induced real anxiety in a seasoned diplomat and soldier, for to do so seems—paradoxically—entirely within the ability and the customary (if not doctrinal) rights of his slave community.

This essay, then, contributes another layer of understanding to our knowledge of power and society in the colonial New Mexican borderlands, to comparisons with other Spanish borderlands, and by extension to the British colonies in North America as well. A series of cases follows the "repertoires of contention" by which the genízaro caste negotiated its status vis-à-vis colonial legal and economic structures between 1700 and 1821. These cases suggest that, as the Bourbon reforms of 1765–1821 liberalized provincial society and economy by relaxing travel constraints, exempting the province from taxation, and increasing specie circulation, genízaro autonomy and vulnerability concurrently increased. This study, then, illustrates the volatile relationship between subordinate communities and those formative colonial states that both exploited and depended upon the former for survival and growth. It also suggests that, although New Mexico stood far from the political upheavals of the American Revolution, its position amid the larger transformations of the Atlantic world produced social phenomena not unlike those erupting east of the Mississippi.[7]

Although not rent by revolutionary upheavals, colonial New Mexico did experience moments of tangible social destabilization. This ambiguous frontier saw both the creation and constant renegotiation of a "borderlands political economy," wherein Indians and Spanish colonists alike came to some understanding of the production and distribution of wealth, as conditioned by the social relations of power.[8] So dependent were Spanish colonists

---

7. See Charles Tilly, "Collective Violence in European Perspective," in Ted Robert Gurr, ed., *Violence in America: Protest, Rebellion, Reform,* II (1979; Newbury Park, Calif., 1989), 62–100, esp. 95; for the Bourbon reforms in New Mexico, see Frank, "From Settler to Citizen," esp. 86–165.

8. For an in-depth treatment of this political economy, and its reliance upon a distinctive slave system for its integrity, see James F. Brooks, "Captives and Cousins: Slavery, Kinship, and Community in the Southwest Borderlands" (forthcoming).

and their Indian neighbors, both Pueblo and *bárbaro* (nomad), on a flexible and oft-changing network of commercial and military exchanges, that peoples like Bustamante's genízaros, who maintained links to all three groups, came to occupy an intermediating space simultaneously marginal and central. Disputes between *los indios genízaros* and their Spanish "masters" reveal that, within this mutually constructed political economy, the region came to express a distinctive sense of *derecho vulgar* (customary justice) that functioned with some autonomy from Spanish colonial *ley* (law in its formal sense) and *doctrina* (the written opinions of jurists), yet reverted to formalism when protagonists thought it suited their interests.

If, as has been argued, much of the legal culture of northern New Spain involved a community-level search for *equidad,* or a communally defined sense of fairness often construed in terms of *"dar a cado uno lo suyo"* ("to give to each his own"), customary justice in colonial New Mexico took this one step further.[9] There came to exist in the colony a widely shared sense that local communities had earned the right to regulate their own affairs, especially regarding intragroup disputes and everyday economic enterprise, yet also to have their complaints heard with fairness by colonial magistrates when intercaste conflicts arose. The genízaros and some of their lower-order vecino neighbors, although technically in the power of their Spanish masters and administrative elites, served as indispensable actors in the military and commercial functioning of the colony, especially in her relations with *los indios bárbaros.* As a consequence, when engaging in extralegal collective action or claiming "traditional" communal (whether Indian or slave) rights, they often exerted influence well beyond what their status might imply. When genízaros were subject to the law as individuals, however, their social and juridical status left them nearly defenseless. Neither Spanish, Pueblo, nor heathen Indian, genízaros dwelt in a shadowland at the interstices between law and power. This investigation of their experience shows the range of agency available to peoples who—although crucial to the political economy of the borderlands—remained socially and legally marginal until the upheavals of 1810–1821 rewrote the "modalities of rule" in effect in northern Mexico.[10]

This borderlands political economy underwent considerable change over time, especially in the period between 1780 and 1821 as the Bourbon reforms and an incipient commerce with Americans intruded on its workings. Most

9. Cutter, *Legal Culture of Northern New Spain,* 31–43, 159 n. 16.
10. Christopher L. Tomlins utilizes the concept of "modality of rule" to capture both the particular autonomy of "law" in situational contexts and its "constant structural relationship with the contexts in which it is located" (*Law, Labor, and Ideology in the Early American Republic* [Cambridge, 1993], chap. 1). This mutually constitutive relationship between law and society lies at the crux of my argument.

evident was a gradual bifurcation in the regional economy between a "colonial" sector, controlled by governors and an emerging class of merchants and sheep ranchers, and an "indigenous" sector involving customary trade with Indians like Navahos, Utes, Comanches, and Kiowas. Whereas the colonial sector might see genízaros and poor vecinos as prime candidates for labor dependency in farming, stockraising, and manufacturing, their central role in the indigenous economy, by which commerce some elites profited as well, set the two sectors in real tension. Within these changing and ambivalent political economies, the weak and the powerful alike developed new tactics and strategies of contention that required a constant reworking of notions of justice and the applicability of law. And, although these dynamics encompassed all the various social and cultural groups of New Mexico, their workings may be detailed most clearly, and ironically, in the historical experience of Bentura Bustamante's people.

Neither "Spanish" nor "Indian," los genízaros have attracted significant scholarly attention in recent years. Much of the debate centers on whether these peoples constituted a racialized and degraded social category imposed from without by Spanish authorities or, in time, developed an internally generated positive "ethnic" identity. The answer lies somewhere within this dualism, but we must start by looking at how the people came to exist in the first place.

As noted earlier, the Recopilación of 1681, while reiterating the ban on Indian slavery first set forth in 1542, served to reinforce just war doctrines of enslavement. But it also encouraged Spanish subjects to redeem indigenous captives from their captors, baptize them into the Catholic faith, and acculturate them as new "detribalized" colonial subjects. These *indios de rescate* (ransomed Indians) were "saved" from slavery among their heathen captors and therefore owed their Spanish redeemers loyalty and service in exchange for the cost of their ransom. Both defeated enemies and redeemed captives came to carry the appellation "genízaro" in New Mexico. These servile peoples then fell under the slavery laws that had originated in Las Siete Partidas in 1265, doctrines noteworthy for their liberal position that "all of the laws of the world should lead towards freedom." Under these regulations, slaves were conferred rights in marriage and against maltreatment and were allowed to hold property, testify as plaintiffs or defendants, and pursue manumission. Of course, application of such principles fell far short of the ideal, for African and Indian slave alike.[11]

11. For Africans, see Colin A. Palmer, *Slaves of the White God: Blacks in Mexico, 1570–1650* (Cambridge, Mass., 1976), esp. 84–118; for the provisions of Las Siete Partidas, ibid., 85–87, esp. 86.

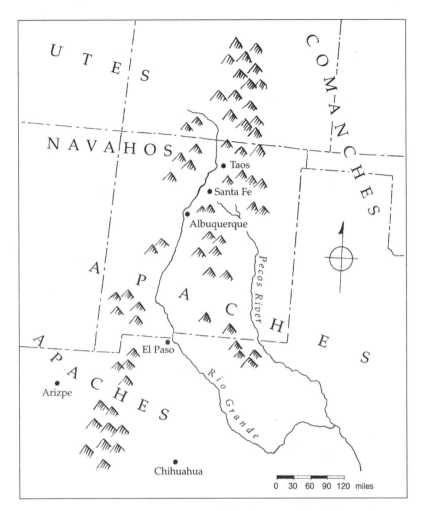

FIGURE 1. The Greater New Mexico Borderlands. *Drawn by Stinely Associates*

Enslavement of Indians under the just war doctrine was rampant during the seventeenth century but tapered off after the reconquest of New Mexico between 1692 and 1696 as the Spanish sought alternative diplomatic routes to pacification of the nomadic Indians. Redemption of captives from Kiowas, Comanches, and Navahos, however, increased in scale during the eighteenth century. These occurred in roughly two forms; either through formal "ransoming" at annual trade fairs *(ferias* or *rescates)* or through small-scale bartering *(cambalaches)* in local villages or at trading places on the Great Plains.[12] Throughout the eighteenth century, Spanish church and secular

12. Trade fairs at Taos, Pecos, and Picuris Pueblos had long fostered the exchange of bison meat for corn, beans, and squash between Plains Indians and the Rio Grande

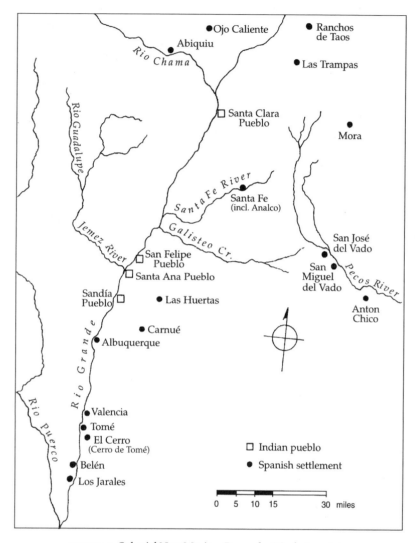

FIGURE 2. Colonial New Mexico. *Drawn by Stinely Associates*

authorities vied for control of this trade, variously blaming each other or local alcaldes mayores for the "saddest" of this commerce. In 1761, Fray Pedro Serrano chided Spanish governors, who, "when the fleet [was] in," scrambled to gather as many horses, axes, hoes, wedges, picks, bridles, and knives in order to "gorge themselves" on the "great multitude of both sexes" offered for sale. Fifteen years later, Fray Anatasio Domínguez reported that

Pueblos, and might have included some exchanges of people as well. For theoretical and empirical cases, see the essays in Katherine Spielmann, ed., *Farmers, Hunters, and Colonists: Interaction between the Southwest and the Southern Plains* (Tucson, Ariz., 1991).

the Comanches brought to Taos for sale "pagan Indians (of both sexes, children and adults) whom they capture from other nations." The going rate of exchange, which seems to have held quite steady until the mid-nineteenth century, was "two good horses and some trifles" for an "Indian girl from twelve to twenty years old." Male captive boys brought a "she-mule" or one horse and a "poor bridle . . . garnished with red rags." The general atmosphere, according to Domínguez, resembled a "second-hand market in Mexico, the way people mill about."[13]

In the early nineteenth century, trade fairs declined, owing to several factors—Plains Indians' determination to avoid possible exposure to Euroamerican disease, attempts on the part of New Mexican villagers to escape taxation of their trade, the geographical expansion of the borderlands economy—to be replaced with smaller, more frequent, on-the-spot bartering. Judging from extant New Mexican parochial registers, between 1700 and 1850, nearly three thousand members of nomadic or pastoral Indian groups entered New Mexican society as indios de rescate, indios genízaros, criados, or huerfanos (slaves, servants, or orphans), primarily through the artifice of "ransom" by colonial purchasers.[14] Ostensibly, the debt of ransom would be retired by ten to twenty years of service to the redeemers, after which time these individuals would become vecinos. In practice, these people appear to have experienced their bondage on a continuum that ranged from near slavery to familial incorporation.

Evidence from the eighteenth-century genízaro community of Abiquiu on the Rio Chama and Hispano settlements northward in the San Juan River system suggests that most genízaros achieved familial assimilation in the households of their masters through the Spanish institution of compadrazgo, or godparenthood. In this sense, genízaros gradually influenced and became a part of a larger Hispano identity group in northern New Mexico. Alternative explanations have asserted a more narrowly circumscribed "ethnic" genízaro identity, based on the existence of several relatively homogeneous and endogamous genízaro settlements in the Rio Grande valley, or have emphasized exploitation, enslavement, and social alienation. Ramón Gutiérrez,

13. "Report of the Reverend Father Provincial, Fray Pedro Serrano . . . to the Marquis de Cruillas . . ." (1761), in Charles Wilson Hackett, trans. and ed., *Historical Documents Relating to New Mexico, Nueva Vizcaya, and Approaches Thereto, to 1773* (Washington, D.C., 1937), III, 486–487; Fray Francisco Atanasio Domínguez, *The Missions of New Mexico, 1776*, trans. and ed. Eleanor B. Adams and Fray Angélico Chávez (Albuquerque, N.M., 1956), 252. See also Amando Represa, "Las Ferias Hispano-Indias del Nuevo México," in *La España ilustrada en el lejano oeste* (Valladolid, 1990), 119–125.

14. Since only some 75 percent of baptismal registers still exist, the actual figures are probably considerably higher. See David M. Brugge, *Navajos in the Catholic Church Records of New Mexico, 1694–1875* (Tsaile, Ariz., 1985), 2; for breakdown by tribal derivation and date, see 22–23.

for example, argues that the genízaros were "slaves and *criados* . . . who had no genealogical ties to the Hispano community, who were dishonored by their status as thralls, and who were deemed socially dead amid men and women of honor."[15] Gutiérrez offers numerous cases of complaints brought by genízaros against their Spanish masters, charging labor exploitation, cruel discipline, and sexual misuse, and buttresses these with characterizations drawn from two contemporary observers, Fray Domínguez and Fray Juan Augustín de Morfí, both of whom show contempt for the caste. Domínguez, writing in 1776, claimed that the genízaros were "servants among our people," unable to speak Spanish "without twisting it somewhat," whose "weak" characters turned them into "gamblers, liars, cheats, and petty thieves." Reporting on the state of the province in 1778, Morfí (who never actually visited New Mexico and drew his information from interviews) characterized the genízaros as landless "on account of their poverty, which leaves them afoot and without arms . . . they bewail their neglect and they live like animals."[16]

A deeper look into the genízaro experience reveals even more complexity and variation than heretofore proposed and suggests that we must sift our analysis through a finer mesh that captures power distributions at all levels of society in colonial New Mexico. The view that, beneath the level of Spanish elites, ethnic boundaries between Spanish and Indian societies eroded under the pressure of kinship and interdependency suffices only so long as we recognize that they did so within a context of unequal and often contested power. The "ethnic identity" position finds some support but requires refinements that include those villages where genízaros and vecinos shared residence, often under the same roof. Although such cases imply easy social mixing, evidence also points to asymmetrical power relations even at the household level. Likewise, Gutiérrez's dichotomy between honorable *españoles* and dishonored genízaros may have been the ideal of elite Spanish ecclesiastics like Domínguez and Morfí but probably reflects prescriptive

15. Ramón A. Gutiérrez, *When Jesus Came, the Corn Mothers Went Away: Marriage, Sexuality, and Power in New Mexico, 1500–1846* (Stanford, Calif., 1991), 188. For more on the debate over the *genízaros*, see Swadesh, *Los Primeros Pobladores;* "The *Genizaro*," chap. 10 of Gilberto Espinosa and Tibo Chavez, *El Río Abajo* (Albuquerque, N.M., n.d.); Chávez, "Genizaros," in Alfonso Ortiz, ed., *The Handbook of North American Indians* (Washington, D.C., 1979), 198–200, IX, *Southwest;* Robert Archibald, "Acculturation and Assimilation in Colonial New Mexico," *NMHR*, LIII (July 1978), 205–217; Stephen M. Horvath, "The *Genizaro* of Eighteenth-Century New Mexico: A Re-examination," in *Discovery* (Santa Fe, N.M., 1977), 25–40; Russell M. Magnaghi, "Plains Indians in New Mexico: The Genízaro Experience," *Great Plains Quarterly*, X (Spring 1990), 86–95.

16. See Domínguez, *Missions of New Mexico*, trans. and ed. Adams and Chávez, 42, 126, 208, 259, quoted in Gutiérrez, *When Jesus Came, the Corn Mothers Went Away*, 189. For Morfí, see Marc Simmons, trans. and ed., *Father Juan Augustín Morfí's Account of Disorders in New Mexico, 1778* (Isleta Pueblo, N.M., 1977), 34–35, quoted in Gutiérrez, 189.

anxieties about the existence of a *mestizo* caste, neither Spanish nor Indian, that was all too important to the colony's survival. Troubled by evidence of social and cultural mixing in distant villages, administrators and churchmen proved eager to find ideological devices by which genízaros could be subsumed within the fragile Spanish hegemony. Questions remain, therefore, especially around the origins of the genízaro category in colonial New Mexico, the quality of day-to-day relationships between genízaros and lower-order New Mexican vecinos, and the nature of their servility in terms of regional notions of customary justice.

Regarding their origins, the genízaros of New Mexico fit into a much larger framework of borderland conflict and accommodation available within the Spanish world than previously recognized. Between 1529 and 1830, Spain (and much of Christian Europe) suffered almost continuous harassment from the Ottoman corsairs of North Africa's Barbary Coast. In addition to plundering, these raiders seized Christian captives by the score, either as prisoners of war or in attacks on coastal settlements. Held as slaves and hostages by the Moors, these captives were pawns in a great rivalry between Islam and Christianity. Their ransom was achieved through the efforts of two orders of religious redemptionists, the Mercedarians and the Trinitarians, who undertook the raising of *limosnas* (alms) for ransom and negotiated for captive repatriation.[17] Thus, while Spanish colonists in New Mexico were obtaining thousands of Indian captives at the Taos and Pecos rescates, their counterparts in Spain were rescuing thousands of Christians from the presumed horrors of captivity among the infidels. And just as the riches obtained through ransom proved crucial to the economies of North Africa, so did the purchase of captives fuel extension of the market economy into native North America.

Many of these indios de rescate came to be known as genízaros in New Mexico, but just why is unclear. The internal politics of the Barbary States yield clues to this puzzle, however. Within the Ottoman Empire, real local power lay, although nominally, with the Janissary Corps, the "slave armies" raised by the Ottomans through the tributary demands of the *devshirme* ("levy of the boys") imposed upon their Balkan subjects. Although the Balkans had few natural resources to offer, they did contain large populations from which mercenary armies could be raised. Supplementing these levies were renegade Christians from the northern Mediterranean, who found adventure and prestige in the renowned military prowess of the Janissaries. These Janissaries (from *yeñi çeri,* "new troops"), known as "los geni-

17. For origins of the Redemptionist orders in the medieval period, see James William Brodman, *Ransoming Captives in Crusader Spain: The Order of Merced on the Christian-Islamic Frontier* (Philadelphia, 1986); for the later era, see Ellen G. Friedman, *Spanish Captives in North Africa in the Early Modern Age* (Madison, Wis., 1983).

zaros" in Spanish, had been created in the fifteenth century, as Ottoman rulers found native Turkish troops too often owed allegiance to local chiefs and throne aspirants rather than to the expanding Muslim state.[18] This clarifies the twin meanings ascribed to the term *genízaro* in Spanish: first, as a subject people descending from parents of alien nations or races, and second, as prestigious military units that owed a particular loyalty to the crown and that ostensibly stood above the petty intrigues of court politics.[19]

These two aspects found expression in the genízaros of New Mexico as well, contributing to the trouble scholars have experienced in defining their role in the colony. Both "slaves" and "soldiers," genízaros certainly occupied a low status in the colony yet also proved crucial in colonial defense and ultimately acted as slave raiders themselves.[20] Colonial New Mexico, rent from within by conflicts between secular and religious authorities and between españoles and mestizos, and threatened from without by the inscrutable politics of contending indios gentiles, was fertile ground for the development of a "slave soldiery."[21]

The earliest reference to genízaros in New Mexico seems to occur when

18. For the origins of the Ottoman Janissaries, and their relation to slavery and servility in Middle Eastern and Muslim thought, see Cemal Kafadar, *Between Two Worlds: The Construction of the Ottoman State* (Berkeley, Calif., 1995), 17–18, 112; Bernard Lewis, *Race and Slavery in the Middle East: An Historical Enquiry* (Oxford, 1990), 11–14, 62–71; for their role in the Barbary States, see Andrew C. Hess, *The Forgotten Frontier: A History of the Sixteenth-Century Ibero-African Frontier* (Chicago, Ill., 1978); John B. Wolf, *The Barbary Coast: Algeria under the Turks, 1500–1830* (New York, 1979).

19. Fray Angélico Chávez, "Genízaros," in Ortiz, ed., *Handbook of North American Indians*, 198–199, IX, *Southwest*.

20. For a campaign against the Sierra Blanca Apaches by fifty-five *genízaros* in 1777 that yielded a score of captives, see Cavallero de Croix to Governor Medinuetta, July 2, 1777, in *SANM*, II, no. 701, roll 10, frame 701. Comparatively, this ambiguity is less unique than it seems. The enslavement of women, and the military mobilization of captive men and male children, often went hand in hand not only in the Ottoman Empire but in Africa and Asia as well. For comparative cases, see Wendy James's treatment of Ethiopia, "Perceptions from an African Slaving Frontier"; for the Sudan, see Douglas H. Johnson, "Sudanese Military Slavery from the Eighteenth to the Twentieth Century," both in Leonie Archer, ed., *Slavery and Other Forms of Unfree Labour* (London, 1988), 130–141, 142–156; for Asia and Africa compared, see Jack P. Goody, "Slavery across Time and Space," in James L. Watson, ed., *Asian and African Systems of Slavery* (Berkeley, Calif., 1980), 16–42. This seems especially true in cases where complex cultural and political subdivisions threatened centralization of power, and rulers needed both concubines and soldiers who were "free" of kin and factional obligations. Claude Meillassoux terms these "symplectic [societies] . . . whose *heterogeneous social components* are not amalgamated but are held together by various compulsive *alliances* which can carry out some functions of centralizing power." "By replacing free men with slaves, the masters could protect themselves from ambitious relatives or rebellious subjects; and at the same time they could protect themselves from these henchmen, by granting them differentiated privileges which divided them among themselves and further attached them to their master" (*The Anthropology of Slavery: The Womb of Iron and Gold* [Chicago, 1991], 64, 140, 344).

21. France V. Scholes, *Church and State in New Mexico, 1610–1650* (Santa Fe, N.M., 1937), vol. VII of Historical Society of New Mexico, *Publications in History*.

Carlos de Sigüenza y Góngora stated that Diego de Vargas employed a genízaro guide during the *reconquista* of 1692 and that in his progress north-ward he had liberated seventy-four *"mestizos, y genízaros,"* who then enjoyed "the freedom to return to their brothers, relatives, and spouses."[22] This sug-gests that the category might have existed in the province before the revolt as a way of distinguishing between a generalized mestizo population and those families involved in military service. Pueblo Indian auxiliaries were also occasionally termed "genízaros," probably more descriptive of their military role than any "enslaved" status. The Spanish Colonial Census of 1750 enu-merated genízaros separately from the Pueblo Indian population when they comprised 4 percent (154 of 3,809) of the Spanish colonial population. The majority were concentrated in the Plaza de los Jarales in Belén and the Barrio de Analco in Santa Fe, but seventeen genízaro families resided along-side vecino families in Ranchos de Taos and San Juan de los Caballeros.[23]

These census data suggest a second refinement, namely, the presumed "landlessness" of the caste. After an initial appeal for lands near Sandía Pueblo was refused in 1733, census reports confirm that groups of genízaros received land grants for settlement near Belén in 1740, at Ranchos de Taos in 1750, at Las Trampas in 1751, at Abiquiu and Ojo Caliente in 1754, at San Miguel de Carnué in 1763 and San José de las Huertas in 1765, at Socorro near El Paso del Norte in 1773, at San Miguel del Vado in 1794, and at Anton Chico in 1822.[24] Spanish colonial authorities had a strategic objective in these settlements, namely, to establish "buffers" on the frontier between nomads and villages in the Rio Grande valley. Far from being landless, genízaros occupied key posts in the colonial defense perimeter.[25]

22. Don Carlos de Sigüenza y Góngora, *Mercurio Volante . . .* , trans. and ed. Irving Albert Leonard (Los Angeles, 1932), 128; Campaign journal of Don Diego de Vargas Zapata Luján Ponce de León, Jan. 8, 1692, in J. Manuel Espinosa, trans. and ed., *First Expedition of Vargas into New Mexico, 1692* (Albuquerque, N.M., 1940), 263.

23. In his 1705 campaign into Navaho country, Captain Roque de Madrid referred to his Jemez Pueblo auxiliaries as *genízaros*. See Rick Hendricks and John P. Wilson, trans. and eds., *The Navajos in 1705: Roque Madrid's Campaign Journal* (Albuquerque, N.M., 1996). For the census statistics, see Census of July 12, 1750, in Virginia Langham Olmsted, comp., *Spanish and Mexican Censuses of New Mexico, 1750 to 1830* (Albuquerque, N.M., 1981), 47–48.

24. For these dates, see "Declaration of Fray Miguel de Menchero, May 10, 1744," in Hackett, trans. and ed., *Historical Documents Relating to New Mexico,* III, 401; Olmsted, comp., Spanish Colonial Censuses of 1750, 1760, and 1790, New Mexico State Records Center; Las Trampas Grant, in *SANM,* I, no. 975, Records of the Surveyor General of New Mexico, report no. 27, roll 13, frames 254–440; Swadesh, *Los Primeros Pobladores,* 38; Andrew T. Smith, "The Peoples of the San Antonio de las Huertas Grant, 1767–1900," New Mexico State Records Center; "Description of . . . the Settlement at El Paso del Norte . . . in 1773," in Hackett, trans. and ed., *Historical Documents Relating to New Mexico,* III, 508; E. Boyd, "The Plaza of San Miguel del Vado," *El Palacio,* LXXVII, no. 4 (1971), 17–26.

25. Magnaghi, "Plains Indians in New Mexico," *Great Plains Quarterly,* X (Spring 1990), 88. Gutiérrez also makes note of this military role (*When Jesus Came, the Corn Mothers Went Away,* 305–306) but does not attempt to integrate the paradoxical information into

But other settlements featured a mix of caste residents, which would seem to have bearing on the relative legal and social autonomy of genízaros. The village of San José de las Huertas, in the Sierra de Sandía east of Bernalillo, offers such an example. The land grant petition of 1765 contains the names of eight families, both español and genízaro. By 1767, the village had increased to twenty-one families of mixed caste status. In its early years, "there was much intermarriage with Indians of San Felipe, Santa Ana, and Sandia [Pueblos]," and villagers who died were buried in the *campo santo* at San Felipe. This alliance with nearby Pueblo people suggests that there was a range of variation in peripheral communities and that ethnic alliances were often negotiated at the local level, whatever the desires of the elites in Santa Fe.[26]

The Spanish Colonial Census of 1750 taken in Ranchos de Taos displays another blending of caste groups. Of the village families, 37 percent were considered Spanish, 26 percent *coyotes* (Spanish-Indian descent), and 35 percent genízaros. The census taker reported nine Spanish households of fifty-seven persons, six coyote households of fifty-five persons, and eight genízaro households of twenty-five persons. Even the Spanish households showed a blurring of caste relations; the house of Antonio Atiensa included his coyota wife María Romero, their son Domingo Romero *(castizo,* the Spanish colonial term for mestizo), and the widow Juana with her daughter Manuela, no doubt *criadas*. Likewise, the house of Juan Rosalio Villalpando, an important español, included his wife María Valdes and their six children, all of whom are termed coyote, suggesting that María might have been an india de rescate. Pablo Francisco Villalpando's household contained three female and two male *servientes,* two of whom carried the family name. Mixing might have crossed class as well as caste lines in some village families.[27]

The fact that the census arranged households by caste reveals a conscious concern about such status on the part of Spanish administrators, but the data also demonstrate how informally these categories may be arranged at the village level. Census findings from a cluster of plazas at Belén show yet another pattern. In 1790, the third plaza, "Nuestra Señora de los Dolores de los Genízaros," contained thirty-three households, all designated as "genízaro," a strong indication that in some cases homogeneous communities developed among some indios de rescate. But the adjacent second "Plaza de Jarales" held thirty Spanish, twelve mestizo, four coyote, and two genízaro households. The marriage patterns from these communities reveal little caste-

his earlier characterizations of "dishonored thralls." He suggests, however, that, with movement to frontier outposts, genízaros "finally had an independent space in which to express their own identity" (305).

26. Smith, "The Peoples of the San Antonio de las Huertas Grant," in New Mexico State Records Center, 37.

27. See Olmsted, comp., *Spanish and Mexican Censuses of New Mexico,* 47–48.

anxious endogamy; of the twenty-eight unions, only one is español-española. Six marriages involved genízaro-genízara, and five mestizo-mestiza. The remaining sixteen show a crossing of caste lines. In most of these, hypogamy seems the rule, with women marrying men of lower status. Children of these unions, for example genízaro-coyota, seem to follow the father's status and are later enumerated as genízaros. Thus, some genízaros did have genealogical ties to the vecino community, contrary to the segregation presumed by Gutiérrez. Within households, intercultural mixing became even more complex, as servientes (many the illegitimate children of the *patrón)* designated "coyotas" or *de color quebrado* (of broken color) cast the purity of the family line into doubt.[28]

Whatever their residence pattern, as military slaves genízaros played crucial roles in the defense of the province. From 1744 forward, when Fray Miguel del Menchero commended the genízaros of "Cerro de Tomé" for the "great bravery and zeal" with which they patrolled the "country in pursuit of the enemy," these auxiliary soldiers utilized their knowledge of the geographic and cultural landscape of the borderlands to preserve the colony. Their military indispensability would provide them some leverage within the social and legal constraints that governed their condition.[29]

Genízaros did more than defend the frontiers against surrounding indios bárbaros. They also mobilized to protest encroachments on their communal lands by colonial *estanceros* (stockraisers). In October 1745, two genízaros of Belén brought a complaint before Viceroy Don Pedro Cebrian y Agustín in Mexico City, claiming that intrusions on the lands of their *pueblo* (village) by Diego de Torres, Fulano Barreras, and Antonio Salazar had forced many members of their community to abandon that place, thereby leaving the southern marches of the colony undefended. Furthermore, a grant issued in 1740 to Torres and thirty-one others (among whom was Don Nícolas de Chaves, alcalde of Albuquerque) "was illegal and should be null and voided . . . since the land in question included Indian *Pueblos.*" Assisted in preparing their complaint by the lawyer Francisco Cordova in Mexico City, the plaintiffs Antonio Casados (Kiowa Apache) and Luís Quintana (Apache) claimed membership in the Pueblo of Our Lady of Belén. Casados stated that, "as a young Apache, he was sold into the household of Francisco Casados" before settling in the Belén area in the household of Captain Torres, where he had "paid off his ransom" and joined the genízaro community. There, he "became a war captain of the *genízaros.*" Quintana had

---

28. Analysis drawn from Horvath, "The *Genízaro* of Eighteenth-Century New Mexico: A Re-examination," in *Discovery,* 25–40.

29. See "Declaration of Fray Miguel de Menchero," in Hackett, trans. and ed., *Historical Documents Relating to New Mexico,* III, 402.

apparently been expelled from the colony some years before but, having met his countryman in Mexico City, now sought "to return to his land."[30]

With the assistance of Cordova, Casados and Quintana deftly nuanced legal details by situating their claim within the tradition of royal protections granted Indian pueblos, thereby sidestepping the question of their social or juridical status as genízaros. The strategy worked, at least for a time. The viceroy ordered Governor Codallos y Rabal to hold hearings in Santa Fe to clarify the question of ownership—or suffer a 1,000-peso fine. When the day of the hearing arrived, Casados marched to the villa with "seventy Indians from all the different Pueblos" in his entourage. But Codallos seized this opportunity to accuse Casados of "inciting all of the friendly Pueblos against the Spaniards," and, based on the fact that the genízaro had gone outside the province "to file his charges before the Viceroy without license or permission from proper authorities," he ordered Casados held in the military guardhouse. Here we see the ambivalent status of genízaros in close focus: sufficiently bold and knowledgeable to journey to Mexico City and recruit to sympathies of the viceroy under the principles of Indian law, in New Mexico Casados remained a "public and notorious fugitive" subject to arrest and confinement as little more than a slave.[31]

Governor Codallos called a series of Spanish witnesses who impugned the validity of Casados's complaint, suggesting that "since he has acquired a certain degree of high intelligence" he had become a troublemaker in the community. Don Nícolas de Chaves came forward to claim that on his authority as alcalde he had given "possession to the Spaniards" in 1740 and that the "twenty or so Indians" resident thereon were only so "with the consent of . . . Diego de Torres."[32] Casados, probably brought before the court in chains, was allowed to testify only through a court-appointed interpreter, despite his fluency in Castilian. Even then, the governor cut off his statement and proceeded to cross-examine with sole emphasis on Quin-

---

30. "Order of Viceroy, Count of Fuenclara," Oct. 20, 1745, "Declaration of Antonio [Luís] Quintana," Feb. 12, 1746, in Antonio Casados and Luís Quintana, "Genízaros: Proceedings against Fulano Barreras, Diego de Torres, and Antonio Salazar over Lands at Puesto de Belén," in SANM, I, no. 183, roll 1, frames 1302–1327. For a discussion, see Stephen Michael Horvath, Jr., "The Social and Political Organization of the Genízaros of Plaza de Nuestra Señora de Los Dolores de Belen, New Mexico, 1740–1812" (Ph.D. diss., Brown University, 1979), 180–181, in New Mexico State Records Center; Ebright, "Advocates for the Oppressed: Indians, Genízaros, and Their Spanish Advocates in New Mexico," NMHR, LXXI (October 1996), 317–320. Casados's statement that he had "paid off his ransom" suggests that, at least in some cases, unfree labor in New Mexico more closely resembled indentured servitude than chattel slavery. No documentary evidence has yet come to light describing formal indenture contracts between captives and their Spanish ransomers like that hinted at by Casados.

31. "Obedience and Writ of Codallos y Rabal," Feb. 11, 1746, in SANM, I, no. 183.

32. "Declaration of Don Nícolas Chaves," Feb. 19, 1746, ibid.

tana's flight from the colony, asking no questions regarding the Indian (or genízaro) rights to the arable lands at Belén. He proceeded to collect considerable testimony in favor of the Torres claim from members of the Spanish community, who also spoke unanimously to the seditious nature of Casados's complaint. With the Spanish claim thus bolstered and the genízaro complaint apparently discredited, the governor forwarded his findings to the viceroy. Unfortunately, the viceroy's decision on this case has not survived. But it may be significant that in 1749 the genízaros of Belén again brought a complaint, this time against Don Nícolas de Chaves for "allowing his livestock to foul their *acequias*." Petitioning in this instance through ecclesiastical channels, rather than secular courts, they won a ruling whereby Chaves was instructed to "build bridges and protect the springs from his cattle." This case suggests that, whatever the resolution to the Casados/Quintana claim three years before, the ability of genízaros to mobilize as a community and assert their rights as wards of the crown or church still allowed them some measure of power in the face of local opposition.[33]

In cases where genízaros acted individually, without support from a larger community, their legal and social marginality proved crippling. Some ten miles south of San José de las Huertas, in Tijeras Canyon, the village of San Miguel de Carnué (del Laredo) featured mixed social composition. In 1763, Governor Vélez de Cachupín gave an agricultural grant to seventeen families, among whom were ten españoles, three coyotes, and the families of the genízaros Gregorio Montoya, Francisco García, and Bartolo Anzures. Five years later, Montoya and García stood accused of stealing eight cattle from Zia Pueblo. As the facts of the case became known, it became clear that the Spanish *teniente de alcalde* (deputy mayor) Cristobal Jaramillo had put them up to the crime, since livestock was in short supply in the village. Although they had acted in the interests of the community, their vecino neighbors failed to come to their defense. The genízaros were put to low-paid labor until the Zia owners were compensated, but Jaramillo went unpunished. The larcenous spirit of these socially mixed villages might have been democratically distributed, but egalitarianism did not apply when courts chose to enforce the law.[34]

But the power of extralegal collective action to shape customary justice at the local level continued despite the constraints of colonial law. A careful look at Bentura Bustamante's complaint illustrates this persistence. In 1776, Carlos III finally approved a massive reorganization of New Spain's northern

33. "Petición de Los Genízaros de Belén," Mar. 28, 1749, in Archdiocesan Archives of Santa Fe, reel 52, frames 68–72, in New Mexico State Records Center.
34. "Diligencias criminales contra los jenízaros de Carnué," in *SANM*, II, no. 636, roll 10, frame 400; see discussion in Swadesh, "Archaeology, Ethnohistory, and the First Plaza of Carnue," in *Ethnohistory*, XXIII (Winter 1976), 31–44.

frontier into the *Provincias Internas* and appointed Teodoro de Croix as comandante general. Aimed at promoting immigration and expanding the economy in the northern provinces, the creation of new or relocation of existing presidial defenses composed one aspect of Croix's strategy. Croix selected Juan Bautista de Anza, fresh from success in establishing the presidio at San Francisco in Alta California, as governor of New Mexico. As part of his military reorganization of the province, Anza considered several options. He proposed that the scattered *poblaciones* associated with the settlements like Santa Cruz de la Cañada and San Buenaventura de Chimayo be consolidated into fortified plazas capable of defense against Indian attacks and in which the unruly settlers might better have their behavior monitored by church and state. He also considered complete relocation of the capital and presidio to a new site on the Rio Grande between Santo Domingo and Cochiti Pueblos. Barring that, he proposed a less dramatic move of the Santa Fe presidio from the north bank of the Rio Santa Fe (where it remains today in the form of the "Governor's Palace") to higher ground on the south side, where the Barrio de Analco clustered around the Church of San Miguel. This barrio had long embraced the lands and homes of Santa Fe's genízaro population, which in 1780 numbered some 142 individuals in 42 families, or 12.25 percent of the town's population. Anza's plans would have included resettlement of many "lower order" vecino residents in the new capital and relocation of the Analceño genízaros to frontier settlements, which Bustamante termed "gateway of the enemy Comanche."[35]

Although Bustamante's complaint was never specifically stated, other evidence makes clear that Anza's relocation plans lay at its root. The genízaro petition was part of a larger protest against consolidation and reorganization that illustrates how the interests of settler society and those of their putative slaves could converge at least momentarily to transcend barriers of race and caste. Bustamante and his companions probably arrived in Arizpe with a larger party of twenty-four petitioners led by Manuel de Armijo and José Miguel de la Peña, who had fled Santa Fe in May after offending Governor Anza by their own refusals to agree to relocation. Also among that party traveled Cristobal Vigil and Salvador Maestas, representing La Cañada and Chimayo respectively. Thus four different communities found themselves sufficiently distressed at Anza's reorganization schemes to send emissaries

---

35. For reorganization of the Interior Provinces, see Weber, *Spanish Frontier*, chap. 8; for Anza's proposals, see *SANM*, I, no. 1118, roll 6, frames 149–160; for genízaro occupation of Analco, see Domínguez, *Missions of New Mexico*, trans. and ed. Adams and Chávez, 42; Fray Juan Augustin de Morfí, "Geographical Description of New Mexico" (1782), in Thomas, trans. and ed., *Forgotten Frontiers*, 92; see also Anza to Croix, May 26, 1780, ibid., 177; Petición de Bentura Bustamante, June 20, 1780, in *SANM*, I, no. 1138, roll 6, frames 323–325.

across some five hundred miles of uncharted territory to plead for their repeal.[36]

Each community expressed different grievances. The citizens of Santa Fe, according to Armijo and Peña, had labored too long and hard to build irrigation dams and acequias, to maintain the chapel, and to till their fields to surrender them now to abandonment. They complained too that Anza's prohibition against the sale or purchase of Indian servants, whom Anza claimed they treated like "infidel slaves," deprived them of the additional profits and labor with which to make good the relocation. The outlying villages of La Cañada and Chimayo, on the other hand, found Anza's orders to congregate vexing in that to do so would distance them unnecessarily from their fields and orchards. Anza later told the comandante general that this concern was trivial; rather, their resistance emerged from a general disposition toward "separation and solitude" that came from the "old custom of living dispersed . . . in order to enjoy greater liberty" and participate in illicit Indian trading.[37]

Bustamante's genízaros argued somewhat differently. Although his people did not wish to abandon their communal lands or their centrality in military affairs, foremost among their fears over relocation stood the danger of "losing their women and children" to capture by Comanche raiders, a peril that had plagued frontier settlements since the colony's inception. The genízaros of Analco knew the pattern of reciprocal slave raiding all too well, for they were one consequence of the trade and often took *cautivos* themselves during their campaigns against los indios bárbaros. Years of military service and coresidence with colonial New Mexicans had made them devout Catholics and loyal subjects, yet Anza's expulsion and relocation plan left Bustamante's people only two alternatives—to "endure their burdens and travails" or to depart the colony altogether.

The latter option raises intriguing questions about just how the Analceños conceived of themselves as a community. Bustamante thrice employed the term "Nación" in his appeal, once declaring his genízaro peoples as an "Indian Nation, all united in due conformity," again when he threatened that they might seek refuge in their "lands and Nation," and finally when he claimed that in military service for the Spaniards they "betrayed our own Nation." That Bustamante described Comanches as "enemies" and that, by

36. "Manuel de Armijo y José Miguel de la Peña," June 2, 1780, Document 5, Sender Collection, roll 1, frames 27–38, New Mexico State Records Center; for Vigil and Maestas, see Anza to Croix, Jan. 12, 1781, in *SANM*, I, no. 1118, roll 6, frames 149–160; for Croix's reception of the petitioners, see Croix to Anza, Jul. 29, 1780, in *SANM*, I, no. 1260, roll 6, frames 949–959.

37. Document 5, Sender Collection, roll 1, frames 27–38; Anza to Croix, Jan. 12, 1781, in *SANM*, I, no. 1118, roll 6, frames 149–160.

1780, Anza had implemented a strategy of taking war to the Sierra Blanca and Lipan Apaches suggest that the betrayal his genízaros felt might have derived from a common Apache descent. Indeed, Apaches comprised some 65 percent (675 of 1,045) of Plains Indians baptized in New Mexican parishes between 1730 and 1780, and perhaps the Analceños represented a concentration of these in a single barrio. Yet it also seems possible that the unified community of which Bustamante spoke grew among peoples of diverse cultural backgrounds sharing similar historical experiences and united by Catholicism, military service, coresidence, and an ascribed servile status. Thus their "Indian Nation" might have been writ larger within and without their minds, meaning any that were simply not Spaniards. Whether Bustamante's threat meant literal desertion and apostasy or merely temporary flight to the Plains while Anza reconsidered his decision remains unclear. It does hint that these genízaros had not entirely severed their familial and cultural connections to their native kinspeople who presumably remained willing to take them in to their rancherías.[38]

Bustamante's people did not need to risk fugitive status, however, for Anza reported to Croix in 1781 that Analco was not sufficiently expansive or well watered to support a new presidio. His preferred plan, relocation of the capital, hung in abeyance for lack of funds and by 1787 would be largely unnecessary. He still fumed that his intended expedition to open a route between New Mexico and Sonora had to be abandoned due to the "malicious and needless flight of the settlers of this Villa," but he appeared heedless to the irony that the path had been trailblazed by the mixed group of renegade vecinos and genízaros the previous year. For a few months, at least, the Spanish citizenry of New Mexico and the genízaros of Analco found common cause. The latter seemed willing to take extraordinary risks in their search for an autonomous social space, however circumscribed, and to protect the interests of their families and growing sense of community.[39]

The troubles of 1780 do point to an emerging array of shared interests between genízaros and lower-order vecinos that occurred in parallel with expansion on the borderlands economies. Consequent to the unauthorized departure of citizens and slaves to Arizpe, Anza had reported to Croix his inability to persuade the citizens of the province to form a *cordón* (trading caravan) to Chihuahua that would have cooperated with his Sonoran expe-

38. Petición de Bentura Bustamante, in *SANM*, I, no. 1138, roll 6, frames 323–325. The phrases at issue are, in order, "compañeros que semos de dicha Nación Yndios todos unidos en devida conformidad"; "o nos iremos a buscar alivio a nuestra tierras y Nación"; and "quando hemos salido a Campaña hemos entregado a nuestra propia Nación." For Apache baptisms, see Brugge, *Navajos in the Catholic Church Records*, 22–23.

39. Anza to Croix, May 26, 1780, in Thomas, trans. and ed., *Forgotten Frontiers*, 177; Morfí, "Geographical Description of New Mexico," ibid., 92, 374 n. 28, 379–380 n. 59; see also Thomas, trans. and ed., *Teodoro de Croix and the Northern Frontier of New Spain, 1776–1783* (Norman, Okla., 1941), 107–108.

dition. He attributed this reluctance to the lack that season of "the formal trading for hides with the pagans," which occurred only every two years. He explained that such a fair "stimulates and makes up the largest part of the trade of this province," without which the settlers felt a cordón to be fruitless. As drought and famine persisted in the province, and with a smallpox epidemic just beginning, local economic conditions would become dire. It is little wonder that genízaros and vecinos alike found neither relocation nor a major trade and military expedition appealing. In December 1780, many of the lower social order pursued an alternative strategy. Probably guided by genízaro scouts like Bentura Bustamante, more than two hundred men, women, and children from the colony took to the eastern plains on a buffalo hunt, returning to their homes with 450 loads of meat.[40]

These seasonal *viajes* would become commonplace in the nineteenth century, a phenomenon that points to the manner in which genízaros worked within an expanding borderlands economy to elevate their status in New Mexican society. By 1800, Governor Fernando Chacón relied almost exclusively on genízaros or repatriated New Mexican captives as scouts and explorers onto the Plains. In June of that year, eager to get a sense of American designs on the West and to explore trade opportunities with the Cheyenne and Sioux, he dispatched the trilingual José Miguel Zenguaras, two Taos Indians, and four genízaros (with their wives) on a reconnaissance toward the Missouri. In November, Comandante José Manuel Ochoa of El Paso del Norte requested from Chacón "a force of the strongest and most warlike Taos and *genízaros*" to scour the Sierras Magdalenas, San Mateos, and Piñones for Apache depredators. Eight years later, following Zebulon Pike's arrest in the San Luis Valley, Comandante Nemesio Salcedo formalized their rising status by creating an official Tropa de Genízaros, whom he then sent onto the Plains to monitor American solicitations of Pawnee friendship and to affirm the faith of the Spanish alliance with the Comanches.[41]

The people of eighteenth-century colonial New Mexico certainly organized their society around concepts of honor, but to argue that "Spaniards revelled in their honor only because they lived among genízaros who were dishonored by their enslavement" glosses over growing divisions within colonial society and emergent alliances between New Mexicans and neighboring indios gentiles. The claim that genízaros and other conquered Indians were now "the enemy within," against which the Spanish could define

40. Thomas, *Forgotten Frontiers*, 177; Don Bernardo de Miera y Pacheco, "Plana de la Provincia Interna de el Nuebo Mexico . . . ," in Domínguez, *Missions of New Mexico*, 2–3.

41. Chacón to Nava, June 10, 1800, Ochoa to Chacón, Nov. 30, 1800, both in *SANM*, II, nos. 1490, 1519, roll 14, frames 548–549, 658–659; José Manrique, draft of a report for Nemesio Salcedo y Salcedo, Nov. 26, 1808, in the Pinart Collection, Bancroft Library, University of California, Berkeley.

their cultural integrity, overlooks the multiple roles played by this slave soldiery. As culturally diverse "slaves," they did provide an example of social subordination and impurity against which españoles could define their *calidad* (quality). As skilled soldiers and scouts, however, they clearly received a measure of respect and occasional success within the customary justice of New Mexico. They, too, developed a sense of honor that derived from their military prowess. In 1793, for example, when Marcos Sánchez of Tomé was arrested for abusing his concubine, he protested, "I am a *genízaro*, unworthy of such base treatment!" These countervailing tensions between formal caste subordination and tactical indispensability would grow, especially as the era of Bourbon reforms spurred economic growth and class divisiveness within New Mexico.[42]

Although the genízaros of Analco resisted expulsion in 1780, in the following decades relocation and resettlement would occur. Land and water shortages in the Rio Grande valley, confidence in the stability of the New Mexico–Comanche alliance negotiated between Governor Anza and Comanche captain Ecueracapa in 1786, and the vigorous economic exchange that followed that treaty all promoted frontier expansion. As settlers of peripheral outposts, genízaros and lower-order vecinos extended the Spanish presence in the borderlands and elaborated their own autonomous strategies in the pursuit of wealth and security. These strategies recognized that cultural hybridization offered village society opportunities that rigid cultural differentiation did not, but such strategies also held the seeds of conflict between borderlanders and their colonial overlords.

In his 1794 instructions to incoming governor Chacón, Don Fernando de la Concha offered a caution about the political consequences of easy relations between vecinos, genízaros, and los indios bárbaros.

> The inhabitants [of this province] are indolent. They love distance which makes them independent; and if they recognize the advantages of union, they pretend not to understand them, in order to adapt the liberty and slovenliness which they see . . . in their neighbors the wild Indians.[43]

Frontier settlement met the objectives of Spanish administrators in that mixed genízaro-vecino outposts provided a skilled military presence on the traditional gateways to the colony. Yet these *llaneros* (plainsmen), as they came to be called, showed little inclination to congregate in fortified plazas

42. Gutiérrez, *When Jesus Came, the Corn Mothers Went Away*, 196, 206, 306.
43. "Don Fernando de la Concha to Lieutenant Colonel Don Fernando Chacón, Advice on Governing New Mexico" (1794), trans. Donald E. Worcester, *NMHR*, XXIV, no. 3 (1949), 236–254, esp. 250.

and commit themselves to a settled farming life. Instead, they proved a constant irritant to their superiors. While maintaining a village-based cultural profile, borderlanders began to move freely across the plains, traveling seasonally to hunt buffalo as *ciboleros* or trade as *comancheros*. In doing so, they came to wear their cultural affiliation lightly, living as Spanish *labradores* (farmers) during periods of planting and harvesting only to slip comfortably into a nomadic life when fat buffalo or barter beckoned in the autumn.

Although their "liberty and slovenliness" dismayed Spanish elites, their knowledge of the borderlands proved so valuable that the authorities had to grant allowances for both travel and settlement beyond the pale of colonial control. During this period, we see the establishment of key villages east of the Sangre de Cristo Mountains: San Miguel del Vado in 1794, San José del Vado in 1803, Mora in 1818, and Anton Chico in 1822.[44] Not coincidentally, each petition for a village grant included names of men designated as genízaros, for these people had long served in the vanguard of intercultural negotiation. In reaching out to their Comanche neighbors, New Mexican llaneros drew upon a century of intercultural exchanges—whether violent or commercial—to develop new strategies for exploiting opportunities on the plains. Cultural hybridity and looser, more flexible village organization were among these innovations.[45]

The fifty-two residents of Sante Fe who petitioned Governor Chacón for a grant of vacant land on the Pecos River on September 1, 1794, illustrate the blending of tradition and innovation. Led by Lorenzo Márquez and Domingo Padilla, both vecinos, the petitioners included thirteen genízaro heads of families, all of whom claimed that, although they had "some small pieces of land" in the Barrio de Analco, water shortages and overcrowding made it "impossible for all of us to enjoy its use." They had already reconnoitered (and probably farmed seasonally, given the use requirements in Spanish land law) a fertile valley twenty miles downriver from Pecos Pueblo, where there lay enough land not only for themselves but also for "as many in the province who are destitute."[46]

44. For the dates, see Boyd, "The Plaza of San Miguel del Vado," *El Palacio*, LXXVII, no. 4 (1971), 17–28. Although the official grant for the village of Mora was not issued until 1835, in 1818 three hundred residents petitioned Santa Fe for a resident priest. For Anton Chico, see Michael J. Rock, "Anton Chico and Its Patent," in John R. and Christine M. Van Ness, eds., *Spanish and Mexican Land Grants in New Mexico and Colorado* (Manhattan, Kans., 1980), 86–91.

45. Since by 1822 caste designations like *genízaro* were no longer used in official record keeping, for Anton Chico it is necessary to trace the genízaro lines by following the village's first settlers from San Miguel and San José in family chain migrations down the Pecos River.

46. San Miguel del Vado Grant, Surveyor General of New Mexico Records, no. 119, roll 24, frames 595–740, New Mexico State Record Center. For the deathblow this outpost dealt to Pecos Pueblo's role in intercultural trade, see John L. Kessell, *Kiva, Cross, and Crown: The Pecos Indians and New Mexico, 1540–1840* (Albuquerque, N.M., 1987), 415–421.

Chacón confirmed the grant at San Miguel del Vado with the understanding that, at the end of two years, all able-bodied men must possess firearms
(only twenty-five of the petitioners did at the time—the others had bows and
arrows), muster regularly, and build the requisite fortified plaza. The settlers,
however, felt little urgency to do so. The first baptismal entry for a vecino of
El Vado dates from 1798, when the Pecos Pueblo Indian Juan de Dios Fer-
nández married María Armijo, daughter of grantee Juan Armijo. Grantees
Márquez and Padilla, however, had appeared as *padrinos* (godparents) in the
Pecos baptismal books in the early 1780s, which suggests that the Analceños
had probably been sojourning on the plains and farming the Pecos bottoms
for some time before making their petition.[47] They had apparently experienced few problems with the nomadic Indians. Since the effort and expense
of building a fortified adobe plaza and equipping themselves with firearms
was probably beyond the means of these families, the risk seemed reasonable
given the rewards of inserting themselves as middlemen in the plains trade.

Outgoing governor Don Fernando de la Concha had already warned
Fernando Chacón to beware the emergence of easy relations between villagers and "wild Indians." Concha had grudgingly allowed the intercourse to
grow, he explained, "with the idea of acquiring a complete knowledge of the
waterholes and lands in which [the Comanches] are situated. Moreover, the
presidial troops needed remounts, and "the only way to acquire horses of
good quality cheaply is to . . . barter with the Comanches . . . the cost of each
[being] eight pesos, more or less." By the beginning of the nineteenth century, Comanches had become the principal horse traders on the southern
plains, and New Mexicans proved a hungry market for these mounts. The
difficulty in regulating this trade, however, evoked increasing anxiety in
colonial administrators.[48]

Concha offered cautions about the general character of these villagers as
well. "Under a simulated appearance of ignorance or rusticity they conceal
the most refined malice. He is a rare one in whom the vices of lying and
robbing do not occur together." These character traits he attributed to "the
dispersion of their settlements [and] the bad upbringing resulting from this,
the proximity and trade of the barbarous tribes." The governor noted that
the civilian militias upon which the province depended for defense functioned virtually free from military authority, "always disturbing the Province whenever it suited them in the purpose of gaining their own ends," a
chaos deriving from a "lack of obedience, wilfulness, and desire to live
without subjection and in complete liberty, in imitation of the wild tribes
which they see nearby." With no little exasperation, he suggested that "the

47. San Miguel del Vado Grant, Surveyor General of New Mexico Records, no. 119, roll
23, frame 599, New Mexico State Records Center; Kessell, *Kiva, Cross, and Crown*, 418.
48. "Advice on Governing New Mexico," trans. Worcester, *NMHR*, XXIV, no. 3 (1949),
251.

removal of more than two thousand labradores to another area" would be "very useful to the society and the state." Social stability could only be attained by "a new system of regulations and . . . a complete change in the actual system of control," especially the creation of a stable commercial agriculture and imposition of military discipline within the militias.[49]

His successor fared no better in imposing order on the borderlands. By 1803, Governor Chacón reported failure in promoting commercial agriculture in the province: "The majority of its inhabitants are little dedicated to farming, [contenting themselves] with sowing and cultivating only what is necessary for their sustenance." It seems that informal and illegal trade with Indian groups, conducted in good part by genízaro bordermen, occupied most New Mexicans. In marked contrast, he praised "the Pueblo Indians who compose a third of the population, [who] develop large fields that are cultivated in common, so that they can take care of widows, orphans, the sick, [and the] unemployed." Noting that only the Pueblos produced a surplus and thus "never feel the effects of hunger," he affirmed by implication their readiness for formal market participation should a more reliable trade be established between the province and the Chihuahua market centers. The governor's interest in developing an export economy was not simply a bureaucrat's endorsement of promarket Bourbon reforms. Since Chacón had held the tithe rental contract for the province from 1796 to 1801, his personal income had probably suffered from the vecino population's fascination with informal commerce, an issue that would come to a head just a few years later.[50]

Chacón also complained of the "natural decadence and backwardness" of the provincial economy, where "internal commerce is in the hands of twelve or fourteen merchants . . . neither properly licensed nor well versed in business matters." Ninety percent of commercial exchange was conducted "on credit . . . exacerbated by the lack of money in circulation." Even worse than this commercial core were "the rest of the citizenry [who] are so many petty merchants . . . continuously dealing and bartering with whatever products they have at hand."[51]

Ironically, "formality prevail[ed]" only "in the trading carried on with the nomad Indians *(Naciones gentiles)* that being a give-and-take business conducted in sign language." In exchange for New Mexican manufactures like

49. Ibid., 243–244.
50. The tithe rental contract, by which holders received a percentage of the 10 percent ecclesiastical tithe on annual increase in all agricultural products and livestock, was a much-sought-after privilege, since it was perhaps the best legal way to accrue income in addition to an administrator's wages. Governors usually won this contract, which aligned their interests with a managed, measurable economy. See Frank, "From Settler to Citizen," 166–210.
51. Simmons, "The Chacón Economic Report of 1803," *NMHR*, LX, no. 1 (1985), 81–88, esp. 87.

saddlebags, bridles, bits, iron goods, textiles, and agricultural products both raw and processed, the "nomads give Indian captives of both sexes, mules, moccasins, colts, mustangs, all kinds of hides and buffalo meat." New Mexican villagers indeed produced a local agricultural surplus and practiced weaving, leatherworking, and blacksmithing but were more inclined to use that surplus in exchange with Plains peoples than to accept the low prices consequent to risky overland shippage and the uncertain markets of Chihuahua.[52]

When it became clear that much local production went into the plains trade rather than south along the *camino real,* efforts were made in both Mexico City and Santa Fe to stem the leakage. Early in 1805, the viceroy decreed that all goods bartered by New Mexicans at the annual trade fair in the San Bartolome Valley would be free from the payment of the 6 percent *alcabala* (tax) required of other provinces. In June, Chacón's successor, Joaquín del Real Alencaster, convened a junta in Santa Fe to discuss methods of improving manufactures and mining and redirect existing production toward the Mexican trade. Although a lack of capital limited any significant invigoration of the textile or nascent mining industries, Alencaster attempted, first, to build up local sheep flocks by prohibiting their sale to Navahos, and second, to gain at least indirect revenue from the broader Indian trade through a licensing system. Both directives produced consequences that would confirm the worst suspicions of his predecessors.[53]

Late in the autumn of 1805, the vecinos of San Miguel and San José del Vado gathered near their new church, ostensibly to discuss raising alms for the upcoming Fiesta de la Señora de Guadalupe. But *teniente de justicia* Juan Antonio Alarí suspected otherwise and managed to eavesdrop on the meeting. Alarí discovered that "all of their conversation," led by Don Felipe Sandoval, involved the governor's recent interference with the Comanche trade. He also learned that Sandoval, *hermano major* of the Virgin's *cofradía* (lay brotherhood), intended to incite the settlers to reject the order and "go to trade with the heathens as is customary." Furthermore, Sandoval claimed that the citizens of La Cañada and Rio Arriba would support their action. Fearing insurrection, Alarí broke up the meeting "with staff and cudgels" and took Sandoval, José García de la Mora, and Victor Vigil of Rio Arriba into custody.

52. Ibid, 87.
53. Junta report on economic development (incomplete), June 17, 1805, in *SANM,* II, no. 1844, roll 15, frames 656–657. For the importance of reciprocal trade in sheep and captives between Navahos and New Mexicans in the pastoral borderlands west of the Rio Grande, see Brooks, "Violence, Justice, and State Power in the New Mexico Borderlands, 1780–1880," in John M. Findlay and Richard White, eds., *Power and Place in the North American West* (Seattle, Wash., 1999), 23–58.

When news of the men's arrest circulated throughout the province, en-
raged bands of citizens from outlying villages converged upon the capital. To
diffuse tensions, the governor quickly convened an investigation of the grievances beneath the scandal. Numerous respondents confirmed general dissat-
isfaction with the governor's restrictions on their customary Indian trade. It
quickly became clear that limitations on commerce with Comanches constituted only one complaint and that Sandoval's agents had circulated a letter
throughout the province urging a general disobedience. García de la Mora
himself complained of the Chihuahua caravan's uncertain timing and rewards, the governor's "lamentable decision" to prohibit the sale of sheep to
the Navahos, and the forced collection of "hundreds of *fanegas* [2–3 bush-
els]" of grain to feed the presidial soldiers in the capital. As "many men on
foot or horseback" bore down upon the capital, Alencaster released the in-
surgents from jail and forwarded the proceedings to Comandante Salcedo
for review. He preferred a charge of sedition against Sandoval, but Salcedo
failed to act upon his recommendation. By 1810, in fact, Sandoval found himself appointed protector de indios of the Pueblo Indians of the province.[54]

At first glance, we might see this case along a continuum of successful
extralegal collective actions in the interest of customary justice, from the
Belén defense of 1746 to Bustamante's action of 1780. But at San Miguel del
Vado we see asymmetries in justice reminiscent of the prosecutions of genízaro cattle thieves at San Miguel de Carnué in 1768. Unlike Sandoval, whose
vecino status probably protected him, other men from San Miguel suffered
severely in the aftermath of the unrest. Even while the investigations of the
vecinos were under way in Santa Fe, Lieutenant Alarí took four more men
into custody. Francisco *el Comanche,* Francisco Xavier *de nacion Aà* (Pawnee), José María Gurulé *de nacion Caigua,* and the genízaro Antonio María
were charged with seditious activities among *los gentiles,* especially the Comanches.[55] Alarí claimed that the men, in disregard of the governor's licensing directives, had visited the camps of Comanche General Somicuiaio,
speaking "very badly of the Spanish, and the Governor." Spreading rumors
and "a thousand lies," including the accusation that customary gifts for the
Indians might not be forthcoming, the men also acquired "hides, meat, and

<hr>

54. For the short-lived insurrection, see "Sumaria informacion indagatoria sobre com-
bocatoria, commocion, y escándolo cometido entre los vecinos de las jurisdicciones Te-
nencia el Pecos, y Alcaldia de la Cañada, deciembre 6–24, 1805," in *SANM,* II, no. 1930, roll
15, frames 1043–1098; Kessell, *Kiva, Cross, and Crown,* 434–435; for Sandoval's appointment, see Cutter, *Protector de Indios in Colonial New Mexico, 1659–1821,* 82–86.

55. Although James H. Gunnerson argues that the Aàs were Crows in *Ethnohistory of the
High Plains* (Denver, Colo., 1988), 49–50, in this case, Elizabeth A. H. John's identification
of the "Aàs" as the "Aguages," or Panismahas (Pawnee) seems most probable. See *Storms
Brewed in Other Men's Worlds: The Confrontation of Indians, Spanish, and French in the
Southwest, 1540–1795* (Lincoln, Nebr., 1975), 592.

other goods" from the Indians. Alexandro Martín, a New Mexican captive
returned by Comanche captain Tosapoy in 1786 at the conclusion of the
Spanish-Comanche Peace Treaty and now "interpreter to the Comanches,"
corroborated Alarí's testimony, claiming the men's activities resulted in
"great harm to the peace." Frustrated as to what measures he could take to
castigate these "baptized and Christian Indians," Alencaster sent them by
military escort to the Assessor-General of the Provincias Internas in Guadalajara, warning of the risk they "might flee and go to live among said Indians,
and upset the Peace." The resolution of this case remains unclear, but in 1807
Antonio María was arrested for vagrancy in Chihuahua, then sent north to
Santa Fe to work off his punishment in service at the presidio.[56]

The disturbances of 1805 point to the extent to which New Mexicans of
several classes and castes depended upon open trade with los indios gentiles
for their economic well-being and the degree to which the borderland economy had come to function within a widely shared sense of customary justice. Borderland villagers felt the Indian trade was their trade and deeply
resented administrative interference. They demonstrated their outrage in
the same fashion that Antonio Casados, Luís Quintana, and Bentura Bustamante had in previous decades—by mobilizing their communities in extralegal public protest and coupling that with appeals to customary rights.
Their actions also point to the astonishing cultural complexity and caste
interdependence of borderland villagers. The "seditious" activities at San
Miguel del Vado involved respectable vecinos like Felipe Sandoval, his com-
padre from the northern villages of the Rio Arriba, genízaros like Antonio
María, and mysterious transcultural social marginals like the Comanche
Francisco, the Pawnee Francisco Xavier, and the Kiowa José María Gurulé.[57]
Provincial grievances went beyond Alencaster's attempt to regulate the
plains trade and included both his prohibitions against the sale of sheep to
the Navahos and the responsibility of the local populace to maintain a
relatively ineffective presidial troop.

Although many details remain obscure, the general condition of the province at the beginning of the nineteenth century seems one of barely restrained entrepreneurial frenzy of a decidedly heterogeneous type. When

56. "Diligencias criminales contra Francisco el Comanche, Francisco Xavier, José María
Gurule, y Antonio María . . . 2 diciembre 1805–28, marzo 1806," in *SANM,* II, no. 1931, roll
15, 1099–1117. On the punishment of Antonio María, see Isidro Rey a Real Alencaster, Mar.
2, 1807, in *SANM,* II, no. 2043, roll 16, frame 315.

57. Gurulé's Kiowa identity is questionable in that governor Chacón reported in 1804
that the Yamparika Comanche captain Guanicoruco claimed him as his son. Chacón
countered that Gurulé was, in fact, a Skidi Pawnee genízaro, once a captive of Guanicoruco, whom Chacón had settled in 1794 as an agent for the Comanches in San Miguel del
Vado. Gurulé's "unruly conduct, cheating, and horse thieving" had led to his replacement
by Alejandro Martín, the former captive of Tosapoy. See Kessell, *Kiva, Cross, and Crown,*
429–430, esp. 430.

Don Alberto Maynez succeeded Alencaster in 1808, he wisely relaxed his predecessor's restrictions, and this energy again expanded outward. Soon the borderland villages would be filled with seasonally nomadic ciboleros and comancheros who connected with the maturing "raiding economies" of Kiowas and Comanches to lay the groundwork for the market-driven livestock economy that would emerge after 1840. In so doing, they would ultimately draw the negative attention of military modernizers and capitalist developers in the 1870s.[58]

But the disturbances and resolutions at San Miguel del Vado also point to the limits of collective action to shape customary justice in the search for equidad, and they allow for some more general observations about the functioning of power in colonial borderlands. The uprising did produce some of the desired corrections in trade policy, but the social marginals who played such a central role were punished where vecinos were not. The four men sent to Guadalajara may have simply been contrabandistas caught in the act, yet they appear indicative of a larger pattern. It may be that expanding economic opportunities on the plains—coupled with liberal social tendencies in the Bourbon reforms—loosened caste constraints while simultaneously scattering tightly knit (and caste-constrained) genízaro communities in a centrifugal fashion. Economic interdependency and shared interests failed to translate into social and legal equality. Caste might have had little salience in day-to-day relations or might even have helped to organize, along with class interests, some aspects of community resistance, but it never lost its capacity under the law to become a tool of unequal justice when courts so wished.

Throughout the Americas, moments when changing political economies fractured sociolegal structures of domination and allowed indigenous and subordinated peoples to develop new repertoires of contention occurred with growing frequency in the late eighteenth century. At the same time that Bustamante laid his challenge before Teodoro de Croix, Bourbon military reformers in Sonora, Chihuahua, and Coahuila were settling soldier communities along Mexico's northern frontier. By the nineteenth century, these would—owing to their distance from colonial legal control and their pivotal role in the borderland economy—become the seedbed for a staunchly independent and revolutionary "norteño" identity.[59] Far to the south, the "raid-

58. This period is treated in Brooks, "Captives and Cousins." For the general outlines of the transition, see Thomas D. Hall, Social Change in the Southwest, 1350–1880 (Lawrence, Kans., 1989).

59. See Ana María Alonso, Thread of Blood: Colonialism, Revolution, and Gender on Mexico's Northern Frontier (Tucson, Ariz., 1995); Daniel Nugent, "Two, Three, Many Barbarisms? The Chihuahuan Frontier in Transition from Society to Politics," in Donna J. Guy and Thomas E. Sheridan, eds., Contested Ground: Comparative Frontiers on the Northern and Southern Edges of the Spanish Empire (Tucson, Ariz., 1998), 182–200; Brooks, "Captives and Cousins."

ing economies" of Indian peoples in the pampas borderlands of South
America were shifting from subsistence to ever-wider networks of market
exchange that included many hundreds of human captives in their commerce. This socioeconomic transition would elevate Indian groups like the
Araucanians and Ranqueles to the status of militarized "tribes," alternately
solicited as allies or attacked as enemies by the formative Chilean and Argentine states that claimed their territory.[60] American Indian groups east of the
Mississippi also sought new strategic space in the unstable imperial landscape but found their options increasingly limited to tactical maneuvering
within the new United States as their former French and British allies withdrew from overtly supportive roles. In most cases, the strategic openings
closed all too quickly, and renewed arts of domination and conquest asserted
themselves. But, for other peoples, the destabilizations of the 1780s held
more lasting promise. Men and women of the white farming frontiers found
power structures of the fledgling republic vulnerable, if to a limited extent,
to their political and economic demands.[61]

Despite their many and manifest differences, the foregoing contestations
over power in colonial borderlands all involved, at some level, law as an
instrument of domination and a tool for resistance. To borrow from the
work of one of the editors of this volume, and to substitute the concept of
"borderlands" as spatial and social producers of contingency in place of his
emphasis on work and employment, we might say that borderlands "furnished a prime site for instability or dissonance between dominant context
and lived experience . . . where, as a result, weaknesses and contradictions in
the institutional and imaginative fabric of the rule of law . . . might be likely
to show up with particular clarity." Bentura Bustamante might have said it
differently, but the meaning would have been inescapably clear to his lis-
teners in Arizpe that June morning.[62]

60. See Susan M. Socolow, "Spanish Captives in Indian Societies: Cultural Contact
along the Argentine Frontier, 1600–1835," *Hispanic American Historical Review*, LXXII, no.
1 (February 1992), 73–99; Kristine L. Jones, "Comparative Raiding Economies: North and
South," Thomas D. Hall, "The Río de la Plata and the Greater Southwest: A View from
World-System Theory," both in Guy and Sheridan, eds, *Contested Ground*, 97–114, 150–
166.

61. Colin G. Calloway, *The American Revolution in Indian Country: Crisis and Diversity
in Native American Communities* (Cambridge, 1995); Andrew R. L. Cayton and Fredrika J.
Teute, eds., *Contact Points: American Frontiers from the Mohawk Valley to the Mississippi,
1750–1830* (Chapel Hill, N,C., 1998). On opportunities for white people in the 1780s, see
Thomas P. Slaughter, *The Whiskey Rebellion: Frontier Epilogue to the American Revolution*
(Oxford, 1986); Alan Taylor, *Liberty Men and Great Proprietors: The Revolutionary Settlement on the Maine Frontier, 1760–1820* (Chapel Hill, N.C., 1990); Taylor, *William Cooper's
Town: Power and Persuasion on the Frontier of the Early American Republic* (New York,
1996).

62. Tomlins, *Law, Labor, and Ideology*, 34.

Customary Laws of Marriage

Legal Pluralism, Colonialism, and Narragansett Indian Identity in Eighteenth-Century Rhode Island

The law reflects a logic of literacy, of the historical archive rather than of changing collective memory. . . .

Indian life in Mashpee—something that was largely a set of "oral" relations, formed and reformed, remembered in new circumstances—had to be cast in permanent, "textual" form. The Indians on the stand had to convince a white Boston jury of their differences without conversation or—as happens in prac-tice—living nearby, struggling to work out who is who. The plaintiffs had to represent themselves through scripted exchanges with attorneys, statements for the record, proceedings witnessed, passively and objectively, by jury members with no right to enter, to ask, or to venture an opinion.

JAMES CLIFFORD, "Identity in Mashpee," *The Predicament of Culture*

I N OCTOBER 1766, prompted by the adultery of his wife Mary, Thomas Ninegret sued for divorce in Rhode Island's Superior Court of Judica-ture. At first glance, nothing seems unusual about this case. But the Ninegrets' situation was special. Mary Ninegret was described in court documents as a mulatto, whereas Thomas Ninegret was denoted as the *sachem* (political leader) of southern Rhode Island's Narragansett tribe. This group of perhaps a thousand Indians based in southern Rhode Island's Narragansett plantation country had survived the devastating King Philip's War of 1675–1676. They retained a large block of lands stretching across the

I thank colleagues at the 1995 Law and Society Association Summer Institute, the fellows in residence at the John Carter Brown Library (Spring 1996), Elinor Abbott, Sally Engle Merry, and Laurel Thatcher Ulrich for their support during the writing process. In public presentations of this work, I benefited from the comments of Kathleen M. Brown (IEAHC Annual Conference, Ann Arbor, Mich., June 1995), Michael Zuckerman ("The Many Legalities of Early America" conference, Williamsburg, November 1996), and members of the Huntington Library's American Legal History Research Seminar. Catherine Albanese, Trevor Burnard, Patricia Cohen, Eve Darian-Smith, Cornelia Dayton, Jonathan Glick-stein, Laura Kalman, Martha McNamara, John Majewski, Bruce Mann, and Christopher Tomlins, as well as James Horn and the two anonymous readers of this volume, offered thoughtful reactions to drafts. The research was supported by grants from the Phillips Fund of the American Philosophical Society and a National Endowment for the Human-

southern half of Rhode Island, which were controlled by the sachem.[1] Ninegret's position as the head of this prominent Indian family only fueled salacious gossip: when Mary's English lover, Benjamin Cross, saucily owned his adultery (he boasted that he had "had the Carnal Knowledge of her Body a hundred Times"), he described his partner not as "Mary," a specific woman; rather, it was the body of "the Indian King's Wife" that he had "known." In one blow, Cross linked the adultery both to Ninegret the cuckolded husband and to Ninegret the personification of Narragansett sovereignty.[2]

Of course, such jests and boasts carried political weight—Mary's adultery signaled Thomas Ninegret's obvious inability to control his own household, much less a sovereign nation, and Ninegret's opponents seized their opportunity to discredit the sachem. In 1768, Narragansetts included the marriage on a list of grievances against Ninegret. Along with his unprecedented alienation of tribal lands and his extravagant life-style, they complained that their ruler had wedded Mary "without the approbation of the tribe" and in violation of the customs attending sachems' marriages.[3]

What is most interesting here is not the divorce, which appears to have proceeded routinely. Rather, it is the way in which the "customs" surrounding sachems' marriages surfaced as an important issue. As historian John

---

ities residential research grant at the John Carter Brown Library, Brown University, Providence, Rhode Island.

This essay is reprinted, in different form, from Ann Marie Plane, *Colonial Intimacies: Indian Marriage in Early New England* (Ithaca, N.Y., 2000), chap. 6.

1. *T. Ninegret v M. Ninegret*, October 1766, Rhode Island Superior Court of Judicature, Newport, R.I. (hereafter cited as Newport, SCJ, Rhode Island), Supreme Court Judicial Records Center, Pawtucket, R.I. (hereafter cited as SCJRC). Some important modern works on Indians in New England after the war include Colin G. Calloway, ed., *After King Philip's War: Presence and Persistence in Indian New England* (Hanover, N.H., 1997); Daniel R. Mandell, *Behind the Frontier: Indians in Eighteenth-Century Eastern Massachusetts* (Lincoln, Nebr., 1996); Jean M. O'Brien, *Dispossession by Degrees: Indian Land and Identity in Natick, Massachusetts, 1650–1790* (New York, 1997); William S. Simmons, *Spirit of the New England Tribes: Indian History and Folklore, 1620–1984* (Hanover, N.H., 1986); population estimate from John Wood Sweet, "Bodies Politic: Colonialism, Race, and the Emergence of the American North—Rhode Island, 1730–1830," 2 vols. (Ph.D. thesis, Princeton University, 1995), I, 16.

2. Alexander Huling, deposition, October 1766, in *T. Ninegret v M. Ninegret*, Newport, SCJ, Rhode Island (SCJRC).

3. See Mary Beth Norton, *Founding Mothers and Fathers: Gendered Power and the Forming of American Society* (New York, 1996), 74–75; Petition of John Shattock to King George III, May 1768, cited in Sweet, "Bodies Politic," I, 79–82, esp. 80. On the larger opposition, see William S. Simmons, "Red Yankees: Narragansett Conversion in the Great Awakening," *American Ethnologist*, X (1983), 257–260, esp. 259. See also Paul R. Campbell and Glenn W. LaFantasie, "Scattered to the Winds of Heaven—Narragansett Indians, 1676–1880," *Rhode Island History*, XXXVII (1978), 72–74.

Wood Sweet notes, Thomas Ninegret certainly had flouted "tribal traditions of pedigree, communal assent, and public ceremony," all considered routine in marriages of "his father's generation."[4]

But, in fact, those very customs had themselves been defined through lengthy litigation, mostly over who would control Narragansett land reserves. During a series of eighteenth-century suits, Rhode Island's courts gathered testimony about Narragansett marital practices. Nothing in New England's seventeenth-century legal experience can compare to this eighteenth-century search for Narragansett "custom."[5] Witnesses, jurors, and judges engaged in an extended act of history-making, inventing and reinventing traditions of Narragansett "royal" marriage. The resulting written, statutelike customs—"invented traditions"—were then imagined to have determined legitimacy and succession in the past, replacing the actual negotiation and contestation of that past. The body of "customary law" that resulted eventually informed contemporary ethnographic writing.[6]

Such an elevation of custom into law has long been recognized as a hallmark of colonial legal systems in Africa and Asia, and such systems of customary law have been widely studied in nineteenth- and twentieth-century contexts. As Sally Engle Merry notes, most anthropologists accept that "customary law itself was a product of the colonial encounter" and that "the notion of an unchanging custom or even customary law was a myth of the colonial era." The Narragansett cases show that similar processes, heretofore unexamined, also occurred in the North American colonies.[7]

4. Sweet, "Bodies Politic," I, 80. Sweet notes that these traditions had been hotly contested.

5. I discuss this pluralistic seventeenth-century legal system in my book, *Colonial Intimacies: Indian Marriage in Early New England* (Ithaca, N.Y., 2000), esp. chap. 3. Missionaries established separate courts for Christianized Indians. This dual system developed an Indian magistracy that expanded to many other Indian towns after King Philip's War. See also Yasuhide Kawashima, *Puritan Justice and the Indian: White Man's Law in Massachusetts, 1630–1763* (Middletown, Conn., 1986).

6. See Terence Ranger, "The Invention of Tradition in Colonial Africa," in Eric Hobsbawm and Terence Ranger, eds., *The Invention of Tradition* (Cambridge, 1983), 211–262. Ranger argues that traditions regarding customary law, land rights, and political structure were created by Europeans and Africans together (237). Such innovations were most "far-reaching" when "Europeans believed themselves to be respecting age-old African customs" (250). In fact, "once the 'traditions' . . . were written down in court records . . . a new and unchanging body of tradition had been created" (251).

7. Sally Engle Merry reviews the anthropological literature on customary law in her essay "Legal Pluralism," *Law and Society Review*, XXII (1988), 869–892, esp. 869–870, 875. On customary law and marital disputes, see Martin Chanock, *Law, Custom, and Social Order: The Colonial Experience in Malawi and Zambia*, African Studies Ser., XLV (Cambridge, 1985), chaps. 8, 10, 11.

Anthropologists who have explored customary law in the later British Empire generally dismiss the American case as irrelevant—see, for example, Bernard S. Cohn, "Law and the

Because the English were the clear victors in the struggle with New England's indigenous peoples, their concern for the intricacies of Narragansett marital custom seems strange. Why, as late as the mid-eighteenth century, would they suddenly undertake the laborious task of translating, determining, and transcribing these Indian controversies? In general, English courts did not hear such matters. Indian marriage was part of a sovereign Indian realm, in which sachems, missionaries, or elders held more sway than English magistrates.[8] The answer may lie in the wider process of legal professionalization that marked the period. Several eighteenth-century cases involved testimony about sachems' lineages and marriages. The Narragansett country had seen at least one earlier investigation of custom "a Bout 30 or 40 years Past," when William Champlin, Sr., Joseph Hull, Captain John Hill, and Captain John Mason "Went into Connecticut Government and there got Evidences from the Sachems and Ancient Indians for to Prove Old Ninegret the Father to the late Charles Deced. [Ninegret II] Heir to his fathers Country." The "Evidences" were "Carried to a Cort of Enquiry Held at Capt. John Elderedges in Kings Town Wch Evidences prov'd [Ninegret II] to be the Eldest Son of his Father."[9] Even earlier, in the 1710s, the island of Chappaquiddick was engulfed in controversy over its sachem's legitimacy, prompting English courts at Edgartown and Plymouth to take testimony about seventeenth-century marriages. It was in this period too that the Uncas family, descendants of the ambitious Mohegan sachem who assumed leadership in eastern Connecticut after the Pequot War of 1636–1637, found itself embroiled in a long-running controversy between two pretenders to the Mohegan sachemship. However, although title disputes had provoked some collection of history and "custom" in the late seventeenth century, the notable Anglicization of the law and the increasing formality of eighteenth-century legal proceedings might have combined with a shortage of open

---

Colonial State in India," in June Starr and Jane F. Collier, eds., *History and Power in the Study of Law: New Directions in Legal Anthropology* (Ithaca, N.Y., 1989), 140–148. Cohn asserts that the indigenous people of British America "were quickly subjugated, relocated or decimated," and what " 'native' problem" remained required "little in the way of legal or administrative innovation" (131).

8. The English court records of Plymouth Colony, its successor counties in Massachusetts, and Rhode Island Colony reveal no instances when English courts intervened in disputes directly involving Indian marriages. The courts did recognize the validity of Indian marriages. For example, in one noted case from Plymouth in 1674, Robin, an Indian man, made a claim to lands "which he ought to have in right of his wife, the daughter of Napoietan"; cf. Nathaniel B. Shurtleff, *Records of the Colony of New Plymouth in New England*, 12 vols. (1854–1861; rpt., New York, 1968), V, 140 (hereafter *RCNP*).

9. William Champlin, deposition, Sept. 5, 1743, in *C. Ninegret v S. Clark*, action of appeal, September 1743, Newport, SCJ, Rhode Island (SCJRC). This might have been the challenge brought by Joseph Garrett, cousin to Ninegret II, in 1699; see Howard M. Chapin, *Sachems of the Narragansetts* (Providence, R.I., 1931), 94.

lands to ensure that customary law was written into the official record. Thus, the exploration of these cases has much to say about the evolution of customary law before the more heavily studied nineteenth century.[10]
The Narragansett cases also reveal that English law could shape Indian identities in colonial America. Eighteenth-century Narragansett customary law was used by different people to advance their own ends—by the English, who wanted to determine who legitimately held titles to tribal lands; by the different members of the Ninegret family, who sought to promote their own interests; by the Narragansett opposition, who used custom to build a case against the Ninegret family. The articulation of custom also reasserted Narragansett status as freeborn Indians in a society that increasingly associated native or African ancestry with enslavement. Customary law collection raises key questions for colonial historians about the formation of ethnic identity, the effects of colonialism, and the cultural diversity of early American marriage, as well as the role of law in shaping each of these.
Of course, Narragansett testimonies also force us to think about the nature of historical knowledge and historical texts in much the same way that anthropologists have reflected upon their relationship to ethnographic subjects.[11] The customs collected from Narragansett witnesses are often our only account of native practices, but they certainly cannot be treated naively as direct representations of that experience. The narratives of custom are found in highly structured depositions, shaped by English lawyers. One never really sees the eighteenth-century Narragansetts, only their reflection in court records. In this essay I listen carefully to the testimony of the many deponents; I try to reconstruct the marriages of the Ninegret sachems, and I

10. Cf. Ann Marie Plane, "Legitimacies, Indian Identities, and the Law: The Politics of Sex and the Creation of History in Colonial New England," *Law and Social Inquiry*, XXIII (1998), 55–77. See also F. M. Caulkins, *History of Norwich, Connecticut, from Its Settlement in 1660, to January 1845* (Norwich, Conn., 1845), 162–163; Plane, "Colonizing the Family: Marriage, Household, and Racial Boundaries in Southeastern New England to 1730" (Ph.D. diss., Brandeis University, 1995), 162–164. Early deeds sometimes recorded the seller's genealogy in order to prove that he (or she) could legitimately offer land for sale; see James Warren Springer, "American Indians and the Law of Real Property in Colonial New England," *American Journal of Legal History*, XXX (1986), 47.
On professionalization, see John M. Murrin, "The Legal Transformation: The Bench and Bar of Eighteenth-Century Massachusetts," in Stanley N. Katz and John M. Murrin, eds., *Colonial America: Essays in Politics and Social Development*, 3d ed. (New York, 1983), 550–553. See also Cornelia Hughes Dayton, "Turning Points and the Relevance of Colonial Legal History," *William and Mary Quarterly*, 3d Ser., L (1993), 9–11. On land, see Kenneth Lockridge, "Land, Population, and the Evolution of New England Society, 1630–1790," *Past and Present*, no. 39 (April 1968), 70–73.
11. Cf. James Clifford, "Introduction: Partial Truths," in James Clifford and George E. Marcus, eds., *Writing Culture: The Poetics and Politics of Ethnography* (Berkeley, Calif., 1986), 1–26. See also the discussion and critique of Clifford in Lila Abu-Lughod, *Writing Women's Worlds: Bedouin Stories* (Berkeley, Calif., 1993), 1–42, esp. 3–15.

describe the many cultural contexts that shaped these historical acts. In so doing, I show the ways in which the discourse of customary law proved enduring in ethnographic renderings of Narragansett culture—both those of the eighteenth century and of the twentieth century as well.

I. The Cases

The collection of marital customary law arose during a series of legal battles for control of the Narragansett lands.[12] At issue was the legitimacy of the potential successors to sachem Charles Ninegret, Sr. When Charles died in 1735, he had been living with a Narragansett woman named Kate, who had just borne him a son, Charles, Jr. Charles, Sr. also left a younger brother, George (who later fathered the cuckold Thomas). At first, power was shared between George and Kate, who acted on behalf of her son. But, by 1738, relations had broken down.[13] In 1742, George seized sole authority over tribal lands, and Kate sued—first attacking his tenant (Samuel Clark), then his guardian (Joseph Stanton), and then George himself. The courts upheld George's authority to sign leases and sell lands, but, upon his death in 1746, controversy arose again about who should succeed him—George's son (Thomas) or Kate's son (Charles, Jr.), each a minor represented by his mother. Another round of litigation followed, as Thomas Ninegret's mother, known as Sarah Queen, sued George Ninegret's guardians and tenants to secure her son's legitimacy—and won.[14]

The stakes were high. For either Kate Ninegret or Sarah Queen, hanging on to the sachemship for her son would bring financial security rare in a world where many Indian women and children lived in a constant state of debt-peonage or servitude. But for ordinary Narragansetts the struggle eventually forced the sale of crucial subsistence lands. In the 1740s the enthusiasm of the Great Awakening sparked a nativist-Christian movement that

12. I am especially indebted to John Sweet for alerting me to the existence of these cases several years ago and to Steven Grimes of the Supreme Judicial Court Records Center in Pawtucket for his assistance in using them. Although Sweet's dissertation does not discuss customary law, he does talk about the "false analogies" set up between "traditional customs" and "English alternatives." I argue that the apparent separation between these realms is itself illusory, for traditional customs could not exist without the English analogies. See Sweet, "Bodies Politic," I, chap. 1, esp. 60.

13. George's mother, grandmother, and great-aunts had turned against Kate, and two English guardians feared that Charles, Jr. would be murdered if George were not formally recognized as regent. See Joseph Stafford, deposition, August 1746, in *T. Ninegret v S. Clark*, August 1746, King's County Inferior Court of Common Pleas, Kingston, R.I. (hereafter cited as King's CCP) (SCJRC); see also order of General Assembly, May 1738, 17–19, in copy of *C. Ninegret v S. Clark*, February 1742/3, King's CCP, in file papers of *C. Ninegret v J. Stanton*, action of appeal, March 1743, Newport, SCJ, Rhode Island (SCJRC).

14. See, for example, jury bill, in *T. Ninegret v S. Clark*, August 1746, King's CCP (SCJRC).

served as the focus of native resistance to the rule of Thomas Ninegret and his English guardians. When Thomas Ninegret moved to take control of his lands at age twenty-one, the New Light minister Samuel Niles and other Narragansett leaders organized opposition to his rule. Charles, Jr. made a final bid to unseat his cousin in the 1750s but ultimately settled for a lump-sum payment in return for a quitclaim to native lands.[15] His title secured, Thomas Ninegret still had to face ruinous debts due to many creditors, including his lawyer, the local landowner Christopher Champlin. This situation provoked opposition among the nativist forces who would eventually complain of customary improprieties in his marriage to Mary, as part of their attempt to bring the Ninegret family's rule to an end.[16]

Customary law, first collected in the 1742 and 1743 cases between George Ninegret and Kate Ninegret, remained important in later actions. This essay focuses on evidence recorded early on, especially from the first two suits, because it was there that custom was initially invoked. These cases set the pattern for customary law collection in the forty-year controversy.[17] At least seventy people gave evidence in the various land actions, and many of these told their story in case after case; depositions from earlier actions were often admitted as evidence in the later ones as well. Even contemporaries found the paper trail tough to follow. At one point, the superior court clerk himself admitted confusion as to which documents belonged with which case. Accused by Charles, Jr. and his supporters of having neglected to make a copy of the court documents, Thomas Ward averred that "he had already given them a Coppy of the case as it was done by James Martin, the former Secretary," though "he had since discovered some papers in his Office that he verily thought belonged to sd Case."[18]

---

15. Simmons, "Red Yankees," *American Ethnologist*, X (1983), 259, 261–265; see also Campbell and LaFantasie, "Scattered to the Winds of Heaven," *Rhode Island History*, XXXVII (1978), 73; Sweet, "Bodies Politic," I, 60; Joseph Crandall, Esq., deposition, June 4, 1760, in Christopher Champlin Papers, box 9, Rhode Island Historical Society Archives, Providence, R.I. (hereafter cited as RIHS).

16. See Sweet, "Bodies Politic," I, 103–108. For a list of some of the money owed to Champlin, totaling several thousand pounds, see "The Estate of Thomas Ninegret . . . to Christopher Champlin" (1752–1757), in Champlin Papers, box 9, RIHS. By the 1770s and 1780s, the conflict would be influenced by the new antimonarchist models active on the larger Anglo-American scene, as mentioned in Sweet, "Bodies Politic," I, 18, 90.

17. The first action began in King's County Court of Common Pleas as *C. Ninegret v S. Clark*. Samuel Clark, a tenant whose lease had been issued by George Ninegret, was quickly replaced as defendant by Joseph Stanton, one of George Ninegret's English guardians. When an appeal to the superior court of judicature failed, Kate Ninegret and her lawyer, James Honyman, attacked George directly in *C. Ninegret v G. Ninegret*, February 1743, King's CCP (SCJRC).

In addition to Sweet's account, see Simmons, "Red Yankees," *American Ethnologist*, X (1983), 257–260; Campbell and LaFantasie, "Scattered to the Winds of Heaven," *Rhode Island History*, XXXVII (1978), 72–74; Chapin, *Sachems of the Narragansetts*, 96–103.

18. Charles Bardine alleged that Ward said this; see Charles Bardine, deposition, August

Such confusions only highlight the difficulty for historians trying to sort out this controversy centuries later. This essay first examines the structure of testimonies regarding customary law, and then the analysis turns to the structure of actual marital practices as reconstructed from the depositions, practices that included polygyny, divorce, and concubinage even as late as the 1730s. Next, it explores the racial and social context in which witnesses argued about the "traditional" Narragansett rules regarding "royal blood" and succession to the sachemship. "Custom," as defined in law, became closely linked to eighteenth-century understandings of Narragansett and, more generally, Indian culture. The dispute suggests the intricate connections between the traditional and the contemporary. The cases were an eloquent response by natives to their increasing impoverishment and racialization.

II. The Witnesses

The determination of customary law was important because common-law rules of succession differed from Narragansett leadership practices. Arguments about the marriages of Charles Ninegret, Sr. would not influence the later marital unions of his kinsmen, but they did determine who might legitimately succeed him. Thus, lawyers cited "custom" to bolster their clients' claims to office. Testimony offered in the Narragansett dispute is quite typical of customary law in other colonial settings. The oldest witnesses, usually but not always Indians, were the ones most often quizzed about Indian customs, giving histories of events that had occurred a generation or more earlier. Some events became the site of controversy and were told and retold in depositions; others were never in dispute.[19]

As always, attorneys for both plaintiffs and defendants were instrumental in shaping witnesses' testimony about tradition. Indeed, Narragansett customary law was heavily shaped by the English common-law tradition, which envisaged the law itself as a body of custom made into law through precedent.[20] Witnesses often hedged their bets by offering both "customary" and

1749, in *C. Ninegret v T. Ninegret*, c. 1747, King's CCP (SCJRC). The copy would have allowed Charles, Jr. to sue Thomas Ninegret for money he won in a 1746 legal victory.

19. In the 1743 cases, the issue of Kate Ninegret's lineage was hotly debated. Witnesses disagreed over her family's connection to other New England sachems or, in the idiom of the time, whether she had any royal blood. But among points of custom that were not controversial, all agreed that the presence of royal blood in both parental lines was essential for any sachem's heir (see discussion below).

20. Peter Fitzpatrick, *The Mythology of Modern Law*, Series in Sociology of Law and Crime, ed. Maureen Cain and Carol Smart (New York, 1992), 60–61. Fitzpatrick argues, however, that, through the work of commentators like Blackstone, common law is transformed from custom into positive law. He also traces to the Enlightenment the identifica-

"common-law" definitions of marriage. If the distant customs described by elderly Narragansetts seemed too untrustworthy, jurors might find a greater certainty in the demonstrable actions of the sachem. Thus, for example, witnesses were asked about the gifts that Charles Ninegret, Sr. had given to wife Betty Coyhees (shoe buckles and calico), debts that wives contracted on the sachem's account, whether the woman had tended him in sickness as a wife should, and whether Ninegret had taken her "abroad" with him and "would bring her Home again."[21] The final proof, as in any intestate death, might be found in showing whom the sachem had "owned" as wife and son in his lifetime and who retained his goods when he died (Kate's partisans favored this line of argument).[22] By the time that Thomas Ninegret became the sachem, his lawyer was arguing that he had inherited the sachemship and the sachem's estate both according to Narragansett custom and "accord[ing] to the Course of the Common Law."[23] As these examples show, English and Narragansett practices of marriage came together in a fertile mixture. Because of this hybridity, it is important to explore the shape of these problematic testimonies before analyzing their content.

Thompson

The 1743 testimony of an old Indian man known by the single name of Thompson was the first deposition among the file papers of the first action. He was apparently the lead witness in Kate Ninegret's challenge to her

---

tion of custom "with the savage and with those small-scale remnants of a recalcitrant past yet to be transformed in modernity." "It is produced by implacable habit and is everything that the reasoned will is not" (60).

21. Joseph Clark, deposition, Sept. 5, 1743, in *C. Ninegret v S. Clark*, September 1743, Newport, SCJ, Rhode Island (SCJRC). When Charles Ninegret, Sr. asked Enoch Kinyon's wife to "Give him Sumthing To Take" in an illness, both Kinyons went to his wigwam and there saw Betty Coyhees "Tend him as his Wife." Also, Kinyon reported that he "often heard the Indians say that they was Marr[i]ed." Enoch Kinyon, deposition, ibid. On Ninegret's taking her abroad, see Sam Niles, deposition, August 1743, in *C. Ninegret v S. Clark*, August 1743, King's CCP, in file papers of *C. Ninegret v J. Stanton*, March 1742/3, Newport, SCJ, Rhode Island (SCJRC), 61.

22. Numerous witnesses made this claim. For example, see John Harrey, deposition, in *C. Ninegret v S. Clark*, September 1743, Newport, SCJ, Rhode Island (SCJRC). In the late 1740s, proponents of Charles, Jr., introduced into evidence copies of the written will of Ninegret II (father of Charles, Sr.), dated Mar. 15, 1716, along with depositions from the English witnesses to the will. This document, following English models, mentioned only one wife (the mother of Charles and George) and clearly spelled out that Charles, Sr. was to inherit, whereas George was to receive only a lump-sum payment and control of a smaller portion of land. See will of Ninegret, Mar. 15, 1716/7, copied from the original, Feb. 3, 1747, in *C. Ninegret v T. Ninegret*, c. 1747, King's CCP (SCJRC).

23. Thomas Ninegret, complaint, August 1746, in *T. Ninegret v S. Clark*, King's CCP (SCJRC).

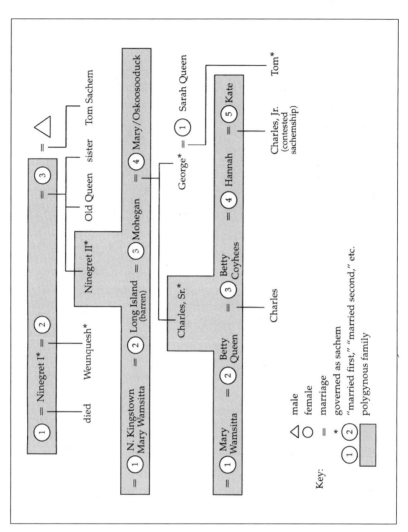

FIGURE 1. Ninegret Genealogy. *Drawn by Stinely Associates*

brother-in-law's authority.[24] Although this text is written as a narrative, the phrasing suggests that it was produced through dialogue; many of Thompson's statements appear to be responses to questioning, presumably by a judge or a lawyer and probably by a translator as well. His testimony typifies the collection of customary law throughout the Narragansett controversy.[25]

The deposition had at least three parts. In the first, Thompson vigorously attacked the idea that an earlier wife of Charles Ninegret, Betty Coyhees, might have produced an heir. He denied that the sachem had ever "kept House together" with Coyhees, and he claimed, with stronger emphasis than grammar, "nor he never heard they were married together." Betty's son, Thompson said, was commonly "called a Bastard among the Indians."[26] Thompson asserted the authority of his recollections by noting that he had "lived several years with the said Sachem Charles near abo[u]t the Time the said Charles the son of Bettey was born."[27]

Thompson drew upon memory to set the record straight about the sachems' marriages. He recalled that "old Ninegret" (Ninegret II, father of Charles Ninegret, Sr.) had several wives "about the time that Charles and George his Sons were born." He listed three: "Mary the Daughter of Wamsitter the Black Sachem," "one from long Island of the royal Blood," and "one from Stonington [Connecticut] of the royal Blood [Oskoosooduck, also known as Mary] who was Mother to Charles the late sachem and his Brother George." When pressed, Thompson acknowledged that Old Ninegret had practiced polygamy, as Mary Wamsitta his "first wife was alive and lived with the said Ninegret after Charles and George were born [to a later wife]." Thompson then strengthened his words by appealing to "custom"; he asserted that "according to the Indians Customs their Sachems might have as many wives as they would" (see Fig. 1).[28]

Having established a precedent (Old Ninegret's example) and a rule (the appeal to custom), Thompson sketched a marital history for Charles Nine-

24. It was the first deposition copied into the complete case record presented to the superior court.

25. Thompson, deposition, in *C. Ninegret v S. Clark,* copy in *C. Ninegret v J. Stanton,* March 1742/3, Newport, SCJ, Rhode Island (SCJRC), 24–28. Because many Narragansetts still did not speak English in the 1740s, George Babcock, a prominent local resident and culture broker in many legal actions, often interpreted for the court. See case summary, ibid., 68–69; summons of George Babcock, Aug. 7, 1746, in *T. Ninegret v S. Clark,* August 1746, King's CCP (SCJRC).

26. The son was described as "now . . . a Servant to Mr. George Babcock" (the translator for the court); see Thompson, deposition, in *C. Ninegret v S. Clark,* copy in *C. Ninegret v J. Stanton,* March 1742/3, Newport, SCJ, Rhode Island (SCJRC), 25. Thompson had also heard that the sachem had beaten Toby Coyhees, Betty's father, "for saying the said Bettey's Child was the said Charles's."

27. Ibid.

28. Ibid., 25–26.

gret, Sr. According to his deposition, Charles was "first married to one of wamsitters Cousins of the royal Blood who died soon after, and afterwards married to one of Tom Sachems Daughters named Bettey." Thompson claimed legitimacy for this match by noting that the marriage "was according to the Custom of the Indians by paying a dowry"; he also acknowledged, by implication, that Charles had been married to Kate.[29]

Finally, in response to questioning, Thompson laid out a list of customs that, in his memory, governed the relationship between the tribe and their sachem. The first seven looked like this:

The tribe could depose a sachem who was too arbitrary or tyrannical;

if there were several of the same degree of "royal blood," the tribe had always chosen the eldest child to be sachem, preferring males over females;

the tribe might finally determine any dispute about the sachemship "by appointing or Choosing a Sachem";

in earlier times, the tribe would "appoint out of the royall Blood who the Sachem should marry but latterly they have lost that";

there was no instance of "a real marriage according to the Custom of the Indians" between a sachem and any who were not "of the royal Family";

it was, however, "common for Sachems to have Wives from among the common Indians," but the children of such unions could not hope to succeed their father;

no elder son had ever been "put by" in favor of "a Younger Brother or remote Relation."

The beauty of this list lay in its seeming objectivity—it read like a catalogue of unalterable rules.[30] But two final items anchored these abstract laws to the current controversy. First, Thompson claimed that Kate, the last wife of Charles Ninegret, Sr. was "of the royal Blood at Block Island," because he "knew her Father and Grand Father." Second, in response to a final question, he noted that "the Sachems might marry a Wife out of any forreign tribe provided she be of the royal Blood." In other words, Thompson meant that the marriage between Charles Ninegret, Sr. and Kate was valid, and their child was of blood sufficiently royal to enable him to rule.[31]

Other deponents followed the old man. One by one, they told their sto-

29. Ibid., 26.
30. Ibid., 26–27.
31. This addendum was also signed with a mark (ibid., 28).

ries, mainly eyewitness accounts and recollections. Their repeated testimony, sometimes rendered in a question-and-answer format by the court
clerk, embellished the stories and elaborated themes. The motifs of Thompson's testimony gained prominence through repetition: had Betty Coyhees
ever really married Charles? Was Kate of the royal blood at Block Island?
Each deposition helped to build the collective historical narrative, painstak-
ingly shaping the events of everyday life into legal evidence as "custom."
Thompson served as the group's historian: when James Robin also testified
that Kate was "of the Blood royal at Block Island," he admitted under questioning that "he had his Knowledge from old Thompson." Another deponent, named John Thompson (who might have been the son of the old
man), said that he could not remember who had told him Kate was connected to the Block Island sachems, but "he has heard so ever since he can
remember." Another strong supporter of Kate, Sam Puckhee, reported that
his information about her lineage came from "two old Indians that are now
dead."[32] The attorneys seem to have challenged each man about his knowledge of Kate's ancestry, but the men's vagueness, instead of weakening their
case, might have cloaked their claims in the aura of tradition, ancient knowledge, and collective memory.

When the witnesses were pressed, though, more prosaic links emerged.
Dorothy Sneahew, after describing the marriage of Kate and Charles in
detail, later revealed under questioning that she was Kate's sister. It turned
out that James Robin "lived with Samuel Clark" (as a laborer or tenant),
whose lease was itself the main point at issue in the suit.[33] And, in response
to a final question, John Thompson acknowledged that "Catharine [Kate] is
Aunt to this Deponant." Did this make the older Thompson a close kinsman
of Kate as well? What weight, then, would the court give to his critical
testimony about her royal blood? At least one spectator of the 1743 trial was
suspicious and asked "that ould Indian Tomson . . . what Made him tell such
a big lie," that "Cate was [kin] to the high Blood at Block Island[?]" Thompson attempted to curtail further questions by answering stoutly that he had
"herd so, and was Bid to say so."[34]

32. James Robin, deposition, June 17, 1742, in court [August 1743], ibid., 36–39; John
Thompson, deposition, Sam Puckhee, Jr., deposition, August 1743, ibid., 40, 42.

33. Dorothy Sneahew, deposition, ibid., 29; Tacy Saunders, deposition, Sept. 2, 1746,
King's CCP, in Champlin Papers, box 9, folder labeled "Indian Deeds (Depositions) 1746,"
RIHS. In listing the men at the coronation of Charles Ninegret, Jr., Saunders included
"James Robins who lives with Samuel Clark Esq., the original Deft. sued in the Case." The
other men present were Sam Puckhee and Kate's "two Sons" (49).

34. John Thompson, deposition, August 1743, in C. Ninegret v S. Clark, copy in C. Ninegret v J. Stanton, March 1742/3, Newport, SCJ, Rhode Island (SCJRC), 41; Sarah Sampson,
deposition, Sept. 5, 1743, in C. Ninegret v S. Clark, action of appeal, September 1743,
Newport, SCJ, Rhode Island (SCJRC).

Wootoniske

The defense introduced its own version of custom and history, a version that followed Thompson's in all but a few respects. Wootoniske, sister to Ninegret II, was its lead witness. She too offered history; she too draped the weight of oral tradition around her testimony, saying that she had her understanding of royal blood "from her Mother"; and she too outlined a history of succession, the rules governing marriage, and the rituals carried out at coronations and weddings. Like Thompson, she stressed that all the wives of Ninegret II had been "of the Blood royall."[35]

Wootoniske differed from Thompson in one key area. Her account of Charles Ninegret's marriages distinguished between different types of marriage: those that involved a dowry and tribal consent, and those that did not.[36] She testified that there had been neither dowry paid nor tribal consent obtained when Charles married Betty Coyhees and, later, Kate, two wives who had borne him sons. In Wootoniske's view, then, neither marriage was of the right type or with the right woman to produce the next sachem.

For whatever reasons, perhaps aided by Wootoniske's testimony, the defense carried the day, for the English jurors found in favor of George Ninegret and the defendants, both in an initial verdict and upon appeal. The legal rulings against Kate and Charles Ninegret, Jr. allowed George Ninegret and his son Thomas to exercise the authority of sachem, although Kate would continue to challenge their legitimacy.[37] Thompson's and Wootoniske's testimony, however, had laid out the main lines along which subsequent battles would rage.

35. Wootoniske, deposition, August 1743, in *C. Ninegret v S. Clark,* copy in *C. Ninegret v J. Stanton,* March 1742/3, Newport, SCJ, Rhode Island (SCJRC), 53–57.

36. Ibid., 56–57. She noted that, when Charles married Betty Queen, the daughter of Tom Sachem, "a Dowry [was] paid according to Custom." But, although she thought that Charles, Sr. "took Bettey Cawheese to Wife and had a Child by her," she said he did not pay "any Dowry for her," and "he took sd Bettey of his own Mind and not by the Consent of the Tribe." Such consent, according to all the deponents, would have been indicated by the collective offering of bridewealth from Charles Ninegret to Toby Coyhees, Betty's father. Likewise, she testified that "she supposes that Charles was married to Catharine, but it was not with the Consent of the Tribe and that there was no Dowry paid according to their Custom. . . . That none of the Tribe consented to . . . [this] marriage except [perhaps] Catharine's Relations."

37. The defense also submitted additional custom and history in a combined deposition made in November of 1742 by Sompauwat (a man aged seventy-three), Konckemotousow (a woman aged seventy-five), and the Old Queen (aged seventy-two, sister to Ninegret II); see their testimony in *C. Ninegret v S. Clark,* February 1742/3, 17, 25, 26, 34, 35, copy in *C. Ninegret v J. Stanton,* March 1742/3, Newport, SCJ, Rhode Island (SCJRC), 49–51.

III. Marriage and Its Uses

These legal documents offer stunningly intimate descriptions of marriage ceremonies between eighteenth-century sachems and the women they married:

[They] set together on a Mat on the Ground in order to Be Marr[i]ed . . . and We saw the old indianes Stand By them and Talk to them."

And after they was married the Indians built the sd Sachem a Wigwam and . . . [I] hath often Times seen them lodge together as man and wife.

Q. was there any Dowry (as the Indians call it) Given?
A. yes Amongst the rest I gave some.[38]

Such descriptions hint at diverse practices heretofore unexplored in studies of early American marriage. Can Narragansett social practice be reconstructed from these highly compromised texts?[39]

In documenting the unions of Charles Ninegret, Sr., of his brother George, and of their father Ninegret II, the court inadvertently recorded some of the best surviving evidence of polygyny (one husband/multiple wives) and endogamy (in-group marriage) among the Narragansett elite, as well as different types of marriages, and the lengthy processes that produced nearly all marriages in this indigenous society even after several generations of English colonization.

The fact that each of Charles Ninegret's wives had a different experience of marriage reveals a great deal about the continuum of practices available to Narragansetts, particularly to the Narragansett elite. One way to make sense of the various marriages that the witnesses described is to look at what each type did for Charles Ninegret, his wives, and, more generally, Narragansett sociopolitical arrangements.[40] For the Narragansetts, as Wootoniske sug-

---

38. Christopher Champlin and Hannah Champlin, deposition, Sept. 5, 1743, in *C. Ninegret v S. Clark*, action of appeal, September 1743, Newport, SCJ, Rhode Island (SCJRC); Joseph Coyhes, deposition, November 1742, in *C. Ninegret v S. Clark*, copy in *C. Ninegret v J. Stanton*, March 1742/3, Newport, SCJ, Rhode Island (SCJRC), 63; James Niles, deposition, August 1746, in *T. Ninegret v S. Clark*, August 1746, King's CCP (SCJRC).

39. Pluralistic marital practices have been recognized among the colonists, of course. For example, ordinary people sometimes divorced themselves, through desertion or by renunciations either written or spoken; see Dayton, *Women before the Bar: Gender, Law, and Society in Connecticut, 1639–1789* (Chapel Hill, N.C., 1995), 116–117.

40. This reading accepts longtime anthropological insights about the functions of marriage. See Laura Bohannan's classic functionalist study, which categorizes different types of marriage in terms of whether they transfer jural rights through the payment of

gested, not every "lawful" wife of a sachem would become a queen. Yet Ninegret's marriages had a logic of their own that it is important to recuperate from the obscuring effects of colonialism, whose influence is visible in the promiscuous abandon with which English and native practices combined in these unions.

Mary Wamsitta

Charles Ninegret seems to have taken his first wife, Mary Wamsitta, soon after he became sachem. She might even have been his own stepmother, the first wife of his father, still living with Ninegret II when that sachem died.[41] This marriage was approved by tribal members, who collected the "dowry" (bridewealth) that the sachem then gave to his bride's family. A marriage to his father's widow (or even her close kin) could have secured his legitimacy as his father's heir: he would literally have taken his father's place. The practice of marrying a predecessor's widow might have been echoed at Charles's death, when Kate stayed on in the Ninegrets' English-style house with her brother-in-law, George, the newly crowned sachem. Although a man's marriage to his brother's widow might offend English sensibilities about incest, in the context of Narragansett royal endogamy, such a marriage might have been regarded with favor, as signaling a continuity of leadership.[42] At the very least, Kate's sharing the sachem's house symbolized the

---

goods and services (bridewealth) by the husband's lineage to the bride's; see "Dahomean Marriage: A Revaluation," *Africa*, XIX (1949), 273.

41. Deponents could not agree about her: Sarah Tom said she was "one of Wamsetter's Daughters" (33); James Robins said Charles married "Mary the daughter of Wamsitter" (39). Thompson claimed that Charles Ninegret married "one of Wamsitters Cousins," whereas Ninegret II married Mary Wamsitter, the daughter of Wamsitter the Black Sachem (25, 26); Wootoniske said that Ninegret II's first wife was a "Squaw from North Kingstown" (55); all in *C. Ninegret v S. Clark*, February 1742/3, copy in *C. Ninegret v J. Stanton*, March 1742/3, Newport, SCJ, Rhode Island (SCJRC). The early-twentieth-century historian Howard M. Chapin identifies Charles Ninegret's wife Mary as a probable niece to the first wife of Ninegret II (*Sachems of the Narragansetts*, 94, 96); there are, however, many documented examples of such marriages to close kin in Narragansett, Niantic, and other New England Indian genealogies, including one marriage between an aunt and a nephew; see William Burton and Richard Lowenthal, "The First of the Mohegans," *American Ethnologist*, I (1974), 595.

42. In 1691, Samuel Sewall recorded that "the marriage of Hanna Owen with her Husband's Brother is declar'd null by the Court of Assistants," and Owen was punished (Dec. 25, 1691, in M. Halsey Thomas, ed., *The Diary of Samuel Sewall, 1674–1729* [New York, 1973], I, 285). The 1656 Rhode Island incest statutes prohibited marriages "to the degrees prohibited by the laws of England"; see John Russell Bartlett, ed., *Records of the Colony of Rhode Island and Providence Plantations in New England* (1636–1663; Providence, 1859), I, 334.

Writing in the 1930s, Chapin reports that people were scandalized by George's living with the "Queen Dowager." As there is no discussion of this in the period documents, the

union of interests between George Ninegret and his dead brother's heir. Some seventeenth-century sachemships were in fact shared between two leaders, one senior and one junior, often an uncle and nephew. This practice faded in the eighteenth century as native sachemships began to conform more closely to English monarchies.[43]

Betty Queen, the Daughter of Tom Sachem

According to different reports, either Charles separated from Mary Wamsitta or she died. In any case, this marriage never became controversial; sometimes the witnesses even forgot to mention it. In 1728, Charles Ninegret married again. Joseph Coyhes remembered that, near planting time, he was "invited" to a wedding between Charles and Betty, "publick Notice being given of a Marriage." Joseph recalled that the whole tribe was "Consulted with Concerning the Marriage and they all agreed to [it]." Someone made "a gathering among the Indians and they gave Money [bridewealth] to the said Sachem in all a Considerable sum as the manner and Custom is when a Sachem marries in order for him to bestow on his Wifes Parents or Friends." Then the two were married "according to the Custom of the Indians Marrying." Betty was only fourteen years old. Afterward, the tribe "built the said Sachem a Wigwam," where the pair lived for "near about half a year." Coyhes was a frequent visitor and therefore could confidently claim that he had "often Times seen them Lodge together as Man and Wife."[44]

Betty was a close cousin to her new husband.[45] In marrying her, Charles made his own contribution to the intricate endogamous networks of relatives that lay at the foundation of the political life of southern New England's Indians. Genealogy alone was never sufficient to assure the sachemship; contenders had to build a following. In-marriage meant that there were always several potential candidates of suitable family connections in any given community; it also discouraged competition among them by forging alliances between royal factions. Over time, endogamy consolidated an elite group who, after Europeans arrived, were described as being of "high" or

---

"scandal" might have been more important to later Victorian historians (Chapin, *Sachems of the Narragansetts*, 98).

43. Narragansetts might have understood George's "regency" for the child, Charles, Jr., in such terms; cf. Neal Salisbury, *Manitou and Providence: Indians, Europeans, and the Making of New England, 1500–1643* (New York, 1982), 147–148, on power sharing between the seventeenth-century Narragansett sachems Canonicus and Miantonomo; see also Burton and Lowenthal, "First of the Mohegans," *American Ethnologist*, I (1974), 595.

44. Joseph Coyhes, deposition, Nov. 17, 1742, in *C. Ninegret v S. Clark*, February 1742/3, copy in *C. Ninegret v J. Stanton*, March 1742/3, Newport, SCJ, Rhode Island (SCJRC), 62–63. Whether Joseph Coyhes was related to Betty Coyhees is uncertain.

45. Her father, Tom Sachem, and Ninegret II were half-brothers, sharing the same mother.

"royal" blood. Special rituals such as the collection of bridewealth from the tribe accompanied marriages among this group, potentially fitting the children of such matches for the sachemship.[46]

If formal marriages could occur only between individuals drawn from the elite (those of royal blood), then suitors like Charles Ninegret would sometimes have had to go courting outside their own nation. When asked "whether the Marriage of the Sachems with those of the Royal Blood (so called) was confin'd to their own Tribe or not," one witness answered, "When they had none of their own they fetch'd them from other Tribes." This royal exogamy (out-marriage) forged larger regional links, above the level of the village and tribe.[47] Read in this light, Charles Ninegret's marriage to Mary Wamsitta, kin to the "Black Sachem," takes on a new meaning, because it assured a continued alliance between Ninegret's and Wamsitta's people.[48] The second marriage, to his cousin Betty Queen, solidified relationships within the Narragansett royal family, a link that was further strengthened when Charles's brother George Ninegret later married another daughter of Tom Sachem, Sarah Queen.[49]

Betty, Daughter of Toby Coyhees

Charles Ninegret's remaining unions were different, revealing the ways in which marriage might link the royal family to more ordinary Narragansetts. Witnesses testified that Charles formed at least two and possibly three important attachments between 1730 and 1735. One of his councillors, Sam Niles, remembered that he helped Charles to negotiate his marriage with Toby Coyhees's widowed daughter, Betty. According to some accounts,

46. Among the closely related Mohegan peoples, multiple kinship connections created a tangle of relationships that allowed an ambitious individual to reconfigure genealogy and claim lineal rights (Burton and Lowenthal, "First of the Mohegans," *American Ethnologist,* I [1974], 595). The negotiation inherent in apparently fixed genealogical reckoning is noted in John L. Comaroff and Simon Roberts, *Rules and Processes: The Cultural Logic of Dispute in an African Context* (Chicago, 1981), 39–41. On the Europeans' descriptions of native endogamy, see Kathleen J. Bragdon, *Native People of Southern New England, 1500–1650* (Norman, Okla., 1996), 140–143, 158–161.

47. Samuel Niles, Jr., deposition, August 1746, in *T. Ninegret v S. Clark,* August 1746, King's CCP (SCJRC); cf. Eric S. Johnson, "Allies, Enemies, and In-Laws: The Politics of Marriage and Alliance in Seventeenth-Century Native Southern New England," paper presented to the Society for American Archaeology, 56th Annual Meeting, New Orleans, La., April 1991, 11.

48. Chapin says that Wamsitta was "the 'black sachem' who lived near Wickford [R.I.]" (*Sachems of the Narragansetts,* 94), a different person from Wamsutta, the son of Massasoit and older brother of Metacom (King Philip), who was active in the 1660s in the Pokanoket homelands; see *RCNP,* III, 192.

49. Sarah Queen was also known as Sarah Ninegret, Sarah George, and, upon remarriage, Sarah Anthony.

Charles was already living with Betty when the negotiations began. With Toby's consent obtained, Charles dispatched Niles to get some rum from John Hill's house. Then the pair "took each other to be Husband and Wife according to the Custom of the Indians in the Presence of all the Indians that were there and before her [Father] Tobey Cawheese who was one of the Indians Justices." During their time together, Charles gave her gifts ("a Calico Gown, a Silk Bonnet, a Pair of Silver Shoe Buckles, and many other Things"), "and when he went abroad he often carried her with him and would bring her Home again." The use of an Indian justice and the mention of English trinkets both signal the hybridity that defined eighteenth-century Narragansett marriages.[50]

Handsome Hannah

Eventually, Charles and Betty Coyhees parted, for, when a "mulatto" neighbor, Rose Sash, next saw Charles, he brought with him another woman, known to the community as "Handsome Hannah." When Sash inquired "Why he had Not Brought his Wife with him to See us," Charles replied, "Here I have Brought Hannah." Handsome Hannah might have enticed Charles with her charms or, as one Englishman claimed, by her promise to keep him in the English style. As Enoch Kinyon reported, Hannah convinced Charles that Betty Coyhees "Did Not Keep him Clean and Did Not Under Stand how to Live in a English hous and if hee Would Leave the aforesd Bettey, the sd Hannah Would Keep his hous and Live with him." Hannah bore Charles at least one son, although, of all five women involved with the sachem, she alone never seems to have married him. A few deponents referred to her as his wife, but she herself claimed only to have lived with the sachem.[51]

Kate

Handsome Hannah herself remembered that, "after I left [Charles], I Left Kate with him but [whether] they was Marryed or Not I Dont Know." A number of witnesses said they saw Kate and Charles married by Jo Cheets, whom they called "the Indian justice." Kate's sister, Dorothy Sneahew, claimed that "the said Justice made Proclamation among the Indians that the said Sachem

50. Sam Niles, deposition, James Niles, deposition, August 1743, in *C. Ninegret v S. Clark*, copy in *C. Ninegret v J. Stanton*, March 1742/3, Newport, SCJ, Rhode Island (SCJRC), 57–59, 60, 61.

51. Rose Sash, deposition, Enoch Kinyon, deposition, Handsome Hannah, deposition, Sept. 5, 1743, all in *C. Ninegret v S. Clark*, action of appeal, September 1743, Newport, SCJ, Rhode Island (SCJRC).

was married according to their Custom, which Marriage . . . was partly
according to the Indian and partly according to the English Custom."[52]

Charles Ninegret's marriages exhibited a striking diversity of function and
purpose. All agreed that the first two—to Mary Wamsitta and Betty Queen—
fulfilled the community's definition of a royal marriage. Charles's relationship with Handsome Hannah was equally unproblematic; although a few
witnesses called her his wife, most seemed to recognize that their union had
been both entered into and ended without public ceremony and was not
thought to be a formal marriage. Perhaps it never became controversial
because no claim to sachemship was made for Hannah's children. But the
arranged union with Betty Coyhees and the union with Kate became the
focus of intense dispute among deponents giving customary law testimony
in 1743, including Thompson and Wootoniske. And, in each dispute, some
hybrid ceremony was claimed to have solemnized these unions of partners
who were already living together. Indeed, each bride was already "big with
child" when the ceremony took place.[53] The emphasis of the court on marriage as defined by a ceremony contravenes the importance of the much
longer processes that might have defined Narragansett marriages.[54] Wootoniske's testimony reveals the impoverishment of English legal definitions
of marriage, in which one might only be married or not.[55] She argued that,
although Charles might have indeed married Betty Coyhees and Kate, he
never did so by a path that would allow any of their children to inherit the
sachemship.

52. Handsome Hannah, deposition, ibid.; Dorothy Sneahew, deposition, in *C. Ninegret
v S. Clark,* February 1742/3, copy in *C. Ninegret v J. Stanton,* March 1742/3, Newport, SCJ,
Rhode Island (SCJRC), 28–29; others include the deposition of James Robin, June 17, 1742,
in court [August 1743], ibid., 36–39.

53. For example, in James Niles, deposition, 1743 (speaking of Betty Coyhees), in
C. Ninegret v S. Clark, February 1742/3, copy in *C. Ninegret v J. Stanton,* March 1742/3,
Newport, SCJ, Rhode Island (SCJRC), 58. John Harrey said that Kate had a child "a Little
After sd Wedding." See deposition of John Harrey, Sept. 5, 1743, in *C. Ninegret v S. Clark,*
action of appeal, September 1743, Newport, SCJ, Rhode Island (SCJRC). Charles told
William and Experience Bassett, "My wife Cate was Bigg before I was married to her"
(William and Experience Bassett, deposition, ibid.).

54. Such a "processual character of marriage" is well known to ethnographers; see, for
example, Comaroff and Roberts, *Rules and Processes,* 67, which describes marriages that
are finalized by bridewealth payments only when the union's grown children want to
marry. They write: "The definition of everyday unions is intrinsically ambiguous and
negotiable for much of their duration. . . . A union, if it lasts, ultimately *becomes* a
marriage when, with the removal of ambiguity [through payments], its sociopolitical
content is determined."

55. Notable exceptions to this statement would be those fornication presentments in
which English men and women received lesser sentences for being under contract, but not
fully married, or the rare divorces of bed and board.

These five unions offer us a glimpse of the considerable pluralism of marriage in colonial New England. Different sets of rights were transferred
through a sachem's marriage with the consent of the tribe and the payment
of "dowry" than were conferred by marriages unmarked by such formal,
customary rituals. The legal documents that reveal this complexity, however,
are products of English legal idioms of lawful ceremony and divorce—
idioms that obscure the polygynous undertones of Charles Ninegret's many
marriages.

IV. "Of the Most Royal Blood"

The "customs" collected by eighteenth-century lawyers required that, for a
sachem's marriage to produce a legitimate heir, not only must certain rituals
be performed but the sachem's partner must also be of "the royal blood."
Even in the seventeenth century, English observers had used that phrase to
describe the elite classes of New England's indigenous society. In 1695, Matthew Mayhew recorded the observation that bloodlines, rather than birth
order, were most important in determining a sachem's heir, "the Blood
Royal, being in such Veneration among this People, that if a Prince had issue
by divers Wives, such Succeeded as Heir who was Royally descended, by the
Mother, although the Youngest."[56] Kate's lineage thus became a central issue
in the earliest court hearings as her opponents launched a full-scale attack
on her pretensions to nobility.

But royal blood had taken on new significance by the mid-eighteenth century—after a full century of slavery, the introduction of African labor to the
region, and the development of new conceptions of race, so the controversy
surrounding Kate's claims to nobility must be grounded in the social complexity of its time.[57] In fact, one must look well beyond the courtroom and
its exposition of apparent custom. In the colonial world, Indian marriages
could no longer be defined without reference to English ones; Narragansett
sachems could no longer function without reference to English kings; and
Narragansett identities could no longer be forged without reference to the
nascent racial ideologies and ethnic complexities of southern Rhode Island.

Although Thompson and others testified to Kate's royal blood, several
witnesses refuted these claims. Jenny Chaugum thought that Handsome

56. Matthew Mayhew, *The Conquests and Triumphs of Grace: Being a Brief Narrative of
the Success Which the Gospel Hath Had among the INDIANS of Martha's Vineyard (and the
Places Adjacent) in New-England . . .* (London, 1695), 14.
57. John Comaroff and Jean Comaroff argue for historical ethnography that grounds
"subjective, culturally configured action in society and history"; see *Ethnography and the
Historical Imagination,* Studies in the Ethnographic Imagination (Boulder, Colo., 1992),
11.

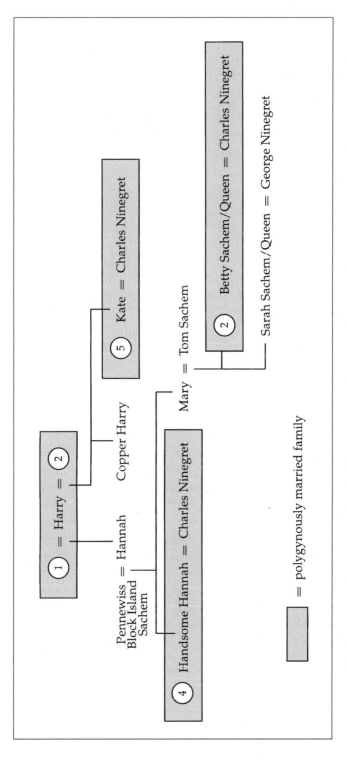

FIGURE 2. Kate Ninegret's Claim to Royal Blood. *This is a patri-centered genealogy that was confirmed in the testimony of Cogemetasco, an elderly Narragansett woman. See the deposition of Copper Harry and the deposition of Cogemetasco, both taken Sept. 2, 1743, before William Clark, both in C. Ninegret v. S. Clark, action of appeal, Newport, SCJ, Rhode Island (SCJRC), file papers. Drawn by Stinely Associates*

Hannah was connected by birth to the sachems of Block Island, but that Kate was "not of the royal Blood nor never reputed to be . . . or any ways akin to the royal Blood." Chaugum "was acquainted with [Kate's] Ancestors . . . [but] they were not any Ways related to the royal Family as ever She heard of." "Copper Harry," who described himself as Kate's brother, also testified against her, offering a detailed lineage—later corroborated by another witness—that showed only tenuous links to the royal blood.[58] This genealogy revealed that Kate was in fact connected to Pennewiss, the Block Island sachem, through marriage (see Fig. 2), but there is some evidence that Narragansetts reckoned kinship through matrilineal descent. If so, then Kate would have had no link by either birth or marriage to Pennewiss, just as Jenny Chaugum had asserted (see Fig. 3).[59] Here, then, is a clear case in which English observers might interpret certain genealogical claims as valid, yet Narragansetts would perhaps see no link at all. The disjuncture might have allowed enterprising plaintiffs such as Kate to make a claim that seemed plausible in an English court, even though it would have seemed ridiculous according to Narragansett practice.

Kate's claims to royal blood did not take on such importance solely because of some timeless custom. Rather, one can here glimpse the social realities of the world in which Narragansetts lived. Benjamin Cross boasted to his compatriots that he had "played with" the Indian sachem by "playing with" Thomas Ninegret's mulatto wife, at once asserting political, racial, and

58. Jenny Chaugum, deposition, August 1743, in *C. Ninegret v S. Clark*, February 1742/3, copy in *C. Ninegret v J. Stanton*, March 1742/3, Newport, SCJ, Rhode Island (SCJRC), 48–49, esp. 48. Copper Harry was a member of the young Thomas Ninegret's council and therefore a strong partisan of George (complaint of Sarah Ninegret et al. to the General Assembly, Aug. 21, 1747, in *C. Ninegret v T. Ninegret*, c. 1747, King's CCP [SCJRC]). He barely disguised his biases behind the aura of custom, recounting that "if there be two brothers [Charles and George] of the high Blood and the Eldest brother [Charles, Sr.] is made Sachem and he has a wife of Low Blood [Kate] and has a Child by her [Charles, Jr.] and then Dies it is the Custom of the Indians to prefer the Brother [George] before the Child [Charles] of the Deceased sachem." Although he conceded that he had never encountered such a case of preferring the brother to the son before, Harry explained that "he was young but I have heard that was the Custom." See Copper Harry, deposition, Sept. 2, 1743, in *C. Ninegret v S. Clark*, action of appeal, September 1743, Newport, SCJ, Rhode Island (SCJRC). The elderly Cogemetasco was the corroborating witness.

59. Mostly, the office of sachem seems to have descended patrilineally, but oral testimony in the nineteenth century suggested that the Narragansetts reckoned kinship matrilineally; see William S. Simmons and George F. Aubin, "Narragansett Kinship," *Man in the Northeast*, IX (1975), 21–22, 24. They find that "seventeenth century Narragansett society was characterized by patrilineal transmission of political office and tribal identity." "Within this structure, but independent of it, may have been a system of exogamous matrilineal clans which were important in the regulation of marriage" (30). In either case, two or three of Charles Ninegret's unions were with women connected through birth or marriage to the Block Island Sachem Pennewiss; this is yet another example of the types of multiple kinship links that were built by endogamy and either polygamous or serial marriages to related partners.

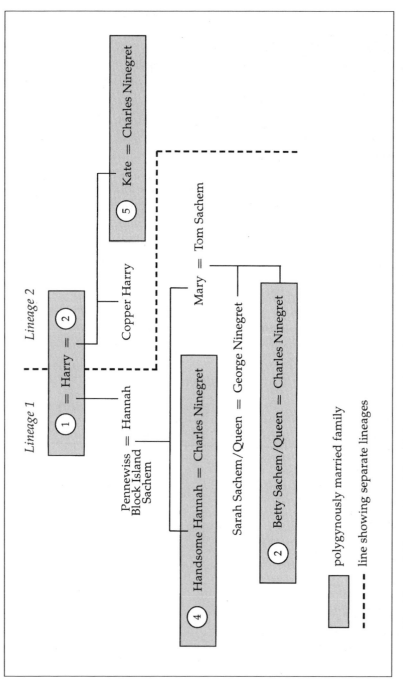

FIGURE 3. Kate Ninegret's Lineage. *Traced through the maternal line, this genealogy shows that Kate would have had no close link to Pennewiss. Drawn by Stinely Associates*

sexual dominance in a world where individual Indians were increasingly in danger of being cast as "mulatto" or "Negro" or as unfree.[60] By the same token, the Narragansetts turned the English courts into a platform from which they asserted a continuing and unbroken Indian identity. Their testimony can thus be read as a powerful act of resistance, perhaps a major motive for some deponents.

The Narragansetts lived in one of the most racially mixed areas in colonial New England. As Edward Channing noted in his early study of southern Rhode Island, by the mid-eighteenth century enslaved people probably accounted for one-third to one-half of the total population, "a proportion to be found nowhere else in New England." In the 1730 census, the town of South Kingstown had 965 white, 333 "Negro," and 223 Indian residents. The neighboring town of Charlestown, the seat of the Narragansett sachems, was listed as 40 percent African American in 1755. Of course, the census categories undoubtedly included a great number of people of mixed ancestry as well.[61] Debt-peonage ensnared many Narragansett men and women, and, at the same time, their contacts with African slaves and servants rose. Children of African men and Narragansett women claimed an Indian ethnic and legal identity through their mothers but discovered that it was all too easy to be deprived of one's birthright. For some, bloodlines could be all that stood between freedom and slavery. Indeed, Jenny Chaugum's daughter, Sarah, described in court documents as a "Molatto," found herself wrongfully enslaved by some enterprising merchants in neighboring New London, Connecticut. She won her freedom, but only after suing these Connecticut merchants in the Rhode Island courts and emphasizing her mother's status as an Indian (and, presumably, free) woman.[62]

60. Struggles by Indians to set themselves apart from Africans were quite common among eastern Indian groups, in both the North and the South; for a statement of the problems, see James H. Merrell, "The Racial Education of the Catawba Indians," *Journal of Southern History*, L (1984), 363–365; see also Karen I. Blu, *The Lumbee Problem: The Making of an American Indian People* (New York, 1980), 24–25.

61. Edward Channing, *The Narragansett Planters: A Study of Causes*, Johns Hopkins University Studies in History and Political Science, 4th Ser., no. 3 (1886), 10. The 1755 census may have grouped Indians and "Negroes" together; see Robert V. Wells, *The Population of the British Colonies in America before 1776: A Survey of Census Data* (Princeton, N.J., 1975), 97. Census of 1730 cited in Elisha Reynolds Potter, "Early History of Narragansett," Rhode Island Historical Society, *Collections*, III, 114, cited in Channing, *Narragansett Planters*, 10. For Charlestown, see William D. Piersen, *Black Yankees: The Development of an Afro-American Subculture in Eighteenth-Century New England* (Amherst, Mass., 1988), 15. See also Lorenzo Johnston Greene, *The Negro in Colonial New England, 1620–1776* (New York, 1942), 88, on the rapid rise in the African American population of this county from 1708 to 1755.

62. For a distinction between race and legal status, see Lawrence R. Baca, "The Legal Status of American Indians," in William C. Sturtevant and Wilcomb R. Washburn, eds.,

Many ordinary English people had a low opinion of Indians, made all the
more so by their increasing association with the enslaved African population. Such attitudes were exemplified early in the century by Sarah Knight,
who remarked in her travel narrative about southern Connecticut:

> There are every where in the Towns as I passed, a Number of Indians
> the Natives of the Country, and [they] are the most salvage of all the
> salvages of that kind that I had ever Seen: little or no care taken (as I
> heard upon enquiry) to make them otherwise. They have in some
> places Landes of their owne, and [are] Govern'd by Law's of their own
> making;—they marry many wives and at pleasure put them away, and
> on the least dislike or fickle humour, on either side, saying *stand away*
> to one another is a sufficient Divorce.

Mistress Knight had little interest in understanding the meaning of native
marriages to the men and women themselves, as her real intent was to liken
Indians' "salvage" polygamy to the liberal divorce climate in colonial Connecticut.[63] So, too, Roger Larkin glossed all Narragansetts as "black" when
he asserted, "I never heard by white or black but that the Sachems held their
Right . . . by Heirship." In his view, the eldest was always preferred as sachem
"whether high Blood or not if married according to their Custom." Larkin
stressed that no "bastards" might inherit office.[64] As did Sarah Knight, many
English observers must have concluded that, given the conditions of their
parents' marriages, most Indian children were often no better than bastards,
at least in the eyes of English law. Although Narragansetts doubtless understood legitimacy differently and few native deponents used the term "bastard," English attitudes nevertheless influenced the way that Narragansett
and English deponents understood Charles Ninegret's marriages.

This complicated social context profoundly shaped Narragansett testimonies. One need think only of Thompson, who was "bid" (by whom?) to

---

The Handbook of North American Indians, IV (Washington, D.C., 1988), 230–237. On
Jenny Chaugum's daughter, see *Sarah v Edward Robinson,* September 1734, Newport, SCJ,
Rhode Island (SCJRC), record book B, 481. This action began in a King's County justices
court, proceeded to the inferior court of common pleas (January 1734), and thence to the
superior court. The file papers at the SCJRC, pulled by John Sweet, contain copies of these
other hearings.

    63. [Sarah Kemble Knight], *The Journal of Madam Knight* [1704] ([1825]; rpt., New York,
1935), 39. She scolded, "Indeed those uncomely *Stand aways* are too much in Vougue
among the English in this (Indulgent Colony) as their Records plentifully prove."

    64. Roger Larkin, deposition, Sept. 5, 1743, in *C. Ninegret v S. Clark,* action of appeal,
September 1743, Newport, SCJ, Rhode Island (SCJRC). Was native testimony about custom weighted differently than that of the English? In the 1743 Narragansett cases, native
deponents, both men and women, outnumbered the English on both sides in the trial at
the county level, but, when the case was appealed to the superior court of judicature, the
new witnesses were mostly English and male.

allege that Kate Ninegret was of royal blood, to see the influence of colonial hierarchies on supposedly objective evidence. The examples are numerous: from the objections of Kate and her son to having an Indian sworn as interpreter in their suit—for fear "that an Indian was not to be depended upon in Point of Veracity as an interpreter equal with an English Man"—to the court's concern, after 1746, to ascertain that the Indians ("known" by the English to be prone to drunkenness) had not been "disguised with drink" at any of the important moments of decision—at the coronation of George or Thomas, at the various marriages, or even at the moment in 1760 when Charles Ninegret, Jr. finally signed away his sachem's rights to his cousin Thomas.[65]

Of course, the English players in the controversy were never disinterested observers either. At least three deponents reported that George Babcock, a local culture broker and translator for the court, had instigated the wedding between Charles and Kate, orchestrating a "traditional" ceremony in order to ensure that the son Kate already carried would be able to inherit Charles's "Estate after him."[66]

Another English intermediary was Joseph Stanton, long a legal guardian or "trustee" to the Ninegret family. Stanton was the descendant of an interpreter for the United Colonies of New England who had turned his negotiating skills to good account in the first English attempts to gain Indian holdings in the Narragansett country. At the time of the Ninegret controversy,

---

65. Kate's objection, although rendered in the way that English jurists would have understood it, might have been based either in the Ninegrets' concern that the particular Indian interpreter would be biased or that, in this racial context, any Indian's interpretations would not stand up upon appeal. See case summary, in *C. Ninegret v S. Clark*, August 1743, copy in *C. Ninegret v J. Stanton*, March 1742/3, Newport, SCJ, Rhode Island (SCJRC), 68–69. On concern over the Indians' drinking, see Joseph Crandall, deposition, June 4, 1760, in Champlin Papers, box 9, folder labeled "Indian Depositions, 1753–1761," n.d., RIHS. Englishmen might have associated Narragansett coronation ceremonies with contemporary and slightly later "Negro election" festivals of southern New England; see Plane, "'Of the Most Royal Blood': Colonial Redefinition of Narragansett Systems of Governance," paper presented to the Annual Meeting of the American Studies Association, Nov. 7, 1993, Boston. A good review of these festivals is Shane White, "'It Was a Proud Day': African Americans, Festivals, and Parades in the North, 1741–1834," *Journal of American History*, LXXXI (1994–1995), 13–50. For more on colonial attitudes toward Indian drinking, see Peter C. Mancall, *Deadly Medicine: Indians and Alcohol in Early America* (Ithaca, N.Y., 1995), 12.

66. William and Experience Bassett, deposition, Sept. 5, 1743, in *C. Ninegret v S. Clark*, action of appeal, September 1743, Newport, SCJ, Rhode Island (SCJRC). James Robins said Babcock told Charles that he "must call as many of the Indians together as loved him if there was but three four or five and make a good Dinner for them and then choose the best or Wisest among them and he to Marry [you] to Kate." See James Robins, deposition, August 1757, in *C. Ninegret v T. Ninegret*, c. 1747, King's CCP (SCJRC). By several accounts, Babcock held the indenture of Betty Coyhees's child and doubtless benefited financially from this relationship with the Ninegrets; see Plane, "Colonizing the Family," 243–246.

Stanton owned "one tract of four and a half miles long and two miles wide . . . kept forty horses, [and] as many slaves."[67] One wonders to what extent his mastery over black and Indian slaves colored his attitudes toward his Narragansett wards, many of whom were indentured servants or day laborers in the county.

A third Englishman involved was Christopher Champlin, who in the late 1750s tallied £1746 19s. 6d. in debts owed him for his labors as attorney and guardian on Thomas Ninegret's behalf from 1752 to 1756 and an additional five hundred pounds in interest on monies he had advanced to the spend-thrift sachem's creditors.[68] Champlin's windfall suggests that Englishmen might have been the chief beneficiaries of Narragansett customary law, al-though it is difficult at this remove to determine the complete story. Cer-tainly they played a large role, even in such tribal events as the 1735 corona-tion of George Ninegret. This traditional ceremony was organized at least in part by two Englishmen—George Babcock and Colonel John Potter, a trustee. Babcock and Potter made sure that the assembled Narragansetts formed two groups or lines to show their support for either George (the majority) or Charles, Jr. (a tiny minority).[69]

The ability of a man like Babcock to shift his support from Charles, Jr. to George suggests that he understood the realpolitik of Narragansett gover-nance. But some Englishmen stood by Charles, Jr., clinging to a familiar notion of father-to-son succession and, in so doing, reinterpreting southern New England's Algonquian modes of governance along more English lines. For them, descent reckoned patrilineally remained the key factor in deter-mining the legitimate sachem, rather than age, ability, the parent's style of marriage, or the quality of the mother's "blood." Such rigidly deter-mined rules of succession flew in the face of testimony about customary law; Thompson's list of rules, for example, had left the tribe considerable flex-ibility in the determination of a fit sachem, allowing for contest and negotia-tion. Thus, even native customary law, as shaped by English common-law traditions, could not contradict English custom, or it might be disregarded.[70]

67. Wilkins Updike, *A History of the Episcopal Church in Narragansett, Rhode Island . . .*, 2d ed., 3 vols. (1847; rpt., Boston, 1907), I, 216, 525 n. 359.

68. "The Estate of Thomas Ninegret . . . To Christopher Champlin," account, in Cham-plin Papers, box 9, folder labeled "Indian Deeds—Thomas Ninegret 1756–7," RIHS.

69. When most of the crowd formed for George, the new sachem sat in a "Great Chair," Toby Coyhees "made a Speech in Indian and put a Belt of Peege upon George's Head," and then the assembled Narragansetts made offerings of bits of money; see John Hill, deposi-tion, August 1743, in *C. Ninegret v S. Clark*, copy in *C. Ninegret v J. Stanton*, March 1742/3, Newport, SCJ, Rhode Island (SCJRC), 43–45, esp. 43.

70. In her discussion of a study of customary law in Senegal, Merry notes that Euro-peans accepted versions of customary law that "meshed best with their own ideology of land ownership, as well as other legal relations" ("Legal Pluralism," *Law and Society Review*, XXII [1988], 875).

In 1746, common-law rules of inheritance took precedence even though they had lacked effect in the earlier contest, for Thomas Ninegret successfully argued that he ought to succeed his father George, despite the prior claim of Charles Ninegret, Jr. to have inherited from Charles, Sr. Issues of race and money undergirded discourses of English common law and Narragansett "custom." The exact nature of English interests may never be determined, but colonial landowners were so heavily involved in shaping the practice of and testimonies about Narragansett custom that the "traditional" practices set forth in these texts cannot be stripped of their contemporary historical setting. Whether in the discussion of royal blood or in the descriptions of coronations, in eighteenth-century English courtrooms custom was forged in dialogue with English legal concepts, the disputes intertwining the interests of individuals both English and Narragansett.[71] Customary law created the illusion of a separate eighteenth-century Narragansett legal culture: part of a multiple legal order with carefully drawn jurisdictions, separate institutions, and, now, separate rules based in Indian tradition. Yet this separation was only an illusion.

V. Law, Custom, and Marriage in the Creation of Narragansett Identity

The notion of "custom" owed much to the earliest ethnographic writers—most notably, for the Narragansetts, the 1643 account of their culture by Roger Williams, whose descriptions of Narragansett marriage read remarkably like those offered by elderly witnesses a century later.[72] But the eighteenth-century litigation might also have influenced the discussions of native cultures that emerged during and after the controversy. In 1761, the Reverend Ezra Stiles spoke with John Paul, a Narragansett man, about old marriage customs. This thirty-year-old informant remembered seeing a Wedding "accordg to [the] old Indian Way" when he was a "little Boy." The couple was, Stiles recorded, "shut up together a fortnight in a Wigwaum by themselves, the parents only bringing them Victuals." "Then the old Indians bro't a Blanket to the young Squaw, which she receivg., the Peage [wampum]

71. Anthropologists argue that even apparently separate systems are linked, both in their conception and in a hierarchical set of power relations. See June Starr and Jane F. Collier, "Introduction: Dialogues in Legal Anthropology," in Starr and Collier, *History and Power,* 9; Merry, "Legal Pluralism," *Law and Society Review,* XXII (1988), 876.

72. Roger Williams, *A Key into the Language of America,* ed. John J. Teunissen and Evelyn J. Hinz (1643; rpt., Detroit, 1973), 206. For a full discussion of these travel narratives, see Plane, *Colonial Intimacies,* chap. 1. Williams's account suggests that, in the seventeenth century, dowry was offered in all Narragansett marriages—not just those of the sachems: "If the man be poore, his friends and neighbours doe *pummenúmmin teàuguash,* that is contribute Money toward the Dowrie."

was mutually given and exchanged, [which] was to be kept in perpetuum. Then they made a feast, and the old Indians talkt to the couple, rejoyced and made merry and so the Wedding concluded." Given the superficial similarity of some details, this might have been one of the Ninegret weddings, living on in the imagination of Narragansetts as a truly traditional and customary form of marriage. It was only when Stiles pressed him for more that Paul observed that the Indians "now mostly disuse this Ceremony, and are either married according to Eng. Custom or take one another without Ceremony." "[Paul] said he himself was married, that he took his Wife without any formality, except mutual Agreemt."[73] Stiles's account encoded the true and traditional form of Narragansett marriage (by custom) even as it recorded the wider range of practices pursued by eighteenth-century native couples.[74] The minister resolved this contradiction by consigning custom to the past, reporting that mid-eighteenth-century Narragansetts "disused" these older practices.

In much the same way, the Narragansett cases of the 1730s to the 1760s were themselves a history of sorts. They all focused on marriages in the period from the years 1728 to 1735. But, although they recorded the ancient customs, the subsequent marriages of the Narragansett royals became increasingly Anglicized. In 1735, already sensing the importance of a lawful, English ceremony, the newly crowned sachem, George Ninegret, married Sarah Queen before the English justice of the peace and Indian guardian, Joseph Stanton, in a ceremony performed according to the English manner—though in a nod to custom, Stanton did stop to ask whether the match was approved by the tribe. And when Thomas Ninegret wed Mary in 1761, the service was conducted in the Anglican church at Newport.[75] No traditional Narragansett customs influenced these marriages. In the ongoing litigation, past practices were cited only to legitimate or to challenge contemporary political leadership.[76]

73. Ezra Stiles, *Extracts from the Itineraries and Other Miscellanies of Ezra Stiles . . . 1755–1794*, ed. Franklin Bowditch Dexter (New Haven, Conn., 1916), 141–142.

74. See also Stiles's contemporary, Samson Occom, *An Account of the Montauk Indians on Long Island* [1761], Massachusetts Historical Society, *Collections*, V (1798), 106–108. Occom was directly involved in a similar controversy that divided the Mohegans of eastern Connecticut; see Laurie Weinstein, "Samson Occom: A Charismatic Eighteenth-Century Mohegan Leader," in Weinstein, ed., *Enduring Traditions: The Native Peoples of New England* (Westport, Conn., 1994), 95–96.

75. See, for example, John Hill, Jr., deposition, Aug. 4, 1746, in *T. Ninegret v S. Clark*, August 1746, King's CCP (SCJRC); Chapin, *Sachems of the Narragansetts*, 102; Sweet, "Bodies Politic," I, 80. His mother, Sarah, widowed in 1746, remarried four years later, taking an Indian husband, John Anthony, in a ceremony performed by James MacSparran, the Anglican missionary to Narragansett. See Narragansett Parish Register, in Updike, *History of the Episcopal Church*, II, 543.

76. The early testimony took on added authority over time. In the 1750s, some English witnesses appealed to evidences taken a decade earlier as proof that ought to quell further

Perhaps the most important result of the collection of customary marriage law was the codification of Narragansett culture in witnesses' accounts—aided, ironically, by English lawyers and legal idioms. The problem is that the invocation of custom in court implies a static notion of culture, one whose blank facade masks the competing goals of real individuals. But, as one modern anthropologist has noted, "Society and culture, are never 'things,' not even historical things; they are always 'happenings,' always constructions of the present, always in the making."[77] In collecting customary law, Narragansett and English witnesses both helped to create a static, "authentic" Narragansett culture that they thought might serve as a standard.

The body of custom said to have governed sachems' marriages now defined the essence of Narragansett cultural identity, both for men such as Ezra Stiles and for nativists responding to rising racial divisions between whites and people of color. When Thomas Ninegret's tribal opponents complained that he had married a mulatto woman without tribal consent and contrary to the customs of the Indians, they were recalling an earlier world in which, they imagined, sachem and tribe had shared a common interest, and the sachem's marriages had both renewed and displayed that reciprocity. But the custom they invoked contained little room for flexible negotiation of interests. The claims of the witnesses, the arguments of the English lawyers, and the decisions of juries and justices mapped a sort of order onto "Indian" practices of marriage, casting unions as lawful or unlawful, ferreting out statutelike customs and imposing rules upon more organic processes.[78]

While the Ninegret disputes certainly reveal the diversity of marriage in early New England, they also invite our exploration of the colonial context that produced this customary marital law, a world in which arguments over marriage might affect Narragansett sovereignty by chipping away the land reserves that were the nation's main resource. Custom created the appearance of Narragansett unity, even as tremendous internal conflicts propelled the collection of customary law. Custom—always remembered, always

---

dispute. Samuel Perry remembered that he had earlier taken sixteen or seventeen "evidences," which, "according to the Best of my Remembrance . . . did prove the Marriage of Charles Ninegrett . . . to Kate, to be according to the Custom of the Indians"; see Samuel Perry, deposition, Feb. 16, 1756, in *C. Ninegret v T. Ninegret*, c. 1747, King's CCP (SCJRC). Joseph Stafford recalled evidences presented to the General Assembly in 1737 or 1738, proving that "Charles the Son of Catherine and Charles the Sacham . . . was the true and Rightfull heir to the Sachamship and Estate of his father" (Stafford, Aug. 11, 1755, in *C. Ninegret v T. Ninegret*, c. 1747, King's CCP [SCJRC]). See Stafford's other deposition, August 1746, in *T. Ninegret v S. Clark*, August 1746, King's CCP (SCJRC).

77. He adds that culture is always "a social act that must be studied to be understood, not assumed to be natural or a historical given." See Richard G. Fox, *Lions of the Punjab: Culture in the Making* (Berkeley, Calif., 1985), 138. On culture as practice, see Sherry B. Ortner, "Theory in Anthropology since the Sixties," *Comparative Studies in Society and History*, XXVI (1984), 144–160.

78. Merry, "Legal Pluralism," *Law and Society Review*, XXII (1988), 875.

past—had never really existed in such pure form, but it became the most precious of legal commodities. Wielded with skill, customary law could validate marriages where no magistrate or minister officiated (as in Charles Ninegret's first two) and invalidate common-law matches (as in Charles Ninegret's alleged marriage to Betty Coyhees). It could render moot the marriage of a sachem performed according to English law before a magistrate or minister (as in Charles Ninegret's marriage to Kate). Custom might also be invoked in the struggle against a tyrannical or improvident sachem like Thomas Ninegret.

Although these aspects of customary law are well-established features of colonial societies, most scholars have focused on nineteenth- or twentieth-century colonial settings. The Narragansett dispute raises the issue of what connection the early American experience might have had to the more extensive reliance upon customary law in the later British Empire. The Narragansett cases suggest that we must more fully historicize customary law, locating its origins in a particular eighteenth-century moment. It seems clear that, although custom had been collected even earlier in the colonies, it was not written down as customary law until the rising pressures on land resources and the growing professionalization of the law combined in the eighteenth century. The task remains for other scholars, however, to investigate links between customary law in American colonial governance, its implementation elsewhere in the later empire, and, perhaps most fruitfully, its connections to similar customary forms in other European colonies.

The Narragansett cases also reveal the ways that colonial American customary law helped to create a native identity—in this instance, a Narragansett one. In the struggle against the Ninegrets' profligacy, Narragansett opposition leaders appropriated both the language of custom and the idioms of English law, arguing over marriage ceremonies and bloodlines as a way of defending Narragansett sovereignty, tribal lands, and a distinctively Indian identity. Throughout their dispute, marriages, both in practice and in law, proved central parts of the controversy. Like all colonized people, they shaped their resistance with the tools at hand: in this case, the law.[79] But, in so doing, they unwittingly created a rigid identity based on "custom" that

79. Comaroff and Comaroff reformulate hegemony as it is usually understood to allow for contestation and resistance, albeit in the terms of the dominant order. They note, "A critical feature of the colonization of consciousness among the Tswana, and others like them, was the process by which they were drawn unwittingly into the dominion of European 'civilization' while at the same time often contesting its presence and the explicit content of its worldview." Likewise, as Narragansetts attempted to assert a unique Narragansett mode of marriage and inheritance, they did so in courts that proceeded according to the common law—the terms of their resistance were thus those of the dominant colonial order (*Of Revelation and Revolution: Christianity, Colonialism and Consciousness in South Africa*, 3 vols. [Chicago, 1991], I, 25–27, esp. 26).

would constrict the possibilities open to ordinary Narragansetts. While the court searched for rules to apply to past actions, the legal languages of custom-cum-law pervaded contemporary travelers' narratives and local histories.[80]

These cases were perhaps the opening salvo in an ongoing struggle, continuing into the present, in which Indians had to define and explain themselves to outsiders, in the outsiders' own terms.[81] American Indians have continued to face the problem of self-definition through the invocation of tradition. The epigraph for this essay is taken from James Clifford's discussion of the late-1970s federal court trial regarding the tribal status of another southern New England Indian group, the Mashpee Wampanoags. Despite the huge gap in time, there is resonance between the two litigations in which each southern New England Indian group had to defend its cultural integrity and in which each side used Indian testimony about tradition to make its case. Just as in the Mashpee trial, the analysis of eighteenth-century customary law is not about really knowing the "traditional" Narragansetts.

Instead, customary law requires the critical exploration of texts and contexts; as we have seen, the witnesses' testimony, shaped by the conventions of English courts, imposed a lawlike custom and a faceless tradition on a flexible past. The events that these deponents described referred to real practices—chiefly, the cultural, political, and social meanings of royal Narragansett marriage. All of this played out in a dynamic historical context: the world of colonial hierarchies and interested selves that defined the place of people of color in eighteenth-century Rhode Island and encouraged the mad rush for control of remaining open land resources. In engaging all of these factors, we can see the critical role of this sort of colonial legal activity in shaping not only the conflicts but also the cultural identities of early America's people.

---

80. In the twentieth century, the idiom of customary law would fuel the evolution of legal anthropology and the anthropology of marriage; see Comaroff and Roberts, *Rules and Processes*, 132–133.

81. Paul Brodeur, *Restitution: The Land Claims of the Mashpee, Passamaquoddy, and Penobscot Indians of New England* (Boston, 1985); James Clifford, *The Predicament of Culture: Twentieth-Century Ethnography, Literature, and Art* (Cambridge, Mass., 1988), 277–346; Jack Campisi, *The Mashpee Indians: Tribe on Trial* (Syracuse, N.Y., 1991); Calloway, ed., *After King Philip's War*.

PART THREE

Rules of Law

Legal Relations as Social Relations

L EGAL HISTORIANS too often assume that law has social effect without seeking to demonstrate it—or perhaps they simply find investigating law's doctrinal genealogies, institutional structures, cultural manifestations, and ideological consequences sufficiently compelling in itself to render superfluous the social historian's claim that consequences "on the ground" must also be exposed before legal rules can be considered worth examining. Such inattention to demonstrable effects, of course, tends to confirm the social historian's skepticism that legal history can help us understand social formations or social relations. More occasionally, it inspires the alternative and more interesting conclusion that the real significance of law's social being lies in the very lack of apparent determinate effect. Or, in other words, that law's primary social role is not to fashion outcomes but to obscure them—to allow ritual, contradiction, and ambiguity to obfuscate the machinations of the big battalions that operate at deeper levels of historical significance.

This conclusion is not one that is in any sense alien to legal historians, and it is not without plausibility. It suggests lines of inquiry that are proper for early American legal historians to pursue. Yet much of the research presented here would suggest other, more intermediate, positions. Few of the authors represented in this collection would accept law's traditional self-legitimating claims on their own terms, but neither would they treat them as obfuscation. Nor do their conclusions support the dismissal of law as mere epiphenomenon. These essays situate law in appropriate social contexts but refuse to simplify its causal relationship with those contexts. In a word, they eschew simplicities—whether of autonomy, instrumentality, or mystification—for causal complexity.

Of all the essays in this collection, those of Part III attempt to join law most immediately and specifically to particular social contexts. In the first, Christine Daniels explores the colonial intersection of law and labor, specifically in the institution of indentured servitude. Based on archival research in a jurisdiction notorious for the severity of its statutory controls on indentured servants—Maryland—Daniels finds that investigation of case and customary servant law significantly modifies traditional representations of the harshness and arbitrariness of early American master-servant relations. Indentured servitude was a legal relationship with roots in English parish administration of the adolescent poor. Inevitably, given both age and situational disparities, it was hardly a relationship of equals, but it was one whose institutionalized inequalities were defined and administered with some precision, and in which legal institutions, in enforcing rights and obligations on both sides, offered dependent servants reasonably effective channels of redress. In Daniels's account, law contributed to the construction of Chesapeake social relations by providing a crucial institutional mechanism that facilitated the supply of labor and an institutional forum that mediated those relations with relative fairness and predictability. In arguing that juridical observation of custom and precedent, not colonial statutes, was the most significant influence on the form and practice of indentured servitude, Daniels's essay underlines law's institutional and ideological plurality. It also recalls both Gaspar's observations on the importance of English example in the construction of early Caribbean servitude and Konig's analysis of the counterpoint from which law's enduring structure was fashioned.

The second essay, by Linda L. Sturtz, also investigates the social impact of a specific legal institution: the power of attorney. Powers of attorney permitted individuals to designate legal representatives who might, depending on the terms of the delegation, exercise considerable practical legal and economic authority—for example, in the management of property—in the name of the principal. Sturtz focuses on the particular case of married women in propertied, commercially active families, who she argues were enabled by powers of attorney to circumvent the legal constraints of coverture. Historians of the colonial Chesapeake have appreciated that women managed property, but they have concentrated on widowhood as the period in women's lives when such responsibilities were exercised. Portrayal of the social and economic position of married women in colonial Virginia has tended to accept the constraints of coverture and the patriarchal ascendancy of male household heads as an accurate guide to reality. Sturtz argues this is an error. The point of departure for analysis of social and economic activity should not be the presumption that a directing male household head, when present, always enjoyed determinative influence, but rather an appreciation of the family as a complex collective enterprise of differentiated parts in which women often took leading roles. Coverture does not hint at this complexity and thus tends to obscure it. Like the executrix, married women with powers of attorney played active economic roles. By exploring the legal forms that facilitated married women's activity, not only does married women's practical participation in social and economic life become more visible but we also recognize that there existed avenues by which that participation could be pursued in harmony with, not despite, Virginia legal culture.

A similar lesson may be learned from the third essay, by John G. Kolp and Terri L. Snyder. Examining an apparently straightforward relationship between law and social life—franchise law excluded women from voting, therefore women had no particular impact on Virginia political culture—they find a far more complex situation, in which alternative legal routes actually provided women with political presence. Kolp and Snyder read political participation broadly, to comprise a range of phenomena wider than the actual casting of votes or the holding of office. From this perspective, they discover that women influenced local political culture in important and measurable ways. Women, for example, could exploit their nonparticipant status to electioneer with a legal immunity that no participating male could claim. More important, because male participation was hedged by property qualifications, women could and, they demonstrate, did settle land on male family members with the specific intent of enabling them to meet franchise property tests, in effect creating voters who could in turn be expected to advance their patron's interest. As in Sturtz's case, both aspects of women's political activity caution against too facile a reading of a clear social outcome from an apparent legal condition of exclusion; the condition can be turned to advantage (electioneering), or its effects can be somewhat countermanded by invoking another perfectly legal mechanism (property transfers). Again as in Sturtz's case, the logic of the maneuvers that the research uncovers is greatly enhanced if we see that the unit of sociolegal action is not the (male) individual but the family. Both essays propose that the social and legal absorption of women by men suggested by coverture and franchise ineligibility is too simplistic a picture, that both men and women behave on behalf of and to maximize the interests of an ongoing collectivity (the family) and, as important, find appropriate legal mechanisms to facilitate that maximization.

In the final essay of this section, Holly Brewer undertakes a broad examination of the legal creation of childhood and its attendant attributions of legal incompetence to children. In the early seventeenth century, children, even as young as four or five years old, were considered capable of engaging in actions of legal consequence: testifying in courts, assenting to contractual commitments. By the end of the eighteenth century, they weren't. This shift, Brewer argues, reflected the influence of an increasing concern in contemporary legal and epistemological debate over the reason and capacity of all those who exercised even personal legal rights and thus serves as an instance of a larger transformation in understandings of the conditions under which humans would be allowed to pursue their own interests and affect the interests of others. The returns to be gained from studying the legal construction of a shift with such momentous social and political significance as this are, one may think, obvious, and surely sufficient to convince the skeptical social historian who contests law's capacity to register effects on social behavior. What Brewer is examining here is the creation of the fundamental distinction between those whose acts have consequences and those whose acts do not. Yet, in its explorations of the rituals of testimony and signature and the hesitant evaporation of the minor's imputed capacity to act on his or her own behalf, Brewer's examination also reveals all the ambiguities and contradictions and distortions implicit in the way different jurisdictions and institutions pick their own routes through that same general sociopolitical transformation—precisely the conditions of legal discourse and development that obstruct the imputation of clear social effects to legal phenomena. Brewer's essay illustrates both sides of the sociolegal conundrum: both the self-evidence, to the legal historian, of the importance of the exercise, and the difficulty, to the social historian, of tying effect to cause.

"Liberty to Complaine"

Servant Petitions in Maryland, 1652–1797

S INCE THE LATE nineteenth century, historians have examined servitude as a labor form in the Anglo-American colonies. Early works
on the political and legal status of bound labor, based heavily on
statute law, were written in an atmosphere permeated with ideas of
American exceptionalism; most focus on the original—indeed (as they argued) unique—nature of colonial indentured servitude.[1] During the first
half of the twentieth century, scholars placed growing emphasis on the
economic side of servitude as well. Their works were hybrids of legal analyses, again based on statute law, and macroeconomic analyses of labor needs
in the Anglo-American colonies. Implicit or explicit views of class conflict
and struggle informed these portraits, and historians often used statutes and
court procedures to emphasize the obviously unequal power relations between masters and servants.[2] These works framed historical studies written
between the late 1940s and the late 1970s that traced the origins of slavery in
the United States to the exceptional structure of indentured servitude.[3]

I wish to thank Jack P. Greene, Susan Juster, Michael Kennedy, participants in the Michigan Seminar, William G. Shade, Christopher Tomlins, and Lorena S. Walsh.

1. Such works were influenced by the prevalence of bound labor during the colonial
period, a general interest in sociopolitical institutions during the nineteenth century, and
the availability of bodies of colonial statute law. Examples include James Curtis Ballagh,
*White Servitude in the Colony of Virginia: A Study of the System of Indentured Labor in the
American Colonies* (Baltimore, 1895); John Spencer Bassett, *Slavery and Servitude in the
Colony of North Carolina* (Baltimore, 1896); Eugene McCormac, *White Servitude in Mary-
land, 1634–1820* (Baltimore, 1904); Samuel McKee, *Labor in Colonial New York, 1664–1776*
(New York, 1935); Cheesman A. Herrick, *White Servitude in Pennsylvania: Indentured and
Redemption Labor in Colony and Commonwealth* (Philadelphia, 1926). Warren B. Smith's
White Servitude in Colonial South Carolina (Columbia, S.C., 1961) was completed as a
doctoral dissertation in 1915.

2. See, for example, Marcus Wilson Jernegan, *Laboring and Dependent Classes in Colonial America: 1607–1783* (Chicago, 1931); Abbot Emerson Smith, *Colonists in Bondage:
White Servitude and Convict Labor in America, 1607–1776* (Chapel Hill, N.C., 1947). Richard B. Morris, *Government and Labor in Early America* (New York, 1946), used both case
and statute law and concluded that seventeenth-century county courts ameliorated statute
law for indentured servants (474).

Please note that, throughout the text, the word "master" can encompass males and
females.

3. See, for example, Carl N. Degler, "Slavery and the Genesis of American Race Preju-

Legal analyses have implied a rigid social construction of servitude as well, another factor with its basis in statute law.[4] As historians of slavery, marriage, and other sociolegal relationships have demonstrated, however, custom and precedent, not statutes, established colonial institutions. They varied considerably over time and from place to place, depending in great part on regional negotiations between masters, husbands, and fathers, who engaged with the legal system, and their various dependents, who usually did not.[5] In fact, to posit this relationship as one based on the needs of only two parties vastly oversimplifies it. Most legal institutions involving dependents evolved in the settler societies of Anglo-America from peculiar circumstances affecting specific regions, including demography, duration of settlement, climate, the economy, customary rights established in individual cases between masters and servants, emphases on various aspects of English and possibly other legal systems, and doubtless additional factors as well.

The historiographical emphasis on statutes rather than case and customary servant law has exaggerated the powerlessness of servants and their duties to their masters. Masters' responsibilities to their dependents remains unexplored. In theory, the law gave masters broad latitude over the lives of their servants; in practice, masters worked under conventions and constraints imposed by courts, communities, and servants themselves. Historians have mistaken the theoretical control masters had over servants for the exercise of that control, have assumed that masters generally did not recognize duties to their servants, and have argued that a legal system controlled

---

dice," Comparative Studies in Society and History, II, no. 1 (October, 1959), 49–66; Oscar Handlin, Race and Nationality in American Life (Boston, 1950), 3–29; Edmund S. Morgan, American Slavery, American Freedom: The Ordeal of Colonial Virginia (New York, 1976); Winthrop D. Jordan, "Modern Tensions and the Origin of American Slavery," Journal of Southern History, XXVIII (1962), 18–30. This is not meant to be an exhaustive list.

Twentieth-century economic analyses used a variety of sources to create a macroeconomic picture of servitude. They considered masters' needs for laborers, the cost and price of servants relative to other labor, and the economic niches servants filled before and after the massive importation of slaves. Works on this topic have been as rigorous as the data allow. See, for example, David W. Galenson, White Servitude in Colonial America: An Economic Analysis (New York, 1981); Galenson, ed., Markets in History: Economic Studies of the Past (Cambridge, 1989); Farley Grubb, "Servant Auction Records and Immigration into the Delaware Valley, 1745–1831: The Proportion of Females among Immigrant Servants," American Philosophical Society, Proceedings, CXXXIII (1989), 154–169; Grubb, "Immigrant Servant Labor: Their Occupational and Geographic Distribution in the Late Eighteenth-Century Mid-Atlantic Economy," Social Science History, IX (1985), 249–275.

4. Darrett B. Rutman and Anita H. Rutman, A Place in Time: Middlesex County, Virginia, 1650–1750 (New York, 1984), esp. 128–163; Sharon V. Salinger, "To Serve Well and Faithfully": Labor and Indentured Servants in Pennsylvania, 1682–1800 (Cambridge, 1987).

5. Terri L. Snyder, "Legal History of the Colonial South: Assessment and Suggestions," William and Mary Quarterly, L (1993), 18–27, posits that an examination of cases, as opposed to statutes, would clarify the agency of dependents.

by masters, indifferent neighbors, and a wide social gap between dependents and independents supported masters' abuse.[6] This historiographical confusion stems primarily from debates over the origins of English indentured servitude and its successor, slavery. Scholars who emphasize masters' abusiveness and servants' powerlessness make teleological arguments that anticipate the more rigid and hierarchical slave systems that followed servitude in plantation colonies and the legal practices that supported them. This argument fails to illuminate the subtleties and negotiations inherent in relationships between seventeenth- and eighteenth-century masters and servants. Ironically, moreover, scholars have begun to question the rigidity of laws regarding the treatment of slaves in the eighteenth century and have argued that New World slave systems, in their infinite plasticity, resulted from negotiation between masters and slaves over customary rights and responsibilities.[7]

Legally and structurally, indentured servitude was based on English poor apprenticeship. Servitude was not, as some historians have argued, a "new labor system" with no forebears, nor was it a form deliberately created to degrade "true" English craft apprenticeship.[8] Poor apprentices in seventeenth-century England were usually adolescents bound to serve a master for a number of years until they reached their majority. Customary indentured

6. This is particularly true for historians of colonies south of Pennsylvania. Abbot Emerson Smith, for example, wrote five decades ago that "courts seem always to have accepted the word of the master," whereas Darrett and Anita Rutman emphasized the indifference neighbors displayed toward their abuse; even free people were evidently so deadened by life in the New World they were "compelled by their own plight to ignore" that of servants. See Smith, *Colonists in Bondage*, 268; Rutman and Rutman, *A Place in Time*, 136–138, esp. 138. See also Morgan, *American Slavery, American Freedom*, pp. 108–130, 250–270; Warren M. Billings, "The Law of Servants and Slaves in Seventeenth-Century Virginia," *Virginia Magazine of History and Biography*, XCIX (1991), 45–62. James Horn discusses servants' passivity and powerlessness in an economic context in *Adapting to a New World: English Society in the Seventeenth-Century Chesapeake* (Chapel Hill, N.C., 1994), 64–69, and Kathleen M. Brown adds a gender dimension in *Good Wives, Nasty Wenches, and Anxious Patriarchs: Gender, Race, and Power in Colonial Virginia* (Chapel Hill, N.C., 1996), 149–154. This note is meant to illustrate, but does not exhaust, the literature.

7. Smith argued that few colonial courts tried to "distinguish a servant from a slave" (*Colonists in Bondage*, 270), while Billings argues that courts conflated the two deliberately ("The Law of Servants and Slaves," *VMHB*, XCIX [1991], esp. 58–62). Scholarly works that emphasize negotiations between master and slave include the essays in Ira Berlin and Philip D. Morgan, eds., *Cultivation and Culture: Labor and the Shaping of Slave Life in the Americas* (Charlottesville, Va., 1993).

8. Quotations from Allan Kulikoff, *Tobacco and Slaves: The Development of Southern Cultures in the Chesapeake, 1680–1800* (Chapel Hill, N.C., 1986), 39–42; Kulikoff, "The Transition to Capitalism in Rural America," *WMQ*, XLVI (1989), 134. For pauper apprenticeship and servitude, see Horn, *Adapting to a New World*, 253–256, 287–288. Scholars of early nineteenth-century apprenticeship do not accord English poor law the attention it deserves. See, for example, W. J. Rorabaugh, *The Craft Apprentice: From Franklin to the Machine Age in America* (New York, 1986).

servants—that is, servants who arrived in the colonies without arranged contracts—were also adolescents bound to serve until they reached their majority; they served "according to the custome of this country." Poor children born in the colonies who were bound to serve until their majority were usually called apprentices but received very similar contracts. In fact, the terms "servitude and "apprenticeship" were often used interchangeably by court clerks until about 1690.[9]

Masters of creole apprentices, however, had not invested money in repaying the cost of their charges' passage from Great Britain, a distinction that gave the masters of immigrant laborers a stronger claim to the value of their labor over time. Yet neither masters of apprentices nor those of indentured or customary servants could claim rights in or ownership of either the person or the offspring of their workers. Both servants and apprentices bound in the colonies had to receive some sort of payment or dues for their time, and their contracts had to be executed before a magistrate.[10] Masters of apprentices who wished to end their obligation could not sell their charges but took them to court to be rebound. Neither apprentices nor servants, therefore, worked in a labor institution that rendered them chattel; they were contracted laborers, whether the contract was written or based on custom. Masters purchased, not their persons, but their contracts.[11]

Servants also retained their humanity at law in the form of a vital right; they could petition county courts for redress of their grievances. Any apprentice or servant being "misused" or "grieved" (except convicted felons) could complain "to any one Justice of the Peace of the County where [his or her] Master dwelleth" for relief. Servants, like married women and children, were neither discrete political nor economic persons, but they were discrete

9. These terms, reflecting similarity in the two institutions, are constant. For examples, see William Hand Browne et al., eds., *The Archives of Maryland* (Baltimore, 1887–), III, 134, LIII, 431 (hereafter cited as *Archives)*; for discussion, see Christine Marie Daniels, "Alternative Workers in a Slave Economy: Kent County, Maryland, 1675–1810 (Ph.D. diss., Johns Hopkins University, 1990), 173–199, 287–384.

10. *Archives,* XLIX, 137. The disposition of servant women's illegitimate children reveals that neither masters nor courts assumed that the woman's master was entitled to her offspring. Masters who wished to bind such children executed contracts through the county court. During the early eighteenth century, when concern for racial mixture prevailed, bastard children of white (or mulatto) women were bound for thirty-one years, but such apprenticeships were also done through the court; masters might have received, but could not legally presuppose, a right to such children's labor. See Thomas D. Morris, *Southern Slavery and the Law, 1619–1860* (Chapel Hill, N.C., 1996), 22–24; Daniels, "Alternative Workers in a Slave Economy," 173–200.

11. Lois Green Carr, "The Development of the Maryland Orphans' Court, 1654–1715," in Aubrey C. Land, Lois Green Carr, and Edward C. Papenfuse, eds., *Law, Society, and Politics in Early Maryland: Proceedings of the First Conference on Maryland History, June 14–15, 1974* (Baltimore, 1977), 41–62; Daniels, "Alternative Workers in a Slave Economy," 173–384.

legal persons, not things.[12] The institution of slavery, on the other hand, was based on property law. Masters owned, not the value of a slave's labor, but the slave herself and her offspring; slaves generally could no more appear before an Anglo-American court than the cattle they tended or the swine they slaughtered.

Slavery and servitude had coexisted in plantation colonies from the earliest years of settlement, although slavery often succeeded servitude as the dominant labor institution. Anglo-American courts had very clear ideas on the distinct boundaries of each. To posit that early modern English people quickly reshaped a labor form in which servants (who were dependent persons) could defend themselves at law into one in which slaves (who were chattel) could not is to underestimate the position of servants and their access to the law within English households and society. Servitude did not evolve into slavery thinkingly or unthinkingly. And servants should not be deprived of the agency they possessed in negotiating within the institution of servitude because of the later influx of African slaves.[13]

County courts, which usually heard cases of disagreements between masters and servants, mediated this negotiation. In doing so, they created local, customarily established standards for the treatment of servants. These standards varied from colony to colony, even from county to county. In fact, individual justices could influence the outcome of certain cases, and a few incidents suggest that some servants clearly perceived that it was to their advantage to enlist one elite patron (a justice) to confront another (a master). Political differences between elites could work to servants' advantage. This form of redress, however, was not nearly as widespread among dependents in English colonies and households as it appears to have been in contemporary Spanish or Portuguese ones. Whereas a few early modern English masters might have held highly stylized and elaborate ideas of honor and dependency, most did not. They were, therefore, willing to accept the court as a public mediator in disputes with their servants rather than seek private redress.[14]

12. Michael Dalton, *The Countrey Justice: Containing the Practice of the Justices of the Peace as well in as out of Their Sessions* (London, 1666), 90.

13. Morris, *Southern Slavery and the Law*, details the respective laws of servitude and slavery in the early colonies (16–57). He argues that "blacks were treated as slaves and separate from white indentured servants from the outset" (41); that it is reasonable to assume that "colonial Englishmen would apply English notions and rules of property law to slaves" (42); and that English villeins and other servants "could go to court and sue persons" (53).

14. The literature on Spanish and Luso-American concepts of household honor is enormous. One important recent work is Sandra Lauderdale Graham, *House and Street: The Domestic World of Servants and Masters in Nineteenth-Century Rio de Janeiro* (Cam-

Still another source of the historiographical confusion over the standing
of servants in Anglo-America results from a misreading of the distinction
between seventeenth-century elites and nonelites. The social gap between
seventeenth-century masters and servants was narrow compared to a more
elaborated society like that of the antebellum South. England's New World
colonies were still social frontiers in the mid-seventeenth century. Con-
sumer culture in both England and the colonies, but especially the latter, had
not yet evolved highly differentiated measures of wealth. Rich people owned
the same goods poor people did; they just owned more of them. Elites,
therefore, could not use consumables easily to illuminate a social hierarchy.[15] Before about 1660 in Virginia and 1680 in Maryland, servants were
often visibly distinguished from their masters as much by age as by signs of
social class.

Seventeenth- and eighteenth-century British political and social theory
was permeated with ideas of dependents and independents. Most people in
Britain and Anglo-America, including married women, children, and servants, were dependents.[16] Dependents had no political standing and related
to legal and governmental authority only indirectly through the person of an
independent male or feme sole who headed a household. An independent
person was responsible both for the control and for the care of his (or her)
dependents. A man's standing within political structures and his recognition
as a person worthy of independence, however, were based not only on how
well he controlled his dependents but how generously and honestly he supported them.[17]

Certainly independents exercised dominion and command over dependents in early modern English societies; legal and social systems had few

------

bridge, 1988). If the historical literature on honor and dependence in the antebellum
South is correct, the seventeenth-century concept of reciprocal obligation between independents and dependents might have been elaborated during the next two centuries into
baroque and highly stylized systems of mutual duties scholars have defined as "paternal-
ism" and "honor." The antebellum system provided public recognition for independent
men who fulfilled their obligations to dependents and equals. The literature on this topic
has burgeoned in recent years. A sampling includes Bertram Wyatt-Brown, *Southern
Honor: Ethics and Behavior in the Old South* (New York, 1982); Steven M. Stowe, *Intimacy
and Power in the Old South: Ritual in the Lives of the Planters* (Baltimore, 1987); Kenneth S.
Greenberg, "The Nose, the Lie, and the Duel in the Antebellum South," *American Historical Review,* XCV (1990), 57–74.

15. Lorena S. Walsh, "Questions and Sources for Exploring the Standard of Living,"
WMQ, XLV (1988), 116–123; in the same volume, Lois Green Carr and Lorena S. Walsh,
"The Standard of Living in the Colonial Chesapeake," 135–159.

16. Linda Grant DePauw argues that only 15 percent of Revolutionary Americans were
politically or legally independent in "Land of the Unfree: Legal Limitations on Liberty in
Pre-Revolutionary America," *Maryland Historical Magazine,* LXVIII (1973), 356–357.

17. Jack P. Greene, *All Men Are Created Equal: Some Reflections on the Character of the
American Revolution: An Inaugural Lecture* (Oxford, 1976), 17–25.

other means of controlling dependent people. Servants especially bore watching—they were often single male adolescents, the people most likely to be lawless in any Western society. They needed strong father figures to control them, lest social havoc result.[18]

But while masters were to control their servants, they also were expected, by courts and by society, to support them adequately, treat them fairly, and often educate them or teach them a trade. If a master failed to do so, he violated the terms of responsibility on which his control was based and gave the lie to his position as an independent man. The idea that colonial masters had a social and personal duty as well as a right to discipline their dependents has heretofore been explained in American historiography primarily as a Puritan religious construction.[19] Masters in the plantation colonies have not been accorded much responsibility for the instruction and care as well as the control of their dependents; they have been relegated to the ahistorical status of anticipating slavery or the sadistic one of perpetrating violence for its own sake. But as the idea of a master's duty had its origins in common—not radical—English social and political thought, it was certainly more widespread and probably stronger elsewhere than it was in the New England colonies.

This essay will argue that many servants understood their legal rights, sought relief for their grievances, and succeeded in their efforts. It will further argue that county courts and the provincial court in Maryland, far from being an instrument of masters' control, were sympathetic to servants' pleas and overwhelmingly adjudicated cases in their favor. By their actions, the courts and the masters and servants who negotiated their positions within them created a local institution of servitude more aware of servants' rights and masters' duties than the current historical literature suggests.[20]

18. As a result, English courts, including those in the colonies, were more reluctant to convict masters of abusing servants than to convict them of violence against other dependents. See J. A. Sharpe, "Domestic Homicide in Early Modern England," *Historical Journal*, XXIV (1981), 29–48.

19. Greene, *All Men Are Created Equal*, 17–21; Morgan, *The Puritan Family: Religion and Domestic Relations in Seventeenth-Century New England* (New York, 1944), 109–132; Philip Greven, *The Protestant Temperament: Patterns of Child-Rearing, Religious Experience, and the Self in Early America* (New York, 1977), 21–150.

20. The essay's evidence was gathered from 261 complaints filed by or on behalf of servants in Maryland between 1652 and 1797: 68 complaints filed in all Maryland county courts between 1652 and 1680; 128 complaints filed in the Kent County court between 1689 and 1797; and 65 complaints filed in the provincial court between 1658 and 1683. The breakdown of complaint by procedure and court was as follows: 132 petitions filed by servants in county courts and 60 at the provincial court; 17 petitions filed by others on servants' behalf in the county courts and 2 in the provincial court; 19 civil suits brought by ex-servants or servants against masters in the county courts and 3 in the provincial court; and 13 county grand jury presentments of abusive or neglectful masters. I used Kent County records for the eighteenth century for three reasons. First, I have combed the

Servants' grievances could come before the county court in one of four ways. First, servants in the colonies, like those in Great Britain, could complain against abusive masters to a justice of the peace. That justice, out of sessions, could choose one of two options. If he thought the complaint had merit, he could bind master and servant to appear before the next county court session. If he considered the complaint unjust, he could dismiss it.[21] Most petitions presented in county courts were heard by justices alone, although a petitioner could request a jury. Nearly four-fifths of the complaints against masters brought to Maryland courts were petitions filed by individual servants. Servants and masters could appeal judgments to Maryland's provincial court, which could uphold or reverse county court decisions.

A servant's friends or relatives could also file petitions on his behalf. This procedure was increasingly common in the late seventeenth and eighteenth centuries for children bound to crafts, husbandry, or housewifery. Such petitions also passed through a magistrate before being heard at the county court.

In two other ways, however, servants' complaints could be heard without a judicial triage. Adult servants sometimes elected to wait until their terms of servitude were completed and to sue their masters in civil court. They primarily sued masters who failed to provide them with freedom dues. Finally, county grand juries sometimes presented masters to the court for abusing servants or failing to educate them. Two types of complaints, therefore, were first heard by a justice sitting singly, whereas two were not.

Petitions were the means whereby a dependent could seek legal redress against an independent and they functioned as a civil suit once presented to the court. The petitioner (the plaintiff) had to prove his or her case by the preponderance of the evidence; if he or she did so, the master (the defendant) paid court costs. Otherwise, the dependents paid the costs. During the 1650s and 1660s, courts occasionally allowed servants simply to "Kneele . . . in open Court and ask forgiveness" when their petition failed because of their "poverty and [in]abillity to make any other satisfaction," but this practice quickly died out. Most servants throughout the colonial period almost certainly paid costs by serving additional time. Many servants retained at-

records of Kent County more thoroughly than those of other counties and have found odd petitions tucked into them in unexpected places. Second, the county retained its petition record for 1739–1757. Such records were not generally retained, and I know of no others in eighteenth-century Maryland. Finally, the county retained its court's Rough Minutes for 1791–1797, which include a record of servants' petitions, although unfortunately not their disposition. I think I have found, therefore, all the eighteenth-century petitions available for at least one county.

21. Dalton, *The Countrey Justice*, 90–92. In Britain, a justice might also send the apprentice to the local house of correction. None existed in the seventeenth-century colonies, however, and some justices may have substituted a whipping.

TABLE 1. Completed Cases

	Entered Cases	Completed Cases	Proportion Completed
County Court, 1652–1797			
1652–1670	48	40	83.3%
1671–1685	19	19	100.0
1686–1720	35	32	91.4
1721–1780	72	61	84.7
1781–1797[a]	21	10	47.6
Overall	195	162	83.1
Provincial Court, 1658–1685			
1658–1670	38	33	86.8
1671–1685	27	26	96.3
Overall	65	59	90.8
Grand overall	260	221	85.0%

a. Includes nine cases from the Kent County Court Rough Minutes, in which case results were never recorded. If these cases are dropped from the sample, the completion rate is 83.5 percent.

torneys to plead their cases; if they were successful, their masters paid the servants' attorney fees. Successful petitions, therefore, cost a servant nothing; unsuccessful ones, especially those presented by an attorney and heard by a jury, could prove ruinously expensive.[22]

The vast majority of servants, however, succeeded in their pleas for redress. Judicial decisions are available for more than four-fifths of all the petitions and other complaints filed by and on behalf of servants (see Table 1).[23]

22. Quotation from *Archives*, LIV, 407. In 1673, justices in Charles County noted that "sev[er]all Attorneyes have undertaken to manage Serv[an]ts Causes agst their Maisters and M[istresse]s" (*Archives*, LX, 496). For successful petitions presented by attorneys whose fees were added to costs, see *Archives*, LX, 108–110, 232–235.

23. Ascertaining the proportion of servants who petitioned for a redress of grievances is extremely difficult, because, first, we have only very rough estimates of the servant population in various parts of early Maryland at various times, and, except for Kent County, I have not found the entire "population" of extant petitions. I will, however, undertake an exercise in statistical guesswork. In the 1660s, Kent County clerks recorded an average of 151 taxables yearly. Taxables included free white men over the age of sixteen and male servants and slaves over the age of ten. If approximately the same proportion of people were male indentured servants as in adjoining Talbot County (.328 percent), then Kent County's population included roughly fifty male servants each year. If 20 percent of these men entered the colony with four-year contracts, and the remaining 80 percent served

Throughout most of the colonial and federal periods, servants won about 90 percent of the petitions they presented at the county courts and about 85 percent of those they presented at the provincial court (see Table 2).[24]

Only between 1671 and 1689 did courts grant fewer than 85 percent of petitions (although petitioners still prevailed in 60 percent of all cases). This reversal demonstrated a reluctance on the part of justices to grant a specific servant request—to be released from indentures—at a specific moment in time: a period of social and political upheaval in Maryland in which servants and poor planters played a large role. This reluctance will be examined in more detail below.

All social historians who trade in court records must come to terms, implicitly or explicitly, with cases that are not presented at court. Servants might have been discouraged by justices, almost always the largest property-holders in the county or the province, from presenting cases against their landholding masters. Grand jurymen, also by definition propertyholders, might have colluded in these efforts to keep propertyless servants in their places and deliberately failed to present servants' wrongs to the courts.

Scattered evidence, however, suggests that neither justices nor jurymen did so. When servant Edward Hotchkiss felt he had been detained beyond the expiry of his indenture, Michael Baysey, his overseer, "told him That if

---

according to the custom of the country and were equally distributed between the ages of ten and twenty-two, their average term length would have been 6.34 years. Just about 16 percent, or eight men, therefore, would on the average have gained their freedom each year. Over the course of the decade, then, eighty servants would have completed their terms, and the county would have maintained a population of fifty, for a total of 130 men. As about 35 percent of servants who had their ages judged in Kent County during the seventeenth century were female, we could assume a female servant population during the 1660s of about seventy women. During the decade, eight male indentured or customary servants and five female ones from the county petitioned for a redress of grievances, suggesting that about 6 percent of male servants and 7 percent of female servants did so. I have previously estimated that between 1 and 5 percent of apprentices in Kent County during the mid-eighteenth century filed petitions (Daniels, "Alternative Workers in a Slave Economy," 319–320). Estimate for Talbot County from Paul G. E. Clemens, *The Atlantic Economy and Colonial Maryland's Eastern Shore: From Tobacco to Grain* (Ithaca, N.Y., 1980), 84 n. 6; Gloria L. Main, *Tobacco Colony: Life in Early Maryland, 1650–1720* (Princeton, N.J., 1982), 102–105. It is reasonable to assume, therefore, that between 5 and 10 percent of servants petitioned for a redress of grievances during their term of service.

24. An eighteen-year period in the late seventeenth century, discussed below, proved the only exception to this rule. If petitions filed from 1671 to 1689 are dropped from the sample, county petitioners had a success rate of 89.6 percent (135 successful petitions of 153 filed) while provincial petitioners had a success rate of 84.8 percent (28 successful petitions of 33 filed). The seventeenth-century date breakpoints used were determined by plotting the available data on a scatterplot and observing the points of discontinuity within the data. The eighteenth-century data showed no breaks until the American Revolution, when county record-keeping was disrupted. I chose 1720 as the date at which Kent planters began to import African laborers heavily.

TABLE 2. Adjudication

	N	Judgments for Defendant (Master)	Judgments for Petitioner (Servant)	Proportion for Petitioner
		County Court		
1652–1670	41	2	39	95.1%
1671–1689	19	8	11	57.9
1690–1720	32	3	29	90.6
1721–1780	61	9	52	85.2
1781–1797	10	0	10	100.0
Overall	163	22	141	86.5
		Provincial Court		
1658–1670	33	5	28	84.8
1671–1683	26	10	16	61.5
Overall	59	15	44	74.6
Grand overall	222	37	185	83.3%

hee thought hee could gett his fredome he had best goe to Mr Preston [a justice]; and his Clerke would draw him a Pet[titio]n to that intent and purpose." Baysey added that "hee would exspect noe service from him, till hee saw wither hee could obteine his ffreedome or noe." When Hotchkiss went to Justice Michael Brooks, his owner James Bowling wrote to Brooks, saying he "should doe well to have him whipt" and should double his time "as a Runaway." Brooks refused and observed "hee had liberty to complaine wth out being tearmed a Runaway."[25]

Brooks's phrase—"liberty to complain"—is significant; it reveals his cognizance of a British jurisprudential culture open to English indentured servants but closed to African and African-American slaves. English servants had assented, through contracts, to their condition and to certain requisites inherent in it. Their contracts, however, did not demand that they accede to unreasonable treatment or give up the protection the law provided against cruel masters. Servants, like other Englishmen, could "not be subjected to any law or power amonge themselves *without their consent:* Whatsoever is more than this, is neither lawful nor durable." It was, instead, "bondage or licentiousnesse" that would "invariably lead to slavery." Servants used the

25. *Archives,* XLI, 179–180.

TABLE 3. Cases Completed in County Courts by Process

	N	Magisterial Triage		Proportion for Servants
		For Master	For Servants	
Petitions by servants	112	15	97	86.6%
Petitions on servants' behalf	14	0	14	100.0
[Overall	126	15	111	88.1]
Grand jury presentments	19	2	17	89.5
Civil cases (juries)	18	5	13	72.2
[Overall	37	7	30	81.1]
Grand overall	163	22	141	86.5%

law to restrain their masters' arbitrary and unlawful power, just as their masters used it to restrain that of the king. English liberty rested on the legal restriction of power, which could be accomplished only by "the old law, the folk law, the good law, the customary law of the community." That law was based, not on "the sovereign's [or master's] command, but the sovereign's restraint." Dependents stood to their masters as independents stood to the king. But even the king's power could be checked by law. Therein lay English liberty, a concept lost neither on magistrates, masters, overseers, nor on servants in the distant regions of Anglo-America.[26]

If justices had exerted pressure to keep complaints from court, the success rate of cases that passed through magisterial triage and those that did not should have been markedly different. Cases heard first by a justice should have been conspicuously more successful if magistrates kept all but the very strongest petitions or the most egregiously cruel masters out of court. In fact, the success rate of cases that passed through a single justice first was only slightly higher than those that did not (Table 3).

Neither do grand juries appear to have shielded masters from their misdeeds. That of Charles County, for example, presented Arthur Turner when his apprentice was "so ill treated in his hows that the voyce of the People Crieth Shame thereat." When the young man came to court, he had a "most Rotton filthy stincking Ulserated [leg]," his clothing was "ragged and torne," and his hair "seemed to be rotted of[f] with Ashes." In fact, the sight of him

26. "Libertye and the Weale Publick Reconciled in a Declaration to the Late Court of Elections in Newtown, the 17th of the 3rd month, 1637," italics in original, Speech of Isaac Wilkins, New York Assembly Delegates, Feb. 23, 1775, both in John Phillip Reid, *The Concept of Liberty in the Age of the American Revolution* (Chicago, 1988), 36, 80 (see also 63).

TABLE 4. Change in Complaints, 1652–1797

	N	Detention/ Sale (%)	Dues/ Wages (%)	Ill- Usage (%)	No Education (%)
1652–1670	87	50.6	34.5	14.9	0
1671–1685	46	60.9	32.6	4.4	2.2
1686–1720	35	28.6	20.0	37.1	14.3
1721–1780	72	36.1	18.1	20.8	25.0
1781–1797	21	47.6	4.8	28.6	19.1
Overall	261	45.2	25.2	18.8	10.8

"loathed all the beholders thearof," a difficult task in 1663; he was freed immediately from Turner's service.[27]

Servants who petitioned the court virtually always adduced one of four reasons for their complaints; the nature of these complaints changed over time (Table 4). Primarily many servants throughout the period complained that they had been detained beyond the end of their indenture or wrongfully sold to a master when they should have been free to make a contract. This complaint was the single most common one among all servants, male and female, Anglo-, Afro-, and native American, throughout the seventeenth and eighteenth centuries.

Between 1671 and 1689, however, servants' requests to be released from their indentures carried dangerous and threatening overtones. By the final three decades of the seventeenth century, freedmen faced declining economic opportunities in the older and most populous areas of the Chesapeake, which resulted in a contraction of suffrage in both Maryland and Virginia. Local economic and political tension, bubbling at least since 1670, coupled with fears of Indian wars and constitutional and religious upheavals, led by the middle of the decade to several Chesapeake rebellions.[28]

27. Grand juries sometimes presented masters on very flimsy evidence (Christine Daniels, "'Blood Will Out': The Test of Blood and Domestic Violence in Seventeenth-Century Maryland," paper presented at the American Historical Association Annual Meeting, January 1995). "Grand Jury Presentments" in Table 3 includes those of the counties' Orphans' Juries, who made some presentments on behalf of apprentices.

28. Lois Green Carr and Russell Menard, "Immigration and Opportunity: The Freedman in Early Colonial Maryland," in Thad W. Tate and David L. Ammerman, eds., *The Chesapeake in the Seventeenth Century: Essays on Anglo-American Society* (New York, 1979), 206–242; Menard, "The Tobacco Industry in the Chesapeake Colonies, 1617–1730: An Interpretation," *Research in Economic History*, V (1980), 109–177; Morgan, *American Slavery, American Freedom*, 180–292; Menard, "From Servant to Freeholder: Status Mobility and Property Accumulation in Seventeenth-Century Maryland," *WMQ*, XXX (1973),

TABLE 5. County Judgments for Servants by Complaint, 1652–1797

	N	Detention/ Sale (%)	Dues/ Wages (%)	Ill- Usage (%)	No Education (%)
1652–1670	41	94.4	94.1	100.0	
1671–1689	19	57.1	66.6	100.0	100.0
1689–1720	32	87.5	100.0	83.3	100.0
1721–1780	61	84.0	90.0	91.7	78.6
1781–1797	10	100.0		100.0	100.0
Overall	163	82.5	88.6	90.7	87.5

William Davyes and John Pate, for example, led a rebellion in southern Maryland in 1676. Although Davyes and Pate were substantial landholders, most of their followers were newly freed servants or poor, disenfranchised men. The list of complaints they sent the proprietor included the restricted access ex-servants had to economic stability and a political voice. The uprising was small and short-lived, but the Maryland Council had the rebels pursued through the province and executed Dayves and Pate.

From 1677 to 1689, the Catholic proprietary government endured a longer and more serious challenge to its authority from Josias Fendall, John Coode, and their followers. Although Fendall and Coode, like Davyes, Pate, and Nathaniel Bacon, were well-to-do, many economically disaffected people joined their movement. Poor planters, craftsmen, and a number of freedmen supported the Protestant Fendall's attack on Maryland's government, which almost led to violence in 1681. Constitutional and religious issues in Maryland then shadowed and echoed those of Parliament and king from the mid-1680s on. In 1689, Coode and a number of other wealthy Protestants led an uprising against the Council, which ended in the overthrow of Maryland's government.[29]

Justices in both county and provincial courts became more suspicious of

---

37–64; Russell Menard, P. M. G. Harris, and Lois Green Carr, "Opportunity and Inequality: The Distribution of Wealth on the Lower Western Shore of Maryland, 1638–1705," *Maryland Historical Magazine*, LXIX (1974), 169–184; Lorena Walsh, "Servitude and Opportunity in Charles County, Maryland," in Land, Carr, and Papenfuse, eds., *Law, Society, and Politics in Early Maryland*, 111–133.

29. Charles M. Andrews, *The Colonial Period of American History*, II, *The Settlements* (New Haven, Conn., 1936), 340–352; Wesley Frank Craven, *The Southern Colonies in the Seventeenth Century, 1607–1689* (Baton Rouge, La., 1949), 360–415; Robert J. Brugger, *Maryland: A Middle Temperament, 1634–1980* (Baltimore, 1988), 35–40; Lois Green Carr and David William Jordan, *Maryland's Revolution of Government, 1689–1692* (Ithaca, N.Y., 1974); Horn, *Adapting to a New World*, 368–380.

TABLE 6. Provincial Judgments for Servants by Complaint, 1658–1683

	N	Detention/ Sale (%)	Dues/ Wages (%)	Ill- Usage (%)	No Education (%)
1658–1670	33	75.0	100.0	100.0	100.0
1671–1683	26	57.9	60.0	100.0	100.0
Overall	59	66.6	86.7	100.0	100.0

servants who claimed that their masters detained them beyond the expiry of their indenture as increasing numbers of freedmen joined rebellions against established government. Although the courts had found for servants in detention cases about 85 percent of the time before 1671, they did so only 60 percent of the time between 1671 and 1689. The increase in political unrest in the 1670s reflected, in part, the inability of the government to accommodate the economic needs of new freedmen in the older settled areas of the Chesapeake. One way, obviously, to keep servants fed, clothed, and away from political uprisings was to keep them under both the care and the control of a master (Tables 5 and 6).

That courts' willingness to detain servants during the 1670s was based on fears of civil unrest is confirmed by the same courts' willingness to free female servants. Whereas only 50 percent of male servants won their petitions for freedom during the 1670s and 1680s, 83 percent of female servants— who were less likely to join civil riots—did so.

Servants of color were much more likely to be detained in servitude than their white counterparts. Although not quite half of all servants complained that their masters had failed to release them after their term was concluded (at least, by their own account) sixteen of eighteen servants (89 percent) who identified themselves as "Negroe," Indian, or mulatto did so. All but one of these people served in Kent County from the middle to late eighteenth century. Certainly African-American and native American servants might have seemed more threatening than Anglo-American servants in a society worried about slave rebellions. But part of this difference should also be ascribed to the increasing presence of permanent or temporary servile labor forms, particularly by the late eighteenth century, that applied only to people of color. Masters and executors, wittingly or unwittingly, could with little effort put indentured servants in other labor institutions that offered fewer legal rights.[30]

30. Other labor forms besides slavery became the province of people of color and generally carried fewer benefits than indentured servitude; they include debt servitude and term slavery. See Daniels, " 'Without Any Limitacon of Time': Debt Servitude in

Although masters might have been more likely to detain such servants, however, county courts did not support them. Twelve completed cases involving petitioners of color survive, most filed in Kent County between 1745 and 1790; all but one were adjudicated for the servant. Cyrius was "held as a slave" in 1753, while Mulatto Judith was "detained as a servant" and Indians Will, Hannah, and Ned were "held as slaves" in 1745. All were freed when they presented their petitions to the justices. Only Indian Mathew was unsuccessful; he had been "taken by the people of Carolina from the Spaniards." Witness William Meeds, who had been "at the taking and selling of many" such laborers, insisted that "all such were slaves during life."[31]

The disjuncture in the courts' treatment of servant petitions during the 1670s and 1680s, however, did not signify a long-term change in servants' positions vis-à-vis the courts (see tables). Servants detained beyond the end of their indentures, moreover, won compensation for their time if they requested it or if the court thought they had earned it.[32]

Other servants were not illegally detained but unlawfully sold in the first place. When French Canadian Thomas D'Ignio was a young boy, for example, he was entrusted to the care of his godfather's neighbor in New York. The neighbor, a Mr. Maneir, promptly took him from New York to Maryland and sold him as a servant, where D'Ignio petitioned the provincial court for his freedom in 1681. He could produce no written evidence of his free status, nor could he immediately present witnesses. The court, however, freed him at once, as in its "Oppinion and Judgment" Maneir "Wrongfully sold" him and "had not any right or title in him as Soe or any otherwaies to Dispose of him." It continued, "Therefore . . . Thomas DIgnio Bee and is hereby acquitted and made free from all servitude." A number of eighteenth-century petitions were similarly judged solely on the servant's oral testimony, such as that of Patrick Suetors, who stated in 1743 that sheriff Hercules Coutts held him as a servant although "in thruth [he] has no pretense of claim to him." The Kent County justices heard Suetor's story and ruled him free.[33]

Maryland's period of social upheaval also prompted the provincial court to punish runaway servants more severely than previously, although it had

---

Colonial America," *Labor History,* XXXVI (1995), 232–250; T. Stephen Whitman, "Diverse Good Causes: Manumission and the Transformation of Urban Slavery," *Social Science History,* XIX (1995), 333–370.

31. Kent County Petition Record, 1739–1757 (hereafter cited as Petitions), 135–137, 266–267; Kent County Bonds and Indentures, 1720–1726, 45–46.

32. *Archives,* XLI, 371, LIII, 600, LIV, 512–513, LXV, 511, LXX, 132.

33. D'Ignio: *Archives,* LXX, 196. The petition does not discuss the length of time he served, but nowhere does the language suggest that it was more than a few months. Suetors: Petitions, 83.

less effect on the actions taken by county courts. By 1661, Maryland's run-away statute, severe compared to those of other colonies, provided that an absconding servant was to serve ten days' time for each day he or she was gone and to be whipped. Despite positive law, however, servants who ran away before 1670 were usually punished as courts saw fit. They consid-ered factors such as the occasion for the servant's flight, whether he or she claimed abuse as a condition, and whether he or she had received corporal correction for running away. County courts, moreover, usually elected ei-ther to whip a servant or to assign additional time, but not both.[34] This variable response to infractions created what might be called customary servant or labor law within each court's jurisdiction. Customary law was based on case-by-case precedents in a given county or area. It did not contradict common law but often ignored statutes.

Kent County justices, for example, questioned Thomas Guinn closely in 1670 to determine his reasons for absenting himself from his master's house for thirty-four days. They inquired as to his cause and whether he had re-ceived any "abuse." When Guinn responded only that his master had "over soaked his Corne to beat," he was slapped with an additional 340 days' time. The same court often preferred swift and summary justice for runaways, however; when, in 1659, Matthew Reade's servant, called simply "Mouse," proved incorrigibly and constantly absent, the court ordered "25 good Sound Lashes" and directed any resident who saw him run away again to "whipp him home againe to his M[aste]r." The court evidently saw little point in ordering additional time for a servant who would not stay home to serve it. Neither was this conundrum lost on some masters. Francis Armstrong, for example, asked the court in 1665 not to require any more time from his runaway servant Roger "Provided that hee doth Run away noe more."[35]

The Charles County court was generally less severe in its treatment of runaways. In 1667, servant David Ralston petitioned the Charles County court for his freedom, claiming that his master Henry Robertson had de-tained him three months beyond the term of his indenture. Robertson produced a memorandum he previously had filed with the court in which he stated on oath that Ralston had run away for two months and seven days during his term. Ralston requested a jury, which found that he had "Served since the Indenture was expired as long time as he had absented himselfe"; in other words, not ten days to one, but one day to one. The court freed Ralston and ordered Robertson to pay him his dues. In 1658, Margaret Pearce's master refused to pay her freedom dues when she ran away. Charles's justices ordered him to do so, and assigned Pearce no additional time, as she had de-

34. *Archives*, II, 149, 298.
35. Kent cases: *Archives*, LIV, 184, 297; Armstrong: ibid., 398.

serted him "only through his abusses." In 1668, Nicholas Emerson appeared before the same court to present his account for runaway time against his servant, Elizabeth Haselton. Emerson had tried to establish a paper trail against his servant by appearing in court whenever she ran away and declaring, on oath, that she had done so. The clerk's laconic entries detail a householder constantly exasperated by his young maid's absence: "the 7th day of July 1665 . . . m[emorand]dum that Elizabeth Hasellton ran away and absented her selfe . . . for the space of sixteen dayes"; June 11, 1667, "M[emorand]dum: Elizabeth Haselton . . . hath absented her selfe from her said Master for the space of 12 dayes"; August 7, 1667, "for the space of 10 dayes." When Emerson appeared to claim Haselton's additional time, however, a jury found against him, after Emerson's other servants and grown stepchildren reported that Haselton had already been either forgiven or punished for her misdeeds. They testified that Haselton "was then pardoned for her running away and after that She run away again and her Mistris tyed her to a bed post and whipped her"; that "Mrs Emanson did beat the defendant for running away"; and that "her mistris tooke her and whipt her." The jury put no credence in Mrs. Emerson's explanation that she had not whipped Haselton for running away but for stealing clothing and therefore deserved compensatory time. The Emersons got no more of Haselton's labor.[36]

Justices in Talbot County used the same rule when John Kinemant requested two hundred additional days from his servant for twenty days' runaway time; as Kinemant had already "beate his [Servant] Until he was awerry," the justices refused the time. Talbot's court, however, adhered more strictly to provincial law regarding servants than did those of other counties and virtually always ordered ten days' service for every day the servant had been gone throughout the 1660s and 1670s.[37]

Although the provincial court often used the ten-days-to-one rule before 1670, it established the custom and precedent firmly between 1673 and 1678 in the face of poor planters' and servants' rebelliousness and discontent.[38] In 1672, for example, John Owen ran away from George Beckwith and was gone fifty days; the provincial court ordered him to serve his master an additional four months' time as compensation, a ratio of about two and one-half days to one. By 1678, however, the provincial court automatically ordered servants to provide ten days' time to one as compensation, even when, as in the

36. *Archives,* LX, 108–110, LIII, 15, LX, 64, 90, 95, 234–235.
37. *Archives,* LIV, 400, 416, 443, 533, 540, 542.
38. Servant runaways were prosecuted as either petitions or civil cases (if the servant had already been freed) with the master as the plantiff and the servant as the defendant. Because these were not servant petitions, they do not constitute part of the database.

case of John Hough, the servant pleaded that he had fled only "in danger of his life what for want of ffood and badd usage."[39]

This increasing severity, however, did not necessarily represent a gradual hardening over time as elites and nonelites became more readily identifiable in Maryland. By 1690, decisions in favor of servant petitions in the Kent County court had risen again to more than four out of five. In fact, the proportion of decisions for servants, though variable, generally increased over the course of the eighteenth century (Table 4). Nor did eighteenth-century courts react differently when elite people were challenged by servants.[40] During the seventeenth century, the provincial court found for servants who challenged elite masters more than 75 percent of the time; during both the seventeenth and eighteenth centuries, the county courts did so more than 80 percent of the time. Challenging an elite master was slightly, but only slightly, less likely to result in a servant's prevailing in court.[41]

Servants who petitioned for their freedom theoretically could be construed as having challenged the first line of political authority in Anglo-America—their masters. Only in times of political rebellion, however, was that challenge threatening enough to require a judicial response.

The other complaints servants adduced in their petitions, on the other hand, did not challenge authority. On the contrary, all were requests for legal redress when their master had not acted responsibly enough as a family governor in one of three ways: by failing to compensate them at the end of their terms, by abusing them physically, or by failing to educate them properly. Although servants prevailed nearly 80 percent of the time in petitions for freedom, they prevailed in more than 90 percent of cases in which their master had failed in his duties.

Many indentured servants and apprentices petitioned the court when their masters withheld their freedom dues; hired servants did so when masters refused to pay them their wages. At the end of a servant's indenture, an informal procedure evidently took place in Maryland to ensure that soon-to-be ex-servants and masters agreed on freedom dues. Servants delivered their half of an indenture to their masters in front of witnesses. The master read the contract aloud, "whereby they [the servant and witnesses] might understand what was therein properly belonging" to the servant "for his

39. *Archives*, LXV, 50, LXVII, 227, LXX, 168, 453, esp. 455.
40. Defendants were considered "elite" if they used one of the following appellations: Captain, Commander, Gentleman, Governor, Mister, or Mistress (as in "Mistress Jones").
41. Raw numbers for provincial court findings were 19 of 25 cases involving elite masters for servants (76 percent); for county courts before 1690, 31 of 37 cases for servants (83.8 percent); for county courts after 1690, 22 of 26 cases for servants (84.6 percent). These numbers are between zero and ten percentage points lower than those for servants petitioning against nonelite masters during the same time periods.

tyme of Service." The servant would then give his or her master or mistress a receipt for the dues. It was a relatively easy procedure, therefore, to discover whether the servant had received his or her dues and simple to require compensation from his or her master.[42]

Servants lodged complaints when masters ill-used them. Most frequently, seventeenth-century servants noted that their masters had corrected them physically "above measure"; that is, their physical punishment had been too great for the infraction they had committed. Female servants were more likely than men to complain of ill-usage, particularly during the seventeenth century; while only 8 percent of all early male servants' complaints listed physical abuse, 38 percent of female servants' complaints did so.

Part of this difference arose from gender boundaries, as mistresses were more likely to assault their maids than their men; servant women, therefore, could be injured by one of two household members, while men were generally, though not exclusively, subject only to their masters' violence. Sarah Evans complained, for example, that "her said Mistris strook" her "three boxes on the eare" when she refused to answer a question, and Sarah Taylor's had slapped her several times while she was in her employ. Although whenever "there had been some falling out . . . [her mistress] sued to her the sd Sarah to be freinds" afterward, Taylor always refused; "shee would not shee scornd it after shee was abused." These examples illustrate the volatility of mistresses' relationships with their teenage maids; they also suggest a relatively narrow social gap between seventeenth-century servants and mistresses. A quick-tempered mistress who begged her maid's pardon does not seem haughty; a stiff-necked young maid who refused it does not seem cowed.[43]

Women servants were also, of course, subject to sexual abuse from their masters or other members of the household; two women complained of sexual assaults, while no male servants did so. Anne Gould, for example, petitioned the Kent County court for compensation from her master, Mr. Owings, in 1656. Gould stated that Owings came to her one night when the overseer was away, threw her on a bed and "forst [her] and had the usse of her bodie, whch was much to [her] greife, beeinge the Custome of weomen was upon her." Owings, moreover, blamed her for her own misfortune, repeatedly asking "what am I the better for thee" and "what the plauge doe I keep thee for" as he raped her. As a final abuse, moreover, he left her with the pox, although "till the tyme shee Receivd this Abusse shee was as well as ever in her liffe." The courts, upon hearing such ac-

---

42. Examples include *Archives*, XLI, 418, LVII, 579.
43. *Archives*, LIV, 181 (Taylor), XLIX, 318–319 (Evans).

counts, proved more likely to find for servants on charges of abuse than on any others.[44]

Other masters, however, took their duties to female dependents seriously. Anne Mardin told her master, William Robisson, that William Wennam had promised her marriage in order to have sex with her. Robisson spoke to Wennam and "deseired" him "to marry his mayd." Wennam refused, and Robisson petitioned the Charles County court "humbly Crave[ing] relife" as Wennam "had dishonored[ed] [his] house." The court—like many of the witnesses, apparently—was confused about the relief it could offer; Mardin was not pregnant, so no child needed support. And in fact there was "no profe of a Carnall Copulation unles hee Coold prove by sufficient evidence that [he] had seene them." Household honor in seventeenth-century Anglo-America was a slippery concept, if indeed it existed at all.[45]

Other women, including midwives, tried to guard maids against the sexual abuses of their masters. Most servants who bore illegitimate children bore them to other servants, who accepted their paternity with more or less grace. But midwives in Maryland, like those elsewhere in Anglo-America, were charged to discover the true identity of bastards' fathers during the mothers' labor. One incident at least suggests they could be zealous in their attempts to uncover masters' abuses. Servant Elizabeth Lockett was brought to bed in 1657, having affirmed throughout her pregnancy that Thomas Bright, a young unmarried planter, was the father of her child. Indeed, she and Bright had betrothed themselves; they had broken a silver coin between them. Each had kept half, agreed to marry, and informed others of their plans. Throughout Lockett's thirty-six-hour labor, the women attending her repeatedly demanded the name of her child's father, but "all that ever she Confest wase that it wase thomas Brights Child." Gossip had evidently suggested otherwise, however, so the midwives further insisted that she tell them what "hur master Dide to hure in the husks in the tobaco house." She cried out "so well as she could" that "hur master Did butt tickell hur," that she "never knew any other mane" but Bright, and that "she never knew hur Master but by his face and Hands." They finally pressured her to pinpoint and describe the night she became pregnant in detail and swore her to it on the Bible.[46]

Nor were female servants necessarily passive victims of male brutality. They occasionally employed one of the traditional weapons of the weak and slandered their masters. Certainly Margaret Mannering did when she ac-

44. *Archives*, LIV, 69.
45. *Archives*, LIII, 133.
46. *Archives*, LIV, 205–211. Breaking a piece of money was evidently part of a contract between a couple that signified they were married or at least betrothed.

cused her master, Thomas Bradnox, of having had "the use of her body and other passages." He pleaded his innocence, however, and finally "in open court she . . . acknowledged to be false . . . her contradictory complaints."[47] Bradnox was a particularly good target for such slanders; he was a brutal and unpredictable man, outrageous even by the standards of a violent time. His behavior was shocking in an independent man with responsibilities and obligations to his neighbors and his dependents. Women servants clearly understood that a cry of "wolf" carried more weight against such a master than it would against a more respectable man.

By the eighteenth century, servants who complained of ill-usage were more likely to mean neglect than violence. In 1742, John Shapley's master failed to clothe him well, "for which reason [he] must go naked or depend upon Charity which is very cold." Ann McManus was "very Barbarously and inhumanly used" by her master "in being denied necessary victuals and clothing and Lodgeing and being burthened with unreasonable labour beyond her strength." Jacob Street complained that "he had been tossicated about from place to place" and had been "a Great Sufferer both for the back and the Belly"; he also suspected that his master was a Roman Catholic, which he adduced as a third point of abuse. Certainly a few masters, like Patrick Johnson's, persisted in "unmercifully beateing" their indentured servants as well as failing to provide them with adequate food, clothing, and housing or forcing them to work too hard. By the mid-eighteenth century, however, servants, both male and female, were more likely to starve or freeze than to be beaten or raped.[48]

Patriarchal domination of the household and the courts did not dissuade women servants from filing petitions. Scholars have estimated that women comprised between 25 and 33 percent of bound servants in Maryland during the seventeenth century, depending on the agricultural economy of the region, a proportion that declined to about 15 percent during the eighteenth century.[49] Women filed more than a quarter of seventeenth-century peti-

47. *Archives*, LIV, 122. Here I assume that slanders proved in court were slanders. Other colonialists have discussed "reputation" and "deviance" in early America, within which this discussion of "responsibility" fits. See T. H. Breen, *Imagining the Past: East Hampton Histories* (Reading, Mass., 1989), 124–137; Mary Beth Norton, "Gender and Defamation in Seventeenth-Century Maryland," *WMQ*, XLIV (1987), 3–39; Laurel Thatcher Ulrich, *Good Wives: Image and Reality in the Lives of Women in Northern New England, 1650–1750* (New York, 1980), 89–99. James C. Scott discusses slander of the wealthy as a traditional tool of the poor in *Weapons of the Weak: Everyday Forms of Peasant Resistance* (New Haven, Conn., 1985), esp. 234–235, 282–285.

48. Quotations from Petitions, 60–61, 103, 194–195, 269. Additional complaints of neglect and occasional violence in Kent County Petition Record, 127; Kent County Court Minutes, 1776–1782, unpaginated, Nov. 26, 1776 (hereafter cited as Minutes); Minutes, 1782–1788, 52, 1789–1797, 326.

49. Paul Clemens estimates about one-third of servants on the Eastern Shore, which was

TABLE 7. Servant Complaints by Gender

	N	Detention/ Sale (%)	Dues/ Wages (%)	Ill- Usage (%)	No Education (%)
Female	46	41.1	32.3	24.4	2.2
Male	176	46.3	23.4	17.1	13.2
Total	222	43.7	27.9	20.8	7.7

tions and about 15 percent of the eighteenth-century ones, proportions that tally closely with their presence in the servant population. Female servants were, in fact, generally more likely to win their cases than were males; 89 percent of women won their cases, while 81 percent of men did so.

In addition to being more likely to claim physical abuse than men, women were more likely to claim their dues had been withheld. On the other hand, they were less likely to be detained than male servants, possibly because they were less valuable field laborers. They were also far less likely to claim they had not received an education according to the particulars of their indentures (Table 7).

Male apprentices to crafts and husbandry and female apprentices to housewifery sometimes complained that they had not been provided with sufficient education, either according to the terms of their contract or "as in right a poor" apprentice deserved. The institution of colonial apprenticeship has not received much attention, and many colonial scholars have considered or assumed that craft apprenticeship was the only "true" form of apprenticeship. This argument, like that concerning slavery and servitude, is historically teleological; craft apprenticeship was indeed the last form of apprenticeship to survive (though in a languishing condition) until the twentieth century. Craft apprentices were certainly the most elite apprentices, in both the education they required and the resources their parents or guardians paid to support them. By the late seventeenth century, however, the apprenticeship of children born in the colonies to agriculture or house-

moving toward a mixed economy, were women during the 1680s in "Economy and Society on Maryland's Eastern Shore," in Land, Carr, and Papenfuse, eds., *Law, Society, and Politics*, 153–171. Walsh estimates that about one-quarter of servants in the tobacco region of the lower Western Shore before 1706 were women in "Servitude and Opportunity in Charles County, Maryland," ibid., 111–133. The proportion of immigrant and creole female servants in Kent County on the Eastern Shore declined during the eighteenth century from about 35 percent to about 15 percent of the servant population (Daniels, "Alternative Workers in a Slave Economy," 200–242). Women's petitions comprised 38 of 144 (26.4 percent) filed before 1700 and 18 of 118 (15.3 percent) of those filed afterward.

work, depending on sex, was a common practice, just as it was in Britain. These children, who were usually though not exclusively poor or orphaned, replaced many of the children and adolescents who had been imported as indentured servants earlier in the century. Apprentices' contracts differed from those of indentured servants only in that they virtually always carried some provisions for education after 1710.[50]

Female servants were less likely to complain of not receiving an education for at least two reasons. First, before 1710, very few girls were promised any sort of education in their contracts. Second, when such promises became common for females during the second decade of the eighteenth century, contracts virtually always specified that the girl was "to learne to read well in her Bible and to be kept to the same so she may read at the age of sixteene or on the day of her mariage." Girls were not to learn writing or arithmetic. Most masters or mistresses could have taught reading themselves, although many may have had to send male apprentices to school to learn to write or cipher.[51]

Failing to receive an education was particularly damaging to craft apprentices, many of whom required considerable formal schooling and, of course, practical instruction in a trade. Maryland's economy supported relatively few craftsmen until the third decade of the eighteenth century. Soon thereafter, apprentices who sought redress for their masters' failures to educate or train them multiplied. James Poole complained that, although he had been a cooper's apprentice for nine years, he "had never been instructed in the trade nor taught to read write and cipher," while Robert Smith, bound as a joiner, had never received "proper instruction whereby [he] is likely to loose his time without Learning his trade." William Bruffitt argued that he had learned nothing of the carpenter's trade from his master Theophilus Randall except "the Drawing of Shingles which [he] conceives to be but a Small Branch if any at all of the Carpenters trade." Nor did Randall send him to school "tho there be a Schoolmaster hard by his plantation and has been for these two years past." Samuel Wilson filed his petition after he had completed his apprenticeship and was struggling as a tailor. He never had been formally taught "to read or write or cypher" and was, therefore, "reduced to very great inconvenience being unable to carrey on his business in a proper manner." Although most servants who pleaded that they had not been educated were craft apprentices, young men and women bound to farming or housewifery occasionally complained as well. Mary Curtis protested that she had "Lived twelve years with John Cracklin who kept me at work at the Hoe

---

50. Daniels, "Alternative Workers in a Slave Economy," 314–384.
51. Daniels, "Alternative Workers in a Slave Economy," 344–356.

and has given me neither learning nor anything else."[52] When the clerk recorded resolutions for these cases, he usually noted that an apprentice's master had been required to make a cash payment to his servant; the servant could use the money to purchase some schooling or to bind himself to another craftsman.

But although the courts generally supported servants' petitions against their masters, some servants, because of their legal status, were at more risk than others. Customary servants who entered Maryland without written contracts were less likely to prevail in their suits than indentured servants for whom contracts had been executed and witnessed either in Britain or in Maryland. Such servants were said to serve "according to the custom of the country," defined in great part by the county courts, which governed their term of servitude, the dues they received, and other conditions. Written contracts were more readily enforced than oral ones, although even customary servants prevailed in seven out of ten cases (Table 8). Customary servants were more vulnerable than indentured servants in several ways. After a master purchased a customary servant, for example, he was to bring the servant into court to have his or her age judged; a servant's term was based on age, as were those of English poor apprentices. In Maryland, the length of the term itself changed occasionally.[53] But no official body had a record of the servant's entry into the colony before the master brought him or her to court. Maryland law required masters to do so within six months of the servant's arrival, but it was to the master's advantage to delay bringing a servant to court if he thought that by doing so he could extend the servant's time; a male servant who appeared to be, for example, fourteen years old would serve seven years whether he were brought to court in February or November of 1655 (as long as life in the tobacco colony had not aged him prematurely).

The provincial court moved strongly against this practice in 1681, when John Staples, servant to Christopher Rousby, protested his continued service as his master had had his age judged tardily. The court agreed that Staples "ought to serve noe longer then from the time of the arrivall of the shipp in

52. Quotations from: Petitions, 8, 15, 137–138; Minutes, 1782–1788, 105, 247. Additional petitions for lack of education include Kent County Court Proceedings, 1716–1718, 92; Petitions, 169.

53. The length of terms of servitude for servants who entered Maryland without contracts changed frequently. In 1654, a law was passed in which people twenty-one years old and older were to serve for four years; those aged sixteen to twenty for six; those aged twelve to sixteen for seven; those under twelve until age twenty-one (*Archives*, I, 352). In 1661, this was amended so that people twenty-two and older were to serve for four years; those aged eighteen to twenty-one for five; those aged fifteen to seventeen for six; those under fifteen until age twenty-one (*Archives*, I, 409, 443, 453, 537). In 1666, all terms were lengthened by a year for all servants except those under fifteen, but, in 1671, their terms too were extended to age twenty-two (*Archives*, II, 147, 335).

TABLE 8. Judgments for Servants by Condition of Servitude, 1652–1797

Status	County (N = 163)	Provincial (N = 59)
Apprentice	90.0	75.0%
Customary	70.4	70.0
Hired	83.3	100.0
Indentured	90.3	76.2
Debt	100.0	100.0
Overall	86.5	74.6%

wch hee was Transported into this Province," although it also noted that it needed some evidence as to the name or date of arrival of that ship. Rousby was a customs official later killed during Coode's rebellion and seems to have been universally disliked. Certainly distaste for Rousby might have contributed to the court's decision, but its precedent was nonetheless established.[54]

But whereas customary servants were vulnerable, they also seem to have been generally cognizant of their rights. They refused, for example, to enter into written indentures that would extend their term of service, even if it meant the security of a written contract. William Knags, who entered Maryland in 1654 without indentures, was about sixteen at the time. According to law, he should have been bound for five years, but his master had purchased him for seven. Knags acknowledged "there was Indentures drawne for his serveing [seven] yeares," but he would "not signe to the same." The jury agreed that "a Servant comeing in at Sixteene yeares of age without Indentures ought not to serve above ffower yeares . . . the plantiff . . . hath . . . compleated his servitude according to the Custome of this Province."[55] Servant Richard Macall, deported to Maryland during Cromwell's campaign against Ireland, arrived as one of a group of very little boys; the "Eldest . . . then was not above tenn years of age," and his mistress asked his master, Thomas Gerard, whether he had also bought "some Cradles to have Rocked them in." His master failed to have their ages judged, however, and, as soon as Macall reached young manhood, he petitioned for his freedom "to see Justice done." Macall lost his petition, being judged at nineteen, but Gerard had his other customary servants' ages reckoned at the same time to eliminate future problems with litigious servants cognizant of their rights.[56]

At least some servants, moreover, knew the laws of more than one region.

54. Archives, LXX, 41; Andrews, Colonial Period of American History, II, 358. County courts were aware of this practice and disciplined masters for it (Archives, LIII, 624).
55. Archives, XLI, 417; also Archives, XLIX, 387–388, 565.
56. Archives, XLI, 476–478, XLIX, 94–95, 122–124, 138. Quotations from first reference.

Matthew Rodham had purchased Joseph Inglesby as an adult in Virginia, where custom required one more year of servitude than in Maryland. After they removed to Maryland, however, Inglesby petitioned for his freedom after only four years. He was granted it, as Maryland courts were "not obleiged to take Cognizance of that Act in Vergenia Concerning Servants Servitudes."[57]

If servants had signed to more favorable contracts than that offered by custom, however, justices upheld their indentures. In fact, they upheld them even if the written contract were no longer in evidence, as long as a free witness could appear or send a deposition to support the servant's claim. At least a few petitioners who ended as customary servants, for example, had originally had indentures. In 1674, Robert Crosman, commander of "the good Shipp called the Antilope of Liverpoole," had carried servants Christopher Williamson and Elizabth Royall into Maryland and sold them to Robert Graham for four years. When Graham attempted to detain them for a fifth, according to Maryland's changeable law of custom, Crosman testified that their term indeed had been only for four years, but their indentures were "accidentally missing."[58]

These procedures for servants' protection conform to those taken by many southern colonial courts in defense of widows' dower rights: servants could claim at least the custom of the country, despite the text of written indentures; they were entitled to more, but not less, on oral evidence. In their dealings with indentured servants, therefore, Maryland courts followed, not property laws, but procedures established for other dependent household relationships.[59]

Maryland colonial courts clearly saw servants as working under contract law, not as chattel. Some servants, moreover, demonstrated the sharp instincts of attorneys as well as an appreciation for their position as contractors. When John Normand bound himself to John Hatton in late 1662, his contract did not include a common boilerplate phrase to indicate that Hatton or his executors could make his indenture over to an assign or heir. After Hatton's death in 1663, Normand appeared before the provincial court, noting that he had contracted to serve only Hatton, "noe assignes or any other prson whatsoever." Normand was so sure of his legal footing that he agreed to pay Hatton's executors double costs and damages if he lost his suit; a jury confirmed his opinion and freed him, noting that the executors had to "stand to" the contract "as it directly lyeth by the words" in the indenture.[60]

---

57. *Archives,* XLIX, 331–332.
58. *Archives,* LXVII, 420. See also LIV, 582.
59. Peter Charles Hoffer summarizes southern widows' dower rights neatly in *Law and People in Colonial America* (Baltimore, 1992), 74–75.
60. *Archives,* XLIX, 82–84.

When Francis Gonby signed on for the colonies as Richard Deaver's servant in 1660, he agreed "to worke att Joyners worke and noe other" and to work for "the full third part of what [his master] should by his Labour gayne" as well as freedom dues. Deaver, however, sold his contract to another master, who soon sold it to a third. His subsequent masters tried to use him in part as a common laborer and refused to pay him one-third share of the profits. The court referred the petition to one of its justices, Henry Sewall, a lawyer trained at the Inns of Court and secretary of the province. Sewall first clarified the question ("If the first importer should sell him to another whither or noe the Last person should not make good that former Condicon?") and answered it: "Yes, If it were to ffive hundred prsons the Last must and should make good that former Condicon." The county courts retained this interpretation well into the eighteenth century. Nicholas Hunt bound himself to William Hall in 1737 for three years. Hall agreed to pay him £3 each year in addition to his dues. Hall sold Hunt's contract to a second master, who sold it to a third, William Wilmer. When Hunt was freed in 1740, Wilmer refused to pay him £9, until the Kent County court ordered him to do so.[61]

It is impossible to imagine a slave's owner making any promises a subsequent owner would be obliged to honor. Owners of slaves had rights in the person, not the contracted labor, of the slave. Indentured and customary servants, on the other hand, were contracted laborers, not property, whether their contracts were written or customary. Some masters assuredly violated those contracts, but the legal ideal, even at the lowest possible level of adjudication, did not countenance the practice.

Nor did courts necessarily give more weight to the written culture of many seventeenth-century masters over the oral culture of many seventeenth-century servants. Servants who entered with written indentures or their masters often had clear cases, but Maryland justices did not hesitate to question or overturn a written contract if they found it suspicious. Dutch servant John De Creyger had served out his time with Captain James Neale when Neale asked him to stay on and help with the next tobacco crop. Creyger was reluctant to do so, but consented in part because Neale withheld his freedom dues. Creyger distrusted Neale (with good reason, as it turned out), "gott a Condition [contract] drawne," and brought it to Neale to sign; the contract provided that Creyger was to receive his freedom dues and a share of the crop at the end of the season. Neale, however, added "I will not performe

---

61. *Archives,* XLIX, 103–104, 140–141; Petitions, 25. Skilled servants like Gonby were about as likely as unskilled servants to win their cases; seventeen of twenty servants (85 percent) who were identified as skilled or learning a skill won cases against their masters.

this Condition" at the bottom of the contract before he signed. Creyger "by Reason I Could not Read it I did belleve" Neale had signed in good faith; when he discovered otherwise, he left Neale's employ. The justices found for Creyger, released him from the contract, and ordered Neale to pay him his dues. In a similar manner, after John Griffith had served out his time with Thomas Paine, Paine refused to give him his freedom dues but managed to persuade "yor poore Ignorant Peticoner to putt his hand unto" "a False Receipt." The provincial court judges dismissed the receipt instantly and ordered Paine to pay Griffith his dues.[62]

By the mid-eighteenth century, many servants could read, but joining their masters in a literate culture did not always protect them from chicanery. John Bryan, for example, signed a contract in 1739 to serve for four years, but his master "rubbed out the word four and put in seven." When his first master sold his contract, Bryan explained the deception to his new master, William Powell. Powell, who had paid for three additional years, nonetheless tried to detain Bryan as a servant; instead, Bryan was freed by the justices in 1743.[63]

Neither was a forced contract a good contract. Owen Sullivan had signed a four-year indenture in Ireland, but "when he was on sea, the captain wanted him to sign an Indenture for five." Sullivan refused, and the captain kept "his allowance of victuals" and threatened to tie the other servants to the longboat if they took food or water to him. What's more, the captain told Sullivan "that nobody would buy him for four years" and that, when they got to Delaware "he would put him in Prison and clapp Irons on him and make him serve his four years there." Sullivan, "being a stranger to the affaires of the country and the want of victuals together," signed a five-year contract, "though it was against his will." The court freed Sullivan immediately.[64]

Cases of master-servant disputes that appeared before a court, of course, were not normative, any more than modern-day cases of domestic violence in police blotters describe normative family life or civil case dockets normative social behavior. But these cases, by example, allow insight into the social roles independents were expected to fill in Anglo-American colonies.

First, servants were not the poor, benighted victims who currently inhabit

62. *Archives*, LX, 344, LVII, 579.
63. Petitions, 78–79.
64. Petitions, 151–152. Such decisions could also work against servants. In March 1682, John Doyly alleged that his master had detained him past his time and adduced a contract he said had been written in Waterford, Ireland, in December 1677. The court examined the document, but found it "noe good Indenture"; Doyly was ordered to serve an additional nine months. Contemporaneous political upheavals, of course, might have influenced the court's decision (*Archives*, LXX, 167).

colonial historiography. Masters and servants were clearly not equal in age, in rank, in status, or in political power, but servants (together with the courts that supported their rights) clearly possessed agency in negotiating and defining the limits of the institution within which they labored. The form of the petition allowed seventeenth- and eighteenth-century servants to proceed against their masters with little cost; magisterial triage evidently screened out only a few weak cases. They also had the same extralegal weapons other politically dependent laboring people used, including slander and false accusation.

Second, servants and slaves held very different places within Anglo-American case law. Justices employed common notions of household dependents' rights, such as those for widows' dower, to structure and create the customary laws and precedents that governed colonial servants with or without written indentures. Widespread ideas about the sanctity of contracts and the terms under which they could be executed contributed to this law as it pertained to servants and apprentices with written indentures. Such ideas, in turn, were embedded in an omnipresent jurisprudential culture in which a person, dependent or no, could be subject to another's power or control only by his or her consent.

Third, the county and provincial court systems must be accorded more influence over master-servant relations than it generally receives. County and provincial justices did not identify reflexively with the interests of elite people to defraud servants and condone their abuse. In fact, it may be a grave error to discuss "elite" status as a clearly recognizable factor on the seventeenth-century American frontier. Practical colonial labor law was created, not by statutes, which were often draconian, but by custom, case, and precedent, which were considerably more sympathetic to servants' needs.

Fourth, the widely held historical notion that servants' legal, economic, or physical abuse was routinely permitted to their masters is not true. Courts, pushed by servants, sought to create labor relationships in which masters undoubtedly controlled their servants firmly—there were, after all, few if any other means of doing so during the colonial period—but also observed their duties and obligations to dependents. Of course, informal procedures, which depended on ideas of reputation and often had their roots in gossip or slander, may have resulted in false convictions. Independents were not, however, habitually allowed to refuse to pay their servants, to fail to educate them if they had undertaken to do so, or to neglect or abuse them. Justices, neighbors, family members, and servants had implicit ideas regarding the treatment of dependents. If masters overstepped their limits, they could and would be called to account for their actions. These limits were, like most standards of social behavior, conditioned locally; a master in Kent County, Maryland, would be held to different standards than one in Sussex, England,

Essex County, Massachusetts, or, for that matter, one in Charles County, Maryland. They were also conditioned temporally; the political and social rebellions of the late seventeenth century caused a decided though temporary swing away from ideals of masters' care and toward ideals of masters' control. But limits on independents' power, negotiated by servants and masters and mediated by law and the courts, did exist.

"As Though I My Self Was Pr[e]sent"

Virginia Women with Power of Attorney

I N 1716, William West planned to leave his Essex County home. Prominent among the arrangements he made for the management of his
affairs during his absence was a grant to his wife, Elizabeth, of a power
of attorney allowing her to do "all my business whatsoever Relating to
me as though I my self was pr[e]sent." Thereby, Elizabeth West, even as a
married woman whom the law defined as a feme covert, gained the authority to manage property and legal matters as she deemed proper. She was not
alone. Judging from this and similar grants in the seventeenth and early
eighteenth centuries in tidewater Virginia, certain colonists did not believe
sex defined or precluded competence in the legal sector. Historians of the
colonial Chesapeake have understood that women managed property but
have concentrated on widowhood as the period in women's lives when they
took on these responsibilities. Even during coverture, however, some Virginia women, especially in families with far-flung economic concerns, handled legal affairs and administered property. Courts recognized married
women's various legal actions by recording powers of attorney.[1]

Not all, or even most, women in colonial Virginia held power of attorney, since it tended to serve the distinctive interests of commercially active
families. Men who granted power of attorney did so primarily when they
planned to be absent pursuing trade or other interests that took them out of
the local vicinity. Thus, the women who possessed power of attorney tended
to be from the relatively prosperous families most likely to have geograph-
ically dispersed economic concerns. Occasionally, power of attorney was

This paper benefited from comments by Amber Ault, Tamara Hamlish, David Konig,
Allan Kulikoff, James Robertson, Chris Tomlins, and the anonymous reviewers for this
volume. The author gratefully acknowledges their advice.

1. Jan. 4, 1715[/6], recorded Sept. 18, 1716, Library of Virginia (hereafter cited as LVA), Essex [Loose] Suit Papers 103-A-1710–103-R-1716, 104-A-1717–104-K-1720. William planned
to leave the colony and granted those powers for as long as he was absent. For widowhood
and legal responsibilities, see Lois Green Carr and Lorena S. Walsh, "The Planter's Wife:
The Experience of White Women in Seventeenth-Century Maryland," *William and Mary
Quarterly*, 3d Ser., XXXIV (1977), 542–571; Daniel Blake Smith, *Inside the Great House:
Planter Family Life in Eighteenth-century Chesapeake Society* (Ithaca, N.Y., 1980). For a
brief discussion of "feme covert" and "feme sole," see below.

assigned to allow a remarrying widow control over her former husband's property. Most women with power of attorney, however, provided their current husband with a responsible local agent authorized to serve in the family's best interests. Still, those grants occurred in situations that concerned only women from propertied families.

A third, anomalous type of power of attorney in the Virginia records developed in an extraordinary case in which the couple established arrangements for distinct control of property in a de facto separation settlement that, the husband hoped, would allow him to establish a new household with a different woman and their children. Although exceptional, this case illustrates the ways that a power of attorney could delineate property relations that distinguished a married woman's authority over property from that of her husband.

Power of attorney permitted women, even married women, with a means to act before the law under specific terms. A husband like William West could designate that his wife had the legal responsibility to act on his behalf by recording his grant to her of a power of attorney. The instructions in such documents varied tremendously in their terms, from very specific, limited powers to more general discretionary authority. Usually men granted power of attorney to their wives in anticipation of travel out of the county, especially if they ventured out of the colony. In granting these powers, the men believed their interests were best served when their wives had the legal authority to pursue the family's business in the local courts.[2]

We know from feminist scholarship how harshly common law limited married women's rights.[3] The colonial concept of marriage, borrowed from English precedent, held that the husband and wife became one person before the law, and "the very being or legal existence of the woman is suspended during the marriage." The law held that the wife was under both the

2. Linda Kerber pointed out that these grants of power of attorney demonstrate the resilience of coverture and the desire of men as well as women to navigate the system of coverture to their own advantage (Kerber, concluding comments, "Many Legalities of Early America" conference, November 1996). The classic discussion of men using women's separate control of property to their own advantage in antebellum Virginia is Suzanne Lebsock, *The Free Women of Petersburg: Status and Culture in a Southern Town, 1784–1860* (New York, 1984).

3. There is an extensive literature on women's oppression under common law and the mitigation of that through equity. This essay touches on that oppression briefly, but the author assumes that individuals interested in the topic have been exposed to these ideas. For those unfamiliar with the literature, turn to Mary R. Beard, *Woman as Force in History: A Study in Traditions and Realities* (New York, 1946); Julia Cherry Spruill, *Women's Life and Work in the Southern Colonies* (Chapel Hill, N.C., 1938); Mary Beth Norton, *Liberty's Daughters: The Revolutionary Experience of American Women, 1750–1800* (Boston, 1980); Linda Kerber, *Women of the Republic: Intellect and Ideology in Revolutionary America* (Chapel Hill, N.C., 1980); Marylynn Salmon, *Women and the Law of Property in Early America* (Chapel Hill, N.C., 1986).

"protection" and "influence" of the husband. She was denied the opportunity to make contracts, incur debts "for any thing besides necessaries," sue,
be sued, or make a will. A feme covert had limited opportunity for legal
impact on the world around her. Indeed, she did not exist as a legal actor
independent of her husband. According to *The Lawes Resolutions of Womens
Rights* (1632), for example: "It is true, that man and wife are one person; but
understand in what manner. When a small brooke or little river incorpo-
rateth with Rhodanus, Humber, or the Thames, the poor rivulet looseth her
name; . . . it beareth no sway; it possesseth nothing during coverture. A
woman as soon as she is married, is called *covert*. . . clouded and overshadowed; she hath lost her streame."[4]

Women's relations to property, however, proved far more complex than
the river metaphor suggests. Members of families had various, and often
competing, claims to property held by the family collectively. Rather than
remain in the undercurrent, some women built canals flowing parallel to the
stream and drew off some of its supply. Historians have accepted the view
that powerful Chesapeake women, once they became widows, took on responsibility for the estates of their deceased husbands. Yet the widows who
served as executors of estates were also constrained by the terms their husbands set out in the wills.[5]

Rigid as coverture seems as a legal concept, the distinction ordained
between the feme sole, who had legal capacity, and the married feme covert,
who had none, was not absolute, especially for women in trading families.
Women participated in the economy and knew about legal maneuvers.
From the days of Mary Beard, historians have recognized that common law
alone failed to delineate women's actions and that colonists defined, redefined, and evaded limitations through a variety of formal and informal
means. Statutes and common law served as a type of prescriptive literature,
but colonists attempted to discover ways of sidestepping those guidelines.[6]
Common law itself provided even a feme covert with a degree of agency in
the courts by permitting her to act under power of attorney. This essay

4. William Blackstone, *Commentaries on the Laws of England* (Oxford, 1765–1769), I,
430; *The Lawes Resolutions of Womens Rights; or, The Laws Provision for Women . . .*
(London, 1632), reprinted in Sylvia R. Frey and Marian J. Morton, eds., *New World, New
Roles: A Documentary History of Women in Pre-Industrial America* (New York, 1986), 92–
94, also cited in Spruill, *Women's Life and Work*, 340.

5. Amy Louise Erickson, *Women and Property in Early Modern England* (London, 1993),
166. Widows could renounce wills of husbands who left them less than their legally
established dower rights.

6. For a recent discussion of the variety of legal and economic activities of women in
colonial America, see Joan Hoff, *Law, Gender, and Injustice: A Legal History of U.S. Women*
(New York, 1991), esp. 82–90. Hoff points out that the "relatively lenient attitude" toward
women resulted, not because the colonial period was "less patriarchal," but because
women were substituting for dead or absent husbands or other male relatives (88).

explains how. The activities women undertook in court under powers of attorney demonstrate that a spectrum of possibilities was open to women under colonial law.[7]

Although Virginia widows' economic activities are well known, it is clear that, during both marriage and widowhood, many women managed economic and legal affairs and propertied women actively pursued their economic and legal concerns. We know, for example, that even after marriage a very limited number of women in the southern colonies acquired feme sole trader status as a means to maintain their public autonomy. In Virginia, it appears that powers of attorney provided colonists with another means of according women legal agency. That agency could be restricted or extensive, according to the designs of the parties. At one end of the spectrum, a power of attorney could grant a woman legal authority to undertake a specific task. In such cases women were confined to following directions outlined by men, gaining the status of what Laurel Ulrich has termed the "deputy husband." This provided women no real initiative or autonomy and merely confirmed the patriarchal nature of family authority.[8]

An example of power being delegated to take limited action is Elizabeth Dale's case. In April 1667, Elizabeth Dale granted to Edward Mosse "the same power that I have from my husband," to record an agreement made "between us" concerning some land. In that instance the power apparently extended to a single transaction and might have been undertaken for convenience, to streamline the land transfer. In any event, Dale refused to undertake the power but instead assigned it away immediately. Women could be the preferred family representative in court, but, like other representatives, women could also be left with very limited discretionary authority.[9]

At the other end of the spectrum, a few women won greater freedom to act according to their own wishes, without direction. They seized large-scale

7. For a more extensive discussion of women's options, see Linda L. Sturtz, "'Madam and Co.': Women, Property, and Power in Colonial Virginia" (Ph.D. diss., Washington University, 1994), 69–178, 277–355.

8. Salmon, *Women and the Law of Property*, 44–49, 55–57; Laurel Ulrich, *Good Wives: Images and Reality in the Lives of Women in Northern New England* (New York, 1982), 36.

9. LVA, York County, Virginia, Deeds, Orders and Wills (hereafter cited as York DOW), book 4, Apr. 10, 1667, 129.

Individuals acting under power of attorney, including married women acting on behalf of their husbands, were different from professional lawyers, referred to as "Mercenary attorneys" in early Virginia statutes. Lawyers who served professionally were prohibited in Virginia in 1645 and were suspect in the early years of settlement. See act 7, November 1645, in William Waller Hening, ed., *The Statutes at Large: Being a Collection of All the Laws of Virginia, from the First Session of the Legislature, in the Year 1619 . . .* , 13 vols. (Richmond, Va., Philadelphia, 1809–1823), I, 302. There were few professional lawyers in the seventeenth-century colonies and, in colonies where lawyers were allowed to practice, the legislatures limited what a lawyer could earn for a case. See Peter Charles Hoffer, *Law and People in Colonial America* (Baltimore, 1992), 40–42.

independent authority for a longer period of time. In the mid-seventeenth century, when the colony was still fairly new, married women acted on be- half of their families as part of the everyday mechanics of operating a busi- ness. James Perry observed that on the Eastern Shore of Virginia "women frequently acted on their own or in behalf of their husbands in and out of the county courts." Similarly, in York County, Mary Smith recorded an obligation in court "by order of her husband" once in October 1647 and again in December 1647. Apparently she did so in both instances without the benefit of a power of attorney, since none was recorded.[10]

In the York County court, women acted as attorneys in numerous cases. Elizabeth Disarme appeared for her husband in November 1679. Alice Page received the confession of J. Mathews in a debt suit in January 1675 while serving as attorney for her husband. Frances Weeks was given power of attorney from her husband in February 1666 and confessed judgment for a debt in January 1668. Anne Clopton served as attorney for her husband in 1681. Charles Bryan made his wife, Susanna Bryan, his attorney to collect his debts, though the records reveal no more details on what she managed. In other tidewater counties, too, women in the seventeenth and early eigh- teenth centuries obtained power of attorney from their husbands. For exam- ple, in Charles City County, Warham Horsmonden made his wife his at- torney with broad powers to make and receive all debts and "to arrest sue and imprison any Debt'r and at her pleasure againe to release and Discharge, and to do all and every such act and acts [——]ing and giving as I my selfe could were I personally here present." Were she to die in his absence, the plantation's overseer was to take her place.[11]

Some of the grants of power of attorney from husband to wife included

10. James R. Perry, *The Formation of a Society on Virginia's Eastern Shore, 1615–1655* (Chapel Hill, N.C., 1990), 81; York DOW 2, Oct. 26?, 1647, Dec. 16, 1647, 287, 312. Both were cases of Smith's confessing judgment, a procedure by which a debtor gives "direction for entry of judgment against him in the event he shall default in payment" (Henry Campbell Black, *Black's Law Dictionary* [St. Paul, 1990], 259–260).

11. Local authorities could also use the procedure of recording a power of attorney as a means of extending short-term credit. When Winifred Martin purchased goods from an estate sale, the court granted her credit by declaring her to be acting as attorney for her husband, but no document indicating that her husband granted power of attorney ap- pears in the record. She confessed judgment before Capt. Thomas Barber, justice of the peace, with securities from Robert Bee and John Young (York DOW 12, Nov. 19, 1702, 58). She had no specific instructions from her husband. Instead, she seems to have purchased ribbons, ruffles, women's clothing, and jewelry, either for her own consumption or resale (see Cope Doyley's estate inventory, York DOW 12, Nov. 19, 1702, 59–65). Granting Martin a power of attorney, technically from her husband, provided an expedient means for the justices to extend a married woman credit. For Bryan's power of attorney, see York DOW 4, July 25, 1670, 299. For Horsmonden's, see Oct. 4, 1656, original order book, 63, in Beverley Fleet, abstr., *Virginia Colonial Abstracts*, X, *Charles City Co. 1655–1658* (Baltimore, 1961), 48–49.

specific instructions from the husband, leaving the wife little room for discretionary action. Husbands who lacked confidence in their wives' abilities appointed men as assistants to the wife in managing the family legal affairs. In 1669, Samuel Plowright, "surgeon," requested that two men assist his wife "in my business whatsoever that belong to me" and recorded the request in the court documents. Sometimes women with power of attorney, in turn, delegated authority to a male representative or even to their own attorneys. Ann Dixon, wife and attorney of William Dixon, appointed James Crabtree her attorney to represent her in an action "between me" and Samuel Dowse in York County. Despite her receiving the suit indirectly, through a power of attorney, she considered the suit her own and continued to do so even after she subsequently turned her authority over to a third party. In this second transfer, she limited her attorney's action to one specific case and retained control over all other business.[12]

Single transactions could involve multiple appearances at the courthouse. Jane Mountford (also Mountfort) acted in court as attorney for her husband, Thomas, in numerous instances over a long period of time. In 1689 she sold the remainder of a term of service for a boy, William Marshall, to John Hatton, but the Mountforts subsequently blocked Hatton's attempt to resell the boy by claiming Hatton had not completed the terms of the bargain. Hatton sued the Mountforts, unsuccessfully, and the court ordered Hatton to fulfill the terms of the contract. Similarly, Jane Mountfort faced a further suit and countersuit as attorney for Thomas Mountfort that both concluded in nonsuits, though the cases were subsequently reintroduced and continued. A seemingly simple transaction required Jane Mountfort to make numerous court appearances before the affair was over.[13]

Husband-to-wife powers of attorney demonstrate that family property was understood to be the responsibility of several members of the kin network, not just the male head of household. Especially when men had to undertake extensive travel to maintain a family business, proximity to courts became a primary motive for assigning a family member of either sex power of attorney. Thus, within trading families with economic concerns that extended beyond a single county, women with power of attorney were most apt to appear.

Local knowledge and proximity could make a wife the best representative for the family. Sarah Harrison's letter of attorney from her husband, Robert

12. Plowright's request recorded in York DOW 4, Mar. 10, 1668/9, 229, made Jan. 16, 1668, witnessed by Elizabeth Maunders. Plowright seems to have died "probat in cur," also in 1668. Dixon's power of attorney granted to Crabtree in York DOW 5, Sept. 19, 1672, 24. Ann was apparently illiterate: she signed with an "x." See York DOW 5, Sept. 19, 1672, 21.

13. York DOW 8, Nov. 7, 1689, Mar. 24, 1689/90, 327, 410. Jane Mountfort was involved in other suits both with her husband and individually.

Harrison, a carpenter, recorded that he was "late in York Town" but granted her power to act, apparently in his absences. Robert Harrison delineated the extensive power he granted to his wife to oversee their business; she could sell the cattle and household goods, collect debts by bills, bonds, accounts, "or otherways," and she could sell their house "and Lot or Lotts" in York-town. On the very day the power of attorney was recorded, the court heard cases that concerned her.[14]

The practice was hardly limited to Virginia or the Chesapeake. Jamaican records suggest that, shortly after the English capture of the island, women served in courts under powers of attorney from unrelated and related men, but most commonly on behalf of husbands. Within the specific context of Virginia, the career of Elizabeth Jones demonstrates the various legal activities of women with power of attorney. Jones obtained power of attorney from Richard Jones, her husband and a planter, when he left Virginia. Elizabeth was to "act in all ways," assisted by Richard's friend George Light. Richard Jones's trust in his wife and only his wife is revealed in the terms of the power of attorney, which indicated that the estate was to remain un-altered if Elizabeth died before he returned to the colony. She began her legal activities a month after the power was recorded and won a suit against a tardy debtor who had refused payment to her husband. By invoking the power of the court, Elizabeth succeeded in obtaining payment for a bill her husband had been unable to collect. Later cases provided her with more experience in the courts.[15]

George Light, the friend appointed to help Elizabeth Jones, did not appear in the records for this particular case. Less than two years later, the relation-ship between Light and Jones took a turn for the worse. By December 1660, Richard Jones was dead, and Elizabeth acted as his executor. At that junc-ture, Light claimed the estate owed him "severall somes of money" and that Elizabeth owed him eight pounds in payment for Light's work as a carpenter in building her a tobacco house. The court appointed a group of "viewers" to examine the completed tobacco house and, after hearing the report and Light's deposition, ordered Elizabeth Jones to pay the reduced sum of £5 for the house. A month later the court heard Jones's own deposition that she had paid most of the debt. After examiners reviewed the accounts, the court

14. York DOW 11, Feb. 24, 1701/2, 573–574. The letter was witnessed by two women, Hester Sessions and Mary Curtis.

15. Spanish Town, Jamaica, Island Records Office, Deeds, liber 1, Old Series, f. 15, Sept. 17, 1665: Margary Dogg attorney for her husband, Edward Dogg; f. 33, Feb. 16, 1664/5: Sarah Barker attorney for her husband, Thomas Barker. For a woman serving for some-one other than her husband, see Spanish Town, Jamaica Archives Office, 1B/11/1/1, Patents Liber, 1661–1665, f. 33v: Margery Pullon for Michael Peterson to collect debts from Zach-ary (Dolinquet?) for a half a share in the ship *Bridget,* May 26, 1663; York DOW 3, Apr. 24, 1658, 26; York DOW 3, June 24, 1658, 27; York DOW 3, Dec. 20, 1660, 100.

settled the dispute between Light and Jones, ordering Jones to pay him £1.5.6 for what remained on the accounts according to her deposition.[16]

It is uncertain whether Jones, in granting power of attorney to his wife, was indicating that he trusted her ability to handle the family business. At the very least, however, Elizabeth Jones's actions under power of attorney exposed her to the family's trade affairs and allowed her to gain practical knowledge about the legal system. In either event, Jones knew how to manage family affairs well before she became a widow: her first accounts, presented in 1660 for goods and services she purchased in 1658, indicate she acquired them "in the time of hir husband Richard Jones being gone for Eng[land]."[17]

By the end of 1661, Jones, now her husband's relict and executor, initiated a long and, according to the court's own description, highly complicated suit over a debt owed by one Richard Longman, Sr. As an executor, she had many of the same responsibilities (and restrictions) she possessed before her husband died, when she acted under a power of attorney. As a widow, she faced Longman's son and John Achley, who described himself as a factor for "his Master" Longman, over obligations each claimed the other owed. The court declared the case "a business of great concernment and difficulty." Jones presented interrogatories to pose to Longman and his associates about the twenty-eight hogsheads of tobacco consigned to Richard Longman, the price obtained for the tobacco in London, the costs incurred in selling the tobacco, and the payments credited to the Jones accounts. In January 1662, the court ordered two examiners to go to the home of James Bray to examine the accounts and receipts in the case. The suit, listed with Longman as plaintiff and Jones as defendant, concluded in March, the court balancing the accounts in Longman's favor. Jones's obligations totaled £374.2.2, and her credits totaled £353.0.9. Jones then turned to pressing a suit against John Whiskin for the proceeds of tobacco her husband had sent through him to Longman, claiming Whiskin had taken an excessive share of the proceeds. She won the suit and also asked that she not be responsible for the costs in the suit brought by Longman. It appears, then, that the discrepancy in the suit arose, not from Longman's underpayment, but from Whiskin's gouging the Jones family.[18]

The progress and variety of Elizabeth Jones's activities in the York County

16. York DOW 3, Dec. 20, 1660, Jan. 25, 1660/1, Feb. 25, 1660/1, 100, 104, 110.

17. York DOW 3, Feb. 25, 1660/1, 112: purchases made of Robert Aldred totaling £4.16.6 included liquor, cinnamon, bread, tailor's work, a coffin for her son, and maintenance work on a saw. She paid £1.10.0 and left the rest on account owed to Aldred.

18. York DOW 3, Oct. 31, 1661, Dec. 20, 1661, Dec. 21, 1661, Jan. 25, 1661/2, 134, 137–138, 142–143, 145. For case initiated against Whiskin, see York DOW 3, Apr. 24, 1662, 162. For reference to Jones's debt to John Whiskin for four days' attendance as a witness in the case, see York DOW 3, Mar. 10, 1661/2, Apr. 24, 1662, 152, 162.

court demonstrate the significance of a woman's actions within a family's transatlantic business and why it was necessary for women to use the courts to try to protect those interests. Although women were most visible in the courts as widows, where they acted in their own names, their participation in the exchange network could begin before widowhood. Indeed, for women who had no experience with the courts, serving as an attorney could provide the transition toward taking more responsibility for family affairs later in life. "Mrs" Anne Calthorpe was summoned to court as attorney for her husband, Colonel Christopher Calthorpe, to answer the suit of James Bray for a debt of four hundred pounds of tobacco due by bill, evidence of community awareness of Anne Calthorpe's responsibilities. A month later, Christopher was dead, and Anne Calthorpe was named administrator of the estate. In families with property, women with written power of attorney took responsibility for business in the courts, which included presenting receipts and demanding evidence for the prices of tobacco sold overseas. Competent women could learn about business earlier in their lives, before they became widows.[19]

Trading enterprises, especially those requiring ties to other counties, to other colonies, or even back to England, benefited from the combined efforts of members of extended families. The ways that women exercised powers of attorney in the local courts show how women served as local representatives in larger, kin-based trade webs. Elizabeth Vaulx, a particularly visible woman within a mid-seventeenth-century family trade network, operated in several tidewater county courts but was especially active in the York County court. Vaulx, born Elizabeth Burwell, sister of Major Lewis Burwell, married Robert Vaulx, one of four brothers who immigrated to Virginia and became merchants dealing in trade between the colony and mother country as well as to Holland. They lived on a five-hundred-acre York County plantation complete with its own warehouses. Robert Vaulx frequently traveled to England to manage his business and to defend himself in lawsuits, and it was for this reason that Elizabeth's active hand in the business became visible in the county courts in Virginia.[20] She received power of attorney from her

19. York DOW 3, Mar. 10, 1661/2, Apr. 24, 1662, 151, 161.

20. See chaps. 2 and 3 of Sturtz, "Madam & Co." See also Jacob M. Price, "One Family's Empire: The Russell-Lee-Clerk Connection in Maryland, Britain, and India, 1707–1857," *Maryland Historical Magazine*, LXXII (1977), 176. Robert Vaulx, a leading merchant of London, married Elizabeth Burwell, sister of Lewis Burwell (see *WMQ*, 1st Ser., XIV [1905–1906], 178). He owned Vaulx's Hall plantation on the west side of Queen's Creek. His brothers Humphrey, Thomas, and James also immigrated to the colony. James Vaulx's son, Robert, settled in Dorchester County, Maryland, and Robert's son Robert settled in Westmoreland County (*WMQ*, 1st Ser., III [1894–1895], 14). For a bond for tobacco shipped to London and Holland, see York DOW 2, Feb. 5, 1646/7, 219. For Robert's owning a share of a ship, see York DOW 2, [May 25, 1648], 377. One of the brothers, Humphrey

husband, who then traveled to London, where he continued to receive tobacco shipped from Virginia. In his absence, she managed some of the
Virginia side of the family enterprise, particularly matters situated in York
County. She oversaw repayment on a sizable number of debts and occasionally appointed her own attorney to represent her in cases.[21]

In addition to the trading business, she began managing substantial land-
holdings both in York County and in northern Virginia. The extended Vaulx
network placed family members and unrelated representatives in various
locations in the colonies and mother country to supervise exchanges of
English finished goods for colonial products. Family records indicate that
Elizabeth Vaulx corresponded with these representatives in other counties.[22]
On at least one occasion, she traveled to England herself, leaving her accounts in the hands of an agent. Before long she returned to Virginia and
handled more cases, including a dispute that was ultimately sent to the
General Court in Jamestown.[23]

The Vaulx family had extensive commercial concerns in other tidewater

<hr />

Vaulx of New Kent County, Virginia, served as Robert's attorney in some York cases after
Elizabeth Vaulx died (York DOW 9, July 24, 1691, 44–45). For a description of the Queen's
Creek plantation, see deed of sale to Peter Temple, York DOW 7, Oct. 17, 1685, 169; York
DOW 3, May 9, 1659, 55.

21. Power of attorney written Sept. 6, 1656, by Robert Vaulx in London, her "Ever honrd.
and Deare husband," and recorded as part of her own grant of power of attorney to Robert
Bournes in York DOW 3, May 9, 1659, 55, document dated May 6, 1659. For record of
tobacco shipped to Robert Vaulx in London, see York DOW 3, June 24, 1661, 119. For
Elizabeth Vaulx in York County courts, see York DOW 3, Feb. 25, 1657/8, Feb. 24, 1658/9,
May 9, 1659, 17, 50, 56.

22. See York DOW 3, Dec. 21, 1657, 9, for certificate granted to Elizabeth Vaulx for 400
acres for transportation of eight people. Robert received 2,000 acres in Westmoreland,
Nov. 16, 1657, Patent Book Four, 172, cited in Nell Marion Nugent, *Cavaliers and Pioneers:
Abstracts of Virginia Land Patents and Grants* (1934; Richmond, Va., 1992), I, 366. Robert
received a land certificate for 3,100 acres in return for the importation of sixty-two people
(York DOW 3, Apr. 4, 1659, 51). In 1657, by a conveyance authorized by her husband,
Robert Vaulx, "gent.," Elizabeth sold 400 acres of land to her "well beloved kin" John and
Charles Woodington. The land was part of a tract of 6,000 acres and was sold on the
provision that John and Charles seat the land (York DOW 3, Oct. 26, 1657, 4, document
dated Oct. 6, 1657). By this means Elizabeth was able to settle her relatives on land near her
own substantial parcel, ensuring that someone she could rely on would keep watch over
her holding. This strategy seems in keeping with that of other women who were absentee
landlords of large tracts of land under speculation. In 1653, Anna Bernard, a woman
writing to preserve her holdings, thanked Walter Brodhurst for seeing that her land was
settled to prevent escheat. She was unable to come to Potomac until the ships returned,
but offered 100 acres to "any honest man" to seat the land (Anna Bernard to Mr. Walter
Brodhurst, letter proved Feb. 20, 1653, in "Extracts from Northumberland County Records," *WMQ*, 1st Ser., IV [1894–1895], 77–78). Elizabeth Vaulx accomplished the same task
by granting her "kin" small parcels of her lands.

23. On trip to England, see York DOW 3, May 9, 1659, 56; York DOW 4, Aug. 24, 1665,
29–30. See also York DOW 4, Apr. 24, 1666, June 25, 1666, Aug. 24, 1666, 60, 69–70, 98.

counties. Although men with power of attorney managed some of this other business, Elizabeth Vaulx retained a hand in the northern Virginia affairs. When one purchaser was interested in a plantation, she was told that she should "speak to Mrs. Vaulx" to see if the land was available. Mrs. Vaulx, if willing to sell, sent the patent and orders to a local representative to lay out the land. The extended family seemed to place members in various locations to receive the goods imported from England and to export tobacco, fur, and other colonial products. Elizabeth Vaulx predeceased her husband in 1666. All of her extensive legal actions, then, occurred during her marriage, since she was never the widow or relict Vaulx.[24]

Into the eighteenth century, protecting a family's collective interests in trade and property demanded the efforts of women, both sole and covert, as well as the management of the men, to advance the family's well-being. Two generations after Vaulx's cases, the geographic location of the frontier had moved away from the tidewater region, and family efforts to acquire land farther west required that Virginia women again participate in legal affairs when husbands left the home region for extended periods to pursue their interests. Elizabeth Cabell provides us with an example of a woman who left extensive records documenting the ways in which she advanced the Cabell fortunes in the 1730s and 1740s. Elizabeth worked closely with her husband, William Cabell; fragments of letters reveal her active hand in family business. A receipt indicates she paid their quitrents and legal fees. In her correspondence, she described both selling a slave and her interest in the proceedings of the local court.[25]

William Cabell, like Robert Vaulx, had business that took him out of the colony. When William left Virginia for Britain in 1735, he left his wife, Elizabeth, power of attorney "for the better managem[en]t" of his affairs. William consoled his wife about his extended absence, reassuring her that

24. Westmoreland County Deeds and Wills, LVA, July 10, 1655, I, 37. For description of land sale, see deposition of John Quisenberry, aged eighty years, about the event that took place "about fifty years ago," Jan. 31, 1707/8, in John Frederick Dorman, abstr., *Westmoreland County, Virginia, Deeds, Patents, etc., 1665–1677* (Washington, D.C., 1975), part 4, 51. There are several references to Vaulx in Lancaster County. See Beverley Fleet, ed., *Lancaster County, Record Book No. 2, 1654–1666* (Richmond, Va., [1937]), Apr. 27, 1659, 185, and June 1, 1663 (recorded June 22, 1663), 265. For Vaulx's death, see Bruton Parish Death Register, Oct. 5, 1666, in York County Project, Master Biographical File, Colonial Williamsburg.

25. The Cabell family name was also recorded under different spellings: Cabbell, Cabel, for example. Elizabeth's business records are from a small packet of waxed paper entitled "signatures of Mrs. Elizabeth Cabell" in the Cabell Family Papers Collection, University of Virginia (hereafter cited as UVA), special collections accession number 5084, box 1, file: "Scraps and fragments, August 24, 1741 to January 16, 1772." The fragments, no more than one inch by three inches in size, all include Elizabeth Cabell's signature and are clipped to exclude the rest of the letter. The cited text comes from the obverse of fragment 2a.

she should not "think it occasioned by want of Respect" but that the delay was only to improve "both our Interests." He asked her to pay an account from Major William Mayo, suggesting she turn to her father or "Richard" to pay it off "to prevent a Sute." The business in Britain required his full attention and prevented him from returning, but he hoped that in the meantime "your and my other attorneys Prudent care will Cary my bisn[es]s on with the same life as tho I was with you."[26]

The relative power of Elizabeth and the other attorneys in managing the land then became part of a protracted legal dispute itself. Elizabeth sought to protect the family's business in a long-running lawsuit with the Carrington and Mayo families over the management of a tract of land. The Cabells claimed Elizabeth was to serve along with William Mayo and George Carrington, and her husband reported that he had granted the two men the power of attorney mostly to "aid and assist" Elizabeth. She was to have the "principal managem[en]t of the family's affairs." Mayo claimed that Cabell originally did not plan to leave the "principal managem[en]t of his affairs to his wife" and that Cabell had added her name to the letter of attorney only after Mayo's "earnest request."[27]

By August 1739, Elizabeth Cabell reported that Mayo and Carrington had undermined her efforts. She wrote to Edward Barradall, a prominent Virginia lawyer, to ask for advice in the case. She forwarded Barradall a copy of her husband's grant of power of attorney and related the recent turn of events. She complained that Mayo wanted to collect fees he was owed as a land surveyor, so, even though he had an interest in the case, he "artfully" confessed a judgment that indebted Cabell to him at the local court. He did this without Elizabeth's "knowledge, consent, or presence," despite the fact she was a party in the power of attorney. All this happened to Elizabeth's "great surprise." She concluded her request for help from Barradall by saying, "If such an extraordinary proceeding as this is justyfiable, I must submitt to it"; otherwise, she wanted to retain Barradall to act on her behalf.[28]

Barradall apparently agreed to take the case and advised Elizabeth Cabell to enter an injunction, which she agreed was acceptable when she wrote him

26. For Cabell's business in Pennsylvania, see Cabell Family Papers, UVA, acc. no. 5084, box 1, folder [1745], Statement of George Carrington; for business in Great Britain, see Cabell Family Papers, UVA, acc. no. 5084, box 1, folder c. 1745, rough draft in *Cabell v Mayo;* William Cabell to "Loving Wife," Jan. 19, 1736, Warminster, in Cabell Family Papers, UVA, acc. no. 5084, box 1, folder William Cabell, three letters, 1736–1737. Cabell also asked her to "keep My poore children close to their books."

27. Cabell Family Papers, UVA, acc. no. 5084, box 1, folder c. 1745, rough draft in *Cabell v Mayo;* Cabell Family Papers, UVA, acc. no. 5084, box 1, folder 1731–1768, *Cabell v Mayo.* The power of attorney was dated Aug. 27, 1735.

28. She spelled his name "Barradil" and her own name as "Cabbell." Elizabeth Cabell, Goochland, to Edward Barradall, Williamsburg, Aug. 23, 1739, Cabell Family Papers, UVA, acc. no. 5084, box 1.

again, two months later. She also asked whether she actually needed to attend the case "at Town," which she preferred to avoid. The case was heard and appealed to the General Court in 1744, where the accounts were settled in Cabell's favor. Other matters remained in dispute between the Cabell, Mayo, and Carrington families into the 1760s, when the case was continued against Mary Mayo and her children after William Mayo's death.[29]

Elizabeth Cabell accepted a significant amount of power and responsibility when she served as attorney in her husband's absence, and her work made an impact on the family's economic success. The cases that went to court indicate the grounds on which that power might be questioned: Was the power of attorney left equally to all three or, instead, to her individually with a veto power over the other two, who were to serve her as advisers? Apparently either option was possible, but William and Elizabeth took the stance that the power ultimately remained in her hands. This is not surprising, since, in this particular dispute, the family would benefit more by claiming the coattorneys possessed no power to proceed without her approval. Still, for the Cabells, delegating the power over immense tracts of land to Elizabeth during William's protracted absence seemed an acceptable division of labor in a family with transatlantic trade concerns. "Temporary widowhood," the situation where a capable woman took over the family business in wartime, could exist in peacetime as well if a husband were absent for equally long periods of time because of economic obligations. Perhaps here "economic widowhood" would be more descriptive. Some of these "economic widows," like Elizabeth Vaulx, never became widows in fact.[30]

Powers of attorney granted to women in family trade networks allowed colonists with commercial interests to preserve a family's prosperity by having competent women in place to oversee the operations of the business at various points in the network. However, in other instances, the practice of men's granting their wives power of attorney might have had an alternative function; instead of commingling legal identities, power of attorney could permit the separation of the two spouses' legal identities.

A common reason for a woman to seek a legal identity independent from

29. Elizabeth Cabell, Goochland, to Edward Barradall, Williamsburg, Oct. 15, 1739, Cabell Family Papers, UVA, acc. no. 5084, box 1, folder Oct. 15, 1739; Cabell Family Papers, UVA, acc. no. 5084, box 1, Mar. 20, 1744. On Oct. 31, 1745, the General Court, sitting in chancery, completed a subsequent final reckoning including the fees and determined that Cabell owed £34.15.3 plus costs, and Carrington gave a receipt for payment on May 20, 1746. For subsequent disputes, see decision of the Cumberland Court, Jun. 23, 1767, Cabell Family Papers, UVA, acc. no. 5084, box 1, folder June 23, 1767.

30. Norton used the phrase "temporary widowhood" to describe capable women who took over family business over the course of the War for Independence in *Liberty's Daughters*, 215–224.

that of her husband was to protect the interests of her children from earlier marriages. The demography of early Virginia meant that women often had multiple family allegiances resulting from a series of marriages. A responsible widow with children could seek, on remarriage, power of attorney from her new husband as a means to keep interests of a first family and its children distinct from the claims of the woman's second, or subsequent, husband. In these instances, a married woman could appear in court independently from her current husband. Women's legal identities were not singular and fixed but can be conceived of as existing along a spectrum of legal statuses. Marriage to a new husband did not completely obliterate the woman's link to her previous husband and their children. Even during marriage, the boundaries between the restrictive prescriptions of feme covert status and the legal freedom of the feme sole were less absolute than those fixed categories would suggest.

Women who used power of attorney in this manner were similar to those who used prenuptial agreements to keep family property distinct. With power of attorney, a remarried widow could manage assets acquired during a previous marriage without the new husband's active intervention. She also could watch over property that she perceived as hers. In December 1666, Elizabeth Woods, the remarried widow of Robert Frith, received power of attorney from her second husband, John Woods, to enable her to collect debts. She had children from her marriage with Frith and took the precaution before marrying for the second time to obtain a prenuptial agreement to protect her children's interest. She did this by demanding a performance bond from her new husband and by requiring him to acknowledge that he was indebted to her or her heirs for the land she owned. Woods promised to deliver the land and cattle to her children when they came of age. Furthermore, if the children died before reaching maturity, Elizabeth was still left with the right to dispose of the property. Elizabeth supervised her family's business, especially after Woods's death. A deposition in a 1675 proceeding indicates that she "knew viewed and accepted" an account concerning a debt.[31]

Other women followed similar paths during widowhood. The career of Susannah Brookes Vergett Davis, an apparently illiterate woman, demonstrates how powers of attorney worked for remarried women. She was granted the administration of the estate of her first husband, Thomas Brookes. Less than a year later, after she had married Job Vergett, she was

31. York DOW 4, Nov. 14, 1666, 123, recorded Dec. 20, 1666; York DOW 3, May 31, 1658, 31, recorded Jun. 24, 1658; debt to Richard Awborne, York DOW 5, Apr. 26, 1675, 110. John Woods was dead by Feb. 24, 1670/1 (York DOW 4, 312). For married women's separate ownership of specific types of minor property (paraphernalia and pin money) in English history, see Susan Staves, *Married Women's Separate Property in England, 1660–1833* (Cambridge, Mass., 1990), 147–149.

sued because she had not returned an inventory of Brookes's estate and because the court had received reports that much of the estate had been "disposed of imbezelled and wasted" at the orphans' expense. Susannah Vergett first confessed judgment "in open court" on behalf of her husband, Job Vergett. Her representing her current husband in the July 1669 court by power of attorney must have been merely a continuation of her supervision of the first husband's estate. The court's written comment that she pursued legal business "in behalf of her husband" simply protected the creditor from any later claim by Susannah's current husband that his wife had no right to take on the debt for her family. By September 1672, Job was dead, too, and two months later, Susannah Vergett, "relict of Mr Job Vergett dece[ase]d and relict of Mr Thomas Brooks dec[ease]d," efficiently presented inventories of the estates of both of her dead husbands at the same court before leaving the county.[32]

In these cases, Susannah Vergett's power of attorney allowed her to continue her already-initiated legal affairs without the meddling, or perhaps much interest, of her new husband, Edward Davis. She returned to the court again in February 1679/80 when Davis appointed her his attorney to conduct business in the York court. She and Elizabeth Brookes, probably her daughter from the first marriage, leased out land. The Davis power of attorney might have been recorded to give her the legal capacity to do so. The fact that mother and daughter cosigned the lease suggests that this was property from the Brookes marriage. Davis might well have seen this as primarily his wife's business.[33]

Susanna's powers of attorney from her various husbands seem to have allowed her to pursue her management of her deceased husbands' estates. Property from one nuclear family could continue to be seen as a unit and identified with those family members even after the widow remarried. By this means, a ghost family and its property continued as an entity even after the father died and the mother remarried, leaving the mother responsible for directing its management. As the thrice-widowed Susanna Brookes Vergett Davis demonstrated, a woman could manage business from a previous marriage, evidence indicating the courts had some perception of a woman's possessing separate property and retaining power over it, even during a subsequent marriage. A woman or her family could attempt to preserve a separate economic identity or to use legal mechanisms to gain a measure of

32. York DOW 4, June 24, 1668, Mar. 10, 1668/9, 186, 227. Vergett confessed judgment to John Cooper for 1,293 pounds of tobacco and cask. York DOW 4, July 26, 1669, 251; York DOW 5, Sept. 19, 1672, Nov. 25, 1672, 30, 32.

33. York DOW 6, Feb. 24, 1679/80, 205; York DOW 1, Mar. 5, 1679, 518, recorded Jan. 24, 1694. The ninety-nine-year lease was for five thousand pounds of tobacco and payment of the annual quitrent.

control over property. Property interests, rather than being defined individ-
ualistically for either women or men, could be seen as a bundle of assets held
by a family, with both women and men involved in their management.

Powers of attorney thus ranged from restrictive, onetime instructions that
allowed the appointed attorney little autonomy to grants that gave women
relative independence. A final, extraordinary, and well-documented example, that of Jane Parke, demonstrates that power of attorney could, even
more dramatically, function effectively as a separation agreement in a time
and place where absolute divorce with right to remarriage was impossible to
obtain. In the first power of attorney that Daniel Parke granted to his wife
Jane (Ludwell) Parke, he provided her with limited legal identity; a later
power allowed her a de facto separation agreement that gave her extensive
authority over property and legal affairs. Her legal career demonstrates how
far a woman could go in exercising power over property, sometimes out of
necessity and often to the chagrin of the men in the family.[34]

In 1689, Daniel Parke II, "gentleman" of York County and later governor
of the Leeward Islands, made his "deare and loveing wife," Jane Parke, along
with his brother-in-law, Major Lewis Burwell of Gloucester, his attorney to
collect all debts that were due then or later. Before being designated as
attorney, Jane Parke's court experience was limited to her making oath to a
will in 1688. As attorneys, Jane Parke and Lewis Burwell initiated two suits in
late 1689 and early 1690.[35] In September 1690, Daniel Parke added another
attorney to manage his affairs in Virginia, but Parke's instructions indicated
that the new attorney should, "if need be," receive directions from Jane Parke
and Lewis Burwell. During this time, Jane responded to several suits, including payment of a fine on behalf of a servant, who had given birth to a bastard
child and faced a whipping if she could not pay the fine. She appeared more
frequently after Daniel once again left her in charge of his affairs when he left
for England in April 1697. Daniel did not designate an assistant for her this
time, but her discretion was more limited because she received no authority
to sell or dispose of his land or slaves without his specific instructions.[36]

While acting as sole attorney for her husband, Jane Parke both initiated

---

34. For discussion of separation in England, see Erickson, *Women and Property in Early
Modern England*, 124–128. Lawrence Stone, *Road to Divorce: England, 1530–1987* (Oxford,
1990) discusses the exceptional and expensive nature of English parliamentary divorce.

35. York DOW 8, Dec. 13, 1688, July 24, 1689, Sept. 24, 1689, 184, 188, 307, 311 (against
James Whaley); York DOW 8, Nov. 7, 1689, Dec. 18, 1689, Jan. 24, 1689/90, Feb. 24, 1689/90,
324, 352, 371, 389 (against Thomas Ballard and John Weyman).

36. York DOW 8, Sept. 24, 1690, 485; York DOW 10, Sept. 24, 1697, Oct. 11, 1697, 462, 470.
The servant was Elizabeth Burnell. The fine, paid to the parish, allowed Burnell to be
exempt from whipping. York DOW 11, Mar. 24, 1698, 23–24, written Apr. 27, 1697. Parke
called on another woman, Elizabeth Archer, to be one of the four witnesses to the power of
attorney.

and defended herself in various suits concerning debts and obligations. She worked, not always successfully, to advance the family's position. She rented land to William Gibbs and sued him when he failed to pay.[37] Like other colonial parents concerned with creating an estate to support and advance the position of their children, she invested in livestock. She purchased cattle from a man named Thomas Steare and employed him to care for the stock. She cultivated corn on her land and purchased an additional sixty-two acres. She sold slaves, but on one occasion she was sued for damages by a purchaser who claimed she sold slaves who had already won their freedom. In this particularly long trial, the jury agreed with her accuser and awarded the plaintiff the cost of the slaves and damages against her.[38]

In another suit, she had more luck in resolving business her husband had initiated earlier. In this case Daniel Parke, before his departure, hired James Ming to survey land, and Ming claimed payment. A Parke attorney, Stephen Thompson, said the action was invalid. Ming countered, saying that, on July 20, 1702, Jane Parke, in her role as wife and attorney of Daniel, asked Ming to wait for payment until the next fleet arrived, at which time she would be able to pay him. She still did not pay, and Ming initiated a suit. The court dismissed the case, making Parke's stalling techniques effective.[39]

Jane Parke's career came to an end when she predeceased her husband in 1708. She might, at first glance, appear to be like other women married to prominent men with political or economic interests overseas, but the Parkes were not the epitome of the charming colonial couple. Daniel Parke clearly had transatlantic business, and Jane Parke, like Elizabeth Vaulx, played a part in her family's undertakings. The testimony in the Ming case revealed that Jane Parke used delaying tactics to hold off creditors. Only her disputed business shows up in the court records, but it demonstrates her many roles. Both alone and with the assistance of other attorneys, Jane Parke participated in the legal and economic activities of the county, advancing her

37. York DOW 11, Dec. 24, 1700, 379: Jane Parke's action of debt against Isabell Peling and Mary White was not prosecuted and was dismissed; York DOW 11, Feb. 25, 1700/1, 387: assigned Robert Cobbs as plaintiff against Use Gibson for debt, not prosecuted, dismissed; York DOW 12, Mar. 24, 1704/5, 321: Jane Parke recorded as defendant in Ejectione Firme, a legal action for recovering or trying titles to land. See entries for "ejectment" and "ejectione firme," in Black, *Black's Law Dictionary,* 516–517; York DOW 12, Feb. 25, 1702/3, Jan. 24, 1703/4, 96, 163: William Gibbs, by his attorney Orlando Jones, confessed judgment to Jane Parke, attorney to Daniel Parke, for the sum of 637 pounds of sweet-scented tobacco and cask.

38. York DOW 11, Mar. 25, 1700, 236; York DOW 13, Mar. 24, 1707/8, May 24, 1708, 125, 141; York DOW 12, Mar. 9, 1705/6, May 24, 1706, 394, 408. The plaintiff in the slave case summoned two witnesses, Arthur Marcenburgh and Winifred Sergeton, who were paid for eight days' attendance at the court as witnesses against Jane Parke.

39. York DOW 13, Jan. 8, 1706/7, 33. James Ming countered by appealing to the General Court. Unfortunately, those records have been destroyed.

business when she chose to do so and protecting assets when necessary, just as Elizabeth Vaulx had done fifty years earlier.[40] Daniel Parke's absence from the colony was due to his service as governor of the Leeward Islands, and his wife did not accompany him there. For good reason, it appears. In his will Daniel Parke acknowledged a female companion and child in the Leeward Islands and left that family land and other property.[41] In the context of this shadow life, the power of attorney that Daniel twice granted to Jane Parke takes on a distinctive meaning. In other families, powers of attorney indicate the ways that women played a part in trade networks. Jane Parke's powers of attorney, especially the second, seem to have served as an effective separation agreement. In a colony that allowed no absolute divorce, a separation agreement delineating rights and obligations of each party was the best that this unhappy couple could hope for.[42] The 1697 Parke power of attorney allowed Jane Parke enumerated but relatively wide powers. She had the right to manage all of the plantations, lands, slaves, stock, and all other real and personal estate in Virginia, with the exception of selling or giving away the land. This last clause proved irrelevant, because she added to the acreage rather than disposing of any real estate. In effect, this power of attorney allowed Jane Parke much of the power of a separation agreement but without the complications. Daniel hoped that distance and the sexual double standard would allow him the freedom to start a new family in a fashion that was no more and no less effective than if he had obtained a separation. He did not entirely succeed, however, and a protracted dispute after his death prevented him from disinheriting his Virginia daughters.[43]

40. Jane Parke's death recorded in Bruton Parish Death Register, 1708, in York County Project, Master Biographical File, Colonial Williamsburg; York DOW 11, Jan. 25, 1699/ 1700, 282–283.

41. Several generations of women in this family might have learned to be independent and justifiably suspicious of their husbands, since all seem to have sired parallel families. Daniel Parke openly provided for his mistress, Katherine Chester, and her daughter, Lucy. It is possible Daniel Parke was merely following his father's example in starting a parallel family (York County DOW 8, document dated Sept. 28, 1687, recorded Mar. 25, 1689, 239). In the third generation, Daniel's white son-in-law, John Custis, freed Jack, whom he identified as "my Negro boy" born of "my Negro Wench Young Alice." See Jo Zuppan, ed., "Father to Son: Letters from John Custis IV to Daniel Parke Custis," *Virginia Magazine of History and Biography*, XCVIII (1990), 81–100. The father's close ties to his son are apparent in his will, where he mentioned a portrait made of his son. The Parke-Custis families found ways to evade increasing legal constrictions defining race as well as gender.

42. It is interesting to note that the Parkes' daughter resorted to an informal agreement during one of the many disputes she had with her own husband. The daughter's agreement was not recorded as a power of attorney but as an enumerated list of each party's obligations (fragment of an agreement between John Custis and Frances [Parke] Custis, [June] 1714, box 1, packet 1, loose papers, Northampton County Court Clerk's Office).

43. York DOW 11, Mar. 24, 1697/8, 23–24. More on the Parke family in the Hardwicke

Further evidence demonstrates that the Parkes's marriage had broken
down by 1707 and that Daniel was also alienated from his daughters. In that
year, Jane's family discussed Governor Parke's attempt to disown his daughters on the pretext of being offended at their marriages. This, according to
Jane's relatives, was merely an excuse, which "saves him the trouble of finding" another reason to quarrel with his children. Jane's family believed Parke
would welcome news that his wife was dead. More immediately, Jane's family was concerned that she "[wa]s in want," though she said "nothing of
shame" in her treatment by her husband. She had some slaves, and "7 or 8
working hands may keep a single body from starveing being well employed,"
but the soil of the plantation was already worn out. The family agent attempted to protect Jane Parke's interests and offered suggestions for providing for the daughters. Still, the governor's vindictive will and complicated
family life plagued his Virginia daughters and their families well into the
next generation. The Parke power of attorney seemed to provide this family
with a means of maintaining themselves in an age before divorce, despite the
actions of a problematic patriarch.[44]

Not all women who acted under power of attorney did so as representatives
for family members. Although Virginia women acting under power of attorney most commonly did so on behalf of their husbands, others did
business for unrelated men who were pursuing commercial interests in
England. In 1683, Anthony Hall, a former resident of Virginia, "now of the
Boogge in England Gent," made Rebecca Hethersall, a widow living in York
Old Fields, his attorney to collect all his Virginia debts. Because she possessed property both in Virginia and England and had used the court successfully to collect debts in her own suits in the 1680s, her reputation as
a litigant no doubt appealed to Hall. She lived up to that reputation when
she successfully defended Hall in a debt suit in 1684. Similarly, Mrs. Mary
Croshaw appeared as attorney "and in behalf of Mr Thomas Holder" in a
suit initiated by Jonathan Newell. Elizabeth Duke served in Prince George
County in 1722 as an attorney for John Woof, a London merchant who had
legal business in Virginia.[45]

Papers, DCCCLXIX, printed cases, British Library, Add. MSS 36,217, ff. 161r–171r. A 1733–
1754 dispute raged between Parke's Virginia daughter and son-in-law, Lucy and William
Byrd, and Parke's heirs in the Leeward Islands concerning ownership of land and slaves.
See Virginia Colonial Records Project Survey Report no. 11408, Virginia Historical Society
(hereafter cited as VHS).

44. Philip Ludwell, [Sr.], London, to Philip Ludwell of "Green Spring," Dec. 20, 1707,
James City County, Virginia, Lee Family Papers, VHS, Mssl L51, f. 51 (microfilm).

45. Jan. 4, 1715[/6], recorded Sept. 18, 1716, LVA, Essex [Loose] Suit Papers 103-A-1710–
103-R-1716 and 104-A-1717–104-K-1720. For Hethersall's power of attorney and subsequent

The most intriguing cases of power of attorney held by women remain those granted from husbands to wives. William Blackstone, in his 1765 *Commentaries on the Laws of England*, confirmed and delineated the proper procedure of a wife acting as attorney on behalf of her husband, and he claimed her doing so "implies no separation from, but is rather a representation of, her lord [the husband]." Women's acceptance of power of attorney, even while under coverture, allowed them to learn about finances and legal procedure and to oversee portions of the family business.[46]

By the time of the War for Independence, colonists and residents of the mother country were reconsidering the position of women under the law. Even before the eighteenth century, England's growing commercial and colonial enterprises during the early modern period complicated legal notions of property, and these changes, not surprisingly, affected women's property rights. When Lord Mansfield, chief justice of the English Court of King's Bench from 1756 to 1788, heard the case of *Ringsted v. Lady Lanesborough* in 1783, he decided that, if a married woman behaved as a single woman for commercial purposes, the merchants and others dealing with her should be able to sue and be sued by the acting-as-sole woman. Trading interests were the heart of Mansfield's innovative approach to women's property rights. English borough customs also formally or informally treated married women as feme sole traders, producers, and providers of credit. The English cases on feme sole trader status were not clear-cut in the late eighteenth and early nineteenth centuries, but, for Mansfield, the residence of

---

litigation, see York DOW 6, Feb. 26, 1682/3, Feb. 4, 1683/4, 470, 560. Note the terms of the marriage agreement Rebecca Hethersall made on behalf of her daughter, Rebecca Wythe, when Wythe married John Tiplady (York DOW 8, July 24, 1690, 471). For Croshaw, see York DOW 4, June 24, 1668, 196. For Duke, see Dec. 4, 1722, transcript in Jane Morris, *The Duke-Symes Family* (Philadelphia, 1940), 62.

46. Blackstone, *Commentaries on the Laws of England*, I, 430–433. Does this make the wife "deputy lord," rather than "deputy husband?"

North Carolinians seemed to use powers of attorney as well, and women there sometimes had legal "careers" during which they became involved in subsequent lawsuits in the process of managing estates and protecting their own business. See Linda L. Angle, "Women in the North Carolina Colonial Courts, 1670–1739" (M.A. thesis, University of North Carolina, 1975), 48–65. Similarly, Hoffer points out that, in West Jersey, attorneys were "not trained lawyers at all, but men—and women—of affairs." However, with the rise of the legal profession, he argues, West Jersey women lost access to legal process. There, women became decreasingly significant figures in legal processes during the 1720s and 1730s, when serving as a professional attorney became a profitable enterprise. Simultaneously, women were prevented from becoming professional lawyers by being denied access to training in lawyers' offices and licensing by the colony's superior courts. Hoffer found that the rise of the legal profession "went hand in glove with the increasing complexity and frequency of litigation" at precisely the time that women were refused access to that more formal training (*Law and People in Colonial America*, 63–64). In a vicious circle, the untrained representative could no longer successfully represent family interests in court, and women could not gain admission to more formal means of education that allowed them to become attorneys-at-law.

one spouse abroad made acceptance of feme sole trader status more palatable. Beginning in 1800, however, English judges began a conservative reaction against Lord Mansfield's claim that married women behaving as femes sole should be considered as such by the courts.[47]

Following Independence, at least one prominent Virginia man also reconsidered the nature of women's public status. The jurist St. George Tucker, in his annotated version of Blackstone's *Commentaries*, published in 1803 to assist lawyers in the new state of Virginia to understand the law, attacked the construction of women's legal rights under British common law. Tucker disagreed with Blackstone's editorial remarks that the disabilities of coverture were "for the most part intended for her [the wife's] protection and benefit." "So great a favourite is the female sex of the laws of England." Tucker then proceeded to enumerate how English law made unfair legal distinctions between men and women. After the Revolution, according to Tucker's argument, women should be released from the bondage of British common law to enjoy instead the power to protect the interests that their colonial mothers and grandmothers had guarded only under power of attorney. Tucker was not immediately successful, and circuitous routes for protecting women's autonomy remained the norm in post-Independence Virginia.[48]

Colonists sought to redefine the options married women had for controlling property and pursuing their legal interests in various ways in the colonial period, and power of attorney should be seen as only one means for colonists to accord married women power over property.[49] Historians of women in Virginia have pointed out that, in practice, colonists used a variety of methods to avoid the strictest of common-law restrictions that would have limited married women in the colony. The grants of power of attorney to married women are consistent with other trends in women's legal history that Linda Speth, Joan Gundersen, and Gwen Gampel have outlined.[50]

47. Susan Staves, "Chattel Property Rules and the Construction of Englishness, 1660–1800," *Law and History Review*, XII (1994), 123–153; James Oldham, *The Mansfield Manuscripts and the Growth of English Law in the Eighteenth Century* (Chapel Hill, N.C., 1992), 1245–1251; Erickson, *Women and Property in Early Modern England*, 30, 136; Stone, *Road to Divorce*, 155. The imperial reaction to developments in colonial Virginia appears in Sturtz, "Innovation and Tradition in an Imperial-Colonial Contest: Virginia Legislation on the 'Settled and Known . . . Point' of Women's Property Rights," working paper, Harvard University International Seminar on the History of the Atlantic World, Aug. 17–29, 1997.

48. St. George Tucker, *Blackstone's Commentaries: With Notes of Reference, to the Constitution and Laws, of the Federal Government of the United States; and of the Commonwealth of Virginia . . .* , 5 vols. (Philadelphia, 1803), II, 445. Note that two pages are numbered 445.

49. Through other procedures, including marriage agreements, women and men tried to find ways to counter coverture. Their attempts sometimes failed, but even failed efforts to create a better position for themselves reveal that women were willing to seek out greater autonomy and improved material conditions. See Sturtz, "Innovation and Tradition in an Imperial-Colonial Contest."

50. Significant articles that deal with married women's property in colonial Virginia include Linda E. Speth, "More than Her 'Thirds': Wives and Widows in Colonial Vir-

Recognizing the role of women's legal status in commercial undertakings as well as seeing women's legal options as existing on a spectrum ranging from severe constraint to relative autonomy allows us to reconsider the nuances of coverture in this one setting within the Anglo-American world. This should allow us to begin explaining the complexity of gender roles in Virginia in ways similar to those pioneered by historians of slavery who have stressed the problematic nature of seeing "slavery" and "freedom" as absolute opposites.[51] Increasingly, historians are beginning to see both that Virginia women inhabited a culturally restricted position and that some women resisted constraints. The variety of powers of attorney that husbands granted to wives suggests that men, as well as women, occasionally saw the advantage of according women power under the law.[52]

---

ginia," *Women and History*, IV (1983), 5–42; Joan R. Gundersen and Gwen Victor Gampel, "Married Women's Legal Status in Eighteenth-Century New York and Virginia," *WMQ*, 3d Ser., XXXIX (1982), 114–134.

51. The literature on this subject is extensive, but, for a theoretical overview, see Stanley L. Engerman, "Slavery, Serfdom, and Other Forms of Coerced Labour: Similarities and Differences," in M. L. Bush, ed., *Serfdom and Slavery: Studies in Legal Bondage* (London, 1996), 18–41.

52. For recent work on women in colonial Virginia as "actors" who were the "empowered weak," see Irmina Wawrzyczek, "The Women of Accomack versus Henry Smith: Gender, Legal Recourse, and the Social Order in Seventeenth-Century Virginia," *VMHB*, CV (1997), 5–26.

Women and the Political Culture of Eighteenth-Century Virginia

Gender, Property Law, and Voting Rights

O N JUNE 27, 1787, Anne Holden of Accomack County, Virginia, made nearly identical deeds to Joseph Boggs and Elijah Milbourne. In consideration of her "natural love and affection" for them, Holden gave each man twenty-five acres of land, specifying that the property enable them to "vote at the Annual Elections for the most Wise and Discreet men who have proved themselves real friends to the American Independance." After a year and with a house on it, the twenty-five acres were precisely the amount necessary to qualify Boggs and Milbourne as voters in Virginia's elections. Holden gave the same gift of land for the same purpose to John and Frank Boggs. Her gifts were unusual, if not singular, in eighteenth-century Virginia. Although white women, particularly elite women, made gifts of real and personal property to family and friends throughout the colonial period, such an explicitly expressed linkage between a gift of land from a woman and the enfranchisement of a man was rare.[1]

Anne Holden's gifts raise questions about the political value of white women's property in eighteenth-century Virginia. Strictly speaking, franchise law placed white women, along with free blacks, unpropertied whites, slaves, and native Americans, outside the political arena; coverture restricted married women's independent control over property. Yet, despite their legal disabilities, women's dependency under the law and their resources in prop-

The authors wish to thank Christopher L. Tomlins, Bruce Mann, James Horn, and several anonymous reviewers for their advice and suggestions. They are also grateful to Linda K. Kerber for her generous and sustaining encouragement of their study of early American women's history. Finally, they dedicate this chapter to the late Sydney V. James, in acknowledgment of his wisdom and guidance in directing their doctoral dissertations at the University of Iowa.

1. Accomack County, Virginia, Deeds No. 6, 1783–1788, 448–449, Library of Virginia (hereafter cited as LVA). Joseph Boggs might have been Anne Holden's cousin, for her father's will mentions a kinsman William Bogg, and John and Frank were Joseph Boggs's brothers. The relationship of Holden to Milbourne is uncertain. See Ralph T. Whitelaw, *Virginia's Eastern Shore: A History of Northampton and Accomack Counties*, 2 vols. (Richmond, Va., 1951), II, 818–819, 1281–1285.

erty enhanced the political prospects of adult male household heads. As with men, women's ability to influence political culture depended not only on their legal status but also in no small amount on their statutory and customary rights in property.

Women's relationships to the political culture of eighteenth-century Virginia can best be understood through an expansive concept of political participation. Clearly, women could not vote or hold office, two traditional gauges of political activity. Yet, as Linda K. Kerber has argued in her work on citizenship, such narrow definitions ignore the political relationships of a range of individuals, regardless of their formal connection to the franchise. In eighteenth-century Virginia, free white women, officially outsiders to political processes, had a measurable influence on local politics. Although not de jure members of the local political culture, they were de facto members in a variety of ways.[2]

The relationship of women to the political culture of eighteenth-century Virginia and the role of property rights in that relationship can be explored in several ways. The development of Virginia's franchise law shows how political participation became legally linked to property rights as well as distinctions based upon race, age, and gender. There were, in fact, political advantages of women's resultant legal dependency, and women's electioneering activities highlight these advantages and offer important clues why women like Anne Holden might have used their property to enfranchise male relatives. A review of the legal status and property rights of women and the House of Burgesses' interpretation of those rights, coupled with a detailed examination of a single community, Accomack County, reveals the complex ways in which women's property contributed to male enfranchisement and voting. Political participation in some parts of eighteenth-century Virginia, we argue, was a "family" attribute, one formally exercised by adult white male householders but promoted and materially supported by female members of the family.

2. In discussing women and citizenship in the early Republic, Linda K. Kerber cautions against a narrow construction of citizenship, arguing that, if "discussions of citizenship be limited to claims to voting and office holding by women, then the early republic offers us mostly silence" ("The Paradox of Women's Citizenship in the Early Republic: The Case of *Martin vs. Massachusetts*, 1805," *American Historical Review*, XCVII [1992], 354, reprinted in Kerber, *Toward an Intellectual History of Women* [Chapel Hill, N.C., 1997], 269). Although we are adopting a more expanded understanding of political participation for our study of the pre-Revolutionary period, the political participation examined here should not be confused with republican citizenship. Citizenship of all kinds, particularly female citizenship, was irrelevant before the American Revolution. Women as well as men were subjects, although the English used the terms "subjects" and "citizens" interchangeably. Only with the advent of the Revolution did the concept of volitional citizenship develop. See Joan R. Gundersen, "Independence, Citizenship, and the American Revolution," *Signs*, XIII (1987–1988), 59–63.

I. Franchise Law

Franchise law—the series of statutes that detailed the requirements for voting—placed women outside of the polity, a seemingly apolitical status, and
defined those men eligible to participate in elections. The colony of Virginia,
in fact, began with no specific franchise and gradually developed a set of
requirements based upon a stake-in-society concept, in which only permanent and economically productive members of the community enjoyed full
political rights. We do not know precisely who voted in Virginia in the 1620s
and 1630s, but, by 1646, and probably before, all freemen could participate in
the election of burgesses. In 1655 the legislature restricted the franchise to "all
house keepers whether freeholders, lease holders, or otherwise tenants" but
with the provision "that this word house keepers . . . extend no further than
to one person in a family." A year later, however, the Assembly (reflecting
perhaps the leveling spirit of the English Commonwealth) decided it was
"something hard and unagreeable to reason that any persons shall pay equall
taxes and yet have no votes in elections" and repealed that part of the earlier
act restricting the franchise to house keepers.[3]

The Assembly reversed itself in 1670, and, for the first time, the law
included property requirements as part of the county franchise: only freeholders and house keepers subject to levies could vote. The Assembly debarred freemen—free white men lacking property—because they had "little
interest in the country [and] doe oftner make tumults at the election to the
disturbance of his majesties peace, than by their discretions in the votes
provide for the conservation thereof." These regulations disappeared, and
freemen gained recognition briefly during Bacon's Rebellion in 1676, but
property requirements once again became the rule with Bacon's demise.
With the reestablishment of the freehold requirement, Virginia's franchise
rested solidly on the possession of property until well into the nineteenth
century. Most of the legislation after 1680 sought only to clarify earlier acts.[4]

In 1684, tenants with life leases became freeholders, and for the first time
the law clearly stated that a person could vote in any county in which he
possessed a freehold. In 1705, a further definition of the term *freeholder*
included "every person who hath an estate real for his own life or the life of
another or any estate of any greater dignity," thus clarifying what types of
tenants could participate in elections. The amount of property remained

3. William Waller Hening, ed., *The Statutes at Large: Being A Collection of All the Laws of
Virginia, from the First Session of the Legislature, in the Year 1619* . . . , 13 vols. (Richmond,
Va., Philadelphia, 1809–1823), I, 333–334, 403, 411–412. A 1658 law combined provisions of
the 1655 and 1656 acts including the affirmation that all freemen could vote (I, 475).
4. Ibid., II, 280, 256, 380–381.

unspecified in these early laws, and presumably a freehold or life lease on just a few acres made the holder a member of the electorate.[5]

By 1735, and probably before, individuals obtained small parcels of land for the sole purpose of enlarging the pool of potential voters. In York County, for example, the sheriff apparently executed nineteen such leases just before the 1735 election, and in King George County one of the candidates and his associates did the same. Immediately following the resolution of the disputed York election, the House of Burgesses instructed the Committee of Privileges and Elections to prepare a bill "to prevent making fraudulent Freeholds." The resulting law specified that a freehold of either one hundred acres of unimproved land or twenty-five acres with a house must be held for at least one year prior to an election. This 1736 law governed election procedures for the rest of the colonial period.[6]

While the 1736 law and its predecessors defined the freehold requirement, additional regulations restricted the franchise by sex, race, age, and religion. It is perhaps a commonplace to state that women in colonial Virginia did not have direct access to the franchise themselves, but the law did not specifically exclude women from voting until 1699, with the passage of "an act for prevention of undue election of Burgeses." Joan R. Gundersen suggests that the Burgesses excluded propertied women from the franchise in response to female voting, and, according to Robert J. Dinkin, Virginia was the only colony to exclude specifically women from the franchise. However, we know of no seventeenth-century female freeholders attempting to vote or complaining of disfranchisement.[7] The 1699 act declared its "true intent and meaning . . . that no woman sole or covert, infants under the age of twenty

5. Ibid., III, 26, 240.

6. H. R. McIlwaine and John Pendleton Kennedy, eds., *Journals of the House of Burgesses of Virginia*, 13 vols. (Richmond, Va., 1905–1915), *1727–1734, 1736–1740*, 2, 251, 256, 282–283 (hereafter cited as *JHB*); Hening, ed., *Statutes at Large*, IV, 475–478. In 1762 and 1769, the House of Burgesses attempted to reduce the required number of unimproved acres to fifty and to shorten the possession time of such property, but neither act received approval in England. See Hening, ed., *Statutes at Large*, VII, 518–530, VIII, 305–317.

7. Statutes in other colonies used language—"he," "male," or "freeman"—that clearly excluded women (Robert J. Dinkin, *Voting in Provincial America: A Study of Elections in the Thirteen Colonies, 1689–1776* [Westport, Conn., 1977], 30; Gundersen, "Independence, Citizenship, and the American Revolution," *Signs*, XIII [1987–1988], 64–65). The *Virginia Gazette* carried reports of widows voting in the colony of New York (Parks's *Virginia Gazette* [Williamsburg], June 24, 1737). In 1787 Hannah Lee Corbin complained that she was forced to pay taxes but had no hand in writing the laws or electing those who did. Her complaint was made to her brother Richard Henry Lee, the head of the Virginia delegation to the Continental Congress. He agreed that she should be able to vote in local elections. Like Anne Holden, Corbin was influenced by emergent republican ideology. See Louise Belote Dawe and Sandra Gioia Treadway, "Hannah Lee Corbin: The Forgotten Lee," *Virginia Cavalcade*, XXIX (1979–1980), 75–76.

one years, or recusant convict being freeholders shall be enabled to give a vote or have a voice in the election of burgesses anything in this act to the contrary notwithstanding." A 1723 statute disfranchised free blacks, mulattoes, and native Americans, although probably few members of these groups voted before this date.[8]

Franchise law determined who might be political participants—propertied white men—and distinguished them from political nonparticipants such as women, the young, African Americans, native Americans, and the nonpropertied. Despite such formal disfranchisement, women participated in the political culture of eighteenth-century Virginia, engaging in a range of activities that included nearly everything except the formal casting of votes. When these activities became an integral part of a highly competitive local political culture, both the men and women of enfranchised households acquired a heightened sense of the import of voting and elections.

II. Women and Political Culture

Anne Holden's deeds to the four men in 1787 suggest both a desire to define a political role for herself and an ability to shape the construction of the political community. Like other women who demonstrated their commitment to the Revolution by disorderly demonstrations, fund-raising, and boycotting and by sending sons and husbands into battle, Holden's gifts of land reflect a form of patriotism and loyalty to Revolutionary principles. If women who sent their husbands and sons to war expressed their "surrogate enlistment in a society in which women did not fight," then Anne Holden's gifts can also be seen as an expression of her "surrogate enfranchisement" in the gendered political culture of the new Republic. Before the Revolution, however, women lacking Anne Holden's resources as well as women for whom issues of republican citizenship were far afield participated in the local political culture of Virginia. Such participation suggests that women in some places possessed a heightened awareness of political issues and processes that might have encouraged them, like Holden, to think of their properties in political as well as economic terms.[9]

8. Hening, ed., *Statutes at Large*, III, 172, IV, 133–134. Imperial authorities reluctantly accepted the voting prohibition against nonwhite propertied males but not surprisingly accepted without question the sanctions against propertied women. See Dinkin, *Voting in Provincial America*, 33; Kathleen M. Brown, *Good Wives, Nasty Wenches, and Anxious Patriarchs: Gender, Race, and Power in Colonial Virginia* (Chapel Hill, N.C., 1996), 219–222.

9. Linda K. Kerber, " 'History Can Do It No Justice': Women and the Reinterpretation of the American Revolution," in Ronald Hoffman and Peter J. Albert, eds., *Women in the Age of the American Revolution* (Charlottesville, Va., 1989), 16–26 (quotation on 22). On gendered citizenship, see 34–42.

Treating freeholders, or providing them with lodging, food, and liquor, was common at Virginia elections, and women were often at the center of such entertainments. Women could be simple spectators at treating, but on occasion they were active participants. At elections where women received or provided treats, candidates were shielded from charges of impropriety. Precisely because they were legal dependents and political outsiders, the presence of women effectively transformed a potentially damaging political event into a simple gathering, channeling women's legal dependency into an effective political strategy.[10]

On August 31, 1734, for example, John Champ, a candidate for election in King George County, along with a Mr. Skinker, went to the local courthouse, where they found four freeholders and twenty women, among whom they distributed four bottles of wine. The sheriff, having received the writ of election on August 27, initially scheduled the election for Wednesday, September 4, but on Friday, August 31, he moved the election up to September 2. The election was contested on both grounds: treating was illegal anytime after the sheriff issued the writ, and the sheriff's changes in the election date were unusual. However, the Committee of Privileges and Elections concluded that the wine was not given with an intent to buy votes and confirmed the election, giving treating a very narrow legal construction. Arguably they did so because women were a majority of the crowd, overwhelming the freeholders five to one, and no harm was done, since women could not vote. In this case, the presence of women served as a sort of damage control, allowing the candidate to beat the charges of illegal treating.[11]

In another instance from Prince George County, both women and slaves acted in ways that deflected charges of election irregularities from a candidate. In 1752 Stephen Dewey was elected as a burgess, but the election was contested on charges of illegal treating. The committee heard from one male witness who reported that Mrs. Dewey, the candidate's wife, told him that she provided lodging, food, and liquor for nearly eighty freeholders who stayed with the Deweys while on their way to the election. The deponent noted that on the

> day of the last Election of Burgesses, for that County, a great number of the Freeholders thereof, supposed to be near Eighty who all, except a very few, lived remote, some Thirty, and others more, Miles from the Court-House, went to the Dwelling-House of the sitting Member, the

10. It was illegal to give or promise money, gifts, food, drink, provisions, entertainment, or any kind of present or preference in exchange for votes (Hening, ed., *Statutes at Large,* III, 243). For a detailed examination of the frequency, distribution, and legal ramifications of treating, see John Gilman Kolp, *Gentlemen and Freeholders: Electoral Politics in Colonial Virginia* (Baltimore, 1998), 28–32.

11. *JHB, 1727–1734, 1736–1740,* 208–209.

Earth being then covered with Snow, and the Weather excessive cold, where they continued 'til the next Day, and during that Time were kindly and hospitably entertained by the sitting Member, who gave them sufficient Meat, and Drink, lodged as many of them as he could, and gave them some Drams of Rum in the Morning; at which Time, as one Witness deposed, the sitting Member's Wife Said, she had been so employed ever since the Night before, but that the sitting Member, or any Person for him, did not invite them to come there, nor then, nor at any other Time, sollicit any of them to vote for him; that much the greater Part of them did vote for him, and intended so to do, before they went there.[12]

Other witnesses disagreed about the scene on election day: some said that the freeholders were drunk in the morning, and others declared that most voters were sober. One freeholder claimed that he voted for Dewey because he had been at the Dewey's the night before the election, and added:

On the Day of the Election, the Wife of the sitting Member, employed one Drury Thweat, a neighbor, and Friend of her Husband, to go with some of his Negroe Servants, and [fetch] an Hogshead of Punch . . . [which] was carried to the Court-House, ordered it to be placed about an Hundred Yards from the door . . . in the Absence of the said Drury Thweat, several Persons drank of the said Punch, by the Invitation of one of the sitting member's negroe-Servants, who told them, that those who had voted, or would vote, for his master might drink as much as they pleased; and that . . . Mr. William Hall, a very young Man, who is a Son of the sitting member's Wife, and another Person, intreated several Persons to drink of the said Punch; . . . but that the sitting member did not know of, or order their doing so; and when a Person asked whether he might not have some Punch, declared that none ought to be drank before the Poll was concluded; and that the Friends of the sitting member, when they were informed that some Persons were drinking his punch, immediately went to the Hogshead, and having pulled the Cock, stopped it up.

The Elections Committee found that Mr. Dewey was fairly elected.[13]

Mrs. Dewey's role in the election was a type of active political campaigning that women, particularly candidates' wives, could engage in with impunity. Women who distributed liquor and provided food and lodging did so because victualing was a traditional female role and because their performance of these tasks freed the treating from charges of illegality. The legal

12. *JHB, 1752–1755, 1756–1758*, 50.
13. Ibid.

dependency of Mrs. Dewey shielded both herself and her husband. Surely it was not simply coincidental that Mrs. Dewey remarked that *she* had been victualing and lodging the freeholders, just as she made sure that it was by *her* orders that the punch be taken to the courthouse. Of further significance were the "negroe-servants" who invited the crowd to drink the punch: as political outsiders, any actions taken by them would not shade the victory of Stephen Dewey. Predictably, the candidate himself was absent from all of the election day activities. All told, the Deweys presented a form of political masquerade: precisely who organized this charade must remain a matter of conjecture, but the ruse involved the candidate's family and dependents. Even the Elections Committee of the House of Burgesses participated, finding that the candidate had committed no violation. Like the committee's earlier decision in the Champ election, they used a narrow legalism, the candidate's absence of intent to treat, in making their ruling. Ultimately such decisions encouraged political outsiders—Mrs. Dewey, the slaves—to assume important and effective roles in the political process. Political culture in Virginia was wide enough to admit such seeming outsiders, whose actions depoliticized a series of events that could have invalidated Dewey's election.[14]

During elections, women with a talent for campaigning, like Mrs. Dewey, transcended their status as political outsiders and enjoyed a degree of influence they otherwise did not possess. Female electioneering in England and America was not widespread, but women could be found "publicly and openly active at the foundation level of politics in managing interests and in the electioneering that such management required." Yet the *Virginia Gazette* often treated the entry of women into the masculinized political sphere with ridicule or satire. In 1737 a report of two widows voting in New York included the swipe that "these two ladies will be chosen constable for the next year," representing women in electoral politics and public service as an absurdity. This was an implicit warning against the full-fledged entry of women into political culture. A 1769 story, linking female disorderliness with their political participation, described two female English "freeholders" who came to blows over their respective candidates. After brawling, one emerged with "the honour of two black eyes and a bloody nose." A second report in the same year joined women's influence in politics with corruption and male weakness. The story described the courting of a barber, Suds, by two candidates. Both candidates patronized Suds, coming to him for shaves and tipping him generously, but his wife prevented him from

14. Although the preparation and serving of food and drink was certainly a traditional domestic role for women, surviving evidence shows at least as many men engaged in such activity as women. In the Dewey election dispute, the entire house voted to confirm that Dewey had been elected. The motion passed fifty-three to seven. See *JHB, 1752–1755, 1756–1758,* 50.

making a choice for either man. Only after one candidate visited Suds for a second shave and left another tip did Suds's wife give her consent. He voted "as his wife and interest dictated."[15]

For the most part, print culture reinforced the incompatibility of women with public culture, depicting their attempts at politics as frivolous or linking them with petty corruption and narrow self-interest. The portrait of elections given in Robert Munford's *Candidates* (1770) is a less harsh representation of women's interests in local politics, although he too suggests that women's political interests, like men's, were often merely self-serving. Yet Munford allowed the possibility of women's political concerns and made the franchise of equal concern to wives and husbands.

Munford's drama presents several types of candidates. As the play begins, the incumbent candidates, Worthy and Wou'dbe, face reelection, but Worthy, who represents the values of gentility, deference, property qualifications, and experience, has retired. Wou'dbe, who shares Worthy's values toward political representation but lacks his social status, must run against three other candidates, all of whom are corrupt and inferior to the incumbents, making ridiculous promises and gifts of liquor to the freeholders. The comedy relies on satire to make its criticisms of political culture, and it concludes with Worthy coming out of retirement and the best men winning the election. Although historians disagree whether the play offers a realistic or simply a hopeful view of elections, it does provide useful commentary by an insider on political life in Virginia in the eighteenth century.[16]

. The *Candidates* portrays a highly competitive election, with candidates vying both through reason (Wou'dbe) and through impropriety (Sir John Toddy, Mr. Strutabout, and Mr. Smallhopes) for the votes of the freeholders. In act 2, several freeholders and their wives gather at a racetrack to discuss the candidates, and the exchanges between the voters and their wives are instructive. For example, Lucy notes that Wou'dbe was a good choice, be-

15. Edmund S. Morgan, *Inventing the People: The Rise of Popular Sovereignty in England and America* (New York, 1988), 190; Parks's *Virginia Gazette*, June 24, 1737; Rind's *Virginia Gazette* [Williamsburg], July 20, 1769; Robert E. Brown and B. Katherine Brown, *Virginia, 1705–1786: Democracy or Aristocracy?* (East Lansing, Mich., 1964), 138–139.

16. Those accepting the play as an accurate but satirical portrait of elections throughout Virginia include Jay B. Hubbell and Douglass Adair, "Robert Munford's *The Candidates*," *William and Mary Quarterly*, 3d Ser., V (1948), 217–225 (analysis), 227–257 (text of *The Candidates*); Charles S. Sydnor, *Gentlemen Freeholders: Political Practices in Washington's Virginia* (Chapel Hill, N.C., 1952). To the contrary, Richard R. Beeman sees it as a description of the "contentiousness and disorderliness" of the Virginia Southside as well as the author's hope that this region will one day assume the stable and genteel political world of the lower tidewater ("Robert Munford and the Political Culture of Frontier Virginia," *Journal of American Studies*, XII [1978], 169–183; "Deference, Republicanism, and the Emergence of Popular Politics in Eighteenth-Century America," *WMQ*, 3d Ser., XLIX [1992], 407–408). All citations to the play refer to Hubbell and Adair's edition.

cause "he's mighty good to all his poor neighbours." When Twist, her husband, reminds her, "Wife, you and I, you Know, could never agree about burgesses," Lucy responds, "If the wives were to vote, I believe they would make a better choice than their husbands." Twist teases her: "You'd be for the funnyest—wou'dn't you?" The husbands in *The Candidates* satirize the political wisdom of their wives.[17]

Similar exchanges occur between Catherine and her husband, Stern, and Sarah and her husband, Prize. Catherine applauds Lucy's sentiments: "Well done Lucy, you are right, girl. If we were all to speak to our old men as freely as you do, there would be better doings." To this, Stern replies, "Perhaps not, Kate." When Catherine reminds him that "Mr. Wou'dbe promised Molly a riband, and a pair of buckles," Stern reluctantly agrees that Mr. Wou'dbe has been a good friend to them but warns that he "can vote for him without your clash." Sarah reminds Prize that Wou'dbe "stood for our George, when our neighbor refused us." Prize agrees that "Mr. Wou'dbe's a man well enough in his neighbourhood, and he may have learning, as they say he has, but he don't shew it like Mr. Strutabout."[18]

In *The Candidates,* wives give allegiance to political candidates who have supported the local neighborhood through small gifts, charity, and loyalty. Each woman is impressed with Mr. Wou'dbe's neighborliness and refers to acts centered in the realm of the household. Munford seems willing to concede that women have a legitimate interest in candidates on the basis of issues that concern families. Wou'dbe's deference to the women and their husbands, evidently exercised not only during election campaigns but at all times, impresses the women as well. Despite Wou'dbe's genteel status, he is genuinely friendly with his constituency, which includes women as key members. Munford presents women as politically astute: Lucy and Sarah, with their intimate knowledge of the neighborhood, are portrayed as able to influence prudently the political choices of their husbands. The play admits the possibility that women have legitimate and positive roles in political culture.

Yet, although women may wisely influence their husbands, Munford exhibits definite antipathy toward the idea of their direct participation in the political process. Ultimately women are too irrational or frivolous to vote soundly. When Twist teases Lucy that she would be for the "funnyest" candidate, she replies, "Yes, faith; and the wittiest, and prettiest, and the wisest, and the best too; you are all for ugly except when you choose me." Furthermore, the play includes several allusions to Lucy's sexual improprieties with Wou'dbe, echoing the satirical representations found elsewhere in print

17. Munford, *The Candidates,* 240.
18. Ibid., 240–241.

culture and conflating female political behavior and sexual disorderliness. Such responses were typical when women openly supported political candidates and thereby transformed their role in society.[19]

The Candidates provides competing representations of women's political participation. In one sense Munford levels the same accusations at men and women. He suggests that men guided by exceedingly narrow self-interest or a lack of reason vote no better than women, who are apt to vote superficially. At the same time, he suggests that, if freeholders follow the lead of women and give careful consideration to the candidate's behavior and local issues, their choices can be trusted. The play carefully circumscribes the roles women might play in political culture, but it does not assume that women's political interests are any less legitimate than those of men.

Women's legal dependency could deflect attention from election improprieties. In limited ways, women treated, canvassed, and campaigned on behalf of favored candidates. Virginia's print culture often treated the intersection of women with political culture with derision, supporting women's exclusion from the masculinized public sphere. While legitimizing women's local political interests, *The Candidates* also presented reasons for sustaining their legal and political dependency.

Yet, however it might have been represented in print culture, women's legal dependency was clearly advantageous to candidates and freeholders in treating and elections. More important, these varied, though informal, political activities demonstrate that women in certain locales were cognizant of their political role within families and communities. Where competitive elections occurred with regularity and freeholders made real choices between candidates, women had an opportunity to make an even greater impact. Here, their dependency under coverture mingled with their property rights as married women, allowing them to enfranchise the men in their lives overtly, covertly, and sometimes accidentally.

III. Women's Property and the Franchise

The system of coverture, part of Virginia's common-law inheritance from England, transferred a woman's legal identity to her husband upon marriage. Husband and wife assumed a unity of person, a partnership that expressed "one will" to the outside world. Hence, married women could not act as their own agents at law and had no independent property rights, unless these were secured before marriage in a separate trust. Coverture and

19. Morgan, *Inventing the People*, 196–200.

traditional interpretations of the economic and political unity of husband and wife were significant when men laid claim to the franchise.[20]

In eighteenth-century Virginia, that political unity meant, among other things, that men could gain the franchise through their curtesy interests in the property of their wives. Coverture provided this benefit. The property a woman owned before marriage or inherited during marriage was understood to be her separate estate, but under coverture her husband held extensive rights in this property. He was entitled to manage her property and to profit from its use, but, despite these curtesy rights, a husband could not waste or alienate it without her consent. If the couple remained childless, the wife retained absolute rights to her own estate, and, upon her death, it returned to her family. If the couple had children, however, the husband retained curtesy rights in his wife's lands even after her decease—his interest was sustained as long as he was alive, superseding the interests of children of the marriage.[21]

Married women could escape the disabilities of coverture through a mechanism of equity law: a marriage settlement, usually in the form of a trust, contract, or jointure. If a woman possessed land and if she or someone acting on her behalf arranged a marriage settlement, then her control over her property could be as extensive as she chose, although her husband had to consent to the terms of the agreement. Such protections for women's separate property were uncommon in eighteenth-century Virginia.[22]

20. Gundersen, "Independence, Citizenship, and the American Revolution," *Signs*, XIII (1987–1988), 67. For other discussions of married women's property and citizenship, see Kerber, "The Paradox of Women's Citizenship in the Early Republic," *AHR*, XCVII (1992), 349–378. For discussions of married women's property rights, see Joan R. Gundersen and Gwen Victor Gampel, "Married Women's Legal Status in Eighteenth-Century New York and Virginia," *WMQ*, 3d Ser., XXXIX (1982), 114–134; Marylynn Salmon, *Women and the Law of Property in Early America* (Chapel Hill, N.C., 1982), 14–40; Linda E. Speth, "More Than Her 'Thirds': Wives and Widows in Colonial Virginia," *Women and History*, no. 4 (1982), 5–41.

21. For married women's property rights, see Salmon, *Women and the Law of Property*, 14–18, 144–145.

22. Ibid., 81–119; Salmon, "Women and Property in South Carolina: The Evidence from Marriage Settlements, 1730 to 1830," *WMQ*, 3d Ser., XXXIX (1982), 655–661.

Landowners in eighteenth-century Accomack County demonstrated disparate understandings of the separate property of their spouses. John West's will, for example, written in 1703, stipulated that his wife, Matilda West, have the disposal of her maiden lands although legally she already had such rights. In another case, Mary Scarburgh Bayly inherited land from her father before her marriage to Charles Bayly, but, when Bayly died in 1716, his will left her inheritance to his son Charles. The widow Bayly filed an objection to the will, claiming that she owned the land in fee simple before her marriage and therefore her husband had no right to will it to anyone. The next year, her father-in-law's will contained a clause stipulating that she could continue to live on the plantation where his son had lived for life, so long as she deeded her property to her son. She did so, thereby

In addition to curtesy rights for husbands and mechanisms for protecting married women's separate property, the law also provided for the widow's dower, usually a one-third share of all real estate owned by the husband during the marriage. Since the law intended that the dower support a
woman during her widowhood, she was given the power to consent to the
sale of any land. The practice of private examination, where justices could
determine that the conveyance was not forced upon her, gave married
women a tool by which they could influence land conveyances: women
could refuse to sign away their dower rights, and courts upheld their right to
do so. Private examination was an imperfect instrument, because it could
not prevent spousal coercion or retaliation. Still, women's right of refusal
could be used to protect the household's best interests: "The ability to keep
property within the family may have saved some women from financial
hardship through the mismanagement or ill will of their spouses." The law
provided wives with the power to protect themselves and their families from
financial strain.[23]

In most cases, women's property served any number of family strategies
designed to improve the fortunes, status, and reputation of the household. A
husband was entitled to use his wife's separate property: he managed it, he
profited from it, and he voted on the basis of his interest in it. Although a
married woman retained certain rights over her property, her husband could
claim his interest in her land to satisfy the property requirement needed for
voting. When he did so, he was simply exercising his curtesy rights.[24]

Franchise law segregated married women from the formal polity, but the
use of their separate property in the service of family interests complicates
our understanding of the relationship of women to political culture. The
political value of female property can be seen in several disputed elections
reported to and decided by the House of Burgesses' Committee of Privileges
and Elections, in which women's property remained at issue in determining
eligibility for the franchise.

In a 1755 election in Elizabeth City County, Thomas Roberts voted "by
virtue of his interest" in the estate of his wife, the widow of William Mallory.
She had a life interest in 100 acres from her deceased husband, and before

---

ensuring support during her widowhood. Similarly, Catherine West Snead had inherited
three hundred acres from her father, which her husband, in 1727, willed to their son,
Smith. She considered the land to be hers, however, and only in 1751 willed it to her son.
See Whitelaw, *Virginia's Eastern Shore*, I, 723–724, II, 61, 959.

23. Salmon, *Women and the Law of Property*, 16–18 (dower and private examination),
146; Salmon, "Women and Property in South Carolina," *WMQ*, XXXIX (1982), 1–2.

24. Although curtesy rights had been long recognized in Virginia, their role in enfran-
chising husbands was not formally mentioned in election law until 1775 (Hening, ed.,
Statutes at Large, IX, 59).

her remarriage she put the land in trust for her children, reserving 25 acres for the use of Roberts until her minor son came of age. Perhaps these 25 acres simply represented a division of the real estate into equal portions for the heirs, but the gift was also the amount necessary to enfranchise her husband. The Committee of Privileges and Elections decided that Roberts could vote. In another election in Elizabeth City County, in 1761, James Cunningham voted "in right of his wife's dower." Elizabeth Servant Cunningham had never received all of her dower interest in lands sold by her first husband, Bertrand Servant, during his lifetime. His will ordered her to sell the remainder of the land and pay his debts, but she renounced the will, presumably suing for her dower interest. Accordingly, the estate administrator gave her an unspecified acreage where she and James Cunningham lived in a "Mansion House." The administrator reported selling 96 acres from Servant's estate and provided the undersheriff's statement that the Servant estate quitrents were calculated on 73 acres. When a "bystander" remarked that "then there were but 23 acres for the Dower," the administrator countered that the remainder was the requisite 25 acres, even though he lacked a precise measurement. The committee ruled that James Cunningham had a good right to vote.[25]

Sons and fathers also battled over women's property. In the same 1761 election, Samuel Dewberry and Samuel Dewberry, Jr. claimed the franchise based upon 190 acres that had belonged to their late wife and mother. Dewberry Senior held the land in right of his deceased wife, although the property was entailed on their son Samuel. Dewberry Junior claimed that, several years earlier, the elder Dewberry had made an oral gift of the land to him, putting him in possession of 145 acres of it, as long as he improved it and paid quitrents on it, which he did for several years prior to the disputed election. The committee voted that the son had no right to vote at the election, probably in part because oral gifts were unenforceable and also because husbands' rights in spousal property superseded those of the children. Without an actual deed from father to son, the father retained full rights and benefits from the property, including the right to vote.[26]

A man who possessed land, however, held a greater claim to vote than a man who held coverture interest in that same land, so long as the two were unrelated. When John Thruston, who married William Dalton's widow, voted in an Elizabeth City County election in 1755, he claimed the franchise based on his curtesy interest in his wife's land. But he had never possessed it. Benjamin Lester had paid quitrents on the same tract of land, cleared it, built a house on it, sold timber from it, and, based on this, claimed the franchise.

25. JHB, 1761–1765, 86–87.
26. Ibid., 86.

The committee ruled on the basis of possession. Although Thruston's claim was a reasonable one, the rights of the possessor superseded coverture interest. John Thruston did not get to vote.[27]

Clearly, county officials took a much more expansive view of electorate eligibility than did the Burgesses' Committee of Privileges and Elections. Local officials, for example, allowed more than one man to lay claim to the same woman's property as a basis for voting. They also permitted seemingly direct violations of statute law governing electors. For instance, in an election in Elizabeth City County in 1755, two free black men, Joseph and Nehemiah Nichols, voted, despite the terms of a thirty-year-old statute that debarred free blacks from exercising the franchise. When these and other local practices resulted in controverted elections, the Burgesses' Committee had the final say over voter eligibility. The committee allowed only one voter to claim his privileges from coverture or dower property: fathers' claims superseded those of sons, but in the absence of other male heirs, claims to coverture or dower property were sustained only through possession. Unsurprisingly, the committee disallowed voters like Joseph and Nehemiah Nichols, who voted in direct violation of statute law. In these instances, local officials defined the franchise relatively loosely, but the committee ultimately defined legitimate claims to the electorate and, therefore, its composition. Moreover, their decisions throw into sharp relief the critical role of women's property in the enfranchisement of their husbands and sons.[28]

As the qualitative evidence demonstrates, women's real property, whether it was theirs absolutely, from their fathers, mothers, or husbands, or whether it was a life-use estate or their dower interest, provided the basis for the enfranchisement of some men in eighteenth-century Virginia. Unlike Anne Holden, most women did not stipulate that their property enfranchise male heirs, although their estates could and did provide voting rights for husbands and sons. What the qualitative evidence does not reveal is the degree of such contributions both across Virginia in general and in specific locales. In Accomack County, the extent to which women made voting possible for their husbands, sons, and male relatives can be explored as well as the reasons why such enfranchisements might have been important family strategies in this and in some other Virginia communities.

IV. Accomack County

One of the reasons candidates and voters bickered in excruciating detail over women's property rights in Elizabeth City and Prince William Counties and

27. *JHB, 1752–1755, 1756–1758,* 359–361.
28. Ibid., 360.

ultimately brought their fight to the House of Burgesses is that both of these counties had highly competitive political cultures in the eighteenth century. Although Elizabeth City offered its citizens a tranquil electoral environment in the first half of the century, by the 1750s longtime burgesses were no longer being automatically and easily reelected. With an electorate of fewer than 150, every eligible male freeholder counted; in 1755, for example, only three votes separated the second-place winner from the third-place loser. Prince William County had an even longer record of elite competition that made freeholders active and desired participants in electoral politics. Beginning with its first election in 1732 and extending into the 1760s if not beyond, the local gentry mounted lively election campaigns that included improper treating of voters with liquor, improprieties by tobacco inspectors, possible early termination of polling by a politically motivated sheriff, and riotous and disorderly conduct by candidates and freeholders. Incumbents met defeat in a third of these contests, and, in several cases, winning and losing candidates were separated by a handful of votes. In these two counties and perhaps in fifteen to twenty more, the competitive level of electoral politics made the use of women's property for male enfranchisement not only relevant to candidates but also a potentially important tool used by families to assure their formal place in the local polity.[29]

Accomack, a tidewater county located on Virginia's Eastern Shore, was one of those highly competitive communities. Agitated early in the century by a controversy involving the membership and responsibilities of the parish vestry, the Accomack political system drew numerous candidates and hundreds of voters into the electoral arena, creating a divisive political climate that often overshadowed the situation that brought it into being. Although a brief hiatus in electoral intensity followed the resolution of the vestry controversy, a second, short-lived, but no less lively dilemma concerning the county court arose that rejuvenated activities in the final decade of the colonial era. Elections became so heated and contentious that often five to seven serious candidates battled over the two available seats; even in by-elections for a single seat, up to four men competed for voter support. The resulting elections not only kept voter turnout high but brought defeat to many incumbents and lengthy petitions to the House of Burgesses.[30] Because Accomack County was probably the most competitive electoral

29. Ibid., 57–58, 73, 81, 352, 359–361; *JHB, 1761–1765,* 20, 73, 86–90, 103–104, 125–130; Elizabeth City County, Virginia, Deed Book E, 8–10, and Deeds and Wills, 1763–1771, 77–77a, LVA; *JHB, 1727–1734, 1736–1740,* 258, 264–265, 306; *JHB, 1758–1761,* 29, 63; Prince William County, Virginia, Deed Book P, 68–73, LVA. Virginia's sixty-five colonial constituencies are evaluated for competitive traits and ranked in Kolp, "The Dynamics of Electoral Competition in Pre-Revolutionary Virginia," *WMQ,* 3d Ser., XLIX (1992), table 1, 666–667.

30. These local political controversies and their impact on the Accomack electoral system are treated in detail in Kolp, *Gentlemen and Freeholders,* 83–114.

constituency in eighteenth-century Virginia, it is probable that, like Anne Holden in the 1780s, local women and men throughout the eighteenth century maintained a heightened sense of the political import of property rights.

Men certainly owned the vast majority of agricultural property in eighteenth-century Accomack, but the land Anne Holden and her female predecessors held contributed significantly to the overall productivity of the local economy and to the wealth of individual families. Representing 10–15 percent of the landowners and controlling more land on average than their male counterparts, women owned nearly a fifth of the county's acreage in the pre-Revolutionary era (see Table 1).[31] Most women inherited lands directly from fathers, but a minority obtained property from their mothers or husbands, and an equal number became owners through deeds, gifts, and other legal mechanisms. As married women under common-law coverture, 60 percent of the female owners surrendered use and management of their properties to the husband. If his skills proved worthy of the task, the family prospered and his personal prestige and reputation in the community increased. Because three-quarters of the men who used their wives' property in this way had no land of their own, they became dependent entirely upon their marriage partners for their economic success and stature in the community.[32]

These men were also dependent upon their wives' land for their initial and often continued membership in the Accomack polity. Some men first became enfranchised through property brought to the marriage by their wives and then later acquired land on their own. In 1706, for example, Elizabeth Bundick inherited 100 acres from her father, John Abbott, which made her husband, George, a member of the electorate for the first time. Later, in 1718, and again in 1731, George acquired additional lands that more than satisfied the franchise requirements, but it was the initial 100 acres that enfranchised him for twelve years. Similarly, Mark Ewell gained coverture rights to his wife's 30 acres in 1722 and then gained his own 400 acres five years later. Even vestryman, frequent candidate, and burgess George Douglas had access to his wife's lands for several years before acquiring modest holdings of his own in 1730. Prudence McDaniel's 75-acre and Patience

31. Similar proportions were found in Charles County, Maryland, where women comprised 14 percent of the landowners in 1782. See Jean B. Lee, *The Price of Nationhood: The American Revolution in Charles County* (New York, 1994), 279.

32. Of the landowners of Accomack County, 73 percent obtained land from parents, 10 percent from brothers, and 6 percent from husbands; wills accounted for two-thirds of the transactions while gifts were 5 percent and deeds 14 percent. These figures and those used in the tables and discussions that follow are based upon analyses of 2,154 land transactions between 1735 and 1775 extracted from Whitelaw, *Virginia's Eastern Shore*. Just over three hundred of these transactions involved women.

TABLE 1. Land Ownership, Accomack County, 1740–1770

	1740	1750	1760	1770
	Landowners			
	(N = 557)	(N = 571)	(N = 573)	(N = 501)
Males	85%	88%	89%	90%
Females	15	12	11	10
	Average size of holdings (acres)			
Males	321	302	280	266
Females	451	397	370	372

Dunton's 60-acre inheritances from their fathers as well as Susan Bowdoin's 500-acre reversion from her brother were the only pieces of property to which their husbands could lay claim. These three men and dozens like them remained legal members of the electorate for fifteen, thirty, or even fifty years based solely on property their wives brought to the marriage.[33]

When it came time to exercise those coverture rights in actual elections, it was men at the bottom of the economic scale who did so with the greatest regularity. Those whose wives brought them vast acres practically ignored the voting process. For example, of the twenty-eight men who held rights to coverture land between 1752 and 1758 and had an opportunity to vote in four separate elections, ten of the thirteen with fewer than 240 acres voted at least twice while only five of the fifteen with more than 240 acres voted, and then only once. Typical of the former group were Thomas Lillistone, who used his wife's 120 acres to vote in three of the four elections, and Jacob Dunton, who participated in all four based upon just 60 acres inherited by his wife. Clearly, men viewed coverture rights in a number of different ways, but those with the most limited and tenuous claims to enfranchisement seemed to have cherished those rights most deeply.[34]

A slightly larger number of men benefited from land belonging to women by obtaining outright title, rather than coverture rights, to these properties. Surviving records are not always clear on familial relationships, but at least

33. Whitelaw, Virginia's Eastern Shore: Bundick, II, 1120; Ewell, II, 1167; Douglas, II, 1344; McDaniel, II, 1222; Dunton, II, 1067; Bowdoin, II, 1244.

34. These twenty-eight men held only coverture land; as far as we can determine, they owned no property of their own. The four contests were the general elections of 1752, 1755, and 1758 and a by-election in 1753. See Accomack County Deeds, 1746–1757, 367–370, 473–476, 623–629, and Deeds, 1757–1770, 52–56, LVA; Whitelaw, Virginia's Eastern Shore: Lillistone, II, 1072; Dunton, II, 1067.

two-thirds and perhaps as many as 90 percent of these transactions occurred between mother and son. The remaining transfers were initiated by sisters, aunts, and grandmothers.

When women willed property to male relatives, they were looking well into the future toward the long-term interests of family members. Usually a mother's death brought land and the franchise to a son for the first time, but occasionally her properties simply added to an already established estate. When Isaiah Bagwell inherited 200 acres from his mother in 1750, they represented his first real property and made him a freeholder for three years before he acquired land on his own. On the other hand, when William Bagge's mother died in 1756, her 200 acres added an important but third parcel to an estate that he had begun in 1745. Most recipients, however, resembled Abel Mears or Peter Parker Copes, who inherited 50 and 200 acres, respectively, from their mothers and, as far as we can determine, obtained no other land during their lifetime.[35]

Mothers no doubt gained considerable satisfaction from knowing that lands they accumulated would help ensure at their deaths the long-term economic and political well-being of sons, yet those choosing to transfer property while still alive might have had the more immediate and short-term interests of their offspring in mind. Although a few heirs were like Isaac Dix, who accumulated considerable property before receiving 112 acres that had once belonged to his grandmother, the vast majority became economically and politically viable only through such deeds and gifts. In 1737, Anne Dickinson deeded her entire 100-acre holdings to her son Richard, which he enjoyed for the next eight years. Similarly, a 100-acre gift from Rebecca Revell to her brother William Coleburn in 1728 and a 45-acre one from Mary Groten to son Solomon in 1771 placed both men within the Accomack electorate for twenty-four and five years, respectively.[36]

Men who inherited or received land directly from mothers and other female relatives took full possession of the properties given to them and thus entered the county electorate as full-blown freeholders. Yet they too exercised their franchise in diverse ways, much like their neighbors with coverture land; some voted as often as possible while others participated irregularly or not at all. Take, for example, the seven men who received land from their mothers in 1751. William Ewell, John Kendall, George Melson, and Daniel Towles immediately used the rights those lands conveyed and voted at the 1752 general election, but only Ewell and Melson continued to do so for the next three elections. Two men, William Wishart and William Onions

35. Whitelaw, *Virginia's Eastern Shore:* Copes, II, 1064; Mears, II, 790; Bagwell, II, 1119; Bagge, II, 779.
36. Whitelaw, *Virginia's Eastern Shore:* Dix, II, 1118; Dickinson, II, 843; Coleburn, II, 783; Groten, II, 763.

TABLE 2. Male Enfranchisement, Accomack County, 1740–1770

	1740	1750	1760	1770
	How Male Property Obtained			
	(*N* = 520)	(*N* = 543)	(*N* = 551)	(*N* = 482)
Transfer from male	80%	81%	82%	81%
Transfer from female	11	11	11	12
Coverture	9	8	7	7
Total	100	100	100	100
	Male Voters and Female Property			
First land from female	19%	18%	17%	17%
All land from female	15	14	14	15

participated in none of the four elections from 1752 to 1758. Daniel Towles was perhaps typical when he used his 250-acre inheritance to vote in three of the four elections.[37]

V. Conclusion

Approximately one-fifth of the landed electorate of Accomack County— about one hundred men at any point in time in the eighteenth century— owed some if not all of their political rights to women (see Table 2). More than half of those dependent upon women obtained property through legal transfers from mothers and other female relatives. A somewhat smaller number utilized coverture rights to the land in which their wives owned or retained interest. Nearly all of this group got their first opportunity for political citizenship through female property, and only a few escaped this dependency. Although they did not always exercise the rights available to them, nearly two-thirds did with some regularity. Overall, approximately 15 percent of the Accomack County electorate remained permanently in-debted to women, mostly their mothers and wives, for their formal political citizenship.[38]

37. Whitelaw, *Virginia's Eastern Shore:* Ewell, II, 1248; Kendall, II, 1336; Melson, II, 1075; Onions, II, 1116; Towles, II, 1385; Wishart, II, 1251.
38. The 20 percent refers to that portion of the electorate who claimed freehold status through permanent attachment to property, theirs or their wives'; it is likely that these same percentages obtain in other counties as well. Another 150–200 men also became

Although operating as legal outsiders, women made vital contributions to the political culture of eighteenth-century Virginia. They treated and campaigned, using their exclusion from the franchise and the legal subordination associated with coverture to shield themselves and candidates from charges of impropriety. When a married woman's property boosted her husband into the electorate, his curtesy interests in her land transformed coverture into a political tool. Similarly, a wife or widow attentive to her separate property could provide gifts of enfranchisement to her sons and male heirs, lending a political dimension to women's inheritance strategies. Women lacked outright membership in the local polity, but their contributions to it reflect the importance families placed on political participation and citizenship in highly competitive counties like Accomack. In this context, citizenship or membership in the formal public culture was an attribute assumed by the head of the household but supported in materially critical ways by wives and mothers.

In post-Revolutionary Virginia, Anne Holden made it possible for four men to become members of the electorate. Her contribution to their membership in the formal public culture reflected the value she placed upon participatory democracy and political membership, if not for herself, then for young men in her neighborhood. Although Holden's counterparts in pre-Revolutionary Virginia did not articulate the link between their property and the membership of their husbands and sons in the political culture, the evidence suggests that their actions were very similar in outcome. Whatever women's intentions, common-law coverture, legal transfers by will and deed, franchise law, and the marriage market kept their property firmly in service to local and family interests. Because it stood to better the economic stature and public influence of their sons and husbands, women's property had a clear political value in eighteenth-century Virginia.

---

enfranchised through life leases, and some of them, like John Simmons of Prince William County, might have benefited from leasing arrangements held or inherited by their wives or other female relatives. The other 80 percent acquired property through inheritance, deeds, gifts, and sales from other men. Women as far as we can determine played no direct legal role in their economic or political stature.

Age of Reason?

Children, Testimony, and Consent
in Early America

I N 1789, twelve-year-old Susannah Brown was not allowed to testify
against the man who raped her, because the Virginia judges thought
her too young. These same judges, however, deemed her old enough
to consent to marry the same man. In 1811, two-year-old Phebe Stuart
placed her mark at the bottom of an apprenticeship contract, indicating that
she consented to her indenture. Why such inconsistency? Are such inconsis-
tencies peculiar to colonial or Revolutionary law? Or derived from the English common law? Answering these two seemingly simple questions, about
which the statutory law said almost nothing, led to the law books that
appeared in lawyers' inventories, that were cited in their cases, that were sold
by their booksellers, and that were published by their printers.[1] The conclusion that slowly emerged was that the common law was changing in England
in response to some of the same forces and ideologies that led to the American Revolution. Indeed, such seemingly private rules defining the status
and abilities of children related intimately to the very public ideology of
revolution.

Scholars have chronicled changing attitudes toward children in Europe
and America during the seventeenth and eighteenth centuries, as reflected,
particularly, in art and literature.[2] Most have argued that there were changes

My thanks to Ruth Bloch, Jim Horn, Bruce Mann, Chris Tomlins, and EATS (Early
American Thesis Seminar at UCLA) for their help with this essay. I would also like to
thank the Littleton-Griswold Fund of the American Historical Association for their aid in
funding the research.

1. See Holly Brewer, "Constructing Consent: How Children's Status in Political Theory
Shaped Public Policy in Virginia, Pennsylvania, and Massachusetts before and after the
American Revolution" (Ph.D. diss., University of California at Los Angeles, 1994), esp.
app. 1 for a discussion of the most popular legal writings in the colonies.

2. Phillipe Ariès, *L'enfant et la vie familiale sous l'ancien regime* (Paris, 1960); John
Demos, *A Little Commonwealth: Family Life in Plymouth Colony* (New York, 1970);
Ross W. Beales, Jr., "In Search of the Historical Child: Miniature Adulthood and Youth in
Colonial New England," *American Quarterly*, XXVII (1975), 379–398; Edward Shorter, *The
Making of the Modern Family* (New York, 1975); Phillip J. Greven, *The Protestant Tempera-
ment: Patterns of Child-rearing, Religious Experience, and the Self in Early America* (New
York, 1977); Lawrence Stone, *The Family, Sex, and Marriage in England, 1500–1800* (New

within the family—that parents gained increasing affection for their children—and changes in perceptions of childhood, a recognition of the innate nature of "childhood" itself. They have identified decreases in child mortality as the main causal force behind these changes, based on the idea that parents could not feel true affection for their children until they knew they would survive. Subsequent scholarship, while acknowledging that perceptions of children did change, has disagreed especially with the idea that the locus of the changes was in parental affection and has shown that the main shifts in identifying childhood do not coincide with changes in child mortality. Virtually no one has explored the legal status of children or the idea that childhood itself could be legislatively defined.[3] Connecting the discussion of children to broad shifts in ideology not only explains origins but helps to delineate the essence of the changes more clearly. The fundamental change related to children was not a recognition of the innate nature of childhood. Rather, modern childhood is a by-product of the Age of Reason, which designated children as those without reason.

What connects the public, republican ideology of revolution to these private transformations of childhood? Legislators and judges began to define children as unreasonable and without understanding. As a consequence, they placed increasing limitations on the validity of children's contracts and their testimony in court. Both restrictions responded to an increasing concern with the reason and capacity of those who exercised even personal legal rights, a capacity that mirrors legal restrictions occurring with respect to public responsibility.

The origins of both transformations lay in the epistemological debates of the seventeenth century, debates not merely over abstractions but over the fundamental ordering of society. Edward Coke, Matthew Hale, and William Blackstone formed part of a broad movement to rationalize, clarify, and reform English law. Their movement toward legal reform constituted an extension of the theoretical debate about the nature and roots of political authority. One of the most important criticisms of monarchical and inherited authority was that it elevated people to positions of power without regard to their ability to exercise power justly. Many republican political

York, 1977); Linda A. Pollock, *Forgotten Children: Parent-Child Relations from 1500–1900* (Cambridge, 1983); Karin Calvert, *Children in the House: The Material Culture of Early Childhood, 1600–1900* (Boston, 1992).

3. On this modern scholarship, in addition to the above, see esp. Pollock, *Forgotten Children*, chaps. 1 and 2, which contain an excellent overview of the scholarship. Those who have at least partially explored the legal status of children include Beales, "In Search of the Historical Child," *American Quarterly*, XXVII (1975), 379–398; Ivy Pinchbeck and Margaret Hewitt, *Children in English Society*, I, *From Tudor Times to the Eighteenth Century* (London, 1969); Robert H. Bremner, ed., *Children and Youth in America: A Documentary History* (Cambridge, Mass., 1970–1974).

tracts sought to replace inherited authority with authority based on reason, merit, and virtue. Increasingly, some of these legal reformers extended these arguments not only to public figures of authority but to the exercise of private authority, indeed, to the granting of even a semipublic voice. They thus extended this emphasis on reason and virtue in much more personal, subtle, and pervasive ways.

Variations in policy between colonies—and over time—illustrate the extent to which children's status was disputed. They reveal the ways in which the issues of childhood and responsibility were contested during the seventeenth and eighteenth centuries, how "consent" itself began to have a different meaning over time, and how broad changes in the common law related to changes in political ideology and religious belief. These examples of, in effect, legal silencing of children reflect broader transitions in attitudes toward consent and personal competency, transitions that did not occur simultaneously or without controversy. Most of all, they offer insight into how differences in individual status could be justified in an increasingly egalitarian legal system.

I. Children as Witnesses

One avenue for exploring the legal status of children is their ability to be witnesses in criminal cases, an ability that protects the victims of crime. Throughout the early modern period, children technically had access to the same protections from assault as had adults (except that parents and others who had authority over individual children were permitted to beat them). The one violent crime for which children received special protection was rape: girls under the age of ten were presumed unable to consent to sexual intercourse, and men proved to have had sex with them could be found guilty of what we now call statutory rape. Although the common law defined rape as sexual intercourse with a woman without her consent, only statutes—from the late sixteenth century onward—defined intercourse as rape even when the girl consented. Since children were singled out by this statute, the cases of statutory rape provide an avenue to explore changing attitudes toward child witnesses (usually the ages of witnesses are not specified).

Limiting a person's ability to testify created situations where, despite corroborating evidence, judges might find an assaulter not guilty. Consider the case of Susannah Brown. In a three-page letter, her father begged the Virginia legislature in 1784 to punish her rapist, to dissolve his daughter's forced marriage, and to prevent similar situations from happening again. Technically, Peter Hopwood, Susannah's assaulter and new "pretended husband," had violated the law. Yet the justices refused to let the twelve-year-old girl testify, and, without her testimony, they decided that they had insufficient evidence to prosecute.

Susannah was a few months under twelve years old when her father and some neighbors hired a "stranger . . . but wearing the semblance of great piety" as a schoolmaster to teach their children for a year. "Soon after she went to school, Hopwood treated her with severity, gave [her] difficult tasks and confined her to the house while the other scholars went to play, under pretense that she had not done her tasks." For a variety of reasons, her father wrote, "long before the year expired, [he] became dissatisfied with him," but Hopwood refused to resign his one-year contract. In June 1783, while Hopwood was still her schoolmaster and only days after Susannah had turned twelve (and could legally consent to marriage), Hopwood raped her while her parents were away. "After having perpetrated the crime he informed her if it ever came to the knowledge of her parents they would treat her with cruelty and contempt, and make her a waiting maid to her sister and if she did not marry him he would publish her to the world as a prostitute that would be despised by everybody and that the Deavil would get her when she died." Six months later, when Susannah was still only twelve, Hopwood finally persuaded her, under threats that he would "publish her to the world as a prostitute," to go with him to be married. The fact that Hopwood committed the rape and initiated the pressure to marry just days after Susannah turned twelve suggests that he was familiar with the law. Since Hopwood was poor and Susannah would probably inherit money and land from her father, it was a potentially profitable arrangement for him.

When Brown discovered the marriage, he questioned his daughter closely, and she told him her side of the story. Brown immediately had Hopwood imprisoned for rape. The evidence for the rape consisted of Susannah's story; that the key to Susannah's room was missing for some days before the parents went away and was later "accidentally" discovered in Hopwood's possession; that Hopwood had forced Susannah to return from her cousins', where her parents had sent her to sleep while they were gone;

> that she returned with tears in her eyes, that he prevented another of her female cousins from coming to sleep with her, that he ordered the servant woman who usually slept in her room with her to sleep in another room. That she was seen in the morning bathed in tears and refused to give an account of her distress. That she uniformly spoke of him with the utmost detestation. That she had been heard to exclaim "No creature knows what the villain has done to me. He has done enough to make me hate him forever." . . . It was further proved that Hopwood had said he had lain with her.

Despite this evidence, however, "a majority of the magistrates [of the Frederick County court] were of the opinion, that the said Susannah ought not to be examined as a witness." "Consequently he was acquitted of the rape there being no positive proof."[4]

Only three witnesses can be positively identified from the official court records: Peter Hopwood (the defendant), David Brown (Susannah's father), and Michael Ireton (a material witness for Hopwood). Although the judges found Hopwood not triable for the rape, they referred Hopwood to a grand jury that was to investigate whether he should be indicted under "4 and 5 Ph. and Mary [the 1558 abduction statute passed during the reign of Philip and Mary] for carrying away the said Susannah from her father without consent." Three months later, the grand jury decided not to indict Hopwood, a puzzling verdict since Hopwood was unequivocally guilty of abduction, having married a twelve-year-old heiress without her father's consent.[5] Perhaps the grand jury was unwilling to enforce the punishment, which was either five years' imprisonment or death. They might have thought the punishment out of proportion to the crime committed. It is interesting that the justices invoked the English statute of 1558 rather than their own late-seventeenth-century statute on clandestine marriages. The main difference was that the Virginia statute specified only that the wife would forfeit her inheritance during her coverture (thus depriving the husband of access to her property).[6] The two laws gave very different punishments for the same crime. The very existence of the different Virginia law hints that the Virginians had not, in 1696, been following the English law terribly closely. Yet the judges' invocation of the English law in 1784 indicates that they valued the English law more highly than the century-old Virginia statute.[7] Their invocation hints at a continuing reverence for English law in the new American states even after the Revolution—the grand jury's failure to indict Hopwood, however, suggests the opposite.

Whatever their larger objectives, the justices had enough doubt about Susannah's ability to testify that they decided not to hear her. There were two possibilities for why the "majority of magistrates" thought that Susannah "ought not to be examined as a witness": first, a wife under some circumstances could not testify against her husband; second, Susannah was too

4. Frederick County, Virginia (FCV), Legislative Petitions, May 29, 1784.

5. FCV Order and Minute Books (1782–1786), 200–203 (Feb. 5–7, 1784), 244 (May 5, 1784).

6. William Waller Hening, ed., *The Statutes at Large: Being a Collection of All the Laws of Virginia, from the First Session of the Legislature in the Year 1619*. . . . (New York, 1819), III, 150–151 (1696). George Webb, *The Office and Authority of a Justice of Peace . . . in Cases Civil or Criminal, and the Method of Judicial Proceedings* . . . (Williamsburg, Va., 1736) cites all three laws: 4 & 5 Phil. & M., c. 8, 39 Eliz. I, c. 9, and the Virginia laws; see 219, 262–263.

7. They might also have thought the Virginia law merely unnecessary, since Susannah's father presumably had control over his property and could disinherit his daughter under the same terms if he chose. The statute was probably only necessary when the property was entailed, the girl was the next beneficiary by a will already implemented, or the daughter had already inherited.

young. But none of the legal guides—either Virginian or English—would have barred a wife from testifying against her husband in this situation. George Webb's *Justice of the Peace,* published in Virginia in 1736, which must have been the standard reference for these judges, claimed that, although in general a wife could not give testimony against her husband, "yet a wife who is an heiress, taken away, and by Threats, prevailed upon to marry the Man, shall be good Evidence against him; and if convicted upon her evidence, he shall be hang'd." Webb referred explicitly to the abduction statute of 1558 whereby it was illegal to abduct any heiress without her own and/or her parent's consent. Yet, on the question of age, Webb implied that those under fourteen were not able to testify. "Any person above the age of fourteen years, and not disabled by law, may be a witness."[8]

Blackstone, whose *Commentaries* were widely read in America after 1770, generally agreed, although he was more sympathetic to hearing the testimony of those under age fourteen.

But where the offence is directly against the person of the wife, this rule has been usually dispensed with: . . . In case a woman be forcibly taken away, and married, she may be a witness against such her husband, in order to convict him of felony. For in this case she can with no propriety be reckoned his wife; because a main ingredient, her consent, was wanting to the contract: and also there is another maxim of law, that *no man shall take advantage of his own wrong;* which the ravisher here would do, if by forcibly marrying a woman, he could prevent her from being a witness, who is perhaps the only witness, to that very fact.[9]

Both Blackstone and Webb thus agreed that wives should be able to testify against husbands when coerced into marriage, especially with a rape involved.

Blackstone held that all witnesses who "have the use of their reason" should be permitted to testify and that the jury "have the opportunity of observing the quality, age, education, understanding, behaviour, and inclinations of the witness" in determining their credibility. He made a partial exception to his guidelines about the reason of witnesses for rape cases, an exception that he coupled with a caution against believing young children.

Infants of any age are to be heard, and if they have any idea of an oath, to be also sworn: it being found by experience that infants of very ten-

8. Webb, *Office and Authority of a Justice of Peace,* 136, 262.
9. William Blackstone, *Commentaries on the Laws of England* (1765), 4 vols. (Chicago, 1979), I, 431. The edition published in Philadelphia between 1771 and 1772 listed 688 subscribers including George Brent, Col. John Hite, James Keith, James Magill, Major Agnus McDonald, the Rev. Charles Thruston, Alexander White, and James Wood, all of Frederick County, Virginia.

der years often give the clearest and truest testimony. But . . . whether the child be sworn or not, it is to be wished, in order to render her evidence credible, that there should be some concurrent testimony, of time, place and circumstances, in order to make out the fact; and that the conviction should not be grounded singly on the unsupported accusation of an infant under years of discretion [under fourteen].[10]

Blackstone's doubts would still have permitted twelve-year-old Susannah to testify. Therefore, Webb's general objection to the testimony of those under age fourteen—as the only general objection that fitted her situation—makes it the most likely explanation for the judges' exclusion of Susannah's legal voice. Webb probably provided their primary legal resource, since it was published in Virginia, and Webb had been a Virginia justice of the peace.

But why the disagreement between Webb and Blackstone? Regardless of the judge's precise motives, this case—and the disagreement among legal commentators—provides an example of a broad phenomenon. By the late eighteenth century, there were significant loopholes in laws for the protection of children: there was some doubt about whether they could testify, and, even when they could, their word was not to be measured against an adult's without, as Blackstone urged, "concurrent testimony." These doubts and exceptions increased dramatically between the seventeenth and nineteenth centuries, as will be shown below.

During the early seventeenth century, young children testified both in England and America, apparently without even the doubts offered by this edition of Blackstone. A published English case from 1606, for example, reveals that two people were convicted of murder on the basis of testimony by an eight-year-old about events she had witnessed when she was four. *The Horrible Murther of a Young Boy of Three Years of Age, Whose Sister Had Her Tongue Cut out . . .* (London, 1606), describes the prosecution of Annis Dell, an innkeeper, and her son for murder. The evidence included the testimony of a tailor (who saw a girl and boy led into a tavern), the body of the boy, and the testimony of the girl. According to her testimony, in 1602 the Dells killed her brother, cut out her tongue so she could not describe what they had done, and left her in a forest many miles away. She wandered and begged for four years until she happened again upon the tavern, where she began babbling and attracted a crowd.

Whereupon the childe was brought before the Bench, and stood upon the Table betweene the Bench and the Jury. Where after that the foresaid knight [Judge] had opened some part of this foule offence, the childe was asked diverse of the former questions: to which she answered as before. The taylor likewise was there, who tolde unto the

10. Blackstone, *Commentaries*, 4 vols. (Philadelphia, 1772), III, 370, 374, IV, 214.

Jurie what he had seene. Then the Jurie was willed to goe togither. . . .
The Jurie staid not long before they returned with their verdite guiltie.

Judges and jury accepted the memories of an eight-year-old about an event
that happened when she was four. Her testimony enabled Annis Dell and her
son to be convicted and afterward hanged.[11]

Other cases from both England and America support this picture of
young children appearing as witnesses, although piecing together the whole
puzzle is somewhat frustrating since ages are so infrequently specified in the
court records. Minutes of trials, in the modern sense, do not exist, and
depositions, which are the most helpful sources in identifying witnesses, are
only sometimes extant. However, in early depositions and court records, the
absence of ages is itself a clue about their relative unimportance.[12] An early
deposition from Accomack County, Virginia, for example, includes the testimony of a boy named William Allinson unproblematically. He was "sworne
and examined in open court" about whether Goodwife Trevellor was guilty
of the murder of her apprentice-girl Elizabeth Bibby.[13] Some evidence in the
trials of witches from Salem in 1692 came from girls, such as that, for
example, of Betty Parris (age nine) and of Abigail Williams (age eleven). Part
of the testimony from these girls was given indirectly through parents or
other adults providing what modern lawyers would call hearsay evidence.[14]
Children's testimony was not exceptional to witchcraft. A study of rape cases
in seventeenth-century court records of Massachusetts found twelve depositions by girls under the age of twelve (many under ten). In another case, in

11. *The Horrible Murther of a Young Boy of Three Years of Age, Whose Sister Had Her
Tongue Cut out . . .* (London, 1606).

12. Some regions seemed to be relatively more concerned about the ages of witnesses.
One such was Essex County, Massachusetts, in whose courtroom young Mehitabel Davis
testified (see below). The court records of Norwich, England, which John H. Langbein has
examined, show a similar concern during the early seventeenth century. See *Prosecuting
Crime in the Renaissance: England, Germany, France* (Cambridge, Mass., 1974), 85–90.

13. Susie M. Ames, ed., *County Court Records of Accomack-Northampton, Virginia, 1640–
1645* (Charlottesville, Va., 1973), 271. It is possible that he was called a boy because he was a
servant. According to the *Oxford English Dictionary,* late-medieval through seventeenth-
century usage of the term "boy" could denote both a male child and a servant. The usage
in this instance is somewhat ambiguous, since Goodwife Trevellor "bidd the boy carry the
Child into the Creeke."

14. See Paul Boyer and Stephen Nissenbaum, *Salem Possessed: The Social Origins of
Witchcraft* (Cambridge, Mass., 1974), 2–3, 6, 210–211. Consider, for example, J. Chitty,
Practical Treatise on the Criminal Law, Containing Precedents of Indictments etc. . . . (London, 1816–1828), I, 590–591: "It was once thought that where the party immediately
injured was an infant of tender years, the parents of the child might be admitted to state
the account he had given of the transaction immediately after it had taken place, and that
the infant might be examined though not sworn; but both these ideas are now rejected;
and it is fully established that if the infant is of competent discretion, he may be sworn,
however, young; and if not, no evidence whatever can be given respecting his assertions."

1680, Mehitabel Davis, a girl who we know was "under ten years old" because her assaulter William Nelson was indicted for statutory rape, testified
to the sexual assault. Her testimony, coupled with his confession and the
testimony of a third person, laid the basis for a guilty verdict.[15]

The first moves toward excluding the testimony of children seem to have
been made in England and then to have slowly and intermittently affected
American decisions. Some judges in England began to question whether
children should be heard during the late seventeenth century. The first
moves in this direction apparently focused on whether those testifying
understood the nature of an oath. Some cases where a judge questioned
whether a particular child could be a witness but then decided to admit his
or her testimony involved witnesses aged seventeen (1679), fifteen (1680),
thirteen (1684), "under twelve" (1710), and "under ten" (1698).[16] About 1700,
the highest courts began to disqualify some children. In a case heard before
the Old Bailey in 1704, which involved a man who had apparently committed rapes upon two young girls, the testimony of a girl aged ten years and
ten months was admitted, whereas the testimony of a six-year-old was not.
The sole authority cited in this case was Sir Matthew Hale's *Pleas of the
Crown* (1678). In 1726, a seven-year-old was prevented from testifying in
what became an often-cited precedent. Her case had first been heard when
she was six but had been dismissed because "Lord Chief Baron Gilbert
refused to admit the child as evidence against [the defendant]." After she
turned seven, the case was tried again and her ability to be a witness debated
at length. The judges concluded that "a child of six or seven years of age, in
point of reason and understanding, ought to be considered as a lunatick or a
madman."[17]

In 1759, the testimony of a ten-year-old girl was heard after great debate
and her rapist executed. Her testimony was supported by the fact that both
she and her mother's seventeen-year-old apprentice, her rapist, had gonor-
rhea. The report of this case is more descriptive than most, containing the
judge's questions and the girl's responses. These reveal that, before admitting
her testimony, the judge made clear that the girl "understood the nature of
an oath."

15. Catharine S. Baker, "Rape in Seventeenth Century Massachusetts," paper delivered at
the Third Berkshire Conference, 1976, 6; *Records and Files of the Quarterly Courts of Essex
County, Massachusetts* (Salem, Mass., 1921), 8 (1680–1683), 15.

16. *Rex v Atkins*, 7 State Trials 241 (1679), *Rex v Giles*, 7 State Trials 1145 (1680), *Rex v
Braddon and Speke*, 9 State Trials 1147 (1684), all in [Great Britain], *A Complete Collection
of State Trials and Proceedings for High Treason and Other Crimes and Misdemeanors from
the Earliest Period to the Year 1783 . . .*, comp. T. B. Howell, 21 vols. (London, 1816–1828);
Young v Slaughteford, 11 Mod 229 (1710), in *English Reports*, LXXXVIII (rpt., London,
1908). The 1698 Old Bailey case was not formally reported but was cited by later decisions.

17. *Rex v Travers*, 1 Strange 700–701 (1726), in *English Reports*, XCIII, 793–794.

Judge: You are going to swear upon the bible; do you know what is the
consequence of taking an oath if you speak falsely?
Child: I shall go to the naughty man?
Judge: What do you mean by going to the naughty man?
Child: Going to the devil.
Judge: Suppose you should speak the truth?
Child: I shall go to God Almighty.

Based on this example, one innovative judge in England in 1795 decided to
postpone a trial until the next court session while the young victim was
"instructed in the mean time by a clergyman in the principles of her duty,
and the nature and obligation of an oath." By the time her case was heard,
she knew how to answer questions about an oath, her testimony was accepted, and her attacker convicted and then executed.[18]

In 1757, a Pennsylvania case of "assault with intent to ravish" listed ten-
year-old Mary Good as a witness, apparently without controversy. The court
did not seem to consider her age important, since it appeared only in the
loose papers and not in the dockets, or basic minutes of the cases that came
before the court.[19] Chester County's records between 1750 and 1820 rarely
listed age, at least with respect to rape and other felony cases. Their lack of
concern with age perhaps can be attributed to the Pennsylvanians' guide to
justices of the peace, which cited Michael Dalton, who specifically allowed
the testimony of children and made no mention of Hale's strictures. That
Pennsylvanians did not alter their rules about children's testimony until very
late shows the jagged pattern of implementation of the changes in ideas
about court procedure.[20]

Even people who did not use the courts regularly seemed to be increasingly aware of the restrictions on children's testimony in criminal cases. In

18. On the 1759 case, see J. M. Beattie, *Crime and the Courts in England, 1660–1800*
(Princeton, N.J., 1986), 129 n. 121. The citation to the 1795 case is rather strange, since it is
discussed only in a footnote to a vaguely relevant case. The proper citation is *Rex v White,* 1
Leach 430, in *English Reports,* CLXVIII, 317. It is a later case than *Rex v White* (1786),
apparently heard in the Gloucester Assizes. The case was cited by, among others, Chitty's
Practical Treatise on the Criminal Law and Matthew Bacon's *New Abridgement of the
Law . . . ,* 1st American ed. from 6th London ed. (Philadelphia, 1813), II, 577. Later cases, in
turn, cited these compilations.
19. See Chester County, Pennsylvania (hereafter cited as CCP) Quarter Sessions Dockets
(hereafter cited as QSD), May 1757, 287 and the loose papers, filed chronologically by year
and then alphabetically by defendant (in this case, Denning).
20. *Conductor Generalis; or, The Office, Duty, and Authority of Justices of the Peace . . .*
(1722; rpt., Philadelphia, 1749), 79. These might have been older children, that is, over the
age of fourteen. For example, a rape/incest case involving Catharine Sentman, prosecuted
in 1818, does not mention her age, although clearly she was still living with her father and
was very probably at least under age twenty-one. See CCP QSD, vol. H (1817–1820), May 4,
1818, 33–35; CCP Oyer and Terminer Docket (hereafter cited as OTD), 59 (August 1818), 62
(November 1818); see also related loose papers filed under "Correy" and "Sentman."

1790, in New Hampshire, Abigail Bailey wrote in her diary that she could not initiate a prosecution of incest against her husband (who had violently raped their teenage daughter in front of the younger children) because the daughter in question was too frightened to testify (she was then aged sixteen) and the eldest of the children who had witnessed the scene was "too young to be a legal witness," although "old enough to tell the truth."[21] Although she does not identify the daughter who was "too young to be a legal witness," and thus we cannot determine the child's age, the fact that Abigail Bailey was conscious of the rules about legal witnesses shows how new attitudes toward children's testimony could permeate popular understandings of legal relationships, defining what came before the court even before judges decided whether an individual child could testify.

By the early nineteenth century, most criminal court decisions in America set fourteen as the minimum age for witness testimony in criminal cases. Depositions taken for murder inquests in Virginia, for example, specified that the witness was of "full age," that is, over twenty-one.[22] Six-year-old Nancy Geer was not allowed to testify in her 1820 rape trial. The judges of the General Court did not even consider her ability to be a witness disputable. They relied on English precedents, referring to such manuals as J. Chitty's *Practical Treatise on the Criminal Law* (1816).[23] Judges retained the ability to make exceptions at their discretion if the child could prove he or she had extraordinary understanding or grasped the nature of an oath. In 1806, a Tennessee judge barred a ten-year-old boy from testifying in the murder trial of his father because, "upon examination, it appeared that he had not any sense of the obligation of an oath, nor of any of the consequences of swearing falsely." Understanding the nature of an oath was one of the key issues in allowing the testimony of younger children.[24] In an 1810 New Jersey case, the child was actually over fourteen years old but appeared to the judge to be

21. Ann Taves, ed., *Religion and Domestic Violence in Early New England: The Memoirs of Abigail Abbot Bailey* (Bloomington, Ind., 1989), 87. Although Abigail Bailey does not describe the rape of her daughter in detail, "I had long before had full evidence to my mind of Mr. B's [her husband's] great wickedness in this matter; and I thought I was prepared to hear the worst. But verily the worst was dreadful! The last great day will unfold it. I truly at this time had a new lesson added, to all that ever before heard, or conceived, of human depravity."

22. For example, see the case against Negro Flora, 1808, FCV, "Inquests on Dead Bodies" file. All three witnesses, Rebecca Whitington, Body Whitington, and Martin Gannet, at the beginning of their depositions, are specified as "of full age."

23. *Commonwealth v John Bennet,* in *Virginia Cases; or, Decisions of the General Court of Virginia, Chiefly on the Criminal Law of the Commonwealth, Commencing June Term, 1815, and Ending June Term, 1826. . . .* (Richmond, Va., 1826), 235–240.

24. See, for example, *State v Morea,* 2 Ala 275 (1841); *Flanegan v State,* 25 Ark 92; *Warner v State,* 25 Ark 447 (1867); *Johnson v State,* 61 Ga 35 (1878); *Moore v State,* 79 Ga 498, 5 SE 51 (1887).

younger. The superior court upheld the judge's decision to exclude him, even though the boy provided proof of his age. They ruled that "his capacity as a witness was a proper subject of discretion in the justice." They reinforced this decision two years later when they upheld a judge's decision to exclude the testimony of a thirteen-year-old boy because the judge questioned the boy's "capacity and understanding."[25]

Some state superior courts held that juries, not judges, should make the final decision but that judges should instruct the juries to carefully consider the qualifications of the witness. In an 1813 Massachusetts case, an eight-year-old was allowed to testify after "the court put sundry questions to him, in order to ascertain the measure of his understanding and moral sense, to most of which he gave rational and pertinent answers." However, while allowing the jury to judge the boy's credibility, the judge cautioned them that "the credit of the witness, which is greatly impaired by his age, is to be judged of by the jury from the manner of his testifying, and other circumstances."[26] The judge's decision to permit such testimony drew on many English authorities, including several of the cases discussed above. In general, however, by the mid-nineteenth century, fourteen years of age for witnesses had become the "prima facie," or "good and sufficient," rule to which some judges allowed occasional exceptions. A California decision of 1858 concluded, "If over fourteen, prima facie, a child is competent to testify; otherwise if under fourteen."[27]

These rules of evidence, however, seemed to apply only to felonies. Ann Weaks, at virtually the same age of twelve and a half as Susannah Brown, was able to testify against her master for ill-treatment only a year later than Brown in the same Virginia courtroom. She was able to do so, most probably, because apprenticeship abuse cases were not technically criminal (it was only a felony if the child died).[28] Thomas Hargis complained about mistreatment at age ten in 1754, as did William Finnichan at age eight, although his mother initiated the complaint on his behalf.[29] By the 1810s, some apprentices ap-

25. 3 NJ L (2 Penning) 930. Sometimes those under age fourteen were allowed to testify, to their own detriment. Twelve-year-old James Guild was convicted of murder—based on his own confession—and hanged in New Jersey in 1828. See *State v Guild*, 10 NJ L (5 Halst), 163–191.

26. *Commonwealth v Hutchinson*, 10 Mass 225.

27. *People v Bernal*, 10 Cal 66; *Century Edition: A Complete Digest of All Reported Cases from the Earliest Times to 1897* (St. Paul, Minn., 1896), L, 114.

28. FCV Minute Books (hereafter cited as MB), 1782–1786, 357 (June 1785) for binding, 372 (August 1785) for complaint. Her complaint was held to be valid and she was transferred to another master.

Age is easily identifiable in these cases because a child's age determined the length of service.

29. FCV Order Books (hereafter cited as OB), Hargis, III, 375 (February 1751) for binding record, which gives his age, and VI, 134 (November 1754) for his complaint. The Finnichan case spans many entries in the order books, but see esp. IV, 378 (February 1753),

peared in the courtroom only via a "next friend," as did William Majors, aged twenty. Still, Majors's example was not the rule, even in the 1810s: Jesse Majors complained at age twelve and Kesia Vass (a black girl) at age nine.[30] Most modern legal authorities have assumed that children have always been excluded from courtrooms.[31] The only two legal scholars who have treated this issue seriously did so in the context of broad surveys of legal history and evidence law. William Holdsworth's encyclopedic early-twentieth-century history of the common law concluded that "infants below a certain age were, like insane persons, absolutely incapable because they 'wanted discretion.'" "It would seem that Coke put this age at fourteen." John Henry Wigmore, from whom Holdsworth drew his analysis, portrayed children's ability to testify as increasing during the eighteenth century. He argued that judges moved from a simple age-based equation to one that inquired more closely into each child's particular abilities.[32]

---

which records his apprenticeship and age (he was then almost four) and VII, 222 (April 1757), which records the complaint and court action. Since the binding records are incomplete for Pennsylvania in the 1750s, the ages of the complainants in these cases in general cannot be determined.

30. FCV MB, III, 252 (February 1811) for binding, III, 299 (June 1811) for initial transfer, V, 252 (June 1819) for complaint in question. The initial complaint of 1811 was also made on his behalf by an adult. Jesse Majors was bound at age five (III, 252 [February 1811]) and complained at age twelve (V, 44, V, 47 [February, March 1818]); Kesia Vass complained at the age of nine and was transferred over a year later (III, 353 [January 1812], IV, 196 [October 1815], IV, 372 [December 1816]).

31. No historians have really examined this issue. Beattie, Barbara Shapiro, and William E. Nelson have commented on children's testimony during this period, but they treat it only briefly in the context of considering broader issues more thoroughly. Although Beattie and Shapiro are somewhat equivocal, they do not comment directly on change over time. Beattie, in particular, notes that the issue of children's testimony seemed in dispute during the eighteenth century. Shapiro and Nelson, to the extent that they addressed this issue, generally seem to agree with the modern legal commentators on evidence law and general legal history, such as William Holdsworth and John Henry Wigmore. See Beattie, *Crime and the Courts*; Shapiro, *"Beyond Reasonable Doubt" and "Probable Cause": Historical Perspectives on the Anglo-American Law of Evidence* (Berkeley, Calif., 1991); Nelson, *Americanization of the Common Law: The Impact of Legal Change on Massachusetts Society, 1760–1830* (Cambridge, Mass., 1975); Sir William Searle Holdsworth, *A History of English Law* (Boston, 1926), IX, 188.

32. Holdsworth, *History of English Law*, IX, 188. Since a pivotal English decision of 1779, Wigmore wrote,

the natural rule has been clearly accepted, that there is NO SPECIFIC AGE below which capacity will always be deemed wanting. The capacity of the infant, therefore, depending upon the circumstances of its understanding as exhibited in each instance, is to be determined by the trial Court. In a few jurisdictions, however, a trace of the old notion is still preserved in a rule that children under a certain age—usually ten or fourteen years—will not be assumed to be capable, so that their capacity must first be shown.

John Henry Wigmore, *A Treatise on the Anglo-American System of Evidence in Trials at Common Law Including the Statutes and Judicial Decisions of All Jurisdictions of the United States and Canada* (Boston, 1923), III, 867–868.

Wigmore seems to have assumed that early-eighteenth-century attitudes typified those of the century before. However, by then the major change had already been introduced—a line had been drawn. The eighteenth century was one of debate over the position of that line. In his study of criminal cases in English courts between 1660 and 1800, J. M. Beattie found little pattern: "There was clearly some confusion in the eighteenth century about the validity of children's evidence." Before Hale's *Pleas of the Crown* (1678), Wigmore cited only one source, Coke's *Institutes* (1628). In citing Coke, he was following several early-nineteenth-century jurists who had sought to find common-law precedents for the exclusion of children. Although the passage Wigmore cited in Coke's *Institutes* did limit the testimony of those without discretion, it concerned who could be witnesses to a particular deed of land, not who could bear witness in a criminal prosecution.[33] Since Coke made clear that different rules applied to different types of legal procedure, the extension of Coke's comment from witnessing deeds to testifying in criminal trials is a stretch at best and a misreading at worst.[34] Coke disqualified witnesses to deeds who were "parties interested," for example, but who were not prevented from testifying in criminal cases (nor would they be now). Consider how empty a criminal courtroom would be if anyone with a stake in the outcome were prevented from testifying. Coke addressed criminal prosecutions in his third volume, where he prescribed no particular qualifications for witnesses.[35] Unlike later commentators, Coke's contempo-

33. Beattie, *Crime and the Courts,* 128 n. 121. The volume Wigmore cited, Coke's *Institutes,* I, described the complex welter of rules surrounding the holding and transfer of property.

  And it appeared by the antient authors and Authorities of the Law; that before the Statute of 12 E. 2. Ca. 2. Processe should be awarded against the witnesses named in the deed, *testes in carea nominatos.* . . . But the delay therein was so great, and sometimes (though rarely) by exceptions against those witnesses, which being found true, they were not to be sworne at all, neither to be joyned to the Jurie, nor as witnesses, (1) as if the witnesses were infamous, for example, if he be attainted of a false verdict, or of a conspiracie at the suit of the King, or convicted of perjurie, of a Premunire, or of forgerie . . . , or convict of felony, or by judgement lost his eares, or stood upon the pillorie or tumbrell, or been stigmaticus branded, or the like. . . . or if the witnesse be an infidell, or of non sane memorie, or not of discretion, or a partie interested, or the like.

His use of the term "discretion" does imply that some witnesses could be excluded who did not have discretion and understanding, so presumably children could be excluded by this rule, at least from being witnesses to deeds (Coke, *The First Part of Institutes of the Lawes of England* . . . [London, 1628], 6). This volume is sometimes called *Coke upon Littleton.*
  34. The only reference he makes about witnesses in courts of common law is in his fourth volume on procedures in different courts, where he states that witness testimony must be "viva voce" (not by deposition but live), that witnesses should take an oath before testifying, and that they must not perjure themselves (Coke, *The Fourth Part of the Institutes of the Laws of England: Concerning the Jurisdiction of Courts* [London, 1644], 279).
  35. The only place where he addressed the issue of witnesses was with respect to cases of

raries would certainly not have conflated the two categories. It is a measure of how eagerly eighteenth- and early-nineteenth-century jurists sought to provide precedent to their interpretations of the common law that they combed through Coke to find a passage that might possibly mean what they wanted him to say. Why would Coke have hidden criminal qualifications about witnesses in a paragraph on the signing of deeds and then put it in a volume on land law?[36]

Although Coke's contemporaries and predecessors said little on this question, it is clear that they allowed children's testimony, even testimony against parents. A range of late-sixteenth-century treatises such as William Staunforde's *Les plees del coron* (1567), William Lambarde's *Eirenarcha; or, Of the Office of the Justices of the Peace* (1581), and Richard Crompton's *L'office et aucthoritie de justices de peace* (1584) placed no limits on who could be a witness. Such books were standard references for judges and those accused of crimes, and many editions, with similar contents, appeared in the sixteenth and seventeenth centuries. Dalton's popular guide of the early seventeenth century (1618), first published a decade before Coke's *Institutes*, made clear that children of any age could testify in criminal matters, even against parents. As proof of their ability, Dalton cited two cases of 1612, one in which children testified against their mother for witchcraft and one in which the testimony of a nine-year-old and fourteen-year-old were heard in open court "upon their oathes."[37]

Hale's popular *Pleas of the Crown*, first published in 1678, contained the first age limits on witness testimony. With respect to capital cases, including felony and treason, where the life of the accused was at stake, he recommended that, although the testimony of those between nine and thirteen should be "allowed in some Cases," normally witnesses should have reached the age of fourteen. In another popular treatise, he suggested that juries, in evaluating witnesses, should consider "the very Quality, Carriage, Age, Condition, Education, and Place of Commorance of Witnesses."[38] His general discussion of "infancy" and age, a discussion that was itself new to a legal

---

high treason, where "it is most necessary to have substantial proof." Following a law of Queen Elizabeth's, he states that there must be "two lawful witnesses" (Coke, *The Third Part of the Institutes of the Laws of England* [London, 1644], 24–26).

36. The first to find the passage was Thomas Wood, *An Institute of the Laws of England; or, The Laws of England in Their Natural Order, according to Common Use*, 6th ed. (London, 1738), 598.

37. Michael Dalton, *The Countrey Justice* (1618; rpt., Amsterdam, 1975), 261.

38. Matthew Hale, *Pleas of the Crown; or, A Brief, but Full Account of Whatsoever Can Be Found Relating to That Subject* (London, 1678), 224; Hale, *The History of the Common Law of England . . .* , ed. Charles M. Gray (Chicago, 1971), 164. In his introduction to this volume, Gray acknowledges the place of this work as a document of the "complex intellectual transformation of the seventeenth century." "The magnitude of that transformation in science and philosophy, religion and political theory, is well recognized" (xiii).

treatise, tried to uncover some sort of natural law. He devoted more effort in this treatise, ironically entitled *History of the Pleas of the Crown* (1736), to discussing Roman law than English. In justifying his extensive discussion of Roman civil law in this "history" of English criminal law, he acknowledged that English laws are "binding by their own authority; yet it must be confessed, the civil laws are very wise and well composed laws, and such as have been found out and settled by wise princes and law-givers . . . and therefore may be of great use to be known." Although Roman laws are not English precedent and "neither I, nor any else may lay any weight or stress upon them," he chose to "here particularly mention them."[39] He then based his conclusions about the legal status of children in England on them as well as on a few scattered and unpublished English decisions, none of which related specifically to witnesses. The most remarkable aspect about Hale's writings on this subject is that he had permitted, without even a question, an eleven-year-old girl to testify in a witchcraft trial over which he had presided ten years earlier. Her nine-year-old sister, Deborah Pacey, did not testify only because she was too sick to come to the court. Instead, Deborah's father testified about the contents of Deborah's visions. It seems that Hale only developed his opinions about children's testimony during the last few years of his life.[40]

Treatises on evidence law quickly incorporated Hale's guidelines as though they had always been common law—indeed, they were treated as custom. The first treatise that dealt solely with evidence law, William Nelson's *Law of Evidence,* appeared in England in 1717 and proved popular in the colonies throughout the century. It said little about the ability of witnesses except that "infants of the age of twenty are good witnesses." Yet he gave an example, when making a separate point, of a man sentenced to be hanged for the abduction of a fourteen-year-old girl based on her evidence.[41] By the second edition of Sir Geoffrey Gilbert's *The Law of Evidence* (1760), a study that greatly expanded on Nelson's initial attempt, the arguments for excluding children under age fourteen had been greatly expanded. Children should be excluded for "Want of Skill and Discernment," because they lack "com-

39. Hale, *Historia Placitorum Coronae: The History of the Pleas of the Crown* . . . , 2 vols (London, 1736), I, 16.

40. *A Trial of Witches at the Assizes Held at Bury St. Edmonds for the County of Suffolk* (1664; London, 1882). The notes from this trial were taken by someone who attended the trial and were published for the first time only after Hale's death.

41. [William Nelson], *The Law of Evidence: Wherein All the Cases That Have Yet Been Printed in Any of Our Law Books or Tryals, and That in Any Wise Relate to Points of Evidence, Are Collected.* . . . (London, 1717), 7, 36–37. The testimony was by Lucy Ramsey, whose age of fourteen is specified because she was an heiress who had been "forcibly taken away" and married informally with an exchange of promises. Her new husband was hanged. Sir Matthew Hale was the judge in this case (*Case of John Brown,* SC 3 Keb. 193).

mon Knowledge," and because they "are perfectly incapable of any Sense of Truth." After making his point about the age of fourteen very precisely, Gilbert backtracked to acknowledge, "There is no Time fix'd wherein they are to be excluded from Evidence, but the Reason and Sense of their Evidence is to appear from the Questions propounded to them, and their Answers to them." Gilbert cited no fewer than ten authorities in justifying children's exclusion. These authorities consisted of three references to writings of Sir Matthew Hale (Gilbert's earliest citation to an English authority), three to cases tried after the publication of Hale's text, one to Justinian's *Institutes* (ancient Roman civil law, discussed by Hale), one to William Nelson's *Law of Evidence*, one to Giles Duncombe's *Tryals per Pais* (1702), which cited only Hale, and one to William Hawkins's *Pleas of the Crown*, which first appeared in 1716 and which drew on Hale.[42] Hale's modifications had had a domino effect: Gilbert, writing in the mid-eighteenth century, could cite ten authorities for his opinion that those without "Reason and Sense" should not be able to testify, most of which explicitly led back to Hale.[43]

Hale's text, however, did not immediately provide the final word; instead, it initiated a debate. Well after the publication of *Pleas of the Crown*, some texts ignored his exclusion of children's testimony, whereas others modified it. The anonymous *Infants Lawyer* (1697) placed no limits on children's testimony and even held that children under age twenty-one could be punished for perjury "if the Infant judicially perjure himself in point of Age, or otherwise," indicating not only that those under age twenty-one testified but that they could be held responsible for it. Dalton's views, which permitted the testimony of children, were cited instead of Hale's by the early- and mid-eighteenth-century Pennsylvania guides for justices of the peace.[44] William Blackstone equivocated between the two: they should be heard but should not necessarily be believed. Yet Hale was the only precedent cited by Blackstone in his discussion of whether children could be witnesses. Later editions

42. See [Sir Geoffrey Gilbert], *The Law of Evidence*, 2d ed. (London, 1760), 146–147; Giles Duncombe, *Tryals per Pais in Capital Matters; or, Some Brief and Useful Observations Relating to Such Tryals* (London, 1702), 23–24; William Hawkins, *A Summary of the Crown-law* (London, 1728), I, 425–426.
43. Perhaps part of the reason Gilbert supported the exclusion of children's testimony was that he was profoundly influenced by Locke's epistemology. Gilbert was also the author of an *Abstract of Mr. Locke's Essay on Human Understanding* (noted by Shapiro, "*Beyond Reasonable Doubt*," 26).
44. *The Infants Lawyer; or, The Law (Both Ancient and Modern) Relating to Infants: Setting Forth Their Priviledges, Their Several Ages for Divers Purposes . . .* (London, 1697), 68. For its prevalence in the colonies during the eighteenth century, see Herbert A. Johnson, *Imported Eighteenth-century Law Treatises in American Libraries, 1700–1799* (Knoxville, Tenn., 1978), 31. Johnson found three copies of this guide in the twenty-two libraries of eighteenth-century lawyers he surveyed. See also Dalton, *Countrey Justice*, 366; *Conductor Generalis*, 79.

of Blackstone, such as that of 1800 (after Blackstone's death and edited by others), removed the passages that suggested children might be heard without taking an oath and excluded the secondhand testimony that a child might have told an adult as hearsay evidence and thus invalid.[45]

While Francis Buller's *Introduction to the Law relative to Trials at Nisi Prius* of 1772 cited Hale as well as two early eighteenth-century cases to claim that "a Child under the Age of ten shall in no Case be admitted," Buller acknowledged that this limitation did cause problems in the prosecution of crimes against children. He carefully encouraged the court to be more lenient toward children's testimony than Hale had suggested in cases where children were the victims of "foul facts done in secret."

> Doubtless the Court will more readily admit such a Child in the Case of a personal Injury (such as Rape) than on a Question between other Parties; and perhaps, in such Case, would even admit the Infant to be examined without Oath; for certainly there is much more Reason for the Court to hear the Relation of the Child, than to receive it at secondhand from those that heard it say so. In Cases of foul Facts done in secret, where the Child is the Party injured, the repelling their Evidence entirely is, in some Measure, denying them the Protection of the Law; yet the Levity and want of Experience in Children, is undoubtedly a Circumstance which goes greatly to their Credit.

Thus Buller sapped somewhat the strength of Hale's arguments, although he cited them dutifully and presented them as the standard opinion.[46] Chitty's *Criminal Law*, which was cited by the 1820 Virginia statutory rape case, explicitly critiqued Hale. Hale, the author claimed, had thought that, "if under nine or then, they cannot be sworn." "But, in modern times, more rational principles have been admitted to prevail. The admissibility of testimony now depends not on the age, but on the understanding of the witness. Children of any age who comprehend the nature of an oath, and are capable of feeling the obligations it imposes, may be admitted to give evidence."[47]

45. Blackstone, *Commentaries,* IV, 214. An 1800 London edition deleted Blackstone's partial qualifier to Hale by deleting his reference to "infants of any age." See the discussion of Susannah Brown's case, above, for Blackstone's original wording.

46. Francis Buller, *An Introduction to the Law relative to Trials at Nisi Prius* (London, 1772), 288–289. In the margin of the volume I examined, the controversy aroused on this point is shown in the handwriting of an apparently English lawyer in 1831. "There is now no determinate age, for the admission or rejection of a child's evidence. Three days ago, a child under six was a witness against Bishop and Williams for murder." This anonymous lawyer also cited Blackstone's *Commentaries*—he apparently had an early or unaltered edition of Blackstone. The volume with this marginalia resides in the UCLA law library.

47. Chitty, *Practical Treatise on the Criminal Law,* III, 314–315. See also I, 590–591; *Commonwealth v John Bennet*, 2 Va. Cases 238.

Actually, since Hale had emphasized the "discretion" of the child and had given age as a guideline to discretion, he would not have disagreed markedly.

Most eighteenth-century legal guides generally agreed with Hale. As shown in the discussion of Susannah Brown's case, Webb's Virginia *Justice of the Peace* offered fourteen as the guideline for the age at which a person could testify. Richard Burn's *Justice of the Peace*, which went through dozens of editions during the eighteenth century and was popular in the colonies, cited Hale and Hawkins to conclude that infants without discretion could be prevented from testifying.[48] Thomas Wood's *Institute of the Laws* (1738) explicitly excluded those "without discretion" from giving evidence in courtrooms.[49] Two guides that were popular and influential in early-nineteenth-century Virginia, St. George Tucker's edition of Blackstone's *Commentaries* (which added Virginia laws) and William Waller Hening's 1795 guide to justices of the peace, both cited Hale as their earliest source for excluding the testimony of children.[50] The first American edition of Matthew Bacon's popular *New Abridgement of the Law*, published in Philadelphia in 1813, although beginning the discussion of "who may be witnesses" by excluding those who do not have "sufficient discretion" or who do not "have a right sense of the sanctity of an oath," allowed that, in some cases, "infants [under fourteen] . . . may be witnesses." His first citation was also Hale.[51]

Whereas earlier treatises advocated the hearing of all evidence, even the evidence of very young children against their parents, the broad historical trend moved away from this simple acceptance toward hearing their evidence but discounting it and then toward excluding the evidence of those under ten or even under fourteen. This transition was especially pronounced in cases where the accused was on trial for a felony. Such cases as that involving Susannah Brown, where the defendant's punishment could be death if convicted of the rape, seem to be among the first to apply explicitly

48. Richard Burn, *The Justice of the Peace and Parish Officer*, 8th ed. (London, 1764), I, 342. Burn did suggest that "an infant of tender years may be examined without oath, where the exigence of the case requires it; which possibly, being fortified with concurrent evidences, may be of some weight; especially in cases of rape, buggery, and such crimes as are practiced upon children."

49. Wood, *Institute of the Laws*, 598. Wood was the first I have found who sought a precedent before Hale. It was he, apparently, who preceded Wigmore in finding the obscure quote from Coke that seems only tangentially relevant (Coke, *First Part of the Institutes*, I, 6b).

50. Hening, *Virginia Justice* . . . (Richmond, Va., 1795), 177–178, 356–357, 453, and see also later editions: *The Virginia Justice: Comprising the Office and Authority of a Justice of the Peace*, 4th ed. (Richmond, Va., 1825), 549–551. He focused on the decision of Chief Justice Raymond (England, 1726) that reversed a 1698 Old Bailey decision. In the earlier case, "Ward chief baron admitted one to be a witness who was under the age of ten years, as the child had been examined about the nature of an oath and had given a reasonable account of it." "But Raymond chief justice" reversed the earlier decision.

51. Bacon, *A New Abridgement of the Law*, II, 576–577.

the guidelines on children's testimony that appeared in legal treatises. This initial exclusion quickly extended to misdemeanors as well as felonies.[52]

Why did Hale introduce such changes? Partly, he was caught in the midst of long-term transformations in procedures in English courtrooms, particularly in the respective roles of witnesses and juries. Only during the fifteenth century did witnesses first start to be used in English courtrooms. Throughout the sixteenth and seventeenth centuries, the lines between the roles of jurors and witnesses were poorly drawn. Before the early seventeenth century, there were virtually no guidelines about who could be witnesses. But these transformations were not destined to follow a particular path. Hale, and common-law reformers like him, shaped the rules for who could be witnesses and how witness testimony should be evaluated at the same time as they shaped evidence law. They did so in alignment with transformations in English epistemology during the seventeenth and eighteenth centuries, transformations that arose, at least in part, from Puritan theology.

During the Interregnum, Hale was a moderate Puritan and consciously connected his religious ideals with an agenda of legal reform. Hale headed a commission—appointed by Cromwell—to revise England's entire legal code. His suggestions for reform included raising the minimum age of marriage and raising the minimum age for jury service from fourteen to twenty-five. After the Interregnum, he continued to be sympathetic with Dissenters; his close friends included such activists as the Nonconformist Richard Baxter (who in turn influenced Locke).[53] Religious Dissenters advocated not only political reform in seventeenth-century England and its colonies but also legal reform. They argued for a particular pattern of legal reform that focused on redistributing the basis upon which authority was allocated. They sought to make laws available for everyone to read and understand, just as they had with the Bible. The significance of Coke's writing his *Institutes* in English, for example, must not be underestimated. He explicitly acknowledged that having the law written in English made the law more accessible and comprehensible to more people.[54] The call for the appearance of treatises in English grew out of the same source as the demands for religious

52. *Rex v Travers* (1726), 1 Strange 700–701.

53. Mary Cotterell, "Interregnum Law Reform: The Hale Commission of 1652," *English Historical Review*, LXXXIII (1968), 689–704. Also see generally Brewer, "Constructing Consent," esp. chaps. 2, 3. On John Locke's involvement in these epistemological debates, see Richard Ashcraft, *Revolutionary Politics and Locke's Two Treatises of Government* (Princeton, N.J., 1986), esp. chaps. 1, 2.

54. Coke, *First Part of the Institutes,* preface. He argues, however, that he does not want to dispense with all of the French and Latin phrases, since they are "vocables of Art, so apt and significant to expresse the true sense of the Lawes, and are so woven into the lawes themselves, as it is in a manner impossible to change them."

services and reading the Bible in English. Having the laws in English would also be one of the main concerns of the Levellers, a group that sought universal political and religious equality.[55] Yet there was a tension built into that goal: it could potentially lead to anarchy by encouraging people to think they might make law as well. To prevent the unfit from misunderstanding and misforming law, Hale was one among many who sought to limit legal access for those whom he deemed unable to exercise properly their understanding. He did this not only theoretically, in his elaboration of Coke's concept of an acquired ability to exercise legal reason, but on an intimately practical level.[56]

That Hale himself was deeply involved in these epistemological debates is revealed especially in his religious writings. He explored the means by which humans acquired knowledge, religious as well as legal. He outlined a theory of knowledge that was similar to but preceded Locke's theory, a fact illustrative less of Hale's significance as a philosopher than of the fact that theories of knowledge were discussed, debated, and elaborated in religious circles during the seventeenth century. Hale focused on the importance of reason in separating humans from animals and of wisdom in separating each human being from any other. "The great PREHEMINENCE that Man hath over Beasts is his REASON: and the great preheminence that one man hath over another is his WISDOM; though all men have ordinarily the privilege of Reason; yet all men have not the habit of Wisdom." He thought it was critical that children learn to read, because it enables them not just to "understand what others have written, [but also] to know what they knew and wrote, and thereby improve their own knowledg and understanding." Hale laid out a theory of knowledge that placed human understanding at its center, that relied on time and sensory perception for the gaining of knowledge from both "artificial" and "natural" sources; for Hale, the development of the human understanding came only with age. And, only with age, then, could one have sufficient understanding to testify.[57]

55. See, among others, Shapiro, "Law Reform in Seventeenth Century England," *American Journal of Legal History*, XIX (1975), 290.

56. Charles Gray, "Reason, Authority, and Imagination: The Jurisprudence of Sir Edward Coke," in Perez Zagorin, ed., *Culture and Politics from Puritanism to the Enlightenment* (Los Angeles, Calif., 1980), 25–66, esp. 30–32. Artificial reason can be characterized as "the natural faculty improved by cultivation." For Hale's perspective, see 32 n. 20. "Hale . . . developed this argument for lawyers especially strongly—very much in the context of asserting that the reason of lawyers is distinctive, as the best reason for particular purposes is always the trained reason of a special craft or profession."

57. Hale, *Contemplations, Moral and Divine by a Person of Great Learning and Judgment* (London, 1676), 17, 486–487. This was his only work published while he was alive; according to the preface, it was published without his consent. See also Hale, *A Discourse of the Knowledge of God, and of Ourselves: I, By the Light of Nature; II, By the Sacred Scriptures* (London, 1788), 2–4.

More important, almost, than why he introduced such changes is why most of the legal treatise writers who followed him accepted his changes so uncritically. His extensive knowledge and writing in the law and his position as chief justice of England between 1671 and 1675 certainly gave him credibility. But the manner in which he made the reforms, the way in which he declared them to be custom, made them difficult to recognize as changes. And, after 1660, Hale was careful not to label himself a reformer. He was conscious that to do so in the period after the Restoration was to give himself a bad name.[58] Hale emphasized that judges should make reforms where they could, "without troubling a Parliament," and that, if Judges did this more, "truly this would go a very great way in the reformation of things amiss in the law." His experiences during the Interregnum convinced him that legal changes should not be introduced without adequately thinking through the consequences: "The business of amendment or alteration of lawes is a choice and tender business, neither wholly to be omitted when the necessity requires, and yet very cautiously and warily to be undertaken." He regarded such revisions as necessary at intervals.[59] So, instead of merely reporting the law, he reformed it. Yet, in the decades and centuries after Hale, the legal treatise writers on these subjects quoted Hale's judgments and assumed he spoke not merely for natural law but for the ancient common law.

The banishment of children from courtrooms formed one part of the development of evidence law during the seventeenth and eighteenth centuries in England. As Barbara Shapiro has shown, the formation of evidence law in the eighteenth century was influenced profoundly by the epistemological theories of John Locke, in particular, but, also, by the late eighteenth century, of David Hartley, Thomas Reid, and others.[60] Although Reid is linked to the Scottish Common Sense School, both he and Hartley elabo-

58. Hale, "Considerations Touching the Amendment or Alteration of Lawes," in Francis Hargrave, ed., *A Collection of Tracts relative to the Law of England from Manuscripts* (Dublin, 1787), I, 266: "Exemplary miscarriages, in the late times, of such as have undertaken reformation both in matters civil and ecclesiastical, hath brought a disrepute upon the undertaking of any reformation in either: so that the very name of reformation and a reformer begins to be a stile or name of contempt and obloquy; so that men are as fearfull to be under the imputation of a reformer of the law, as they would be of the name of knave or fool, or hypocrite."

59. Ibid., 253, 272–273. See also Hale's discussion of Justinian's revision of Roman laws, ibid., 266–267.

60. Shapiro, *"Beyond Reasonable Doubt,"* 25–26, 196. On witnesses, see esp. 187–189. See also William Twining, "Evidence and Legal Theory," in Twining, ed., *Legal Theory and Common Law* (Oxford, 1986), 62–80, esp. 70: "In short, nearly all Anglo-American writers [on evidence law] seem by and large to have adopted, either explicitly or by implication, a particular ontology, epistemology and theory of logic. All of these are closely identified with a particular philosophical tradition, that is English empiricism, as exemplified by Locke, Bentham and John Stuart Mill."

rated on Locke's theories of human development. These ideas about human development emerged from the Dissenting cauldron that Hale helped to stir. As the discussion of Hale's ideas in particular illustrates, however, evidence law was not merely a simplistic outgrowth of Dissenting epistemology—that epistemology led him to try to find an underlying natural law by searching for grand symmetries in different legal traditions. Relying for his precedents in part on the Roman civil law and Catholic ecclesiastical law, he altered ages and standards in order to discern the natural law that fitted with his developing epistemology.[61]

The new attitudes toward human nature and the development of the human understanding that grew out of these debates were neither immediately nor universally accepted. Each individual judge or jury member had a certain degree of latitude in deciding which witnesses to hear and believe, and they made these decisions within what were in some ways flexible guidelines. What, precisely, did "understand the nature of an oath" or "have sufficient understanding" mean? Virginia seemed to be the most careful and thorough in following the English pattern. Massachusetts initiated a somewhat democratic version of these guidelines: the jury, not the judges, would decide about the validity of each witness's testimony, at least by the early nineteenth century. Still, the jury was forewarned to treat children's testimony with skepticism. Apparently because judges in Pennsylvania used a guide for justices of the peace that ignored Hale's guidelines, Pennsylvania continued to hear children's testimony probably at least until the Revolution. Their continued use of the earlier guide may be related to Quaker ideas about an "inner light" in all persons, even children. Their belief in this inner light from God that exists from birth implies that, for Quakers, the understanding of children did not need to be cultivated to the same degree, and that children could speak as truly as adults.

Over the course of two centuries, these debates, and the men whose ideas were formed by them, helped to alter practical and omnipresent rules about such mundane but critical issues as who could testify in a court of law.[62] Excluding the testimony of young children, as well as hearsay testimony from them (through others), meant that laws that had previously protected them from sexual or physical assault did not do so nearly as well. Their voices were legally silenced. As Francis Buller commented about the prob-

---

61. This draws on a minor point made by Shapiro, *"Beyond Reasonable Doubt,"* 187–188. It was these texts, apparently, that first excluded minors under fourteen from testifying in civil cases and those under age twenty in criminal cases, by which Hale was directly influenced.

62. For a good discussion of the increasing protection of children, see Joseph M. Hawes, *The Children's Rights Movement: A History of Advocacy and Protection* (Boston, 1991).

lems with the new orthodoxy in 1772, "In Cases of foul Facts done in secret, where the Child is the Party injured, the repelling their Evidence entirely is, in some Measure, denying them the Protection of the Law."[63]

II. Labor Contracts

Another avenue for exploring the legal status of children—particularly the weight given to their words—is through their ability to make legal contracts. One type of contract, the labor contract, is discussed here, because (as with new regulations on witness testimony) most changes happened without benefit of statutes; they, too, were changes in the common law. In early-seventeenth-century England, contracts for children's labor were of two types, which formed the legal basis for similar processes in the English colonies. The first was a contract directly between the parties, which stipulated a particular wage and set of benefits, often including instruction in a trade. The second was a contract between the vestrymen of the parish (Overseers of the Poor) and the master, which could bind the poor against their will. The one involved the direct consent of the child to labor, and the other avoided the child's consent—just as it avoided the consent of adults—on the basis of poverty. The nature and use of both types of contracts would change.[64] With respect to the first type of compact, there was an increasing consensus, as with contracts for goods, lands, and marriage, that young children should not have to be bound by their contracts.[65] Like marriage contracts, these labor contracts also became conditional on parental consent during minority. The minimum age to form a binding labor contract inched upward between the seventeenth and nineteenth centuries, with different states following different rules. Since labor contracts involving children were often apprenticeships where the child learned a trade and was taught to read, write, and cipher, if the contract was voidable at the child's wish, then masters or mistresses might be less willing to invest in the child in the early years in order to fulfill the contract. This voidability without liability thus effectively limited the opportunities for children to make their own contracts. The increasing belief that these contracts could be void at the request

63. Of course, even in the earlier period, crimes against very young children would always have been more difficult to prosecute, since below age one or two they literally could not speak, and slightly older children would not have known the law so could not make a direct appeal for its protections.

64. On changes in labor law generally during this period, see Robert J. Steinfeld, *The Invention of Free Labor: The Employment Relation in English and American Law and Culture, 1350–1870* (Chapel Hill, N.C., 1991); Christopher L. Tomlins, *Law, Labor, and Ideology in the Early American Republic* (Cambridge, 1993); Karen Orren, *Belated Feudalism: Labor, the Law, and Liberal Development in the United States* (Cambridge, 1991).

65. For other types of contracts, see Brewer, "Constructing Consent," chap. 3.

of the child encouraged the use of parents as coguarantors as well as the apprenticing of children by the vestry or county courts, which could circumvent the problem altogether. As part of a broad strengthening of notions of custody, parents began to be given a kind of property right in their children and, in some states, even sold their labor.

The Elizabethan Poor Law (1563), which authorized involuntary labor contracts, allowed vestrymen to imprison any poor girls or boys who refused to bind themselves to labor until they consented. Children between ten and eighteen could be bound apprentices to husbandry "as the parties can agree" until the "age of one and twentye yeres at the least," or to skilled trades for seven years. "No person shall by force or color of this [statute] bee bounden to enter into any Apprenticeshippe other then suche as bee under the age of one and twentye yeres."[66] Adults could also be forced to work but could be bound only for periods of one year. This law was but the first in a long series of laws that placed restrictions on children's ability to form their own contracts, and its basic provisions were repeated in legal manuals popular in the English colonies.[67]

Statutes of Elizabeth I made clear that labor contracts signed by apprentices of any age were valid and enforceable "as amply and lardgly to every Entent as yf the same Apprentice were of full Age at the time of the making of suche Indentures."[68] The text of the law added this clause "because ther hath bene and ys some Question and Scruple moved, wether any person being within [the age] of one and twenty yeres . . . shoulde bee bounden accepted and taken as an Apprentyce." It made the above comment, "any lawe, usage or Custome to the contrary notwithstanding." Even in the sixteenth century, there were questions about the abilities of those under a particular age to make binding contracts for apprenticeship, at least outside of London, where the custom of London made them binding. This legislation would be repeated in legal guides over the next two centuries.[69] Parental consent to these contracts was not much of an issue, although certainly to be bound to better trades required a payment to the master, which a child would have had difficulty paying without parental support.

Several examples illuminate the way these two competing guidelines

66. 5 Eliz. I, c. 4; Paul Slack, *Poverty and Policy in Tudor and Stuart England* (London, 1988); A. L. Beier, *Masterless Men: The Vagrancy Problem in England, 1560–1640* (London, 1985); Paul Griffiths, *Youth and Authority: Formative Experiences in England, 1560–1640* (Oxford, 1996), esp. chap. 7.

67. 5 Eliz. I, c. 4, cited by many later treatises such as William Lambarde, *Eirenarcha; or, Of the Office of the Justices of Peace* ([1581]; rpt., Amsterdam, 1970), 370; Wood, *Institute of the Laws*, 52.

68. 5 Eliz. I, c. 4, 5.

69. Ibid. For example, see Wood, *Institute of the Laws*, 13: "An apprentice shall be bound by his Indenture, notwithstanding his Nonage."

worked in practice. In effect, in the eyes of both English and colonial authorities, poverty tended to invalidate the need for individuals to consent; their consent was obviated both legally and, sometimes, as will be shown below with kidnapping, illegally but with the complicity of English authorities. Between 1617 and 1622, the City of London sent three boatfuls of children to the colony of Virginia, accompanied by agreements with the Virginia Company about their term of service. These children were all poor "vagrants," mostly boys, and ranged in age from eight to sixteen. One of these children was Nicholas Granger. He arrived in Virginia at the age of nine in 1619 and was one of the few to survive his apprenticeship. When asking for a second batch, the Virginia General Court requested that all children be over age twelve. Some scheduled for the second batch revolted and were "obstinate" about not wanting to go to Virginia. That they were sent anyway may be interpreted as a lack of concern about children's consent to contracts. However, the City of London, it turned out, needed the children's consent to convey them to Virginia. To circumvent this, the City had to obtain the special permission of the Privy Council, which granted the request for two reasons: that the transportation would be to the youths' benefit (on the grounds that they would obtain land when their service finished) and that these children were rogues and vagabonds. James I described them as "divers idle young people." Because these children had "noe ymploymente" and were seen to have no legitimate means of supporting themselves, they were forced to enter a labor contract—in this case, one across the ocean.[70] This episode reveals the deep truth about contemporary treatment of the poor: children could be bound without their consent under Elizabethan poor laws. In fact, in the early seventeenth century, children over age seven were held responsible for their own poverty. Their status as poor, more than their status as children, invalidated their consent.[71]

---

70. Robert C. Johnson, "The Transportation of Vagrant Children from London to Virginia, 1618–1622," in H. S. Reinmuth, ed., *Early Stuart Studies: Essays in Honor of David Harris Willson* (Minneapolis, Minn., 1970), 137–151, esp. 148; Grace Abbot, *The Child and the State: Select Documents, with Introductory Notes,* I, *Legal Status in the Family: Apprenticeship and Child Labor* (Chicago, 1938), 196, citing *The Records of the Virginia Company of London . . .* , 4 vols. (Washington, D.C., 1906–1935); Abbot E. Smith, *Colonists in Bondage: White Servitude and Convict Labor in America, 1607–1776* (Chapel Hill, N.C., 1947), 147–151. The Virginia General Court's request is reprinted in Abbot, *The Child and the State,* I, 195–198. See also Pinchbeck and Hewitt, *Children in English Society,* I, 106; Johnson, "Transportation of Vagrant Children," in Reinmuth, ed., *Early Stuart Studies,* 144.

For James I's comment, see Pinchbeck and Hewitt, *Children in English Society,* I, 106. For other, similar examples, see James Horn, *Adapting to a New World: English Society in the Seventeenth-Century Chesapeake* (Chapel Hill, N.C., 1994), 62–65, 253–255.

71. A directive from Chief Justice Popham issued at the beginning of the seventeenth century stated that all vagrants over seven were to be whipped and sent to their proper place of settlement (determined by a complicated equation of place of birth and last

Clearly, however, not enough servants could be obtained legally with the aid of local authorities, whether City of London officials or parish officers in charge of the poor laws. But English authorities did, for most of the century, turn a blind eye to a thriving trade in what would come to be called, by midcentury, "kidnapping." Thousands of people, both children and adults, were kidnapped, to be sent to the colonies and sold as servants during the seventeenth century. English court records are full of complaints: such theft of persons was technically illegal, but it was a crime only lightly punished with a small fine, and that obtainable only when an individual brought suit and, usually, captured the kidnapper as well. A variety of statutes sought to prevent kidnapping by securing the consent of all immigrants, especially young ones. Barbados required in 1661 that servants under fourteen years of age "have a certificate from the parish stating that they had emigrated with their own consent or at their own request" (though it is not clear that this was enforced). Massachusetts and Pennsylvania heard a few petitions from such kidnapped persons and sometimes released them.[72] Seventeenth-century Virginians, however, condoned the practice, passing laws about how long such servants who arrived without contracts should serve—laws that, with every iteration, increased the length of service. The first law, passed in 1643, directed "such servants as shall be imported haveing no indentures or covenants either men or women if they be above twenty year old to serve fowre year, if they shall be above twelve and under twenty to serve five years, And if under twelve to serve seaven years." By 1666, those over age nineteen

residence), whereas those under that age could be sent, with their parents, to their parents' parish. See Pinchbeck and Hewitt, *Children in English Society,* I, 100–101.

  Similar directives appeared in many legal treatises of the seventeenth and eighteenth centuries but began to specify age fourteen instead of seven. According to the Pennsylvania *Conductor Generalis,* 219, those over fourteen should be sent to the their parish (place of legal settlement), whereas those under fourteen should be sent to their parents' parish. This clearly derived from an older policy that punished those over fourteen for "begging or wandering." "If any such person, as is declared to bee a Roage, Vagabonde, or sturdy Beggar, by the Statute [14 Eliz. I, c. 5] being above the age of fourteene yeares, shall bee taken begging, or wandering, or missusing hymselfe, contrary to that act . . . (they should be sent to gaol until next general sessions)." See Lambarde, *Eirenarcha,* 192, 244. See also Pinchbeck and Hewitt, *Children in English Society,* I, 97.

  Yet children of fourteen or probably even much younger seem to have been committed to "Houses of Correction," in the 1820s and afterwards, just as many had temporary residences in poorhouses and workhouses in the earlier period, before being bound apprentices. On the later period, see John R. Sutton, *Stubborn Children: Controlling Delinquency in the United States, 1640–1981* (Berkeley, Calif., 1988), 69–71; Allen Steinberg, *The Transformation of Criminal Justice: Philadelphia, 1800–1880* (Chapel Hill, N.C., 1989), 179–180. Steinberg gives evidence of mass arrests of children for begging in the 1850s and 1860s. Unfortunately, he does not offer particular ages, nor does Sutton.

  72. Richard B. Morris, *Government and Labor in Early America* (New York, 1946), 340 (Morris's paraphrase, citing Hall, *Acts of Barbados,* 35), 341–345.

had to serve for five years, whereas those under that age had to serve until
they reached age twenty-four; for those aged "under twelve," who would
have had to serve seven years by the 1643 act, that meant an additional six or
more years of service. Virginia judges assessed their ages. So, in 1679, "James
Browne a servant coming in without indentures consigned by Mr. William
Smith of London to Captain Francis Page . . . is adjudged eleven years of age
and is ord. to serve according to act," which meant he had to serve thirteen
years.[73] By forcing such persons to labor for long terms without contracts,
Virginians were permitting kidnapping of English subjects—of adults as well
as children—and completely ignoring whether those persons had consented
to that labor. (The similarities to the capture and sale of Africans in Virginia
are striking.)

   To prevent such practices, English courts set up some policies to ensure
that those taking ship for the New World had chosen to go, but they seem to
have been weakly enforced. The first prosecution of kidnapping began during the Civil War, seemingly amid heightened tensions between Parliament
and the king. In 1643, Elizabeth Hamlyn was committed to Newgate Prison,
where she was to be whipped, "for taking of diverse little children in the
street and selling them to be carried to Virginia." In 1645, Parliament enacted
an ordinance that those who "in a most barbarous and wicked Manner steal
away many little children" should be pursued and publicly disciplined.
When four-year-old Richard Harnold, heir to eight hundred pounds a year,
was stolen and sent to Virginia in 1657, the courts seemed more concerned
than over most poor children. With the Restoration, the penalties seem to
have relaxed considerably, despite the institution of a formal registry of all
outgoing passengers and sending "serchers," or English officials, to visit
servant ships before they left to determine whether anyone was on them
against his or her will. If the children "had been properly signed on," that
is, if they had consented to go, then "the parents could not distress ship
owners" but must let them go to the colonies.[74]

   Enforcement of the antikidnapping laws gained some teeth in the 1680s,
but kidnapping was still fairly widespread, and only lightly punished,
through the first half of the eighteenth century. In 1682, Charles II ordered
that persons over twenty-one should bind themselves as servants in the
presence of a justice of the peace and that those under twenty-one could bind
themselves only with the consent of parents or masters. If they were under

---

73. Hening, ed., *Statutes at Large*, I, 257 (1643), 441–442 (1658), II, 113–114 (1662), 240
(1666). York County Records Project, citing DOW (6) 112 (Aug. 24, 1679). Many other such
cases appear.
74. Peter Wilson Coldham, "The 'Spiriting' of London Children to Virginia, 1648–1685,"
Virginia Magazine of History and Biography, LXXXIII (1975), 280–287, esp. 281, 286; Morris, *Government and Labor*, 342, 344; Smith, *Colonists in Bondage*, 73.

fourteen, their parents or masters had to be present at the making of the new contract. Although renewed under James II, this order was only sporadically enforced. In 1717, in response especially to pressure from merchants, who feared being sued by irate masters deprived of apprentices or wives deserted by husbands, Parliament issued its first proclamation on the subject, one that reaffirmed Charles II's original order. Those over fifteen had to give assent in person to a magistrate, which would make their binding irrevocable; those under that age apparently had to have their parents present as well.[75] Significant evasion of these acts was still occurring in the eighteenth century, however. That children were still coming into Virginia without indentures in 1705, for example—and serving until age 24—is revealed by an act of that year concerning tithables. A pamphlet published in London in 1715 announced that two kidnappers had been discovered, caught, and were awaiting trial. Only through the endeavors of parents were they discovered. These two ship captains, named Azariah Daniel and Edward Harrison, seemed to prefer boys between the ages of ten and twelve. Two boys of "about the age of twelve," kidnapped by Daniel, had been found "bound in a garret." Meanwhile, the others he had kidnapped had already been placed aboard ships. The father who had tracked down the other captain, Harrison, had found him too late: Harrison had put his son on a frigate that had already departed for Barbados. Harrison admitted to putting "above 150 more aboard several other ships in the said river bound to his Majestys Plantations." In other locales, such as Aberdeen, Scotland, in the 1740s, the judges colluded with those who captured boys under fourteen, in particular, giving them false contracts that stated parent and child consented.[76]

The evidence from the shipping records and a few contracts in the colonies shows that children were consenting to their own contracts, although not always. In 1634, a servant in Plymouth Colony agreed to serve a master for twelve years until he turned twenty-three, so he was eleven when he bound himself. One study of the Middlesex registrations of 1683–1684 found children as young as eleven putting their mark to such contracts. Sometimes, at least in Virginia, parents seem to have consented for their children. Six-year-old Elizabeth Bartlett's apprenticeship contract was signed only by her mother and her new master in Virginia in 1701.[77] Is this failure to

---

75. Morris, *Government and Labor*, 340. Although the contracts were identical in other respects for persons of all ages, the contracts of servants under age twenty-one were more likely to include training in a trade or education (David Galenson, *White Servitude in Colonial America: An Economic Analysis* [Cambridge, 1981], 200–203).

76. Hening, ed., *Statutes at Large*, III, 259; *The Grand Kidnapper at Last Taken. . . .* (London, [1715]); Coldham, *Emigrants in Chains: A Social History of Forced Emigration to the Americas of Felons, Destitute Children, Political and Religious Non-conformists, Vagabonds, Beggars, and Other Undesirables, 1607–1776* (Baltimore, 1992), chap. 7.

77. Lawrence William Towner, "A Good Master Well Served: A Social History of Servi-

consider her consent part of a transition to parental consent? Due to her very young age? Or a reflection of Virginia's rather cavalier approach to consent to labor in the seventeenth century? Regardless, it's clear that, during the late seventeenth century, the contracts of even those under fourteen were still valid, but becoming less necessary, and parental consent was beginning to be required instead.

By the eighteenth century, the various colonies had begun to follow very different policies in response to growing doubts about the ability of children to make contracts. A comparison of various apprenticeship contracts from Virginia and Pennsylvania during the eighteenth and early nineteenth centuries reveals that Pennsylvanians put a higher value on the consent of the child, of whatever age, as well as that of the parent. Not only were Virginia's children much more likely to be bound by vestry (or, after the Revolution, Overseers of the Poor) on the basis of poverty, where their consent was considered to be invalidated, but children were much less likely to sign other labor contracts in Virginia. In fact, the only two contracts I found where boys explicitly signed their own indentures were from the 1750s; in later contracts, children of both sexes were bound only by their parents, and their consent was not an issue.[78] In Pennsylvania, on the other hand, children usually signed their contracts, regardless of their age. In all of the cases where children were under fourteen, a parent or other family member signed the contract as well. In one case, two-year-old Phebe Stuart's mark appeared next to her name at the bottom of the contract. In two others, a four-year-old and a five-year-old signed their own contracts. Nine-, ten-, and twelve-year-olds also signed their own apprenticeship contracts.[79] Even the wording of the contracts in Virginia and Pennsylvania was different. In nearly all the Pennsylvania contracts, the words "doth voluntarily, of his [or

---

tude in Massachusetts, 1620–1750" (Ph.D. diss., Northwestern University, 1955), 69. Unfortunately for my study, Towner's extensive survey of servants and apprenticeship was not concerned generally with questions of consent. See also Galenson, *White Servitude*, 76; YCRP, citing DOW (11) 528.

78. Indenture of Thomas Pollard, dated June 14, 1751, aged seventeen (no parents, guardians or others signed), indenture of John Tucker, dated July 20, 1753, age unspecified (both he and his mother signed), Lancaster County, Virginia, Apprenticeship Records. My sample of apprenticeship contracts not authorized by the Overseers of the Poor (OOP) is fairly small for Virginia: I could only find seven with which the OOP were not involved, several of which came from Lancaster County. Since the apprenticeship contracts themselves were not formally kept, this is of course only a fragmentary sample. Still, it seems that the OOP increasingly authorized most apprenticeships in Virginia.

79. Contracts of Phebe Stuart, Oct. 15, 1811, David Wilson (age four), June 27, 1818, James Keegan (age five), Dec. 19, 1748, record 32020, Hannah Field (age twelve), June 27, 1811, record 32812, Lydia Morton (age nine), June 24, 1822, Johnson Walters (age ten), July 10, 1814, Benjamin Webb (age ten), Aug. 3, 1775, all in Chester County Historical Society (hereafter cited as CCHS), Pennsylvania, Apprenticeship Records (hereafter cited as AR).

her] own free will and accord, put himself apprentice to . . ." appeared, even, for example, in the apprenticeship contract of four-year-old David Wilson. The exact wording of his contract read: "This indenture witnesseth that David Wilson . . . by and with the approbation of his father James Wilson . . . hath put himself and by these presents doth thereby put, place, and bind out himself."[80] In Virginia, however, wording appeared differently: instead of the consent of the child, the contract laid stress on the consent of a parent. "Nicholas Hardin . . . hath of his own free will put and by these presents doth bind *his son* Henry Hardin apprentice."[81]

Several cases illustrate the developing tensions over children's consent in Pennsylvania. In 1748, two guardians petitioned the Pennsylvania court, praying the court to allow them to bind two orphan boys. "Rich Richard and David Richard, two of the children of the deceased being minor yet being obstinately inclined, refuse to be bound to trades pursuant to the direction of their late father's will or to follow any other employment whatsoever, which in the method they are in must inevitably end in their ruin." The guardians promised to bind them only to such masters as the boys "may judge proper or convenient to them" but could not legally do so, in Pennsylvania, without a court order authorizing them to bind the orphans. There is no record of their age, yet they were both called "minors," which in 1741 probably meant under age twenty-one. In Pennsylvania in 1753, seventeen-year-old Thomas Ralph petitioned the court that he should be released from the indenture he had signed two years previously with one Arthur Kennedy, in Ireland, who used "many persuasions and fair promises, to entice your petitioner to leave his parents, and go to Pennsylvania." He was only fifteen years old at that time, and his parents "knew nothing of the agreement." He also noted that the master to whom Kennedy had sold him had forced him to sign a new indenture with more time on it. The court ignored the issue of parental consent but responded to the claim about a coerced second contract and made him serve his master only until the time first set.[82] Clearly, they thought that a fifteen-year-old did not need the consent of his parents in order to enter a binding agreement. In 1811, Elizabeth Rope petitioned the court that she was bound apprentice by a man who claimed to be, but was not, her guardian, at the age of fifteen, without her consent, to learn the art of housewifery. Her new master and mistress beat her severely, and she asked

80. Contract of David Wilson, June 27, 1818, AR, CCHS; for an earlier contract, see that of a different boy with the same last name, Robert Wilson (1732), "with the advice and consent of his mother and father in law Joseph Stringer and Mary String[er] . . . of his own free and voluntary will and accord put and bind himself" (CCHS AR).

81. Indenture of Henry Hardin (age eleven), Jan. 20, 1787, FCV AR.

82. Petition of Thomas Ralph, in CCP Quarter Session Indictments (hereafter cited as QSI), May 1753.

to be dismissed from the apprenticeship on the grounds that neither she nor the appropriate person had consented to the indenture.[83]

In Virginia in 1789, however, a boy was released from his contract— despite the fact that his master had paid for his passage from Ireland—on the grounds that his parents had not consented. Eighteen-year-old Humphrey Murphy petitioned the court to be set free from his apprenticeship because he had signed his own indenture when "about" age thirteen in 1784 in Ire- land, without his father's consent. The court, after examining his indenture, which contained his own mark at the bottom (as well as that of Timothy Parker, to whom he had originally indented himself), released him from his service on the grounds that he had made the contract "when a minor and uncapable of entering into any transaction obligatory." Murphy's master, who had bought his indenture, was apparently astounded at the verdict and appealed to the Frederick district court, where the lower court's judgment was upheld.[84] Thus, the labor contracts of those under fourteen, at least, were held to be invalid in Virginia in 1784. Indeed, the court's blanket use of the term "minor" indicates that, had he been under age twenty-one when he signed the contract, it would also have been voidable at his wish.

By the early nineteenth century, in most states, the decision rendered by the Virginia court came to be typical.[85] A Massachusetts statute of 1794 held that parental consent was necessary to the labor contracts of all those under age twenty-one, but that, if the child were over fourteen, his or her consent was needed in addition. If the father were not living, or if the child were illegitimate, the mother could bind the child. If the child had no parent, then a legal guardian could bind him or her. If a child also had no guardian, then he or she could request to be bound by the town selectmen if over age fourteen.[86] In other words, some adult always had to consent, and, if a child was under fourteen, then that adult would provide the sole authorization. In some states, in fact, it began to be considered normal for a father to have the right to the labor of his children, including the profits arising therefrom. Two contracts from Connecticut in 1815 show fathers binding out several of their children to the Slater Cotton Mill and having the right to their wages, although one father agreed to give his two oldest sons one-half their wages.[87]

83. Complaint and Petition of Elizabeth Rope, CCP QSI, November 1811.

84. *Murphy v Magill,* FCV Ended Causes, June 1789. See also FCV MB, 1786–1790, June 1789, 281–282.

85. See generally the *Century Edition,* XXVII, 1120–1122. There seems to be little dispute on this issue in the nineteenth century. None of the state cases that upheld a minor's right to dissolve his or her labor contract in the nineteenth century appeared in Pennsylvania.

86. *The Revised Statutes of the Commonwealth of Massachusetts, Passed November 4, 1835 . . .* (Boston, 1836), 494.

87. Slater Company Records, University of Connecticut Library, nos. p2243 (March 1815), p2245 (May 1815). Thanks to David Zonderman for this reference.

The contracts do not specify ages, but the newly accepted rule was that fathers had the right to their children's labor until the children reached twenty-one. The case that best illustrates Pennsylvania's exceptional stand—even better than the very young children's signatures to labor contracts—is the 1793 Pennsylvania supreme court decision of *Respublica* v. *Catharine Keppele*. In this case, Peter Dehaven bound his ward Benjamin Hannis, aged ten, to Catharine Keppele for five years, for which Keppele paid Dehaven. The judges agreed that guardians should not have the right to bind their wards as servants and that even parents should not be able to bind their minor children as servants. Although they granted that "a parent may have a right to the personal service of his child," they held that "no parent can make his child the servant to another," since such a contract "cannot be for [the child's] benefit."[88] They thus implied that the child must always consent as well and specified that the "personal service" of a child could not translate into selling the child's service. The justices in Pennsylvania set a completely different precedent at this juncture, separating their policy decisively from that of Massachusetts and Virginia, who were wrestling with the same questions.

A broad change thus occurred in the ability of children to consent to their own labor contracts. Whereas, in the Elizabethan period, the labor contracts of children under fourteen were held to be valid and unavoidable, even at the child's own request, by the late eighteenth century, courts were beginning to uphold the father's, mother's, or guardian's ability to make a labor contract for a child rather than that child's own ability. Contracts signed only by minors began to be held invalid. This change did not happen overnight but appears to have begun in the seventeenth century with the first laws that required parental consent to labor contracts for those under twenty-one. The process of change on the individual level can be seen in the notes made in the margins of the practice book of a man who would later become a Massachusetts supreme court justice. Young Theophilus Parsons, when first learning the law in 1775, copied out a form, or precedent, for an action of covenant broken against an apprentice for which the injured master could obtain damages. After copying out the routine form, which served as the basic pattern for masters seeking damages, however, he wrote in the margin: "Quere whether this action his [against] the [person] who was a minor when he sealed the deed?" In other words, Parsons questioned whether the master had the right to damages if his apprentice were a minor when he signed his apprenticeship contract. If not, of course, no action or damages were possible, because the minor would be able to annul the contract at his

88. *Respublica v Catharine Keppele,* Jasper Yeates, I, 233–237.

own discretion.[89] These are the questions that began to haunt all of contract law as it began to cohere into a unified body of thought in the eighteenth century. Under what circumstances could a minor's contract be valid and enforceable? If a father consents for his children in the political arena because his children cannot sufficiently exercise their understandings, as the republican political theorists had argued, should he not consent on their behalf to other contracts as well?

Locke's *Two Treatises of Government* (1689) distinguished adults who could reason from the children who could not. "Children, I confess, are not born in this full state of Equality, though they are born to it. Their parents have a sort of Rule and Jurisdiction over them." Locke referred to children as "weak and helpless, without Knowledge or Understanding." The parents' task is to "govern the Actions of their yet ignorant Nonage, till reason shall take its place." "Though I have said above," he continued, " 'That all Men by Nature are equal,' I cannot be supposed to understand all sorts of Equality. Age or Virtue may give men a just Precedency."

> Thus we are born Free, as we are born Rational; *not that we have actually the Exercise of either: Age, that brings one, brings with it the other too. And thus we see how natural Freedom and Subjection to Parents may consist together, and are both founded on the same Principle. A child is Free by . . . his Father's Understanding, which is to govern him, till he hath it of his own. The Freedom of a Man at years of discretion, and the Subjection of a Child to his parents, whilst yet short of that Age, are so consistent, and so distinguishable."*[90]

Thus, for Locke, until children attained reason, that is, until they reached an "age of discretion," they should be dependent on their parents and subject to their will. He elaborated on these ideas in *Some Thoughts concerning Education* and *An Essay concerning Human Understanding*, both of which described the lengthy process a child undergoes in order to develop the ability to reason, what Locke called "reflection," or the ability to "abstract" generalizations from particular observations. Locke held that these abilities were essential to participatory citizenship.[91]

Consider the similarity between that passage from Locke's *Two Treatises*

89. Theophilus Parsons, "Precedents Book of the Massachusetts Law, 1775," MS at Harvard Law Library, Cambridge, Mass. See also Nelson, *Americanization of the Common Law*, 199 n. 47. He found several examples in late-eighteenth-century Massachusetts where the contracts of apprentices were held to be invalid on the grounds that the parent or guardian had failed to sign the indenture.

90. John Locke, *Two Treatises of Government*, ed. Peter Laselett (Cambridge, 1947), 304–308.

91. For more on republican theories and childhood (including my comments on the debate between republican and liberal theories), see Brewer, "Constructing Consent," chap. 1.

of Government and the following quote from an 1807 treatise on the law of contract. Samuel Comyn's popular treatise on contract law began by stating, "All contracts with infants, except for necessaries, are either void or voidable: the reason of which is, the indulgence the law has thought fit to give infants, who are supposed to want judgment and discretion in their contracts and transactions with others, and the care it takes of them in preventing them from being imposed upon or overreached by persons of more years and experience."[92]

It is no coincidence that the "rise of contract" in the law accompanied the rise of republican political ideas and institutions, since both relied on consent. The legal category of childhood (technically "minority," "nonage," or "infancy") was redefined during this period, partly in response to changing ideas about the personal qualities that a person needed in order to make a political contract. The qualities necessary for the making of formal legal contracts began to center increasingly on the "full development" or "maturity" of understanding. In the early seventeenth century, before this redefinition, even those under age—generally fourteen—could consent to covenants of all varieties. In order for the contract to be valid, every person making the covenant actually had to consent in words or writing, regardless of age, even if that consent was only a mark at the bottom of an apprenticeship contract or the prompted words spoken by a seven-year-old in a marriage ceremony.

The law of contract, as we now know it, was influenced profoundly by eighteenth-century attitudes toward natural law and political theory and gained the central place in the common law it now occupies only in the late eighteenth and early nineteenth centuries. The first treatise that elaborated the centrality of a law of contract in its own right was written by John Joseph Powell, *Essay upon the Law of Contracts and Agreements* (1790). One measure of the increasing importance of contract law is the rise of assumpsit actions, that is, contract suits based only on the oral promises between two partners but unaccompanied by any corroborating actions. Such suits drew on what became the core conception of contract law, "the idea that a contractual liability can be *created*—out of nothing as it were—by a promise, or at least an exchange of promises." The biggest change, however, occurred with respect to the adjudication of contracts: judges began to focus increasingly on the intent of the parties contracting and less on the fairness of the contract.

92. Samuel Comyn, *A Treatise of the Law relative to Contracts and Agreements* (London, 1807), I, 148. Children may still make contracts to purchase goods or services or to buy or sell land in many states. Their contract, however, is voidable at their own wish any time before they reach the age of majority (usually twenty-one). A modern legal scholar therefore advises that, practically speaking, children should not have this right, and property left to them should be managed by a trust or a guardian and not by the child (Robert H. Mnookin, *Child, Family, and State: Problems and Materials on Children and the Law* [Boston, 1978], 217, 681).

Once intent was given priority, it put greater stress on the capacity of those contracting.[93]

Blackstone, the most influential English jurist on late-eighteenth- and early-nineteenth-century American law, adapted the common law to highlight ideas of contract. Although he was conservative in some ways, he adjusted the common law to conform more closely with Enlightenment epistemology in order to pacify critics of the English legal system.[94] Blackstone's metaphorical crowning of custom was moderated by the weight he gave to reason and natural law. Not only did Blackstone cite such philosophers as Grotius, Pufendorf, Locke, Barbeyrac, and Montesquieu, but he held specifically that custom that did not conform with reason was invalid. Any precedent that contradicted reason was not a precedent, simply not law. Discussing this aspect of Blackstone, David Lieberman summarized:

> When the judges discovered a previous judicial opinion of the law to be "contrary to reason, much more if it be contrary to the divine law," they declared "not that such a sentence was bad law, but that it was not law, that is that it is not the established custom of the realm." And since a determination "contrary to reason" was "not law," "our lawyers are with justice so copious in their encomiums on the reason of the common law; that they tell us that the law is the perfection of reason, that it always intends to conform thereto, and that what is not reason is not law."

Thus, according to Blackstone, a precedent that did not conform with what a judge thought the law should be could be ignored.[95]

He openly incorporated republican political theory, especially the emphasis on consent and contract, into his synthesis of the common law. As an influential scholar on the rise of the law of contract has noted, "Blackstone [was] an important propagator of social contractarianism in the Locke tradition. If anybody was needed to convert Locke's ideas into an influential tool for lawyers—and perhaps none was needed, for every educated lawyer must have read Locke—this part was played by Blackstone."[96] Yet Blackstone discussed only briefly the rules of contract with regard to property and

93. P. S. Atiyah, *The Rise and Fall of Freedom of Contract* (Oxford, 1979), 102–103, 139; Nelson, *Americanization of the Common Law,* esp. 136–144; Morton J. Horwitz, *The Transformation of American Law, 1780–1860* (Cambridge, Mass., 1977), esp. 160–210.

94. Duncan Kennedy, "The Structure of Blackstone's *Commentaries," Buffalo Law Review,* XXVIII (1979), 205–382.

95. Lieberman, *The Province of Legislation Determined: Legal Theory in Eighteenth-Century Britain* (Cambridge, 1989), citing Blackstone, *Commentaries,* I, 69–71, 76–77. Lieberman also cites other legal treatise writers who gave similar opinions, including Hale, *History of the Common Law,* 45–46.

96. Atiyah, *Rise and Fall of Freedom of Contract,* 59, 215–216.

treated this issue separately from other contractual relations. The common law in the nineteenth century would make contract ever more integral.[97]

Blackstone was alone in neither his increasing references to the importance of individual consent nor his alliance of custom with reason. The Revolutionary-era lawyers tended to conflate custom with reason, and reason by the eighteenth century was itself equated with natural law theory and political theory.[98] Thus, custom did not always mean past precedent. Custom sometimes created a past in order to justify a future. As J. G. A. Pocock rather tactfully described this tension as it emerged in the early seventeenth century, "Custom was . . . always immemorial and always up-to-date."[99]

III. Age, Consent, and Power

The young children of six or seven years who testified in court, the four- and five-year-olds who made their crude marks at the bottom of apprenticeship contracts seem to be participating in what we would regard as meaningless rituals. Yet such testimony and assent were not meaningless. At the beginning of the seventeenth century, the law vested a measure of authority in the testaments and personal covenants of persons however young. Gradually, in fits and starts and with much controversy, a semiconsistent pattern of rules for valid testimony and contracts emerged. This controversy can be seen in the different policies followed by Virginia, Massachusetts, and Pennsylvania as well as in reversed judgments and disputes within popular legal treatises. These rules developed the same ideas captured in early modern political and natural law theories. Choice came to depend on judgment and the ability to form intent. Those who have no judgment or understanding cannot and should not exercise choice. Judgment comes with experience and education. Children should be protected until they can fully exercise choice of their own.

97. Ibid., 102–103, referring to Blackstone, *Commentaries* (1772), II, chap. 30, III, chap. 9; see also III, 215–216.

98. James Q. Whitman, "Why Did the Revolutionary Lawyers Confuse Custom and Reason?" *University of Chicago Law Review*, LVIII (1991), 1321–1368. See also, generally, J. R. Pole, "Reflections on American Law and the American Revolution," Peter Charles Hoffer, "Custom as Law: A Comment on J. R. Pole's 'Reflections,'" Bruce H. Mann, "The Evolutionary Revolution in American Law: A Comment on J. R. Pole's 'Reflections,'" all in *William and Mary Quarterly*, 3d Ser., L (January 1993), 122–175.

99. J. G. A. Pocock, *The Ancient Constitution and the Feudal Law: A Study of English Historical Thought in the Seventeenth Century* ([1957]; Cambridge, 1987), 15, 241. The general change that Pocock describes in this volume is a shift in appeal with regard to political and legal theory, from the reliance on a simpler understanding of custom and tradition to a blending of those two factors with reason. Even the appeal to the English Constitution was transformed during the seventeenth century as it became not merely (or even purely) immemorial, but also rational.

Pennsylvania seems to have adopted its own path with respect to both the mutual signing of apprenticeship contracts and continuing to hear children's testimony in criminal cases. The transformations in Virginia, on the other hand, seem to be the most dramatic: they sanctioned kidnapping of their (English) labor force in the seventeenth century, ignoring issues of consent altogether, regardless of age, but, by the late eighteenth century, advocating freeing an indentured servant who consented to a labor contract when he was thirteen but whose parents did not. Consent had become much more important to them, and they had internalized rules about what constituted valid consent. Policy in all three colonies and states was profoundly influenced by the English cases and legal treatises that gradually adopted some of the new perspectives during the seventeenth and eighteenth centuries.

Many collections of the common law were written by men who actually sought to shape the common law, who were active reformers. This makes the common law difficult to identify at any given point, yet, despite the interpretive difficulties this admission raises, it is critical that this constant reshaping be acknowledged. Coke, Hale, and Blackstone, the three most frequently cited legal compilers of the seventeenth and eighteenth centuries, all actively molded the common law in order to make it conform to reason and to turn it into a coherent system. Very gradually, their treatises affected the proceedings in American courts not only because American justices of the peace or lawyers read their books but because American judges and treatise writers chose to cite these earlier judges as precedent. Each of these three authors openly acknowledged that he sought to make the law conform to reason; each ignored precedents that did not fit with his revision and reduction of the common law. Although they justified reforms on a theoretical level, they rarely acknowledged the alterations they made on the level of specific discussions and revisions of particular issues. Coke and Hale, particularly, have to be seen in light of the religious and political conflicts in England in the seventeenth century. Both served as members of Parliament multiple times, and, while there, sided with what could be termed the Puritan, or Nonconformist, faction, actively seeking to revise legal procedure. The fact that the legal treatise writers who followed Coke and Hale cited them merely as compilers of the common law has led to a variety of distortions. As one scholar has rather tactfully put it, "Hostile contemporaries were aware, and legal historians cannot help becoming so, that accuracy was sometimes the loser [in Coke's attempts to create a coherent synthesis]; Coke's power to shape the law under color of reporting it was to exceed his expectations."[100]

100. Gray, "Reason, Authority, and Imagination," in Zagorin, ed., *Culture and Politics from Puritanism to the Enlightenment,* 27; see also Stephen D. White, *Sir Edward Coke and "The Grievances of the Commonwealth," 1621–1628* (Chapel Hill, N.C., 1979), 16, 14, 46, 80;

Although the shift in children's ability to testify and to form contracts did not happen suddenly with the American Revolution, as did other specifically legislated changes, the intellectual roots behind these shifts are the same as those that lay behind the Revolution. The epistemological debates of the seventeenth and eighteenth centuries were not merely abstract theorizing about religious faith, human potential, and the laws of nature. They were central to Lockean and republican political ideology. Although earlier Christian authors such as Thomas Aquinas had introduced the concept of an age of reason, and classical authors such as Aristotle had similar concepts, seventeenth-century Continental natural law theorists and English Dissenters and revolutionaries, upon whom Hale and other legal reformers drew, developed this concept, granting it much greater definition and weight. The separate status of childhood is in many respects a consequence of this emphasis on an age of reason, a new distinction that arose as a critical part of the new basis for political legitimacy.

The United States Constitution, for example, established much higher ages for holding elective office than had obtained either in English or in earlier colonial precedent: they set twenty-five for the House of Representatives, thirty for the Senate, and thirty-five for the president; meanwhile, to give only one example, teenagers had routinely been elected to Parliament in seventeenth-century Britain.[101] During the intense debates over this question during the Constitutional Convention, delegates made points such as the following by George Mason of Virginia: "He would if interrogated be obliged to declare that his political opinions at the age of 21. were too crude and erroneous to merit an influence on public measures."[102] Whereas this might seem simply a statement of "fact," it was instead a statement intertwined with Revolutionary ideas that attacked aristocracy and set up new standards of competency. Young persons, indeed very young persons, could and did hold power when power was allocated on the basis of inherited right, as the delegates to the Constitutional Convention, and Revolutionary pamphlet writers such as Paine, had explicitly condemned. They preferred that those who held public power should rest their authority on virtue and reason, attributes that came only with age. Their positions were not born suddenly with the American Revolution. They were expressed in different forms and to different degrees by New England Puritans, by the Puritans

---

Pocock, *The Ancient Constitution*, 268–269: "Coke's habit of citing as maxims what it is hard to find so cited before was not altogether as outrageous as it might appear. The ongoing reason of the courts contained custom but was not limited to it; it need not cite custom, but might do so whenever it saw fit."

101. See Brewer, "Constructing Consent," chap. 2.

102. Wilbourn E. Benton, ed., *1787: Drafting the U.S. Constitution*, 2 vols. (College Station, Tex., 1986), I, 242.

under Cromwell, by the supporters of the Glorious Revolution such as Locke and Algernon Sidney, and they were embodied in much of what we have come to call the Enlightenment. Yet these ideas would transform not only the basis of political power but the basis of personal power, as this essay illustrates. They would do this explicitly, with the transformation of statutes—and, implicitly, in transformations much more difficult to trace—by rewriting the common law.

Martha Minow summarizes the chasm that characterizes the division in modern law between "persons who are mentally competent and persons who are not."

> The competent have responsibilities and rights; the incompetent have disabilities and perhaps, protections. The competent can advance claims based on principles of autonomy; the incompetent are subject to restraints that enforce relationships of dependence. These "two tracks" of legal treatment reflect the traditional Western idea that responsibility follows only from voluntary, knowing, and intelligent choice. Mental competence signifies the ability to appreciate the consequences of one's actions, to protect oneself from manipulation and coercion, and to understand and engage in transactions of property and commerce.

Although Minow, speaking from the perspective of today, can write of the "traditional Western idea that responsibility follows only from voluntary, knowing, and intelligent choice," we have seen that such sharp distinctions were not traditional in the eighteenth century. These distinctions developed gradually as a consequence of the law's focus on "voluntary, knowing, and intelligent choice."[103]

103. Martha Minow, *Making All the Difference: Inclusion, Exclusion, and American Law* (Ithaca, N.Y., 1990), 126.

PART FOUR

Rules of Law

Legal Regimes and Their Social Effects

THE FLUIDITY AND DIVERSITY characteristic of early American legal regimes during the seventeenth century was succeeded in the eighteenth by an explicit crystallization and routinization of doctrine, practice, procedure, and administration. Legal historians have had resort to the term "Anglicization" to characterize these eighteenth-century trends, suggesting a generalized turn throughout the English colonies toward an increasingly uniform legal culture, modeled on and influenced by that of eighteenth-century England—professionalized, formalized, committed to the technicalities of common-law practice and procedure. The essays in Part IV help to illustrate this transformation, flesh out its institutional embodiments and dynamics, and explore its meaning in particular institutional settings.

In the first essay, Cornelia Hughes Dayton presents seventeenth-century New Haven Colony (1639–1665) and its legal regime as an exemplification of the capacity of the early mainland environment to accommodate quite distinct ideologies of governance—in New Haven's case, a Calvinist legality of godly living. Odd or aberrant when viewed from the perspective of Anglo-American legal history and church-state relations, New Haven's legal regime fitted comfortably the practice and magisterial style of European jurisdictions inspired by John Calvin's consistory in mid-sixteenth-century Geneva. In particular, Dayton shows how the implementation of Calvinist principles governing immorality and domestic relations in New Haven's courtrooms had major consequences for gender relations, resulting in a substantially enhanced legal presence for women. Because similar conclusions are suggested by research on European Calvinist jurisdictions, Dayton proposes that, once placed within the spectrum of post-Reformation confessional ideologies—Lutheranism, Calvinism, Catholicism, the smaller radical sects—Calvinism represented a distinct form of patriarchy, one whose overarching emphasis on universal God-fearing moderated the traditional social relations of patriarchy in certain significant respects. Dayton's conclusion traces the end of the configuration of Calvinist morals enforcement and a distinctive Calvinist patriarchy amid the eighteenth century's wider reorientation of state attention toward servicing the circulation of peoples and goods throughout an increasingly expansive and pluralistic North Atlantic commercial world. Pluralism, the circulation of peoples, meant diversifying communities and progressively less interest in using (or capacity to use) legal means to enforce confessional discipline. Meanwhile, commerce, the circulation of goods, precipitated concomitant demands for greater consistency of rules and decision making across hitherto diverse legal orders. It also precipitated a legal system that gave primacy to the enforcement or mediation of economic transactions. Centering the North Atlantic's law on commerce meant an increased impetus toward its Anglicization, while the simultaneous dilution of Calvinist legal culture reinforced the normality of unpoliced male-centered social relations. Patriarchy became ordinary.

In the second essay, William M. Offutt, Jr. undertakes a methodical examination of the terms of early American legal systems' social authority, which also offers a systematic illustration of the trends detected by Dayton. Early American history reveals something of a paradox—that colonial legal regimes played roles of critical social importance, yet had available to them only modest coercive resources. What then were the conditions of acceptance of their rules? Offutt's answer focuses on the acceptance and transmission of legal values. Longitudinal litigation analysis provides a means to measure acceptance of court authority over certain subjects and among certain social groups by revealing differential levels of adherence to legal norms in the law-using population. Offutt hypothesizes that cases handled routinely without in-court conflict or with predictable outcomes indicate high propensity to adhere to the prevailing legal norms and thus substantial effective authority for the legal regime implementing those norms; cases with greater levels of in-court conflict or unpredictable outcomes indicate a lower propensity to adhere and, correspondingly, lower levels of effective authority. Applying the hypothesis to Middle Colony litigation patterns, civil and criminal, in the late seventeenth and early eighteenth centuries, he finds that high and increasing levels of adherence characterized litigation over economic transactions (contracts and debts), that medium to low levels characterized litigation over social transactions (primarily moral and social transgressions), and that litigation over the protection of property rights enjoyed the lowest levels of consensus. Offutt shows that the analysis can be extended in several ways. Comparison across colonial lines, particularly in the case of litigation directly implicating legal authority, affords a comparative measure of different colonial legal regimes' social stability. Stability can also be measured by examining variation in participation and adhesion to legal authority across different elements of the colonial population. The Middle Colony Dutch, for example, showed a propensity for involvement in litigation on subjects governed by high levels of adherence to norms, but their participation levels fell dramatically, amounting to a withdrawal from (English) legal authority. Swedish settlers' litigative involvements followed a similar track. Women's participation also declined over time and also differed in that women's litigative involvements were concentrated in the subject areas exhibiting medium to low norm adherence. Methodologically, the same analysis could be extended to many other groups. Substantively, Offutt's findings suggest that the period saw decided shifts in the behaviors considered appropriate for efficient resolution through litigation, accentuating the economic at the expense of the moral, a development that saw certain groups of actors disappear from the realm of legal participation altogether. One reason for this was the growing influence of English legal culture. By moving increasingly into an Anglocentric legal orbit, colonial mercantile and landowning elites were able to draw upon the authority of the metropolitan "core" to resolve their own disputes while pushing other social groups to the legal periphery. By the end of Offutt's period, court business concentrated on those closest to the center of colonial society. "It was no longer deemed necessary to negotiate with those on the periphery, nor to encourage their participation," but only to control them.

The third essay, by Richard Lyman Bushman, takes up the question of law's place in eighteenth-century society and economy from a distinctive angle. Using Orange County, North Carolina, as a site, the essay probes the deep and intimate involvement of technical legal processes and instruments in the quotidian rhythms of a rural economy. Although he replicates Offutt's concentration on norm adherence, Bushman, unlike Offutt, does not pursue the subject through a study of litigation and its outcomes. Rather, his goal is to recover the texture and sociocultural meaning of legal routines. He shows how law, whether as text, discourse, process, or authoritative institution, did not merely order economic life, in the sense of regulating its transactions, but actually called its constituent elements and concepts into being. Law in Bushman's analysis is literally a process of social construction, one that thereby creates a dense web of mutual dependencies among a population, its legal institutions, and those institutions' rules. To function successfully, law depends on the trust generated by the sharing of beliefs and values and, equally important, by the suspension—through procedure, rhetoric, ritual, and the elaboration of strategic fictions—of disbelief. Bushman probes the resilience of those conditions of success by examining Orange County's courts at a moment of extreme vulnerability, namely the North Carolina Regulator uprisings of the late 1760s. But, if the examination demonstrates that disbelief could assert itself with highly disruptive consequences, it also demonstrates that the assertion would likely be temporary.

The courts were agents of the propertied, and farmers as the privileged class of owners benefited from judicial authority. They could imagine no tenable existence without a judiciary to sustain them.

The final essay, A. G. Roeber's examination of charity law, reflects on the relationship between legal institutions and the conceptualization of social life on a broader canvas: that of state formation in the northern colonies. Roeber renders problematic what observers writing in a Lockean tradition may take to be self-evident, namely the identification of the task of legal regimes ("the state") as protection of private rights—such as the individual right to dispose of property as the holder thinks fit—and simultaneously the fulfillment of certain public responsibilities, such as oversight of the general welfare. First, while moderns may think of property as necessarily private and state institutions as public, this distinction was far less precise in the eighteenth century, when states might better be envisioned as fuzzy private-public amalgams and when, as Offutt's investigation has already indicated, ideological consensus over the meaning of property rights was not as developed as one might have supposed. Charitable giving, for example, created institutions that were quasi-public in role but quasi-private in operation and that sought privileged quasi-state embodiments as trusts and corporations. Charitable giving was hence appropriately subject to legal oversight, in the exercise of which courts might analyze the purpose of the giving and its legal embodiment in relation to their conceptions of what the ideological purposes of the law (and the state) were. Second, of increasing importance in that debate as the eighteenth century progressed, Roeber argues, was the question whether the law embraced Christian content and purposes, and if so whether on that account it should overrule individual intent in order to pursue instead a Christianized conception of the general welfare. With increasing frequency over the latter part of the eighteenth century and into the nineteenth, he shows, debates erupting over the identification of *salus populi* and the state's police role in realizing it revealed that profound and lasting tensions between religious purpose and liberal individualism, between a Christian republic and freedom to devise, were deeply embedded in the processes of American state formation.

Was There a Calvinist Type of Patriarchy?

New Haven Colony Reconsidered
in the Early Modern Context

CENTRAL THEME in the field of American legal history has been
the fate of English legal institutions once they were transplanted
to North American settings. Rather than engage directly with an
older literature that focused on the transmission of the common law to America, the essays in this collection approach the topic of early
American legal development with a broader set of analytical questions.
Characterizing the place or reign of English law among the many legalities of
early North America means asking about state and class formation, intercultural exchange and accommodation, and crystallizing ideologies of ra-
cialism and gender hierarchy.[1]

This essay addresses, in terms of place, only a small patch in the quilt of
North American legal cultures. In terms of time, it is concerned with the
earliest decades of English colonization. New Haven Colony lasted only
from 1639 until 1665, when it was absorbed into Connecticut, but, under the
leadership of its governor, Theophilus Eaton, and its principal pastor, John
Davenport, the colony earned the reputation as the New World jurisdiction
where a Puritan program of legal and moral reform was most thoroughly
implemented.[2] From a bird's-eye view of England and its colonies, New

My thanks go to Mark Valeri, Margaret Hunt, Richard D. Brown, John M. Murrin, and Lee
Palmer Wandell for helpful advice.

1. For an overview of the older literature, see Herbert Alan Johnson, "American Colo-
nial Legal History: A Historiographical Interpretation," in Alden T. Vaughn and George
Athan Billias, eds., *Perspectives on Early American History: Essays in Honor of Richard B.
Morris* (New York, 1973), 250–281.

2. Perry Miller called New Haven "the most exclusively and aggressively" Puritan colony, explaining that Massachusetts Bay Colony "contained too many other elements
besides Puritanism" to be so categorized (review of Isabel MacBeath Calder, *The New
Haven Colony*, in *New England Quarterly*, VIII [1935], 582). Calder declared: "More than
any other colony in New England, it represents the goal toward which the most orthodox
wing of the Puritan party was striving" (*The New Haven Colony* [New Haven, Conn.,
1934], vi). For elaborations that focus on law, see John M. Murrin, "Magistrates, Sinners,
and a Precarious Liberty: Trial by Jury in Seventeenth-Century New England," in David D.
Hall, John M. Murrin, and Thad W. Tate, eds., *Saints and Revolutionaries: Essays on Early
American History* (New York, 1984), 170–182; Cornelia Hughes Dayton, *Women before the
Bar: Gender, Law, and Society in Connecticut, 1639–1789* (Chapel Hill, N.C., 1995).

Haven, with its profile of rejecting juries, banning lawyers, offering nearly inquisitorial power to presiding magistrates, and systematically punishing immorality, appears an aberration in the longue durée of Anglo-American law, a fringe regime doomed to collapse into secular orthodoxy. But, viewed from other angles, early New Haven was not so odd.

As William Offutt's essay in this volume makes clear, in its utopian aspirations and in many of its approaches to the law, New Haven Colony joined company with other fledgling European outposts in the New World that were founded according to Reformed or Quaker principles.[3] Yet looking to Continental Europe provides an even more pertinent context for the legal orientation of the Puritan colony: New Haven Colony can legitimately be seen as one of many Calvinist legal regimes that took their inspiration from the moral governance John Calvin brought to mid-sixteenth-century Geneva.

Calvinism has loomed large, of course, in scholarly portraits of seventeenth-century New England. Calvin's theological principles, as interpreted by Puritan divines in England, laid the foundations for the distinctive structure of the New Englanders' "tribalistic" Congregational churches, their covenant theory, and their preparations for experiencing conversion, passing tests for church membership, and facing death.[4] Although historians acknowledge that Calvin's special emphasis on discipline was carried out in early New England churches, we rarely bring Calvin into our discussions of the enforcement of morals in the secular courts. I do so here in the interests of affirming the profoundly religious mindsets of many early colonial lawgivers and of reawakening legal scholars to the important parallels and links between Reformation Europe and New World legal frontiers.

Because my focus is on the consequences for women and gender relations that followed from the implementation of Calvinist principles in courtrooms in New Haven Colony and on the Continent, I am venturing into the scholarly debate on whether the Reformation enhanced the status of women. Yet, rather than posit overarching calculi of better-or-worse, we may find that a more rewarding way to address the intertwining of religious belief, legal culture, and gender relations in the early modern period is to identify different styles and strands of patriarchy operating in various parts of the West.[5]

3. William M. Offutt, Jr., "The Limits of Authority: Courts, Ethnicity, and Gender in the Middle Colonies, 1670–1710," below.

4. Perry Miller, *The New England Mind: The Seventeenth Century* (1939; rpt., Boston, 1954), esp. 92–97, 366–370; David D. Hall, *The Faithful Shepherd: A History of the New England Ministry in the Seventeenth Century* (Chapel Hill, N.C., 1972). On "Puritan tribalism," see Edmund S. Morgan, *The Puritan Family: Religion and Domestic Relations in Seventeenth-Century New England* (New York, 1966), chap. 7.

5. For summaries of the debate, see Jeffrey R. Watt, *The Making of Modern Marriage: Matrimonial Control and the Rise of Sentiment in Neuchâtel, 1550–1800* (Ithaca, N.Y., 1992),

It should be possible to map out a typology of patriarchal regimes corresponding to the different sorts of confessional societies found across the spectrum of Lutheranism, Calvinism, Catholicism, and radical sects that marked the post-Reformation European world. This essay delineates the distinctive elements of what we might call a Calvinist brand of patriarchy. It ends by offering a speculative framework for why Calvinist reform regimes, stamped as they were with a particular ideology of gender, were everywhere eclipsed.

In both Calvinist Geneva and Puritan New Haven, the defining experience of any resident's legal encounter was an intense, one-on-one conversation with a particular authority figure of renowned religious zeal, formidable persuasive powers, and international repute. John Calvin played this role in mid-sixteenth-century Geneva as the pastor (and highly trained lawyer) who sat at the head of the bench of cleric judges of the Consistory, the primary disciplining body for the city and surrounding rural parishes. In New Haven, one hundred years later, Theophilus Eaton was the awe-inspiring governor and chief magistrate before whom miscreants quaked. For both Reformed Geneva and Puritan New Haven, the identity and destiny of the city were bound up with the leadership skills and personal fate of the chosen leader. Moreover, both Calvin and Eaton were unusual in their times for their emphatic and effective insistence on regulating morals. And each man's dominance over law, politics, and residents' behavior lasted for about two decades—long enough to link each city's name to a lasting reputation for sobriety.[6]

It would be fascinating to know whether Theophilus Eaton modeled his New World magistracy on John Calvin. He and his brother had owned "eleven stout folios by Calvin," perhaps including the *Institutes of the Christian Religion,* which were evidently given to New Haven to serve as a town library on Eaton's death. Perhaps as a genteel Londoner moving in Puritan circles or as a merchant traveling in northern Europe in the 1610s and 1620s Eaton had heard stories about Calvin's role as morals enforcer when disci-

---

11–14; Sherrin Marshall, ed., *Women in Reformation and Counter-Reformation Europe: Public and Private Worlds* (Bloomington, Ind., 1989), 1–7.

6. The Consistory bench also consisted of annually elected lay elders. See Robert M. Kingdon, "The Control of Morals in Calvin's Geneva," in Lawrence P. Buck and Jonathan W. Zophy, eds., *The Social History of the Reformation* (Columbus, Ohio, 1972), 7. On Calvin's superior legal expertise and skills on the bench, see Kingdon, *Adultery and Divorce in Calvin's Geneva* (Cambridge, Mass., 1995), 17. Calvin dominated the Consistory from its establishment in 1542 to his death in 1564. Eaton acted as governor and presiding magistrate of New Haven from the first court session in October 1639 until his death in 1658.

pline was at its peak of effectiveness in Geneva during the 1550s and 1560s.[7] By persuading the city government in 1541 to create a consistory as a standing committee, Calvin was determined to change the face of Geneva from a city in which prostitution, premarital sex, and bitter domestic quarrels went unchecked to a zone in which the residents walked in godly ways. Unless he was sick or traveling, Calvin invariably was present at Consistory sessions and acted as spokesman for the other members.[8] The disciplining body worked by first visiting an evildoer privately in an attempt to secure penitence and a promise of reform. When this was not effective, the man or woman was called before the Consistory and "subjected to vehement tongue-lashings, at which Calvin was particularly adept." Thus, Calvin and his fellow morals enforcers relied principally on the oral reprimand—ritualized scoldings—to remind sinners that God and his earthly agents were watching them. Undoubtedly, the words of the famous French minister in chastizing transgressors circulated around the town and villages so that the great man's oral retributions grew into elaborated legends. But when miscreants refused to show penitence, the Genevan Consistory, unlike similar courts in other jurisdictions, had the power to punish sinners with temporary excommunication (a term typically lasting under one year). By the time of Calvin's death, the Consistory was handing out an average of six excommunications per week.[9]

7. Samuel Eliot Morison, *The Intellectual Life of Colonial New England* (Ithaca, N.Y., 1960), 145–146; Franklin Bowditch Dexter, *A Selection from the Miscellaneous Historical Papers of Fifty Years* (New Haven, Conn., 1918), 223–234.
  The Marian exiles, who returned home from Geneva in 1559, were one obvious source for such stories. Furthermore, editions of Calvin's works translated into English outnumbered translations in all other European languages put together; this figure testifies to the profound impact of Calvin on reformers in the Elizabethan church (Francis Higman, "Calvin's Works in Translation," in Andrew Pettegree, Alastair Duke, and Gillian Lewis, eds., *Calvinism in Europe, 1540–1620* [Cambridge, 1994], 87–99). For an early New England probate inventory that listed Calvin's *Institutes,* see George Francis Dow, ed., *Records and Files of the Quarterly Courts of Essex County, Massachusetts,* I (Salem, Mass., 1911), 413.
  8. Calvin consolidated his control over discipline in a 1555 showdown with secular magistrates (Kingdon, "Control of Morals," in Buck and Zophy, eds., *Social History of the Reformation,* 11–12; William G. Naphy, *Calvin and the Consolidation of the Genevan Reformation* [New York, 1994], 167–235). On lax morals enforcement in Geneva prior to 1542, see Kingdon, "Control of Morals," in Buck and Zophy, eds., *Social History of the Reformation,* 4–6. On Calvin's attendance, see E. William Monter, "The Consistory of Geneva, 1559–1569," *Bibliothèque d'humanisme et renaissance,* XXXVIII (1976), 470; Kingdon, "Calvin and the Establishment of Consistory Discipline in Geneva: The Institution and the Men Who Directed It," *Nederlands Archief voor Kerkgeshiedenis/Dutch Review of Church History* (hereafter cited as *NAKG/DRCH*), LXX (1990), 163, 166. Kingdon notes that Calvin also shaped the decrees of the institution by exercising practical veto power over the lay elders selected for the Consistory (166–167).
  9. Kingdon, "Control of Morals," in Buck and Zophy, eds., *Social History of the Reformation,* 10; Monter, "Consistory of Geneva," *Bibliothèque d'humanisme et renaissance,* XXXVIII (1976), 471, 476, 484; Kingdon, *Adultery and Divorce,* 18. On Calvin's sermons, see

Theophilus Eaton, in contrast to Calvin, was a strictly secular magistrate. His bench meted out oral admonitions, fines, whippings, and the occasional, terrifying sentence of execution by public hanging, but not religious sanctions. However much the governor might have wrapped himself in the mantle of a zealous reformer in the Calvinist tradition, he was not an ordained minister and was unable to instill fear in the hearts of New Haven's sinners from both the bench and the pulpit as Calvin could. Eaton exercised moral suasion because of his reputation as a learned and pious pillar of the gathered church and because of his close association with New Haven's minister, John Davenport, who was in effect cofounder of the tiny colony with Eaton.

As governor, Eaton could not only shape the laws passed by the General Court, but he also could act as *"the Terror of evildoers"* at two stages in the criminal justice process. When a person was suspected of a crime, he or she was first summoned before Eaton to be grilled in a preliminary examination. Not only was the setting intimidating—Eaton's "stately and costly" house was bedecked with luxurious furnishings and totems of learning and worldliness—but the governor, through his demeanor, countenance, and voice, projected an "ungainsayable *Authority*," according to Cotton Mather. At the formal court session, which took place in the meetinghouse, the accused individual faced Eaton again; this time the governor was sitting at the head of a bench of magistrates and town deputies. Here, all decrees were handed down by the bench; the colony had dispensed with juries because they were seen as unscriptural and impractical. Thus, in its domination by one figure, in its essentially inquisitorial approach, in its primary focus on moral breaches, and in its presumption that pious authority figures could discern the truth and cajole confessions from sinners, the New Haven Colony judicial system was quite similar to the Genevan Consistory.[10]

Naphy, *Calvin and the Genevan Reformation*, 153–162. As Monter puts it, the Consistory, though "not technically a tribunal," came to act like a court in the realm of immorality ("Women in Calvinist Geneva [1550–1800]," *Signs*, VI [1980–1981], 190). It was effectively the court of record convoking transgressors for misdeeds like Sabbathbreaking, illicit sex, breach of the marriage covenant, and domestic or neighborly quarreling, while it turned over to the secular courts incorrigible criminals and persons accused of the most serious crimes (Kingdon, "Control of Morals," in Buck and Zophy, eds., *Social History of the Reformation,* 10). On the Consistory's unusual power of excommunication and the controversy it engendered, see Kingdon, "Control of Morals," in Buck and Zophy, eds., *Social History of the Reformation,* 11; Monter, "Consistory of Geneva," *Bibliothèque d'humanisme et renaissance,* XXXVIII (1976), 477; Naphy, *Calvin and the Genevan Reformation,* esp. 185.

10. Cotton Mather, *Magnalia Christi Americana: Books I and II,* ed. Kenneth B. Murdock (Cambridge, Mass., 1977), 257; Samuel Maverick, "A Briefe Discription of New England and the Severall Townes Therein, Together with the Present Government Thereof," Massachusetts Historical Society, *Proceedings,* 2d Ser., I (1884–1885), 245; Elizabeth Tucker Van Beek, "Piety and Profit: English Puritans and the Shaping of a Godly Marketplace in the

In the quest for legitimacy, Eaton in New Haven was at an advantage: he was founding a colony and able to attract as settlers Puritan families who shared his vision of a godly community. Calvin, as a Frenchman who made a rocky start in Geneva in the late 1530s, faced considerable political resistance until he squelched his political foes in 1555 and thereby gained much stronger support for extensive moral disciplining.[11] John Knox, visiting Geneva in 1556, claimed that, as a result of Calvin's influence and the Consistory's oversight of morals, the behavior of Genevans had changed dramatically. Knox called the city "the maist perfyt schoole of Chryst that ever was . . . since the dayis of the Apostillis" and announced that in no other place had he seen "manners and religion so sincerely reformed." Given the number of morals infractions that continued to come before the Consistory, Knox's assessment was undoubtedly too optimistic. But scholars of the Reformation agree that Calvin, through the power of his intellect, the messages of his sermons and catechism lessons, and the purging of his political enemies, succeeded in persuading Genevans to change their behavior—to internalize self-discipline and to manifest outwardly their sobriety. A final measure of Calvin's success can be seen in the wide imitation of the institution of the Consistory by jurisdictions on the Continent that embraced Calvinism officially.[12]

New Haven Colony" (Ph.D. diss., University of Virginia, 1993), 449–459. The grandeur of Eaton's mansion and several others in early New Haven was a rarity in North America at that time. On New Haven Colony's judicial procedures, see Gail Sussman Marcus, " 'Due Execution of the Generall Rules of Righteousnesse': Criminal Procedure in New Haven Town and Colony, 1638–1658," in Hall, Murrin, and Tate, eds., Saints and Revolutionaries, 99–137. On the inquisitorial process and truthtelling, see Kingdon, Adultery and Divorce, 22–23.

11. Naphy, Calvin and the Genevan Reformation, documents how Calvin's attempt at dominance in Geneva was enmeshed in factional politics and continually contested by the city's ruling classes and bourgeoisie who resented the growing influence of French religious refugees. Even after Calvin emerged "triumphant" after the 1555 elections, the petit conseil, one of the governing bodies in Geneva, often gave out much lighter sentences to criminal defendants than the pastors would have advocated (see esp. chap. 7).

12. John Knox to Mrs. Locke, Dec. 9, 1665, in David Laing, ed., The Works of John Knox, IV (Edinburgh, 1855), 240. On Calvin's role in inducing changed behavior, see Naphy, Calvin and the Genevan Reformation, 153, 155, 228–230; Kingdon, "Calvin and the Establishment of Consistory Discipline," NAKG/DRCH, LXX (1990), 167–168. According to Kingdon, the effect was long-lasting: well into the seventeenth century, the number of out-of-wedlock births in Geneva remained very low (167).

On Calvinist jurisdictions in Europe, see Kingdon, "Calvin and the Establishment of Consistory Discipline," NAKG/DRCH, LXX (1990), 161; Watt, The Making of Modern Marriage, 49–54. Outside of Switzerland, imitations of Calvin's Consistory took different names: classis, synod, presbytery, or session, for instance. On international Calvinism in general, and for a record of changed moral behavior in a Calvinist Scottish community, see Alastair Duke, "Perspectives on International Calvinism," in Pettegree, Duke, and Lewis, eds., Calvinism in Europe, 1–20, esp. 15.

The experiment in godly living and governing that was New Haven Colony can be seen as a last bright flame in the Protestant reform tradition inspired by Calvin. The success of Eaton and Davenport's regime can be gauged by the extraordinary discipline most New Haveners exercised over their own temptations and the extent to which they accepted the strictures of their leaders. Eaton's political and moral strength seem never to have waned: the male electorate persisted in choosing him as governor annually until his death, and miscreants haled into court rarely resisted his upbraidings, even in the wake of the scandal of his wife's 1645 excommunication for heresy.[13] Not only did New Haven implement a "purer Puritanism" than any other Puritan New England colony, but the colony's inhabitants in the 1640s and 1650s generated a "phenomenally" low rate of violence, acrimony, and sexual misconduct. Of course, New Haven Colony was a dramatically smaller jurisdiction than the city of Geneva: it was made up of at most 2,500 European settlers, compared to about 20,000 in Geneva at Calvin's death. Small population along with the settlers' shared ideological values helps explain why New Haveners did not try to evade the magistrates' efforts to root out sin: almost no defendants or witnesses fled when summoned to court, and very few suspected criminals had to be jailed before trial. The most dramatic hallmark of Eaton's skills in getting his people to repent their sins and cleanse the colony of guilt was the strikingly high confession rate: 85 percent of defendants admitted their guilt before conviction. Despite the presence of a cluster of rowdy, non-Puritan ironworkers on the outskirts of town, along with handfuls of disobedient servants or restless, libidinous, male youths and a clutch of outspoken religious dissenters who were banished or chose exile, settlers in the tiny New Haven Colony communities showed a remarkable degree of consensus about their God-given mission to lead morally upright lives.[14]

13. Eaton presided over almost every pretrial examination and court session, 1639–1658. For treatments of the Anne Eaton case, see Dayton, "Excommunicating the Governor's Wife: Religious Dissent in the Puritan Colonies before the Era of Rights Consciousness," in John McLaren and Harold Coward, eds., *Religious Conscience, the State, and the Law in Anglo-American History: Historical Contexts and Contemporary Significance* (Albany, N.Y., 1999), 29–45; Mary Beth Norton, *Founding Mothers and Fathers: Gendered Power and the Forming of American Society* (New York, 1996), 165–180.

14. Mark Valeri, "Religion, Discipline, and the Economy in Calvin's Geneva," *Sixteenth Century Journal*, XXVIII (1997), 127; Marcus, "'Due Execution of the Rules of Righteousnesse,'" Murrin, "Magistrates, Sinners, and a Precarious Liberty," in Hall, Murrin, and Tate, eds., *Saints and Revolutionaries*, 104–105, 108, 122, 132–133, 136, 175–176. On the efficacy of summonses, compare New Haven with Geneva (Kingdon, "Calvin and the Establishment of Consistory Discipline," *NAKG/DRCH*, LXX [1990], 163).

On the "dysfunctional family" who worked at the iron mines, see Norton, *Founding Mothers*, 27–38. For 1646 trials against dissenters and for recurring reprimands of certain servants and youths, see Charles J. Hoadly, ed., *Records of the Colony and Plantation of New*

Calvinist Geneva's reputation as a stricter enforcer of morals than Lutheran or Catholic jurisdictions stemmed in large part from the authorities'
approach to punishing the two sexes. The occasional disgruntled comment
of a convicted man confirms what is revealed by statistical analysis of the
records: rigor in prosecuting sexual misconduct was achieved because men
were pursued as assiduously as women. Parity in punishing men and women
for fornication and adultery not only was stipulated in the laws but was also
followed in sentencing by both the Consistory and the secular courts. In
short, what was unusual about this Calvinist regime was not just its refusal
to turn a blind eye to immorality but also its rejection of the double standard. When a peasant called Geneva's ministers "the cruellest in the world,"
he was underscoring their surprising betrayal of their own sex. Genevan
women might not have agreed with another rural inhabitant who, perhaps
satirically, claimed that the Consistory had established on earth a "paradis
des femmes," but many confessors to fornication or adultery might have
appreciated the fact that they stood before the bench and took their punishment of a few days in prison on bread and water alongside their male
lovers.[15]

In areas beyond illicit sex, Genevan justice also scrutinized and penalized
men's irregular behavior. Scores of men (and more men than women) were
reprimanded and excommunicated for persistently quarreling with their
spouses; when wife-beating was proven, husbands could be sent to jail and
fined. Like jurisdictions across Western Europe, Geneva prosecuted more
women as witches than men; however, it "had an unusually low conviction
rate" for witchcraft, and "it punished men . . . relatively more severely than
women." In the seventeenth century, women were more likely to be executed
for another sex-linked crime, infanticide, than witchcraft, but we can think
of these sex-based punishments as being offset by the slightly higher number
of men put to death for sodomy.[16]

The Genevan regime did not altogether eradicate double standards that

Haven from 1638 to 1649 . . . (Hartford, Conn., 1857) (hereafter NHCR, I), 38, 77–78, 81,
242–257, 435; Hoadly, ed., Records of the Colony or Jurisdiction of New Haven, from May,
1653, to the Union . . . (Hartford, Conn., 1858) (hereafter NHCR, II), 138; Franklin Bowditch
Dexter, ed., Ancient Town Records (New Haven, Conn., 1917–1919), I, New Haven Town
Records, 1649–1684 (hereafter NHTR), 451, 461, 499.

15. R. Po-Chia Hsia, Social Discipline in the Reformation: Central Europe, 1550–1750 (New
York, 1989), 124–125; Kingdon, "Calvin and the Establishment of Consistory Discipline,"
NAKG/DRCH, LXX (1990), 160; Monter, "Women in Calvinist Geneva," Signs, VI (1980–
1981), 190–193; Jane Dempsey Douglass, Women, Freedom, and Calvin (Philadelphia,
1985), 105. Naphy points out that men came under more scrutiny from the Consistory
from 1546 on (Calvin and the Genevan Reformation, 109, 111).

16. Monter, "Women in Calvinist Geneva," Signs, VI (1980–1981), 196–197. On the
punishment of wifebeaters by the Neuchâtel consistory, see Watt, The Making of Modern
Marriage, 148–152.

brought harsher judgments to women. Widows petitioning to remarry, for example, were often denied if their desired spouse was significantly younger, but similar requests by widowers were granted. In the Consistory's earliest years, when concern over religious practice and weeding out Catholic rituals was highest, more women than men were cross-examined and reprimanded on grounds of suspected heterodoxy. Most telling, perhaps, of the Protestant commitment to uphold gender hierarchy was Calvin's refusal to allow divorce on cruelty grounds. Protestant reformers were willing to desacralize marriage and to reward abandoned or jilted wives with the right to remarry, but they continued to believe that wives were to some degree guilty in violent marital disputes and that magisterial reprimands were sufficient to restrain an intemperate family patriarch.[17] Outside the legal sphere, Calvin and his allies did little to increase the economic and educational opportunities for Genevan women. In his sermons, Calvin avoided "traditional misogynistic themes" while stressing Christians' obligations to uphold God's "order"—that women play a supportive but clearly subordinate role to men. Thus, left largely unscathed in Calvin's Geneva were the structural and ideological props of a patriarchal society that made women's fates dependent on marriage and men.[18]

By holding men accountable for their immoral and ungodly acts, Calvin had not subverted patriarchy, but he had succeeded, for a few decades in Geneva, in dulling some of its harsher legal consequences for women. After 1590, the double standard began once again to infiltrate Geneva's secular courts and affect how they handled adultery cases. Male agitation over the equal application of the newly harsh adultery laws to the sexes led to a climate in which cases were not pursued or women were banished while their male partners were simply fined. Yet into the 1700s the Consistory persisted in disciplining people for premarital sex and tracking down fathers of children born out of wedlock. The final showdown between irate male

17. Monter, "Women in Calvinist Geneva," *Signs*, VI (1980–1981), 193; Jeffrey R. Watt, "Women and the Consistory in Calvin's Geneva," *Sixteenth Century Journal*, XXIV (1993), 429–435. More frequent persecution of women might have reflected, not simply a bias among judges and accusers, but a behavioral distinction, for possibly more women than men continued to be attracted to Catholic rituals. For a review of Reformed jurisdictions reluctant to grant divorces purely on cruelty until the eighteenth century, see Watt, *The Making of Modern Marriage*, 157–159, 228–230. On the handling of quarreling spouses, see Watt, "Women and the Consistory," *Sixteenth Century Journal*, XXIV (1993), 436–437.

18. Monter, "Women in Calvinist Geneva," *Signs*, VI (1980–1981), 199–205; John H. Bratt, "The Role and Status of Women in the Writings of John Calvin," Charmarie Jenkins Blaisdell, "Response to Bratt," in Peter De Klerk, ed., *Renaissance, Reformation, Resurgence: Papers and Responses Presented at the Colloquium on Calvin and Calvin Studies . . .* (Grand Rapids, Mich., 1976), 9, 21. See also Douglass, *Women, Freedom, and Calvin*, esp. 10, 46–51, 107; Mary Potter, "Gender Equality and Gender Hierarchy in Calvin's Theology," *Signs*, XI (1985–1986), 25–39.

citizens and righteous clerics came in the 1760s, when Voltaire championed
the cause of a fop sentenced to public genuflection in a fornication-paternity
case. With the ministers unable any longer to insist on their way, the magistrates gave in to public pressure and abolished public humiliation as a
punishment for men's extramarital escapades.[19]

As colonial historians of British America attempting to gauge the impact
of the Reformed principles on women's encounters with the law, we can
recognize that, in the case of New Haven Colony, two reformist traditions
were at work. One was inspired by Calvinist religious fervor. In ferreting out
all forms of immorality, pursuing a single standard for women and men,
making provision for full divorce, fashioning the capital code on Mosaic law,
and giving greatest priority to truthtelling and confession, Governor Eaton
and his fellow lawmakers followed the path forged so forcefully by Calvin.
The second strain of reform present in New Haven was inspired by Puritans'
disgust with the contortions and costs of the English legal system. When
New Haven leaders decided to simplify pleading, abolish writs and lawyers,
or permit wives to testify in their husbands' civil disputes, they were implementing a program of legal reform advocated (largely in vain) in England by
a variety of commentators, some from Dissenting circles, some not.[20]

The colony's leaders believed that disputants who could not settle their
differences privately or before arbitrators should be able to argue their case
face-to-face in court, using everyday language, introducing any material
they feel relevant, and calling any witness who can speak to the issues. The
simplification of legal rules in Eaton's colony had the general effect of increasing access to the courts by women and other groups who would have
found the English common-law courts intimidating and too costly. In its
gendered dimension, this was an unintended consequence, since the Puritan
scheme for legal reform contained no explicit call for improving women's
legal status. The informality of pleading, the banning of lawyers, and the
equitable remedies favored by judges, however, encouraged women and all

19. Monter, "Women in Calvinist Geneva," *Signs,* VI (1980–1981), 192–193. Voltaire's
resistance to the Consistory in the case of the fop Robert Covelle took the form of ordering
his own valet to introduce Covelle as "M. le Fornicateur" (193 n. 15).

20. G. B. Warden, "Law Reform in England and New England, 1620 to 1660," *William
and Mary Quarterly,* 3d Ser., XXXV (1978), 668–690. To the eyes of sixteenth-century
jurists, procedures in Reformed Geneva, both in the Consistory and in the secular courts,
must have departed significantly from previous practices. Kingdon concludes that the
Consistory drew on a mixture of sources so that its law consisted of "rough applications of
principles drawn from Scripture, more survivals of Catholic canon law than the consistory members would admit, some survivals of Roman civil law, and principles of custom
law drawn . . . from France" and Geneva ("Calvin and the Establishment of Consistory
Discipline," *NAKG/DRCH,* LXX [1990], 165). The job of teasing out what aspects of the
Consistory's practices were departures from canon law I leave to Reformation specialists.

those not learned in the law to bring complaints to court without fearing that their mistakes and ignorance would lead to failure and expense.[21]

This climate for disputation had two effects for New Haven women. First, women were clearly present as direct parties to debt and other private law disputes more often than they would be in later decades when common-law guidelines were followed more rigidly. Quantification of this pattern is next to impossible, since civil cases were recorded haphazardly and vaguely in this era. My rough estimate is that women must have participated in 20–30 percent of civil disputes in the years 1639–1665. This means that many individual New Haven women grew accustomed to being at court sessions and that, to male observers, women were familiar figures in court. Compare the New Haven Colony period to the 1720s, when legal procedures became more technical and when economic and demographic change made civil litigation more formal and routinized: by then, women's participation had dropped to 10 percent. Second, in the interest of getting at the truth of a dispute by including all pertinent testimony, the colony's judges ignored the common-law rule prohibiting spouses from testifying for one another. It was possible in New Haven's earliest courts for male litigants to ask their wives to recall for the court critical conversations and actions that had originated a debt or led to an impasse over repayment. On some occasions, women verified the incidents recollected by their spouses; at other times, they spoke of sales, purchases, or agreements they had made on their own.[22]

Thus, in the earliest decades of settlement, women's economic roles were *not* invisible but rather were acknowledged publicly in the discourse that filled the courtroom and made its way into official records. Because of the informality dictated by Puritan legal tenets, the pre-1666 records convey the realities of economic life for early New England women and men much more clearly than records of any later period. New Haven was not alone in this. Richard B. Morris notes that several seventeenth-century colonial juris-dictions influenced by Protestant reform ideology flouted the common-law rule incapacitating spouses' testimony. Furthermore, in its inclusion and acknowledgment of married women's economic activities, New Haven's le-gal system was not unlike that of New Netherland, where women (including wives) participated in 26 percent of the 195 debt cases recorded for 1663.

21. Dayton, *Women before the Bar,* 27–31.
22. Ibid., 84. On the common-law prohibition, see William Blackstone, *Commentaries on the Laws of England* (1765–1769; rpt., Chicago, 1979), I, 443; and William Hawkins, *A Treatise of the Pleas of the Crown . . .* , 2d ed., 2 vols. (1724–1726; rpt., New York, 1972), II, 431. For examples of wives testifying in suits involving a wide range of economic trans-actions, see Dexter, ed., *NHTR,* I, 29, 157, 162, 262–263, 305; Hoadly, ed., *NHCR,* I, 330, 416–417, II, 276–284, 382, 396.

Under the Dutch regime in New York, access for women was broad, not so much because of simplified rules but because of the civil law's adherence to community property principles and traditions of spouses' collaborating in trade or leading independent business lives. Just how widespread this higher profile for women in civil disputes was in seventeenth-century British America, and just what ideological and structural factors determined it, are questions that need attention by legal historians.[23]

In the area of regulating marriage, New Haven Colony adopted many of the approaches followed by Calvin's Consistory. Puritans rejected separations from bed and board as "popish invention[s]" contrary to nature; they believed that only full divorce with permission to remarry ought to be granted. The divorce law, cast in gender-neutral language, set forth limited grounds: adultery, desertion, and impotence. Eager to reconcile quarreling couples, the magistrates were ready to punish men who scorned community standards by abusing their wives, but divorces on cruelty grounds were not even considered. Despite their more open embrace of divorce relative to Catholic and Anglican canon law, both the Geneva and New Haven jurisdictions heard very few divorce petitions. Perhaps the need for divorce was dampened in these populations because Reformed ideology inspired spouses to turn away from behaviors that broke up marriages; or perhaps potential petitioners were hindered by the unfamiliarity or stigma of the process. During New Haven Colony's twenty-six-year existence, only two residents (both women) took advantage of the law. However, the spirit and letter of the policy lived on, offering to eighteenth-century Connecticut women a remedy that wives in other colonies could rarely obtain.[24]

Indeed, Puritan approaches to divorce are best examined in the decades from 1665 to 1710 in Connecticut, the jurisdiction that replaced New Haven. It was then that the first significant number of petitions was considered. In this period, Connecticut magistrates, in the name of equity and morality, often ruled against the grain of the English common-law tradition that gave nearly absolute rights to husbands and fathers. In several property distributions and one custody award that accompanied divorces granted to women, the judges showed themselves willing to abrogate customary male rights—

23. David E. Narrett, *Inheritance and Family Life in Colonial New York City* (Ithaca, N.Y., 1992), 48–49; William M. Offutt, Jr., *Of "Good Laws" and "Good Men": Law and Society in the Delaware Valley, 1680–1710* (Urbana, Ill., 1995); Deborah A. Rosen, *Courts and Commerce: Gender, Law, and the Market Economy in Colonial New York* (Columbus, Ohio, 1997).

24. For the 1656 New Haven Colony divorce law, see John D. Cushing, ed., *The Earliest Laws of the New Haven and Connecticut Colonies, 1639–1673* (Wilmington, Del., 1977), 28. On divorce in sixteenth-century Geneva, see Monter, "Consistory of Geneva," *Bibliothèque d'humanisme et renaissance*, XXXVIII (1976), 473–474; and the case studies in Kingdon, *Adultery and Divorce*.

custody of all children, two-thirds of the marital property—when a husband's behavior had been particularly immoral and aggressive. Moreover, when men demanded divorces after their wives had left their households in protest of mistreatment, judges manifested great reluctance to proclaim the woman the guilty party and leave her bereft of property and access to her children. Instead, they tried to mediate by, first, accepting testimony that the woman had sought shelter with neighbors or family only after severe provocation or being "turned out" and, second, nudging fuming husbands to reform their tempestuous behavior and effect a reconciliation. Thus, rather than rule reflexively in favor of male demands, the seventeenth-century magistrates listened carefully to aggrieved wives' stories and brought to their decrees a skepticism regarding husbands' claims to righteousness—a skepticism informed by the Puritan emphasis on human depravity. In the next century, the meaning that judges assigned to a wife's act of estrangement changed radically, and their shift to scrutinizing and punishing "deserting" wives marked a judicial commitment to making husbands' rights more absolute.[25]

In the criminal sphere, New Haven Colony judges strove to implement a single standard. They were motivated by a strongly held belief that godly behavior should be the measure for *all* inhabitants, male or female, wealthy or servant. Confronted by handfuls of youths charged with fornication before marriage, Eaton and his peers succeeded in persuading both men and women to confess. Even though the magistrates were emphatic about applying punishments (whippings and, later, fines) in an evenhanded manner, in practice they more often than not sanctioned the man's receiving a harsher sentence. Slander cases provide a further measure of the seriousness with which the authorities viewed male sexual misbehavior. Sexual slander constituted the same proportion of men's suits and women's suits in this period, and men who had been falsely charged with sexual impropriety found their slanderers soundly rebuked in court. The Puritan practice relative to premarital sex—a low rate of premarital pregnancy, miscreants willingly confessing, and equal punishments for men and women—persisted in New Haven until 1690. Then, in a major cultural shift, men began to evade charges or plead not guilty, and judges, less inspired by Puritan principles and more attuned to a growing English emphasis on stricter rules of evidence regarding paternity, began to countenance the emergence of a double standard.[26]

25. For wife-desertion cases and cases in which magistrates granted an innocent wife more than one-third of the marital property, or prohibited a divorced father from taking custody of children, see Dayton, *Women before the Bar,* 121–130.
26. For a fuller explication of the New Haven Colony cases involving fornication and lascivious carriage and the shift at the end of the 1600s, see ibid., 173–207, 293–294.

The New Haven magistrates' readiness to scrutinize men's behavior was most dramatically apparent when women raised charges of rape or sexual harassment. Instead of adopting the skepticism that English legal culture harbored toward women who brought rape charges, Theophilus Eaton invariably relied on a key biblical passage to explain his predisposition to believe a woman's word. Deuteronomy 22, he explained, showed that, in "the case of a rape, . . . there is no witnes onely the testimoney of the maid and the effects found upon her; the damsell cryed and there was none to save her: then none but herselfe to testifye, yet that was accepted." Ready to believe that "a young girle . . . [would not] bee so impudent as to charge such a carriage upon a young man when it was not so," Eaton also depended on the broad, probing judicial interrogations so central to his juryless system to expose when an accuser was dissembling or hiding her own complicity. In sexual assault cases, the magistrates focused on the various accounts of the incident itself, not on the previous character or truthtelling habits of the parties. That a young servant girl, Susan Clarke, "had been taken . . . in some untruthes" on other matters did "not prove that she tells untruth" when charging a fellow servant, Ellis Mew, with attempted rape. Conversely, just because Mew had not been caught in falsehoods beforehand, he could very well be, like the biblical figure Gehazi, covering his sin on this occasion.[27]

Before 1700, the New Haven authorities followed the double-headed, reformist script of depending on women's stories to seek the truth and vigorously enforcing moral codes for all. In this period, when almost all sexual assault cases that came to the courts involved attempted violations of women who knew their assailants, the conviction rate came close to 100 percent. Puritan magistrates emphatically articulated their design to "make punishment exemplary," first, for men who carried on with "filthynes and boldnes" and, second, in more muted fashion, for women who had concealed such crimes or (in harassment cases) had encouraged the dalliance in any way.[28] Race rather than gender or class moved the magistrates to initiate a two-tier system: in the handful of cases in which youthful, white women charged an Indian or African man with fornication, the bench treated the incidents as rape by severely punishing the "wicked" defendants and refraining from punishing the young women. After 1700, judges followed another sort of script. Their growing reliance on English legal treatises and more formal evidentiary standards meant that women's charges were treated much more skeptically, especially when they accused native white men. The bias of the

27. Dexter, ed., NHTR, I, 152, 182.
28. Ibid., 32. For similar emphatic statements from the bench, see ibid., 183; Rex v Arthur Teague (August 1667), New Haven County Court Records, book I, State Archives, Connecticut State Library, Hartford (hereafter CSL), 12; Records of the Colony of New Haven, orig. MS, IB, CSL, 331.

system toward associating nonwhites and outsiders with punishable, coercive sex grew even stronger.[29]

It would not be credible to argue that in either Eaton's New Haven or Calvin's Geneva patriarchy was erased by the impulses of moral and legal reform. Calvinists supported evenhandedness in the treatment of the sexes only to the extent to which it encouraged more godliness in the general population and made patriarchs themselves more godly by squelching male licentiousness and husbandly tyranny. To Calvinist groups, following in the footsteps of the apostles dictated no alteration in the essential props of Western patriarchy: the institution of marriage in which women were expected to defer to men's proper governance, a polity in which men represented women and children to the state, an economic structure that afforded women few avenues to independent livelihoods, and a cultural belief in women's intellectual and emotional inferiority. In New Haven Colony, while Eaton and Davenport might have respected women's capacity for godliness and acknowledged their essential economic roles in a frontier setting, they had no interest in subverting the inherited, hierarchical gender system. Their rejection of the double standard in fornication cases—and their abhorrence of bawdy and satirical jesting that often targeted women—flowed, not from a conviction that women were oppressed, but from other strong intolerances, including revulsion at seeing any sinner go unpunished and hearing the sanctity of marriage impugned.

When it came to adultery or witchcraft, colony leaders were prepared to believe the worst of women. Choosing a definition of adultery that would remain on the books in Connecticut for two centuries, New Haven Colony lawmakers followed the narrow Old Testament concept that adultery was an act committed with a married woman. Thus, married men who had affairs with single women were exempted from adultery's penalties. Nor were New Haven's magistrates more immune than their counterparts in Massachusetts Bay from the implicit belief that women were more prone than men to the most damning sin of all—renouncing God in order to serve Satan. Like Geneva under Calvin, New Haven Colony experienced a significantly lower rate of witchcraft accusations than neighboring jurisdictions, but the identification between witches and women was still very strong. Moreover, the colony's most prominent leaders staked out clear positions condemning dissident

29. *Rex v Margaret Trowbridge* and *Rex v Mary Butler* (November 1691), New Haven County Court Records, book I, CSL, 194; *Rex v Cush* (November 1692), New Haven County Court Records, book I, CSL, 202. For a fuller discussion of sexual harassment and sexual assault cases, see Dayton, *Women before the Bar,* 177–180, 234–243. From 1666 to the end of the eighteenth century in Connecticut, rape was a capital crime. But, in the seventeenth century, thirteen of fifteen defendants were charged with a lesser crime such as attempted rape and punished with severe whippings. For the increased bias after 1700, see Dayton, *Women before the Bar,* 243–274.

women. Davenport, while in Boston in 1637, had supported the proceedings against Anne Hutchinson. And Eaton complied with the 1645 excommunication of his wife, Anne Yale Eaton, for her unorthodox opinions. Through these postures and others, they linked themselves to centuries-old European ideas about the inferiority and necessary submission of the female sex.[30]

The juxtaposition of New Haven Colony, the most Calvinist legal regime in the New World, with mid-sixteenth-century Geneva, the "mother and . . . model" for almost all other Calvinist communities in Europe, dovetails with the long-running debate on the Reformation's impact on women. Historians of early modern Europe who write on this topic generally focus on certain important areas—changing lay and ministerial views of celibacy and marriage, the closing off of convents and the worship of female saints for Protestant women, and the extent of women's preaching and publishing.[31] The spheres of legal practice and ecclesiastical discipline have not been brought to the fore as much as other topics in part because systematic studies of Consistory records have only recently got underway. My aim in this essay has been to synthesize the existing scholarship on how Calvinist discipline was actually enforced, in the hope of integrating law into our discussions of the varieties of patriarchy that existed in the early modern West.[32]

By highlighting the many similarities between Calvin's Geneva and The-

30. Carol F. Karlsen, *The Devil in the Shape of a Woman: Witchcraft in Colonial New England* (New York, 1987). Four witchcraft cases were launched against one married couple and two individual women during New Haven Colony's existence. On female dissenters, see Calder, *New Haven Colony,* 36; Murrin, "Magistrates, Sinners, and a Precarious Liberty," in Hall, Murrin, and Tate, eds., *Saints and Revolutionaries,* 172. For telling comments by Calvin on women who improperly assumed public positions as prophets or teachers, see Bratt, "Role and Status of Women," in De Klerk, ed., *Renaissance, Reformation, Resurgence,* 4–6.

31. Kingdon, "Calvin and the Establishment of Consistory Discipline," *NAKG/DRCH,* LXX (1990), 169; Merry E. Wiesner, *Women and Gender in Early Modern Europe* (Cambridge, 1993), 179–217; Miriam U. Chrisman, "Women and the Reformation in Strasbourg, 1490–1530," *Archiv für Reformationgeschichte,* LXIII (1972), 143–168; Natalie Zemon Davis, "City Women and Religious Change," in Davis, *Society and Culture in Early Modern France: Eight Essays* (London, 1975), 65–96; Steven Ozment, *When Fathers Ruled: Family Life in Reformation Europe* (Cambridge, Mass., 1983).

32. Similarly, scholars interested in the confessional state have tended not to make women and gender their primary focus (Hsia, *Social Discipline*). Douglass noted in 1985 that a full consideration of Calvin's position on women and gender would need "to deal seriously with . . . practice," but much of the research had not been done (*Women, Freedom, and Calvin,* 8). For an update on the monumental project that Kingdon is directing on the Genevan Consistory records, see Kingdon, "The Geneva Consistory in the Time of Calvin," in Pettegree, Duke, and Lewis, eds., *Calvinism in Europe,* 21–34). Note that Watt's article on these newly transcribed registers covers only the years 1542–1544 ("Women and the Consistory," *Sixteenth Century Journal,* XXIV [1993], 429–439).

ophilus Eaton's New Haven, this essay suggests that there existed in the period 1540–1700 a Calvinist brand of patriarchy. This type of legal regime had two defining elements. The first ingredient was magisterial success at prosecuting all immorality that came to light, including sexual assault, and implementing a single standard in punishing men and women in almost all areas. The second key element was reconfiguring the regulation of marriage such that domestic violence was taken seriously, husbands were held accountable for irresponsibility, and full divorce was made available on adultery and desertion grounds. Recent and ongoing research in the court and consistory records of Reformed cities (such as Neuchâtel and Augsburg) and explicitly Calvinist jurisdictions (Emden and communities in the Palatinate and in Scotland) finds these two elements strongly present, despite variations in enforcement.[33]

In essence, members of early modern Calvinist communities committed themselves, because of their religious convictions, to holding men as well as women, rich as well as poor, accountable for sinful behavior. This had the effect of reorienting some of the traditional aspects of patriarchy. Eliminating the double standard undercut men's sense of sexual entitlement to women's bodies, just as sanctioning divorce and penalizing wifebeaters relieved some women from continuing dependence on sinful men. Calvin and the leaders he inspired made no brief for altering the familiar economic, political, and social rules of gender hierarchy, but in giving a distinctive shape to the sphere of law and moral discipline they moderated the face of patriarchy.

In making this argument about the blunting of patriarchy, I could be interpreted as combining the viewpoints of two other historians. Among those who argue that on balance the Calvinist or Reformed approach led to at least a temporary amelioration of women's experiences are E. William Monter and Steven Ozment. Monter asserts that the most telling change in women's lives came through Calvin's particular stance on regulating morals and sexual behavior, whereas Ozment emphasizes the right to full divorce and its implicit endorsement of companionate marriage, since this reform had the most lasting effect. My own study of that peculiarly Puritan colony of New Haven confirms both of their conclusions but also invites us to

---

33. Watt, *The Making of Modern Marriage*, 106, 155–159; Lyndal Roper, *The Holy Household: Women and Morals in Reformation Augsburg* (Oxford, 1989); Kenneth M. Boyd, *Scottish Church Attitudes to Sex, Marriage, and the Family, 1850–1914* (Edinburgh, 1980), 5–9. My approach is to think of Calvinist jurisdictions as a subset of Reformed ones. Scholars of Reformation Europe tend to use the label "Reformed" broadly, to refer to regimes based on the teachings of Luther, Calvin, and other Protestant reformers. Some opt for the term "Reformed" to avoid association with those in the sixteenth century who used "Calvinist" as a pejorative label (see Duke, "Perspectives on International Calvinism," in Pettegree, Duke, and Lewis, eds., *Calvinism in Europe*, 4 n. 12).

inquire how different types of patriarchy coexist in neighboring, kindred societies and how economic, legal, and cultural forces combine to change the internal logic of particular patriarchies. And it is the processes of change that deserve the creative, interpretive energies of historians. What follows is my own speculative offering of a framework that might help to illuminate the forces that eclipsed the Calvinist legal regimes of the early modern West along with their insistence on restraining patriarchal power.[34]

Posing the question of what caused the passing of Calvinist regimes such as those headed by Calvin in Geneva and Eaton in New Haven is perhaps not so different from asking why any utopian community—any experiment in radical, social change—comes to an end. One local factor is often the death or departure of the founding magistrate or pastor around whom the community of believers had rallied. And, indeed, in the cases we have examined, New Haven Colony as a political entity was snuffed out a few years after Eaton's death in 1658, while Calvin's death in 1564 was followed by an immediate increase in excommunications under the leadership of Theodore Beza before a decline in the enforcement of moral discipline. But the waning of Calvinist discipline that occurred in all Reformed communities on different schedules between the end of the sixteenth and the end of the eighteenth centuries can be ascribed to larger forces than a single leader's compelling personality.

Whether we are examining Zurich, Basel, Emden, Scotland, Geneva, or New Haven, we find a common trajectory: Calvinist principles gradually ceased to drive a concerted regulation of morals *either* because clergy along with like-minded, pious magistrates lost their central role in shaping and enforcing law *or* because ideological and demographic shifts prompted clerics to handle discipline differently. Although we tend to associate the fate of Reformed jurisdictions with secularization, more important factors were the population movements and the increasing religious pluralism of the early modern world. Of course, it was these forces—migrations, displacements, and religious turmoil—that permitted Calvin's Geneva, Eaton's New Haven, and all the "stranger" churches of Continental Europe to exist in the first place. Yet the political and economic forces that moved Europeans

---

34. Monter, "Women in Calvinist Geneva," *Signs*, VI (1980–1981); Ozment, *When Fathers Ruled*, 99. See also Nancy L. Roelker, "The Appeal of Calvinism to French Noblewomen in the Sixteenth Century," *Journal of Interdisciplinary History*, II, no. 3 (1972), 403–413. Linda K. Kerber also called for a focus on the processes of change in "Separate Spheres, Female Worlds, Woman's Place: The Rhetoric of Women's History," *Journal of American History*, LXXV (1988–1989), 9–39. For an eloquent plea for feminist historians to study the "many varieties" of "historical patriarchies," see Judith M. Bennett, "Feminism and History," *Gender and History*, I (1989), 252–273, esp. 261; Bennett, *Ale, Beer, and Brewsters in England: Women's Work in a Changing World, 1300–1600* (New York, 1996), esp. 152–157.

around the Continent and across the Atlantic worked in tandem with the initial splintering force of the Reformation to doom orthodoxies like those of Calvin and Eaton. As adults within increasingly heterogeneous communities developed strategies that allowed them to worship as they pleased, no public leader, no matter how fervent, could hope to implement a program demanding rigorous behavioral change in any group larger than the members of a gathered church.[35]

Capitalism was a second, momentous force impinging on Reformed communities. As local economic relations were reconfigured to facilitate the transatlantic and eventually global circulation of goods, both household strategies and legal business changed too. Courts that lavished most of their attention on morals regulation, offered ad hoc, equitable remedies for civil disputes, and depended on local knowledge to hand out sentences were ill suited for the growing number of commercial actors who, in settling transactions made over large geographical distances, needed a legal system that generated predictable outcomes. A cruder way to put this is that, from the viewpoint of the secular state, protecting a dispute resolution system that greased the wheels of the expanding Western economy was more important than perpetuating confessional discipline. Individual churches or frontier utopian villages might adhere to strict discipline, but these communities could no longer expect to supply the organizing ethical principles for the majority in pluralist, commercial states.

Laypeople, notably male householders whose decisions were paramount in propelling families to go into exile or to cooperate with consistories, were implicated not just in the origins but also in the eclipse of Calvinist regimes. Remember that John Calvin and Theophilus Eaton had combated differential standards of discipline based not simply on gender but also on rank. Not just servants but members of wealthy, well-connected families had been hauled into court to publicly acknowledge their sins. It was individuals from these ranks who eventually mounted effective resistance to strict discipline— resistance that varied in motives, form, and timing from place to place. As the Calvinist impulse waned, the regulation of moral behavior became more and more selective, with prosecutions or new administrative agencies targeting the laboring classes and, in the case of North America, nonwhites.[36]

By the late eighteenth century, and long before in many instances, once-Calvinist communities had abandoned the distinctive principles of the single standard, strict scrutiny of male irresponsibility, and reliance on media-

---

35. William G. McLoughlin, *New England Dissent, 1630–1833: The Baptists and the Separation of Church and State,* I (Cambridge, Mass., 1971); Boyd, *Scottish Church Attitudes,* 11.

36. Boyd, *Scottish Church Attitudes,* 11; Dayton, *Women before the Bar,* esp. 12–13, 65, 188–216, 225–230.

tion and local knowledge to resolve disputes. Such policies, which were intended to create not gender equality but rather the most God-fearing society possible, could not survive at the state level. The only ingredient of Calvinist legal regimes to survive in eighteenth-century statecraft was the policy of granting full divorce to both men and women. We can view this as fitting both for an intellectual age that championed the self-liberating powers of reason and for a new nation in which lawmaking was imbued with universal Protestant values rather than those of individual sects. For the next century and beyond, agitation against the double standard and against social codes that turned a blind eye to domestic violence and sexual assault no longer would come from revered magistrates but from marginalized grassroots activists. Indeed, it was the same pluralism that doomed the Calvinist regimes of the sixteenth and seventeenth centuries that provided a basis for the women's and civil rights movements of the modern era.[37]

37. Charles Taylor, *Sources of the Self: The Making of the Modern Identity* (Cambridge, Mass., 1989); Robert A. Ferguson, *The American Enlightenment, 1750–1820* (Cambridge, Mass., 1997). Norma Basch argues that, although nineteenth-century Americans embraced the Reform principle of granting divorce, they would hedge it about with an ever-increasing set of rules and qualifications so that its moral premises became more and more ambiguous (*Framing American Divorce: From the Revolutionary Generation to the Victorians* [Berkeley, Calif., 1999]).

The Limits of Authority

Courts, Ethnicity, and Gender in the
Middle Colonies, 1670–1710

W HEN DISCUSSING the legal systems of various Anglo-American colonies, historians commonly stress the elites' quest for authority, and with good reason. Colonial courts possessed extremely modest abilities to compel obedience. Law was only one of a number of discourses available for colonial elites and colonial peoples to choose from in order to make sense of their lives and regulate their societies. By necessity as well as in emulation of practices in England, courts as local institutions would have to rely heavily on widespread participation of the populace (particularly but not exclusively adult male property owners) to serve in various roles and to use courts to resolve disputes, civil and criminal. Authority, not merely defined by power but also requiring institutional legitimacy, involved a measure of consent that had to be conferred by nonelite members of society. Elites could attempt to influence these social negotiations in ways that would attract desirable issues and participants into legal processes, that would influence outcomes in desirable directions, and that would peripheralize topics and groups of less importance. To the extent that such consent was achieved and involved affective notions of justice and acceptance of underlying values, one can speak of a legal consensus supportive of authority.[1]

One successful method for measuring whatever consensus underlay colonial court authority depends on longitudinal litigation analysis. Close anal-

I wish to acknowledge Joyce Chaplin, James Horn, Bruce Mann, John Murrin, William Nelson, John Reid, Christopher Tomlins, the New York University Law School Legal History Colloquium, the Columbia University Seminar on Early American History and Culture, and the anonymous readers of this volume for their assistance and helpful comments.

1. Jack P. Greene, *Pursuits of Happiness: The Social Development of Early Modern British Colonies and the Formation of American Culture* (Chapel Hill, N.C., 1988), 200; Christopher L. Tomlins, *Law, Labor, and Ideology in the Early American Republic* (Cambridge, 1993), 16, 21, 49, 51; Mary Beth Norton, *Founding Mothers and Fathers: Gendered Power and the Forming of American Society* (New York, 1996), 11–12; Joyce Oldham Appleby, *Liberalism and Republicanism in the Historical Imagination* (Cambridge, Mass., 1992), 159; Lawrence M. Friedman, *The Republic of Choice: Law, Authority, and Culture* (Cambridge, Mass., 1990), 211.

ysis of the records of legal behavior can measure the relative strength or weakness of legal authority over specific subject matters (authority over what) and the relative participation by various demographic groups (authority over whom). Changes in legal behavior over time and differences in legal behavior between colonies can then be traced using a common yardstick. Thus, a statistical history of colonial litigation, covering both civil and criminal outcomes, can identify the edges and the trends of legal consensus among various disputes and groups. The numbers generated indicate social processes and social change as well as the impact of legal processes and doctrinal change on particular groups of litigants.[2]

Measuring and comparing levels of colonial legal authority cannot be achieved directly. Legal records cannot generally reveal the affective elements of a consensus in a society, the psychological attachment felt by members of a society to legal rules and institutions. Consensus often manifests itself implicitly by restricting the range and intensity of conflict, but silence in the records as to hostility may also betoken a submission by one party to realities of power, a sullen or resentful restraint of conflict rather than any positive attachment.[3] What the records can reflect is what I will call the legal *adherence* that is necessary for any legal consensus, and without which legal

2. The promise of quantitative litigation analysis, as practiced by proponents of the "law and society school," has been its claim to mine docket data for "how people relate to the law, about how the legal process operates, about the role that law plays in society, and about how these phenomena change over time (Richard Lempert, "Docket Data and 'Local Knowledge': Studying the Court and Society Link over Time," *Law and Society Review*, XXIV [1990], 321–322). Yet these claims have been accused, often by some of the practitioners, of failing to take into account constraints of class, ethnicity, and power; of ignoring cultural contexts and applying modern interpretations anachronistically; of ignoring the links between legal institutions and their communities; of ignoring political implications in favor of process concerns; and, more generally, of practicing positivism. See ibid., 322; Barbara Yngvesson, "Making Law at the Doorway: The Clerk, the Court, and the Construction of Community in a New England Town," *Law and Society Review*, XXII (1988), 409; Frank Munger, "Afterword: Studying Litigation and Social Change," *Law and Society Review*, XXIV (1990), 595–599; Lynn Mather, "Dispute Processing and a Longitudinal Approach to Trial Courts," *Law and Society Review*, XXIV, no. 2 (1990), 357; Christopher Tomlins, review of *Of "Good Laws" and "Good Men": Law and Society in the Delaware Valley, 1680–1710*, by William M. Offutt, Jr., *Law and History Review*, XVI (1998), 421. Quantitative measures of litigation can be used as markers for inferences regarding social relations and legal authority, which can then be confirmed or refuted by careful examination of the legal culture, politics, power, and community relations. This approach is best suited for "studying the effects of processes that make legally significant relationships and meanings contingent and to studying actors whose power uniquely fits them to exert [or lose] influence over the longer run." See Munger, "Afterword," *Law and Society Review*, XXIV (1990), 600.

3. Edward Shils, *Center and Periphery: Essays in Macrosociology* (Chicago, 1975), 169. Actor-oriented perspectives, such as those employed in this and other research, have begun to generate theories (such as microeconomic, cultural orientations, or "thematizations") that may bridge the gap between the "objective" viewpoint of the observer/historian and the ambiguous and contingent beliefs of the participant. See Munger, "Afterword," *Law and Society Review*, XXIV (1990), 599.

authority could not have been established. Adherence does not equate with obedience, for a party may recognize a rule governing conduct and yet refuse to obey it. Rather, adherence here refers to an understanding of legal categories and rules governing behavior and an understanding of likely legal strategies and outcomes. High levels of adherence existed when the legal rule governing an issue in potential conflict was clearly recognized by the actors involved, when the facts in the underlying social transaction were not in dispute, and when the parties felt able to predict the likely application of rule to facts by a legal institution. Adherence reveals mitigated and regularized conflict, a willingness to conform behavior or acquiesce in the outcome regardless of personal attitudes toward the law or result. A classic example of adherence would be where a debtor, facing a lawsuit for a sum certain he knows is due, would settle out of court with his creditor or confess judgment in court, forgoing further conflict by being able to predict accurately that a court would decide against him. Logically, no legal consensus on a subject could be found without also finding evidence of legal adherence.

The social significance of choices made in county courts—by litigants as well as legal decision makers—dwells in their implications for legal authority. Courts were critical social institutions in all colonies, established on arrival or soon thereafter by the first English settlers to transmit a colonial elite's values throughout the settlements. Elites spent extraordinary amounts of time and effort contending over the proper distribution of jurisdiction among courts and over who would control court personnel. Courts were an arena (in many times and places, the primary arena) for presentation and resolution of social conflicts, within which members of different social groups could contend. Simplification, by design in New England and the Delaware Valley and by necessity in other regions, combined with a fusion of functions (criminal, civil, administrative) to create a wide-ranging forum available initially to lawyers and laypeople alike. In such a setting, a primary goal of the legal elite would be to achieve and maintain legitimacy through popular usage of courts and popular acceptance of legal decisions based on legal norms.[4]

Beyond what a court had to do to achieve and maintain authority against direct attack, choices made in litigation and prosecutions reflected the limits of consensus. First, case outcomes reveal how much adherence has been achieved on particular subjects. The lower the level of adherence, the less

---

4. G. S. Rowe, *Embattled Bench: The Pennsylvania Supreme Court and the Forging of a Democratic Society, 1684–1809* (Newark, Del., 1994), 19–62; Gary Nash, *Quakers and Politics: Pennsylvania, 1681–1776* (Princeton, N.J., 1968), 166–167, 229–230, 264–267; Rhys Isaac, *The Transformation of Virginia, 1740–1790* (Chapel Hill, N.C., 1982), 88–94; David Thomas Konig, *Law and Society in Puritan Massachusetts: Essex County, 1629–1692* (Chapel Hill, N.C., 1979), xiii, 124, 188–191; Richard J. Ross, "The Legal Past of Early New England: Notes for the Study of Law, Legal Culture, and Intellectual History," *William and Mary Quarterly*, 3d Ser., L (1993), 34–35; Shils, *Center and Periphery*, 4–10.

likely a consensus existed, marking the subjects on which legal authority had its weakest reach. In such circumstances, competing discourses (religion, community, notions of informal justice) were more likely to have held decisive influence. Levels of adherence on issues and the ranking of important issues may change over time, marking potential changes in authority. Second, cases reveal which groups in a society participated in or avoided courts and how involved they were in particular categories of disputes. Bringing conflicts to court may help integrate a diverse society and provide courts with chances to exercise authority, but the pattern of who brought cases and with what results indicates whether that potential was realized, and for whom.[5] It is this essay's contention that groups' social standing may be accurately mapped by their presence, over time, in cases ranked by levels of legal adherence. To wit, those of high social standing will participate more often in cases of higher adherence; those of lower social standing will participate more often in cases with lower adherence levels. Over time, a group can be seen as becoming more central socially by having more cases in topics of high adherence or becoming more peripheralized by having cases in areas of lower adherence—or by having no cases at all.

This analysis relies on both civil and criminal litigation from courts of the Middle Colonies in the period from the 1670s to the early 1700s. Cases from four county courts in the Delaware Valley for 1680–1710, the Mayor's Court of New York City for 1674 through 1675 (akin to a county court), and the supreme courts of New York (1691–1704) and New Jersey (1704–1710) have been compiled. Other historians have also mined New York civil and criminal cases; although those other scholars employed diverse categorization schemes, their results can be reconfigured to analyze legal adherence and group participation.[6] The result suggests an intercolonial framework to

5. Konig, *Law and Society in Puritan Massachusetts*. Konig's formulation of the integrative role of law in colonial society is the starting point, as it has been for many recent colonial law and society analysts. This paper attempts to measure the realities of integration; an integrative role is thus a necessary, but not a sufficient, condition for social consensus through law.

6. *Records of the Courts of Quarter Sessions and Common Pleas of Bucks County, Pennsylvania, 1684–1700* (Meadville, Pa., 1943) (hereafter cited as *Bucks Courts*); H. Clay Reed and George J. Miller, eds., *The Burlington Court Book: A Record of Quaker Jurisprudence in West New Jersey, 1680–1709* (Washington D.C., 1944) (hereafter cited as *Burlington Courts*); *Records of the Courts of Chester County, Pennsylvania*, I, *1681–1697* (Philadelphia, 1910) (hereafter cited as *Chester Courts*, I); *Records of the Courts of Chester County, Pennsylvania*, II, *1697–1710*, transcribed by Dorothy Lapp (Danboro, Pa., 1972) (hereafter cited as *Chester Courts*, II); Transcription of the Minute Book, Quarter Sessions/Common Pleas, no. 1, 1686–1713, Gloucester County, N.J. Gloucester County Historical Society, Woodbury, N.J. (hereafter cited as *Gloucester Courts*); Kenneth Scott, ed., *Minutes of the Mayors Court of New York, 1674–1675*, New York Historical Manuscripts (Baltimore, 1983); Minutes and Rules of the New Jersey Supreme Court, 1704–1715, New Jersey State Archives, Trenton, N.J., 1704–1710 examined (microfilm) (hereafter cited as *New Jersey Supreme Court*); Paul M. Hamlin and Charles E. Baker, eds., *Supreme Court of Judicature of the Province of*

compare and synthesize the findings of the varied legal histories regarding Anglo-American colonies. It also suggests a method by which legal history can speak clearly to colonial historians on the transmission of values, the creation of legal consensus, the marginalization of certain groups, and the maintenance of authority.

I. Issues in Court

The issues that reached a court reflected only a fraction of the potential number of cases that could have been brought on a given topic, and that fraction changes over time and space. Perhaps if we knew the total number of incidents (murders, thefts, fornications, trespasses on land by cows, getting drunk, breaking contracts, debts unpaid) that occurred in a colonial society, then used the number of cases brought to create a percentage of the total incident pool that came to court, we could prove the intensity of the legal system's interest in resolving each sort of problem. But we can never know that underlying rate of behavior, and that "dark number" makes analysis of litigation and prosecution rates and of changes in an issue's share of a court's docket unreliable indicators of legal focus and consensus. It is the outcomes of those issues brought to court that are known that can reveal whether the necessary conditions for a consensus on particular issues had been met.[7]

A colonial legal system's ability to achieve legal adherence can be measured through two numerical breakdowns of case outcomes. First, the percentage of cases that were completed either by the parties out of court or without a contest on the merits in court reveals the level of routinization and predictability on the subject in dispute.[8] Some of these outcomes reflected

---

New York, 1691–1704: The Minutes, Annotated, II (New York, 1959) (hereafter cited as *New York Supreme Court Minutes*); New-York Historical Society, *Collections for the Year 1912* (New York, 1913) (hereafter cited as NYHS, *Colls.*); Douglas Greenberg, *"Persons of Evil Name and Fame": Crime and Law Enforcement in the Colony of New York, 1691–1776* (Ithaca, N.Y., 1974); Deborah A. Rosen, *Courts and Commerce: Gender, Law, and the Market Economy in Colonial New York* (Columbus, Ohio, 1997); Eben Moglen, "Settling the Law: Legal Development in New York, 1664–1776" (Ph.D. diss., Yale University, 1993); Thelma Wills Foote, "Black Life in Colonial Manhattan, 1664–1786" (Ph.D. diss., Harvard University, 1991).

7. Peter Charles Hoffer, "Honor and the Roots of American Litigiousness," *American Journal of Legal History*, XXXIII (1989), 297–298. Cornelia Hughes Dayton, *Women before the Bar: Gender, Law, and Society in Connecticut, 1639–1789* (Chapel Hill, N.C., 1995), 189–193, comes closest to the dark number regarding fornication by examining the number of children born within eight months of marriage, compared to the number of prosecutions.

8. These measurements are not the only ones that could reveal adherence; analysis of the efficiency with which courts disposed of issues (that is, speed or delay) and analysis of the ease or difficulty of enforcing judgments also would be revelatory (John Murrin, com-

the affective notion of consensus, as where parties reached an agreement, but might not have reflected voluntary assent to the law as much as recognition of power. Some creditors required debtors to confess judgment as a recording device or as a condition for receiving credit in order to facilitate later collection.[9] But such exercises of economic power fitted the definition of legal adherence, where both parties knew the rule pertaining to the transaction, where the facts were not in dispute, and where, critically, the result of any court contest over the transaction was predictable. Conceding defeat did not mean the losing party liked the result, only that a clear legal rule governing the circumstances had been transmitted that the loser recognized and that he or she acceded to. Parties might alter their behavior to take advantage of legal predictability, as in creditors' requiring debtors to sign written notes or bonds instead of book accounts. Cases could become increasingly low-intensity and routine as filing suit or charging a defendant becomes a bargaining chip designed to induce the recalcitrant to come to terms. Contrariwise, issues possessing this sort of legal adherence can lose it, particularly in times of social stress; declining predictability reflected in litigants' increased willingness to fight in court would imply a breakdown of legal consensus on the issue.[10]

Legal issues are rarely, if ever, completely predictable in their outcomes, and parties are not always accurate predictors; therefore, perfect legal routinization (100 percent uncontested resolutions) is unlikely. For the percentage of cases that were contested, the opinions of third parties—decision makers—must be included. Thus, the percentage of contested cases won by the plaintiff (civil) or prosecution (criminal) constitutes a second measure

ments, "Many Legalities of Early America" conference, Williamsburg, Va., Nov. 23, 1996). Such measures should and will be employed systematically in subsequent research based on this model—a review of cases already analyzed did not alter the basic outlines of the levels of adherence for each issue.

Civil disputes could include nonsuits of plaintiffs or defaults or confessions of judgments by defendants; criminal cases might involve confessions by defendants, uncontested summary judgments and fines, dismissals and discharges, and ignoramuses. An ignoramus was a jury's declaration of insufficient evidence for an indictment.

9. My thanks to John Reid and Bruce Mann, who separately informed me of this phenomenon.

10. Lawrence M. Friedman and Robert V. Percival, "A Tale of Two Courts: Litigation in Alameda and San Benito Counties," *Law and Society Review*, X (1976), 269–272, 286–287. For example, more routine use of courts to collect debts from fishermen in the 1700s did not generate resistance among the losers (who did not contest the actions), reflecting a recognition of the legitimacy of the legal system's role. See Daniel Vickers, *Farmers and Fishermen: Two Centuries of Work in Essex County, Massachusetts, 1630–1850* (Chapel Hill, N.C., 1994), 164–165. In the Delaware Valley, peace bonds (recognizances) were used as a bargaining chip to improve behavior and prevent crime. See Paul Lermack, "Peace Bonds and Criminal Justice in Colonial Philadelphia," *Pennsylvania Magazine of History and Biography*, C (1976), 174–177.

of adherence, which incorporates the notion of contingency in evaluating legal choices; not all participants evaluate their situation vis-à-vis the law correctly or even rationally. This second percentage reveals the predictability of in-court decisions by judges or by jurors (who represented white male property owners of middling status whose participation and consent were critical to legal authority).[11] If the outcome was highly predictable in favor of the plaintiff/prosecution, going to a full in-court trial involving the monetary costs of witnesses, additional court fees, and perhaps lawyer's fees, along with a potential public humiliation, probably reflected a miscalculation by the defendant. On the other hand, lower success rates for plaintiffs/prosecutions in contested cases denote a lower level of predictability and a higher role for contingency in the parties and the decision makers' evaluations of the law involved, the relevant facts, and their legal meaning.[12]

For the purposes of this essay and to facilitate cross-colonial comparisons, litigated subject matters have been grouped into four categories that ignored the permeable boundary between "civil" and "criminal" in colonial courts. First will be those cases that directly implicated legal authority, followed by three categories of civil and criminal cases that showed similar levels of adherence in early Delaware Valley outcomes: economic transactions, protection of "body and soul," and property. Evaluation of New York's cases reveals a similar pattern, although the comparison is hampered by unstandardized categorization and thus must be regarded as more tentative.

On establishing authority, elites within Pennsylvania, New Jersey, and New York faced similar problems in the late 1600s: ethnically and religiously diverse populations; the supplanting of one regime by another (sometimes several times), which necessarily brought into question the legitimacy of the new regime; the lack of established and customary relationships of authority and privilege. The fragility of these regimes was exemplified when, to protest the new governor and justices, potential jurors and appointed constables in Gloucester County, West Jersey, boycotted court sessions for nearly two years. No civil or criminal business could be transacted during such court avoidance, and only a new set of justices could restore court authority and

11. Konig, *Law and Society in Puritan Massachusetts*, 164; Darrett B. Rutman and Anita H. Rutman, *A Place in Time: Middlesex County, Virginia, 1650–1750* (New York, 1984), 90–91, 144–147; Konig, "Country Justice: The Rural Roots of Constitutionalism in Colonial Virginia," in Kermit L. Hall and James W. Ely, Jr., eds., *An Uncertain Tradition: Constitutionalism and the History of the South* (Athens, Ga., 1989), 72–73; Offutt, *Of "Good Laws" and "Good Men": Law and Society in the Delaware Valley, 1680–1710* (Urbana, Ill., 1995), 52–60.

12. Usually, the onus for continuing a contest was on the defendant. Unworthy plaintiffs were weeded out by nonsuits or ignoramuses. Furthermore, in order to file a case, plaintiffs/prosecutors had already jumped a psychic threshold in the sense of feeling wronged, and they had already fitted that wrong into a legal category cognizable by courts. Logically, plaintiffs should win more often than they lose, regardless of cause.

legitimacy. Thus, at the core of the legal elite's efforts would be prosecutions designed to protect court authority: for civic contempt (refusing to serve or appear in official roles) as well as for contempt of authority, defamation of legal officers, abuse of legal processes (such as perjury), and the rare but sensational treason and sedition offenses.[13]

Comparisons of the Middle Colonies' legal adherence levels in such cases reveal the relative authority granted elites. All three colonies handled civic contempt cases with summary judgments and fines, and these were nearly 100 percent uncontested in each jurisdiction.[14] Efforts to compel performance in various legal jobs (juror, constable, highway duty) reflected courts' acknowledgment of their need for participation from white men of middling status; periods of political instability such as the early 1690s when Penn's charter was lifted or the Gloucester County boycott noted above showed an increased frequency of civic contempt as courts struggled to maintain their authority.[15] Nonetheless, a high level of adherence in all jurisdictions reflects an acknowledgment of court power over this issue, even while a consensus might have been lacking.

It was in the remainder of authority cases that intercolonial differences emerged. In Delaware Valley county courts, 79 percent of all contempt of authority and criminal defamation cases with known outcomes were handled without an in-court fight, and 95 percent of all such cases that went to trial ended in conviction. In contrast, the New York supreme court from 1691 to 1704 disposed of only 50 percent of authority cases out of court, but 83 percent of trials resulted in convictions. The cases in New York were much more serious than those in Delaware Valley county courts, including two prosecutions for high treason and several for fraudulent election of aldermen in New York City. Although in some cases judges had to pressure juries to reach the "proper," authority-confirming verdict, nonetheless New York courts were able to obtain convictions.[16]

13. Nash, *Quakers and Politics; Gloucester Courts*, 198–215; Alan Tully, *Forming American Politics: Ideals, Interests, and Institutions in Colonial New York and Pennsylvania* (Baltimore, 1994); John E. Pomfret, *Colonial New Jersey: A History* (New York, 1973); Richard P. McCormick, *New Jersey from Colony to State, 1609–1789* (Princeton, N.J., 1964); Patricia U. Bonomi, *A Factious People: Politics and Society in Colonial New York* (New York, 1971); Michael Kammen, *Colonial New York: A History* (New York, 1975); Wayne Bodle, "Themes and Directions in Middle Colonies Historiography, 1980–1994," *WMQ*, 3d Ser., LI (1994), 355–364.

14. Of the 114 civic contempt cases for which verdicts were recorded in Pennsylvania and New Jersey county courts, only one was contested (unsuccessfully).

15. Offutt, *Of "Good Laws" and "Good Men,"* 193–196, gives a fuller treatment of the meaning of civic contempt. Norton, *Founding Mothers and Fathers*, 329, divides crimes against authority cases similarly, calling civic contempt "neglect of duty" to differentiate from challenges to authority ranging from contempt to treason.

16. The Delaware Valley information comes from 101 completed authority cases. Of the 12 completed New York cases, 4 were dismissed before trial (including all the prosecutions

The least adherence was shown by New Jersey's supreme court in its first six years under royal control (1704–1710). Only seven of seventeen authority cases (41 percent) with known outcomes were uncontested, and, of the ten cases that went to a jury, nine resulted in acquittals (a 10 percent conviction rate). Whether the defendant was a friend or an enemy of the royal government did not matter; convictions could not be obtained. Thus, John Hollinshead, accused of sedition for scandalous words against Governor Cornbury, Thomas Killingsworth, accused of calling the Church of England "a Carnall church," and John Harrison, accused of scandalous words against the chief justice, were all acquitted. But when a "runaway" grand jury indicted friends of the government such as Jeremiah Basse and Peter Sonmans on various charges of perjury and altering records, they, too, were acquitted (Basse by acclamation with the jury not leaving the room).[17]

Of the three Middle Colonies, the level of adherence suggests royal New Jersey as weaker in core authority than New York (despite their sharing the same governor in this period), with Pennsylvania courts possessing still greater authority. This ranking agrees with a modern finding of "slightly more tension over the legitimacy of provincial and county government in New York than in Pennsylvania."[18] Legal adherence in authority cases may thus be a more reliable measure of authority than the number of cases or the percentage of the docket filled by these authority cases.

The issues that achieved the highest adherence involved economic transactions, such as contracts and debts. County court jurisdiction extended only over those transactions deemed significant—small causes (less than two pounds in value) were to be handled out of court by single justices of the peace without a jury. Transactions valued at more than twenty pounds in New York and ten pounds in Pennsylvania could be appealed to a supreme court; otherwise, the county court judgment was final. In New York, the supreme court was also available for original jurisdiction over causes valued at more than twenty pounds.[19] Thus, the more at stake in a transaction, the

---

for fraudulent elections) and 2 involved guilty pleas. Of 6 trials, 5 ended in jury convictions—the one acquittal involved bribery. See New York Supreme Court Minutes, 58, 81–87, 88–89, 92, 98, 104, 137, 182; Adrian Howe, "The Bayard Treason Trial: Dramatizing Anglo-Dutch Politics in Early Eighteenth-Century New York City," WMQ, 3d Ser., XLVII (1990), 57–89. In the wake of the Glorious Revolution, Jacob Leisler led an uprising in New York against suspected Catholic officials and was ultimately hanged. The sharp and bitter political divisions between Leislerian and Anti-Leislerian forces were reflected in jury selections; legal adherence by no means meant affective legal consensus in such a polarized setting.

17. New Jersey Supreme Court, 7, 27, 36, 46, 50, 52, 61, 74, 75, 79, 80; Pomfret, Colonial New Jersey, 125.

18. Tully, Forming American Politics, 365.

19. Staughton George, Benjamin M. Nead, and Thomas McCamant, eds., Charter to William Penn, and Laws of the Province of Pennsylvania, Passed between the Years 1682 and 1700 . . . (Harrisburg, Pa., 1879), 131, 219; James T. Mitchell and Henry Flanders, eds., The

more legal options litigants received and the "better" the expected rendering of legal values pertaining to their dispute. Furthermore, the social stratum to which a party belonged did not determine whether one's expectations in an economic transaction would be enforced. Access to court was open to all involved in a significant transaction, and, at least in Delaware Valley courts, outcomes of in-court contests were a function of the type of transaction and not the status of the parties.

Economic transactions brought to the law reform courts of the Delaware Valley revealed a striking level of adherence regarding the protection of plaintiffs' expectations. Where causes of action (under English common law) were recorded, plaintiffs overwhelmingly brought disputes as either actions in Debt or Case. In Debt, 81.9 percent of cases brought were resolved without a contest, and of those contested, plaintiffs won 84 percent. In Case for economic transaction disputes, 75.7 percent of cases were resolved without a contest, and of those contested, plaintiffs won 74.8 percent. Adherence was slightly higher in Debt because of the written instruments often sued on in Debt, which made proof easier and limited defenses. Combined, Case and Debt saw 78.1 percent of cases uncontested, and 76.8 percent of contested cases were plaintiff victories. In other contested cases where no cause of action was recorded but evidence clearly indicated a contract or debt, plaintiffs won 84.4 percent, making the combined plaintiff victory rate for all cases identified with a contract or debt 79.7 percent.[20]

There is evidence from other jurisdictions that such adherence strengthened over time; that is, core legal values regarding significant economic transactions influenced individuals to adjust their behavior to take advantage of the adherence. As debt litigation grew enormously in New York City from the 1690s to the 1750s, out-of-court settlement and rates of default grew even more rapidly. Out-of-court resolutions grew from 32 percent of cases in the 1690s to 69 percent in the 1750s, while default rates for those cases with

---

Statutes at Large of Pennsylvania from 1682 to 1801, II (Harrisburg, Pa., 1896), 43, 189; Aaron Leaming and Jacob Spicer, eds., *The Grants, Concessions, and Original Constitutions of the Province of New Jersey* . . . (Philadelphia, 1752), 509–510; *The Colonial Laws of New York from the Year 1664 to the Revolution* . . . , I (Albany, N.Y., 1894), 7, 74, 88, 125, 175, 226–227, 303; Jessica Kross Ehrlich, " 'To Hear and Try All Causes betwixt Man and Man': The Town Court of Newtown, 1659–1690," *New York History*, LIX (1978), 277–305. All three jurisdictions experimented with how to deal with small claims but settled on the two-pound/single justice approach by the 1690s (New York in 1691, West Jersey in 1692, Pennsylvania in 1693). On state supreme court involvements with appeals and original jurisdiction in larger causes, see Rowe, *Embattled Bench,* 35; George, Nead, and McCamant, eds., *Charter to William Penn,* 184, 225; *Colonial Laws of New York,* I, 7, 228–229, 305, 681.

   20. Case could also be brought for noncontract issues such as defamation; these cases were separated out before analysis. Completed cases analyzed here totaled 424 in Case, 276 in Debt, and 169 economic transactions without cause of action specified (869 total). See Offutt, *Of "Good Laws" and "Good Men,"* 104–105.

in-court judgments went from 44 percent to 69 percent in the same period. Overall, the rate of jury trial dropped from 17 percent of all cases in the 1690s to 4 percent of all cases in the 1750s, and the evidence from Richmond County indicated that jury trial was being reserved primarily for nondebt issues. All of these indicate a broadening and deepening adherence regarding contract and debt enforcement in court; that, in turn, encouraged and reinforced a commercialization of economic relations, suggesting that increasing market relationships were not only the cause but also the effect of the predictability of debt litigation.[21]

The same growth of uncontested cases occurred in Connecticut debt actions from 1690 to 1760. The cause of such growth lay in the change of form embodying the debt sued upon. Account books in a neighborly economy based on trust gave way to written instruments (notes and bonds) as credit relationships became more distant and impersonal. As mentioned above, written instruments meant more certainty of recovery for creditors in court because defenses were few and outcomes were predictable, thus reducing contested cases. Uncontested cases for book debts also increased, although only into the 70-plus percent range as opposed to the 90-plus percent uncontested for written instruments.[22] As in New York, adherence and numbers of suits on this issue grew concurrently, suggesting at the least a reciprocal relationship between litigation and commercialization. In the Delaware Valley, however, legal adherence about debt and contract appears to have preceded widespread commercialization. Moreover, it was not until the 1720s and 1730s that the percentage of uncontested cases for debts in Connecticut reached the levels seen in the Delaware Valley twenty years before. Tracing this rise in adherence moves back the timing of the shift away from a static and communitarian legal system and may alter our sense of the time and places involved in the transition to capitalism in rural America.[23]

At lower levels of adherence in the Middle Colonies were issues of "body and soul," of personal expectations in social behavior. This category looks at alleged injuries in social transactions from the standpoint of the plaintiff in civil cases or of the victim (where known) in criminal cases. Unlike economic transactions, courts did look at the status of the victim or the plaintiff

21. Rosen, "Courts and Commerce in Colonial New York," *American Journal of Legal History*, XXXVI (1992), 142, 144, 147–154, 160; Rosen, *Courts and Commerce*, 7, 65–66, 151–153.

22. Bruce H. Mann, *Neighbors and Strangers: Law and Community in Early Connecticut* (Chapel Hill, N.C., 1987), 12–39, 171, 172, 177, 181.

23. Tomlins, *Law, Labor, and Ideology*, 21 n. 11; Allan Kulikoff, *The Agrarian Origins of American Capitalism* (Charlottesville, Va., 1992), 13–33; Charles Sellers, *The Market Revolution: Jacksonian America, 1815–1846* (New York, 1991), 3–33; Rosen, *Courts and Commerce*, 11, 91; Richard Lyman Bushman, "Markets and Composite Farms in Early America," *WMQ*, 3d Ser., LV (1998), 370–374.

to decide whether this sort of issue could come to court. The combination of civil and criminal actions in this category reflects the fusion of functions in colonial courts as well as the victims' control of the prosecution as dictated by statute. Where there was no victim, as in morals cases, the grand jury, often aided by constables, or a prosecutor conveyed the expectations of the legal elite regarding social behavior.[24] In the Delaware Valley, this level of adherence included morality prosecutions (protection of soul), violence (protection of body), and civil defamation (protection of reputation). Overall, 71.5 percent of 404 completed cases were uncontested in court, and, of those 115 cases that went to trial, plaintiffs or the prosecution won 74.8 percent of the time.

These aggregates, showing less adherence on both measures than for economic transactions, obscure certain differences among the elements of this category. The Delaware Valley legal elite achieved more adherence over protecting soul than body, and, although certain groups bore the disproportionate brunt of such prosecutions, no group escaped scrutiny. Of 215 completed morals cases, 81.9 percent went uncontested, as defendants pleaded guilty, submitted to the court, or suffered summary judgments in recorded silence at a greater rate than for any other criminal cause. These courts had not yet undergone the shift experienced in 1690s Connecticut, when men stopped confessing and started using common-law procedures and defenses to contest (often successfully) accusations of sexual immorality. Such a shift to lower legal adherence marked a decline of legal authority over the issue in Connecticut, a decline not yet visible in the Delaware Valley but that had occurred long before in the Chesapeake. Of those few who did contest morals charges in the Delaware Valley, 84.6 percent were convicted; the level of adherence was virtually identical to that achieved on actions in Debt.[25]

However, immoral behavior reflected only one sort of social (as opposed to economic) transaction courts sought to regulate. Court protection of an individual's body or reputation revealed a far lower level of adherence than that found for issues of sexuality, drunkenness, and Sabbath breaking. Criminal prosecutions for violence resulted in uncontested cases 68.7 percent of the time, and, of the contested cases, 69.4 percent were victories for the prosecution. On the civil side, only 45.9 percent of defamation and assault cases were uncontested, with plaintiffs winning the contested cases 70 percent of the time. Establishing legal adherence to the protection of social

24. Ross, "Legal Past of Early New England," *WMQ*, 3d Ser., L (1993), 34–35; Mary Maples Dunn and Richard S. Dunn, eds., *The Papers of William Penn*, I, *1644–1679* (Philadelphia, 1981), 399; John Dawson, *A History of Lay Judges* (Cambridge, Mass., 1960), 121–127, 217–218.

25. Offutt, *Of "Good Laws" and "Good Men"*, 200–208, 229; Dayton, *Women before the Bar*, 173–175, 186, 192–194; Norton, *Founding Mothers and Fathers*, 346–347.

expectations was more problematic than gaining adherence to protect economic transactions.

Adherence was even more elusive regarding the protection of property rights. Here, in criminal cases of theft and in the civil causes of trover and conversion, trespass, and land (sometimes denoted *ejectment*), Delaware Valley's legal core found these issues too ambiguous in terms of the definitions of rights and responsibilities or too contentious to be resolved out of court. Theft accusations were the least likely criminal cause to be resolved out of court before trial or by confession; only 52.1 percent of 121 completed theft cases went uncontested. Similarly, its civil counterpart, trover and conversion, saw only 59.4 percent uncontested out of 32. The most contested property issues had to do with alleged invasions of landed property rights: trespasses and those causes trying to establish either the borders to or the rightful possession of land saw only 37 percent of 73 cases resolved out of court or uncontested in court. In terms of plaintiff/prosecution victories, theft prosecutions succeeded in 70.7 percent of cases, while the comparable civil causes saw only 61 percent success. Overall, this ring had only 47.2 percent of 226 completed cases uncontested, and 65.8 percent plaintiff/prosecution victories, the lowest level of adherence found for any set of legal issues, and, logically, the weakest area of consensus and the weakest realm of legal authority.[26]

The history of land policy provides evidence of the political and cultural difficulty behind achieving adherence to core legal values regarding property. Pennsylvania's law reforms hoped to simplify conveyancing through mandatory land registration, instead of relying on local memory and a chain of documents as under the common law. Lawsuits over land title were to avoid the convoluted legal fictions required by the action of ejectment. Nonetheless, Penn's land policy fell apart in the face of squatting, unregistered transactions, unpaid quitrents, and irregularly surveyed boundaries. In 1687, and again in 1700, Penn established a separate "Court of Inquiry" to resolve land disputes. Although he was forced to return land cases to ordinary courts quickly, to be tried under a welter of different causes of action, Penn's heirs and settlers continued to dispute land titles with no sign of a legal consensus into the 1750s.[27]

26. Offutt, *Of "Good Laws" and "Good Men"*, 104, 222, 229.

27. Dunn and Dunn, eds., *Papers of William Penn*, II, *1680–1684* (Philadelphia, 1982), 223; Roy N. Lokken, *David Lloyd: Colonial Lawmaker* (Seattle, Wash., 1959), 166; *Minutes of the Provincial Council of Pennsylvania, from the Organization to the Termination of the Proprietary Government*, II (Philadelphia, 1852), 358–360; Nash, *Quakers and Politics*, 94–95, 215–217, 227–229; Tully, *Forming American Politics*, 74–75, 82; James T. Lemon, *The Best Poor Man's Country: A Geographical Study of Early Southeastern Pennsylvania* (Baltimore, 1972), 55–57. For more on legal fictions, see Konig, "Legal Fictions and the Rule(s) of Law: The Jeffersonian Critique of Common-Law Adjudication," above.

New York's experience in trying to protect landed property rights was, if anything, worse. "Bitter and continual were the disputes over land in New York," leading to "incessant litigation" and "acrid political controversy" from 1664 to 1776.[28] The English conquerors confirmed Dutch land grants, but ordered the patents renewed under the duke of York. Compliance was spotty. Land registration, implemented as early as 1665 and renewed in 1683, proved ineffective as a means of confirming title and boundaries. "Extravagant" land grants, approved by one governor, were annulled by a second, and then the annulment itself was voided by a third.[29] The New York supreme court's treatment of ejectment cases revealed an almost total lack of adherence. Of ejectment cases with recorded outcomes, only 22.5 percent were uncontested, and plaintiffs were victorious only 51.9 percent of the time.[30]

As a response to this weak adherence, landowners in New York began to change their behavior in ways that mimicked the move to written instruments among creditors. Land as status, the English core legal value, was redefined in practice to land as commodity, just another article of commerce and speculation. The result was "the contractualization of land law in the eighteenth century" in the longer-settled regions of New York, as bargaining and market arrangements took over land law in the form of leases and mortgages. On the geographic periphery, attempted reliance on the common law of land titles led to continuous frustration and contention.[31]

This shift is completely understandable as a response to the failure to create legal adherence (and concomitant failure of consensus) in protecting landed property rights; potential litigants rearranged their behavior in order to get the higher level of protection accorded deals. Land transactions could thus be rearranged by those alert to legal strategy to secure higher predictability and thus higher legal adherence, facilitating the growth of a commercial market in land in the more settled areas.

Thus, as measured by legal adherence, the Middle Colonies' legal elites were far more likely to have achieved consensus and authority over transactional expectations than over ownership rights. That legal values regarding deals carried more influence (whether affectively appreciated or not)

28. Julius Goebel, Jr., and T. Raymond Naughton, *Law Enforcement in Colonial New York: A Study in Criminal Procedure, 1664–1776* (New York, 1944), 206–207.

29. *Colonial Laws of New York*, I, 30–31, 44, 80, 83, 89, 141–142, 412, 524.

30. *New York Supreme Court Minutes;* NYHS, *Colls.*, 41–214. Because of fictional parties, the numbers here must be considered indicative only. Eighty-two ejectment cases were noted over fourteen years, forty-two without result, nine uncontested, fourteen jury verdicts for plaintiffs, thirteen for defendants, and four special jury verdicts (usually for establishing property lines).

31. Moglen, "Settling the Law," 63–102, esp. 82; Daniel J. Hulsebosch, *"Imperia in Imperio:* The Multiple Constitutions of Empire in New York, 1750–1777," *Law and History Review,* XVI (1998), 354, 359.

with average colonists than did core values regarding property, and that such a gap in legal adherence established itself relatively early in the Middle Colonies and widened over time, carry enormous implications for the debate over colonial mentalité. Whether this gap in legal adherence preceded and helped cause the economic and social fluidity of a colonial "pursuit of happiness" through markets and deals or whether that fluidity caused legal adherence to form in response to social needs can best be explored through comparative research using litigation outcomes as markers.

II. Ethnicity and Participation

Arranging the business of courts from higher to lower levels of adherence allows for the synthesis of a wide range of legal research that has heretofore been relatively incommensurable. Measuring various groups' participation in issues with varying adherence and comparing that participation with each group's population and previous participation on those issues can reveal critical information regarding social power and position. In a statistical snapshot, a group that participated in issues of higher adherence at or above its population percentage could be regarded as central to legal authority; a group that participated in issues of lower adherence or that participated generally below its population percentage can be seen as peripheral to legal authority. In the sense of diachronic development, a group that sees a growing percentage of its litigation on issues of higher adherence would be described as becoming legally centered; groups that see an increasing percentage of their participation in areas of lower adherence or whose participation declines or disappears entirely will be termed legally peripheralized. Two ethnic groups—the Dutch in New York and the Swedes in the Delaware Valley—will illustrate how legal adherence combined with participation levels can measure changes in social status and power and reveal limits to court authority.

The behavior of the New York Dutch reveals how a large and socially significant group can become legally peripheralized.[32] Under their own legal system, before 1664, the Dutch were voracious users of courts on a wide range of subjects. In civil litigation, which relied not on juries but on ar-

---

32. The identification of parties' ethnicity rests on the less-than-firm ground of last name analysis. See Oliver A. Rink, "The People of New Netherland: Notes on Non-English Immigration to New York in the Seventeenth Century," *New York History,* LXII (1981), 5–42; David Steven Cohen, "How Dutch Were the Dutch of New Netherland?" *New York History,* LXII (1981), 43–60; Joyce O. Goodfriend, *Before the Melting Pot: Society and Culture in Colonial New York City, 1664–1730* (Princeton, N.J., 1991), 13–15, 63. Last names may be Anglicized, and the ethnic identity, as defined by the individual, may be affected by exogamous marriages. The results below should be considered tentative.

bitrations and bench decisions, an average of more than 300 cases per year were filed in the 1650s and early 1660s for an adult white male population in Manhattan counted at 222 (88 percent Dutch) in 1664.[33] The English take-over changed the legal system gradually, with the duke of York's laws apply-ing first to Long Island, then to Manhattan in 1674, and finally to the whole colony in 1676. The legal validity of Dutch inheritance practices and land tenures was assured at first. Most historians believe that complete Angliciza-tion of the law's substantive content, in the sense of elimination of Dutch legal practices, was achieved in the 1690s.

As time passed, the Dutch became more familiar with the nuances and scope of English law. Furthermore, the Dutch retained significant power in New York City politics and dominated the personnel of the Mayor's Court of New York City long into the 1700s. A. G. Roeber has argued that the Dutch Anglicized in public life, politics, and law relatively easily; logically, the Dutch should have retained a presence in court commensurate with their population and economic standing. Yet they did not.[34]

Rather, the Dutch seem to have increasingly abandoned the courts as forums, resulting in a social Anglicization of court business that was more rapid than doctrinal. John Murrin found such avoidance on Long Island, where the ethnic Dutch, who had previously used English courts, aban-doned the new King's County court in 1684, leaving it with virtually no business. New York's mayor's court records suggest a less drastic but still significant drop in Dutch participation by the mid-1670s. At a time when the Dutch comprised approximately 66 percent of the adult white male popula-tion, only 37.7 percent of plaintiffs were Dutch.[35] By the 1690s and thereafter, the pattern of Dutch participation in court—at far lower rates than their population, their previous participation, or their economic and political significance would have predicted—had been well established.

Douglas Greenberg's study of New York between 1691 and 1776 found that

33. Linda Briggs Biemer, *Women and Property in Colonial New York: The Transition from Dutch to English Law, 1643–1727* (Ann Arbor, Mich., 1983), 93; Goodfriend, *Before the Melting Pot,* 62; Moglen, "Commercial Arbitration in the Eighteenth Century: Searching for the Transformation of American Law," *Yale Law Journal,* XCIII (1983), 136–138.

34. Moglen, "Settling the Law," 18–62, 103–16; Goodfriend, *Before the Melting Pot,* 78, 166 (aldermen were 66 percent Dutch from 1687–1707 and 89 percent Dutch from 1708–1730); see A. G. Roeber, " 'The Origin of Whatever Is Not English among Us': The Dutch-speaking and the German-speaking Peoples of Colonial British America," in Bernard Bailyn and Philip D. Morgan, eds., *Strangers within the Realm: Cultural Margins of the First British Empire* (Chapel Hill, N.C., 1991), 221, 236.

35. John M. Murrin, "English Rights as Ethnic Aggression: The English Conquest, the Charter of Liberties of 1683, and Leisler's Rebellion in New York," in William Pencak and Conrad Edick Wright, eds., *Authority and Resistance in Early New York* (New York, 1988), 73; Goodfriend, *Before the Melting Pot,* 62; Scott, ed., *Minutes of the Mayors Court of New York* (of 122 completed cases, Dutch were defendants in 57.3 percent).

the Dutch appeared as criminal defendants at a far lower rate (13.1 percent) than their population. Greenberg conceded, without explanation, that the Dutch somehow infrequently faced prosecution. Two of his criminal categories, contempt and crimes by public officials, dealt with authority issues that had a high level of legal adherence. Joyce Goodfriend found that 65–66 percent of municipal officers from 1687 to 1730, including those who sat on the mayor's court, were Dutch. Yet only 25.3 percent of contempt cases and 23.6 percent of crimes by public officials had Dutch defendants. The Dutch presence in the issues with lower adherence was even less—in the body and soul ring, they were only 13.2 percent of criminal defendants, and for property crimes, the Dutch were only 4.1 percent.[36] As measured by legal adherence, the Dutch presence in criminal litigation was more central than peripheral (in cases of higher adherence), but overall the Dutch disproportionately avoided prosecution, either because of a strategy of inoffensiveness or because of withdrawal from the legal system.

More persuasive are the statistics regarding Dutch participation in civil cases. In 1695, the Dutch constituted 58 percent of the adult white male population in New York City, declining to 52 percent in 1703. The Dutch comprised 44 percent of the merchants and retailers in 1695 (presumably those who would be most interested in suing on debts) and possessed 59 percent of all taxable wealth.[37] Therefore, it may be inferred that Dutch residents had many deals and much property to protect through litigation, a process they had embraced thirty years before. Furthermore, the Dutch could be assured of litigating in a court where Dutchmen controlled the bench. Yet, in the New York mayor's court of the 1690s, only 27 percent of the litigants were Dutch, approximately half their population rate. The Dutch litigants were sued more than they sued—38 percent appeared as plaintiffs, while 62 percent appeared as defendants. The Dutch were also more likely than the English to settle their cases or default, a practice associated primarily with cases involving economic transactions.[38] The conclusion is inescapable. The Dutch became peripheral to civil litigation, even on those issues where legal adherence was high. When the Dutch did litigate (more often than not involuntarily), they avoided appearing in court. The inference that the Dutch disdained the authority of the English legal system in resolving Dutch grievances is equally inescapable.

36. Greenberg, "Persons of Evil Name and Fame," 41, 47–49, 58, 64–66; Goodfriend, Before the Melting Pot, 78, 166. Greenberg's and Goodfriend's numbers when combined must be considered suggestive only due to their incomplete temporal and geographic overlap. The body and soul prosecutions combine what Greenberg counted as crimes of violence, disorderly houses, and violations of public order.
37. Goodfriend, Before the Melting Pot, 62, 66, 75, 78.
38. Deborah Rosen, "Courts and Commerce: The Formative Period of Legal Practice in New York, 1690–1760" (Ph.D. diss., Columbia University, 1990), 254–255.

Although the New York supreme court's civil jurisdiction covered the
whole province, in 605 supreme court civil cases between 1691 and 1704, the
Dutch comprised only 20.7 percent of plaintiffs and 31.7 percent of defendants. As with the mayor's court, the Dutch were less likely to sue than to be
sued, and, as with the mayor's court, even their rate of appearance as defendants was far less than their population level would predict. Other ethnic
groups showed nowhere near that level of avoidance, and they sued roughly
as often as they were sued. The French, found to be 10–11 percent of the New
York City population in the 1690s, were 8.8 percent of plaintiffs and 7.6
percent of defendants; Jews were 1 percent of the population, 1.3 percent of
plaintiffs, and 1.5 percent of defendants.[39]

Clearly, by the 1690s if not well before, the Dutch had withdrawn most of
their disputes from the legal system. The precise cause—whether they disliked English legal processes or distrusted court personnel (many Dutch
legal officers might have become too Anglicized)—is one of those cultural
context questions that litigation analysis can raise but not answer. A close
analysis of the Bayard treason trial of 1702 found that "the Dutch participants in the trial played low-keyed, even passive, roles" and summarized the
Dutch behavior as a retreat from politics and confrontation.[40] Whatever
presence the Dutch had in court was in areas of higher legal adherence,
indicating concerns close to the center of legal authority. Yet their overall
participation shrank dramatically. By avoiding courts and relying on nonlegal mechanisms for the protection of their transactions, their personal
expectations, and their property, the Dutch apparently peripheralized themselves and tried to deny English legal values much decision-making authority over them. Since it is highly unlikely that the Dutch became less disputa-
tious following the English conquest, the question remains as to how their
disputes were resolved. Some hints of where these disputes might have gone
appear in the preference of the Dutch for arbitration, a system that could
have continued to work within the competing discourses found in the merchant community or within the vital Dutch churches. Regardless, by the
1690s and thereafter, real court authority over legal issues that involved the
Dutch was limited, was less extensive than that expressed over the English.[41]

39. Goodfriend, *Before the Melting Pot,* 62; *New York Supreme Court Minutes;* NYHS,
Colls.
40. Howe, "The Bayard Treason Trial," *WMQ,* 3d Ser., XLVII (1990), 88–89. Dutch
officials, especially in the period surrounding Leisler's Rebellion, often suffered from
identifying too closely with the English. See Murrin, "English Rights and Ethnic Aggression," in Pencak and Wright, eds., *Authority and Resistance in Early New York,* 67–74;
Randall Balmer, "Traitors and Papists: The Religious Dimensions of Leisler's Rebellion,"
New York History, LXX (October 1989), 347–353, 364, 371–372.
41. Jerold S. Auerbach, *Justice Without Law?* (Oxford, 1983), 32; John Aiken, "New

Even in jurisdictions where court authorities went out of their way to assure fairness in process and result, ethnic groups could change their minds about the courts. Residents of New Sweden on the Delaware River in the early 1600s came under New Netherlands jurisdiction, then after 1664 were placed under the duke of York, and, finally, after 1681, came under William Penn. From 1676 to 1681, so-called Swedes (which actually included immigrants from various parts of Scandinavia as well as some Dutch) constituted the entire bench and most of the litigants of the Upland court under the duke of York. In 1681, under Penn, only half the justices were Swedes in the new Chester County, which covered only a portion of the geographic area of the old Upland court. Within two years, following the great Quaker migration to Pennsylvania, there were no Swedish justices left. Yet Quakers' law reforms were designed to encourage all ethnic groups to litigate, simply, cheaply, quickly, and without lawyers, and implicitly promised all groups fair judgments by bench or jury.[42]

An examination of Swedes in litigation in Chester County shows initially a high degree of participation. Swedes used the Chester court extensively through the mid-1690s, appearing as defendants more often than as plaintiffs but, when plaintiffs, suing other Swedes with disproportionate frequency, a sign of trust in courts controlled by non-Swedes. The causes brought for or against Swedes showed their position relative to levels of legal adherence; their cases usually did not involve an economic transaction or attacks on authority. Thus, in court involvement, the Swedes' presence was more peripheral, focusing on personal and property issues with lower levels of adherence. Regarding outcomes, whether as plaintiffs or defendants, Swedes had no statistically different results from other litigants. By the 1690s, on the surface, Swedes were well integrated into the Pennsylvania legal system and fairly treated thereby.[43]

However, Swedes avoided the courts thereafter. Where there had been forty-two Swede versus Swede cases from 1681 to 1695, from 1695 until 1710 there was one. Only five Swedish plaintiffs appeared from 1696 to 1710, following fifty-five in the previous fifteen years; participation by Swedish

Netherlands Arbitration in the Seventeenth Century," *Arbitration Journal*, XXIX (1974), 145–160; Moglen, "Commercial Arbitration in the Eighteenth Century," *Yale Law Journal*, XCIII (1983), 136–138; Balmer, *A Perfect Babel of Confusion: Dutch Religion and English Culture in the Middle Colonies* (New York, 1989).

42. *The Record of the Court at Upland, in Pennsylvania: 1676 to 1681*, in Historical Society of Pennsylvania, *Memoirs*, VII (1860; rpt., Philadelphia, 1959), 9–203 (hereafter cited as *Upland Court*); *Chester Courts*, I.

43. In these instances, Swedes were identified from last name analysis and comparison with lists of Swedes. See *Upland Court*, 77–80; Israel Acrelius, *A History of New Sweden...* (Philadelphia, 1874), 190–193.

defendants declined nearly as precipitously.[44] In light of the evenhanded treatment of Swedes in civil cases, this legal peripheralization is surprising. One possible explanation comes from the legal experience of Swede Derrick Clawson (alias Johnson) of Bucks County. An unknown person was found dead on May 8, 1692; the coroner suggested that he had been murdered about six weeks before. In June, because "a Considerable Quantity of blood on the wall and on the bed" of Clawson appeared about the time of the murder, Clawson was arrested, committed to prison; in questioning along with his wife, he basically denied the allegation. He was not released, but neither was he charged.

Clawson was held until October without trial, when the justices then deferred the trial until spring "to See if Something further might not be discovered." In April 1693, a grand jury, with apparently no additional evidence, indicted Clawson for the murder along with his wife and sister for abetting the crime. Still, the authorities were reluctant to press their circumstantial case to trial, and the Clawsons petitioned the provincial council for being held in prison twelve months (unclear whether this count was accurate) without trial. A provincial court of oyer and terminer was then convened; the jury convicted Clawson, but not the women, and he was sentenced to death, becoming perhaps the first man executed by the anti–capital punishment Quakers. As of May 1694, two years after the murder, Derrick Clawson's widow Britta was back before the council, petitioning to have her husband's property returned to her because of her "very Low condition" with three children.[45]

Assuming that the Delaware Valley Swedes discussed this case among themselves, they were probably dismayed by the treatment of their ethnic kin. The long delay between accusation and trial, the circumstantial nature of the case, the defendant's denial, the prosecution of his wife and sister, and his ultimate conviction and execution might have appalled them. Perhaps even more disturbing was the case of Harry, a black slave convicted in 1693 of buggering a cow and sentenced to death, who had his life spared first by the intervention of West Jersey freeholders attending the trial and then by being allowed to escape.[46] A plausible link between the treatment of the Clawsons and the immediate withdrawal by previously participating Swedes from the Quaker legal system exists. Participation changes such as those of the Swedes

44. *Chester Courts,* I; *Chester Courts,* II. Of civil defendants, there were ninety-four Swedes from 1681 to 1695, and only nineteen from 1696 to 1710, all but one of whom faced non-Swedish plaintiffs.

45. *Bucks Courts,* 163, 177, 181–182, 270; *Minutes of the Provincial Council of Pennsylvania,* I, 367–368, 442; Rowe, *Embattled Bench,* 41–42.

46. *Burlington Courts,* 142–143, 148.

and the Dutch illustrate the way groups reevaluated their legal position and might remove themselves and their problems from court authority. Such peripheralization, as with the Dutch, did not mean that Swedes had no more conflicts within or without their community; it did mean, however, that they would turn to other discourses for resolution of those conflicts.

III. Women's Participation

As a group of participants in a colonial legal system, women may not seem comparable to ethnic groups such as the Dutch or Swedes. Unlike Dutch or Swedish men, women suffered from a number of disabilities imposed by English common law that restricted the scope of their participation. As David Konig has noted, although "recourse to the law may not have been solely an instrument of hegemony[,] removal from the law, by contrast, may have been so." Modern analyses of women's position under different colonial legal systems have extensively employed the peripheralization or marginalization metaphor to describe the growth of common-law hegemony in matters of gender. This essay's methodology provides a standard means of comparing women's legal peripheralization among the colonies.[47]

With the possible exception of early Virginia, no colonial jurisdiction found women's behavior a threat to authority necessitating regular prosecution. Donna Spindel reported five cases of women's contempt of authority in North Carolina between 1663 and 1776, Greenberg found sixteen in New York between 1691 and 1776, and Cornelia Hughes Dayton reported a "handful" of such cases in Connecticut (only two between 1710 and 1790). In 1620s Virginia, Kathleen Brown found women vigorously participating in slander cases, some of which were against great men and thus prosecutable as authority offenses. Additionally, gossip networks were seen as potentially undercutting legal power; however, by the late seventeenth century, women's speech offenses had been trivialized and prosecutions were few.[48] Law reform jurisdictions with high legal adherence in authority cases showed little interest in women. Only five women were accused of authority offenses in the Delaware Valley county courts between 1680 and 1710. One Mary Allen,

47. Konig, "A Summary View of the Law of British America," *WMQ*, 3d Ser., L (1993), 47; Rosen, *Courts and Commerce*, 110, 130; Kathleen M. Brown, *Good Wives, Nasty Wenches, and Anxious Patriarchs: Gender, Race, and Power in Colonial Virginia* (Chapel Hill, N.C., 1996), 185–186, 284.

48. Donna J. Spindel, *Crime and Society in North Carolina, 1663–1776* (Baton Rouge, La., 1989), 83; Greenberg, *"Persons of Evil Name and Fame,"* 50; Dayton, *Women before the Bar*, 287, 321–323; Brown, *Good Wives, Nasty Wenches*, 99–100, 148, 185–186; Norton, *Founding Mothers and Fathers*, 334.

for false accusations against Walter Pumphary, was hauled before the Burlington court not only for perjury but also for attempting to suborn others
to perjury. She submitted to the court and was pilloried.[49] In contrast, New
Jersey's supreme court under royal authority apparently could not get wom-
en's words taken seriously at all. In 1706 and 1707, two women were prosecuted for libeling the government and one was prosecuted for perjury;
neither submitted and neither was convicted.[50]

More telling of women's position was their presence or absence in other
cases with high levels of adherence—those involving economic transactions.
Dutch law allowed married women, if they made a prenuptial agreement, to
retain all their property and contracting rights as if they were still single.
Property acquired during marriage was community property, and husbands
and wives often made mutual wills. In New Netherlands courts, these rights
meant it was common to find a woman in a case involving an economic
transaction, either because she retained her legal status to transact, because
she was her husband's legal representative, or because she was a widow
controlling property. Of 195 debt cases in the New Netherlands in 1663, 26.1
percent involved women (75 percent of which related to a woman's own
business activities).[51]

English law and English practices pushed women out of these roles. The
number of female traders in Albany shrank from 46 in the decade before
1664 to 10 in the decade thereafter; the corresponding numbers for New
Amsterdam/New York were 134 in the decade before takeover and 43 in the
decade after. Whereas 80 percent of the Dutch wills in the 1660s were mutual
wills, by the 1690s that percentage had dropped to 7 percent as 93 percent of
husbands followed the English practice of drafting their wills alone.[52] When
this was combined with English legal rules of coverture, the result was a
precipitous drop in women's presence in litigation, particularly regarding
economic transactions. By 1674–1675, women constituted only 10.3 percent
of New York City mayor's court litigants. In the New York supreme court of
1691–1704, women appeared in only 8.6 percent of all cases; in New Jersey's
royal supreme court, that number was 6.9 percent from 1704 to 1710.[53] By the
1740s, women still constituted 10 percent of the plaintiffs but only 3.5 percent
of defendants in New York mayor's court litigation. If only nonexecutor

49. Offutt, *Of "Good Laws" and "Good Men,"* 201; *Burlington Courts,* 58.

50. *New Jersey Supreme Court,* 46–47, 52.

51. Biemer, *Women and Property,* 1–7; David E. Narrett, *Inheritance and Family Life in Colonial New York City* (Ithaca, N.Y., 1992), 42–49.

52. Biemer, *Women and Property,* 7; Narrett, *Inheritance and Family Life,* 83.

53. Scott, *Minutes of the Mayors Court of New York* (21 of 203 litigants); *New York Supreme Court Minutes* and NYHS, *Colls.* (52 in 605 cases); *New Jersey Supreme Court* (14 in 203 cases).

single women (who were not settling their husbands' debts and credits) are included, women constituted 6 percent of plaintiffs and 2 percent of defendants.[54]

As opposed to New York, Connecticut, operating under a Puritan brand of law reform, saw women participate far more often in cases involving economic transactions. Between 1670 and 1719, 17 percent of all cases in New Haven County court involved women, and, of the cases that involved debt, women were present in 15 percent.[55] By analogy, one would expect the law reform jurisdictions of the Delaware Valley to have a similar presence of women litigants, but that was not the case. Only 9.3 percent of cases in Pennsylvania and West Jersey between 1680 and 1710 involved women litigants. In those cases, there was no statistically significant difference in results between men and women, indicating that, once their transaction reached court, women's causes were considered fairly. However, going to court over economic transactions was rarer for women in the Delaware Valley than in New Haven.[56]

Reforms instituted by the Delaware Valley's legal elite might have worked against women's presence in court over economic transactions more than those instituted in New Haven. Women's role, both as producer and trader, was essential to both the family and the colonial economy, but the female economy was often confined to neighborly networks engaged in small trades (in monetary value) or trading of goods in kind. Whereas men's account books aggregated debts over a number of transactions to exceed the jurisdictional limit, such record keeping by women of their trading was apparently quite rare.[57] In Connecticut, county courts retained concurrent jurisdiction over such small causes (less than forty shillings), merely allowing a justice of the peace to hear such causes out of court. Women thus had a choice of forums, and their small debts could become part of the court records. But, in Pennsylvania, as of 1683, all small causes less than forty shillings were to be handled by justices out of court; West Jersey passed the same requirement in 1692. These different jurisdictional rules may account for why women's transactions appeared more often in court under Connecticut's law reforms than in the Delaware Valley.[58]

54. Rosen, *Courts and Commerce*, 96–97.
55. Dayton, *Women before the Bar*, 84–85.
56. Offutt, *Of "Good Laws" and "Good Men,"* 93–98, 129–137.
57. Dayton, *Women before the Bar*, 58; Laurel Thatcher Ulrich, *Good Wives: Image and Reality in the Lives of Women in Northern New England, 1650–1750* (Oxford, 1980), 13–50; Ulrich, *A Midwife's Tale: The Life of Martha Ballard, Based on Her Diary, 1785–1812* (New York, 1990), 5–35; Sara M. Evans, *Born for Liberty: A History of Women in America* (New York, 1989), 28; Kulikoff, *Agrarian Origins*, 30–32.
58. Dayton, *Women before the Bar*, 38; Mann, *Neighbors and Strangers*, 7; George, Nead,

It is in cases protecting body and soul expectations, issues that achieved a middle level of adherence, that Delaware Valley women appeared most often. As either offenders or victims, Pennsylvania and West Jersey took women seriously. Although half of all women accused of any crime faced morals charges (which included liquor, swearing, and Sabbath violations as well as issues of sexuality in the Delaware Valley), men accounted for more than 80 percent of the total accused of morals offenses. In fornication, adultery, bastard, clandestine marriage, and cohabitation cases, women were rarely charged alone, as the offending male was most often prosecuted alongside the female. In outcome, men and women were also equal; of those convicted, both men and women submitted, pleaded guilty, or were summarily fined 80 percent of the time. Not all men appreciated this equality. When Katherine Knight named Charles Thomas in court as the father of her bastard child, he grudgingly admitted it, was ordered to be whipped twenty times to her ten, and was additionally ordered to marry her. When Thomas swore and stomped off after his sentencing, the court added a five-shilling fine. As in seventeenth-century New England, morality was not for women only in the Delaware Valley.[59]

Legal authority protected Delaware Valley women's physical integrity as well. There were, in criminal accusations, ten attempted-rape cases and one rape accusation in the thirty years studied; additionally, one man brought a civil defamation action concerning reports of his rape attempt. Of the ten attempted-rape cases, there were no acquittals—six ended with the defendant's guilt (in five cases he submitted and was whipped, in the sixth, which might have only been a threatened rape, he was fined), two were removed to another court because the defendant was a slave, once the defendant fled, and once—after damning testimony—the record was too torn to discern the verdict. It is probable that these cases reflected only a small fraction of the incidence of rape and attempted rape. Nonetheless, in similarity to Connecticut's courts of the seventeenth century and in strong contrast to the Chesapeake, Delaware Valley courts redefined English legal values in their willingness to trust women.[60]

---

and McCamant, eds., *Charter to William Penn*, 131, 219; Mitchell and Flanders, eds., *Statutes at Large*, II, 43, 189; Leaming and Spicer, eds., *Grants, Concessions, and Original Constitutions of New Jersey*, 509–510.

59. *Bucks Courts*, 21; Dayton, *Women before the Bar*, 159–224; Norton, *Founding Mothers and Fathers*, 336, 346.

60. *Bucks Courts*, 75–76; Bucks County Combined Common Pleas and Quarter Sessions Docket, 1684–1731, Historical Society of Pennsylvania, Philadelphia, 375 (2 cases), 385; *Chester Courts*, I, 163, 328, II, 39; *Burlington Courts*, 55, 127; *Gloucester Courts*, 52–53; Dayton, *Women before the Bar*, 246; Brown, *Good Wives, Nasty Wenches*, 193, 207–210.

The Burlington rape trial of Charles Sheepey in 1688 made the legal validation of women's words apparent. Elizabeth Hutcheson testified that Sheepey had once before tried to rape her while she slept when they both were at her father's house with a large group. She had grabbed his hand after he grabbed her knee and elbow, then she called to the maid to bring up a candle; Sheepey quickly returned to his bed before anyone else saw anything. Elizabeth wanted to complain to her father, but most of the household thought she had only dreamed it, so, rather than anger her father, she kept quiet. Sometime later, when Elizabeth and her sister Martha had returned to their own house with Sheepey, they were so afraid that they tried to get a neighbor's daughter to come home with them. Failing that, they tried to stuff some clothes in the door to keep it shut against him. Nonetheless, according to Elizabeth and Martha's testimony, Sheepey got in and grabbed Elizabeth's hands. She struggled and cried out, Martha awoke, and, despite the fact that "they both with all their strength strive to resist and repulse the said Sheepey, yet hee did then against the will of her the said Elizabeth force the said Elizabeth and with his yard had the use of her body by carnall Copulation."[61]

Sheepey pleaded consent. His first court statement related that he told fortunes, that Elizabeth wanted her fortune told and "would doe any thing for him, if hee would." Sheepey claimed that he had "Carnall knowledge" of Elizabeth at least four times (with particular locations described) and that "Shee was always as willing as hee." Then followed five men's testimony or depositions, virtually all of it hearsay, some supporting Sheepey, some supporting the Hutchesons. Sheepey again claimed consent. Finally, five wives of leading West Jersey men (including one ex-governor and three current justices of the peace) declared that they had "made it their businesse to search Elizabeth Hutcheson" regarding the state of her body. Their conclusion: that Sheepey "hath greatly wronged her in saying" that she had consented, that "What hath beene done, by the said Sheepey, hath beene forcibly." Sheepey then for the third time claimed her consent.

The jury found Sheepey guilty; he was whipped for an hour at a cart's tail as it was driven through town. Following that, Sheepey was to be kept in irons for three months in prison, made to work for his bread, and whipped in a similar manner once each month. After his release, for the next twenty-one months (seven courts), he was to be whipped at each quarterly court session. It is fair to say that the women in this case were believed, particularly in view of the court's and jury's acceptance of the wives' testimony that reflected their special expertise regarding women's bodies. It is also fair to say

61. *Burlington Courts,* 76.

that other women victims were believed from the results of the attempted-rape cases.[62]

Free white women also could have other aspects of their physical well-being protected in court. Stephen Nowell was accused of striking his own wife and Elizabeth White; he was found guilty after his wife testified against him. Joseph Smallwood was presented by the grand jury for "beating and Intolerably abusing his wife" after he had to post a peace bond eight months earlier designed to stop his abuse. Richard Burges, accused of "Selling of his wife" (selling her goods) and not taking suitable care to maintain her, consented to make good whatever the court ordered for maintenance. Not all those accused of harming women were successfully prosecuted, sometimes because witnesses or even the victim did not appear.[63] Nonetheless, protection of free white women's bodies was part of the legal agenda. Courts did not, however, extend the same solicitude to black women. Leading Quaker James Wills could beat his slave woman to death and then have a 1688 Burlington jury exonerate him despite gruesome testimony by his white neighbors. John Neve could rape the slave Mingo's wife, and Mingo would be whipped and sent to prison for reporting it.[64]

Where there were limits to protecting white women through criminal process, civil cases could be used. Martha Wheeler was beaten savagely by Daniel Brinson as he alleged her to be a beast and the Dutchman's whore. The case appeared as a civil action of assault and battery where Wheeler's very wealthy husband Gilbert asked for five pounds' damages and an acknowledgment of the great wrong done his wife. The harm was magnified because, although he had previously let her manage "both of his publique and private affaires," she was now "Incapable of managing the affaires" in his absence. Apparently, Gilbert received satisfaction out of court, because the case was withdrawn.[65] Women were valued for their economic abilities as well as their reputations, both deserving protection; however, whether Martha was satisfied by her husband's suit and settlement (coverture required him and not her to be the plaintiff) remains unknown.

Protection of property showed the weakest adherence generally, yet, when women eluded coverture through widowhood, Delaware Valley courts would protect their property. Widows could have their land protected against adverse claims to the title or encroachments against boundaries, and they could

62. Burlington Courts, 77–80. Such acceptability in a public legal forum of women's expertise over reproduction and women's bodies was also found in New England and Virginia. See Norton, Founding Mothers and Fathers, 206.

63. Bucks Courts, 306–307, 336, 340, 346, 350, 362; Gloucester Courts, 170–172; Chester Courts, I, 21.

64. Burlington Courts, 56–57, 254–255.

65. Bucks Courts, 37–38.

sue to enforce their claims to animals. Even married women who had property stolen would see justice done alongside male victims of the same thief; all would receive restitution fourfold.[66] Yet Pennsylvania's laws esteemed economic transactions more than property rights, especially women's property. Penn himself had redefined common law before he left England: land could be made liable to pay debts. Because husbands could make deals without wives' involvement, her dower right in land was subject to execution for transactions beyond her control. Furthermore, Pennsylvania established that no woman could recover dower rights in land that was acquired and then sold during coverture even if she neither signed nor consented to the sale. Until 1770, Pennsylvania did not even examine a wife privately regarding land transactions that affected her dower.[67] Married women were pushed out of court regarding property in order to safeguard men's expectations in economic deals. Higher adherence in such cases therefore indicated more routine, a routine that could be maintained by keeping contentious women's property questions out of court.

For colonial women, changes in participation at various levels of legal adherence outlined dramatic changes in status. New York women were moved out of economic transaction cases within a few years of the English takeover and thus were marginalized in a growing market economy that relied on routine use of law for predictable results. Law reform in the Delaware Valley offered a mixed blessing, with women's participation aided only on issues concerning body and soul. Diminishing prosecutions of moral offenses in the eighteenth century would erode this advantage. Law reforms in Connecticut, based more heavily on a religious vision, undermined the patriarchy of common law and opened up more areas for legal participation during much of the 1600s, although women would never participate proportionate to their numbers in regard to authority or economic transactions. However, the late 1600s and early 1700s saw a shift toward Anglicized legal practice in Connecticut as women were pushed toward the periphery. Fewer women appeared in the litigated economy, paternity issues became contested and then moved out of court and into a hearing before a single justice, attempted-rape indictments disappeared for seventy years, accused rapists were acquitted, and women were involved in fewer slander suits. Women's behavior became less a public concern, as "privatization" (a competing

66. *Burlington Courts,* 14, 170; *Chester Courts,* I, 372–373 (widow lost). A thief robbed from Mary Grub a shirt and tallow, from Mary Gosling a shift, handkerchiefs, and stockings, and from nine other victims. See *Burlington Courts,* 64–65.
67. George, Nead, and McCamant, eds., *Charter to William Penn,* 100; Dunn and Dunn, eds., *Papers of William Penn,* II, 222; Mitchell and Flanders, eds., *Statutes at Large,* II, 210; Marylynn Salmon, *Women and the Law of Property in Early America* (Chapel Hill, N.C., 1986), 24–25.

rhetoric in many ways) evolved to control middle-class women's lives. Virginia saw a similar progression, especially in areas involving women's words such as slander and sexual morality, as gossip networks became an expression of women almost wholly outside of court.[68]

What these litigation histories shared were two patterns: first, women's participation began at low level in cases of high adherence and then declined because of increased legal Anglicization and increased market relations from which women were excluded; second, where women's participation in a legal issue began in a colony at a higher rate, as with issues of body and soul, the level of adherence started to decline first, followed by a decline in the number of cases and women's role in them. Women and their concerns were peripheralized and privatized by courts as men and their market relations became more central to the law's authority in colonial British America, a result whose pace and pattern can best be detected and compared through litigation analysis for these and all other colonies.

IV. Conclusion

These intersecting models, one that examines legal adherence on various issues and one that overlays groups' participation in those issues over time, can, by systematizing the treatment of legal issues and legal participation, synthesize the meaning of inclusion, avoidance, or removal from the law's issues for additional groups in additional colonies. The withdrawal of critical social groups from their previous levels of legal participation, such as farmers in North Carolina's Regulation, could produce catastrophic losses in court authority.[69] Servants in Maryland could take advantage of general legal adherence by framing their disputes in contract; however, social and political upheaval would reduce such adherence and thus the ability of servants to gain positive outcomes in their petitions. Women in Virginia could subvert coverture by gaining powers of attorney from their husbands; the effect and significance of such powers can then be traced by participation of such women in issues of higher adherence.[70] The social position of blacks, In-

68. Rosen, *Courts and Commerce*, 95–110, 130; Dayton, "Was There a Calvinist Type of Patriarchy? New Haven Colony Reconsidered in the Early Modern Context," above; Dayton, *Women before the Bar*, 49–53, 84–88, 159–161, 192–194, 206–207, 218, 232–234, 246–248, 286–288, 304; Brown, *Good Wives, Nasty Wenches*, 185–191, 285, 287.

69. Richard Lyman Bushman, "Farmers in Court: Orange County, North Carolina, 1750–1776," below.

70. Christine Daniels, "'Liberty to Complaine': Servant Petitions in Maryland, 1652–1797," above; Linda L. Sturtz, "'As Though I My Self Was Pr[e]sent': Virginia Women with Power of Attorney," above.

dians, members of various occupations, the poor, ethnic groups, and denominations (among others) can be traced over time by the amount of their legal participation and by the location of that participation within a ranking of issues based on their legal adherence.

As discussed here, courts employing law reforms and non-English legal principles seem to have been more inclusive of peripheral groups; returning to values contained in common law not only Anglicized the content of the law but also the legal participants. Courts in the Middle Colonies attempted to assert authority over a wider variety of behavior and to include a wider cross-section of peripheral groups in their earlier years than they did later. Court authority over the whole spectrum of social behavior ironically might have shrunk as adherence regarding economic transactions grew. The widely noted litigation explosion of the 1700s seems to have occurred in contract and debt causes that concurrently showed increased adherence, marking such concerns as central to legal authority and perhaps limiting the legal resources available for individuals or the elite to address other issues.[71] Courts became more specialized in dividing functions between civil and criminal, and they became more complicated, technical, and dominated by lawyers, thus pricing some litigants out of court. The spectrum of issues voluntarily brought into court narrowed over time, peripheralizing legal discourse as issues previously subject to public legal authority such as sexuality became more subject to the authority of "privatized" discourses such as gossip.

The spectrum of people who voluntarily came to court also narrowed. When colonial legal values and practices moved closer to metropolitan legal values and practices, groups like women, non-English ethnic groups, and the poor either withdrew or were pushed out to the legal periphery, leaving court business increasingly focused on the interests of elite groups such as merchants and large landowners. This social replication of English law occurred much sooner than has been suggested elsewhere—around the turn of the eighteenth century, in many places—and implied that law was a leading indicator for the replication of English life observed in eighteenth-century colonial culture and society. Courts now responded more exclusively to the needs of those closest to the center of colonial society; it was no longer deemed necessary to negotiate with those on the periphery or to encourage their participation. Through other means, the periphery then only needed to be controlled.

More speculatively, the center-periphery metaphor, now generally em-

---

71. The explosion took slightly different forms in other colonies. See Konig, "Summary View of the Law of British America," *WMQ*, 3d Ser., L (1993), 43.

ployed by colonial historians in its geographic sense, may be integrated into colonial legal history in a sociological sense to outline the pace and pattern of the transmission of legal values over time, over places, over groups.[72] Edward Shils defined a sociological core as the central value system of a society, set by an elite and expressed through a network of institutions. Less powerful segments of the society constitute a periphery. The central value system and its institutions successfully achieve a substantial amount of consensus even among peripheral groups in any functioning society. "Consensual action derives from the common adherence to laws, rules, and norms. It is supported by attachment to the institutions which promulgate and apply the laws and rules." The successful transmission of elite values may be identified by the degree of adherence that prevails as one moves outward from the core toward the social periphery, to discover where "attachment to the central value system becomes attenuated" and authority diminishes.[73]

Historians concerned with what J. R. Pole has called "the sociology of consent" to colonial legal authority thus can connect, in theory, observed behavior and internalized values and can map the relative social positions of groups on a center-periphery scale through the adherence and participation shown in litigation behavior.[74] Only by analyzing evidence of surrounding community and cultural factors, only by examining the power of competing discourses at given points can such hypotheses about the affective levels of

72. Bernard Bailyn, *The Peopling of British North America: An Introduction* (New York, 1986), 112–114; Greene, *Pursuits of Happiness;* Greene, *Peripheries and Center: Constitutional Development in the Extended Polities of the British Empire and the United States, 1607–1788* (Athens, Ga., 1986); David Hackett Fischer, *Albion's Seed: Four British Folkways in America* (New York, 1989), 3–11; Greene, "Interpretive Frameworks: The Quest for Intellectual Order in Early American History," *WMQ,* 3d. Ser., XLVIII (1991), 515–530. Only Fischer utilized legal history extensively, but with little on the significance of law in courts (*Albion's Seed,* 189–199, 398–410, 584–595, 765–776). Movement of English legal rules and practices to the colonies has long been a subject of research; see Zechariah Chafee, Jr., "Colonial Courts and the Common Law," Julius Goebel, Jr., "King's Law and Local Custom in Seventeenth Century New England," both in David H. Flaherty, ed., *Essays in the History of Early American Law* (Chapel Hill, N.C., 1969), 53–120; John M. Murrin, "The Legal Transformation: The Bench and Bar of Eighteenth-Century Massachusetts," in Stanley N. Katz, ed., *Colonial America: Essays in Politics and Social Development* (Boston, 1971), 415–449; David Grayson Allen, *In English Ways: The Movement of Societies and the Transferal of English Local Law and Custom to Massachusetts Bay in the Seventeenth Century* (Chapel Hill, N.C., 1981); Ross, "Legal Past of Early New England," *WMQ,* 3d Ser., L (1993), 39–41. Legal historians have begun to use an overall colonial model to inform their research: see Hulsebosch, *"Imperia in Imperio,"* Law and History Review, XVI (1998), 322–379.

73. Shils, *Center and Periphery,* 3–47, 164–179, esp. 10, 168–169; Greene, *Peripheries and Center,* ix. Ross has noted the need for legal historians to concentrate on such peripheral groups' relationship to the core legal culture ("Legal Past of Early New England," *WMQ,* 3d Ser., L [1993] 35–37).

74. J. R. Pole, comments, "The Many Legalities of Early America" conference, Williamsburg, Va., Nov. 24, 1996.

consensus be accepted or rejected. Colonial women's historians have done such work and confirmed hypotheses of peripheralization suggested by litigation patterns. Center-periphery can thus provide a common framework for identifying through litigation patterns the social movement of all groups (toward center or periphery) and the social movement of legal values among the various colonies.

Farmers in Court

Orange County, North Carolina, 1750–1776

NYONE STUDYING FARMERS in early America must go to court, as the farmers themselves did so often throughout their lives. As young farmers, they registered deeds to their first lands or received inheritances from their fathers at court; as old men, they passed on farms to their children. At every stage, they went to court to sue for debt or be sued, to petition for mills or taverns, to have roads laid out and repaired, and to register cattle marks. In most places, county courts imposed the taxes assessed to the farmers' names on the tax lists. If a farmer kept no diary or account book and saved no letters, as few did, court documents are about the only record of a farmer's life. To recover the lives of the great mass of farmers, a historian of farming must come to terms with the deeds, wills, and debt cases now stored in court archives.

Ordinarily we mine this mountain of records for what we take to be the gold: such nuggets of information as the amount and value of the property exchanged, the number and value of debt cases, the locations of debtors and creditors, the division of property among children, the value and types of objects in estate inventories, and similar kinds of information that can be used to reconstruct the social organization and the economic workings of the rural economy. The information extracted from court records, after arduous and ingenious refinement in the mills of the historians, accounts for a large part of what we know about rural life.

But in mining the ore and refining the gold, we can lose sight of the mountain from which the data were taken. That immense pile of legal texts stacked in the archives represents something beyond the price of land or the contraction of debts. Taken together it amounts to a cultural system, a set of deep routines, a vast map of social interactions and human purposes. Like all texts, judicial texts create worlds peopled with characters and specifying habits of living, actions, dangers, and rewards. The farmers who came to court to conduct their business entered those worlds and became players in

I am grateful to Christopher Tomlins and Bruce Mann for inviting me to the "Many Legalities of Early America" conference and for their astute editorial advice in preparing the paper for publication. The groundwork was laid during my tenure as a fellow at the National Humanities Center.

their intricate plots. If we restrict our researches to a limited number of outcomes of the farmers' days in court, we lose sight of this complex textual world that encompassed them as much as the physical world of fields, barns, and fences. Court texts constructed both farms and farmers in the largest sense of producing identities and formulating imagined worlds in which farmers lived portions of their lives. By looking at the records as complete texts, we get at these broader meanings of court documents.

To grasp the full meaning of the texts, we must realize that farms and farmers were constructed by words and thoughts and did not consist solely of their physical beings. Although the notion of texts' producing social reality may seem perverse, the idea of court records' producing farms is much more obvious. We are obviously mistaken to think of farms as composed solely of soil and the works of human labor inscribed on the earth. The total farm, besides being a fixture on the land, also existed in the mind and had mobile segments that could exist far from the site of the farm itself. A migrating farm family carried essential ingredients of a farm in their wagon. The knowledge of agriculture borne in their heads was as important as the land in creating a farm, as was the resolve to work the land, their own bodies inured to hard labor, and their tools, seeds, and stock. These vital portions of the whole farm system traveled in the wagon train even before the farm was located and purchased.[1]

Just as essential parts of a farm were detached from the earth and existed in the farmer's imagination, so the farm existed in court records. The physical construction of a farm was only one manifestation of the farm idea. The farm existed in courthouse documents as essentially as it existed on the earth. Courts made farms from texts. The representations of the farm in deeds, wills, inventories, and promissory notes affected its shape, size, and ownership as much as fencelines or cleared fields. The documentary farm in the court records at times even overruled the physical farm formed by long labor on the land. An execution for debt could snatch away animals, tools, and acres; a paper description of a boundary could shift a property line between neighbors. The words scrawled on diagrams in the courthouse often preempted the farm laid out on the landscape. The court's job was to preserve, interpret, and enforce the documentary farm that was created in those papers.

Farmers themselves were constructed in the courts, just as their farms were. The court records gave form to a documentary farmer as well as a documentary farm, rural identity consisting as much of marks on paper as of marks on the land. We sometimes think of the farmer as essentially a producer who cleared land, fenced, plowed, planted, weeded, harvested, and

---

1. I am indebted to Claudia Bushman for the concept of a migrating farm.

marketed crops. We conjure that picture mainly from what we know of farmers today, projecting back their work to a time of simpler tools and restricted sources of power—helped by historical reconstructions like Old Sturbridge Village. But, if we based our ideas of farming on the remaining records where farmers are named and their actions recorded, we would also think of them in court, involved in legal transactions. We actually have more records of farmers at court than there are accounts of them working the soil. Not that farmers spent all their time in court; the documents record only a few brief moments in their long lives. But, basing our judgments on the surviving records, we would envision farmers as transactors as much as producers. We would see them locked in the embrace of their property, striving to deploy it through space and time. The entire farm enterprise rested on property, a fictive construction of the court, and the farmer had to attend to his property as conscientiously as he worked his land. Viewing the farmer from the perspective of the court documents, we see him as transactor, a propertyholder who had to define, protect, and disperse property in court.

By looking at farms and farmers as they are represented in these texts, we can begin to explore the mountain of court records in a more holistic way. The texts produced specialized worlds wherein the management of property occupied center stage, and to reconstitute the farmer's life we must enter those worlds with him. But the records also represent the court itself. The court was the stage where the farmer transacted his legal business. To recover farmers' lives, we must look at the county court as farmers encountered it, for it was the place where farmers most directly confronted the state. The court's rulings invaded farmers' lives when property was transferred, a will was probated, or a debt was collected—times when a farmer's economic fate hung in the balance. At these moments, when farmers came face to face with state power, rural political culture was generated, tested, and remolded. Besides forming the farmer as a transactor, court records and court experience were the dominant influences in the formation of the farmer as a political subject.

The political beings constructed by their experiences at court were complex fabrications, richly inscribed with ideas about government institutions, political motivation, and the sources of danger. Farm political culture included unconscious assumptions about the broadest conceptions of state power. We have wanted to know farmers' sentiments about the Revolution or the United States Constitution, specific issues at certain times in the eighteenth century. But in court the idea of legitimacy itself was on trial. The courts implicitly raised the question of why individuals should submit to government and, more particularly, to court rulings that deprived them of life, liberty, and property. Why should the men on the bench have such immense power over people on the other side of the bar, awarding the property of one man to another, sentencing persons to imprisonment, and even taking away life? Why should an individual acknowledge this awesome authority in emissaries of a remote and feeble government?

The question, rarely asked by any parties to a court case, forces itself upon us once we recognize that courts themselves were textual productions. The court records produced the court in the same sense that they produced documentary farms and farmers, the court being even less physical than the farm. It was wholly an imaginary fabrication, another specialized world constructed for the purpose of enforcing laws and protecting property. The clerk's minutes described a scene and characters and devised actions, with farmers named as players in the court's little dramas. Whether farmers liked it or not, these judicial concoctions became a field of endeavor for them like their pastures and barnyards. The question is, Why did they go along with the fiction when they had so many causes to complain? In virtually every court case, one of the parties was disappointed and suffered a loss of some kind. The courts could be seen as repeatedly generating natural enemies. Why did opposition not arise more frequently? Why the nearly universal support for an invasive institution resting on a flimsy foundation—mere words on paper? By answering these questions, we come to know farmers as political subjects constructed through their court experiences.

To enrich these investigations of the courts, I have selected my examples of court texts from Orange County, North Carolina, in the second half of the eighteenth century, when the legitimacy of the courts was brought into question. During the Regulator controversies, beginning around 1766, farmers objected to the management of the Orange County courts and, after a seesaw exchange of declarations and warnings with court officials and eventually the governor, confronted a contingent of government troops in 1771 at the Battle of Alamance, in which lives were lost on both sides. The Regulator controversy produced an unusual spinoff document in the commentary of Hermon Husband, the spokesman for the Regulators during Orange County's struggle with county court officers in the late 1760s. Husband, an untutored, irrepressible, prickly farmer and agitator, compiled a decade's worth of petitions, pleas, and complaints in a disjointed narrative that he called *An Impartial Relation of the First Rise and Cause of the Recent Differences in Publick Affairs*, published in 1770. His account balances the routine documents in the court archives with a story of violent resistance to court officers.

The burden of Husband's grievance was the abuse of power by sheriffs, clerks, justices of the peace, and lawyers, who were all said to charge excessive fees and extract unwarranted taxes. The protests grew from 1766 on, until in 1770 Husband and the furious farmers drove the offending officials from the court. To restore order, Governor William Tryon sent troops to Orange County in May 1771 to meet more than two thousand aroused farmers. At Alamance Creek, government soldiers confronted a crowd of farmers and demanded surrender of their arms. When they refused, shots were fired, and at the end thirty men lay dead. *An Impartial Relation* was published before the violence had broken out, but Husband's writing captured the anger that brought the affair to its desperate conclusion. After a hundred pages of frustrated fuming against the evildoers, he likened the farmers to Balaam's asses and the officials to Balaam's children riding on the asses' backs. Pitifully the animals cry out: "Are not we thine asses, upon which thou has ridden ever since we were thine?" Did the complaint sum up farmers' feelings about courts?[2]

In a coda following this outcry, Husband claimed that before the outbreak the farmers had considered a boycott. They resolved, he reported, "If the government was against us, and we could get redress no way, we would, rather than rise in riots, agree not to go to law at all, but leave our Differences to arbitrations." The farmers briefly contemplated informal mediation but, in the end, did not take that course. Through their miseries, they never stopped coming to court. After the Battle of Alamance, the government instituted a few modest changes, and the courts continued as before. During the Revolution, when the courts could have been reformed, the most radical proposal was for lower fees and the election of clerks and sheriffs. Both failed in the state constitutional convention, and the courts carried on without modification. County courts, though often criticized, were as solidly entrenched as any institution of government. The Regulator movement causes us to ask, Why were the courts so stable in rural political culture despite the anger they aroused? Why were centuries-old forms of rural justice able to continue largely unchanged through two decades of revolutionary transformation?[3]

2. [Hermon Husband], *An Impartial Relation of the First Rise and Cause of the Recent Differences in Publick Affairs, in the Province of North Carolina . . .* , in William K. Boyd, ed., *Some Eighteenth Century Tracts concerning North Carolina* (Raleigh, N.C., 1927), 331. The Regulators have been much examined in search of their social motivations, which are not the focus of this essay. A clearheaded account, along with relevant bibliography, can be found in A. Roger Ekirch, *"Poor Carolina": Politics and Society in Colonial North Carolina, 1729–1776* (Chapel Hill, N.C., 1981), 164–208.

3. [Husband], *Impartial Relation,* in Boyd, ed., *Eighteenth Century Tracts,* 331; Ekirch, *"Poor Carolina,"* 206–207; Elisha P. Douglass, *Rebels and Democrats: The Struggle for Equal Political Rights and Majority Rule during the American Revolution* (Chapel Hill, N.C., 1955), 127–128, 133. The only significant change after 1776 was to allow any three justices of the peace to sit as a county inferior court rather than require there be at least one specially designated justice of the quorum. See R. W. Herring, "The Early Judicial System of the State of North Carolina, and Its Relation to the Proprietary and Royal Systems," *North Carolina Journal of Law,* I (July 1904), 360.

Up to the moment of disruption and immediately after, the standard, formulaic court documents were dutifully entered in the records. From them we can partially reconstruct the conventional textual worlds in which farmers figured as transactors. In the crisis years, the court came as close to dissolution as at any time in the eighteenth century. If judicial legitimacy was ever questioned, it was then. In the documents from these years, we are able to explore the limits of rural skepticism about courts and examine the basis of the farmers' usual allegiance. Together, the years of stability and the moment of disruption in Orange County give us a broad view of court culture, allowing us to ask what the mountain of court texts meant to farmers.

I

After the organization of Orange County in 1752, the first item on the docket was the request of several persons to "have their several Marks recorded." Not the signature marks of illiterate men, these marks identified cattle roaming at large on unfenced lands: "Henry Bedingfield a Crop and two Slits in the right ear and a halfmoon under it and a Swallow fork under it, Brand RHB." Marks allowed animals to graze in the woods for most of the year, returning to the owner, if at all, for the brief span when winter vegetation did not grow. Not until roundup and slaughter did the farmer pay much heed to the animals, and thus he was freed to concentrate on corn and vegetables for home consumption and on market crops like wheat. This efficient grazing system depended on turning animals into property with unique marks for identification at the roundup, and the court registered the crucial marks.[4]

Farmers came to court for practical help of this kind. County courts laid out roads, ordered out work crews for construction and repair, and appointed overseers to check on upkeep. The courts licensed tavernkeepers and public ferrymen. Deeds were registered in court, debts collected, wills probated. Farmers called as jurors and constables added to the numbers at court. Orange County court days drew scores of farmers to Hillsborough, the county seat, to conduct public or private business at the quarterly sessions. Of the 739 heads of household named on the 1755 tax list, 59.9 percent were also named in the court minutes for 1752–1761, even though many 1755

4. "Orange County, North Carolina Court Minutes, 1752–1761," book I, transcription of the original minutes by Weynette Parks Haun (Durham, N.C., 1991), 1. Haun's scrupulous transcription, based on long experience with eighteenth-century handwriting, is the best way to consult the minutes. The transcription is in the collection of the North Carolina State Archives and is available directly from Haun at 243 Argonne Drive, Durham, NC 27704-1423. The original is Minutes of the Court of Pleas and Quarter Sessions of Orange County, N.C., 1752–1766, 3 vols., North Carolina State Archives, Raleigh. All Orange County records, unless otherwise noted, are in the North Carolina State Archives, Raleigh.

residents left the county before the end of the period and the names in the minutes do not include those on deeds and wills. Only a rare farmer stayed away for long. No information in the almanacs was more useful than the court day schedule.[5]

Migrating farmers first came to court to register a deed, the initial documentary representation of the farm. Beginning at midcentury, the North Carolina piedmont attracted thousands of migrants from Virginia, Maryland, and Pennsylvania, doubling the population between 1750 and 1770 and raising the colony from seventh in size to fourth by the time of the Revolution. For the first decade of Orange County's existence, from 1752 to 1762, 91 titles on average were entered each year. After the end of the Seven Years' War, constraints burst, and migration skyrocketed. From 1763 to 1765, the average number of title entries rose to 410, before leveling off in the next three years to an average of 142 per year. Most of these newcomers came to court to register their deeds.[6]

Even squatters wanted secure titles if they could get them, as can be seen from Hermon Husband's defense of one group of them. Seven years before settling in 1762, Husband came to Orange County as an agent for ten Maryland investors who planned to purchase land. What he found was an unworkable land system that forced people to squat. He wrote a long letter to John Carteret, Earl Granville, the English proprietor of the tract that included Orange, complaining of the obstacles in the way of land purchase. Husband reported that "numbers of honest industreous people" arrived in Orange after a journey of hundreds of miles and then faced another two-hundred-mile trip to the land office in Edenton to purchase land. Unable to face this ordeal, they were "obliged to employ themselves as industreously as possible on any piece of land they can meet with, for one, two, or three years before they can procure stock and grain to sustain their famalies." They wanted the land entered and surveyed and did not like working unpurchased land, but distance and an uncooperative land agent hampered them. The new arrivals were about to leave, Husband reported, because

5. "North Carolina Orange to Wit: A List of Tythables for the Year 1755." The index for the court minutes is in "Orange County Court Minutes," trans. Haun, I. In addition to official business, court days were an occasion for private business and pleasure, for trading horses and selling chickens, for drinking and gaming. Sleepy towns changed into bustling centers at court times. In the South especially, no public institution, not even the churches, attracted more interest. See Joseph A. Ernst and H. Roy Merrens, " 'Camden's Turrets Pierce the Skies!': The Urban Process in the Southern Colonies during the Eighteenth Century," *William and Mary Quarterly*, 3d Ser., XXX (1973), 549–574. See also Darrett Rutman and Anita Rutman, *A Place in Time: Middlesex County, Virginia, 1650–1750* (New York, 1984), 87–93, 125–127.

6. Ekirch, *"Poor Carolina,"* 231–232; Harry Roy Merrens, *Colonial North Carolina in the Eighteenth Century: A Study in Historical Geography* (Chapel Hill, N.C., 1964), 53–55; Orange County Registration of Deeds County Court, 1752–1793, part I.

Granville's agent made it hard to obtain a title. "The people in generall are become heartless and quite careless to improve their lands or buildings," and instead talked of "a flight to some new place." Husband said this reaction "was ever the case where they have not a shure foundation and title in those American parts."[7]

Land titles meant everything to farmers and were doubtless scrutinized, even though, we must assume, they were rarely produced by farmers themselves. Lawyers, clerks, and justices wrote out deeds and conveyances. Many farmers could not write their own names, much less compose a legal document. But even illiterate farmers knew the contents of the deeds. They listened as they were read to be sure the acreage on the ground corresponded to the property in the deed. Some learned enough to be appointed justices of the peace without legal training, solely on the basis of experience in court where they absorbed the language that figured so powerfully in their lives—language so affecting that, even for those who remained on the margins of the court, it constituted rural identity as authentically as texts written in the person's own hand.

These documents were deeply personal. When the signature was affixed, a deed or a promissory note captured a portion of the maker's will. The most potent writing on any document, the signature signified the surrender of will to the paper. In that instant, the person irrevocably concurred in the sale or purchase of property or in a promise to pay a debt. No reconsideration or change of circumstances reversed the agreement. Thereafter a portion of the person's will resided, not in his mind, but on the signed paper in the courthouse, given away to a written text. An active person might deposit scores of such surrenders in the court records, thereby transferring many parts of himself into these scattered writings. The effect was scarcely less with those who signed only two or three times in a lifetime, or with a mark. Each signature left a part of the person in the text.

The texts themselves, brief and stilted as they might be, contained a world. A deed, a promissory note, or a will each represented a society, the wording of the document framed to suit the purposes of the court in the action of the case. The document reduced society and personality to essentials, to the abbreviated qualities required for the recorded transaction. The text's world was framed on a field where the issue of the case—rightful ownership, payment of debt, or execution of a will—was being contested, and representation had to be stripped for maximum effect in addressing the primary issue. Though specialized, truncated, and highly stylized, the texts represent

7. Ekirch, " 'A New Government of Liberty': Hermon Husband's Vision of Backcountry North Carolina, 1755," *WMQ*, 3d Ser., XXXIV (1977), 639–640. For a resort to violence to protect titles, see Ekirch, *"Poor Carolina,"* 138, 140–142.

recognizable worlds where farmers lived out important fragments of their lives. A legal document crystallized experience in a peculiarly intense and focused form, sharply defining critical passages in a rural life.

What worlds, then, existed inside the classic court documents, deeds, promissory notes, probate records, and wills? What passages were farmers expected to navigate when they went to court?

A

The world of the deed is primarily a landscape. The deed describes the land, not the people who come to purchase and sell. Where the people came from or where they are going is of no concern to the deed. On the other hand, the deed describes the land in detail, including its history. A deed from John Cate, Sr. to John Cate, Jr. January 25, 1772, writes a history of the parcel being sold, describing it as "part of a tract of Land that Joseph Aldrige purchasd. of Earl Granville and by him Conveyd. to the sd. John Cate Senior." The whole body of deeds together form a landscape history of the county in which the descent of property from owner to owner can be (and by title searchers is) reconstructed. This is not an ecological history of animals, plants, and birds, an agricultural history of crops and buildings, or a social history of squabbles over control; it is a property history of bounds, sizes, and owners. The landscape is mapped with property lines and nothing else. Trees and streams figure only as they mark the boundaries of ownership.[8]

Persons achieve significance on the bounded landscape only as owners. The society of the deed is devoted solely to the exchange of property. In this world, possession of land and buying and selling are all that give a person existence. Nonpossessors—the large population of women, children, servants, laborers, and slaves—are nearly invisible. Occasionally women are possessors, and more often children, but infrequently. The male possessors are the players in this world. Women and children are dimly visible as "heirs and Assigns," but they are always "his" heirs and assigns, extensions of the possessor's persona. The deed projects a future in which the land passes down through the generations of the possessor's family, keeping the owner and his property at the center of attention. The central human activity in the deed is to possess and exchange property, in the past and interminably into the future.

The deed world is one of movement and change. Tracts of land large and small pass from one owner to another like ships moving from port to port. And the voyage is not free of danger, as the deeds tell the story. There is the question of the seller's true intent. It is not enough to say John Cate, Sr.

8. John Cate, Sr. to John Cate, Jr., Jan. 5, 1772, Orange County Deeds, 1755-1927, Ad-Ca.

agrees to sell the land to John Cate, Jr. He "doth Give grant Bargin and sell infeofe Release and Confirm unto the sd John Cate Junr. his Heirs and Assigns forever a Certain tract or parcel of Land." So many forms of selling can be imagined by the lawyers that seven words are need to cover all the rights and limitations and to truly divest John Cate, Sr. of all forms of ownership. Moreover, Cate, Sr.

> for himself his heirs and Assigns forever Doth Covenant and grant to and with the heirs and all and every other person or persons and his or their heirs any thing having or Claiming in the sd. premises Above Mentioned or any part therof shall and will warrant and forever Defend.

Cate must promise on behalf of himself and everyone connected with him that he will defend the title being passed to Cate, Jr. The lawyers envision challenges coming over the horizon at some future date and make Cate, Sr. promise to fight them off.[9]

The courts try to stabilize the constant movement in the world of the deed, offering protection during the passage of property from owner to owner. One way was by conducting business in the open. On the back of the Cate deed is written: "The execution of the within Deed was duly proved in open Court by the Oath of John Pyron and Ordered to be Registred." The phrase "in open Court," always included in descriptions of registration, implied that the court construed itself as a public space. Here any challenge to Cate's ownership could be entered; and, having thus exposed itself to counterclaims, the deed was more secure. Other court documents began with the words "Know all men by these presents," similarly construing the court as a public space. By construction, all men were considered present at the reading of the document, even if court was held in a tiny room in a remote place with a dozen people in attendance. In a formal sense, presentation in an open court notified the whole world of the commitment in the text. Courts embodied the most pervasive and ancient of public spaces in the Anglo-American tradition and perhaps the precedent and model for subsequent public spaces given over to contests and debate.[10]

B

The landscape recedes from view in the promissory note, the document behind debt suits, the largest single category of court cases.[11] The action in the text takes place over time rather than in space.

9. Ibid.
10. Michael Warner, *The Letters of the Republic: Publication and the Public Sphere in Eighteenth-Century America* (Cambridge, Mass., 1990), 34–43.
11. The calculation of the number of debt cases assumes that most items called "trespass on the case" involved debt. Students of the courts agree that this is a fair assumption. "The

I promise to pay or cause to be paid unto John Amstead his Hairs or assigns the Just and full Sum of three hundred pounds current Money of North Carolina on or before the first Day of October next ensuing the date hereof for Value received as Witness my Hand and Seal this 11th Day of August 1792. Andrew Burke.

Money is lent on one day, and the borrower promises to return the amount at a specific later time. The note controls an exchange of money in the future rather than the exchange of property on the landscape. The parties again are owners, but the possession is money, not land, and the dimension is time, not space.[12]

The futuristic quality of the note is in keeping with a common purpose for borrowing: to develop the farm or to provide for children. Farmers were projectors; they had to live in the time ahead. Crops were planted in the expectation of growth and harvested many months later after passing through all the havoc that weather, pests, and disease could wreak. Still further into the future, many years ahead, the farmer foresaw the development of his land: forested acres cleared, fences built, swamps drained, parcels added, herds enlarged, buildings constructed. He foresaw entirely new farms for his children, at nearby sites or in remote areas. His life depended on events hard to foretell, indifferently regulated, and yet necessary for him to project if he were to have any control over the future. The promissory note reveals the farmer in his futuristic orientation, in the critical act of promising, hoping, and trusting.

Unlike deeds, promissory notes bound borrowers and lenders for a period of time and so created a little society of debtors and creditors within the larger society. Deeds had no time dimension. The sale of land occurred in the seconds when the signature was affixed, and the link between the parties lasted only for the moment of transaction. The promissory note tied lender to borrower for months or years. The key act for both borrower and lender is the promise. I will pay, the signer of the note says, resting the entire transaction on both parties' confidence in the borrower's ability to fulfill. Both trust in the borrower's accurate prediction of what he can and will do

---

most common type of civil suit brought before the county court was the action of 'trespass on the case,' often referred to simply as an action of 'case.' Trespass on the case was a universal action for personal wrongs and injuries inflicted without force. The plaintiff used this action to obtain a remedy for damages he suffered from a broken contract, slander, negligence, or deceit. The most frequent basis for an action of case was a debt or obligation arising from a breach of contract" (Paul M. McCain, *The County Court in North Carolina before 1750* [Durham, N.C., 1954], 54–55).

12. Orange County Promissory Notes, n.d., 1773–1819. Promissory notes for Orange County are found in Orange County Civil Action Papers, n.d., 1771–1781; Orange County Promissory Notes, n.d., 1773–1819.

months or years in advance. While the note was in effect, each had an interest in the other, the debtor had an obligation, and probably both had fears. A lender could demand payment at an embarrassing time; a borrower could fail to pay. Yet the notes said nothing of fear and anger, reducing the bond to purely financial and temporal terms—I will pay this much in this time—but, in the world of the note, the web of credit relationships, extending through time, was made visible.

C

The estate sale returns to the instant transaction of the deed, leaving behind the time dimension of the promissory note. But, in place of the land or money in deeds and promissory notes, records of estate sales emphasized things—hoes, chairs, clothing, bushels of corn. The sales dealt with a deceased person's movable estate, consisting of all the tools and furnishings in house and barn as well as the animals, slaves, and crops. Such items were not always itemized in wills, as real estate was, and so, to manage distribution among the heirs, the sales disposed of the goods and added the receipts to the cash balance. A clerk of the court oversaw the sale, recording each item sold, the purchaser, and the price and prepared a list for inclusion in the probate file.

At the sale, the wife and children of the deceased often purchased items against their inheritances, but non–family members attended and bought goods too. At the estate sale of Ephraim McCaleb in Orange County in November 1770, five family members, including the widow, purchased goods, and thirty-three others bought from one to five items, the prices ranging from a few pennies to ten pounds.[13]

The estate sale, like the inventory of goods made during probate, reveals the farmer amid his many possessions, the large numbers of small items that were scattered through house and barn. Women, who were active at estate sales, had their own array of goods, clothes, utensils, bedding, and chairs. Besides having practical uses, these objects extended men and women into their possessions, elaborating their material identities. Farm people worked with tools, never with their hands alone. Tools mediated action on the natural world of soil, crops, animals, raw food, or fiber. Skillets, flails, churns, stills, yokes, spinning wheels, and carts extended the body into tasks of housekeeping and husbandry. Of all the legal documents, the estate sale offers the best glimpse of the work that occupied farm people every day of the year.

The old pots, chipped dishes, axes, and hoes that appeared on most of the

13. Orange County Estates, 1758–1785, 251–253.

lists can only be imagined as a ragged assemblage of objects. In Orange County at midcentury, few farmers owned display objects. McCaleb, a fairly well-off tobacco planter, had only eight pewter plates to go with his wooden trenchers. Although he owned a walnut table and chest, no ceramic table dishes connected him with rising genteel styles. The rest of the list named only utilitarian items: a dough trough, sidesaddle, pot and pot hooks, piggin, chest, handsaw, curry comb, drawing knife and auger, branding iron, and saddle tree—objects that came together piecemeal over a lifetime, as McCaleb himself went to estate sales or bartered with neighbors. He would have known each item and inventoried each in his mind so that he knew what tools he had for each task, the whole comprising his material world.

At death, McCaleb's assemblage of objects was disassembled. At the sale buyers came to add to their own assemblages of things, each with an inventory of current possessions in mind, ready to fill in gaps. Beyond a few basics, they had no model of a complete inventory to go by, judging from the diversity of estate inventories, and no nearby store stocked everything a farmer needed. Collecting tools called for improvisation. A farmer had to pick up items when he could, in estate sales like McCaleb's, or by barter. The assemblage assumed new shapes from month to month, as items came and went, until family and friends cannibalized the collection at death. If the deed and the promissory note project a flow of land and money about the county, the estate sale implies household objects and farm tools moving from hand to hand, the boundaries of the inventories always being refigured, extending and contracting the farm family's material sense of itself, its efficiency at farm tasks, and its visible identity in the community.

D

Finally, the will brought these stories and operations to a culmination for the individual while guaranteeing their continuance in the lives of the next generation. Death marked the end of a person's collection of objects, and similarly death was a turning point in all the stories recorded in court documents. Death dropped like a cleaver across the worlds of deeds, notes, and estate sales. Although settlement could take years, at death, ownership of land ended for one person and had to be started up again with others; debts were ordinarily paid off; and the movable estate was dispersed. Both space and time were changed. Dividing a farm among the heirs gave the landscape a new shape, and, if not divided, the land had a new owner. By settling debts, the probate of the will dissolved the little debtor-creditor societies that extended through time to the due date of the note. The departure of a landowner, debtor-creditor, and owner of tools disrupted relationships that then had to be reconstituted in a new way.

Responsibility for organizing this reconstituted society fell, not to the heirs, but to the dead person himself, since the heirs and the probate court only carried out his will. The will was necessarily a complex family document that had to take into account the age, health, marital status, and character of his children, the viability of the farm if divided, the testator's sense of justice, past gifts to heirs, and innumerable idiosyncratic considerations. All these had to be weighed and the testator's intention reduced to who got what. In 1790, John Armstrong of Orange County gave his son, William, two hundred acres, his daughter Elisabeth a plantation of one hundred acres, his daughter Mary forty pounds, his daughter Margret a brown mare with saddle and bridle, and his daughter Rachel maintenance for life from the land left to William and Elisabeth. Armstrong's wife, Margret, was to receive all the income from his land until the older children came of age and, thereafter, one-third.[14]

The justice of those divisions, with one daughter getting a plantation of one hundred acres and another girl one brown mare, can never be understood outside of particular circumstances in John Armstrong's family. For whatever reason, Armstrong assigned plantation properties to two children, making them possessors in a society of landowners, and gave one daughter a nominal gift and the other support but no land. The two hundred acres William received was "the tract of Land wherein I now Live." By assigning the requisite property, John made William a planter like himself. Elisabeth would be a more attractive bride with one hundred acres of land in possession, the potential wife of another substantial planter. On these two, John fastened his hopes for perpetuating a family of possessors into the next generation.

The task of reconstituting society was a heavy burden for a single document to bear, and, even with the court's assistance, the will could never master all contingencies. Armstrong's intentions for his family were subverted by uncertainties outside his control. Who composed the family, for example? John's wife was foremost in the family so long as she was his wife. He awarded her all the income from the estate until his children came of age, "the better to inable her to pay my Debts and Raise and Scool my Children." To that point she was a substitute husband, managing the family's affairs, but "should she Marry it is my will that She only hold and injoy one third of the Lands . . . and money now Left her by me and the other Two thirds to be Equally divided among my Children." Marriage to another man partially removed Margret from the family, stripped her of control of the estate, and devised two-thirds of the property to the children. Armstrong's plans for his family had to provide for a reconfiguration of the family itself.

14. Will of John Armstrong, filed in Orange County Wills, 1753–1937.

In the face of such difficulties, the intention of the court, the legal system, and all of society was, nonetheless, to put the testator squarely in control. In the world of the will, he was in charge of the future. The court made every effort to honor the will and to enforce the testator's purposes, even though he was gone. The landowner was responsible for propagating society, constituting the form of the next generation. Although intestate laws stated the legislature's sense of how to configure society, those laws gave way before the will of the testator. The text he produced, in combination with all the other wills in the court archives, mapped the future structure of society. The burden and power of perpetuating society was given over to the largely male landowners, who, like John Armstrong, designated the all-important possessors of the next generation. Although often subverted by contingencies beyond their control and by contests among the heirs themselves, the men of property in each generation remade society—usually in their own images.

What are we to make of these court documents and the textual worlds they bring into existence? What do the deeds, the promissory notes, the estate papers, and the wills all add up to? To conclude they add up to one thing would surely be an error, a distortion of their meaning for the farmers who entered the various worlds of the texts. Each text led down its own path to distinctive configurations of space, time, and social interaction, and the farmer coming to these paths in the woods took them all. His life situation made him an actor on all these textual landscapes, a figure in all their histories.

But, if each text is idiosyncratic, taken together the court documents do give us the farmer as man of property, counteracting a temptation to view farmers more narrowly as mere heads of household production. Ownership of property made every farmer large and small a transactor who bought and sold land, borrowed, lent, assembled, dispersed, and at the end dispensed his property to heirs and assigns. The court was a site for managing property, a place where court officials facilitated negotiations with other propertyholders, bringing order and rudimentary justice to the transactions and making the court an adjunct to the marketplace. In all its proceedings, the court defended propertyholders—if need be, against the king. Rather than arousing adversaries against itself, the court joined with farmers to expedite the movement of property from person to person and down through the generations. Court texts formed the time-space continuum in which the great cause of property had its existence.

II

As the mediators of property, the courts exercised daunting power over the lives of farmers. Courts handed down judgments that took property from one person and gave it to another, that confiscated household goods to pay a debt, that favored one heir to the disadvantage of another. In North Carolina, three justices of the peace sitting in a quarterly inferior court of common pleas, often without a jury, determined the economic fates of litigants for years to come.

Why did farmers hand their economic destinies over to a few men sitting on a bench, particularly in the first decade of Orange County's existence, when nothing prepossessing invested justices with personal authority?[15] A Virginia merchant visiting the Orange County seat in 1753 was taken aback by the unsavory characters he met there until he learned they were justices of the peace. There "were sundry people assembled and their appearance did not prejudice me much in their favor. But I soon understood they were Justices of this Court which disapated our fears a little." Only the justices' titles calmed the visitor's concern about the rough company. The Virginian went on to say that the houses in town were built of logs, some not caulked, and the room where he stayed had no windows. No one in the little county seat looked distinguished, and yet, from this collection of disheveled persons, the justices were selected, raised to the bench, and given authority to decide the fates of their countrymen.[16]

These men received only feeble ideological support. The legislation organizing courts was surprisingly laconic about reasons and justification. The introduction to one act for the "establishment of Inferior Courts" simply said they "would be of great service and General Utility in the several Counties within this Province," or, with equal brevity, "Whereas, it is necessary for the due administration of Justice, that Courts should be established . . ." The draftsmen of the legislation assumed that courts were necessary and useful and made no attempt to locate them in a grand scheme of politics.[17]

And still these simple justices were vested with the mysterious authority of government, lifted above their fellows, and given power over life and prop-

---

15. This batch of North Carolinians was nothing like the auspicious personages who presided in tidewater Virginia's courts. See A. G. Roeber, *Faithful Magistrates and Republican Lawyers: Creators of Virginia Legal Culture, 1680–1810* (Chapel Hill, N.C., 1981), 45–77. For England, see E. P. Thompson, "Patrician Society, Plebeian Culture," *Journal of Social History*, VII (1973–1974), 382–405.

16. Quoted in William Doub Bennett, "Introduction," in "Orange County Court Minutes," trans. Haun, I. The same was largely true everywhere in North Carolina. "There is no difference to be perceived in Dress and Carriage," Governor George Burrington complained in 1732, "between the Justices, Constables and Planters that come to a Court, nor between the Officers and Private men, at a Muster" (quoted in Ekirch, *"Poor Carolina,"* 39). As time went on, the better-educated, better-dressed, and better-connected figures, of course, took over. The point is that courts could be made before the justices had these qualities.

17. Walter Clark, ed., *The State Records of North Carolina*, XXIV, *Laws 1777-1788* (Goldsboro, N.C., 1905), 36, XXV, *Laws 1789–1790 and Supplement, Omitted Laws 1669–1783* (Goldsboro, N.C., 1906), 405.

erty. Authority was invested less by ideology than by a series of ritual gestures enacted in the court at the installation of the officers. In the early years
of Orange County, the clerk recorded a once-a-year ceremony in which the
commission was read and the justices swore the appropriate oaths. In subsequent years, no mention was made of this ceremony, perhaps because the
clerk left it out rather than because the routine was overlooked. The law
required all new justices to take the oath on pain of a hundred-pound fine.[18]

I have found no copy of the justice of the peace commission; the minutes only say: "At the house of James Watson Esqr. on tuesday the 2d. day
of July Anno Dom 1754 was read and published a Commission of the peace
and Dedimus Potestatum Directed to the Honorable"—then followed the
names of ten members of His Majesty's Council and seventeen local men—
"Constituting and appointing them Justices of the peace for and within the
County aforesaid." The minutes for 1757 spoke of a commission "from his
Excellency Arthur Dobbs Esqr. Governor and Commander in Chief." Presumably the commission came from the governor, written as word from
him, and signed with his name. The commission must have referred to the
king, for the commissioned individuals were henceforth called "his Majesties Justices." By some political magic, the authority of the king crossed
the water and, by way of a paper signed by the governor, was carried to
Orange County and bestowed upon these common men. They were henceforth called "the Worshipful Samuel Watson James Dickey, James Alli-
son . . ." Physically speaking, a sheet or two of paper, writing with a signature
and seal, and a few spoken words brought into existence a court bearing
royal authority to dispose of liberty and property. The will and purpose of a
king three thousand miles distant, a king who never saw the men's names,
were conveyed via the governor to the tiny village of Hillsborough in the
hills of North Carolina. By action of that paper, seventeen farmers and
backwater merchants, men of only slightly greater wealth and education
than most, were transformed into justices and vested with the mysterious
authority of government. Most impressive, the people of the county, with no
known exceptions, willingly suspended disbelief and conformed to the illusion of this fabulous documentary fabrication.[19]

By law, the justices took the oaths appointed by Parliament and subscribed to the "Oath of Abjuration" against the Pretender. They repeated
and subscribed to "the Test," indicating they were communicants of the
Church of England. The wording of the parliamentary oaths was not included in the legislation, but the specific oath of the Justice of Peace was:

18. Clark, ed., *State Records of North Carolina*, XXIV, 288. For Virginia's court day
ceremonies, see Roeber, *Faithful Magistrates and Republican Lawyers*, 74–80.
19. "Orange County Court Minutes," trans. Haun, I, 12, 18. See also I, 5, 66.

You shall swear that as Justice of the Peace in the County of —— in all Articles in the Commission to you directed, you shall do equall Right and Justice to the Poor and to the rich, After your Cunning, Wit and Power and According to Law, And you shall not be of Counsel of any Quarrel hanging before you. You shall not let for Gift or other Causes, but well and Truly you shall do your Office of a Justice of the Peace as well within your County Court as without, And you shall not take any fee, gift or Gratuity, for anything to be done by virtue of your Office. And you shall not Direct or cause to be directed any Warrant by you to be made to the Parties, but you shall direct them to the Sheriff or Bailiffs of the said County or other the King's officers or Ministers or other indifferent Persons to do Execution thereof.—So Help You God.

Based on a traditional oath, almost all of these words had a single purpose: to strip the entering justice of private interests. As he heard the parties to the case, he was not to heed their wealth, which might distort his judgment, nor was he to counsel either party. He was not to accept any gratuity that could be construed as a bribe. In other words, he had to repress every desire for personal advantage, to purge himself of self-interest. Confidence in the court rested, not on ideology, but on a belief in virtuous justices.[20]

The investment and purification of the justices by commission and oath took on quasi-religious overtones. The term "worshipful" and the appeal "So Help Me God" gave a religious aura to the courtly rituals. In the same spirit, the architecture of the courtroom resembled the structure of a church. The bar before which pleading took place served as an altar rail. Behind its protective boundary, acts of power were performed by those vested with authority from on high. The bar set both priest and judge apart from ordinary men. The people on one side of the bar observed or pleaded their cases; on the other, the mighty exercised authority on behalf of God or the king. Both priest and justice were physically elevated above the floor where the people sat. In some eighteenth-century courthouses, the platform was raised by as much as three feet, and in the simplest by at least a few inches. The courthouse and the commission changed farmers of less-than-inspiring qualifications into "worshipful" justices empowered to dispose of liberty and property.[21]

At first, North Carolina counties made do without courthouses and held court in private dwellings. To dignify court proceedings, the legislature in 1722 required a courthouse at least sixteen by twenty-four to be con-

20. Clark, ed., *State Records of North Carolina*, XXIV, 287–288.
21. Roeber, "Authority, Law, and Custom: The Rituals of Court Day in Tidewater Virginia, 1720–1750," in Robert Blair St. George, ed., *Material Life in America, 1600–1860* (Boston, 1988), 422–426. For comparisons to religious rituals, see 435 n. 15.

structed in every county. Orange County justices ordered the construction
of a courthouse during the first court session in September 1752, when the
county was in its infancy. They called for a building thirty-two by twenty-
two feet, nearly twice the size required by law, with an eleven-foot-pitch
shingled roof, weatherboarding, and inside finishing, making it doubtless
the most imposing building in the county. When Hillsborough was laid out
on the classic central square pattern, the courthouse was given the central
place of honor. Physically, the town revolved around the courthouse, and,
since most main roads angled toward Hillsborough, so did the county as a
whole. Although the planters were keenly sensitive to excessive taxes, no one
objected to the expensive new courthouse or to its central siting. In the next
century, North Carolina courthouses became ever larger and more elegant, a
source of local pride rather than contention. If courthouse architecture was
meant to overawe people, they were at least passively complicit in manufacturing the illusion.[22]

The illusion carried over into the language of the court minutes. Although
the first justices might not have been imposing figures personally, as the
visiting Virginia merchant reported, the first clerk of the court knew how to
write formal court language. He began with perfect confidence in a clear
Italian hand:

At a Court of Common Pleas and Quarter Sessions begun and held for
the sd. county at the house of Mr. John Gray on Eno River on the
Second Tuesday in September being 19th. said Month in the Year of our
Lord 1752 Before the Worshipful his Majesties Justices to keep the peace
in and for the said County . . .

Every entry was written with the same certainty, with virtually no cross-
outs, deploying the technical language of the law. The presence of a clerk
who knew the terms and syntax of court language partially accounts for the
easy erection of courts. Although not common, fluency in court language,
like skill in surveying, must have been widespread. The large number of
courts meant there were jobs for those who managed to learn the court
lingo. Plenty must have qualified, for no county lacked a clerk who could
sustain the court by writing in the authoritative language.[23]

In doing its job, the court language created a stylized judicial society, just
as other legal documents—deeds, promissory notes, and wills—called little
paper worlds into existence. The court officers, the leading figures in these

22. Hen. Potter, J. L. Taylor, and Bart. Yancey, eds., *Laws of the State of North-Carolina,
Including the Titles of Such Statutes and Parts of Statutes of Great Britain as Are in Force in
Said State . . .* (Raleigh, N.C., 1821), II, 116; "Orange County Court Minutes," trans. Haun,
I, 2; Catherine W. Bishir, *North Carolina Architecture* (Chapel Hill, N.C., 1990), 172.
23. Minutes of the Court of Pleas and Quarter Sessions, 1752–1766, 3 vols., I, 1.

judicial societies, were the creations of the language in the commissions. Until a legal document constituted them, the officers were ordinary men with no legal existence in the court.

> Mr. Underhill Produced to this Court a Commission from his Excellency Gabriel Johnson Esqr. late Governor to William Churton, Gent Constituting and appointing him public Register of this County which being Considered by the Court and it appearing that Mr. Churton is unable to attend at present Ordered that the said commission be in full found, provided he give Security agreable to Law next Court.

Churton then became something he was not before, a public register, and within court society took on a new identity. For most officers, the court records acknowledged no other identity than the one that the commission created. In Churton's case, he was permitted one extraneous label: "gent." Traditionally, gentlemen were civil officers by nature with an official place in court. But, for everyone else, wealth, experience, family, and character went unmentioned, even though they doubtless weighed heavily in the appointment, since a higher social position was meant to enhance a justice's political authority. But, once a man was in place, the minutes constructed a fictive court society wherein the commission was everything and social position nothing.[24]

That same stripped character applied to the persons who came to court. All plaintiffs, defendants, petitioners, and jurors existed in the minutes solely as names: Marmaduke Kimbrough, William Blackwood, James Mc-Gowin, Joseph Tate, Thomas Lovelatty, Richard Crunk, William Martin, Timothy Tyrrel. Each name stood in the records without social markings, each one presumed officially to be the same as every other, all without distinctive social character. Appearance, wealth, skill, eccentricities, reputation, piety, learning, and temperament, qualities many in the courtroom knew well, were obliterated in the minutes. People simply "appear" in court, with no history or personality, all equal before the law. The records reduced them to their roles as legal actors and, despite the names, made them entirely impersonal.

In a further linguistic gesture of anonymity, the justices themselves are almost invisible. After the beginning of the session, they are never mentioned by name or title. The "court" takes action, not the justices as individuals, and certainly not the actual personalities who had been made into justices. Most of the time, not even the court is named as the acting subject of the sentence. The minutes read, "Ordered that James Daniel be appointed Guardian to John Gouge an Orphan," or, in the case of a deed proved in

24. "Orange County Court Minutes," trans. Haun, I, 2.

open court, "Ordered to be Regestered." The most potent authorities in the court are totally effaced, acting with complete impersonality.[25]

Impersonality was part of the illusion that upheld public trust in the court's proceedings. The faceless officers resemble the impersonal writers of eighteenth-century political pamphlets studied by Michael Warner. The court, like the political pamphlets, existed in a public space where all had free access as speakers or observers. All was done in the open, under public scrutiny, to accomplish the public good. In these textually constructed spaces, the social characteristics of the actors counted for nothing. The pamphlet writers performed anonymously, hiding even their names. In court minutes, people existed only as names, all on an equal standing. The officers of the court existed only as officers, not as great planters or merchants, not as pious Quakers or doubters, not as poor or rich, but only as clerks, justices, or attorneys. This artificial construction created a socially neutral environment for public business. Long before the eighteenth-century pamphlets appeared to monitor government, the courts served as a rhetorical arena for accomplishing the public good.[26]

The artificiality of the court personae was evident to all. The entirely fictive nature of judicial impersonality was perfectly transparent. The justices donned their masks in public. All watched as they listened to their commissions, took their oaths, and ascended to the bench. No one was fooled by the proceedings. Observers knew the officers' social identities in the world outside the courtroom and never forgot who they really were, large or small planters, debtors or creditors, Quakers or Baptists. The officers' temptations were known to all, even as they were sworn to treat poor and rich alike and to expect no personal gain from their decisions. In view of the discrepancy between court identity and the social self in the world outside, the question of whether court officers would render impartial justice was always open. Would they act impersonally as the court records implied, or would their social identities overpower their impartiality?

The oaths of office testified to temptation's power; officers swore to pay no heed to wealth and to take no personal interest in the parties to the suit. To guarantee their virtue, bonds were required of many officers, such as constables and sheriffs, who handled taxes, fees, and county payments, along with the register of deeds. Lawrence Thompson, the Orange County sheriff in 1765, and five others bound themselves to pay Governor Dobbs one thousand pounds sterling unless Thompson "shall well and truly Collect and Receive all such Publick Taxes and Dues" and pay the same to such persons as the law directed. Constables were bound by lesser sums to "well and truly

25. Ibid., I, 124.
26. Warner, *Letters of the Republic*, 35–43.

execute and perform the office of Constable according to law." The bonds and oaths were candid efforts to prop up the fiction of socially effaced and virtuous functionaries and, taken another way, testimony to the ineradicable force of the self-interested social self. The makers of the oaths and bonds and the governors and officials who sent them out knew as well as Husband and the malcontents about the temptations of judicial office. Governor Josiah Martin, who visited the western counties in the wake of the Regulator uprising, concluded that dishonest officers had subjected the people to "every sort of rapine and extortion." The presumption that the commission from the king transformed specific social personalities into impersonal court officers who would dispose of liberty and property impartially was known by all to be false.[27]

On this shaky foundation, the commission from the king and governor constructed the court system. The wonder is that court officers exercised their immense power so peaceably most of the time. Criticisms and disruptions were few and far between. No one questioned the paper train of commissions, seals, and oaths that conveyed royal authority from Westminster to Hillsborough. The fabulous fabrication of judicial authority was left stolidly in place. When it was disrupted in Orange County in 1770, Husband and the Regulators struck at the fault made visible in the commissions and oaths themselves. The Regulators attacked the weak spot that bonds and oaths were meant to mend: the disjuncture of the personal and the impersonal in court officers.[28]

The uprising began in 1766 after the tidal wave of immigration struck Orange County following the Seven Years' War. In the years from 1763 to 1765, the number of new land titles entered into the court records rose fourfold. Newcomers, who had risked their lives and fortunes on a move, flooded Orange County. They purchased as much land as possible, wanting all they could get before prices rose. The median-size tract purchased was between 250 and 300 acres, huge farms by northern standards. At the same time, the newcomers needed capital to stock the farms, construct buildings and fences, purchase seed and tools, and cover all the expenses of getting started. Debt was inevitable, and so was failure to pay. A huge load of debt cases placed immense pressures on the system; the number rose from 7 in 1755 to 111 in 1765, and the total number of cases increased from an average of

27. Orange County, County Court Minutes (Court of Pleas and Quarter Sessions), August 1762–August 1766, part 1, 278–279; Orange County Constables' Bonds, 1786–1814; Governor Martin quoted in Marvin L. Michael Kay, "The North Carolina Regulation, 1766–1776: A Class Conflict," in Alfred F. Young, ed., *The American Revolution: Explorations in the History of American Radicalism* (DeKalb, Ill., 1976), 104.
28. For an example of a protest after Independence, see *The Independent Citizen; or, The Majesty of the People Asserted against the Usurpations of the Legislature of North-Carolina, in Several Acts of Assembly, Passed in the Years 1783, 1785, 1786 and 1787* (n.p., 1787).

68 a year between 1753 and 1762 to 280 a year between 1763 and 1765. Farmers, living on the edge of disaster, had many reasons for anger and frustration. Husband spoke for this tense population.[29]

The Regulators' objections were never directed at the creditors who lent the money and were using the courts to collect. Nor did they attack court procedures or the ideological foundation of the courts. The royal commissions, the laws constituting courts, and the legitimacy of government itself were never at issue. The Regulators focused their animosity on a single target: the malfeasance of the officers. They were charged with using the powers of their offices to pursue their own interests and, primarily, to charge exorbitant fees contrary to law. Husband began with the justices and lawyers who lived by their fees, gradually expanded the attack to include the sheriffs who collected taxes, and eventually criticized the governor for requiring the legislature to build him a palace. Husband went from a strictly local to a broadly provincial critique, but always the accusation was the same. Officers were governed by personal interests. "What can be expected from those who have ever discovered a Want of good Principles, and whose highest Study is the Promotion of their Wealth; and with whom the Interest of the Publick, when it comes in Competition with their private Advantages, is suffered to sink?—nothing less than the Ruin of the Publick." Everything promised in the minutes, commissions, and oaths had failed.[30]

The rights and powers of the court, the authority of its officers, or even its reality made up from purely symbolic gestures was not brought into question. Instead, Husband limited his charges to the weak spot identified in the court documents themselves: the danger of self-interest. The bonds and oaths of office contained the very accusations that Husband directed with such animosity against Edmund Fanning and Governor Tryon. The bond to "execute faithfully and well" implied the same wrong that Husband believed was being enacted daily in the courts. He asked nothing more of justices than was contained in their oath not to accept gratuities for performing their duties. Common people did not have to be instructed by literate readers of Cato's Letters or Bolingbroke's Patriot King to recognize the subterfuges of self-seeking officeholders. The fear of corruption was part of a broad public culture that extended to remote courthouses on the edges of empire and infused the institution of government that ordinary farmers knew best—the county courts.[31]

29. James P. Whittenburg, "Planters, Merchants, and Lawyers: Social Change and the Origins of the North Carolina Regulation," WMQ, 3d Ser., XXXIV (1977), 226, 232.

30. [Husband], Impartial Relation, in Boyd, ed., Eighteenth Century Tracts, 262–266, 301–304.

31. For the early history of court political culture, see Wilfrid Prest, "Judicial Corruption in Early Modern England," Past and Present, no. 133 (November 1991), 67–95; Whittenburg, "Planters, Merchants, and Lawyers," WMQ, 3d Ser., XXXIV (1977), 215-238.

Farmers, we can hypothesize, learned their political principles at court the way they learned their theology at church. The court instilled habits of thinking about the state as the church taught people about God, as much by common practices and underlying attitudes as by explicit doctrine. The court minutes assumed a domain of impartial justice where personal interests were totally suppressed, and officers, jurors, plaintiffs, and defendants were reduced to names, equal before the law and, in the case of officers, impartial in administering it. In the idealized space of the court minutes, ambition and greed never tainted the discourse of justice. And, all the while, the parties in the courtroom knew perfectly well the particular desires, the idiosyncrasies, the histories of sharp dealing or bad luck, the religious preferences, the family needs of every person in court. Below the calm surface of the court minutes, as the participants knew, public interest and self-interest did battle. That was the lesson imparted in the only institution that matched the church in its systematic impact on a farmer's life. From the practices and assumptions of court society, farmers learned that the court, and by extrapolation the state, could never escape the contest between personal advantage and the public good.

III

The records of the Orange County Regulation have been searched for clues to the dynamics of power in the North Carolina piedmont: Who were the oppressors, who the victims? Who controlled government and the economy? Who suffered from that control? The research has not yielded firm conclusions. Can we say that the conflict pitted poor farmers against rich farmers when Husband himself owned nine thousand acres? More likely, as James Whittenburg has argued, farmers resented the merchants and lawyers who took over county offices in the 1760s, ousting farmers who previously were in control. Husband despised the lawyer Edmund Fanning, a 1757 Yale graduate who moved to Orange in 1759 and soon occupied a number of key offices.[32]

But even this rivalry fails to explain everything that happened. Husband's resentment was not universal among farmers. As the agitation began, a majority of them elected Fanning to the legislature, and, during the Regulation, many sided with the government and its merchant-lawyer allies. Moreover, whatever animosities aroused the Regulators did not last for long. The social divisions of the Regulation did not foreshadow whig and tory factions

32. For an argument in support of economic class differences, see Kay, "North Carolina Regulation," in Young, ed., *American Revolution*, 84–103. Evidence placing the Regulators more in the middle of society and drawing from every rank is in Whittenburg, "Planters, Merchants, and Lawyers," *WMQ*, 3d Ser., XXXIV (1977), 219–220.

in the Revolution, nor did Regulators take a consistent position on state constitutional issues after Independence. Perhaps the Regulation is best understood as a temporary flare-up, a time when extraordinary population growth placed heavy pressure on government, igniting a brief flash of angry mistrust.

In the long run, the pressures that disrupted the county subsided, and the court went back to normal. Stabilizing forces took over once again. They prevailed because the court protected vital social interests. Taken as a whole, the court records manifest a far more fundamental divide in rural society than the one that temporarily set Orange County residents against one another: the difference between propertyholders and nonpropertyholders. The most powerful elements in provincial society needed the judicial order to sustain that division. Property gave the court its reason for being. Virtually every page in the court records tells of the propertyholders' dominance in the county—men over women, fathers over children, and owners over nonowners. Every court document had the underlying purpose of enforcing the wills of owners. Through the courts, his majesty and all his subjects accepted the invisible lines dividing the earth into property, whereby the farmers' little kingdoms were constituted. Propertyowners dominated society so completely that no one could conceive of an alternative. Everyone thought that the right to property was natural, a part of the fixed structure of moral reality. How else could people know what land to farm and what was theirs to use? Without property, there was only chaos. And sustaining, abetting, and advancing the cause of property were the courts.[33]

The courts supported the hierarchy of landed power, expanded it, repaired it, and made it work. Hermon Husband's proposal to circumvent the courts with informal arbitration foundered on the farmers' own needs as transactors. Courts were as essential to rural life as barns and fences. A proposal to abandon the courts could only be a gesture of momentary frustration. All farmers were complicitous in the maintenance of judicial legitimacy in the knowledge that, without courts, their farms had no existence. The courts propagated the illusion that property was real. They were machines for manufacturing property, producing the fundament of power in rural society. For most practical purposes, farmers, like farms, had no existence apart from the courts. No wonder farmers stuck by the courts even through troubles as disturbing as Orange County's Regulation.

Inevitably, then, the courts went back to normal after the Battle of Alamance. The Regulation was a tiny perturbation in an otherwise stable cultural system. But the significance of the outburst should not be minimized.

33. In 1780, 29 percent of the Orange County households owned no land (Ekirch, *"Poor Carolina,"* 224–225).

The farmers' resistance was a sign of a potential instability. Like an atom, the court contained explosive forces that held it together or could blow it apart. The court had the power to obliterate a farm and sometimes did. Execution of debts could lead to sheriffs' auctions where tools were sold off or land was taken. Disputes over wills brought family feuds to court, where old angers were played out, and the respective wealth of brothers and sisters for years or even generations was decided upon. The courts dealt with the most powerful antagonisms in rural society, forever playing upon the farmer's fundamental fear of losing his property. And the courts did it all within a framework constructed by a few words on paper. The Regulation showed how the court could be brought down like a house of cards by a handful of distressed men who blamed their troubles on court officers. The protest scared the governor into calling out troops, knowing that the legitimacy of government itself was at stake. Even though the farmers sank back into passive compliance after Alamance, defeated more by their own need for courts than by the soldiers, rulers were reminded that government depended on consent of the people and could collapse when they willed otherwise. Courts were productions of communal belief and evaporated into the air when belief faltered.

The court went back to normal because the explosive powers in the court were also binding forces. Farmers' complicity in the fictions of the court began with their involvement in the worlds conjured in the court texts. The landscapes and chronologies of deeds, promissory notes, and wills were as real to farmers as their labors on the land. The textual worlds of the court were their worlds, the sites where they functioned as transactors. Farmers needed courts to live out those vital episodes in their lives when they purchased land, sold it, borrowed money, or passed property to children. And, once absorbed into the worlds made at court, farmers of necessity adopted the sustaining judicial fictions. They could imagine no tenable existence without a judiciary to keep propertyowning farmers in place as masters of the earth.

The Long Road to *Vidal*

Charity Law and State Formation
in Early America

OES ANY ONE DESIRE that the old times in religion should
return?" queried John Sergeant before the United States Supreme Court in January 1844. "What was the spirit that led to
burning the convent near Boston? Precisely this. Religious acrimony now destroys property, if it does not doom to the stake."

The case Sergeant was arguing, *Vidal et al.* v. *Girard's Executors,* commonly referred to as the *Girard Will* case, may seem an odd starting point
from which to call for a reassessment of our understanding of law, religion,
and state formation in early America. Though justly famous among legal-
constitutional scholars, the contest over the 1831 will of Stephen Girard,
the wealthy Philadelphia merchant-banker, is generally unfamiliar to early
American students of law or religion. Further, historians of early American
religion have paid little attention to the specific problem the *Girard Will* case
best illustrates: the complex intersection of charity law with religion and
state formation. Explications of church-state separation and reflections on
the blasphemy statutes of the early states have acknowledged a belief that has
never really vanished in the popular mind: namely, that America was a
Christian republic. But charity law plays no role in these investigations. Nor
has the interminable wrangle over "liberal" and "republican" state formation ever admitted a role for charity law in that debate.[1]

The author wishes to thank the anonymous readers, the coeditors, Kathryn Burdette, and
Professor Richard Ross for criticism and suggestions on earlier drafts of the essay.

1. *Vidal et al.* v *Girard's Executors,* 2 Howard's Reports US 127, 169–170 (1844). On
America as a Christian republic, see for example Richard R. John, "Taking Sabbatarianism
Seriously: The Postal System, the Sabbath, and the Transformation of American Political
Culture," *Journal of the Early Republic,* X (1990), 517–567; Stuart Banner, "When Chris-
tianity Was Part of the Common Law," *Law and History Review,* XVI (1998), 27–62. On the
debate over "liberal" and "republican" state formation, see Knud Haakonssen, "From
Natural Law to the Rights of Man: A European Perspective on American Debates," in
Michael J. Lacey and Knud Haakonssen, eds., *A Culture of Rights: The Bill of Rights in
Philosophy, Politics, and Law, 1791 and 1991* (Cambridge, 1991), 19–61. The assumption
guiding this essay is aptly summarized on 46: "Liberalism is a nineteenth-century construct that is best kept out of these discussions . . . the natural-law and duty framework . . .
could provide a certain assimilation of republicanism."

The omissions are regrettable. Charity law rests at the center of state formation because charity poses nakedly the question of how social responsibility for the welfare of others shall be conceived of in a polity and how property shall be used in the name of that pursuit. Is social welfare a public or a private responsibility, a state-regulated or a self-defined concern? Nor could such questions be put to eighteenth-century North Americans without their also asking whether inherited religious definitions of "public" or "private" charity should provide conclusive answers. This essay proposes the thesis that, in pursuing their cherished freedom to devise property as they saw fit, North Americans unwittingly rejected another set of equally cherished values located in religious conviction that the state had a responsibility to construct a just, Christian society. That conviction would have required an American charity law that gave close scrutiny to the religious intent—and, hence, the desired social outcome—of private charitable trusts and incorporated societies.

By the 1790s, American religious convictions in favor of charity were in conflict with another set of objectives, liberty in property within state formation. The outcome confirmed earlier legal developments that had encouraged private property acquisition and complete freedom over its devise. That confirmation, in turn, doomed the more restrictive law of charity and the heightened "police" role that some new states had embraced in pursuit of an America composed of Christian republics. Yet, half a century would elapse before this clash—and its outcome—became fully apparent in the *Girard* case.[2]

The long road toward that clash can best be followed by contrasting New England's example with New York's and, especially, Pennsylvania's.[3] With this in mind, the essay first reviews the *Girard* case, then provides some

2. Stephen A. Marini, "Religion, Politics, and Ratification," in Ronald Hoffman and Peter J. Albert, eds., *Religion in a Revolutionary Age* (Charlottesville, Va., 1994), 184–217; see also Stephen Botein, "Religious Dimensions of the Early American State," in Richard Beeman, Stephen Botein, and Edward C. Carter II, eds., *Beyond Confederation: Origins of the Constitution and American National Identity* (Chapel Hill, N.C., 1987), 315–330.

3. In Virginia, Thomas Jefferson's antipathy to religious bodies' acquisition of realty accounted for his state's hostility to incorporating churches and its prohibition of religious trusts. Partly because of this Virginia hostility, the thrust of American charity law evolved in the former colonies to the north of the Old Dominion.

Jefferson's essay denying the relationship between Christianity and the common law, although possibly written in 1764, was not published until 1827 and added considerably to the then-emerging controversy only a few years before the *Girard Will* case began its stormy way through the courts. See Gilbert Chinard, ed., *The Commonplace Book of Thomas Jefferson* (Baltimore, 1926), 57–59, 351–362; Bernard Schwartz with Barbara Wilcie Kern and R. B. Bernstein, *Thomas Jefferson and Bolling v. Bolling: Law and the Legal Profession in Pre-Revolutionary America* (San Marino, Calif., 1997), 49–57. For cases, arguments, and literature on trust law and the churches, see Dallin H. Oaks, *Trust Doctrines in Church Controversies* (Macon, Ga., 1984), 42–72.

context via a brief discussion of the alternatives that North Americans inherited and "received" from English and Continental legal traditions. Following that is an analysis of Pennsylvania's legal history of charity law that eventually gave rise to the *Girard* case; and, finally, part IV offers suggestions for research to promote a more comprehensive view of religion, state formation, and the development of an American law of charity.

I

Both Stephen Girard's intent in his will and the controversy that followed its execution are deceptively simple. Girard arrived in America in June 1776. A successful merchant-banker, he played no public role in the Revolution and devoted his early career in North America to the pursuit of liberty in property. Despite his wealth and probanking posture, Girard was no Federalist. Indeed, his sympathies for the French Revolution—specifically, his distaste for religious indoctrination—perhaps account for the proviso of his will that became so controversial. After settling modest sums on distant relatives (he had no direct descendants), Girard left the bulk of some seven million dollars in trust to the city of Philadelphia to fund an orphan boys' school. Notoriously, the will forbade any religious minister or ecclesiastic to set foot on the school's grounds, much less to offer religious instruction to the orphans.

It was on this proviso that the suit by Girard's collateral heirs turned.[4] The heirs' suit complained that the trust was uncertain of enforcement because of its vagueness, and the city was not legally empowered to accept the devise. But the real issue was joined on the question of Girard's intent, which could not be squared with the inherited, or traditional English, definition of a charitable trust. His heirs contended, unsuccessfully, that this trust law required testators to conform their intents to a recognition that Christianity was an integral part of the law of Pennsylvania.[5]

That Christianity was part of Pennsylvania law had been settled in the blasphemy case *Updegraph v. Commonwealth.* Abner Updegraph was con-

4. John Bach McMaster, *The Life and Times of Stephen Girard: Mariner and Merchant*, 2 vols. (Philadelphia, 1918), I, 212–224, 294–295, 372–376.
5. Robert A. Ferguson, "The Girard Will Case: Charity and Inheritance in the City of Brotherly Love," in Jack Salzman, ed., *Philanthropy and American Society: Selected Papers* (New York, 1987), 1–16, esp. 6–10. Technically, the object of charity, not the intent of the donor or creator of the trust, defines how a court determines the legitimacy of a trust—but the origins of charitable uses in England simply took for granted the existence of a Christian kingdom, hence the difficulties for North Americans; see below. For more on the *Girard Will* case, see Lawrence M. Friedman, *A History of American Law* (New York, 1973), 224; Banner, "When Christianity Was Part of the Common Law," *Law and History Review*, XVI (1998), 41–43, esp. 41; 43 US 127, 133 (1844).

victed of blasphemy in 1822, and, in 1824, the Pennsylvania supreme court found that Pennsylvania's laws rested upon divine and natural law and cited Justice James Wilson's law lectures in support of the decision. That position was also settled law in New York, where Chancellor James Kent took the same view as Wilson for similar reasons. Natural law and divine (or revealed) law were contained in the common law.[6] To rely upon British common-law "custom" alone threatened the new American republic with instability and uncertainty. Seeking pillars upon which state formation could safely rest, Kent argued that the sanctity of property and American liberty had to be made timeless and universal. Repulsed by the alternative model implied by the French Civil Code, he fell back on a quasi–natural law tradition with Christianity at its root. The Revised Statutes of New York reflected Kent's eulogy of lawyers and judges as interpreters of the American common law, but at the base of their interpretive acumen, he urged, must lie the bedrock of an emerging American common law: Christianity.[7]

Like his jurisprudential ally Supreme Court Justice Joseph Story of Massachusetts, Kent had once favored the almost absolute testamentary liberty the Supreme Court would eventually uphold in confirming Girard's will. Indeed, Story wrote, "it is in cases of wills . . . that we most usually find provisions for public CHARITIES; and to the consideration of this subject, constituting, as it does, a large and peculiar source of Equity Jurisdiction," he devoted considerable attention. Despite his approving the refusal of Americans to "receive" English mortmain statutes and their severe limitations on devises of realty to charities, however, Story, like Kent, loathed the Second Great Awakening and viewed the growing institutional presence of Roman Catholicism in North America with apprehension.[8] Customary testamen-

---

6. For a discussion on *Updegraph v Commonwealth*, see J. William Frost, *A Perfect Freedom: Religious Liberty in Pennsylvania* (University Park, Pa., 1993), 132–134. For Wilson's explication, see "Lectures on Law," vol. I of Robert Green McCloskey, ed., *The Works of James Wilson*, 2 vols. (Cambridge, Mass., 1967), 94–96, 126–167, 232–241, 356–368; Mark David Hall, *The Political and Legal Philosophy of James Wilson, 1742–1798* (Columbia, Mo., 1997), 35–89.

7. J. R. Pole, "Reflections on American Law and the American Revolution," *William and Mary Quarterly*, 3d Ser., L (1993), 123–159, esp. 151–152. On the growing conflict between the appeal to custom and the appeal to more rigorous standards of judicial evidence, see James Q. Whitman, "Why Did the Revolutionary Lawyers Confuse Custom and Reason?" *University of Chicago Law Review*, LVIII (1991), 1321–1368. On Kent's beliefs, see Carl F. Stychin, "The Commentaries of Chancellor James Kent and the Development of an American Common Law," *American Journal of Legal History*, XXXVII (1993), 440–463; Perry Miller, *The Life of the Mind in America* (New York, 1965), 186–194.

8. Literally, the "dead hand," mortmain originally referred to lands alienated to medieval religious houses, thus excluding their use by living descendants of the donor; by extension later, the restrictions applied to other corporate forms. For Story's remarks, see Joseph Story, *Commentaries on Equity Jurisprudence, as Administered in England and America*, 2 vols. (1836; rpt., Boston, 1839), II, 389.

tary freedom, Story wrote, might need to be reined in "to check an unfortunate propensity, (which is sometimes found to exist under a bigoted fanati-
cism), the desire to acquire fame, as a religious devotee and benefactor, at the
expense of all the natural claims of blood and parental duty."[9]

Here, then, was the exquisite dilemma: in forming the new American
state, conservative religious and patrilineal family defenders like Kent and
Story needed to rely on the authority of the state to further religious and
social welfare, but, at the same time, such intervention served to compromise complete freedom of individual property rights.

By virtue of hindsight, academic historians of law and religion have dismissed the dilemma as insignificant since reputable scholars long ago concluded that, as classical American legal thought took shape in the nineteenth
century, state governments avoided intrusion into market and property
relations. The states could and did regulate "private" lapses in morals and
mores by attacking lotteries and alcoholism and by promoting free public
education. But they shied away from endorsing formally the definition of an
individual state as a Christian republic beyond apparent encouragements to
charitable trusts and incorporated benevolent societies.[10]

The shearing of the law of property, business, commerce, and the market
from regulation of mores and a law of charity, however, was anything but
clear or inevitable in colonial or early state law.[11] In 1819, for example, the
supreme court ruled in *Trustees of the Philadelphia Baptist Association* v.
Hart's Executors against a charitable bequest written in Virginia for the
indefinite use of Pennsylvania Baptists. (The decision turned on narrow
technical grounds—namely, that, since Virginia had repealed the Elizabe-

9. Story, *Commentaries on Equity Jurisprudence*, II, 436.
10. For examples on marriage law and orphan legislation, see Michael Grossberg, *Governing the Hearth: Law and the Family in Nineteenth-Century America* (Chapel Hill, N.C.,
1985), 103; Lillian Laser Strauss and Edwin P. Rome, *The Child and the Law in Pennsylvania*
(Philadelphia, 1943), 1 [*Commonwealth v Addicks*, 5 Binney 520 (1813)].
11. I am positing an ongoing interest among North Americans in a "police" tradition of
civil society that envisioned Protestant religious teachings on the importance of free male
heads of families combined with the state's moral obligation to control real and movable
property for the general welfare. For an alternative view, see Christopher L. Tomlins, *Law,
Labor, and Ideology in the Early American Republic* (New York, 1993), 89–96. For a summary of the early-nineteenth-century patterns sketched here, see Herbert Hovenkamp,
Enterprise and American Law, 1836–1937 (Cambridge, Mass., 1991); "Law and Morals in
Classical Legal Thought," Fulton Lecture, University of Chicago Law School, May 15, 1996;
William J. Novak, *The People's Welfare: Law and Regulation in Nineteenth-Century America* (Chapel Hill, N.C., 1996), 105–113, warns against assuming lack of interest by states for
exercising vigorous police oversight of corporations and charters, but does not discuss
charity law. For a survey of recent work on state formation, see Richard R. John, "Governmental Institutions as Agents of Change: Rethinking American Political Development in
the Early Republic, 1787–1835," *Studies in American Political Development*, XI (1997), 347–
380.

than Statute of Charitable Uses, charitable trusts could not be valid if they were attempted via wills written in such a jurisdiction.) In Virginia and Maryland, this decision rendered charitable trusts invalid just as incorporation of religious societies was becoming heavily restricted; but, in neighboring Pennsylvania and New York, charitable trusts and incorporated societies were defended for their religious intent and the resulting good to state and society they portended.[12]

II

In England, the legal form of public charity, notably the poor laws, was relatively stable in the seventeenth century. Poor-law legislation of 1601–1603, the Elizabethan summary of a deeper medieval tradition that distinguished the worthy from the idle poor, focused attention upon parish and county authorities and institutions as the proper legal context where charity would be dispensed. Varying in specific provisions, North American poor laws reflected this public charity tradition, differing only slightly from the Elizabethan model. Before the eighteenth century, public charity law attracted no significant American attention.

A sizable shift in parliamentary regulation of private charity, or benevolence expressed by individual propertyholders, occurred, however, between the 1690s and the 1730s. English law presented a complex set of doctrines and options that proved troublesome for North Americans learning of their full import just before the outbreak of the imperial crisis. The clue that eluded colonials later struggling to understand English private charity law lay in the turf wars that had been waged between common-law and ecclesiastical (and, after the Reformation, chancery) courts. Ecclesiastical courts had claimed the right to administer the effects of deceased persons since the ninth century; royal courts checked ecclesiastical jurisdiction from extending to realty. Real property descended at death according to common-law rules of inheritance; personalty could be distributed according to the decedent's will, administered by church courts. Before 1540, real property could not be devised (left by will), but it was freely alienable (transferable to another), with the common law establishing the rules by which transfers were to be done. Royal

12. Louis Hartz, *Economic Policy and Democratic Thought: Pennsylvania, 1776–1860* (Cambridge, Mass., 1948), in his discussion of the mixed corporation, neglects an analysis of corporation laws as they applied to charity groups beyond a brief observation on Pennsylvania's 1791 statute (38–39), on which, see below; on the implication of *Hart's Executors*, see Oaks, *Trust Doctrines*, 42–48; Carl Zollmann, *American Civil Church Law* (New York, 1969), 25–26, 38, 62–63; Howard S. Miller, *The Legal Foundations of American Philanthropy, 1776–1844* (Madison, Wis., 1961); Irvin G. Wyllie, "The Search for an American Law of Charity, 1776–1844," *Mississippi Valley Historical Review*, XLVI (1959–1960), 203–221.

courts had won a major victory in 1285 as the original Statute of Mortmain limited devises of personalty for church uses. Now, in 1540, the Statute of Wills allowed two-thirds of a decedent's real property to be devised. Both the Statute of Wills and a series of later mortmain statutes carried forward these benefits for propertyholders and restrictions on the church.

As chancery courts increasingly eclipsed ecclesiastical courts, they assumed the latter's equity functions, revealing an important distinction. Charitable corporations were governed, like all corporations, by common law; charitable trusts, by equity. The Statute of Charitable Uses (1601) closed loopholes chancery courts had allowed as they assumed some of the duties formerly exercised by the ecclesiastical courts. It also listed exactly what purposes were permissible for the establishment of a charitable trust: relief of poverty, advancement of education and religion, and the promotion of public health and welfare—all obvious hallmarks of a Christian commonwealth. As such, charitable trusts, unlike private trusts, were not subject to the Rule against Perpetuities.[13] A charitable trust would remain inviolable until its purpose had become impossible, impracticable, or illegal. The courts were obliged to carry out "as nearly as possible" (cy pres) the intent of the original trust unless one of those three obstacles arose and required its elimination.

Charitable trusts existed side by side with chartered or incorporated societies of various sorts. The charters always lay open to revocation should the society fail of its public purpose. These included the foundling hospitals, charity schools, societies to reform manners, and workhouse societies that sprang into being between the English Reformation and the late seventeenth century, largely emanating from London example. Chancery courts might have exercised jurisdiction over charitable trusts, but British legal experts debated well into the eighteenth century whether these courts could also investigate and control incorporated charitable societies. If a religious corporation held property at law, the property was not held in trust. Still, property could be devised to an individual who held it in trust for a religious corporation, rendering such a trustee open to investigation by chancery.

Between the 1690s and the 1730s, and summarized in the 1736 Mortmain Act, British authorities turned a stern eye on gifts in wills or trusts that

13. Stemming from the *Duke of Norfolk's* case (1682), this was an attempt under the law of conveyances to protect the "remainder" or right to reclaim the interest in land after a donor had given it for a limited time for someone else's enjoyment. Remainders could be protected by trusts, but the rule insists that a limit of twenty-one years marks the time during which this "remainder" must actually become active; the twenty-one years began at the decease of those alive when the estate was created. See Frederick G. Kempin, Jr., *Historical Introduction to Anglo-American Law in a Nutshell* (St. Paul, Minn., 1990), 149–154; Sir William Blackstone, *Commentaries on the Laws of England: A Facsimile of the First Edition of 1765–1769*, 4 vols. (1765–1769; facs. rpt., Chicago, 1979), II, 163–178, 398–399.

endowed hospitals or charity schools, severely restricting the reception of land *ad pias causas* (for charitable purposes). This trend of "centrality of inheritance over benevolence," although imperfectly understood, shaped charitable trusts and incorporated societies in North America.[14] The muddle of religious "establishment" in the colonies further guaranteed hesitation among those urged to scrutinize charitable intent within the emerging imperial oversight of the eighteenth-century colonies.

The first systematic wrestling with the appearance of both private and public charity began in New England, predictably, because of the Puritan clergy's reflections upon Christianity's obligation to reflect the love of God in doing. New England divines devoted considerable effort to answering the query posed by the lawyer to Jesus of Nazareth in the parable of the Good Samaritan (Luke 10:29): Who is my neighbor? Their response reflected centuries of European Christian anguish. The short answer remained: first, the immediate members of family and kinship, then the congregation and town, and the community in widening and weakening ripples thereafter. Whether in early modern England, New England, or on the European continent, charity began at home. It rarely extended to strangers, the strolling poor, or military deserters, all of whom posed dangers to the established, but precarious, social and economic order.

The inherited patterns of European public charity left the exact dimensions of private charity, especially charitable trusts or incorporated charitable societies, less certain. Both Peter Dobkin Hall and Conrad E. Wright have traced the religious origins of a New England tradition that kept tight control over trusts and charitable corporations well into the nineteenth century, refusing the latter discretion in dispensing charity without close state supervision. The cy pres doctrine guaranteed the states' capacity to redirect trust funds once the original purpose of a trust became problematic. New England's charity law reflected the teaching that Puritan divines shared with most medieval and early modern Christians. The public authority of the prince or state emanated from revealed and natural laws that maintained order encouraging charity toward one's neighbor. The laws of the well-ordered state channeled the growing numbers of both corporations and trusts toward social ends intended to conserve the familial household, including servants and dependents, and to ward off the uneducated and the under- or chronically unemployed.[15]

14. Donna T. Andrew, *Philanthropy and Police: London Charity in the Eighteenth Century* (Princeton, N.J., 1989), 12–73, esp. 47. For the broader trends sketched here, see Gareth Jones, *History of the Law of Charity, 1532–1827* (Cambridge, 1969), 16–92; Kempin, *Historical Introduction*, 129–179.

15. Peter Dobkin Hall, *Religion and the Origin of Voluntary Associations in the United States* (New Haven, Conn., 1994); see also Hall, ed., *Inventing the Nonprofit Sector and*

Scholars have long speculated on the relationship of wealth to moral obligation in New England, particularly whether Puritans had difficulty reconciling the acquisition of wealth to corporate and communitarian religious obligation. Stephen Innes and Christine Heyrman have both reviewed the ancient debate and argued that worldly success and religious faith were quite compatible in seventeenth-century Puritan communities. Neither, however, notices the explosion in private-law instruments and litigation that challenged the sufficiency of older, smaller circles of private charity, perhaps because the intrusion of strangers, lawyers, and novel ways of resolving economic and social conflict produced no immediate debate over the innovations of charitable trusts and incorporation of religious societies.[16]

Despite the "decline" in strict seventeenth-century federal theology, the sociopolitical and legal residue of Puritan theology remained quite potent (as David Konig's research suggests). In the 1740s, New Englanders still perceived moral and religious implications embedded in the disposition of private property and in related issues of debt and usury. How people "secure and enforce their promises" revealed itself in Massachusetts's adoption of writs of case (special assumpsit and *indebitatus assumpsit)* that punished those failing to pay debts on time. Creditors were just as strictly enjoined from practicing usury. This nexus of religious belief, concern for social welfare, and willingness to control private property dealings should have led the provincial governments into shaping trusts made by deed or will, that is, genuine charitable trusts. Hall, Konig, and Wright discern a New England tradition of charity law where such a development should have emerged by the 1730s. Why, instead, did this occur only much later?[17]

The answer is rooted in Massachusetts's and Connecticut's handling of

---

Other *Essays on Philanthropy, Voluntarism, and Nonprofit Organizations* (Baltimore, 1992), 23–25; Conrad Edick Wright, *The Transformation of Charity in Postrevolutionary New England* (Boston, 1992), 3–47; Robert Middlekauff, *The Mathers: Three Generations of Puritan Intellectuals* (New Haven, Conn., 1970), 273–276, 305–311; Richard F. Lovelace, *The American Pietism of Cotton Mather: Origins of American Evangelicalism* (Grand Rapids, Mich., 1979). On the European, pre-Reformation origins of the debates over private and public responsibilities for charity, see Margo Todd, *Christian Humanism and the Puritan Social Order* (Cambridge, 1987). For a good bibliography and overview from the perspective of various European studies, see Carter Lindberg, *Beyond Charity: Reformation Initiatives for the Poor* (Minneapolis, Minn., 1993).

16. Stephen Innes, *Creating the Commonwealth: The Economic Culture of Puritan New England* (New York, 1995), 70–73, 229, 309; Christine Leigh Heyrman, *Commerce and Culture: The Maritime Communities of Colonial Massachusetts, 1690–1750* (New York, 1984). On the litigation explosion, see Bruce Mann, *Neighbors and Strangers: Law and Community in Early Connecticut* (Chapel Hill, N.C., 1987); Peter Charles Hoffer, *Law and People in Colonial America* (Baltimore, 1992), 50–55.

17. David Konig, "The Virgin and the Virgin's Sister: Virginia, Massachusetts, and the Contested Legacy of Colonial Law," in Russell K. Osgood, ed., *The History of Law in Massachusetts: The Supreme Judicial Court, 1692–1992* (Boston, 1992), 81–115, esp. 103.

public charity law. Both colonies had followed English example in public charity law by erecting workhouses and institutions for dealing with the poor beyond the vicinage by the 1730s.[18] Neither colony, however, moved to "receive" the 1736 Mortmain Act or to restrict religious charitable trusts. Desire to avoid sectarian controversy may offer one plausible explanation. After the apostasy of former Congregational clergy at Yale College in September 1722, aggressive Anglicans pressured authorities in Britain to declare the de facto establishment of congregational churches illegal in favor of the Church of England. Accepting the justness of the claim, Anglican authorities nevertheless declined to pursue the demand. Opening the question of religious establishment would have demanded a wholesale investigation of the intent of testators who had made bequests via wills and deeds to further the interests of dissenting congregations and the corporations of Harvard and Yale Colleges.

Furthermore, although British authorities quietly accepted the de facto existence of New England intestacy laws based on custom *(Phillips* v. *Savage,* Massachusetts, 1733), colonies—themselves the creatures of charters of incorporation—were not universally thought capable in their turn of incorporating educational and charitable institutions. If one injected the question of establishment into such uncertainty, even setting aside incorporation that was governed by common-law rules, who was competent to judge the law of charitable trusts in New England? During the crucial decades 1722–1752, just as growing socioeconomic pressures forced novel legal mechanisms upon debtor-creditor relationships, neither governors nor assemblies cared to question publicly whether the poor in the burgeoning population might be rescued by incorporated benevolent societies or through genuine charitable trusts. Instead, fierce battles over the legality and footing of land and silver banks reflected growing socioeconomic tensions in New England. Political as well as religious prudence dictated that charity law questions be left as much as possible within local and denominational bounds.[19]

18. On Connecticut, see Edward Warren Capen, *The Historical Development of the Poor Law of Connecticut* (1905; reprint, New York, 1968), 59–63, 84–85. Mann, in *Neighbors and Strangers,* suggests that the technical change in the nature of pleas from general issues to pleas in abatement and demurrer reflects more abstract principles of law in defining debtor-creditor relationships; by implication, the same emotional distancing between dependents and property holders seems evident in the attempt to erect a central poorhouse and the debates over the need for workhouses, which, however, failed for lack of adequate financial support. See also Peter J. Coleman, *Debtors and Creditors in America: Insolvency, Imprisonment for Debt, and Bankruptcy, 1607–1900* (Madison, Wis., 1974), 1–95.

19. Thomas J. Curry, *The First Freedoms: Church and State in America to the Passage of the First Amendment* (New York, 1986), 105–113; Hoffer, *Law and People,* 74–75. On the banking wars and religious-social divisions, see Anthony Gregg Roeber, " 'Her Merchandize . . . Shall Be Holiness to the Lord': The Progress and Decline of Puritan Gentility at the Brattle Street Church, Boston, 1715–1745," *New England Historical and Genealogical Register,* CXXXI (1977), 175–194.

New York's poor law reflected a similar copying of English public charity law. However, New York's reconciliation of religious convictions to the formation of an emerging state proved vexatious. This was not readily apparent on the surface; in the lower counties of New York, where the Anglican Church enjoyed a quasi establishment, any connection between religious faith and legal obligations toward the unfortunate seemed distant indeed in the early eighteenth century. If New York Anglicans had known of Bishop Edmund Gibson's 1727 ruminations upon Christianity and slavery, they could have extrapolated from them a rejection of expansive prerogative powers exercised through chancery in shaping charitable trusts or interfering with wills. Christianity, the bishop wrote, "does not make the least Alteration in Civil Property, or in any of the Duties which belong to Civil Relations; but in all these Respects, it continues Persons just in the same State as it found them."[20]

Yet the New York struggle in addressing charity law was not so simply divorced from religious conviction. To begin with, New York's approach to the English law of charitable trusts was muddled, a situation that apparently stemmed from lack of information about British case law. By the 1770s, decisions made clear that courts of chancery and the attorney general enjoyed no power of supervision over charitable corporations but did exercise supervisory powers over religious trusts by virtue of the crown's prerogative. The effects of the Elizabethan Statute of Charitable Uses remained unclear until the new state received it as incorporation of benevolent societies quickened with the Revolution.[21] Partly because of this imperfect understanding of British law, Stanley Katz argues, no vision of promoting even a vaguely Protestant republic underlay New York's groping toward a law that encouraged testamentary trusts.

Incorporation was technically distinct from trust issues that fell under chancery's jurisdiction, but it nonetheless raised uncomfortable questions rooted in New York's past about what kind of society and what social ends should be promoted by the law. Corporations established by royal charter

20. John C. Van Horne, ed., *Religious Philanthropy and Colonial Slavery: The American Correspondence of the Associates of Dr. Bray, 1717–1777* (Urbana, Ill., 1985), esp. 29–30. For a useful examination on faith, stewardship, and pious manuals among varying Protestant groups, see Eamon Duffy, "The Society of Promoting Christian Knowledge and Europe: The Background to the Founding of the Christentumsgesellschaft," *Pietismus und Neuzeit*, VII (1981), 29–42, esp. 36–37. For a Virginia example explicitly holding up rights in property against "Religious Principles and . . . universal Charity," see Fredrika Teute Schmidt and Barbara Ripel Wilhelm, eds., "Early Proslavery Petitions in Virginia," *WMQ*, 3d Ser., XXX (1973), 133–146, esp. 143–144.

21. That statute (1601) sought to correct abuses that had arisen from the court of chancery's carelessness about demanding oversight to be strictly enforced over trustees and those benefiting from a trust. The statute now enumerated the exact purposes a trust could have and erected a royal commission to correct past mistakes.

and based on an outright gift of crown lands—not the result of purely private benevolence or desire for incorporation—had touched off explosive political debates in New York during the 1750s precisely because of religious beliefs. William Livingston's attack on Anglican efforts to dominate the founding of King's College asserted the necessity of a legislative act to incorporate that body, thus assuring a controversial role for religious beliefs when charitable trusts and religious corporations came to be discussed a generation later. Livingston's attack also raised the volatile question of whether legislative intent, reflecting a majority's religious convictions, could be countermanded by magisterial or judicial decisions.[22]

Social and economic pressures guaranteed controversy about private religious benevolence just as the debates over New York's college erupted (as Deborah Rosen has documented). Docketed cases became backlogged, resolution was delayed, and debt, libel, and assault and battery causes increased sharply in New York's common-law courts between the 1730s and the 1750s. The rise of the Anglophone New York bar during the previous two decades had also eclipsed formerly distinctive Dutch testamentary procedures. To achieve speedy resolution of commercial disputes and to avoid contesting of wills, the procedural, internal logic of New York's common-law courts constrained potential litigants and herded them in the direction of more uniform patterns of testation and devisal of real and personal property. In the courts of the lower counties, one can perceive a near replication of the New England pattern of standard promise enforcement.[23]

Between 1748 and 1754, New York's public charity took on institutionalized form in the first poorhouses. But, although rural areas still managed to depend on local taxes for poor relief until the 1750s, public charity began to collapse as communities were riven by Presbyterian-Anglican disputes in the aftermath of the Great Awakening. Unable to rely on local consensus for establishing tax rates, New York's public charity faltered. By the time the

22. Milton M. Klein, ed., *The Independent Reflector; or, Weekly Essays on Sundry Important Subjects More Particularly Adapted to the Province of New-York . . .* (Cambridge, Mass., 1963), 32–38.

23. Deborah A. Rosen, "The Supreme Court of Judicature of Colonial New York: Civil Practice in Transition, 1691–1760," *Law and History Review*, V (1987), 213–247, esp. 220–235. On the New York Dutch, see Roeber, " 'The Origin of Whatever Is Not English among Us': The Dutch-speaking and the German-speaking Peoples of Colonial British America," in Bernard Bailyn and Philip D. Morgan, eds., *Strangers within the Realm: Cultural Margins of the First British Empire* (Chapel Hill, N.C., 1991), 229–235; Herbert Alan Johnson, *The Law Merchant and Negotiable Instruments in Colonial New York, 1664 to 1730* (Chicago, 1963), 4–14; Adriana van Zwieten, "The Orphan Chamber of New Amsterdam," *WMQ*, 3d Ser., LIII (1996), 319–340. See also Rosen, "Courts and Commerce in Colonial New York," *American Journal of Legal History*, XXXVI (1992), 139–163; Ronald E. Seavoy, *The Origins of the American Business Corporation, 1784–1855: Broadening the Concept of Public Service during Industrialization* (Westport, Conn., 1982), 9–21.

statute of 1770 was passed, New Yorkers since 1732 and in renewals of a
statute for the relief of poor debtors were used to the description of the
unfortunate as "proper Objects of public compassion." But legislators could
put no public money at the churches' disposal for funding compassion.
Public poor laws' dysfunction reflected both religious acrimony and growing anxiety about the laboring and wandering poor; private charity in the
form of incorporated societies and charitable trusts lagged even further
behind, testifying to the religious diversity and animosity that had characterized New York for most of its history.[24]

New York's legislature prohibited devises of land to corporations altogether in 1788, appearing to restrict the growth of charitable corporations.
As subsequent case law demonstrated, however, legislators allowed the chancery court to adjudicate the details of charitable trusts, perhaps from the
desire to prevent religious acrimony from spilling over into public policy
debates in the dominant common-law courts, where decisions over real
property were firmly lodged.

New York's wrestling with charity law casts useful comparative light on
Pennsylvania's, not least because it has furnished the substance for Katz's
analysis of the law of charitable trusts. Unlike Hall, who sees New England's
experience extending to colonies like Pennsylvania similarly influenced by
religious settlements, Katz perceives a "near autonomy" of developing charity law in eighteenth-century New York—and, by implication, elsewhere.
New York moved to the forefront of developing incorporated charitable
societies while Pennsylvania opted, he argues, for a liberal or permissive
policy toward the intent and purpose of charitable trusts. Katz further argues that the piecemeal adjudication of conflicting social, economic, and
political objectives created a charity law with little or no cohesive ideology.
Neither "restrictive" nor "permissive" patterns describe the peculiar tensions that pitted the defense of private property acquisition and devise
against Kent's vigorous chancery court defense of social welfare cast in terms
of Christian charity.[25]

Far from being merely autonomous, New York's treatment of charity law
actually allowed the expansive growth of equity law in Kent's hands. He and
his associates aggressively defended the religious purposes of charity law and
concluded, not unreasonably, that Christianity was part of the common law
and of equity, where the law of charitable trusts mitigated common-law

24. Coleman cites the New York statute's identification of the imprisoned poor as
worthy of public compassion (*Debtors and Creditors,* 113); on the collapse of county relief,
see Robert E. Cray, Jr., *Paupers and Poor Relief in New York City and Its Rural Environs,
1700–1830* (Philadelphia, 1988), 36–66, 91–92, 101.

25. Stanley N. Katz, Barry Sullivan, and C. Paul Beach, "Legal Change and Legal Autonomy: Charitable Trusts in New York, 1777–1893," *Law and History Review,* III (1985), 51–89.

restrictions that might impede laudable social welfare goals. By 1806, a statute gave the chancellor power to preside over property held by religious corporations. Upon their application, he could order sale of real estate belonging to them or with their consent dictate how money derived from the sale of such lands could be used. Until the 1850s in New York, a doctrine of implied trust applied to the trustees of religious corporations even if these had formally been incorporated at law; in the words of one scholar, it had to follow "that equity has jurisdiction over them."[26]

New York exercised considerable watchfulness over both trusts and religious corporations, as had New England. However, unlike the legislators in either New England or Pennsylvania, New Yorkers moved between 1788 and 1828 to restrict trusts and uses. The revisers' explanation to the legislature reflected deep suspicions of attempts to circumvent the common law for the "interests of the church." Plausibly, the revisers were interested only (as Katz believes) in simplifying the law of real property. Yet the emerging legislative hostility toward both Roman Catholics and some Protestant groups rather suggests growing tension between religious and social welfare purposes defended in New York's equity courts, and the legislature's promotion, via aggressively secular common-law revisers, of a simplified and secular law of descent, devises, and, ultimately, charity.[27]

Yet neither the New England nor the New York struggles with private charity law completely clarify that of Pennsylvania, whose state formation provided Louis Hartz with an early example of liberality in religion and property. Pennsylvanians, too, struggled over two principles: the state's duty to protect liberty in property and its obligation to promote social welfare in a godly commonwealth. New York's Livingston, in arguing for a college in New York, had pointed to Pennsylvania's "rising Prosperity," expressing admiration for "the impartial Aspect of their Laws upon all Professions . . . their vast Importation of religious Refugees . . . their Strength and their Riches," little realizing that in just this mix of religious opinion and wealth lay the dilemma charity law encompassed in state formation.[28]

III

Pennsylvania's Quaker origins, which guaranteed deep suspicion of "police" and magistracy, explain much of the colony's and commonwealth's ap-

---

26. Ibid., 59–64; Zollmann, *American Civil Church Law,* 49–54, esp. 54.

27. Ibid., 64–66, esp. 66. One can only wonder at the authors' conclusion at 64 that the legislature proceeded "for reasons wholly unrelated to any public policy concerns relating to charity."

28. Klein, ed., *Independent Reflector,* esp. 183 (Mar. 29, 1753, continuation of "Remarks on Our Intended College").

proach to charity law. Unlike New York, Pennsylvania ended a brief flirtation with chancery powers vested in a court of equity in 1735. Quaker memories of confrontation with unfriendly judges in England led to general hostility toward magistracy, which in turn allowed for private benevolence among their fellow believers. Not only Quakers, of course, but other denizens of Penn's colony exhibited a narrow understanding of, for instance, how charitable trusts would work in the colony. Francis Daniel Pastorius's *Young Country Clerk's Collection*, compiled between 1698 and 1710, contained two forms for trusts. Both, however, assumed an "in-house" ability of Quakers (for whom they were intended) to control property and its uses for monthly meeting via trustees. If Pastorius's unpublished manuscript exercised influence upon later developments, his mistrust of magistracy and chancery may have set the precedent: "A wicked Magistrate is a wolf made leader of the fold. [He] will not protect us in our Lives, Liberties and estates."[29]

Pennsylvania's equity jurisdiction lay initially with the justices in the courts of common pleas and the supreme court in accordance with the proprietor's instructions. Legislative attempts to control equity were blocked in 1711 and 1719 before a final equity court was established in 1720. The chancery court ended altogether in 1736, its duties absorbed by the supreme court.[30]

From the 1680s, the chancellor's power manifested itself in Pennsylvania's orphan's court, which sat in each of the counties. It was here that investigation into trustees of real or personal property held for orphans or minors developed a quasi tradition of equity law. The essential jurisdictional and procedural nature of these courts did not change from 1713 until 1832. The laconic manner in which Quakers ran the loan office after 1723 and their avoidance of taxation and liberality in advancing loans encouraged local propertyholders to assume additional financial burdens associated with the care of orphans and dependents.[31] As in New England, prosperous Pennsylvanians pursued debts in the form of bonds and mortgages, no longer book debt, using the same writs of case and constructing wills to favor the perpetuation of households headed by males. How many of the "worthy poor" deserved charity before midcentury proves impossible to estimate, despite

29. Alfred L. Brophy, "'Ingenium est fateri per quos profeceris': Francis Daniel Pastorius's *Young Country Clerk's Collection* and Anglo-American Legal Literature, 1682–1716," *Roundtable: A Journal of Interdisciplinary Legal Studies*, III (1996), 638–734, esp. 664; for the trust forms, see 676, 707–708.

30. Craig W. Horle, *The Quakers and the English Legal System, 1660–1688* (Philadelphia, 1988), 187–188, 260–274; Curry, *First Freedoms*, 79–82; Craig W. Horle et al., eds., *The Papers of William Penn*, IV, *1701–1718* (Philadelphia, 1987), 702–703; Thomas Richard Meehan, "The Pennsylvania Supreme Court in the Law and Politics of the Commonwealth, 1776–1790" (Ph.D. diss., University of Wisconsin, 1960), 53–62; Pole, "Reflections on American Law," *WMQ*, 3d Ser., L (1993), 151.

31. Alan Tully, *Forming American Politics: Ideals, Interests, and Institutions in Colonial New York and Pennsylvania* (Baltimore, 1994), 288–295.

efforts to distinguish the "absolute Poor, who *must be* supported" from productive subjects temporarily in need.[32] The Pennsylvania Assembly intentionally excluded charity from the purview of the courts. In 1731, the assembly passed a law that provided for quasi incorporation of religious societies. These quasi corporations were only minimally defensible, their trustees not unlike those named in a deed or will. The common-law courts exercised a vague kind of equity jurisdiction over these quasi corporations. Five years after the passage of the law, Pennsylvania's chancery court collapsed, encouraging interested parties to apply directly to the assembly for charters and effectively blocking judicial oversight. The assembly encouraged leaving gifts for the use of religious and educational groups; dependent tenants on lands were allowed to guard against an insecure future by making improvements. Pennsylvania paid no attention to the 1736 Mortmain Act. As long as the rough objective of promoting a godly society could be discerned, the legislators approved donations, gifts, and other "uses" via testaments, deeds, and, supposedly, charitable trusts.[33]

In Pennsylvania, the same rough dates as in New York—1748 to 1754—are an index of increased concern for public charity in the form of settlement laws and poorhouses. The upturn in the economy at that time created a demand for cheap labor, which argued against a too-strict enforcement of settlement laws or collection of monies by Overseers of the Poor.[34]

Pennsylvania's public charity took shape with the opening of the alms-

32. Mary M. Schweitzer, *Custom and Contract: Household, Government, and the Economy in Colonial Pennsylvania* (New York, 1987), 21–34; on the loan office policies, see 116–130. On the "worthy poor," see John K. Alexander, *Render Them Submissive: Responses to Poverty in Philadelphia, 1760–1800* (Amherst, Mass., 1980), 7. The standard survey of Pennsylvania Quakers and charity remains Sydney V. James, *A People among Peoples: Quaker Benevolence in Eighteenth-Century America* (Cambridge, Mass., 1963), 205–215, on the work of Anthony Benezet and the background leading to the founding of the Pennsylvania Hospital and the Bettering House illustrating the mix of private contributions and public funds.

33. Schweitzer, *Custom and Contract*, 218–219. For a discussion of the 1731 act and supporting literature, see Roeber, *Palatines, Liberty, and Property: German Lutherans in Colonial British America* (Baltimore, 1993), 259–261; Zollmann, *American Civil Church Law*, 61–63.

34. New Jersey provided generous allowances to debtors threatened with falling into the ranks of the working poor, another index of Quaker coolness toward magistracy and indifference toward nonperformance by debtors. Such practices diverged sharply from promise enforcement as documented in New England and the lower counties of New York. Indeed, when William Paterson undertook a revision of New Jersey law, the long-standing prodebtor sentiments of the assembly showed in its reluctance to insist on enforcement of specific performance; chancery jurisdiction languished for lack of regulation until 1799. See James Leiby, *Charity and Correction in New Jersey: A History of State Welfare Institutions* (New Brunswick, N.J., 1967), 7–20; Coleman, *Debtors and Creditors*, 131–138; William M. Offutt, Jr., *Of "Good Laws" and "Good Men": Law and Society in the Delaware Valley, 1680–1710* (Urbana, Ill., 1995), 308–311; John E. O'Connor, "Legal Reform in the Early Republic: The New Jersey Experience," *American Journal of Legal History*, XXII (1978), 95–117.

house in 1730, a tradition of outdoor seasonal relief similar to the poorhouse. Overseers of the Poor exercised near-absolute authority over recom-
mending candidates for relief and determining who received food. The
incorporation of these local overseers in 1749 as quasi trustees allowed private gifts to flow through their hands. Yet, as late as 1765, only one-quarter of
the money needed for Philadelphia relief alone came from private donations. The Bettering House of 1767 fused the almshouse and a house of
employment for dependents, who comprised 15 to 20 percent of the town's
inhabitants. Managers of the Contributors to the Relief and Employment of
the Poor functioned as a board of directors in what we would call a private
corporation operating in the public interest. Some twenty-one private acts
passed by the Pennsylvania Assembly between 1760 and 1776 relieved debtors
who might have become objects of public charity.[35]

The founding of the St. Andrew's Society by immigrant Scots in 1749 signaled that more recent arrivals in the colony deemed public charity efforts
inadequate. Already evident among Quakers, limited private charity groups
like the St. Andrew's Society offered immediate but temporary relief from
unemployment, disease, fire, or imprisonment. A decade later, incorporation of a society to relieve widows and orphans of deceased Presbyterian
clergy underscored a conviction among Pennsylvania clerics of private charity's growing importance. All such efforts remained, as had Pastorius's draft
of trust forms, specific to a religious confession or tradition.[36]

The charity school, that private charity identified with Puritan and dissenting groups in Britain, flourished under Quaker auspices in Pennsylvania
as well. Effectively "chartered" in 1754 and created by the German Society in
England, the schools were supported by private Dutch and Scottish collections, the last such project founded in North America. The charity school
also laid the groundwork for debates over social welfare and the mix of
public and private responsibility over property and its uses. The society
named six trustees in Pennsylvania, to whom a supervisor of the schools
answered. At each location, another layer of deputy trustees superintended
local details. Supported by private donations, the schools brought together
Anglican, Lutheran, Reformed, and Moravian supporters. German Lutheran pastors asked that public charity funds be funneled into the venture;
in one community, a petition to hold a lottery in support of the schools
surfaced by 1759.

35. See Stephen Edward Wiberley, Jr., "Four Cities: Public Poor Relief in Urban America, 1700–1775," (Ph.D. diss., Yale University, 1975), 64–72, 175–177 tables 6.2, 6.3; Alexander, *Render Them Submissive*, 43, 65–60, 87–108.

36. Alexander, *Render Them Submissive*, 128–129; Ned C. Landsman, *Scotland and Its
First American Colony, 1683–1765* (Princeton, N.J., 1985); Eric Richards, "Scotland and the
Uses of the Atlantic Empire," Maldwyn A. Jones, "The Scotch-Irish in British America,"
both in Bailyn and Morgan, eds., *Strangers within the Realm*, 67–114, 284–313.

By the early 1760s, the large number of German-speakers provoked concern among Anglophones, and support for the charity schools project aroused renewed worry. Disputes over the protection of testamentary gifts to churches as well as struggles manifesting deep distrust of trustees and their powers erupted within these quasi-incorporated religious societies. Local court records and congregational minutes among German Reformed and Lutherans reveal considerable hostility against trustees, their poorly understood legal status, and their obligations to the public power that created the quasi corporation. For their part, these worthies came to resent fellow congregants and, although they sometimes wrote wills containing modest bequests to local schools or congregations, established no charitable trusts.[37]

German clerics joined their Presbyterian and Anglican counterparts in the perception that private charity needed to supplement public charity. Seasonal outdoor relief—traditionally given to women in Pennsylvania— now shifted from informal almsgiving and local charity to encouraging able-bodied males to obtain basic literacy and training to become productive. This shift toward education as a key form of charity extended especially to the children of the working poor, dovetailing with the founding of parochial schools conducted in German among Lutherans, Reformed, and Moravians. Heinrich Melchior Mühlenberg's visit in 1757 to preach in the almshouse in Philadelphia revealed only nine German-speakers among the four hundred residents. By 1774, however, his parish had initiated its own private charity drive to relieve poor widows and single women while successfully expanding its parochial school. Unfortunately, broader plans for a seminary to train pastors, begun a year earlier with a much publicized lottery, failed.

As the imperial crisis deepened, money donated from Europe and held in trust for the benefit of Lutheran congregations provoked demands that pastors operating as trustees divulge more fully the uses to which these donations were put. After the Revolution, these disputes threatened to spill

---

37. The only legal handbook available to German-speakers provided a survey of the orphans' court, summarized the public poor laws, and explained in some detail how to write a will but provided neither explanation nor definition of a devise that could be held in trust and avoided speaking of corporations altogether ([David Henderson], *Des Landsmanns Advocat, das ist: Kurzer Auszug aus solchen Gesetzen von Pennsylvania und England* . . . [Philadelphia, 1761], 36–37, 55–56, 107–108, 114–123). Charles H. Glatfelter, *Pastors and People: German Lutheran and Reformed Churches in the Pennsylvania Field, 1717–1793,* 2 vols., II (Breinigsville, Pa., 1981), 308–326, reviews the literature on the charity schools project. The only hint about such matters is a cryptic note that a devise of realty to a child still unborn is valid (116) but without discussion otherwise of how devises *(Vermächtnisse)* could be made via will or deed and held in trust. For details on German private-law understanding of trusts, see Roeber, *Palatines, Liberty, and Property,* 258–266, 377–378 n. 40, 402 n. 31. A more detailed explication of both German Lutheran and Catholic struggles with charity law on both sides of the Atlantic will be provided in Roeber and Georg Fertig, *Troublesome Riches: Catholic and Lutheran Stewardship and the Law of Charity in Transatlantic Perspective* (forthcoming).

into the court system, intensifying debates over how private charity and concern for the broader public welfare should involve state regulation of property and its uses. The conviction that free schooling under religious auspices ought to link private charity to state support for advancing the common good survived the Revolution and was seriously affirmed in the new commonwealth.[38]

As the colonial regime collapsed in the mid-1770s, Pennsylvania's supreme court under Thomas McKean faced renewed legislative pressure—from an assembly striving to maintain complete control over incorporated societies—to define trust law more carefully. In a series of cases that came before the court, one can discern, first, that the focus of the law of property became clearer; second, that the legislature continued to dominate the courts and to assume that it was promoting charity within an at least vaguely Christian society. Perhaps most important, however, courts and the legislature began to understand that, technically, the law of charity looked at the object of charity, not the intent of the donor. This discovery further intensified the debates. To ask about the object of public and private charity necessitated reflection on social welfare, on what kind of police powers should exist, and on justification for those police powers' control of property on behalf of a law of charity.[39]

The assembly continued to incorporate charitable societies; McKean and his colleagues routinely reviewed the charters without commentary on the scope or duties of trustees. Reflecting both its own authority, and citing the "repugnance" of an original charter of incorporation to the Scots Presbyterian Church that implied subordination to a "foreign body," the assembly vacated that charter and issued one more in accord with the dignity of an independent commonwealth. But Pennsylvanians reacted in horror at discovering Virginia law passed that same year altogether dismissed religious

38. Karin Anne Wulf, "A Marginal Independence: Unmarried Women in Colonial Philadelphia" (Ph.D. diss., The Johns Hopkins University, 1993), 147–198. For Mühlenberg's observations, see W. J. Mann, B. M. Schmucker, and W. Germann, eds., *Nachrichten von den vereinigten Deutschen Evangelisch-Lutherischen Gemeinen in Nord-America, absonderlich in Pennsylvanien . . .* , 2 vols. (Allentown, Pa., 1886), I, 1208–1210, Halle Reports; Roeber, *Palatines, Liberty, and Property*, 278–282; on the proposed seminary, lottery, and discussion of the central importance of free education for the poor, see Kurt Aland, ed., *Die Korrespondenz Heinrich Melchior Mühlenbergs aus der Anfangszeit des deutschen Luthertums in Nordamerika . . .* , IV (Berlin, N.Y., 1993), 487–492, and 518–522 for Mühlenberg's plea (1773) for an orphanage and a retirement home for pastors, schoolteachers, and their widows instead of plans for seminaries or colleges.

39. The following paragraphs will cite cases from S. J. Dallas, *Reports of Cases Ruled and Adjudged in the Courts of Pennsylvania, before and since the Revolution* (Philadelphia, 1790); Alexander Addison, *Reports of Cases in the County Courts of the Fifth Circuit, and in the High Court of Errors and Appeals of the State of Pennsylvania, and Charges to Grand Juries of Those County Courts* (Washington, D.C., 1800), and the relevant statutes; for an overview, see G. S. Rowe, *Embattled Bench: The Pennsylvania Supreme Court and the Forging of a Democratic Society, 1684–1809* (Newark, N.J., 1994), 184–185, 206–218.

belief's connection to social welfare or state police interest.[40] Indeed, that connection was taken for granted by Pennsylvania's assembly. Furthermore, only two business corporations had been created before the Revolution, the Free Society of Traders and the Philadelphia Contributionship for the Insuring of Houses from Loss by Fire. Even after 1790, to the eve of the Civil War, only 8 percent of charters of incorporation authorized business and manufacturing; the overwhelming majority had a "distinct public-utility or community-interest cast."[41]

Where trust law was concerned, McKean lamented the absence of a chancery court, noting that the law's purpose was to "prevent a failure of justice." "Conscience, that infallible monitor within every judge's breast," he opined, needed its own court, yet no one doubted that "equity is part of the law of *Pennsylvania*." In examining appeals to presettlement English statutes, the Pennsylvania supreme court found that none applied "unless they are convenient," and those enacted after Pennsylvania's charter was granted held only if the colonies were specifically named in them. In treating deeds of covenant, however, the court relied on English formalities, invoking the Statute of Uses and pointing out that, since that statute's passage, "no inheritance, in a covenant to stand seized to uses, or other deed to uses, can be raised, or new estate created, without the words *heirs* ... though the intent of the parties be ever so fully expressed."[42]

When charitable bequests appeared in wills, not in trusts per se, the court reminded attorneys that a legacy, whether under canon law, the law of nations, or equity, had to coincide with the intent of Pennsylvania's colonial legislators: even when "not implicitly adhering to the civil or ecclesiastical institutions," two witnesses to the probate of wills of lands or testaments

40. John Swanwick, *Considerations of an Act of the Legislature of Virginia* . . . (Philadelphia, 1786). See William G. McLoughlin, "The Role of Religion in the Revolution: Liberty of Conscience and Cultural Cohesion in the New Nation," in Stephen G. Kurtz and James H. Hutson, eds., *Essays on the American Revolution* (Chapel Hill, N.C., 1973), 197–255.

41. On the 1786 reincorporation statute, see James T. Mitchell and Henry Flanders, eds., *The Statutes at Large of Pennsylvania from 1682 to 1801* (Harrisburg, Penn., 1896–1919), XII, 1776–1786, 258–260. The later hostility expressed in Pennsylvania courts to Roman Catholic episcopal control over incorporated parishes was already clear in the language here applied to Scots Presbyterians: Pennsylvania found it "highly derogatory" of its sovereignty "that the legal estate, use or benefit of any real property within this state should depend or should be supposed to depend upon or be under the control of any person or persons, or body of men without this state, whether they pretend to civil or ecclesiastical authority." On the patterns of incorporation, see Novak, *People's Welfare*, esp. 106; George David Rappaport, *Stability and Change in Revolutionary Pennsylvania* (University Park, Pa., 1996), 144–145. That little coherent ideology shaped legislative debates over bank incorporation is the argument of Hans Eicholz; see "The Bank of North America and the Transformation of Political Ideology in Early National Pennsylvania" (Ph.D. diss., University of California at Los Angeles, 1992).

42. *Pollard v Shaaffer*, 211, 214 (1787), *Morris's Lessee v Vanderen*, 64, 67 (1782), *Vanhorn's Lessee v Harrison*, 137, 139 (1785), all in 1 Dallas's Reports.

were essential, a strict application of English precedent that overturned a looser interpretation from Montgomery County's Registry of Wills. Only a year earlier, in 1787, the court had pointed to the intent of a testator as the "pole star" in how wills were to be read as long as intent did not clash with settled law. If technical terms had been omitted, they were to be supplied from the "manifest . . . words and expressions in the will." Using a common exception to the Statute of Frauds (1678), the court in another case read a constructive trust, noting that, if fraudulent purposes were later discovered in a deed where only parol proof of intent had existed, fraud committed in obtaining a conveyance allowed the courts to declare: "The grantee may be considered as a mere trustee."[43]

If English doctrines brought property devisal and simple bequests into focus, and if legislators still watched incorporation carefully for signs of social benefit, the cases of breach of truth, covenant enforcement, and specific performance that came before the court still did not clarify the law of charity. To a degree, this was no oversight. In 1779, the assembly had attempted to expropriate the Penn family lands and demanded an opinion from McKean. Were these lands outright grants to the proprietary family or, as the assembly claimed, gifts in trust for their use, a trusteeship and use now transferred to the people of the new commonwealth? McKean sidestepped the potentially explosive reaction to a judicial attempt to define an area of law long jealously guarded by the legislature. Instead, he granted protection to the Penns' private lands but remained silent on broader principles about the circumstances under which trusts under a cy pres doctrine could be declared no longer valid or practicable.[44]

Charitable trusts per se were not at risk in the debate over the Penn family lands, nor did they produce case law before the supreme court prior to 1790. Nor did public charity law change dramatically when, in 1788, Overseers of the Poor acquired control over the disbursement of charity at the expense of the former managers of the public poor law, wealthy Philadelphia Quakers who were still the object of hostility. Two years later, legislators again defeated an attempt to revive the court of chancery, reaffirming their control of incorporation and the determination of private charity's connection to state interest in promoting social welfare.[45]

43. *Lewis v Maris,* 278, 283 (1788), *Busby v Busby,* 226, 226 (1787), *Lessee of Thompson et ux. v White,* 424, 427 (1789), all in 1 Dallas's Reports.

44. On the Penn lands case, see Meehan, "Pennsylvania Supreme Court," 237–240; Rowe, *Embattled Bench,* 154–156. "Specific performance" refers to a bill in equity that forces actual fulfillment of a contractual obligation according to the prior, precise terms the parties have agreed to.

45. On the unsuccessful attempt to revive chancery courts at the time of the adoption of the 1790 constitution, see Anthony Laussat, Jr., *An Essay on Equity in Pennsylvania* (1826; rpt., New York, 1972), 26–31.

Appropriately—and prophetically, given Stephen Girard's will that would endow an orphan boys' school—public support for charity schools touched off the debates between the rights of property devisal and the goal of promoting social welfare in a Christian republic. In 1787 and 1788, Pennsylvania's legislators turned to extant charity schools run by Quaker, Episcopal, German Lutheran, and German Reformed churches to provide education for poor children. Land grants in the western parts of the commonwealth subsidized their efforts.[46]

By 1791, incorporation of charitable societies was supposed to move out of the assembly; prospective parties were directed to the attorney general and the supreme court, who would determine whether such groups—and testamentary bequests left to their use—operated in the public interest.[47] Albert Gallatin's Society for the Establishment of Sunday Schools, founded a year later, seemed to reflect both the commonwealth's support for incorporating religious societies and its assumption that these had a public interest. In 1794, a sweeping statute assaulted gaming, violation of Sunday rest, profanity and blasphemy, and other affronts to the moral quality of society. The conviction that the common law of Pennsylvania should reflect broadly Christian patterns of behavior seemed quite clear.[48]

Two years later, growing sectarian strife and resulting public opposition to the mix of public and private charity school efforts produced a bill in the legislature to fund public schools. Quakers, Lutherans, German Reformed, and Anglicans denounced this assault upon what they considered a settled point in Pennsylvania law: religious charity schools, subsidized by gifts of state lands, provided practical training for and inculcated morals in the poor children of a Christian republic. While German Lutherans read Pastor J. H. C. Helmuth's denunciations of the proposal, Alexander Addison in a 1799 grand jury charge argued for the "Importance of Public Institutions for Instruction." Addison, like Helmuth, took for granted the state's interest in

46. Glatfelter, *Pastors and People*, II, 509–512; *A Retrospect of Holy Trinity Parish as a Souvenir of the 125th Anniversary of the Foundation of the Church* (Philadelphia, 1914), 36–38; Mitchell and Flanders, eds., *Statutes at Large*, XIII, 182–184, 333–334. Alexander, *Render Them Submissive*, 142–159, misses both the statutes and the roles denominations played in providing a mixed private/public charity.

47. Peter Dobkin Hall, *The Organization of American Culture, 1700–1900: Private Institutions, Elites, and the Origins of American Nationality* (New York, 1982), 124, citing E. Digby Baltzell, speculates that Philadelphia's elite hesitated in the face of Pennsylvania's religious and ethnic heterogeneity to develop a settled law of charity; see Baltzell, *Puritan Boston and Quaker Philadelphia: Two Protestant Ethics and the Spirit of Class Authority and Leadership* (New York, 1979), 369–374. The argument for a conscious crafting of a charity policy is in Miller, *The Legal Foundations of American Philanthropy*, and Wyllie, "Search for an American Law of Charity," *Mississippi Valley Historical Review*, XLVI (1959–1960), 203–221; for the 1791 statute, see Mitchell and Flanders, eds., *Statutes at Large*, XIV, 50–53.

48. Mitchell and Flanders, eds., *Statutes at Large*, XV, 110–118.

promoting "instruction, both in religion and literature . . . under protection of government, and without violation of the rights of conscience and freedom of will, regulated by law, and supported by public authority." Addison thought New England's mix of public police interest and private charity exemplary; by contrast, Pennsylvania, "either from parsimony, peculiarly censurable when indulged to defeat an useful purpose, or from the difficulty of combining in one direction the opinions of many," had not decided how to regulate private property. Instead, his fellow citizens indulged "a zeal for liberty, more excusable than intelligent" and left the task of promoting "piety, knowledge, and national liberty" "to the discretion of individual liberality or interest."[49]

Some doubted whether the Christian society that was being encouraged included Roman Catholics. Catholic attempts to join their schools to the list of those providing education to the poor had been rebuffed in 1790. Bishop John Carroll made plain for wealthy gentry Catholics their obligation to place "sacrifice of a property" first in order that "charity towards the poor and ignorant" would be possible through a rational exercise of "domestic economy" and avoidance of debt.[50] German Roman Catholics who had founded Holy Trinity Parish in May of 1788 might have agreed with the sentiment but not with episcopal interference in their control of their corporate property. Following Protestant practice and precedent, they insisted that their trustees also held the right to nominate what priest would serve them, the parish, and the orphanage they built to succor survivors of the recurrent yellow fever epidemics. From late 1796 to March 1798, the supreme court heard inconclusive arguments and issued writs (including one threatening attachment for contempt against Bishop Carroll) in a vain attempt to sort out the distinction between trustee rights over incorporated property and the rights of an ecclesiastical superior—nowhere mentioned in the articles of incorporation. Could the purpose of the corporation be achieved if a priest had been named without episcopal consent? Protestants were not comforted when Carroll chided Philadelphia's Catholic parishioners for "exchanging the doctrines of the Catholic Church for those of Luther and C[al]vin." For the courts, the task seemed less clear than to Carroll that one could easily

49. Roeber, "Citizens or Subjects? German-Lutherans and the Federal Constitution in Pennsylvania, 1789–1800," *Amerikastudien/American Studies*, XXXIV (1989), 49–69; Roeber, "The von Mosheim Society and the Preservation of German Education and Culture in the New Republic, 1789–1813," in Henry Geitz, Jürgen Heideking, and Jürgen Herbst, eds., *German Influences on Education in the United States to 1917* (Cambridge, 1995), 157–176; Roeber, "J. H. C. Helmuth, Evangelical Charity, and the Public Sphere in Pennsylvania, 1793–1800," *Pennsylvania Magazine of History and Biography*, CXXI (1997), 77–100; Addison, "Importance of Public Institutions for Instruction," March Sessions, in Addison's Reports, 313–314 (1799).

50. Pastoral letter, May 28, 1792, in Thomas O'Brien Hanley, ed., *The John Carroll Papers*, 3 vols. (Notre Dame, Ind., 1976), II, 43–52, esp. 48–49.

separate trustee responsibility to the larger social welfare as defined or implicit in the charter of incorporation—including the establishment of salaries for priests and schoolmasters—from definitions of "spiritual authority" over such corporations.[51]

A testamentary trust made by a dying priest to provide for his permanent
successor illustrated such complexities even more sharply. How could one
reconcile the intent of a decedent erecting a trust via his will to the broader
objectives of charity and ascertain which social welfare benefits validated the
trust? The thrust of Pennsylvania's law toward respecting the "pole star" of
testator intent was quite clear. Yet, in this case, the executors of the trust had
agreed to accept Father Franciscus Fromm, who on his own initiative had
occupied house and lands left in trust by the deceased priest, Theodorus
Browers. The executors sued for ejectment when they discovered Fromm lay
under episcopal censure. With some asperity, the court lamented "that people will apply to ignorant men to write wills and other papers affecting
property." Deploring the absence of a court of chancery to superintend trust
execution, the court upheld the verdict for the plaintiffs and opined that it
would have been better "to apply to the legislature to vest the estate in
trustees for the uses of the will."[52]

Rejecting a claim advanced by Fromm's aggressively anti-Catholic attorney that the deceased Father Browers had merely "intended" that a priest
be there to say mass, the court also fled from being drawn into intricate
arguments over episcopal authority or over whether, once the executors had
accepted Fromm, they had lost their authority over the real estate upon
executing their duties as trustees. As these cases attracted notice, German
Lutherans and Catholics exchanged pamphlets denouncing undue influence
exercised on a dying woman and the bequest purportedly left to one or the
other of their confessions.[53] Watching such incidents, the wealthy baker to
the Continental army Christopher Ludwig, before dying in 1800, wrote his

51. For general background, see Dale B. Light, *Rome and the New Republic: Conflict and
Community in Philadelphia Catholicism between the Revolution and the Civil War* (Notre
Dame, Ind., 1996), 24–39; Vincent J. Fecher, *A Study of the Movement for German National
Parishes in Philadelphia and Baltimore, 1787–1802* (Rome, 1955), 9–57; Hanley, ed., *John
Carroll Papers*, II, 201.

52. *Lessee of the Executors of Theodorus Browers v Franciscus Fromm*, 1 Addison's Reports
PA 362, 368 (1798).

53. Ibid., 371; Friederick Valentine Melsheimer, *Brief eines Priesters der römischen Kirche
und die darauf ertheilte Antwort* . . . (Baltimore, 1796); [Rev. Francis Xavier Brosius], *Antwort eines römisch-catholischen Priesters an einen Friedensliebenden Prediger der luther-
ischen Kirche* (Lancaster, Pa., 1796). On the religious acrimony of the 1790s, see Henry F.
May, *The Enlightenment in America* (New York, 1976), 197–277; on the "autonomy and
popular sovereignty" beliefs of Americans, see James T. Kloppenberg, "The Virtues of Liberalism: Christianity, Republicanism, and Ethics in Early American Political Discourse,"
Journal of American History, LXXIV (1987), 9–33, esp. 10; Nathan O. Hatch, *The Democra-
tization of American Christianity* (New Haven, Conn., 1989), 17–46, 210–213.

will to establish in trust the Philadelphia Society for the Establishment and
Support of Charity Schools. This was a nonsectarian trust instead of one that
could have endowed the Lutheran poor relief society and the parish school,
both of which his pastor J. H. C. Helmuth regarded as prime opportunities
for private and public charity on behalf of poor children.[54]

IV

These cases—and many others that blossomed in the 1790s—exposed Pennsylvanians' conviction that Christianity was part of a common law that
should generously support religious and charitable trusts and incorporated
societies for promoting the public welfare. Yet, as the cases also showed,
courts shied away from defining what the precise dimensions of that Christian society should be. How could private charity be shaped or property
rights modified without a tighter definition of the specifically Christian—
and hence doctrinal—basis of the law to justify the social welfare objectives
the state wished to promote? Partly, the tense relationship of Pennsylvania's
courts to a legislative tradition hostile toward "magistracy" accounts for the
silence. But legislators had, by 1791, attempted to remove themselves from
constantly incorporating charitable societies and showed even less interest in
crafting legislation that would have avoided such unpleasantness as that
caused by the Fromm testamentary trust. Renewed sectarian strife also gave
both jurists and legislators pause. Nonetheless, the option Stephen Girard
would exercise in his will remained unthinkable for some time to come.

   In the controverted literature on American state formation, Lockean and
neoliberal writers continue to emphasize the law's expansive capacity to
affirm a colonial tradition of subjective rights tied to the idea of ownership
of property by title.[55] Given Locke's relative silence on charity law, few
scholars have asked how the American affirmation of liberty in property
could be reconciled to their equally cherished attempt to affirm "the moral
dimension of rights . . . especially in relation to public service," which
remained more often implicit than systematically argued. Had he lived, and
not died in disgrace, Pennsylvania's James Wilson would have insisted on the

---

54. See "Kurze Geschichte der männlichen Wohltäthigkeits Gesellschaft," Lutheran Archives Center H10/P5/M6/L5; for the published rules, see *Die Gesellschaft für Unterstüt-
zung der redlichen hülfsbedürftigen Haus-Armen . . .* (Philadelphia, 1790). See also William
C. Kashatus III, "The Inner Light and Popular Enlightenment: Philadelphia Quakers and
Charity Schooling, 1790–1820," *PMHB*, CXVIII (1994), 87–116; Bruce Allen Dorsey II,
"City of Brotherly Love: Religious Benevolence, Gender, and Reform in Philadelphia,
1780–1844" (Ph.D. diss., Brown University, 1993), 15–86.
   55. Elizabeth V. Mensch, "The Colonial Origins of Liberal Property Rights," *Buffalo Law
Review*, XXXI (1983), 635–735, esp. 655–658.

broad moral rights of Christian communal interest over naked individual rights to property's devise. Pennsylvanians might have understood Wilson's law lectures; if so, they declined to entrust their courts with intrusive powers over private property. At the same time, while suspicious of corporate monopoly and wary of the Bank of North America, the vaguely pro-Christian sympathies of Pennsylvanians found expression in watchful statutes of incorporation that demanded a public interest definition of corporations in general while encouraging religious corporate bodies.[56]

Historians most critical of Lockean theories of state formation have also missed the mark.[57] The rise of a laboring class provoked both an upsurge in Universalism and evangelical groups among the "lower sorts" in Pennsylvania. Unarguably, many of these struggling workingmen and their families were unconvinced of "liberal" ideology. Yet in neither case did Universalists or evangelicals argue that property in one's labor had Christian as well as legal standing. Nor did the Antifederalist and later Democratic-Republican political forces mount a successful assault on common-law or equity practices in the Commonwealth. The assault failed because the courts had been warned off restricting the developing law of property descent and devise. Legislative suspicion guaranteed an inconspicuous profile to courts and especially to experts in equity when questions arose about police powers that could plausibly shape either religious trusts or the property of religious corporations for public social welfare.[58]

Ordinary Pennsylvanians assumed that blasphemy statutes and support for charitable trusts and incorporated religious societies accurately reflected their conviction that theirs was a Christian commonwealth. Roman Catholics fitted awkwardly into this world, of course, and contests over their incorporated property or trusts that advanced their particular version of

56. James H. Hutson, "The Emergence of the Modern Concept of Right in America: The Contribution of Michel Villey," *The American Journal of Jurisprudence: An International Forum for Legal Philosophy*, XXXIX (1994), 185–224, esp. 220–221.

57. Thomas A. Horne, *Property Rights and Poverty: Political Argument in Britain, 1605–1834* (Chapel Hill, N.C., 1990), 201–251. For an interesting attempt to tie Locke's property theory to natural law, not common-law doctrine, see Michael P. Zuckert, *Natural Rights and the New Republicanism* (Princeton, N.J., 1994), 247–288, 295–297; for the largely negative assessment of Locke's (and liberalism's) view of charity as Christian moral obligation, see John Marshall, *John Locke: Resistance, Religion, and Responsibility* (Cambridge, 1994), 318–326.

58. Jennifer Nedelsky, *Private Property and the Limits of American Constitutionalism: The Madisonian Framework and Its Legacy* (Chicago, 1990), 246–254. Most of the excellent research on this topic comes from students of Gary B. Nash; see his *The Urban Crucible: Social Change, Political Consciousness, and the Origins of the American Revolution* (Cambridge, Mass., 1979); Alexander, *Render Them Submissive;* Billy G. Smith, *The "Lower Sort": Philadelphia's Laboring People, 1750–1800* (Ithaca, N.Y., 1990); Ronald Schultz, *The Republic of Labor: Philadelphia Artisans and the Politics of Class, 1720–1830* (New York, 1993).

Christianity remained the source of unease. The religious acrimony that surfaced in the 1790s climaxed in the infamous riot that destroyed St. Michael's and St. Augustine's Catholic churches in Philadelphia a half-century later, just three months after the *Girard* decision was handed down. Religious acrimony, as Sergeant argued, could destroy property. Liberalism triumphed by default over custom, since both state and national judiciaries refused to debate precise doctrinal justification for the state's social welfare interests when confronted with controversies involving religious corporations or charitable trusts.

This entire story of state formation from the 1760s to the 1820s remains an underdeveloped area for students of American legal and religious history. North American religious history, around which so much of charity law inevitably developed, urgently needs integration into collateral legal history themes. Both will inevitably have to acknowledge regional differentiations in this story. A closer examination of where property concerns and religious belief intersected or conflicted requires probing the specific objectives of religious trusts and incorporated societies, bearing in mind the gender and race of purported recipients. We know something about dower rights in general and the shift in the poor laws' treatment of women. Yet how such legal rights or changes were integrated into the religious beliefs of both men and women remains largely a mystery. The same silence surrounds the question of who was reached by private charity and how ethnic and racial barriers placed informal restraints upon both the law and religious intent as benevolence actually came to be administered. The intricacies of transferring charitable bequests from Continental donors and systems into American trustees' hands is also still imperfectly understood.

The Pennsylvania example sketched above partly confirms the argument that the law of charity developed in North America without a cohesive ideology. Yet, surely, the deep tension between the two sets of cherished values we have been exploring here suggests an alternate line of inquiry to a New York story of a nearly autonomous and accidental evolution of the law of trusts. There is undoubtedly some truth to this version of what happened; indeed, Pennsylvania does not fit the New England model of charity law either. But academic historians of the law and of religion need to be wary of their own ideological blinders and internally directed discussions of state formation or of law and society. The perennial belief—usually expressed outside the academy—that America could have been a Christian nation and perhaps once was needs serious attention, even if legal and religious historians tend to be impatient with the claim. Only by opening up the complex areas of conflict between sets of belief such as those noted here can historians reach beyond their understanding of these disputes and engage a broader audience and its anxieties. Only by seriously examining the legitimacy of competing objectives that investigation of the early law of charity reveals can we clarify our own intents and perspectives. The ongoing ideological and cultural disagreement over the state's police interests in issues of broad social welfare versus the rights of private property more than justify our best efforts to understand those disagreements' roots in early American religious and legal history.

AFTERWORD

The Death and Transfiguration of
Early American Legal History

O   NE OF LIFE'S many small epiphanies came to me at the conference from which the papers in this volume are drawn, when
I heard myself described by a young historian whose work I
admire as "a traditional legal historian." Despite my quickly
determining that the speaker did not intend "traditional" as a euphemism
for "old," I nonetheless had to admit, after furtive glances in mirrors both
real and intellectual, that what was once trumpeted as the "new" legal history is now middle-aged. One might even argue that it is dead, a prospect
about which I admit ambivalence.[1]

The blending of social history and legal history into the new legal history
is well known, thanks largely to Stanley N. Katz, whose commentary, with its
occasional undertone of lament, has made him the Greek chorus of early
American legal historiography.[2] The new legal history is, or was, a sociolegal
history—a study of law and society that treated law as one social institution
among many and sought to explain legal change in terms of social and
economic change. It was an approach that initially found more congenial
affiliation with the sociologists and anthropologists of the Law and Society
Association than with the doctrinal and institutional legal historians of the
American Society for Legal History, although the latter association subsequently shook off its torpor and regained its vitality.

The range of possibilities within sociolegal history was reflected in its
patron saints: James Willard Hurst, Max Weber, and, for some, Karl Marx.
In truth, this was not a very wide range, despite the obvious distinction of
the pantheon. Although their work inspired scholars to venture beyond the

1. See Peter Charles Hoffer, "Custom as Law: A Comment on J. R. Pole's 'Reflections,'"
William and Mary Quarterly, 3d Ser., L (1993), 160–167, esp. 161.
2. See Stanley N. Katz, "Looking Backward: The Early History of American Law,"
University of Chicago Law Review, XXXIII (1966), 867–884; Katz, "The Problem of a
Colonial Legal History," in Jack P. Greene and J. R. Pole, eds., *Colonial British America:
Essays in the New History of the Early Modern Era* (Baltimore, 1984), 457–489; Katz,
introduction to "Forum: Explaining the Law in Early American History—a Symposium,"
WMQ, 3d Ser., L (1993), 3–6.

bloodless world of legal doctrine and procedure, it also established the economy as a principal focus of sociolegal history, thereby reducing the larger field of law and society to a subset, law and economy. With the exception of Lawrence M. Friedman, the early sociolegal historians rarely looked beyond economic issues to questions of social structure, community, or religion, not to mention race or gender—although, to be fair, the latter two are coins of a later realm. These first steps outside the "law-box," to use Robert W. Gordon's memorable image, were, to be sure, liberating and exhilarating.[3] They revealed a legal history that made the realist bent of then-contemporary legal scholarship seem less a cynical aberration than a confirmation that law had never stood apart from economic interest. This was hardly a revelation to historians. One must remember, however, that those inside the law-box were lawyers, whose professional training emphasized analytical precision, intellectual focus—and, coincidentally, a blindered, self-referential view of the world. It would be churlish to chide them for not seeing more to law and society than the ties between law and economy, but one must nonetheless acknowledge the limits of their vision.

In the 1970s, the new legal history of early America held out the prospect of a more textured methodology than the new legal history of the nineteenth century. The latter quickly became dominated by attempts to prove or disprove the "Horwitz thesis." Morton J. Horwitz posed exceptionally stimulating, provocative questions about the relationship between law and economy, but the debate he sparked too often limited itself to the same kind of sources that had previously informed the "internalist" legal histories written from within the law-box. The new legal historians of early America, on the other hand, came of age when early Americanists were on the cutting edge of social history. Thus, not only did they have the vast historiography of the colonial era to build upon; they also absorbed the social historian's passion for studying society from the bottom up as well as the social historian's method of immersing oneself in large quantities of diverse sources, where meaning arose more from patterns than from individual instances. In doing so, they made a virtue of necessity, since they had to work without the appellate court opinions that were so readily available, and therefore so seductive, to their colleagues who studied the nineteenth century. Instead, legal historians mining the colonial period sifted through trial court records and bundles of case files—in addition to the other sources of social history—which, for all their limitations, were much closer to unfiltered legal data.

3. So exhilarating, as Gordon observed, that some who ventured into the wider world to broaden their perspective on law never came back—most prominently, Daniel Boorstin and David Riesman. See Robert W. Gordon, "Introduction: J. Willard Hurst and the Common Law Tradition in American Legal Historiography," *Law and Society Review,* X (Fall 1975), 9–55, esp. 10, 33.

Unlike appellate records, trial records offer glimpses of how law looked to people who were not themselves lawyers or judges: the perspective that most interested social historians of law. The view was less panoramic, but the new legal history of early America looked rather different from the new legal history of the nineteenth century.[4]

The focus of early American legal history has shifted, as the essays in this volume illustrate. Whether it has shifted away from or beyond the questions and methods of the new legal historians remains to be seen. Reading the new legal histories of ten to twenty years ago, one is struck by how lawyerly they were, even as they drew on nonlegal literatures to deepen and broaden their insights.[5] Although the authors were sometimes better lawyers than historians, or better historians than lawyers, they saw the challenge of sociolegal history as how to connect the intricacies of legal substance and procedure to economy and society. No matter how far afield they roamed in search of insight—to letters, sermons, pamphlets, newspapers, diaries, tax lists, petitions, and other sources not stereotypically legal—they always returned to core legal questions that required at least some mastery of the internal dynamics of law to answer.

The essays in the present volume reflect, for the most part, a very different sense of where one should draw connections between law and society. The authors address many of the deepest and most compelling issues of current historiography—gender, ethnicity, family, patriarchy, culture, dependence. In doing so, they have moved well beyond the new legal historians who first defined the field. In the classic division of the world into "lumpers" and "splitters," the new legal historians were lumpers in their depictions of society, however refined their analyses of legal change. By way of contrast, the authors in this volume bring to the study of law and society a much richer, more nuanced understanding of the complexities of society. They partake fully of the grand efflorescence of recent historical scholarship. But their engagement with law is more incidental than central. The inner workings of

4. The field of nineteenth-century American legal history has, of course, changed markedly in the last ten to fifteen years. Sarah Barringer Gordon, Michael Grossberg, Hendrik Hartog, William J. Novak, Robert J. Steinfeld, Christopher L. Tomlins, the late Elizabeth B. Clark, and numerous others have brought religion, labor, women, and the family to the forefront of legal history.

5. Prime examples, which also illustrate the diversity among the "new" legal historians, include Hendrik Hartog, *Public Property and Private Power: The Corporation of the City of New York in American Law, 1730–1870* (Chapel Hill, N.C., 1983); David Thomas Konig, *Law and Society in Puritan Massachusetts: Essex County, Massachusetts, 1629–1692* (Chapel Hill, N.C., 1979); Bruce H. Mann, *Neighbors and Strangers: Law and Community in Early Connecticut* (Chapel Hill, N.C., 1987); William E. Nelson, *Dispute and Conflict Resolution in Plymouth County, Massachusetts, 1725–1825* (Chapel Hill, N.C., 1981). Hartog and Nelson migrated with the terminal dates of their studies and no longer work in the early period.

practice and procedure, the interplay between internal and external pressures for legal change or stability, the continuities and discontinuities between changes in law and in society—all of which require digging deeply into law—play fainter roles in their inquiries. Instead, they take law as a given and examine its effects on whatever surrounds it, much as astronomers observe the gravity pull of unseen celestial bodies. The authors are very much aware of the presence of law, and are much more comfortable with legal sources than earlier historians tended to be, but law itself holds only secondary interest for them.

This is, of course, a bit of an overstatement. Holly Brewer, Richard Lyman Bushman, Cornelia Hughes Dayton, William M. Offutt, Jr., and A. G. Roeber all attend to law with great insight and sensitivity. We have not returned to the time when historians treated legal records, if they treated them at all, simply as sources for social, intellectual, or political history. Not surprisingly, however, the essays that engage law most directly are by the one law professor in the volume, Mary Sarah Bilder, and by David Thomas Konig, who has always been the most lawyerly of nonlawyer legal historians.

Bilder's singularity as the lone lawyer (although not the sole contributor with a law degree) reminds us that legal historians of early America, whatever their training, increasingly work in history departments. Their counterparts in law schools, on the other hand, even those trained in history as well as law, gravitate to later periods, the nineteenth century in particular. This is a striking departure from the time, not too long past, when most legal historians, colonialists included, taught in law schools. Although related to "the professional bifurcation of the field" between legal historians in history departments and those in law schools that Katz described, the division I am referring to is the deeper one of professional affiliation influencing the historian's choice of period.[6] It arises from the intellectual culture of law schools—a culture shaped by the lingering influence of the hoary Pound-Hurst-Gilmore dismissal of the colonial period, by the superficial similarity and familiarity of sources, by the connection of nineteenth-century legal issues to ones that still occupy modern law (giving the former greater value as precedent), by the pressure, and desire, to take sides in the ideological debates that lend excitement and cachet to other fields of legal scholarship, and by the tendency of academic lawyers to judge interdisciplinary scholarship by its relevance to their own contemporary interests. The reasons for the divide, however, are less important than its consequences for early American legal history.

Historians on law faculties identify themselves as legal historians. As a

6. See Katz, "The Problem of a Colonial Legal History," in Greene and Pole, eds., *Colonial British America*, 478.

matter of professional imperative, it is unthinkable that they would do
otherwise. After all, they spend at least as much time, if not more, teaching
property, contracts, family law, trusts and estates, and other law courses as
they do legal history. Law, for them, is not one arrow in a quiver—it is the
quiver, albeit one filled with interdisciplinary arrows. Most of the historians
represented in this volume, on the other hand, probably do not think of
themselves as legal historians first, no matter how much they use legal
materials. This is not to say that they are not doing legal history or that they
are not extending our knowledge of law and society; their contributions here
clearly demonstrate otherwise. Rather, it is to suggest that historians of
early American law risk becoming lumpers in their depictions of law, even as
their understanding of early American society grows ever deeper and more
refined.

F. W. Maitland, still the greatest of all legal historians, understood that
legal history is, at bottom, history rather than law, just as religious history is
not theology and the history of science is not science. His ability to see the
full range of human experience—society, economy, politics, intellect, culture, religion—in the dry technicalities of law remains unparalleled. The new
legal historians aspired to do the same, and they often succeeded, if not as
grandly as Maitland. The "newer" legal historians have also proved capable of discerning broader meaning in technical legal matters; for example,
Brewer's challenging reassessment of entail in Virginia, Dayton's masterly
reconstruction of the changing roles of women within the legal system,
Bilder's splendid reinvention of institutional legal history as a form of cultural history.[7] What is too often missing, however, is an equal marriage of
legal and historical sophistication, a recognition that attention to seemingly
mundane matters of legal procedure and sensitivity to the complexities of
gender, race, culture, class, and the like can complement one another. Some
historians may sympathize with M. H. Smith's comment about James Otis
taking his political stand on the more dramatic writs of assistance case rather
than on an earlier, plainer lawsuit over excessive fees in the vice-admiralty
court—"but what tribune of the people ever made his name by arguing an
indebitatus assumpsit?"—with its implication that great issues must rest on
something more arresting than legal minutiae. But lawyers know that procedure and substance are inseparable, indeed often indistinguishable. One
cannot hope to understand how law operates in and on the world unless one
understands how it operates within itself. Historians who doubt this would

7. Holly Brewer, "Entailing Aristocracy in Colonial Virginia: 'Ancient Feudal Restraints'
and Revolutionary Reform," *WMQ*, 3d Ser., LIV (1997), 307–346; Cornelia Hughes Dayton, *Women before the Bar: Gender, Law, and Society in Connecticut, 1639–1789* (Chapel
Hill, N.C., 1995); Mary Sarah Bilder, "Salamanders and Sons of God: The Culture of
Appeal in Early New England," above.

do well to observe how Konig parlayed the distinction between writs of debt and writs of assumpsit into a revealing study of how the legal and economic cultures of Massachusetts and Virginia differed.[8]

The orientation of the present volume to "legality" rather than "law" is salutary. It opens the playing field and reminds us that law's empire is too far-reaching to be left solely to the interpretation and mediation of lawyers or legal historians. This has, of course, long been a guiding principle of the law and society movement, which first nurtured sociolegal history, but only recently has it been taken up by historians of early America. As the present volume demonstrates, the shift to "legality"—and the concomitant recognition that there can be many legalities—allows historians to avoid the tiresome and ultimately pointless exercise of trying to define law that once preoccupied legal anthropologists and sociologists. It frees them instead to focus on the myriad ways in which people ordered their relations with one another, whether as individuals, groups, classes, communities, or states.

On one level, the leap to many legalities fulfills the dream of the new legal history: to treat law as so deeply embedded in the world that one can look anywhere and see its reflection, or, more precisely, its many reflections, refracted with abundant diversity. On another level, however, it begs a fundamental question, namely, how one reconciles the image of law-as-hegemon with that of subordinate groups creating their own legalities. In the insightful call to consider law as a central actor in the extended processes of colonization that Christopher Tomlins issues in his introduction to this volume, law is Old Man River. It moves inexorably across the landscape—not evenly, by any measure, but constantly and unrelentingly—alternately nourishing, transforming, and occasionally destroying the world it moves through and forcing all who live near it to fashion individual and collective accommodations with its presence. What this "traditional" legal historian does not want to lose sight of is that, no matter how much we study law as a social phenomenon, we must recognize the degree to which it, like great rivers, remains autonomous and try to understand how that autonomy helps make law and legality so coveted even by those who resist them.

8. M. H. Smith, *The Writs of Assistance Case* (Berkeley, Calif., 1978), 330; David Thomas Konig, "The Virgin and the Virgin's Sister: Virginia, Massachusetts, and the Contested Legacy of Colonial Law," in Russell K. Osgood, ed., *The History of the Law in Massachusetts: The Supreme Judicial Court, 1692–1992* (Boston, 1992), 81–115.

NOTES ON THE CONTRIBUTORS

CHRISTOPHER TOMLINS is Senior Research Fellow at the American Bar Foundation, Chicago. He is the author of *Law, Labor, and Ideology in the Early American Republic*.

JAMES MULDOON, Professor Emeritus at Rutgers University, is now an Invited Research Scholar at The John Carter Brown Library. He is the author of *The Americas in the Spanish World Order: The Justification for Conquest in the Seventeenth Century*.

MARY SARAH BILDER is Associate Professor of Law at Boston College Law School. She is the author of "The Lost Lawyers: Early American Legal Literates and Transatlantic Legal Culture," in *Yale Journal of Law and the Humanities*, XI (Winter 1999).

DAVID BARRY GASPAR is Professor of History at Duke University. He is the author of *Bondmen and Rebels: A Study of Master-Slave Relations in Antigua*.

DAVID THOMAS KONIG is Professor of History at Washington University in Saint Louis, Missouri. He is the author of *Law and Society in Puritan Massachusetts: Essex County, 1629–1692*.

KATHERINE HERMES is Associate Professor of History at Central Connecticut State University. She is the author of "Bodies of Liberty: The Making of Legal Institutions in Colonial New England," in *Australian Journal of Law and Society*, XI (1995).

JAMES F. BROOKS is Assistant Professor of History at the University of California, Santa Barbara. He is the author of "Served Well by Plunder: *La Gran Ladronería* and Producers of History Astride the Rio Grande," *American Quarterly*, LII (March 2000).

ANN MARIE PLANE is Associate Professor of History at the University of California in Santa Barbara. She is the author of *Colonial Intimacies: Indian Marriage in Early New England*.

CHRISTINE DANIELS is Associate Professor of History at Michigan State University. She is the editor (with Michael V. Kennedy) of *Over the Threshold: Intimate Violence in Early America*.

LINDA L. STURTZ is Associate Professor of History at Beloit College in Wisconsin. She is the author of *Within Her Power: Propertied Women in Colonial Virginia* (forthcoming).

JOHN G. KOLP is Associate Professor of History at the United States Naval Academy. He is the author of *Gentlemen and Freeholders: Electoral Politics in Colonial Virginia*.

TERRI L. SNYDER is Associate Professor in American Studies at California State University. She is the author of "Legal History of the Colonial South: Assessment and Suggestions," in *William and Mary Quarterly*, 3d Ser., L (January 1993).

HOLLY BREWER is Assistant Professor of History at North Carolina State University. She is the author of "Entailing Aristocracy in Colonial Virginia: 'Ancient Feudal Restraints' and Revolutionary Reform," in *William and Mary Quarterly*, 3d Ser., LIV (April 1997).

CORNELIA HUGHES DAYTON is Associate Professor of History at the University of Connecticut. She is the author of *Women before the Bar: Gender, Law, and Society in Connecticut, 1639–1789*.

WILLIAM M. OFFUTT, JR., is Associate Professor of History at Pace University. He is the author of *Of "Good Laws" and "Good Men": Law and Society in the Delaware Valley, 1680–1710*.

RICHARD LYMAN BUSHMAN is Gouverneur Morris Professor of History at Columbia University. He is the author of many books, including *The Refinement of America: Persons, Houses, Cities.*

A. G. ROEBER is Professor of Early Modern History and Religious Studies at Pennsylvania State University. He is the author of *Palatines, Liberty, and Property: German Lutherans in Colonial British America.*

BRUCE H. MANN is Professor of Law and History at the University of Pennsylvania. He is the author of *Neighbors and Strangers: Law and Community in Early Connecticut.*